TV's M*A*S*H:
The Ultimate Guide Book

Published in the USA by:
BearManor Media
P O Box 71426
Albany, Georgia 31708
www.bearmanormedia.com

ISBN 1-59393-501-3

Printed in the United States of America.
Book design by Brian Pearce.

TV's M*A*S*H: The Ultimate Guide Book

BY
Ed Solomonson
AND
Mark O'Neill

Table of Contents

Dedications

Dedicated to the memory of Michael Alan Tannenbaum, a friend for thirty years now walks in the Heavens. You are sorely missed, my friend.

To my wife, Nava, who's tougher than she appears and who had to endure more than was necessary while I was working on this book.

My daughter, Julia, is not only my source of inspiration, she's the center of my universe.

My parents, Charlie and Marion, for your support never wavered.

Photographer extraordinaire, my brother Steven.

And John Maher, my future son in law and my friend. Thanks for the legal advice, counselor.

Eddie Solomonson

I dedicate this book to the Spindlers, O'Neills and Parkhursts, all of my friends, to the M*A*S*H *ensemble for entertaining us and greatly assisting us with this book, to my enemies and for peace.*

Dad, may the good Lord be taking a liking to you.

Mom, may God be rewarding you for all that you suffered, with such grace. I miss you so much.

To Ann, I love you, and baby makes three.

Thank you, God.

Mark O'Neill

33,741 Americans killed in action during the Korean War.

2,833 Non-theater deaths.

15 other nations joined the United States and South Korea to become the U.N Allied Forces.

3,360 gave their lives.

This book is also dedicated to those who fell in "The Forgotten War," for their sacrifice shall never be forgotten.

Acknowledgments

This book could not have been done, or be even worth doing, without the help and contributions from *M*A*S*H* alumni. We would like to thank, in particular, Larry Gelbart. We are unable to adequately express our heartfelt gratitude for his support and contributions throughout this process, his seemingly never-ending supply of patience, all the correspondence, interviews, phone calls, episode and season comments, and *M*A*S*H* dialog, never before published. It's easy to understand why Larry is held in such high regard, not only from cast members, guest stars, directors and others behind the scenes, but from other writers during his time with *M*A*S*H* and after his departure. We dare not think what this would have been like without Larry's participation.

We would also like to thank Larry's production partner Gene Reynolds who, as Larry, also has a bottomless pit for patience and his ability to recall details of episodes that are now upwards of 36 years old. People are always debating television "duos" in front of the camera. But behind the camera, there was no better duo than Gene Reynolds and Larry Gelbart.

The third person behind the camera who, along with Gene Reynolds, had an uncanny ability for casting the right people for the right role, is Burt Metcalfe. To quote Larry Gelbart, "They have a nose for casting," which has been proved time and time again.

More thanks than we are able to give also go to the following: Alan Alda, Gary Burghoff, William Christopher, Jamie Farr, Mike Farrell, Jeff Maxwell and Wayne Rogers. These people worked long, hard hours and dedicated themselves to bring us the best possible product they could…and they did. Period.

A very special "Thank You" goes to the following who helped us achieve our goal of putting together the most complete guide to *M*A*S*H* episodes with never before published stories and anecdotes: Chris Allo and The Marvel Comics Group, Tom Atkins, Guy Boyd, Amy Brownstein, Josh Bryant, James Callahan, Larry Cedar, Elias Davis, Robert Decker and Gail Edwards, Kenn Fong, Bernard Fox, Harvey J. Goldenberg, Arlene Golonka, Kevin Hagen, Karen Hall, Larry Hama, Richard Herd, Richard Hurst, Ken Levine, George Lindsey, Stuart Margolin, Pat Marshall, Melinda Mullins, Thad Mumford, Michael O'Keefe, Howard Platt, David Pollock, Burt Prelutsky, Eldon Quick, Michael Rodgers,

Rodney Saulsberry, William Self, Sab Shimono, Enid Kent Sperber, Burt Styler, Richard Lee Sung, Erik Tarloff, Stanford Tischler, Father Frank Toste, Jean Turrell-Wright, Joan Van Ark and Loudon Wainwright III. From British Columbia George Hiebert, Aussie Brad Whitford, Barbara Malone, Mike Reyes and Kings Plaza Air Brush.

We would also like to take a minute to thank Ben Ohmart for working with us, never making us feel rushed or pressured, and for allowing us the time needed to put this book together.

This book is by fans, for fans of the timeless television show, *M*A*S*H*. The contents go far beyond anything that has ever been done before. All-new interviews not only feature the creators and stars of the show, but guest stars, writers, technical advisors, a stuntman, and even the former President of 20th Century-Fox.

Episode synopses feature more than just detailed episode descriptions, they include commentary from over 40 *M*A*S*H* alumni, and behind-the-scenes trivia. There's never been another show like *M*A*S*H*, and there's never been a book about the show, like this one.

And now, it gives us great pleasure to introduce the creator and legendary genius behind it all, Mr. Larry Gelbart...

Foreword by Larry Gelbart

Very strange, this assignment: writing a foreword for a book that's devoted to looking backward.

Just for starters, as amazing as the tons of information (actual weight) contained within these covers, the title which the Messrs. Solomonson and O'Neill have chosen for their work is not only inaccurate, it is highly inadequate. To call this tome an "ultimate guide" (to TV's *M*A*S*H)* is to call the Grand Canyon a pothole.

This is a work that leaves "ultimate" in the dust. It is nostalgia on speed. What you're holding in your hands right now is no less than the *ultra*-ultimate guide to the series.

If a fan can be defined as someone who has a strong interest in or admiration for a particular sport, art form, or famous person, then Eddie Solomonson and Mark O'Neill can be defined as being the heavyweight champions of fandom.

The sheer, staggering amount of scholarship they have compiled — from Hawkeye's rantings to the series' ratings — is replete right down to the precise color of the bathrobes the show's leading characters were wearing when they dropped to their cots, exhausted by one too many sessions of "meatball" surgery (indeed, to the surgeons, recognizing the futility of war, a single such session was already one too many).

Lest you think this assemblage is a mere compendium of statistics as dry as the martinis distilled and downed by the "Swampmen," let me assure you that while the book is a veritable Niagara of facts and factoids (tablets which provide facts with a pleasant breath), some of which, nearly four decades on, I have only the dimmest memory of, there are also a great many details within its pages that up until I read them there I never even knew existed.

For instance? After all this time, I was completely clueless as to how Gene Reynolds came to be picked by 20th Century-Fox to produce first, the pilot and then, the subsequent series until I read the William Self interview that that estimable gentleman granted to Eddie and Mark. Talk about getting it straight from the horse's mouth. Way beyond Bill Self there is no part of the animal our intrepid authors ever shied away from talking with.

Their appreciation of the series does not blind them to the many inconsistencies committed by the show's producers and writers (who knew some of us would still be alive this long? I guess some people just have no luck.) To them, these lapses in continuity are just part of the compromises you find yourself making when you're blinded by love.

But don't let me keep you any longer.

What lies before you is a treasure trove and I urge you to start digging in.

I think you'll soon agree that this guide is a great example of what Hawkeye Pierce would unquestioningly describe as being the "finest kind."

Larry Gelbart
Beverly Hills, California

The History of M*A*S*H

It's been over three and a half decades and almost two generations since *M*A*S*H* first aired on television, and it's as popular as ever. The phenomenon began in the late 1960's, with Richard Hooker's novel. From there, it was turned into a hit movie by Robert Altman, in 1970. Two years later, *M*A*S*H* was transformed into a TV show, and immortalized forever by Larry Gelbart and Gene Reynolds. *M*A*S*H* aired once a week for most of its original run. It was syndicated when original episodes were still being produced, and has aired multiple times a day ever since. Currently, between TV Land and The Hallmark Channel, *M*A*S*H* airs at least six times a day. According to TV Land, it consistently ranks among their top five shows. A whole new generation of fans is watching *M*A*S*H*, who weren't even born when the final two-and-a-half-hour movie aired. The ratings record set for that movie has never been broken, and even the outdoor set, in the hills of Malibu, is now being recreated for legions of fans. A few years ago, *TV Guide* named *M*A*S*H* the greatest television show of all time. Even more recently, they named Hawkeye and Trapper as TV's funniest duo.

William Self was the President of 20th Century-Fox Television when *M*A*S*H* premiered:

"*M*A*S*H* probably has been written about more than most televisions shows, but I have never seen an accurate report about how it got started. The reason for this may be due to the fact that none of the executives, cast or crew connected with the show when it went on the air, were around at the very beginning. It began one night when I screened the theatrical film in my projection room for a few friends. I felt that they would enjoy seeing a film that hadn't been released. I didn't know much about *M*A*S*H* but I knew that Dick Zanuck, who was head of 20th Century-Fox, thought it would be a big hit. It is always dangerous to screen a comedy with a small audience. That night was no exception. None of us laughed very often. Nevertheless, by the end of the screening, I was convinced that *M*A*S*H* would make a great TV series. I had had good luck converting other Fox features into series, namely *Peyton Place*, *Voyage to the Bottom of the Sea*, *Margie*, *The Long Hot Summer*, and *12 O'Clock High*. I felt *M*A*S*H* was stronger than any of them. The characters were unique and the theme that appealed to me most was that no matter how much they goofed off, they were always good doctors. The next morning, I called Dick Zanuck, and told him I would like to get the television rights to *M*A*S*H*, after the movie had completed its theatrical run. He said I could have them but I would have a long wait. He was so sure that it would be a big hit (which it was) that he had optioned the next book by Richard Hooker called *M*A*S*H Goes to Maine*, which tells what happened to all the doctors after they went home. He guessed it would be three or four years before *M*A*S*H* was available for television. I forgot about it. Many months later, Dick Zanuck called and asked if I was still interested in *M*A*S*H* for television?

PHOTO COURTESY BARBARA MALONE

William Self, President of 20th Century Fox Television when M*A*S*H *first aired on September 17, 1972. After screening the* M*A*S*H *movie, "I was convinced that* M*A*S*H *would make a great series."*

I said, 'Yes, of course.' It seems Dick did not get a satisfactory script for *M*A*S*H Goes to Maine* and the second feature was canceled. I immediately flew to New York to try to get a network deal for the script and the pilot. I was so sure of the potential success of the series that I told the 3 networks that I would not accept the usual development deal of only a script, with an option to make the pilot. They had to commit to both, going in. Only Fred Silverman of CBS was willing to do that. He said he had a lot of reservations about a project based on a movie that dealt almost entirely with nudity, profanity, blood and sex, all forbidden on television, but he made the deal anyway. He asked who was going to write and produce the series. I had a writer/producer under contract to Fox-TV named Tony Wilson who was very good. I told Fred I would assign Tony to the project. When I returned to Hollywood, I asked Tony to take over the project. He had some reservations. His major concern was that the movie had such a great cast, he felt it would be impossible to find other actors just as good. Nevertheless, he was willing to give it some thought. He ran the movie and read the book. A few days later, Tony came to me with his solution to the problem. He had decided that there were so many great characters in the book, that our TV version wouldn't use any of the characters from the movie! None! I couldn't believe it! Fred Silverman would kill me. I told Tony that his suggestion was impossible and we agreed he should not do the project. I had to tell Fred Silverman of my decision to get a different producer. He agreed. I recommended a producer/director named Gene Reynolds who was under contract to Fox and had produced and directed *The Ghost and Mrs. Muir* and *Room 222*. I felt Gene was a sensitive director who would understand the more serious moments in the series. Silverman said O.K. Gene and I then had to pick a writer. Our first choice was Larry Gelbart. Unfortunately he was tied up in London and couldn't come to America to meet with us. So, Gene and I went to London. We had a great meeting with him and he agreed to become involved. Once Larry delivered the script, which was brilliant, we started casting. It seemed like we considered every actor in Hollywood, until we finally felt we had a great cast. Our main problem was deciding who would play Hawkeye and who would play Trapper. We tested Wayne Rogers for both roles and he was good in both. We then learned that Alan Alda might be interested in playing Hawkeye but he wasn't available to test and he wasn't available to start on the date we were committed to. He was working on a TV movie entitled *The Glass House* and he didn't have a stop date. If we waited for him it would cost Fox a great deal of money. After long discussions, I decided to wait. How lucky! The last big crisis came at the end of the first season on the air. The series hadn't done as well as CBS wanted. Bob Daly, then head of business affairs for CBS, told me the network wouldn't pick up *M*A*S*H* a second season if 20th Century-Fox insisted on getting a firm order for 22 episodes, as called for in the contract. They would only order 13, with an option for nine more. I had nowhere to go. If I let CBS drop the show, I felt I would have little chance to get another network to pick it up. I also knew we didn't have enough episodes to go into syndication and therefore could not recoup our productions overages. I felt forced to go along with CBS's offer. Again how lucky! I often wonder what would have happened if we had not used any of the characters from the original movie as Tony Wilson had suggested, not waited for Alan Alda and not accepted CBS's reduced order for the second season? I suspect *M*A*S*H* would have become only a footnote in the history of television instead of becoming one of television's all-time hits…"

Interviews: The Producers

PHOTO COURTESY LARRY GELBART

Larry Gelbart — Sesasons 1-4 producer, writer, director and executive script consultant.

Larry Gelbart

We would like to take this opportunity to express our profound sadness at the unexpected and untimely passing of Larry Gelbart. During this process, Larry became a friend whose contributions and unwavering support were more than we ever dared to hope. If you were fortunate enough to have crossed paths with Larry, you came away with an admiration reserved for the kindest and most talented among us; you came away with the better part of the exchange. We will forever be grateful for his unending help, guidance and lessons learned.

Ed Solomonson and Mark O'Neill

ES: Do you remember a while back, I had asked you if you watch *M*A*S*H* on TV? You said that you couldn't because you found it too painful with all the cuts and constant interruptions?

LG: Yeah, right.

ES: Now that you have the DVD's, and you're able to see them through, un-cut, in great condition, without the laugh track, now how you feel about watching *M*A*S*H?*

LG: You know what? I don't have the time. I saw one or two of the first season when the DVD came out. It was thrilling to watch the show without the laugh track. I realized how much that device had trivialized the tone of the show.

ES: I'm hearing things I've never heard before.

LG: I know you are. I heard many I'd long forgotten.

ES: I'm hearing Radar's little chuckles and things in the background never heard before.

LG: I'm glad I lived long enough to hear that again.

ES: Someone had once asked about film vs. video, and you were adamant about video. Why would that be? If you were filming *M*A*S*H* today, would you do it on video as opposed to film?

LG: No, no no. I would still do it on film. If you're doing it on tape, you're mostly doing it indoors. You're probably going to have an audience. You're going to have people sitting there watching you do this stuff. Everything is different. The lighting is different, the performance for sure is different. When a performer is performing to another performer, and he's performing for the benefit of the camera instead of an audience that's watching him, you get a motion picture rather than a theatrical type of performance, and that's what we got with these actors and I think that's one of the reasons it holds up.

ES: It's held up all these years.

LG: Just before I called you, I was on the phone with a young woman from the Wall Street Journal and she was talking about it. Did you see that nice piece in the New York Times a few weeks ago?

ES: About "For the Good of the Outfit"?

LG: "For the Good of the Outfit."

ES: Yes.

LG: It was terrific, wasn't it?

ES: Yes. In the first season, before anyone knew *M*A*S*H* would be picked up for another season, I've heard from others and read in some articles but I don't know how true they are. Were people actually saying goodbye to each other, thinking there was not going to be a second season because the ratings were so poor?

LG: No, but people, me included, were thinking "What can I do after the show is dropped?" "Maybe I better entertain a few offers." You have to do that in this business, obviously. You have to look for the next place to land after they push you off the cliff. We were very uncertain. It didn't figure that we would be back.

ES: Apparently not.

LG: Yeah, but nobody said "Goodbye."

ES: How was the mood of the cast with the ratings so poor in the first season?

LG: We were all a little bummed out. We all knew we were doing our absolute best. We thought, "We're not doing the numbers for them. How are they going to bring us back?

ES: Why were there two sets? For the helicopters, you would need an outdoor set. But, being that the movie just gave you the set, it didn't cost FOX or CBS much money to build it. Why wasn't everything done outdoors?

LG: Because it's not just a matter of "Outdoors." It's a matter of the distance from the studio…

ES: Was it that far?

LG: Oh, yeah. It's in a place called Malibu Canyon, so you have to transport everybody there. It's not like everybody driving to the studio and parking their car. They would have to come to the studio and you would have to provide transportation and take them out there and you would have to feed them…

ES: So logistics were prohibitive.

LG: Union requirements made it too difficult and we didn't have the budget. Even if you were shooting outdoors, you would have wound up shooting indoors after a certain time anyway because the light isn't always favorable. You can't control it. After a certain hour, you lose it completely and you find yourself having to quit sooner than if you were filming at the studio. We went out to the Fox Ranch as often as we could. We tried to work there for at least one day per episode but it didn't always work out that way. Or we might shoot some stuff out there that we might use in a forthcoming episode, sort of bank it. You know what I mean?

ES: When did the pilot start?

LG: When did it start filming?

ES: Yes.

LG: In December… When did we go on the air, '71?

ES: '72

LG: We went on in '72?

ES: You went on September 17, '72.

LG: We shot the pilot in December of '71. It's not your legs that go first, it's remembering what the word for legs is.

ES: How does it strike you that the people watch M*A*S*H and we pick out the inconsistencies or errors…?

LG: *(Laughs)* Yeah, right.

ES: …Or things that don't make any sense?

LG: You know, I didn't remember one week to the next, obviously, whether someone's wife was Laverne, or, or…

ES: Shirley?

LG: *(Laughs)* …Or Shirley. That was coming, right? What's the other name…?

ES: Lorraine?

LG: Lorraine, right.

ES: Lorraine and Mildred.

LG: Exactly. Mildred was my cousin Mildred so her name came to me very quickly. Lorraine, I don't know. It was probably from the song, "Sweet Lorraine." Who knew that anybody, not that anybody wasn't paying attention, we knew people were watching, but who knew that we were doubling up on names and relationships?

ES: But nobody ever thought that 30 years later, people were going to be dissecting M*A*S*H.

LG: I thought I'd be dead 30 years later.

ES: Nah, no way.

LG: I thought I'd be safe. I'm reasonably certain there are no re-runs after death. Although with M*A*S*H who can be sure?

ES: You are one of the reasons M*A*S*H was so successful, because you give of your time generously to us on the board *(an internet discussion group)*, you answer people's questions. That should make you feel good and…

LG: It does, indeed.

ES: …We speak in private E-mail and we all…

LG: Oh, do you?

ES: Yeah, sure.

ES: George is the one who put that *(M*A*S*H)* song together *(from our internet group)*.

LG: George is great. The names are not strange to me. I know the names. And where does Brad come from?

ES: Australia.

LG: I have a lot of good friends down there. *M*A*S*H* was extremely popular in Australia.

ES: In England too.

LG: Well, yeah. Australia especially because there are a lot of veterans in that country. England got the best of the series, because England got to see the show without the goddamned laugh track (although once it began showing up on cable there, the dreaded giggle machine had been installed). What they did do in England, in the pre-cable days — I think I wrote about this once, they played all the episodes faster. It has to do with different sound cycles. (Electric cycles) I had my back to the set one day and the dialog was so fast. It wasn't a cartoon, but it was quite different.

ES: *M*A*S*H* on amphetamines?

LG: *(Laughs)* *M*A*S*H* on speed, right. Did you watch any of the guys during the Gulf War? The Gulf War, Take two, that is. They showed wounded soldiers on camera, getting an IV in the field and they're on a cell phone talking to their mothers in Kansas.

ES: It's amazing, isn't it?

LG: Pretty bizarre.

ES: Mr. Gelbart thank you so much.

LG: Larry, Larry. Not Mr. Gelbart

ES: Okay, Larry.

LG: All right, Eddie. It was a pleasure talking to you.

ES: Thank you.

ES: Never take the dissecting of *M*A*S*H* as we find the...

LG: Oh, please. Are you kidding? It's a revelation to me.

ES: That should be taken as the utmost of compliments.

LG: That you're talking about it at all and I'm here to witness it and that you and others who admire the series can finally see it without the laugh track so that you can get a truer appreciation of its true tone and intention. I can't tell you what that's worth to me.

ES: I wasn't sure that I'd be able to watch it without the laugh track after all these years, but after the first minute...

LG: Now you can't go back.

ES: Okay, Larry. I don't want to keep you any longer. Thank you so much.

LG: Gotta go. Incoming!

ES: All right. Thank you.

Larry Gelbart

Conducted by Ed Solomonson, January 20, 2004

ES: You know we're working on this project and...

LG: I think it's amazing that you guys really put it together. Tell me what I can tell you, and I'll try to tell you.

ES: Hiring the writers, were they friends of yours, people that you knew like Jim Fritzell and Everett Greenbaum...

LG: Fritzell and Greenbaum I did know, but friendship was not a factor. They were very experienced guys, with tremendous credits, as you know...

ES: Yes.

LG: There was no cronyism.

ES: So everybody that was hired to write on the show was there by merit.

LG: By merit, and some people I had never worked with, in fact, I'd never heard of because I had been away from California for so long. But, Gene Reynolds had a very good list of people and also has a very good nose for talent. That was very useful.

ES: By the way, Gene is being very helpful with this. Mark has contacted him and...

LG: He's terrific. He's got a very good memory, and he's just a good guy.

ES: Were there any major directing problems?

LG: Gene cast very good directors. He got the best people he could. After a while, when a show is a hit, a director is not really going to tell Alan how to be Hawkeye, and he's not going to tell people how to be funny when they know how to be funny. You can be creative. I don't mean to demean anybody. Guys like Gene and Hy Averback...Extremely creative, and Jackie Cooper. They were people with one eye on the budget and on the schedule and on the sunlight if we were outdoors, and were very good craftsmen. But some were clearly more creative than others. Incidentally, remember that I only speak about the first four years of the series.

ES: I understand. Speaking of the first four years, did you have any regrets after you left? Did you think twice about it — did you say to yourself "Maybe I should have stayed a little while longer"?

LG: Hmmm, yeah, but that's like a baby not wanting to have his diapers changed, you know? (Both laugh) It's very warm and comfortable.

ES: I know Mac had some serious regrets after he left.

LG: Mac had looked like the soul of affability, but he suffered from a lot of stress. A lot of problems. I can't pretend that I knew them all. I wasn't plagued with the same problems. I had my own.

ES: Were they any laugh track problems? It's pretty well publicized you didn't want it and CBS did.

LG: Ultimately, it was not a question of making people laugh at what wasn't funny or making them think an audience was laughing when there was no audience at all. What's come to light with the creation of the DVD is how much the laugh track distorted the tone of the series. It simply trivialized what we were doing.

ES: Were there any major network problems? Did CBS give you a hard time about anything in particular? They didn't want us to see too much blood...

LG: In the Pilot.

ES: Right. Did they ever say "Is this a comedy or a drama?"

LG: They never said "Get funny" or "Get less serious" or somewhere in between more funny and less serious. They were watching with fascination. Certainly, after the first year, after the show took off because they put it in a place where it would attract ratings, they didn't say a whole lot about the show, in general. They had censorship comments on every script, but they pretty much let us alone because they didn't know what we were doing — and whatever we were doing, it was getting them ratings.

ES: The line that you wrote, when Hawkeye goes into Margaret's tent and sees Frank and Margaret he says "Behind every great man is a woman with a vibrator," how did you get that past the censors?

LG: Probably the poor schmuck, who was the censor, didn't know what people did with a vibrator *(both laugh)*. He may have thought we were talking about a foot vibrator.

ES: I think the first time I heard that line, I said "What?"

LG: I think after the first time they let us say it, *I* said "What?" *(both laugh)*

ES: And the line that Frank says to Margaret, "Oh, Margaret, you're my Snug Harbor. I don't know what I'd do if I didn't have you to sail into"...

LG: I don't know *why* they allowed that. I guess they were too busy looking for "Hells" and "Damns"...

ES: They overlooked the obvious.

LG: They were only looking for single entendres.

ES: Larry Linville had some great lines in the show.

LG: Because Larry's character was crazy. His character was crazy. And there's enough of Larry's personal craziness mixed in there too, so that you could make him say far more outrageous things than you can give to anybody else. In "The Interview," when Clete Roberts asked him, "Has the war changed you in any way at all?" And he says, "No, not really." That to me was the man, Larry Linville, beautifully understanding the mind of the idiot he was portraying.

ES: Larry Linville was great.

LG: He was wonderful. He was *wonderful*. He was just too big an engine to fit into one person's life.

ES: "Margaret, all you have to do is speak and it gets my gumption up."

LG: *(Laughs)* Do you have a list of these?

ES: No, this is all from memory.

LG: That's great. To me, the greatest kick is that people quote *M*A*S*H* the way I used to quote the Marx Brothers when I was a kid.

ES: Did you see this as a comedy or a drama or…?

LG: I saw it as something in the spirit of what I had seen on the big screen. Certainly, it's a comedy, a *black* comedy. Not a drama for a second, but blackness implies that we're talking about subjects not generally talked about. Making jokes about death and illness and war and all the other subjects we dread being serious about.

ES: You had brought that out in the first season with "Sometimes You Hear the Bullet."

LG: Yes, well, we sort of found our compass, well, not sort of. We found our, our uh… What's the word I'm looking for?

ES: I wish I knew.

LG: Me too. *(Both laugh)* We found our tone.

ES: That episode shows what it's all about.

LG: That episode also illustrates how a television series works in many cases. That was a script written by Carl Kleinschmitt. In its original form, it just dealt with, what was his name, his character was a writer, Callahan?

ES: Tommy Gillis? Yes, James Callahan.

LG: That's right. He came to camp. He and Hawkeye had a brief reunion, he went off to do what he was going to do and wound up back at the 4077th on an operating table, where he died. Gene and I felt the show should be more than about "just dying." Something positive should result from the man's death. It's not that we wanted a Pollyanna ending, because there certainly isn't one, so we suggested the role of the young Marine, played by Ronnie Howard, as you know…

ES: Right.

LG: That character was woven into the re-write so that when Tommy dies, Hawkeye can send the kid home by betraying him, the kid *thinking* he's betraying him, so Tommy's death wasn't in vain. Because if his death was in vain, maybe the whole war was in vain. Maybe everybody died for nothing. It's a painless sort of message. I don't like messages that either telegraph themselves or are underlined or in Italics or you nudge the audience *"Get it?"*

ES: That's one of my favorite first season episodes.

LG: Mine, too.

ES: So that script had rewrites.

LG: They all had rewrites.

ES: Was there anything that didn't work when you filmed a scene?

LG: Oh, often, sure. But you work that out right there on the spot. You come down to the stage and work directly with the actors.

ES: I got a kick out of your office story where, for four years, you listened to the sound effects for *The Mod Squad*.

LG: And as I'm speaking to you now, there's a helicopter flying over the house.

ES: Over your house?

LG: I can only hope it's friendly incoming. I hope they're just looking and not dropping anything.

ES: If you could go back and change any specific feature of a character, would you do that?

LG: I'd have made Frank a little less silly.

ES: I think Frank became silly in the fifth season.

LG: Well, I'd like to lay it off on somebody else, but know that I share the blame. That's why there would be the occasional show where he would get drunk, try to be one of the guys. That's the one thing I would do. I'd make him a little less inane *before* the fifth season. Just lazy writing. Coasting with what you know works.

ES: The episode, "The Interview" to me, is probably the finest in the whole run.

LG: I won't quarrel with you. (Both laugh) I call it my valedictory episode. It was the very last one I was connected with.

ES: You certainly went out on a high note with that one, and William Christopher made that episode.

LG: I know. That one speech. You know, Eddie, I was watching a rerun the other night. It was maybe the first season or the second season.

ES: Which episode and I'll tell you what season it is.

LG: I don't know. I'll tell you the line, and you'll tell me the episode. Here's the thing. It's hard to articulate. When you do really heavy research on a subject, when you find out the truth of a situation, or people *and* that situation and relationships, very often you can say things that might have actually been said. You know what I mean? You make a connection with the truth. Let me illustrate. In this one particular episode, somebody in the O.R., talking about how cold it is, says, "I don't know whether to close this guy or crawl inside of him."

ES: Trapper.

LG: So, isn't that thought an actual doctor's line? "We warm ourselves on a patient"?

ES: Yes.

LG: That is such a source of satisfaction, to know that what you think you're making up has already been made up, already been said, already been felt. There's a great pride in that.

ES: Well, the message came across loud and clear.

LG: What year was that? It had to be 1, 2 or 3, right?

ES: Yes. I believe it was a second season show. *(The episode and scene in question are "Crisis" from Season 2, Chapter 9, "The Army Comes Through," in the O.R.)*

ES: Why did you leave and what would you have done had you stayed?

LG: I left because, I have the feeling that I've said this at one time or another...

ES: You probably have.

LG: Perry Lafferty, who was the vice president in charge of entertainment for CBS on the west coast, and an old friend, said, "Every time I saw you during this period," because there would be frequent meetings at CBS, he said, "I thought you were going to die." I looked so bad. I was so haggard, involved, obsessed, possessed.

ES: Is it true that you would actually bite the strings off the actor's clothes, take off threads if you saw them loose?

LG: Oh, absolutely, until I became loose myself. (Both laugh)

ES: Well, I can understand the obsession part.

LG: I *was* obsessed. I mean, this was so "my baby" in a way, you know? Everybody thought it was their baby. William Christopher, to this day, thinks that *M*A*S*H* was about a priest in Korea.

ES: That was said on the reunion show.

LG: I said that?

ES: It was either you or Gene who said it and I thought it was hysterical *(actually, it was Alan Alda who said that).*

LG: Anyway, after four years, I was played out. I said in an interview back then, I did my best and I did my worst and everything in between. I didn't want to repeat myself. I didn't want to be the best *M*A*S*H* writer in the world and only be able to write for that one set of characters. I wanted to try other avenues of expression, which I did, and there was no anger, there was no heat, there was no conflict, there was no contention. I couldn't have been treated more respectfully by everybody.

ES: Did anybody ask you to stay?

LG: Everybody asked me to stay, but once I knew I had to go I had to go. Four years was more than plenty.

ES: Did you prefer to write for one combination of actors over another? In other words, did you prefer to write for Henry and Radar or for Frank and Margaret or Hawkeye and Trapper, better than the others?

LG: No. My brain was open 24 hours a day. I loved whoever I was writing for. Each was rich in characteristics; each had a different point of view, each had a different background. It was nice to be able to skip from one to the other, and I didn't favor one over the other. Well, perhaps Hawkeye, making him my microphone, in a way.

ES: The dialog between Henry and Radar, in my point of view, is just superb. When they had a scene together, no matter what it was, it was always wonderful to listen to that.

LG: The big trick in the show was not the writing, I mean the most difficult part was not writing the dialogue. It was getting the idea, structuring the idea, laying out the show in a number of scenes in the first act; then, the second act; then the tag. The actual writing was so natural and easy and a pleasure, that it was addictive. Had I stayed another year or two, I would have never written anything else again.

ES: Radar always managed to make himself seem like he was the C.O. whenever he was talking to Henry.

LG: Absolutely.

ES: There's a scene where Radar slips Henry blank papers for him to sign while he was on the phone. After the call ended, Henry asked if that was a good idea to sign blank papers. Radar told him it must be because he signed them. Henry tore them up, got back on the phone again and Radar slipped him more blank papers to sign. Henry signed them and Radar left.

LG: *(Laughing)* It sounds immodest to laugh. Their scenes felt like classics, almost burlesque in text and execution.

ES: I think it's great that you can still laugh at this, you know? I mean, you put all this together, it's 30 years later, and it doesn't seem to be played out.

LG: They don't date. This is the kind of comedy that has been going on forever; the clerk who's smarter than the boss, the smart fast-moving straight man and con man and the sucker; Bud Abbott and Lou Costello.

ES: Gene and Burt Metcalfe were the ones primarily responsible for casting. Is this correct?

LG: Absolutely. It helped that they were ex-actors themselves. They had a feel for actors who have a feel for material. They were brilliant. Roy Goldman was there from day 1 to day 10,001, whenever it was.

ES: Roy Goldman?

LG: I have special reason to remember Roy. His father in law taught me clarinet when I was a kid in Chicago.

ES: Oh, really?

LG: He was my clarinet teacher.

ES: That's interesting. Do you still play?

LG: I'm looking across my desk at this beautiful clarinet. No. If I play it, I'll trip over my lip — it would fall to the ground. *(Both laugh)*

ES: Is there anything specific you can relate to about *AfterM*A*S*H*, with regard to setting it up, etc?

LG: I'll have to look at my old suicide notes. (Both laugh)

ES: My reasoning for *AfterM*A*S*H*, not being what it was, is that people were expecting *M*A*S*H*.

LG: *We* were expecting *M*A*S*H*. The series needed a top banana, and we didn't have one. That's not to dismiss the actors who were in the cast. They were basically supporting players and you have to be in support of something, and we didn't have that element. If I had to do it all over again (and thank God I don't have to), I would make it an hour show, more dramatic in nature, with comedy overtones rather than the other way around. There are probably 23 or 24 million veterans in the country. There's an audience out there who recognizes what happens in the VA, but I just took the wrong approach.

ES: Mark is the other gentleman who's working with me on this project.

LG: Right.

ES: He asked me to refresh your memory by telling you that he's the cartoonist…

LG: Mark O'Neill.

ES: He wants to know if you prefer "Divided We Stand" over the Pilot episode. By the way, "Divided We Stand" is a classic.

LG: I had had a year's practice by the time I wrote Divided We Stand. I'd been through 22 scripts by then, and there had been a great deal of refinement. The Pilot is like looking at your baby pictures and "Divided We Stand" is like looking at your high school graduation.

ES: It's a great episode ("Divided We Stand").

LG: I think it was a smart move to introduce to people that were seeing it for the very first time.

ES: In "Deal Me Out," the dialog in the Swamp, when they're playing cards is just…

LG: It doesn't stop.

ES: When Klinger tells his story about being trapped in a pay toilet, and how it cost them 4 dollars in nickels to get him out, it's hilarious.

LG: Sometimes, you do a show, you get on such a writing roll, the stuff just pours out. And *good* stuff. That's with John Ritter, right?

ES: Yes, John Ritter was in that.

LG: How old were you when you saw the series the first time around?

ES: In '72, I was 17.

LG: What gets me is the youngsters whose parents weren't even born the first time around. Anyway, enough back patting.

ES: Who made who laugh on the show? Wayne Rogers had laughed at a lot of what Alda had said.

LG: Wayne did, and I was always telling him not to do it that much. There's nothing worse in a comedy routine than having the people doing it, laugh at it. It seems to be a signal to the audience.

ES: Some of his laughter seems very genuine.

LG: It *was* genuine. Wayne's a pushover. I see Wayne at a party, he starts laughing across the room. I don't know if he's remembering something we did, or if he's anticipating what's possibly going to be said. He did laugh. Actually, everyone in the cast had a good sense of humor and a really good sense of humor need that's essential in doing a series. Actors have to remember their lines; they have to remember where to stand, they have to remember what they mean by what they're saying. We used to sit around between takes and talk about the next scene, talk about something or a part of that script, and it was very instructive. It gave them a chance to ask questions further about what it is was they were doing, and I could make some writing changes, as well. It was a wonderful creative climate – and good humor, which is a manifestation of good will, was the touchstone for it all.

ES: In "5 O'Clock Charlie," whenever someone replaced Frank's side arm with a stapler, water gun, a plunger, Wayne Rogers always laughed at that and that's contagious. When I see him chuckling a bit, I laugh at it.

LG: Far more than because of a laugh track.

ES: You come to realize that a laugh track is there for a reason, but when you see somebody on the show, another actor laughing, a genuine laugh at something that was said, its great. When Henry was searching for the money in "I Hate A Mystery"…

LG: The soot.

ES: The soot. When Alda cracks ups, that's a very infectious laugh.

LG: Again, we're talking about classic. Not classic because we did it, but classic because some schmuck's getting injured or looking ridiculous is as basic as it gets.

ES: And he (Mac) had a straight face while he was doing it.

LG: A neat trick, considering he knew what was coming.

ES: In a 1983 book about *M*A*S*H*, you had mentioned filling four black notebooks with story ideas. About how many of those actually ended us as episodes?

LG: I can't tell you. Some might have been episodes, some might have been that one line that Mulcahy did in "The Interview." *That* was in the book. Some were part of a "Dear Dad" or a "Dear Somebody Or Other" episode, where it would just be a thread, rather than a whole episode. But I kept going back to that book as though it was the Daily Word, or the Bible. I just kept looking at it. It's like washing your face several times a day. You refresh yourself. I just kept going back to the well, and if I didn't find an idea, I know enough about how the creative process works to know that some line, or idea that I might read would be the start of another idea. The germ of another idea that might be miles away from whatever was written in the book. But it would have been created because the thought was spurred by a line in the book. Is that convoluted enough?

ES: *(Laughs)* That's just fine. Wayne Rogers had suggested that your writing had moved from short, snappy sketches to longer paced — on scenes. Was that a conscious change?

LG: I don't know. He was probably more objective about what I was doing than I was.

ES: You know, he owns a business here in Brooklyn.

LG: He owns a business everyplace.

ES: He owns a very popular bridal store.

LG: Well, as we know, he's a very brilliant businessman.

ES: Yes.

LG: With bridal, do you mean wedding gowns or horses?

ES: *(Laugh)* Wedding gowns. Or a mail-order bride catalog.

LG: He's a smart cookie.

ES: Yes, he is.

ES: To what extent was the writing process? Was it with a group of writers?

LG: There was no group of writers when I was there. Freelance writers were given assignments, there was no staff, no sitting around a table. You see the credits.

ES: The credits. How does all that work? If you wrote a line in an episode, who would get the credit? How were the credits divided up?

LG: I didn't take the credit for work I did on other people's scripts. It's as simple as that. Once or twice perhaps in four years. Whether it was a line, or a complete rewrite from page one, I didn't "muscle" in on anybody's credit.

ES: In the first couple of seasons, character development became very apparent. How keen was the network on this? Did it spring from your own desire to make the characters more complex, or from the actors wanting more themselves?

LG: It didn't come from the network. It didn't come from the actors. It came from The Old Writer's Building.

ES: Speaking of The Old Writer's Building, you said that Frank's (Burns) home movie was filmed there.

LG: Right around the corner.

ES: Henry's (Blake) home movie was filmed at that cottage as well?

LG: Yeah. First of all, it made sense to film…I don't know if it was at that particular cottage or another one. As I remember, Henry's home movie, there was a lot of outdoor stuff with the birthday party.

ES: Yes. Why was it that MacLean Stevenson got to kiss two men on the show? *(Both laughing)*

LG: I didn't keep track of all the men he kissed on the show.

ES: When Tommy Gillis kissed him, his reaction is classic.

LG: Yes, it is. I think Mac was probably not even acting.

ES: It didn't seem so. It seemed like a natural response.

LG: To go back to the home movies for a second, it makes a lot of sense, or it *made* a lot of sense to just roll out all the equipment from the soundstage and go maybe 300 or 400 feet away, rather than go to some location where you really start getting into some heavy expenses.

ES: If I didn't know that was filmed on the lot, I would have thought that somebody rented out their house for a couple of days to film a scene.

LG: You've got to remember that 20th Century Fox was built in the 20's, and a lot of it is vintage stuff.

ES: Larry, thank you for once again being very generous with your time.

LG: My pleasure. I'm in awe that you guys are pulling this off.

ES: Mark has contacted several people connected with the show…Joan Van Ark…

LG: You know, I did some work with Joan Van Ark. She was in an episode where Hawkeye was engaged to her or something.

ES: He wanted to marry her.

LG: That was the show where there was one scene in her tent…

ES: That was "Radar's Report."

LG: We lost the generator for a second and the lights flickered. That happened while we were filming, and we kept filming. So what we did in post-production was to add the sound of a jet making a low pass over the camp.

ES: You mean that was real?

LG: The blackout was real, the jet fighter was ours.

ES: I always thought that somebody was standing by the switch making them go on and off.

LG: We didn't have time to re-shoot the scene, so we kept it with the flicker in it, but we tried to add something that made it sound like it was a technical problem at the camp, not in the studio.

ES: There was a PA announcement that said "Don't worry folks, it's just the generator again."

LG: Weren't we clever?

ES: If there's anything you need to know, Larry, just ask. (Big laughs here)

LG: Now, that I've got your number, I will. (Both laugh) I'm so embarrassed about misspelling Sidney Freedman.

ES: Oh, yes, that was the other thing I wanted to mention to you. (Laughs) I saw that on the board, but I didn't want to say anything about it.

LG: (Laughing) No big deal.

ES: I figured somebody else was going to pick up on it, and they did.

LG: I have to tell you that, as much as I enjoy it, I sometimes think that my presence on the board is an inhibition.

ES: Why is that?

LG: Well, maybe people don't want to say, "I didn't like this when he was there" or maybe "I shouldn't say I like so much of what was afterwards." Sometimes I feel like I'm a schoolteacher in the corner.

ES: Well, I'm not too sure about that. People have said what they don't care for. I mentioned that I didn't like "Edwina."

LG: Alan hated it too.

ES: Once again, I can't thank you enough for your time.

LG: My pleasure, Eddie. Please give my best to Mark.

ES: I certainly will. Thank you.

Gene Reynolds

M*A*S*H *producer and occasional director for Seasons 1-5, Gene Reynolds left after the fifth season, but served as script consultant for Seasons 6-11. By all accounts, he knew what was funny, when to be funny, and is credited with being a huge guiding force for* M*A*S*H. *Reynolds was instrumental in bringing Larry Gelbart on board. He also contributed story ideas throughout the show's run.*

"Gelbart and I shaped the show. I'd had a lot more experience in television, but Larry was a great writer. I relied on research in *Room 222* and fell back on the same practice for *M*A*S*H.* I found a doctor in L.A. and we discussed what life was like in a *M*A*S*H* unit. I got his permission and recorded the interview. Well, as you pour over an interview, you get stories or even bits of stories as you listen. After I left, Metcalfe did the same thing. There was one position that I took that was correct. Freddie Silverman said, 'why not make it an hour show?' And I said no. Too strong a story tends to fight the comedy. Freddie never really gave up on that. A year later, the beginning of season 2, he came back and wanted me to produce another half hour military show in addition to *M*A*S*H*. He wanted that hours' worth of military show. *Roll Out* never went anywhere [*Roll Out* ran on CBS in 1973-74…and was about a group of supply

Gene Reynolds — producer, director and occasional writer seasons 1-5, creative consultant seasons 6-11.

truck drivers who were African American]. I enjoyed scenes with Radar and Henry. And there was a scene where Hawkeye goes crazy over the same liver and fish they keep serving in the mess tent. Alan Alda (he chuckles)…once you pointed him in a direction he'd take off. I'd seen him in a play, and knew we needed a certain type of guy for Hawkeye. Angry but comedic. Very cerebral. He wanted to meet with Larry and I. After 5 or 10 minutes, he could see we didn't want to make a *McHale's Navy*. I never worked with a more professional actor. Gary Burghoff was extremely gifted. Better than good, as Gelbart used to say. Wonderful talent…a character kids could identify with. Larry Linville was very sweet, not at all like his character. Funny, funny guy. McLean Stevenson was never better before or after *M*A*S*H*. He never should have left. Alan Alda articulated his thought, as Hawkeye, on the folly of war. He was an editorial voice. Alan is a very decent guy and was very welcoming to Mike Farrell. When Wayne left, we just wrote for a different character. 'The Sniper'

is a favorite episode. I really liked it but had to fight for it. It starts out funny...
the Henry and Radar bit. I was very proud of that episode. Once it was being
filmed, the actors kind of took it over and did something different in shooting. I had to go into the editing room to bring the episode back to how I really
wanted it. Jackie Cooper was an excellent director. He knew just what cuts to
make. He was very controlling and driven. I took him aside one day and asked
him to back off the actors. He couldn't. And that ended it. I probably should
have left him alone and just used him less. He was a very talented and comedic
man. He knew just when to cut a scene. It was his idea to show Radar running
back into the shower tent and have his towel fall off. 'Leave one frame in', he
said (Reynolds is referring to the view of Radar's rear end). Jackie Cooper was
one of the best directors. He always went for something special. All directors
labor under the pressure of the clock. The business has gotten even worse in
recent years. As far as directing, you develop your own style. You can see the
personality of the director on film. The director has such control. When I first
started directing, I'd look at some classic films, once a month, to study the work
of other directors. Notably, I studied European directors. They did things a little
differently. Jackie and I were always pressing for that golden moment when the
comedy worked. There were thousands of things I'd do differently. You know,
you always find little things...that shot could have been tighter, etc... Blythe
Danner was wonderful. Mary Wickes...she was a favorite of two wonderful
writers. She'd be massaging her gums and then say..."My gums are singing".
Those 2 writers from 'House Arrest' wrote great stuff. Great whimsy, very light,
silly stuff. Of course, 'Sometimes You Hear the Bullet' was good. For General
MacArthur in 'Big Mac,' I know we wanted a guy with a prominent nose. We
got a guy... not a terribly prominent guy, just a prominent nose (he chuckles).
'Out of Sight, Out of Mind' originated as the concept...Hawkeye goes blind. I
loved that concept. We learned a person could actually have temporary blindness due to an injury and thought this would be a great story, you know, to
have a stove or whatever, blow up in Hawkeye's face...causing temporary blindness. That was the first script that [Ken] Levine and [David] Isaacs wrote. As
creative consultant, we would usually meet at Burt's (Metcalfe) house at night,
once a week, to talk about story lines. I gave a couple of stories... 'Point of
View' was one. I kind of saw the whole thing, you know. I had an image of the
scene opening from a soldier's point of view. Bombs are exploding all around
him, he spins around and collapses. Another soldier comes over to help him.
He's brought to a M*A*S*H unit and he sees Radar's face. I thought this episode worked well. I liked the writers [Ken] Levine and [David] Isaacs. I had a
roommate, and war had just worn him thin. I realized the guy was burned out.
I thought, what if a guy came to M*A*S*H with a great reputation as a doctor,
and just fell apart. Ed Hermann played the part in 'Heal Thyself.' I told his

agent this part was there for him (Ed), not something like an extra... a real role. Occasionally, I watch *M*A*S*H*. But if it's not mine I don't watch it. I always had a crew that was decent. I was always very careful to be aware of what the show was saying... what the particular premise was. Later *M*A*S*H*'s did get sentimental. You have to have a feel for this sort of thing. As a consultant, I'd suggest where they should have gone for laughs and they wouldn't always do it. I remember Potter opening the bottle he'd saved to toast his buddies. Lot of sentimental stuff. I thought it would have been a perfect time to go for a laugh. I thought he should have taken a swig and then gone "BLECCCHHHH!"... and then maybe said something about just kidding or whatever. But they were like "oh no..." I met Bill Jurgensen on *Hogan's Heroes*. I did 67 of those. He was available when we did *M*A*S*H*. I had a wonderful relationship with him. We had the kind of relationship where all he had to do is give me a "look", and I'd say, "What's on your mind, Bill?" And he'd make a suggestion about getting a tighter shot or something. He directed several episodes. We named the character of BJ after Bill. Dominic Palmer was brought in by Jurgensen. He was one of the best cameramen...a really good operator."

Burt Metcalfe

Burt Metcalfe served as associate producer of M*A*S*H *for it's first 5 years. Following the departures of Larry Gelbart and Gene Reynolds, he took over as producer for Seasons 6-11. Metcalfe was also in charge of casting, and made some brilliant casting decisions for the show. Occasionally, he directed and wrote episodes, as well.*

"I don't really have one (a favorite episode), I would have several. 'The Interview,' 'Point Of View'...any episodes that shook up the form are among my favorites. When Gene left, I had already been working right along with him. When Larry left was the biggest change. We had to explore characters more. We talked to a lot of different people when casting for BJ. I had known Mike Farrell from before. We did talk about other actors. With David Stiers, I didn't entertain another actor. I was never home on Saturday nights, but one time had the flu. I knew, of course, that Larry Linville was leaving and I happened to catch *The Mary Tyler Moore Show* and just happened to see Stiers. The following week I called his agent, who I knew. He played with that accent by himself, no one coached him. We used background music briefly and economically in the first few years. But we didn't feel it had the distinctiveness of the *M*A*S*H* theme. We used it less and less. It also got to be lumped in with the laugh track. I mean, why would there be an audience in Korea...or, where would music be coming from. I was always very concerned with pace. I would tell that while we were shooting, and was also conscious of it in editing. You might have had a 27 minute show but had to get it down to 23 minutes. It's even less now. I tried to shoot things fairly and simply. I'd just let the actors do their thing. Maybe that's not really a style. A classic example of how inarticulate syndicators were in editing is in 'The Interview.' At the end of the first act, when Clete Roberts asks each of the actors how this event (war) has changed them, the final response comes from William Christopher. In syndication, that moment was cut. For that moment to be cut is sort of like the ultimate inartistic decision. It was removing one of the truly great moments. I only watch *(M*A*S*H)* if I'm channel surfing and happen to catch it. I have all the tapes, but no DVDs."

The Opening Credits and Theme

What's left of a M*A*S*H *ambulance on the outdoor set in Malibu.*

"Choppers!" Those old choppers that we see in the opening credits of *M*A*S*H* have been coming over the distant hills of South Korea and into our living rooms since 1972. Happily, the choppers are not carrying real wounded, and those hills are not really in South Korea, but in Malibu. However, one truth remains.

The choppers, opening footage, credits and accompanying music by Johnny Mandel has all served to usher in an incredibly rich half-hour of television programming, over and over again. And yet, as much as *M*A*S*H* has been airing non-stop on TV for decades, and now on DVD, viewers may not notice that the opening credits and theme music did change a bit over eleven seasons. Prepare to notice.

Unless you watched *M*A*S*H* when it first aired in 1972, you might not know that extended footage was used for the opening credits of the Pilot. It was edited out for syndication, and didn't show up again until it appeared on the documentary *Making M*A*S*H*, on PBS in 1980. Then, it disappeared again until the DVDs came out.

The extended footage of the opening credits for the Pilot was trimmed down for the second and subsequent episodes of *M*A*S*H*. For the first three seasons, the opening remained the same, with the exception of an occasional short version used in Season 1. We see Radar looking off at incoming choppers, a close up of the choppers against the sky as the title "*M*A*S*H*" appears, an aerial view of the camp as actor's credits appear (this view of camp is either footage from the movie, or was filmed before they refined the outdoor set for the show, as the tents are quite different), nurses and Hawkeye and Trapper running to help the wounded, then two jeeps driving off the helipad with Hawkeye in one and Trapper in the other. (As more actor credits appear) But Season 4 marks a big change in the *M*A*S*H* opener.

The first thing you notice is that the close up of the flying choppers against the sky is replaced with a view of choppers from a more downward looking angle. The letters of the title and credits are noticeably larger. Naturally, these credits also reflected the departure of Rogers and Stevenson, and the arrival of Farrell and Morgan. Also gone is the shot of Trapper running to a chopper. It was replaced, over the next two seasons, with two variations of B.J. footage. And whereas the final, aerial footage showed *two* jeeps driving off the helipad, now only the one with Hawkeye in it was zoomed in on. However, for those who missed Trapper, look closely. His shadow and arm can clearly be seen as a bit of the second jeep still shows. (In effect, Wayne Rogers remained on *M*A*S*H* for its entire-eleven year run)

Jamie Farr's name now appeared on the credits in this, the 4th Season. By Season 5, William Christopher's name appeared on the opening credits, and the guitar strum at the end had been extended to allow more time to show the additional names. Season 6 featured a cast change, and David Ogden Stiers replaced Larry Linville on the credits.

But it was the sixth's season's closing theme that featured the biggest change, for one season only. It began with the guitar strums of the opener, and had a much slower pace. For Season 7, the *M*A*S*H* theme and credits remained pretty much unchanged. The only exception was a new shot of B.J. with his new mustache, replaced the old one. In Season 8, Gary Burghoff left the show. So, Radar looking out at incoming choppers was edited out, and his name was removed from the credits. Only for the episodes leading up to "Goodbye Radar" was his name added in the form of "and Gary Burghoff as Radar." Musically, the first half of the theme took on an ever-so-slightly nasal sound to it. By Season 9, the opening guitar strums at the beginning of the theme were altered drastically. The result was a more synthesized sound, almost harpsichord-like. The music, which accompanied the closing freeze frame, also changed to a higher pitch, starting in this season. For Season 10, the opening guitar strums of the theme reverted back to the original melody. But the overall theme sounded less harmonious. The different musical instruments did not seem to blend as well together, and the parts were more apparent than the whole. Instead of a soft sound in the first half of the theme, it sounded like two flutes. Bridges to changes in tempo were more abrupt. The same thing happened to the theme of *Murder She Wrote* in its final seasons. In Season 11, the opening theme and credits inexplicably imploded. Most of the footage in the middle was chopped out, and the accompanying music was either the traditional theme with the mid-section chopped out, or sounded like an abbreviation of the closing theme. For the latter, the sound of a single helicopter was dubbed in, rather awkwardly. Aside from the fact that Trapper's arm and shadow remained on the show (in the opening credits) for all eleven seasons, one more bit of trivia almost outdoes that. Though George Morgan only played Father Mulcahy in the pilot, he is seen in the opening credits, (running with Hawkeye and others to a chopper) also, for all eleven seasons.

One show, many themes.

Profiles

Alan Alda
Captain Benjamin Franklin "Hawkeye" Pierce
MD, Surgeon

Alan Alda, whose real name is Alphonso Joseph D'Abruzzo, is the son of actor Alphonso Giovanni Giuseppe Roberto D'Abruzzo, better known as Robert Alda and Joan Brown, a past Miss New York Beauty Pageant winner. Born in New York City on January 28, 1936, he married his wife, Arlene Weiss in 1957 and the two have three daughters, Eve, Elizabeth and Beatrice.

Mr. Alda played the role of Hawkeye Pierce on *M*A*S*H* and is the only cast member to appear in every episode of *M*A*S*H*'s 11-year run and has been in such notable films as, *Same Time Next Year* (1978), *California Suite* (1978), *The Seduction of Joe Tynan* (1979), *The Four Seasons* (1981) and *Murder at 1600* (1997).

More recent television appearances include hosting *Scientific American Frontiers* (1993-2005) and appearing in *The West Wing* (2004-2006).

Wayne Rogers
Captain John Xavier "Trapper" McIntyre
MD, Surgeon

Wayne Rogers was born on April 7, 1933, in Birmingham, Alabama. In 1954, he graduated from Princeton University with a degree in history and served in the U.S. Navy before becoming an actor. He married his wife, Amy Hirsh, in 1988, and has two children from a previous marriage.

Mr. Rogers played Trapper John McIntyre on *M*A*S*H* for the first three seasons, (1972-75) but wasn't happy with his character's development as a "sidekick," as opposed to an equal, to Hawkeye. For this, and other reasons, he left the show.

He has appeared in notable television shows such as *The F.B.I.*, *Gunsmoke*, *Gomer Pyle, U.S.M.C.*, and from 1979 to 1982 starred in *House Calls*. He has also guest-starred on *Murder, She Wrote* five times.

Today, Wayne Rogers in on the Fox News Channel show, *Cashin' In* and, in 2006, was elected to the Board of Directors for Vishay Intertechnology, a Fortune 1000 company manufacturing semiconductors and electronic equipment. He also heads up his own company, "Wayne Rogers & Co," a stock trade and investment firm.

McLean Stevenson
Lieutenant Colonel Henry Blake
MD, Surgeon

Edgar McLean Stevenson Jr., "Mac," was born on November 14, 1927 in Normal, Illinois. Son of a cardiologist and the brother of actress Ann Whitney, Mac was also the press secretary for his 2nd cousin (once-removed), Adlai Stevenson II, for the 1952 and 1956 Presidential elections.

After serving in the Navy, he graduated from Northwestern University with a Bachelor's degree in theater arts, and guest starred in *That Girl* (1966), which also featured *M*A*S*H* alumni Stuart Margolin, William Christopher and Harvey J. Goldenberg. Mac also appeared as a magazine editor in *The Doris Day Show* (1968-73), created by *M*A*S*H* writer, Jim Fritzell.

Mac began to establish himself as a comedy writer, writing for *That Was The Week That Was*, in which Alan Alda appeared, and *The Smothers Brothers Comedy Hour*, occasionally appearing in both shows.

Mac had originally auditioned for the role of Hawkeye on *M*A*S*H*, but was convinced to play the "Lovable Henry Blake" from 1972 to 1975. Mac had left the series for his own shows, *The McLean Stevenson Show* (1976-77) and *Hello, Larry* (1979-80), both of which were met with limited success.

McLean Stevenson suffered a fatal heart attack on February 15, 1996, in Los Angeles.

Loretta Swit
Major Margaret Houlihan
RN, Army Careerwoman

Loretta Swit was born on November 4, 1937; 30 years later, in 1967, she shared a stage with Don Rickles and Ernest Borgnine, portraying a Pidgeon sister in a Los Angeles run of "The Odd Couple." In 1970, Ms. Swit appeared in the television shows, *Gunsmoke*, *Mission: Impossible*, *Hawaii Five-0* and *Mannix*. She also appeared in such films as *SOB* (1981) and *Beer* (1985)

Ms. Swit was the host of a cable television wildlife series, *Those Incredible Animals,* and more recently toured in the production of "The Vagina Monologues."

After doing the pilot episode for *Cagney & Lacey*, she wanted to star in the series, but due to contractual obligations with FOX, she wasn't able to. In 1989, she received a star on the Hollywood Walk of Fame. She was also the first *M*A*S*H* cast member to actually visit Korea when she narrated *Korea, the Forgotten War*.

Ms. Swit married actor Dennis Holahan in 1983, who appeared in a Season 11 episode, "U.N., the Night and the Music" as a Swedish diplomat. The two were divorced in 1995. Swit is the only *M*A*S*H* star, besides Alan Alda, to appear in the Pilot and the 2½ hour series finale, "Goodbye, Farewell and Amen." She was Major Margaret Houlihan for *M*A*S*H*'s entire 11-year run.

Loretta Swit is an animal activist as well as a vegan, and also has a line of jewelry sold across the country.

Larry Linville
Major Frank "Ferret Face" Burns
MD, Surgeon

Lawrence Lavonne "Larry" Linville was born September 29, 1939, in Ojai, California and played the "overbearing fusspot" antagonist Major Frank Burns. Despite Mr. Linville's portrayal of the over-the-top greedy and married major who lusted after Major Margaret Houlihan, his fellow cast members describe him as kind, friendly, open-minded and courteous to others. A far cry from the role he played to perfection and a credit to his abilities as an actor.

Mr. Linville left *M*A*S*H* after his five-year contract expired and declined a two-year renewal, citing he had taken the character as far as it could go given how the show changed from largely comedic to one with more dramatically focused story lines. He appeared in a total of 28 movies and television shows, most commonly in *Murder, She Wrote*, and was also in *Fantasy Island*, *The Love Boat*, *Mannix*, *ChiPS* and *Mission Impossible*.

Mr. Linville took ill in the late 1990's, after years of smoking and drinking, and had part of a lung removed in 1998 after doctors found a malignant tumor under his sternum.

One of the most talked about characters on *M*A*S*H*, Linville continues to be a favorite of *M*A*S*H* fans to this day. Linville drew strength from all the fan mail he received and was deeply touched by all. Unfortunately, he passed away in New York City after complications from cancer surgery left him with pneumonia: in a strange twist, he died on April 10, 2000, Harry Morgan's 85th birthday.

Mr. Linville had a daughter, Kelly Linville.

Gary Burghoff
Corporal Walter Eugene "Radar" O'Reilly
Company Clerk

Gary was born in Bristol, Connecticut on May 24, 1943. His acting and music careers began during his high-school years in Delavan, Wisconsin, and in 1967, appeared in an off-Broadway musical, "You're A Good Man, Charlie Brown."

Mr. Burghoff was the only regular from the original *M*A*S*H* film to continue his role of Corporal Radar O'Reilly on the series. He left the series after Season 7, and returned in Season 8 for the two-part, "Goodbye, Radar."

In the 1970's Gary appeared on the game show, *The Match Game*, as a stand-in regular for Charles Nelson Reilly and as a "Special male guest" in Seat 1. Other shows included are *Tattletales* and *Showoffs*, plus an episode of *The Love Boat*. He also starred with Fred Astaire in the TV movie, "The Man in the Santa Claus Suit." (1979) He went on to do the pilot for a television show, *W*A*L*T*E*R*, but only one episode was shown and went unsold. In recent years, Gary has appeared in such plays as "The Last of the Red Hot Lovers."

Besides being an accomplished jazz musician, heading The We Three Trio, he recorded an album, "Just For Fun," and also sings. An avid philatelist (the study of revenue and postage stamps) he starred in a United States Postal Service video for beginning stamp collectors.

Gary, now retired, has three children, and is an avid animal activist and wild-life artist.

Mike Farrell
Captain B. J. Hunnicutt
MD, Surgeon

Mike Farrell, born on February 6, 1939, hails from Saint Paul, Minnesota. When he was two years old, his family moved to California. He attended West Hollywood Grammar School with Natalie Wood and after graduating from West Hollywood High School, he served in the Marines.

Mike had originated the role of Scott Banning on the soap *Days of Our Lives*, and has appeared in the television shows *The Monkees*, *I Dream of Jeannie*, *Banacek*, and *Marcus Welby, M.D.* More recent appearances include *Murder, She Wrote*, *Matlock*, *Mannix*, *Desperate Houswives* and a starring role on the television show *Providence*, from 1999 until 2002.

In 1963, Mike married his wife, Judy, who appeared in several *M*A*S*H* episodes as a nurse; the couple has two children, Michael and Erin (B.J.'s daughter on *M*A*S*H* was named after Erin). Mike and Judy divorced in 1983; in 1984, he married his current wife, actress Shelley Fabares.

Mike Farrell joined the cast of *M*A*S*H* in 1975 after Wayne Rogers left the show, and stayed for the remainder of the series' run.

Harry Morgan
Colonel Sherman T. Potter
Regular Army, MD, Surgeon

Born on April 10, 1915 in Detroit, Harry Morgan, whose real name is Harry Bratsburg, married Eileen Detchon in 1940 and they remained married until her death in 1985. In 1986, Harry married Barbara Bushman, the granddaughter of silent film star Francis X. Bushman, and the two are still together.

Harry Morgan began his 60-year career in 1942 and has a very extensive list of credits to his name. Billed as Henry Morgan from 1942 until around 1959, appearances include *Dr. Kildare*, three episodes of *The Partridge Family*, three episodes of *3rd Rock from the Sun*, five episodes of *The Love Boat* and played Bill Gannon on a 1995 episode of *The Simpsons*.

Before *M*A*S*H*, Mr. Morgan was a co-star on the television show *Pete & Gladys*, portraying Pete Porter in 72 episodes. Also well known as Officer Bill Gannon on *Dragnet*; he played Captain Gannon in the 1987 film adaptation of *Dragnet*.

Harry Morgan as Colonel Sherman T. Potter.

Harry Morgan's first appearance on *M*A*S*H* was in the 3rd season opener, "The General Flipped At Dawn," and it was the only time he appeared on-screen with McLean Stevenson. When Stevenson left the series, Harry Morgan was given the role of Colonel Sherman T. Potter, the new Commanding Officer of the 4077 and remained until the series ended in 1983.

Harry Morgan retired in 2002.

David Ogden Stiers
Major Charles Emerson Winchester, III
MD, Surgeon

David Ogden Stiers has entered his 40th year acting with appearances on *Kojak*, *Charlie's Angels* and *Rhoda*. Also to his long list of credits are eight episodes of *Perry Mason* as Michael Reston, a district attorney, several voices for Disney and a memorable performance as Dr. Timicin on *Stat Trek: The Next Generation*.

Born in Peoria, Illinois, the 66-year-old actor was noticed on *The Mary Tyler Moore Show* by Burt Metcalfe. Metcalfe placed a call to Stiers' agent and the rest, as they say, is history. David Ogden Stiers joined the cast of *M*A*S*H* in Season

6, as Major Charles Emerson Winchester, III, a wealthy, highly educated and skilled surgeon who was a formidable foe for Hawkeye and BJ.

Mr. Stiers brought to his character his love of classical music and has conducted 70 orchestras with over 100 appearances, and is the resident conductor of The Newport Symphony in Newport, Oregon.

Jamie Farr
Corporal Maxwell Q. Klinger
Corpsman, Company Clerk

Jamie Farr, born Jameel Joseph Farah on July 1, 1934, in Toledo, Ohio, is the son of Lebanese-American parents Jamelia and Samuel Farah. At 11 years old, he won a local acting contest with a grand prize of $2.00, and after attending Woodward High School, where he was an exceptional student, he attended The Pasadena Playhouse where a scout offered him a screen test for *Blackboard Jungle*. He won the role of "Santini," a mentally challenged student.

Since regular work was difficult to find, Jamie had taken jobs as a deliveryman, postal clerk, an airlines reservation agent, and worked on a chinchilla ranch.

Jamie became a regular on *The Red Skelton Show* and *The Danny Kaye Show*, and appeared in *The Dick Van Dyke Show*. He also was a regular on *The Chicago Teddy Bears*, which featured Huntz Hall.

Jamie Farr served two years in the army overseas in Japan and Korea after the Korean War ended.

Only called to do a day's work on *M*A*S*H*, it wound up an 11-year stint as a popular corporal wanting a Section 8 discharge and proving his point by wearing dresses. However, this character profile would change later in the series when Klinger became a sergeant; Jamie wanted out of the dresses as he felt his children would be embarrassed at their father wearing dresses on national television on a weekly basis. While on *M*A*S*H*, he was in the movies *Cannonball Run* and *Cannonball Run II*.

Jamie is married to his wife, Joy, and has 2 children, Jonas and Yvonne (Klinger's sister on *M*A*S*H* was Yvonne). He's also a grandfather and, in 1985, Farr received a star on the Hollywood Walk of Fame.

William Christopher
Father Mulcahy

William Christopher, born on October 20, 1934, had attended Methodist Wesleyan University in Middleton, Connecticut, majoring in drama. He met his wife, Barbara O'Connor, on a blind date and the two were married in 1957. Barbara Christopher played Nurse O'Connor in the Season 4 episode, "Dear Mildred" and performed a duet with her husband. William Christopher is believed to be a direct descendant of the American Patriot, Paul Revere.

Television appearances include *The Andy Griffith Show* (in two episodes, one as a doctor and the other as an I.R.S. Agent trying to collect taxes from Aunt Bea after she won prizes on a television show), *Death Valley Days*, *The Patty Duke Show*, *Good Times* and the recurring role of Private Lester Hummel on *Gomer Pyle, U.S.M.C.* Other appearances include *That Girl* and *Hogan's Heroes*, for which Gene Reynolds directed 26 episodes.

Interestingly, William Christopher appeared in the movie, *With Six You Get Egg Roll* (1968) with Jamie Farr, both playing hippies five years before they would reunite on *M*A*S*H*.

William and Barbara Christopher have two sons, John and Ned, and together have written a book, *Mixed Blessings*, about their experiences raising their autistic son, Ned. Much of Mr. Christopher's spare time is devoted to the National Autistic Society and doing public service announcements to raise awareness for autism.

Interviews: The Cast

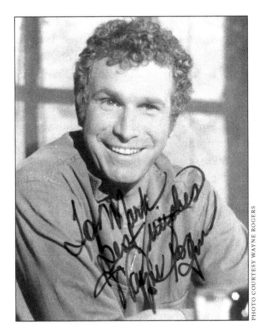

Wayne Rogers

"For the record, I do not watch *M*A*S*H* and in fact I rarely ever did. By way of explanation, at the time we did the work, Alan Alda and I would go to the dailies, meaning we would watch the scenes we had shot on the previous day so that we could learn from our own observation on how to improve those little moments that seem to be second nature. People used to say they thought we improvised the dialogue. In fact, every word was carefully crafted by Larry Gelbart and it was up to us to hone our skills such that it seemed as if we were saying it for the first time. I didn't watch *M*A*S*H* after I left the show, and as a consequence I have no thoughts on the direction the show took. I believe Larry left shortly thereafter, as did Gene Reynolds. I assume the show continued in the vain they originally developed. Nevertheless, if things did change, I was certainly not aware of it. Did I have a favorite director? No. However, there were some who were better than others. But, you would have to understand something about the process of directing to know this. It its simplest form, comedy traditionally is shot with a master and several close ups and the scene is put together in the cutting room. Occasionally, there are directors that know how to use the camera to make a joke play better. One such director was Michael O'Herlihy and another was Hy Averback. But, you must understand that in most television, even though the director is allowed a first cut, such an event rarely takes place and most of the editing is done by the producer. In that regard Gene Reynolds was very adept. Confrontations between Hawkeye and Trapper on one side and Frank Burns on the other were deliberately conceived. It is much easier to write a scene when one party wants something that the other party opposes. In fact, all good drama as well as comedy depends on this. Frank Burns was the quintessential character for the kind of humor M*A*S*H portrayed. About *Divided We Stand* and the use of voice over: since that was 32 years ago, I have not the vaguest idea what Mr. Alda and I talked about. However, we often discussed things that would enhance the mood of the upcoming scene, such that it was preparation for something that would follow. Having directed things before and since, there must have been an episode that I thought I could do well. Directing just for the purpose of directing as an exercise holds no interest for me. If a certain piece of material for which I think I have a visual eye, and to which I have an immediate visual and emotional response when I read it, then I would certainly want to direct it. I am sure there were suggestions I made about my character, some of which were used and some of which were not. I do not recall what they might have been. As a generalization, Alan and I would constantly look for those things that might distinguish us from each other as opposed to two characters speaking with the same voice. For example, Hawkeye was more cognitive whereas Trapper was more impulsive. With regard to comments on humor, Alan and I determined early on that the jokes were being told for each other's benefit, never for the audience. In other words, we would attempt to make those characters in the show around us laugh. Part of the success of M*A*S*H comes from the fact that sanity in the face of horror can best be protected with humor. Best of luck on this endeavor."

Gary Burghoff

"I absolutely adored Larry Gelbart. Larry wrote us all a note that he shouldn't have won the Humanitas Award, when so many others worked on M*A*S*H. And the man I have to congratulate the most is Gene Reynolds. He went very much by the book. And here he hired people that *didn't* go by the book and he let them loose. That takes courage. A lot of directors won't do that. He got the chemistry going. A lot of people say we couldn't have done *M*A*S*H* without Alan Alda. Well, there is a point there, but then, the star of *M*A*S*H* was *M*A*S*H*. But the man we really couldn't have done it without is Gene. Gene's philosophy was that you entertain first and then give your message second. In the feature film, after the football game, we're all singing something on the way back to *M*A*S*H*. The studio actually hired a music director to direct us in singing the song in that scene. In the scene, we are laughing so hard because of the idea that a musical director was trying to direct us. I mean, they didn't realize it was 'supposed' to be chaos. The great thing about TV's *M*A*S*H* wasn't the financial reward, it was about the work. It was about the level of work that could be reached if you took chances. We were walking a thin line. We didn't want to do a Hogan's Heroes. The networks didn't know what to make of us. To us, acting was the ability to communicate thoughts and ideas on an emotional level. I was always trying not to reach Alan or Gene…but you…the people. You realize that the audience's humanity is the same as yours. When Gene directed, he knew funny the instant it happened. He'd laugh. He knew if "he" laughed, it was funny. But also, if you had a dramatic moment he knew if it was false or real. It was the same with Robert Altman. Directors you had problems with were ones who intellectualized, and lost the spontaneity. Gene and Larry leaving *did* contribute to my leaving…no question about it. I felt a huge loss when Gelbart left. His leaving, and then Reynolds, did contribute to my leaving…no doubt about it. A lot of the humor left the set. But it was one of many, many reasons. It wasn't that Alda and Metcalfe didn't do a good job. They were so dedicated. But all of a sudden Larry and then Gene were gone. This should not be at all construed as a criticism of Alan, who was the creative force after they left. In order to do what Alan did, you don't have to be dedicated, you have to be *totally* dedicated. I could see that, like me, he was getting burned out. But he still kept at it. He was that good. But 7 years is a long time. Even our legal system, up until the 70's, didn't like 7-year contracts. People need to be renewed after 7 years. I was filled with all kinds of conflictions during the filming of the (my) last episode. I felt a deep sadness that I had to go. That time of my life was like a crucifixion. Such an emotional time. Anything can happen when Jackie Cooper directs. In "The Sniper," my towel was rigged so it would come off right at the moment I entered the shower tent. I knew what Jackie intended, by having the towel come off, but it was just meant to be fun. I always admired Jackie's work. A lot of directors are resigned to the fact that you can't get the good shot. But Jackie did it. He'd shoot it like a movie. I once suggested to another director, not Jackie, that we could get a great dramatic shot in one instance. But he said, 'no, that would be feature,' meaning like the kind of shot they do in a feature film. And my heart just sank. In terms of warmth and friendship, Linville and

Christopher were the dearest. Linville was the kind of guy you could talk to about anything. Great sense of humor, loved to laugh. Bill Christopher has a spontaneous sense of humor. He has the most original sense of humor of anyone I know. As far as McLean and Harry…in both instances they were like brothers. Harry was solid as a rock, loyal, faithful and always kept us in stitches. McLean was a wonderful disarmer. We'd come around a corner *hating* a scene we just did, and there was McLean, pretending to be a farmer selling tickets to watch his cousin eat a goat. We doubled up with laughter. I learned he was disarming tension. In this way, he was extremely selective as to when to be humorous. He knew exactly how and when to do it, even in a phone conversation. Wayne and Mike…they had one thing in common…they were just nice guys. Wayne had said he wanted to leave. Well, the studio said if you violate your contract you'll never work again. He said, 'What contract?' They went and looked. Wayne had never signed it *(Gary laughs)*. Steve McQueen had told Wayne, when he heard he was going to do a series, 'I hope you're taking your asshole pills.' So, he kind of came on board with a suspicious attitude towards the studios. I thought David Ogden Stiers was a brilliant choice. You couldn't have another Frank, you had to be different. Compliments have to go to Burt Metcalfe, who was brilliant at casting. And Jamie and I were and are friends. Stuart Margolin is one of the best actors I've ever worked with. He never has a false moment, just like Allan Arbus. Margolin is often *so* good, he's not recognized enough for it. Ed Winter was the salt of the Earth as a guy. He was the hardest character to keep a straight face with. In a lot of my scenes with him, he'd come nose to nose with me with one of Flagg's just awful, horrendous threats…you know, saying something like he was going to pull my intestines out through my nose. It was unbearably hard to keep a straight face. Ed had a great sense of humor, because if he saw me starting to go…*he'd* go (laugh). I watched an episode last night. It was one I'd never seen on TV, "Dreams." It was after I left the show. *I loved* "Dreams." I found it fascinating. I loved it. But, it was a little frustrating because I had written a script called "Radar's Dream." In it, you know how they would sometimes show Radar reading comics. Well I had Radar having a dream [where] he became a superhero…just like in his comics. I had Radar actually getting taller, having him walk on unseen 6-inch ramps that inclined on the floor. And, he ends the war, Gelbart loved it and wrote me a letter saying we'll do it. Someone put the kibosh on it. Well, I honestly think that they (some *M*A*S*H* people) honestly thought of me as this man/boy like Radar was. So I think that contributed to my not getting to direct or having a script produced. They always saw me come in as Radar. I had just come from doing *You're a Good Man, Charlie Brown* where I was playing a 5 year old. It was actually a step up to play Radar. I guess I didn't have that persona on the set that I could do it (write or direct). I think Gelbart knew. I look at that script of mine and think, 'this could have flown.' Funny thing is, I'd already had a lot more experience than some of the others on the set. But I just couldn't convince them I was not this man/boy. They let me blow my own bugle. I asked 'how does Reveille go?' So I did it. It sounded terrible but you could tell it was Reveille. The same thing happened in the episode that featured 'No talent night.' They actually hired musicians to play badly for us. Wayne and the rest of us went to them and said 'look, we're comedic actors…we know how to play badly.' And so, we did. We once read a script and kind of let out a collective 'sigh' because it just wasn't funny, or up to par. We saw Gelbart literally re-write the script, cover to cover, in 3 hours, that was an entirely new script. I do know of one instance where I told him he could tie two different happenings together beautifully. And he said 'you're right!" But he got distracted and never found the time for it. Once, we were receiving an award. I walked into the green room and Stiers said, 'Do you know who that is? It's Charles Kuralt.' So I went up to him and said, 'thank you for reinforcing validity for the average person.' The best part of the whole experience of the 2003 *M*A*S*H* reunion was that Allan Arbus approached me and said 'of all the people on the show, you made me feel most at home.' This is after 20 years. He was just so real in that role (as Sydney Freedman). But he knows nothing about psychiatry. When my oldest son, who was six, was sick at Christmas time, I think I had four bucks in my pocket when we were out. Well, I wanted to stop in a hardware store to buy a light bulb. Bear in mind that my son had heard people stop me countless times and thank me for hours of laughter. I had been admiring this etched glass of a hummingbird coming up to a morning glory, but only had those four bucks. On our way out, there was the storeowner with the etched glass piece and he wanted to give it to me for all the times I'd made him laugh. I said I couldn't, but my son said, 'take it dad, you deserve it.' About a week later, he finished his first book. And when the students finish a book, they get to pick something out of the treasure chest at school. Well, my son noticed a crystal goose in the treasure chest. When his mother arrived, she realized, unbeknownst to the teacher, that the crystal goose was worth about 200 bucks. So his mom approached the teacher and said, 'we can't take this.' The teacher pensively took it back because she felt he'd earned it. I called her and asked her if she would instead, trade some wildlife art for it. *'Oh yes,'* she said. Well, the note to my son that came with the goose said 'take it, you deserve it.'"

William Christopher

"There are some (*M*A*S*H* episodes) I like quite a bit. In the first year, I was not a regular and I would have liked to have been. I felt Mulcahy would be useful. I had been on Gomer Pyle, but wasn't a regular there either. Some roles in the first season were very small. "Dear Dad" was especially exciting because it showed they would use me more. I liked "The Interview," and there were some wonderful shows...especially in the early seasons. Henry's desk flying way up overhead...very funny to me. I haven't seen it (*M*A*S*H*) much for a long time. My wife and I don't watch a lot of television. I was working on a play in Halifax, Nova Scotia, and *M*A*S*H* was playing. My wife was flipping around the dial and I said, 'wait a minute' when she got to *M*A*S*H*. I couldn't remember how it all came out. The first time I came on the set to shoot, I was in the operating room. I had a mask on but no glasses. But the next time, I did wear glasses.

PHOTO COURTESY WILLIAM CHRISTOPHER

They dropped the nickname 'dago red' for Mulcahy, but might have called me 'red' once. They didn't want Mulcahy drinking, like in the movie. They called me and asked me to come in for a rehearsal, and the cast was tremendously friendly. They could have done 'some' more of the spiritual part of Mulcahy's work. I suggested that Mulcahy be attracted to a nurse and visa versa. But I envisioned it as much more challenging for Mulcahy than it turned out. That was ok, though, I guess they didn't want to put Mulcahy in a situation where he feels tempted. The one thing that I liked was that they let me play the piano (not that I play very well). It was from the first season, where I (Mulcahy) played a section from *Maple Leaf Rag*. I liked Ragtime. It came out of a conversation with the producers when they asked if I had any talents. They came up with the boxing thing. I had to practice and practice hitting a punching bag (the small kind). You know, there's a rhythm to it. One of the senior crewmembers took me aside to show me how to make a punching bag go. There was one scene where I was supposed to punch someone out. I think that was the year I got hepatitis. They had Loretta do it. I was in that episode where Klinger is pole sitting, but only because they had shot exteriors earlier. They were all likeable people. McLean was very unique. He had an improvisational ability that was fascinating. I was so surprised upon learning he wanted to leave, because he had writers writing for his unique abilities. I was sorry to see him go. Harry brought a different element because of his maturity. I always thought Wayne and Alan had a very good chemistry. I related to Mike very well. He and I had instant rapport and I liked doing scenes with him. Mike felt tremendous pressure. Womanizing was a theme in the early years, and we wanted to shift away from that if we were to keep going. Mike's character helped with that. Having Stiers come changed things quite a bit in that regard. Frank and Hot Lips had been an item. We didn't want to fall into the trap of feeling like we kept on seeing the same movie. New characters changed that. Gene Reynolds was a favorite director. He was a charming guy. Ronny Graham was another sort of far out character we used once. He was usually behind the scenes. I think that maybe because of Alan or the direction the show was taking, we didn't do as much sillier stuff. I would talk to Father Frank Toste about my character from time to time. Not being Catholic, I'd need his advice for Mulcahy. We had just finished shooting at the ranch, and thought we'd go to the Hollywood Parade. I don't remember if we stopped by Gary Burghoff's house or not, but we got to the parade, and somehow I got handed a small bottle of something…to kind of keep me warm. There I was, dressed as Father Mulcahy, tossing out slightly intoxicated blessings. One time, I was sitting opposite Gary Burghoff in the mess tent and Burt Metcalfe was directing. I wasn't aware of it, but I was getting hepatitis. Gary looked at me and said, 'you look terrible, your eyes are yellow.' Well, I had this difficult line and managed to get it out. Then Burt said, 'Do it again, but a little bit faster.' He had no idea how lucky he was just to get the *first* take. Well, I did it again, managed to get it and it was better. I went immediately to the doctor and he told me I had hepatitis. It was a Tuesday morning, I remember, and he told me to go straight home…but to *first* go vote. For the most part, *AfterM*A*S*H* is not worth talking about. I think there was one tragic flaw, it wasn't serious enough. But I was very pleased when I heard they were going to do it. The network wanted a zany comedy, and so the emphasis became trying to make it funny. I thought we should have done an hour show, like *St. Elsewhere*. A lot of veterans came back with problems, but we were doing wheelchair races in the hospital. Larry Gelbart wrote the show that paralleled the Agent Orange problem in Vietnam. The hospital was sort of a joke hospital, not a real one. The pilot did very well in the ratings. The idea that Mulcahy had a drinking problem just didn't seem to work. One of the first things we did was get rid of his hearing and drinking problems. That first season's ratings were very respectable. I think some episodes never even aired. I found it a fascinating challenge to portray the clergy and make Mulcahy as real as possible. The one thing I wanted to make clear was that Mulcahy's faith was tremendously important to him. I was very aware that Mulcahy's presence was useful. I've often said I think I have the distinction of playing a priest longer than anyone on prime time TV. I've received a lot of positive mail from the clergy, and that makes me feel good. And I did save my wardrobe…you know, the hat, glasses, collar, fatigues…"

PHOTO COURTESY MIKE FARRELL

Mike Farrell

"I don't watch television at all if I can help it. If I'm going by the set and the show is on, though, I'll always stop and watch for a while, enjoying the memories. When I do, I'm always touched by seeing my friends and by seeing the quality of the work that was done. Though there were certainly some episodes that missed the high level we were shooting for, the attempt was always there and, when I watch it, it never fails to tug at my heart and always makes me proud. The only suggestion I ever recall making was near the end of my first season when BJ and Hawkeye had a scene about an affair Hawkeye was having with an old flame (played beautifully by Blythe Danner). In it, Hawkeye asked BJ if he disapproved. BJ's response was something like, 'It's not my place to disapprove.' The discussion went on and Hawkeye asked if BJ had ever been unfaithful, to which BJ replied, 'Never.' Hawkeye's next question was, 'Ever been tempted?' BJ's response was, 'Tempted's a different story,' to which Hawkeye rejoined, 'Aha, so you have been tempted.' BJ then said, 'No, I just said it's a different story.' The scene played well and we finished it. Afterward I said to Larry Gelbart or Gene Reynolds something to the effect that I loved playing a guy who was faithful to his wife, but I think it's a mistake to suggest that he's never tempted to stray. What's the meaning of fidelity if there's no temptation? That really wasn't meant as a 'suggestion,' but I thought it was an important point to make about the character. As a result, in the next season, Gene came to me and recalled the conversation and asked how I'd feel if BJ 'fell off the fidelity wagon.' I said it depended on how it was handled. And they handled it well. I suggested the story that became the episode "Yalu Brick Road." I also suggested a story based on 'The Tortoise and the Hare' that had Father Mulcahy run a long-distance race against an athlete from another unit. Alan and I got into a long discussion about the morality of doing a surgery on a hot-shot line officer to get him out of commission and save some young men from being sent into unnecessarily dangerous combat situations. It resulted in changing a story they had already written. I also suggested the story that had Susan St. James come in to play Aggie O'Shea, the combat photographer who fell for BJ — and vice versa. It's hard to direct and act at the same time. In the best of circumstances I think one should do one or the other, but getting the opportunity on *M*A*S*H* was a chance to learn by doing. As far as my 'style' is concerned, it was something like, 'What the hell do I do now?' I don't remember having a bad director, but one has favorites, of course. Gene is one of the best directors in the business. He's smart, very well prepared and very supportive. Alan is terrifically smart and always searching for a way to do something different. Burt was great, Harry was terrific. A director we got to work with a lot who I just loved is Charlie Dubin. A great man and a wonderful talent. I felt cheated when Larry (Gelbart) left because I had only had the pleasure of working with him for one season. He is a genius and his contribution to the show can't be overstated. Gene embodied the spirit of the show in a way no one else did and his decision to leave was very hard to take. Both were great losses, personally and professionally. It felt like losing a limb. I loved watching Gary create Radar with such innocence; I loved watching Jamie work his magic; I loved everything Harry did; I marveled at Loretta; I adored Alan, was charmed by Bill and was astonished by Larry Linville's ability to make Frank real. But the one who could put me away was David Ogden Stiers. I was thrilled to work with all the guest stars. But, I will confess to a bit of a crush on Susan St. James. I loved doing the Radar Goes Home episode where BJ is broken up by the news that his daughter Erin, seeing Radar in a uniform, called him Daddy. Tore me up. Many episodes moved me greatly, but I think my all-time favorite remains the original black and white documentary — style episode called "The Interview." In a situation like that (such as in "Welcome to Korea, Part 2," where Hawkeye and BJ are seen walking and talking on their way to the shower, but you can't hear what they say) there would be no script, so we could talk about anything we chose. It might have been anything at all, but we'd have made sure that whatever it was would convey the proper qualities to work for the shot. Suffice it to say that those eight years were the finest professional experience I could ever hope for and one of my most important personal experiences as well. Thanks."

Jamie Farr

"We had so many wonderful episodes…and in them, wonderful scenes. Memorable scenes…dramatic and comedic. Some say 'Sometimes You Hear the Bullet,' a great show which began to take the series in another direction, is their favorite. Some say "The Interview" with Clete Roberts, is their favorite. I will not commit to either of those. Too many fine moments. I still watch the show and enjoy it. Actually I enjoy it more now than when I first viewed them. The distance has made my heart grow fonder. I marvel at the quality of the series in every aspect. A few times I have even laughed at something I did. As an actor…a critical one, looking back I wished I had made another choice in my delivery in a particular scene. Other times, I surprised myself and made the right one. Overall I was satisfied. As for the rest of the cast…they were always superb. I enjoyed working with Hy Averback. He was so easygoing and never surly or discontent. He had a wonderful sense of humor. I used to call him Mr. Fellini. Charles Dubin was another director who was easy going but always got you to do your best work. All of our guests were terrific to work with. They were so pleased to be a part of our show. We had a great reputation for work ethics and our show was highly thought of in the business. Many actors and actresses wanted to be on the series. It was all very comfortable. And creative.

It was different working with each cast change. Each change was different, but all classic. Different styles, different approaches, different timing…but when you looked at their work…always wonderful. It was different, but the same, when it came to quality. Gary Burghoff is extremely talented in so many fields."

The Camp

The famous mountains in the opening scene of M*A*S*H *(without the choppers).*

After watching *M*A*S*H* for any length of time, one character emerges as an integral, familiar and distinctive part of the show. This character provides the back-drop for all the goings-on, and is not a living person, but is the very camp itself.

There were actually two *M*A*S*H* 4077ths. One was in Stage 9, at 20th Century-Fox Studios, and the other was at the Fox Ranch at Malibu Creek State Park. Much of the set at the Fox Ranch was left standing after the original *M*A*S*H* movie. For television, the hospital building remained largely the same, but the tents were modified. The set up of the hospital building and tents was replicated inside stage 9 for *M*A*S*H*, the series. As Gene Reynolds lamented at the time, he wished he could have been around for the assignment of a sound stage, since Stage 9 was the smallest on the lot. Therefore, the stage 9 *M*A*S*H* 4077th was much smaller than the Fox Ranch 4077th.

Most interior scenes were filmed at Stage 9, but a painted landscape allowed them to film scenes in the compound…making it appear to be outdoors. As the lighting, backdrop and proximity of the tents to each other are quite different at the stage 9 compound versus the Fox Ranch compound, it becomes easy to detect at which location a scene was filmed, after a while. Additionally, there was a bit of an echo on Stage 9, and a slippery floor, as opposed to the outdoor dusty ground of the Fox Ranch.

Interiors of the Swamp were filmed at Stage 9, with the exception of a scene in such episodes as "Dear Dad, Again." Similarly, interiors of the mess tent were also filmed at stage 9, with the brief exception in "Henry, Please Come Home," "Springtime" and "Guerilla My Dreams." Conditions and varying extremes of temperature at the Fox Ranch location were so harsh, they were apparently one of the many contributing factors for McLean Stevenson's departure from the series.

In 1982, the outdoor set in Malibu was completely destroyed by wild fires. This disaster was incorporated into the final movie. The set had to be rebuilt to complete filming. Some of the best views of the 4077th can be seen in long shots from episodes like "Henry, Please Come Home," "Bombed," and an aerial view from a soldier's perspective in "Point of View."

One of the biggest reasons *M*A*S*H* was not filmed entirely outdoors was logistics. Malibu Creek State Park, a.k.a., "The Ranch," was not close by. A number of buses had to be loaded with equipment and crew and was a costly proposition. But once there, as many scenes would be filmed as daylight permitted.

Notes on the Episode Guide

Two of the most widely discussed topics are the inconsistencies in storylines and all things anachronistic in the *M*A*S*H* timeline. We have gone to great lengths to bring these to the forefront and it should not be taken as disparagement or criticism, but rather, the ultimate compliment in a quest for more information. The army of devoted *M*A*S*H* fans can recite passages from memory; they know which episode they're watching moments after the opening theme concludes; they can narrow the season by the cast listed in the opening credits, and they know exactly what's going to happen as the episode unfolds. Some of what's left to be discovered is inconsistencies, events going on in the background, and the many "bumps" in the timeline, as it relates to the Korean War's timeframe.

This has been a tedious, time-consuming and sometimes physically painful experience, but has also been rich in history through research. We not only learned about popular movies and music of the time, who the big movie stars were, who the popular singers and songwriters were, but we also learned about political and military figures, and even learned about some of the products that are still in use and sold in stores today.

Are we nitpicking with some of this? Perhaps just a bit. But nevertheless, if we found something out of time or in error, we noted it.

When *M*A*S*H* aired in 1972, consumer VCRs were years away, longer still for DVD's. Much of what was found has taken over 30 years to uncover. Putting together all the information contained here was a daunting task for a television show that ran for eleven years. Countless hours were spent on research checking and re-checking information in an effort to be as accurate as possible. It's been a long and mind-numbing process, but it's also been fun and we hope you'll agree.

If you find any mistakes, please contact the publisher.

Season 1

While it often takes a TV series several episodes, if not a whole season, to settle in on their stride, *M*A*S*H* was *M*A*S*H* from the opening scene in the Pilot episode. Indeed, it did take a good part of the first season before the producers, writers and actors discovered the ideal rhythm and method by which to tell the stories of the men and women of the 4077th. And, it was almost mid-season before a given episode featured more than one plot. In "Dear Dad," written by Larry Gelbart, Hawkeye describes life at the 4077th at Christmastime in a letter to his dad. Unlike previous episodes of *M*A*S*H*, "Dear Dad" intertwined several plots into one episode. This was unheard of in television comedy, up to that point. This way of storytelling conveyed a sense of realism, and set the standard for future episodes of *M*A*S*H*. Before "Dear Dad," it was Gelbart's wife, Pat Marshall (who will appear in Season 3's "Pay Day") who made the comment to him that a given episode of *M*A*S*H* featured one plot, as though nothing else was going on in camp. Still, there is a certain raw, unpretentious feel and freshness to the early Season 1 episodes of *M*A*S*H*. The comedy was cool and hip, and the backdrop of the war and drama was mixed in, flawlessly. Semi-regulars, subsequently dropped as *M*A*S*H* streamlined (for multiple reasons), added to the sense of this being a real live military base. Corporal Klinger was introduced, various styles of background music were used and classic episodes were born. Among the stellar episodes of season one are "Tuttle," "Dear Dad" and "Sometimes You Hear The Bullet." One of the more noteworthy things about Season One was how the actors seemed to have perfected their characters right from the first moment. This is a credit to the actors, but maybe even more importantly, Larry Gelbart. Season 1 is a delight, and in a *M*A*S*H* category all its own.

The Pilot – 9/17/1972

Season 1 / Episode 1 / Production 1 – Z9522

Columbia House VHS Tape . . . . Welcome To M*A*S*H (Catalog # 3569)
Fox DVD . . . . Season 1, Disc 1

Alan Alda, Wayne Rogers, McLean Stevenson,
Loretta Swit, Larry Linville, Gary Burghoff
(This main cast will remain in place for the first three seasons.)

Written and Developed for Television by Larry Gelbart
Produced and Directed by Gene Reynolds

G. (George) Wood . . . . General Hamilton Hammond
Patrick Adiarte . . . . Ho Jon
Karen Philipp . . . . Lieutenant Dish
George Morgan . . . . Father John P. Mulcahy
Timothy Brown . . . . Spearchucker Jones
Odessa Cleveland . . . . Lieutenant Ginger Bayliss
John Orchard . . . . Ugly John
Linda Meiklejohn . . . . Lieutenant Leslie Scorch
Laura Miller . . . . Knocko
B. Kirby Jr. . . . . Boone
Copyright 1972 – 20th Century Fox Film Corporation

Chapters

1: Korea, 1950 / Main Titles   6: Where's Frank? – 15:41
2: Conduct Unbecoming – 2:38   7: The Raffle – 18:43
3: Ho Jon's Big Chance – 6:08   8: Under Arrest – 20:28
4: Asking for Favors – 8:50   9: Screw-ups In Reverse – 22:38
5: Problems with Frank – 11:21   10: Cast / End Titles – 24:21

Closing Stills

1: Chopper lands on pad
2: Nurses running
3: Jeep carrying wounded from chopper pad
4: O.R.
5: Raffle in Mess Tent

Synopsis: Hawkeye gets word that Ho Jon has been accepted to his college in the States, but needs close to $2,000 to get him there. To come up with the money, Hawkeye holds a raffle where the winner will receive a weekend pass for two in Tokyo, and will be accompanied by a "gorgeous" nurse, but the winner, unfortunately, cannot enjoy the full extent of the grand prize.

Commentary by Larry Gelbart: "Gene Reynolds and Hy Averback were my two favorite directors to work with.

"I wrote the line to indicate how long ago the Korean War seemed in the minds of the American public (on the words seen at the beginning of the show; "Korea — A Hundred Years Ago"). We felt we were carrying on where the film left off, with Hawkeye already very much a part of the 4077th. Trapper John just seemed more colorful than Duke and so we decided to drop the latter and keep the former. While Altman got zilch, Hooker received $500 for each new episode and nothing for reruns. As matters turned out, Hooker's money was pretty much zilch, too. A few of the movie cast was asked to appear in the series. All but Gary Burghoff, of course, turned the idea down. We tried to call the Father Mulcahy character 'Dago Red' in the pilot episode and the CBS censor removed it with the Jaws of Life.

"We were so aware of certain standards even though we didn't have 4 or 5 scripts in the bank. Despite that fact, if we didn't like a finished script after we read it around the table, and this actually did happen once, we threw it out. Came up with another one very fast. You can never get ahead. Never, ever get ahead. At least, it seemed we never could.

The entire budget for *M*A*S*H*, and it wasn't a lot of money then, I mean, it seemed like a lot of money, but it was $225,000 for a whole episode, for my first four years — maybe with minimal raises."

PA Announcements By Jimmy Lydon

Authors' Notes: Filming for the Pilot episode began in December 1971 and as *M*A*S*H* went to air in September 1972, not all 24 episodes were finished.

No laugh track was used, generally, in operating room scenes during the show's 11-year run. This was at the insistence of the producers, however, there are exceptions to this, albeit rare.

Hawkeye has parents. (This will become significant later in the series.)

There are several "only time seen" instances in this episode:

1: *An opening scene before the theme music begins*
2: *An extended opening and hearing Hawkeye during triage at the chopper*
3: *George Morgan as Father Mulcahy (the producers wanted someone a bit more, "quirkier")*
4: *Trapper in a red MD robe*
5: *Trapper's hair parted on the side*
6: *The still in the Swamp with that type of construction*
7: *The camp library*
8: *Margaret in a hospital-white nurse's uniform at Fort Benning*

To Market, To Market – 9/24/1972
Season 1 / Episode 2 / Production 3 – J303
Columbia House VHS Tape . . . . *Bending the Rules (Catalog # 3740)*
Fox DVD . . . . *Season 1, Disc 1*

Alan Alda, Wayne Rogers, McLean Stevenson,
Loretta Swit, Larry Linville, Gary Burghoff

Produced by Gene Reynolds
Executive Script Consultant: Larry Gelbart
Written by Burt Styler
Directed by Michael O'Herlihy

Jack Soo . . . . Charlie Lee
Robert Ito . . . . Lin
G. Wood . . . . General Hamilton Hammond
Odessa Cleveland . . . . Lieutenant Ginger Bayliss
John C. Johnson . . . . .Truck Driver
Copyright 1972 – 20th Century Fox Film Corporation

Chapters

1: *Main Titles*	6: *The Desknappers – 15:12*
2: *Black Market Blues – 0:50*	7: *Locked In – 17:49*
3: *Charlie Lee – 6:38*	8: *The Disappearing Desk – 19:09*
4: *A Deal for A Desk – 10:15*	9: *The Payoff – 24:01*
5: *"General" Lee – 11:22*	10: *End Titles – 25:01*

Closing Stills
1: *Hawkeye & Trapper massage Charlie Lee's back*
2: *"General" Lee in Henry's office having a drink*
3: *Hawkeye & Trapper pray over covered desk*
4: *Hawkeye, Henry, Trapper & Frank looking up at desk*

Synopsis: In the middle of an operation, Ginger informs Hawkeye that they're out of hydrocortisone, and then the doctors discover the supply truck with hydrocortisone has been robbed. When General Hammond refuses to send more, Hawkeye and Trapper are left with one option: The Black Market, only to find out that the medicine will cost them $10,000. Not having that kind of money, they make a deal with Charlie Lee by offering Henry's 100-year-old antique desk in trade.

Commentary by Burt Styler: "I was a freelance writer, sort of a hired gun. In the early days of the show my agent set me up with a meeting with a one-script commitment, as I remember it. I went in, viewed Larry Gelbart's Pilot, and had a meeting with either Gene Reynolds or Larry Gelbart, or both. I told them a couple of thoughts for shows, among them was the concept of dealing in the black market for medicine. They liked that one, said 'go' and I went. I not only had Jack Soo in mind when I wrote the character of the black marketeer, I suggested him to Gene and Larry. As I recall it, they weren't too familiar with his work. I was happy they hired him. The staff, at that time, consisted of Larry Gelbart. I might mention that, in those days...unlike today, shows did not have a platoon of writers. Most had one producer (often the writer-creator of the show) and he or she was the only person you dealt with. Sure, I'd watch the episodes I wrote, and a select few others that I enjoyed. The first time you view one of your own shows, you're overly conscious of every brilliant touch you put in that the director screwed up. If you see it again, after the passage of a little time, it's not so bad. By the third time around, you forget who wrote it, and possibly even enjoy what you're seeing. The people on the show I dealt with were, of course, Larry and Gene...mostly Larry. The recollection I have of him that stands out is what a decent guy and respectful editor he was. He actually went to the trouble of sending me a note, explaining why he was forced to change a few lines or a bit of action for pragmatic reasons, having to do with the budget...making sure I understood it was not some arbitrary whim. I think the letter was longer than the changes. Actually, I was invited to write more M*A*S*H scripts but luckily at that time, I was on a bit of a roll and had a number of other assignments, including pilots. So, though I enjoyed doing the show, I just didn't have the time."

Authors' Notes: There are no PA announcements in this episode.

This is the first of two appearances by Jack Soo, who went on to co-star on *Barney Miller*.

Robert Ito went on to co-star in *Quincy, M.E.*

In the mess tent, Radar calls the bar where Charlie Lee's office is "Madam Koo," but the sign on the bar says "Mama Koo."

The desk in Henry's office is not the same desk Hawkeye and Trapper are seen carrying.

Hawkeye and Trapper are locked in Henry's office and had to cut the back wall down to get out with the desk, but when Henry runs into his office with Frank, the doors are not locked.

This is the only time the C.O.'s office was used and seen for filming at the Fox Ranch set, as Henry's wall was removed and it's clear that they are not on Stage 9.

Requiem for A Lightweight – 10/1/1972

Season 1 / Episode 3 / Production 8 – J308

Columbia House VHS Tape . . . . *The World's A Stage (Catalog # 21039)*
Fox DVD . . . . *Season 1, Disc 1*

Alan Alda, Wayne Rogers, McLean Stevenson,
Loretta Swit, Larry Linville, Gary Burghoff

Produced by Gene Reynolds
Executive Script Consultant: Larry Gelbart
Written by Robert Klane
Directed by Hy Averback

Sorrell Booke. . . . . General Barker
John Orchard. . . . . Ugly John
Marcia Strassman . . . . Lieutenant Margie Cutler
Odessa Cleveland . . . . Lieutenant Ginger Bayliss
William Christopher . . . . Father Mulcahy *(First appearance as Father Mulcahy)*
Copyright 1972 – 20th Century Fox Film Corporation

Non-Credited Appearances. . . . . Dennis Troy, Ralph Grosh, Robert Gruber

Chapters

1: Main Titles	6: The General's Fighter – 13:56
2: The Semi-Nude Nurse – 0:49	7: The Ethereal Approach – 16:02
3: Transferred – 5:25	8: The Big Fight – 18:28
4: Henry's Deal – 6:19	9: A No-Punch Knockout – 22:53
5: Trapper in Training – 11:20	10: End Titles – 25:00

Closing Stills

1: Hawkeye & Trapper in Cutler's tent
2: Trapper runs behind jeep
3: Fighters touch gloves in the ring
4: Trapper knocked down and dazed in the ring

Synopsis: When Hawkeye and Trapper become enamored with a pretty, new nurse, Margaret immediately finds her a distraction and has her transferred. The doctors argue that Lieutenant Margie Cutler has OR skills that are hard to come by, but the only way Henry will overturn Margaret's decision is if one of them takes part in an inter-camp boxing tournament. Hawkeye talks a reluctant Trapper into it, only to find his opponent is much larger and outweighs Trapper by nearly 100 pounds, but Hawkeye, with help from Ugly John, puts a plan into effect to insure Trapper's victory.

Commentary by Larry Gelbart: "The cast never saw any of the scripts until we sat down at the table to read them. There were no black surgeons attached to MASH units in Korea. Ugly John was cast as an Australian in the movie to emphasize the fact that the armed forces in Korea were UN backed."

PA Announcement by Jimmy Lydon

Authors' Notes: The DVD credits Klinger as making the PA announcement. This is incorrect. One reason is Klinger hasn't appeared in the show yet.
　　The use of slow motion photography is used for one of four times on *M*A*S*H*, as Trapper's boxing opponent falls out of the ring. Slow motion was again in "The Trial of

Henry Blake" (it's not supposed to be slow motion, but Klinger's body, while hang gliding, is clearly moving in slow motion), "Follies of the Living/Concerns of the Dead" (as the ghost of a soldier walks through camp), and in "Sons and Bowlers" (when Margaret bowls).

At the show's end (the tag), Trapper says, "I should hope so," in response to Nurse Cutler's comment. We see his face when he says it, but his lips don't move.

This episode marks the debut of William Christopher as Father Mulcahy.

Sorrell Booke, who went on to star as Boss Hogg in *The Dukes of Hazzard* will appear in the next *M*A*S*H* episode, also as General Barker.

Marcia Strassman (Lieutenant Margie Cutler) went on to costar in *Welcome Back Kotter* as Gabe's wife.

The first of Frank's three names appears in this episode, "Maj. Frank W. Burns" and his serial number is RA98672412.

Radar has a cigar in his mouth and also has a Martini in the Swamp (this will become significant later in the series).

Chief Surgeon, Who? – 10/8/1972

Season 1 / Episode 4 / Production 7 – J307

Columbia House VHS Tape . . . . *Hawkeye vs Frank (Catalog # 3771)*
Fox DVD . . . . *Season 1, Disc 1*

Alan Alda, Wayne Rogers, McLean Stevenson,
Loretta Swit, Larry Linville, Gary Burghoff

Produced by Gene Reynolds
Written by Larry Gelbart
Directed by E.W. Swackhamer

Sorrell Booke . . . . General Barker
Timothy Brown . . . . Spearchucker Jones
John Orchard . . . . Ugly John
Jamie Farr . . . . Corporal Klinger *(First Appearance)*
Jack Riley . . . . Captain Kaplan
Linda Meiklejohn . . . . Lieutenant Leslie Scorch
Bob Gooden . . . . Boone
Odessa Cleveland . . . . Lieutenant Ginger Bayless

Copyright 1972 – 20th Century Fox Film Corporation

Non-Credited Appearances . . . . Gwen Farrell, Marcia Gelman

Chapters

1: Main Titles
2: Frank's Form Letters – 0:50
3: Pressing Charges – 3:31
4: The New Chief Surgeon – 6:59
5: Hail to the Chief – 9:32

6: Deep Trouble – 13:54
7: Everybody's Crazy – 17:47
8: Hawkeye in Action – 20:54
9: The Better Surgeon – 24:23
10: End Titles – 25:01

Closing Stills

1: Barker stares at Hawkeye – Deep Trouble
2: Hawkeye – cowboy hat in Mess Tent
3: General Barker arrives
4: Trapper, Hawkeye, Barker, Henry – Klinger naked

Synopsis: When Frank charges Hawkeye with insubordination and lack of military courtesy, he's also upset that, in the operating room, Hawkeye answers everyone's questions and "calls all the shots." But when Henry appoints Hawkeye as the new Chief Surgeon, citing his medical abilities and his certification as a "chest cutter" and general surgery, Frank becomes incensed. Margaret then contacts General Barker, urging him to come to the 4077th. Hawkeye, indifferent to Barker, impresses him during an operation and the General winds up apologizing to Hawkeye, the new Chief Surgeon.

Commentary by Larry Gelbart: "I think the minimal music usage was deft and appropriate. In the first three or five episodes, which have quite a bit of scoring to them, I find it jarring. Klinger was named after a boyhood friend of mine in Chicago, Marvin Klinger, whose parents were Hungarian. Klinger got to be more and more Lebanese (and a native of Toledo) because he was played by a Lebanese from Toledo."

"It was never, never, never intended for Klinger to be played in an effete manner. It was misdirected in that fashion, much to my disappointment, and Gene's. Gene reshot the character's introductory scene without a hint of femininity."

Authors' Notes: According to Gelbart, calling someone "dad" (as Hawkeye referred to General Barker during surgery) was a common slang word of the period. Gelbart used to use it a lot in scripts when he worked for Bob Hope.

Though Klinger is supposed to be naked at episode's end, if you look carefully you can see he has something on below his waist.

There is no dartboard in the Swamp in Chapter 6, but it's there in Chapter 8.

The sinks in the scrub room, in this episode, are in the middle of the room, side by side. This will change from episode to episode. Sometimes they're against the wall.

Jack Riley, who played Captain Kaplan playing poker in the Swamp, later appeared in 29 episodes of *The Bob Newhart Show* as Elliot Carlin.

The Moose – 10/15/1972

Season 1 / Episode 5 / Production 5 – J305

Columbia House VHS Tape. . . . . *Card Tricks (Catalog # 3748)*
Fox DVD . . . . *Season 1, Disc 1*

Alan Alda, Wayne Rogers, McLean Stevenson,
Loretta Swit, Larry Linville, Gary Burghoff

Produced by Gene Reynolds
Executive Script Consultant: Larry Gelbart
Written by Laurence Marks
Directed by Hy Averback

Paul Jenkins. . . . . Sergeant Baker
Virginia Lee. . . . . Young Hi
Timothy Brown. . . . . Spearchucker Jones
Patrick Adiarte . . . . Ho Jon
John Orchard. . . . . Ugly John
Craig Jue . . . . Benny
Linda Meiklejohn . . . . Lieutenant Leslie Scorch
Barbara Brownell. . . . . Lieutenant Jones

Copyright 1972 – 20th Century Fox Film Corporation

Non-Credited Appearances. . . . . .George Simmons, Marcia Gelman

Chapters

1: Main Titles	6: A New Home – 13:40
2: Young Hi – 0:49	7: Trouble – 16:55
3: The Sergeant's Moose – 2:48	8: Young Hi's Brother – 21:11
4: The Captain's Lecture – 6:20	9: A Letter – 24:13
5: Gambling for Moose – 8:33	10: End Titles – 24:58

Closing Stills

1: Sergeant Jenkins and Young Hi
2: Henry and Hawkeye in Henry's tent
3: Young Hi leaves on truck – Hawkeye waving
4: Young Hi touching Spearchucker's face

Synopsis: When Sergeant Baker arrives at the 4077 looking for Henry, he has with him a young Korean girl carrying all his gear, then orders her to find quarters, schedule a shower, polish his boots and arrange for food. Radar informs the doctors that she's called a moose, and was bought from her family for $500, infuriating Hawkeye, Trapper and Spearchucker. Hawkeye orders the sergeant to release the young woman, and when he refuses, Hawkeye arranges for a friendly poker game in which he's guaranteed to win Young Hi's freedom without dishonoring her family.

Commentary by Larry Gelbart: "If I found my voice in Hawkeye, it also found expression through the other characters as well (even the unpleasant ones) A simple rule of thumb: any episode in the first seasons (With the exception of the one-man Hawkeye show) that does not contain a major character, means we chose not to use that character and, contractually, that was okay."

Authors' Notes: There are no PA announcements in this episode.

Radar, while in the shower spying, watches a nurse enter a different shower. There are two showers in this episode.

Radar has a Martini in this episode (this will become significant later in the series).

In Chapter 6, the Swamp on the Ranch set has the dartboard. Later in Chapter 6, the Swamp is on Stage 9 and there is no dartboard.

Hawkeye claims his father always wished he had a sister, but earlier in this episode, he makes a reference to his sister.

This is the only episode where Trapper wears a blue terrycloth bathrobe.

Johnny Mandel's name is misspelled in the closing credits: *M-a-n-d-e-l-l* (with two l's)

Yankee Doodle Doctor – 10/22/1972

Season 1 / Episode 6 / Production 10 – J310

Columbia House VHS Tape . . . . *The World's A Stage (Catalog # 21039)*
Fox DVD . . . . *Season 1, Disc 1*

Alan Alda, Wayne Rogers, McLean Stevenson,
Loretta Swit, Larry Linville, Gary Burghoff

Produced by Gene Reynolds
Executive Script Consultant: Larry Gelbart
Written by Laurence Marks
Directed by Lee Philips

Herb Voland . . . . General Crandall Clayton
Ed Flanders . . . . Lieutenant Duane William Bricker
Marcia Strassman . . . . Lieutenant Margie Cutler
Bert Kramer . . . . Sergeant Martin
Tom Sparks . . . . Corpsman

Copyright 1972 – 20th Century Fox Film Corporation

Non-Credited Appearances . . . . Gwen Farrell, Dennis Troy

Chapters

1: Main Titles	6: Negotiation – 14:05
2: A Documentary – 0:49	7: A New Shoot – 15:39
3: A Star – 2:54	8: The Screening – 16:34
4: Fixing the Movie – 8:29	9: The Yankee Doodle Doctor – 24:00
5: Accused – 12:06	10: End Titles – 24:57

Closing Stills

1: Lieutenant Bricker shooting his movie
2: Hawkeye, Henry, Trapper and Bricker in the Swamp
3: Trapper, Radar and Hawkeye Class A's & shorts
4: Hawkeye, Radar, Trapper – Groucho & Harpo

Synopsis: Hawkeye, less than impressed that Special Services wants to make a documentary on a M*A*S*H unit, gives in and accepts the lead role to prevent Frank from getting it. Not satisfied with the final product, Hawkeye and Trapper destroy the film and Lieutenant Bricker, the director, gives up and leaves. Since Bricker left his gear and film crew behind, Hawkeye decides to make his own documentary, just a little different than what was originally planned.

Commentary by Larry Gelbart: "The cast couldn't wait to get to work during my time with them. There was no nonsense about anyone wanting to work that same way Sinatra did, or Alda sulking in his dressing room, or any other bad behavior. Groucho Marx was and continues to be my chief influence. Passing his style on to Hawkeye was inevitable. I may have mentioned it before, but he (Groucho) loved the series."

PA Announcements by Sal Viscuso

Authors' Notes: Hawkeye impersonates James Cagney saying, "You dirty rat," but Cagney never said this on screen.

Ed Flanders went on to co-star in *St. Elsewhere* as Dr. Donald Westphall. Sadly, Mr. Flanders, suffering from depression, took his own life by a self-inflicted gunshot wound on February 22, 1995. He was 60.

Herb Voland makes his first appearance as General Crandall Clayton, and will return in that role in "Tuttle" and "Ceasefire" in Season 1.

Bananas, Crackers and Nuts – 11/5/1972

Season 1 / Episode 7 / Production 11 – J311

Columbia House VHS Tape . . . . *Cracking Up (Catalog # 3745)*
Fox DVD . . . . *Season 1, Disc 1*

Alan Alda, Wayne Rogers, McLean Stevenson,
Loretta Swit, Larry Linville, Gary Burghoff

Produced by Gene Reynolds
Executive Script Consultant: Larry Gelbart
Written by Burt Styler
Directed by Bruce Bilson

Stuart Margolin. . . . . Captain Philip G. Sherman
Marcia Strassman . . . . Lieutenant Margie Cutler
Odessa Cleveland . . . . Lieutenant Ginger Bayless

Copyright 1972 – 20th Century Fox Film Corporation

Non-Credited Appearances. . . . . Dennis Troy, Marcia Gelman

Chapters

1: Main Titles	6: Psych. Exam – 10:49
2: Fatigued Doctors – 1:09	7: Meeting with Captain Sherman – 15:31
3: The Well Ran Dry – 3:10	8: Tests – 17:42
4: R & R – 4:28	9: Thwarted Again – 24:09
5: Hawkeye Cracks – 5:20	10: End Titles – 25:01

Closing Stills

1: Captain Sherman and Hawkeye
2: Hawkeye in surgical dress and liver in Mess Tent
3: Trapper, Hawkeye and Frank in Swamp
4: Capt. Sherman caught with Margaret

Synopsis: Before Henry leaves to play golf, he denies Hawkeye and Trapper's request for time in Tokyo, leaving the doctors angry and Frank as Acting Commanding Officer. Hawkeye, not one to easily give up, shows up for dinner in the Mess Tent in full surgical dress, including mask, gloves and carrying his own dinner: liver from a North Korean who was, "very clean." But when Frank touches the plate, Hawkeye becomes enraged that Frank ruined his meal and Trapper has Radar bring him back to the Swamp, then talks Frank into letting him take Hawkeye to Tokyo. But Frank later has second thoughts and orders Hawkeye to make himself available for a psychiatric exam.

Commentary by Burt Metcalfe: "I'd always liked Stuart Margolin. I'd first cast him when I first got into casting."

PA Announcement by Sal Viscuso

Authors' Notes: This is the first of two appearances by Stuart Margolin. He'll return in a Season 2 episode, "Operation Noselift" as Major Stanley 'Stosh' Robbins, plastic surgeon. Mr. Margolin went on to win an Emmy Award for his portrayal of Angel Martin in *The Rockford Files.*

Cowboy – 11/12/1972

Season 1 / Episode 8 / Production 9 – J309

Columbia House VHS Tape . . . . *Not A Pretty Sight (Catalog # 21036)*
Fox DVD . . . . *Season 1, Disc 1*

Alan Alda, Wayne Rogers, McLean Stevenson,
Loretta Swit, Larry Linville, Gary Burghoff

Produced by Gene Reynolds
Executive Script Consultant: Larry Gelbart
Written by Robert Klane
Directed by Don Weis

Billy Green Bush . . . . Cowboy John Hodges
William Christopher . . . . Father Mulcahy
John Orchard . . . . Ugly John
Patrick Adiarte . . . . Ho Jon
Joseph Corey . . . . Goldstein
Mike Robello . . . . The Cook
Jean Powell . . . . Lieutenant (Nurse) Baker

Copyright 1972 – 20th Century Fox Film Corporation

Non-Credited Appearances . . . . Dennis Troy, Marcia Gelman, Ralph Grosh

Chapters

1: *Main Titles*
2: *The Cowboy – 1:04*
3: *On the Links – 7:40*
4: *Jeep Attack – 10:13*
5: *Boom! – 13:04*

6: *The Marked Man – 16:22*
7: *The Cowboy's Obsession – 20:20*
8: *A Dear John Letter – 21:36*
9: *Happy Ending – 24:14*
10: *End Titles – 25:00*

Closing Stills

1: *Cowboy in post-op*
2: *Henry with toilet seat around neck ("Boom.")*
3: *Trapper on radio to Cowboy w/ Radar and Hawkeye*
4: *Trapper laughs – Henry splashes drink on himself*

Synopsis: The Cowboy, a chopper pilot flying wounded to the 4077 is wounded himself, but is more concerned that his wife hasn't written him. Hawkeye tries to get him sent home, but Henry doesn't think his wound is too serious and denies the request. After someone shoots Henry's golf ball and a driverless jeep suddenly runs through Henry's tent as he goes to sleep, the latrine explodes with Henry inside. Hawkeye discovers that the Cowboy is also an explosives expert who is up in his chopper with Henry, and Henry does not have a parachute.

Commentary by Larry Gelbart: "The cast also acted as script police, never failing to tell those guest actors who were inclined to insert a word of their own here and there just where they could insert those words."

PA Announcement by Sal Viscuso

Authors' Notes: The clip of Cowboy landing the chopper, plus the clip of Radar riding on the running board of the ambulance will appear in other episodes. A closer look will reveal Cowboy's hat.
This is the only time we see the M*A*S*H Country Club & Golf Links.

Henry, Please Come Home – 11/19/1972

Season 1 / Episode 9 / Production 2 – J302

Columbia House VHS Tape . . . . *Frank's In Charge (Catalog # 3744)*
Fox DVD . . . . *Season 1, Disc 2*

Alan Alda, Wayne Rogers, McLean Stevenson,
Loretta Swit, Larry Linville, Gary Burghoff

Produced by Gene Reynolds
Executive Script Consultant: Larry Gelbart
Written by Laurence Marks
Directed by William Wiard

Timothy Brown . . . . Spearchucker Jones
Patrick Adiarte . . . . Ho Jon
John Orchard . . . . Ugly John
G. (George) Wood . . . . General Hammond
Willaim Christopher . . . . Father Mulcahy
Bob Gooden . . . . Boone
Linda Meiklejohn . . . . Lieutenant Leslie Scorch
Odessa Cleveland . . . . Lieutenant Ginger Bayliss
Bill Svanoe . . . . Aid
Jean Pleet . . . . Nurse
Noel Toy . . . . Mama San
Kasuko Sakuro . . . . Cho-Cho

Copyright 1972 – 20th Century Fox Film Corporation

Non-Credited Appearances . . . . Dennis Troy, Virginia Lee

Chapters

1: *Main Titles*
2: *A Citation of Merit – 0:49*
3: *Goodbye, Henry – 5:38*
4: *The New Boss – 8:10*
5: *He's Got to Go – 12:26*

6: *Help from Henry – 15:03*
7: *Radar's Problem – 17:38*
8: *Henry Takes Over – 21:25*
9: *Back in Command – 24:04*
10: *End Titles – 24:59*

Closing Stills

1: *Hammond addresses unit on "R" compound*
2: *Hawk, Trap, Spearchucker at attention in Swamp FB*
3: *Henry, Hawkeye, Trapper in tub in Tokyo*
4: *Radar's not ill in post-op*

Synopsis: After Henry is transferred to Tokyo Medical Headquarters, Frank, who is 2nd in command, becomes the new CO. As such, he holds a surprise inspection of the Swamp, puts his former bunkmates on report and has armed MP's remove the still, creating an intolerable situation. Knowing how much Radar means to Henry, Hawkeye and Trapper visit him in Tokyo and make him think that Radar has come down with a mysterious illness. Henry immediately returns to the 4077th by chopper, only to discover that Radar was faking it, but takes back his command of the 4077th anyway, much to Frank's dismay.

Commentary by Larry Gelbart: "Over thirty years ago, I was busy working on future scripts for the balance of our first season. I was anxious, of course, having seen some of the show's reviews in advance (*Time* magazine said we were the biggest disappointment of the year), I was anxious to see what sort of ratings we'd get (ratings meaning either an extended run or a death sentence), anxious to see what the public, my friends, my family, my peers thought. We, who were responsible for the show, felt extremely proud of what we had done, but we had no idea whether others would view our work as positively. How could just a few days ago turn so inexplicably into over thirty years? I must get myself a slower calendar."

Authors' Notes: There are no PA announcements in this episode.

According to General Hammond, the 4077th has achieved a 90% efficiency rating, the best of any medical unit in Korea.

This is one of the few episodes featuring the interior of the mess tent at the Ranch location (instead of inside stage 9)

The American Flag on the Ranch compound stands alone. This will change in later episodes, as the flags of the United Nations and South Korea will join it.

This is also one of the very few times two jeeps, serial numbers 18210717 and 18210175 are seen with a canopy. These jeeps are almost exclusively seen without it.

A close-up of Hawkeye and Trapper was filmed on Stage 9. They were supposed to be part of the assembly on the Ranch compound while Henry was given his Special Citation of merit, 4th Class.

Reveille is heard for the first time in this episode.

Radar is seen reading a Captain Savage comic book. This particular comic book, *Captain Savage and his Battlefield Raiders*, episode "To the Last Man," is issue number 10 from January 10, 1969 and cost 12 cents (published by the Marvel Comics Group).

I Hate A Mystery – 11/26/1972

Season 1 / Episode 10 / Production 6 – J306

Columbia House VHS Tape . . . .*The Unexpected (Catalog # 22050)*
Fox DVD. . . . . *Season 1, Disc 2*

Alan Alda, Wayne Rogers, McLean Stevenson,
Loretta Swit, Larry Linville, Gary Burghoff

Produced by Gene Reynolds
Executive Script Consultant: Larry Gelbart
Written by Hal Dresner
Directed by Hy Averback

Timothy Brown. . . . . Spearchucker Jones
Patrick Adiarte . . . . Ho Jon
William Christopher. . . . . Father Mulcahy
Bonnie Jones . . . . .Lieutenant Barbara Bannerman
Linda Meiklejohn . . . . Lieutenant Leslie Scorch
Odessa Cleveland . . . . Lieutenant Ginger Bayliss

Copyright 1972 – 20th Century Fox Film Corporation

Non-Credited Appearances. . . . . .Dennis Troy, Roy Goldman, Marcia Gelman

Chapters

1: *Main Titles*
2: *Winning – 0:50*
3: *Stealing – 2:24*
4: *Tent Search – 8:32*
5: *Court Martial – 11:55*

6: *Surveillance – 13:32*
7: *A Trap – 17:52*
8: *A Bribe – 22:52*
9: *A Parable – 24:38*
10: *End Titles – 25:01*

Closing Stills

1: *Frank and Margaret in Margaret's tent*
2: *All in Mess Tent – Henry missing spoon*
3: *Corpsman and Hawkeye on 9 compound*
4: *Ho Jon shows hands in Mess Tent with Trapper*

Synopsis: Frank's sterling silver picture frame, Margaret's hair brushes, Trapper's watch, Hawkeye's swizzle stick, along with various other's personal items, have all been stolen. To try and put an end to the crime wave at the 4077, Henry conducts a tent-by-tent search and discovers all the stolen items neatly packed away in Hawkeye's footlocker. Hawkeye, now the prime suspect puts a plan into play designed to trap the real thief and later in the Mess Tent, reveals the real culprit.

Commentary by Larry Gelbart: "The actors (with the exception of portions of "The Interview") were never told or encouraged to ad lib lines or business. Not all actors are blessed with improvisational skills. Not all actors are that blessed reciting written material either. There will always be some viewers (just as there were some listeners back in the days of [non-talk] radio shows) who prefer to believe that the personalities they are watching — or hearing — are delivering inspirational, original thoughts rather than those that have been crafted by faceless, off-camera writers. Early days. Scrambling for ideas. For tone. Storyline makes no sense at all, in terms of character issues. I hope to be able to fix it one day. I was working in my office when they shot it (scene where Hawkeye and Trapper laugh, hysterically, at Henry's face with soot). We roared at it, of course, when we all saw the scene in the dailies."

PA Announcement by Jimmy Lydon
PA Announcement by Hawkeye

Authors' Notes: When Hawkeye makes his announcement over the PA, several of the people paged are already heading for the mess tent before or at the exact same moment their names are being called.

Ho Jon makes his way towards the mess tent along with the others, even though his name was not called.

Frank mispronounces Margaret's name as, "Major Houlihand."

According to Frank, he became a doctor because it was the "wish of my dear mother." This will change later in the series.

According to Hawkeye, the year is 1951.

The "Sato-Tannaka" fishing reel Henry gives to Leslie is actually in a Penn Fishing Reel box.

Radar's bear makes its first appearance with a missing left eye.

A dartboard is seen for the first time in Henry's office on the floor to the left of the door.

Germ Warfare – 12/10/1972

Season 1 / Episode 11 / Production 4 – J304

Columbia House VHS Tape . . . . Not A Pretty Sight (Catalog # 21036)
Fox DVD . . . . Season 1, Disc 2

Alan Alda, Wayne Rogers, McLean Stevenson,
Loretta Swit, Larry Linville, Gary Burghoff

Produced by Gene Reynolds
Written by Larry Gelbart
Directed by Terry Becker

Timothy Brown . . . . Spearchucker Jones
Patrick Adiarte . . . . Ho Jon
Karen Philipp . . . . Lieutenant Dish
Bob Gooden . . . . Boone
Byron Chung . . . . P.O.W.
Odessa Cleveland . . . . Lieutenant Ginger Bayliss

Copyright 1972 – 20th Century Fox Film Corporation

Chapters

1: Main Titles	6: A Beer with the Boys – 12:25
2: The Patient Problem – 0:49	7: No Hot Lips – 16:33
3: A New Roommate – 4:07	8: Frank's Condition – 21:15
4: Frank's Donation – 6:11	9: The Test Results – 23:25
5: Jaundice Juice – 9:41	10: End Titles – 24:59

Closing Stills

1: Trap, Hawk, Ho Jon and the POW in the Swamp
2: Hawkeye and Trapper take Frank's blood
3: Trapper, Hawkeye, Frank on "R" compound
4: Radar nailing "out of order" sign on latrine

Synopsis: After Hawkeye and Trapper take a pint of Frank's blood while he's asleep, they give it to a wounded P.O.W. who then begins to show signs of possible hepatitis. To be sure, they need to test Frank further and convince him to drink beer, something that Frank admits he's not able to hold, and it doesn't take long before he needs to use the latrine. Unfortunately for Frank, Radar has nailed the latrine shut, due to "remodeling," and has Frank use a temporary latrine complete with its own bucket.

Commentary by Larry Gelbart: "It was just more fruitful to keep referring to the book than it was to the movie, finding and mining ideas in it the more it was read and reread."

PA Announcement by Jimmy Lydon

Authors' Notes: This is the first episode of the series that ends in a freeze-frame.

The dartboard first seen in Henry's office in the previous episode ("I Hate A Mystery") is now seen on the wall behind Henry's desk and not on the floor. This 2nd location will change as well.

There is a glass cabinet in front of Henry's desk that will not be in that location in future episodes.

Frank's blood type is AB negative.

Frank is seen sleeping on his right side with a shelf and a clock behind him. When Hawkeye and Trapper siphon Frank's blood, he's on his back and his position is reversed — his head is now where his feet were before.

On the Ranch set, Frank says, "I'm fine. I'm completely fine. The last thing I'm gonna give you two ghouls is any of my blood." An echo can be heard delivering this line, even though they're outside. Possible voice-over?

The American flag is still alone on the Ranch compound.

Dear Dad – 12/17/1972

Season 1 / Episode 12 / Production 13 – J313

Columbia House VHS Tape . . . . Dear Dad (Catalog # 10993)
Fox DVD. . . . . Season 1, Disc 2

Alan Alda, Wayne Rogers, McLean Stevenson,
Loretta Swit, Larry Linville, Gary Burghoff

Written by Larry Gelbart
Produced And Directed by Gene Reynolds

Jamie Farr . . . . .Corporal Maxwell Q. Klinger
William Christopher. . . . . Father Mulcahy
Buck Young. . . . . M.P.
Odessa Cleveland . . . . Lieutenant Ginger Bayliss
Bonnie Jones . . . . .Lieutenant Barbara Bannerman
Lizabeth Deen. . . . . .Becky (also the name of Larry Gelbart's daughter)
Bill Kaat . . . . P.F.C.
Gary Van Orman. . . . . .Corporal

Copyright 1972 – 20th Century Fox Film Corporation

Non-Credited Appearances. . . . . Gwen Farrell, Dittsbury
(from "Requiem For A Lightweight")

Chapters

1: Main Titles	6: The Peacemaker – 10:29
2: A Letter Home – 0:50	7: Some Enchanted Evening – 14:38
3: Christmas in Korea – 2:41	8: Doctor Claus – 19:45
4: The Monthly Lecture – 4:54	9: Merry Christmas – 24:10
5: Trapper's Private Practice – 9:25	10: End Titles – 24:59

Closing Stills

1: Henry helps Radar tie box to send home
2: Hawk, Margaret, Frank, Trap at Henry's lecture
3: Mulcahy hit in gut in post-op
4: Frank with hands over Margaret's eyes – her tent

Synopsis: It's Christmas season at the 4077 as Hawkeye writes to his father in the first of three, "Dead Dad" episodes and justifies joking during a 70-hour OR session as a defense mechanism. He brings his father up to date about the people he works with as Radar ships home a jeep, piece by piece. But the Holiday Season doesn't seem to slow down the fighting as Hawkeye, dressed as Santa for the local Korean children, soon finds himself making a house-call from a chopper to save the life of a GI on a hill under fire. Back in the Swamp, exhausted, he wishes his father a Merry Christmas from everyone at the 4077th, even Frank Burns.

Commentary by Larry Gelbart: " 'Dear Dad' was indeed a seminal episode. A few shows into our first season, my wife said she'd like to know more about what was going on at the 4077 beyond whatever the storyline was we were dealing with. She reminded me what a busy place it must have been and thought we could tell more than just one story per script. The result, 'Dear Dad,' was the paradigm for any number of subsequent episodes (not just Dear Somebody letters), in which we told up to a half dozen stories simultaneously and had some or all of them intersect at one point or another. Reading the characters' names at the end was a way of reminding our viewers — and hopefully, any new ones — just who was who. This episode remains one of my favorites, too. Once I became aware (through research) that some enterprising serviceman did in fact mail a jeep to his stateside home, one or several pieces at a time, I knew that we had to have someone do it in an episode — and who was more enterprising than Radar? After that, it became a matter of indicating very specifically where in the episode's script Radar would be seen carrying a steering wheel or whatever jeep component or any other designated item and then somehow paying the whole business off.

I forget which director did that episode, (Gene Reynolds) much as I now forget that show's title, but it was no problem at all to successfully realize that particular vision. I know that whenever I made a gaffe, it was chiefly because I'd forgotten what I'd written previously. (Gelbart, on inconsistencies regarding Hawkeye being an only child) I always thought of the title as a tribute to my own father, who was chiefly responsible for my becoming a professional father. To make someone laugh is no big trick. Any second banana with a banana peel can do that. To make someone feel is a much more rewarding experience."

PA Announcements by Sal Viscuso

Authors' Notes: In the O.R., Trapper mentions, "The Bears beat the Packers, 21-10." Between 1950 and 1953, the Chicago Bears and the Green Bay Packers played a total of 8 games, none of which ended with the score of 21-10 either way:

> 1950: *Week 3 – Packers beat the Bears 31 – 21 at Green Bay.*
> *Week 5 – Bears beat the Packers 28 – 14 at Chicago*
> 1951: *Week 1 – Bears beat the Packers 31 – 20 at Green bay*
> *Week 8 – Bears beat the Packers 24 – 13 at Chicago*
> 1952: *Week 1 – Bears beat the Packers 24 – 14 at Green Bay*
> *Week 7 – Packers beat the Bears 41 – 28 at Chicago*
> 1953: *Week 2 – Bears beat the Packers 17 – 13 at Green bay*
> *Week 7 – Packers and Bears tied at 21 in Chicago*

The sign designating the nurse's quarters is on a separate pole on the Ranch compound as opposed to a sign above the door of the tent on Stage 9.

A rare, early-season appearance where Klinger is wearing regulation fatigues. (With a red bandana his mother sent him for good luck)

Henry's first sex lecture — "Sex and the Family" with Figures A & B.

DVD captioning misspells Albert Schweitzer's name: *S-c-h-w-i-e-t-z-e-r* is incorrect.

Hawkeye is from Vermont in this episode.

A nurse, played by Lizabeth Deen, is named, "Becky," which is also the name of Larry Gelbart's daughter.

Edwina – 12/24/1972
Season 1 / Episode 13 / Production 12 – J312

Columbia House VHS Tape . . . . *The World's A Stage (Catalog # 21039)*
Fox DVD . . . . *Season 1, Disc 2*

Alan Alda, Wayne Rogers, McLean Stevenson,
Loretta Swit, Larry Linville, Gary Burghoff

Produced by Gene Reynolds
Executive Script Consultant: Larry Gelbart
Written by Hal Dresner
Directed by James Sheldon

Arlene Golonka . . . . Lieutenant Edwina Ferguson
Marcia Strassman . . . . Lieutenant Margie Cutler
Linda Meiklejohn . . . . Lieutenant Leslis Scorch
Copyright 1972 – 20th Century Fox Film Corporation

Non-Credited Appearances . . . . Marcia Gelman, Gwen Farrell, Sheila Lauritsen,
Ralph Grosh, Dittsbury *(from "Requiem For A Lightweight")*

Chapters

1:	Main Titles	6:	The Great Lover – 12:49
2:	A Surprise Party – 0:50	7:	The Big Date – 17:30
3:	A Guy for Eddie – 3:58	8:	No More Pretending – 20:42
4:	Cutler's Conspiracy – 6:23	9:	My Kind of Girl – 24:17
5:	Eddie's New Boyfriend – 9:47	10:	End Titles – 25:00

Closing Stills

1: Eddie's party in the Mess Tent
2: Hawkeye and Trapper leave OR
3: Hawkeye picks the short straw
4: Eddie almost killing Hawkeye on date

Synopsis: Lieutenant Edwina Ferguson, a 28-year-old klutzy nurse who runs from her own birthday party when everyone sings, "For she's a jolly good fellow" because she's not jolly and not a fellow. However, she was engaged to a fellow for nearly two years but when he was drafted, he seemed to forget about her and now, nobody at the 4077 wants to date her. But when the nurses refuse to date anyone until someone goes out with "Eddie", Hawkeye picks the short straw and nearly winds up in post-op as a casualty.

Commentary by Arlene Golonka: "Playing her (Edwina) was not very difficult, because I "was" Edwina. She was fun, even though she messed up a lot. My favorite scene was when Edwina got spaghetti all over her face, and eventually pulled down the tent. I loved doing *M*A*S*H*. It was truly fun working with such an incredible cast, a wonderful director, and a brilliant writer/producer. I feel honored and grateful to be a part of television history. I still watch all the reruns, and they are just as funny as when they first aired."

Commentary by Larry Gelbart: "Not one of our shinier half-hours. A good example of how we hadn't found our footing yet. Alda hated it."

Authors' Notes: There are no PA announcements in this episode.

As mentioned by Larry Gelbart, this episode is not one of Alan Alda's favorites.

A list of Edwina's accidents:

1: *Hands Hawkeye forceps instead of clamp in OR (Chapter 6)*
2: *Puts clipboard on bench and Hawkeye sits on it in the mess tent (Chapter 6)*
3: *Tosses salt over right shoulder into Hawkeye's face in the mess tent (Chapter 6)*
4: *Steps on Hawkeye's ankle in the mess tent (mentioned, not seen, Chapter 6)*
5: *Breaks her hair brush in her hair in the nurses tent (Chapter 7)*
6: *Opens nurse's tent door into Hawkeye's head (Chapter 7)*
7: *Splashes drink into Hawkeye's face in the Swamp (Chapter 7)*
8: *Bangs her head into Hawkeye's left eye in the Swamp (Chapter 7)*
9: *Pushes ice cube into Hawkeye's bruised left eye in the Swamp (Chapter 8)*
10: *While dancing with Hawkeye, he slips and his butt lands on the heater in the Swamp (Chapter 8)*
11: *Bangs into a tray of glasses and they break on the Swamp floor (Chapter 8)*
12: *While dancing w/ Hawkeye in the Swamp, he steps on broken glass without shoes, in Japanese slippers (Chapter 8)*
13: *While dancing with Hawkeye, he slips, falls on bunk and shelf falls on his left shoulder (Chapter 8)*
14: *Knocks down soot-filled chimney on Swamp stove onto Hawkeye's head (Chapter 8)*

Love Story – 1/7/1973

Season 1 / Episode 14 / Production 14 – J314

Columbia House VHS Tape . . . . *News From Home (Catalog # 10992)*
Fox DVD . . . . *Season 1, Disc 2*

Alan Alda, Wayne Rogers, McLean Stevenson,
Loretta Swit, Larry Linville, Gary Burghoff

Produced by Gene Reynolds
Executive Script Consultant: Larry Gelbart
Written by Laurence Marks
Directed by Earl Bellamy

Kelly Jean Peters . . . . Lieutenant Louise Anderson
Marcia Strassman . . . . Lieutenant Margie Cutler
Barbara Brownell . . . . Lieutenant Jones
Indira Danks . . . . Lieutenant O'Brien
Jerry Harper . . . . Sergeant

Copyright 1973 – 20th Century Fox Film Corporation

Non-Credited Appearances . . . . Gwen Farrell, Dennis Troy

Chapters

1: Main Titles	6: Intellectual Training – 11:29
2: Radar's Problem – 0:48	7: Margaret's Demand – 17:00
3: A "Dear John" Record – 3:58	8: Love & War – 18:39
4: A Date for Radar – 6:34	9: The Acme Cupid Company – 24:11
5: Love at First Sight – 8:10	10: End Titles – 24:57

Closing Stills

1: Radar meets Louise Anderson
2: Trap, Louise, Hawk, Radar – Mess Tent
3: Margaret and Frank in the Mess Tent
4: Hawkeye and Trapper in Margaret's bed

Synopsis: When Radar is found in the office on top of a filing cabinet in the fetal position and then fouls up a supply requisition, Henry suggests a complete physical workup, and all tests come back negative. Radar hasn't been the same since his fiancé sent him a "Dear John" record to tell him she's marrying someone else, but when a new nurse arrives, it's love at first sight for Radar. The only problem, besides Margaret trying to stop them from being together is the nurse reads books such as "Plato's Republic" while Radar's literary interests are rooted in comic books. Hawkeye and Trapper try to help Radar by introducing him to Tolstoy and Bach, but are met with limited success.

Commentary by Larry Gelbart: "I did work on it. I always thought it was a good show. These men were doctors, far more than they were military types; much more familiar with proctology than they were with protocol."

Authors' Notes: There are no PA announcements in this episode.
The "Dear John" record's blue label is "National."

Tuttle – 1/14/1973

Season 1 / Episode 15 / Production 15 – J315

Columbia House VHS Tape . . . . *Bending The Rules (Catalog # 3740)*
Fox DVD. . . . . *Season 1, Disc 2*

Alan Alda, Wayne Rogers, McLean Stevenson,
Loretta Swit, Larry Linville, Gary Burghoff

Produced by Gene Reynolds
Executive Script Consultant: Larry Gelbart
Written by Bruce Shelly & David Ketchum
Directed by William Wiard

Herb Voland . . . . General Crandall Clayton
Mary Robin Redd . . . . Sister Theresa
Dennis Fimple . . . . Sergeant "Sparky" Pryor
William Christopher . . . . Father Mulcahy
James Sikking . . . . Finance Officer
Captain Jonathon S. Tuttle . . . . Himself

Copyright 1973 – 20th Century Fox Film Corporation

Chapters

1: *Main Titles*	6: *General Hawkeye – 11:18*
2: *Tuttle's Generosity – 0:49*	7: *Where's Tuttle – 14:43*
3: *Who's Captain Tuttle? – 4:18*	8: *The Pride of the Army – 18:25*
4: *Frank Investigates – 6:24*	9: *No More Tuttle – 21:22*
5: *The Tuttle File – 8:22*	10: *End Titles – 25:00*

Closing Stills

1: *Radar, Hawkeye, Trapper make Tuttle file*
2: *Margaret on Henry's phone*
3: *Hawkeye with Tuttle's dog tags*
4: *Henry – "best damn OD we ever had"*

Synopsis: Whenever someone would knock down the garbage or break a window, Hawkeye would blame "Tuttle," his imaginary friend when he was a boy. Tuttle has now been given credit for giving Sister Theresa a crate filled with blankets, powdered milk and penicillin for the orphans. After making a file for Tuttle, Hawkeye realizes that he hasn't been paid in 14 months, and donates all the back pay to Sister Theresa's orphanage, and instructs the finance officer to send all future pay to the Sister as well. But the real problem occurs when General Clayton comes to the 4077 to give a citation to Captain Jonathon S. Tuttle only to discover that Tuttle, who went to do field surgery in a chopper, jumped without his parachute and Hawkeye has to deliver the eulogy.

Commentary by Larry Gelbart: "Captain Jonathan Tuttle, born in 1924, of proud parents Harry and Frieda Tuttle…the names of my mother and father (except for the Tuttle part) Some pre-*M*A*S*H* years ago, while still living in London, I saw a marvelous program on the BBC. It was an English adaptation of a French play; its English title (or should that be Tuttle?) was 'Lieutenant Tenant.' It was the story of a lowly private in the Russian army in Napoleonic times, who volunteered to act as an officer's clerk, even though the private was barely literate. He just wanted to be able to work in a cozy, warm office instead of being out in the freezing cold. The first time he was required to take dictation from the officer, the private, a pen in his totally (or should that be tuttaly?) inexperienced hand, he was in trouble. The officer, writing to another officer, began his dictation, 'My dear Lieutenant…' The private, repeating the word out loud, as he slowly tried to write, 'Lieu-ten-ant,' making the officer impatient, prompting the private to go write faster, he repeated the last two-thirds of the name, 'Ten-ant.' The result was the private started the salutation by writing, 'My Dear Lieutenant Tenant.' The letter was sent out to a totally fictitious officer. What happened next, you can guess, I was so taken with the idea of the play, I checked into its availability for an American adaptation. Other ideas and events intervened, and I never got around to doing one. And, then, along came M*A*S*H…Hawkeye's speech (about Tuttle) was written after we did the exteriors. We just felt that sort of eulogy was necessary. That's why we had to shoot it on the set. At lunch with Tuttle yesterday, I learned that Radar's imaginary friend has had two imaginary implants."

PA Announcements by Sal Viscuso

Authors' Notes: An example of how they used Stage 9 and the Fox Ranch location for filming is Hawkeye arriving with Tuttle's parachute, filmed at the Fox Ranch, and the close up of him giving the eulogy was filmed on Stage 9.

Tuttle's serial number and BJ's serial number (As given by BJ in "The Late Captain Pierce" from Season 4) is 39729966. This is Larry Gelbart's real army serial number.

There is no dartboard in the Swamp in Chapter 2 and it's across from the supply shed on Stage 9. Sometimes it's across from the mess tent.

Radar has a Martini with Hawkeye (this will be significant later in the series) and admits to having an imaginary friend, Shirley, who looks like Radar, only with, "tiny, little breasts."

Radar is also reading the same comic book he read in, "Henry, Please Come Home," a Captain Savage and His Battlefield Raiders episode, "To the Last Man," from 1969.

Tuttle's parents, Harry & Frieda are the names of Larry Gelbart's parents.

The sign indicating the showers has block lettering as opposed to the free-style writing usually seen.

This is the only time Radar's friend "Sparky" is seen on-screen.

Sparky mentions a "Captain Marvel Annual" comic (Captain Marvel's first appearance was in *Whiz Comics* #2, in 1940) and also says, "Shazam." "Shazam" is from Captain Marvel — when Billy Batson, a young radio news reporter says, "Shazam!," he's struck by a magic lightning bolt and transforms into Captain Marvel with the abilities of six mythical figures.

The finance officer, James B. (Barrie) Sikking has had an extensive television and film career, co-starring in such shows as *Perry Mason, Rawhide, Bonanza, Hunter,* and more notably as Lieutenant Howard Hunter in *Hill Street Blues* and as Dr. David Howser in *Doogie Howser, M.D.*

Mr. Sikking was also Captain Styles of the USS Excelsior in *Star Trek III: The Search for Spock.*

The Ringbanger – 1/21/1973

Season 1 / Episode 16 / Production 16 – J316

Columbia House VHS Tape . . . . *Career Advancement (Catalog # 10994)*
Fox DVD . . . . *Season 1, Disc 2*

Alan Alda, Wayne Rogers, McLean Stevenson,
Loretta Swit, Larry Linville, Gary Burghoff

Produced by Gene Reynolds
Executive Script Consultant: Larry Gelbart
Written by Jerry Mayer
Directed Jackie Cooper

Leslie Nielsen . . . . Colonel Buzz Brighton
Linda Meiklejon . . . . Lieutenant Leslie Scorch

Copyright 1973 – 20th Century Fox Film Corporation

Non-Credited Appearances . . . . Ralph Grosh, Roy Goldman, Gwen Farrell,
Dennis Troy

Chapters

1: *Main Titles*
2: *Colonel Buzz Brighton – 0:47*
3: *A Real Ringbanger – 3:22*
4: *Second Opinions – 8:04*
5: *The Degenerate Doctor – 10:35*
6: *Buzz's Bigger Problem – 13:05*
7: *In A Lather – 15:46*
8: *Buzz's Bad Night – 20:01*
9: *Brightening Things Up – 24:25*
10: *End Titles – 24:56*

Closing Stills

1: *Trapper, Hawkeye, Buzz on 9 compound*
2: *Frank taking Buzz's pulse in the Swamp*
3: *Margaret in Buzz's tent*
4: *Margaret, Henry, Hawkeye, Buzz wristlock on Frank*

Synopsis: Margaret recognizes Hawkeye's patient from a picture she saw in *Stars & Stripes:* Colonel Buzz Brighton. The Colonel, evidently a career military man, wants nothing more than to get back to the front lines. What wasn't in *Stars & Stripes* is the fact that Brighton has twice as many casualties as any other regimental commander while gaining only half the ground, and Hawkeye and Trapper initiate a plan that not only keeps Brighton from getting to the front, but will send him back to the States for a couple of months to "cool off."

Commentary by Larry Gelbart: "Another example of Gene Reynolds' and Burt Metcalfe's uncanny, unfailing and creative ability at casting" (on casting Leslie Nielsen).

"Writing requires a comfortable chair and some ideas that you're not comfortable with until you work them out on the keyboard. Logic is required. Abandon. Honesty. Passion. Courage. Mix and serve. Facing the wall was a way of concentrating. There were dozens of people on the sound stage — each one of them was a distraction."

PA Announcement by Sal Viscuso

Authors' Notes: The first mention of Hawkeye being from Maine comes in the operating room when he mentions he was the pickup sticks champion of Southern Maine.

In Chapters 5 and 6, the Swamp on Stage 9 has no dartboard.

In Chapter 6, before Radar sneaks a glass of milk into Buzz's tent, you can see it's already there, in a long shot.

In Chapter 7, Frank is wearing his dog tags in the shower and mid-scene, they're not there.

In Chapter 8, we see the same clip of Radar sneaking milk into Buzz's tent.

Though the movie Airplane is often credited with being Leslie Nielsen's first venture into comedy, this episode appears to be his real first venture.

Mr. Nielsen is from Canada's Northwest Territories. His father was a Mountie and one of his brothers became the Deputy Prime Minister of Canada. Mr. Nielson also has an extensive film and television history, including the movie *Airplane!* and *The Naked Gun* movies. He's also been nominated for many awards, both Canadian and American, and has a star on Hollywood's Walk of Fame.

Sometimes You Hear the Bullet – 1/28/1973

Season 1 / Episode 17 / Production 18 – J318

Columbia House VHS Tape . . . . *Staff Infections (Catalog # 3769)*
Fox DVD. . . . . *Season 1, Disc 3*

Alan Alda, Wayne Rogers, McLean Stevenson,
Loretta Swit, Larry Linville, Gary Burghoff

Produced by Gene Reynolds
Executive Script Consultant: Larry Gelbart
Written by Carl Kleinschmitt
Directed William Wiard

Lynette Metty . . . . .Lieutenant Nancy Griffin
Ronny Howard . . . . Private Wendell / Walter Petersen
James Callahan . . . . Corporal Tommy Gillis
William Christopher. . . . . Father Mulcahy
Fred Lerner . . . . Patient # 1
Chuck Hicks . . . . Patient # 2

Copyright 1973 – 20th Century Fox Film Corporation

Non-Credited Appearances. . . . . John Orchard, Gwen Farrell, Roy Goldman

Chapters

1:	*Main Titles*	6:	*Wendell – 13:44*
2:	*Alone at Last – 0:48*	7:	*A Long Night – 18:32*
3:	*Frank's Back – 4:31*	8:	*Saving A Life – 23:03*
4:	*An Old Friend – 7:10*	9:	*A Purple Heart – 23:44*
5:	*An Appendectomy – 11:06*	10:	*End Titles – 24:59*

Closing Stills

1: *Tommy kissing Henry*
2: *Hawkeye talks to Wendell in post-op*
3: *Margaret, Hawk, Henry, Frank in traction in post-op*
4: *Hawkeye crying*

Synopsis: Tommy Gillis, one of Hawkeye's best friends, pays him a surprise visit and it doesn't take long before they're in the Swamp having martinis with Trapper. After telling Trapper that Hawkeye was the best milk-monitor he'd ever seen and how Hawkeye wrote a poem to a pretty teacher, he tells them the real reason he's in Korea. Tommy, a correspondent, wants to write a book titled, "You Never Hear the Bullet," but wants to write it as a soldier fighting in Korea, not as a correspondent. Tommy's visit is cut short when Hawkeye and Trapper are paged to O.R., and Hawkeye has to say goodbye to his long-time friend. The O.R. is busy, and nothing in Hawkeye's experience could have prepared him for his next patient. He turns to the operating table and sees Tommy lying there after being shot in the aorta. Tommy, too weak to lift his head, confesses that he did hear the bullet. Hawkeye tells him to change the title of his book, but Tommy's pressure is faint and falling, and then he's gone. After the session, Henry finds Hawkeye alone, staring out at the compound, crying. But Hawkeye knows how he can save the life of a 15-year-old who lied his way into the Marines, just so he can get a medal to impress a girl back home.

Commentary by Larry Gelbart: "Somehow, over the years, I have come to remember this as the seventh episode of the first season. It was, as some of you may know a lot better than me, the eighteenth. *(Author's note — this was the 18th episode produced.)* The episodes that preceded it were a mixed lot. Some good, some less so. What was missing was a certain tone and perhaps certain courage. The ideas for the shows came from several sources: from research, from original thoughts that occurred to me, or Gene Reynolds, or from both of us. Not a lot of outside writers (there was no staff — I was the staff) contributed to the idea pool. The show was in its infancy and quite unlike any others that were on the air, so it was difficult for freelance writers to key into us. The original idea for Bullet came from a writer named Carl Kleinschmitt that dealt with a civilian friend of Hawkeye's, a writer, covering the war as a fighting man so he could best tell realistically what going through battle was all about - and paying for that search for truth with his life. That, in itself would have probably made a successful episode. Gene and I wanted to add another element, however. We wanted something constructive to come from the experience, wanted the man's death to mean something. We did not want him to be just one more war casualty. To Kleinschmitt's original outline, we added the character and storyline of the underage Marine who enlisted to prove his manhood, using the experience of Hawkeye's friend to prevent the death of the boy. Besides enriching the episode, the success of the resultant script emboldened us to dig a little deeper with all subsequent scripts. I wish it had been the seventh episode. Who knows what the first might have been."

Commentary by James Callahan: "The opening sequence, in my episode, had me coming in on a stretcher, moaning and groaning. When McLean Stevenson leaned over, I kissed him full on the mouth. It got a big laugh, and McLean's take got an even bigger laugh. So, to top it, the next day he printed a blurb in Variety, saying we were engaged!!

Larry Gelbart, the writer, called me in to congratulate me for my part, and told me that except for the final show, it was the most watched *M*A*S*H* ever. Also, it starred Ron Howard, who borrowed an Orson Welles book I had on the set and, soon after, quit acting to become a director. I'm not taking credit. It was a joy to work on such a good script, with so much talent in each department (acting, writing, directing). Even the technicians seemed to be instilled with the spirit."

PA Announcements by Sal Viscuso

Authors' Notes: Closing still # 3 appears, then suddenly zooms out on the DVD.
Frank applies for the Purple Heart: "Tripped in the mud on the way to the shower."
Frank is seen in this episode wearing two different bathrobes.
The second of Frank's names is mentioned in this episode as, Franklin D. Burns, Major, U.S.Army Reserves. Frank in the U.S. Army Reserves seems to contradict his serial number starting with RA for Regular Army.
Frank's Purple Earring is actually green.
Ron Howard, after a successful television acting career, went on to become one of Hollywood's foremost directors, whose work includes the movies, *Splash, Willow, Cocoon* and *Apollo 13*. Mr. Howard won an Oscar for the movie *A Beautiful Mind*, and his movie *The Da Vinci Code* has earned over $700 million.
James Callahan has an extensive list of credits and has appeared in over 120 movies and television shows, including, *Charles In Charge*. After being diagnosed with esophageal cancer, Mr. Callahan passed away on August 3, 2007.
The authors of this book are deeply saddened at his passing and are grateful for his comments with regard to his appearance in this episode, one of the most talked-about from the first season.

Dear Dad, Again – 2/4/1973

Season 1 / Episode 18 / Production 17 – J317

Columbia House VHS Tape . . . .*Dear Dad (Catalog # 10993)*
Fox DVD. . . . . *Season 1, Disc 3*

Alan Alda, Wayne Rogers, McLean Stevenson,
Loretta Swit, Larry Linville, Gary Burghoff

Produced by Gene Reynolds
Written by Sheldon Keller & Larry Gelbart
Directed by Jackie Cooper

Alex Henteloff . . . . Captain Adam Casey / Sergeant Schwartz
Jamie Farr . . . . Corporal Klinger
William Christopher. . . . . Father Mulcahy
Odessa Cleveland . . . . Lieutenant Ginger Bayless
Gail Bowman . . . . Nurse
Copyright 1973 – 20th Century Fox Film Corporation

Non-Credited Appearances. . . . . Ralph Grosh, Dennis Troy, Roy Goldman,
Gwen Farrell, Dittsbury

Chapters

1: Main Titles	6: Radar O'Reilly – 8:30
2: Dear Dad – 0:49	7: Frank and Hot Lips – 13:37
3: Captain Casey – 2:25	8: Re: Captain Casey – 18:43
4: Father Mulcahy – 4:35	9: No-Talent Night – 21:24
5: The Streaker – 6:08	10: End Titles – 24:58

Closing Stills

1: Hawkeye naked in the Mess Tent with Klinger
2: Trapper asleep – Frank drunk
3: Henry gives Radar father's pen to clean
4: Margaret singing "My Blue Heaven"

Synopsis: In the second of three "Dear Dad" episodes, Hawkeye brings his father up to date on the goings-on at the 4077th, including a new surgeon who is just as good as Hawkeye, and he'll "get him for it." One of the biggest problems faced by the 4077th is boredom, to the point that Hawkeye feels nothing would faze anyone, calling them, "a bunch of zilches" and makes a $50 bet with Trapper that he can walk into the mess tent naked and nobody would even notice him. Hawkeye puts more faith in Radar's ability to read other people's minds and later, Frank gets into an argument with Margaret, and then shocks Hawkeye and Trapper when he wants a double-martini. At 2:45AM, Frank, now drunk and drinking martinis from a beaker, insists on "doing something," but the only thing Hawkeye and Trapper want to do is sleep. Things pick up a little when Radar gets news about Captain Casey, the new surgeon, who's not a captain and worse, he's not a doctor and although he's an excellent surgeon, Hawkeye will not let him near any more patients, but won't turn him in either if he leaves the camp. In closing his letter, Hawkeye thanks his father for sending him his old tuxedo, which he wore on the Charity-No-Talent-Night show. It's now Saturday night; Hawkeye will shower, shave, put on a clean uniform and get some sleep, asking his father to kiss his mother and sister for him.

Commentary by Larry Gelbart: "Alda was wearing jockey shorts. Jockey shorts are jockey shorts with a pocket and please don't ask me what you put in them. They are visible for a split second. Use your pause button, if you've got the video" (on whether or not Alda was really naked as he walked through camp).

PA Announcement by Sal Viscuso

Authors' Notes: In the operating room in Chapter 2, this is one of the very rare instances when a laugh track was used after Hawkeye makes a joke with Ginger.

As Hawkeye adjusts his hat before going out naked, dog tags can be seen hanging below the mirror on the center post. Whose?

Henry's office in Chapter 6 now has the dartboard on the wall by his diploma.

Henry passes Radar on his final exam from the "AAA High School Diploma Company of Dellavin, Indiana." *(There is a Delavan in Wisconsin, where Gary Burghoff went to high school, and in Illinois, but no information for Dellavin, Indiana.)*

Frank is drunk for the first time in the series and confesses that nobody has ever called him "pal" or "buddy" in his "whole rotten life."

Frank's brother gave him the name, "Ferret Face."

Hawkeye mentions to Radar putting his appendix back:

1: *When was it taken out?*
2: *In a Season 3 episode, "Abyssinia, Henry," Radar credits Henry for saving his life by taking out his appendix.*

At the Charity-No-Talent-Night show, Radar's name is seen on the bass drum while he plays. This is the first time Radar plays the drums on-screen. He'll play drums again in the Season 1 finale, "Showtime."

Gary Burghoff is an accomplished musician and is seen on *M*A*S*H* playing a bugle and piano, as well as drums. Playing the bugle and piano off-key was intentional by Gary.

Shortly after leaving *M*A*S*H*, he recorded a jazz album entitled, "Gary Burghoff and his Mardi Gras Celebration Jazz Band — Just For Fun," and in addition to playing the drums, he also sings.

Gary also has written over 100 songs and has won the ASCAP (American Society of Composers, Authors and Publishers) Award for Excellence three times.

Hawkeye, in his letter to his father, has a mother and a sister. This will be significant as the series progresses.

The Longjohn Flap – 2/18/1973

Season 1 / Episode 19 / Production 19 – J319

Columbia House VHS Tape . . . . *Prize Possessions (Catalog # 3773)*
Fox DVD . . . . *Season 1, Disc 3*

Alan Alda, Wayne Rogers, McLean Stevenson,
Loretta Swit, Larry Linville, Gary Burghoff

Produced by Gene Reynolds
Executive Script Consultant: Larry Gelbart
Written by Alan Alda
Directed by William Wiard

Jamie Farr . . . . Corporal Klinger
William Christopher . . . . Father Mulcahy
Kathleen King . . . . Nurse Beddoes
Joseph Perry . . . . The Cook

Copyright 1973 – 20th Century Fox Film Corporation

Non-Credited Appearances . . . . Roy Goldman, Gwen Farrell

Chapters

1: *Main Titles*	6: *Frank's New Underwear – 10:13*
2: *Cold Days in Korea – 0:48*	7: *Klinger's Crime – 15:00*
3: *Hawkeye's Longjohns – 3:03*	8: *Henry's Appendix – 20:44*
4: *Trapper's Bet – 5:32*	9: *Back Where They Belong – 24:05*
5: *Radar's Little Gift – 7:23*	10: *End Titles – 24:56*

Closing Stills

1: *Hawkeye in longjohns*
2: *Trapper loses bet*
3: *Frank in longjohns*
4: *Trapper, Henry in longjohns, Hawkeye*

Synopsis: The Korean winters are cold, but Hawkeye seems unaffected, even singing on the compound, then in the Swamp, he reveals his long underwear. When Trapper sees this, he offers Hawkeye $60 and his kids, but Hawkeye won't give up his long johns, until Trapper starts coughing, and thus begins the journey of the long johns around camp. A trade for food, an armed holdup, a confession and an appendix operation is some of what the underwear goes through before being returned to its rightful owner.

Commentary by Larry Gelbart: "Korea's weather, I seem to recall, is much like New York City's."

PA Announcement by Radar

Authors' Notes: This is the first episode written by Alan Alda.
According to Frank, the password is, "Mickey Mouse has warts."
The cook is not yet played by Jeff Maxwell, but Joseph Perry, who has quite an extensive list of television appearances, including *The Partridge Family, Barney Miller, Bewitched* and *I Dream of Jeannie,* to name a few.
Closing still #3 changes positions halfway through on the DVD.

The Journey of The Longjohns:

1: *Hawkeye's father sent them to him.*
2: *Hawkeye gave them to Trapper because he's sick.*
3: *Trapper lost them to Radar playing poker. Radar won with 2 pairs of 10's.*
4: *Radar traded the cook for a complete leg of lamb with mint jelly.*
5: *The cook gave them to Frank as a bribe so Frank wouldn't bust him down in rank.*
6: *Frank gave them to Margaret after she tells him she wants to re-evaluate their relationship.*
7: *Klinger, after trying to hold up Frank at gunpoint, steals them from Margaret's tent with his bayonet.*
8: *Klinger confesses and gives the longjohns to Father Mulcahy.*
9: *Father Mulcahy gave them to Henry, after sleeping in them the night before, to find the rightful owner.*
10: *After Hawkeye and Trapper successfully take out Henry's appendix, Henry returns them to Hawkeye, as his way of saying thank you for saving his life.*
11: *Trapper starts coughing again in the Swamp, but the longjohns are staying with Hawkeye.*

The Army-Navy Game – 2/25/1973
Season 1 / Episode 20 / Production 22 – J322

Columbia House VHS Tape . . . . *Leisure Time (Catalog # 10995)*
Fox DVD . . . . *Season 1, Disc 3*

Alan Alda, Wayne Rogers, McLean Stevenson,
Loretta Swit, Larry Linville, Gary Burghoff

Executive Script Consultant: Larry Gelbart
Teleplay By Sid Dorfman
Story By Mclean Stevenson
Produced and Directed by Gene Reynolds

William Christopher . . . . Father Mulcahy
Jamie Farr . . . . Corporal Klinger
John A. Zee . . . . Commander Sturner
John Orchard . . . . Ugly John
Sheila Lauritsen . . . . Nurse Hardy
Bobbie Mitchell . . . . Nurse Mason
Alan Manson . . . . Colonel Hersh
Copyright 1973 – 20th Century Fox Film Corporation

Non-Credited Appearances . . . . Gwen Farrell, Dennis Troy, Roy Goldman

Chapters

1:	Main Titles	6:	Calling the Navy – 12:32
2:	The Football Game – 0:46	7:	The Bomb's Owner – 17:56
3:	Under Attack – 3:11	8:	Defusing the Bomb – 19:41
4:	An Unexploded Bomb – 5:44	9:	The Winner – 24:03
5:	Bomb Exam – 9:18	10:	End Titles – 24:57

Closing Stills

1: All listening to the game in the office
2: Henry and Radar in the office
3: Hawkeye and Trapper dismantle the bomb
4: Raining propaganda leaflets

Synopsis: Just as the Army kicks off the Army-Navy game, the camp comes under attack, and they must now deal with an unexploded shell in the compound. After checking around, Henry finds out from Naval Command in Seoul that the bomb belongs to the CIA, but they won't tell anyone their business. From a bunker in the compound, Henry relays instructions through a bullhorn as Hawkeye and Trapper nervously attempt to dismantle the unexploded shell, until Henry makes a critical mistake leaving the doctors less than two minutes to get away, but it's too late. The bomb explodes sending hundreds of leaflets in the air as it turns out to be a propaganda bomb telling the enemy to give up, that they can't win.

Commentary by Larry Gelbart: "In those days, a hundred bucks seemed like a thousand." (On Radar's comment about there being "almost a hundred bucks, here")

Commentary by Gene Reynolds: "McLean came in with the story for The Army Navy Game."

PA Announcement by Sal Viscuso

Authors' Notes: The game on Henry's radio is announced as, "The 53rd Gridiron Classic."

The 53rd Army-Navy game was played in 1952 (in "I Hate a Mystery," it's 1951, according to Hawkeye), in Philadelphia's Municipal Stadium, roughly equidistant from West Point and Annapolis. The final score of that game was Navy 7, Army 0. The following games were played at Municipal Stadium in Philadelphia:

1950: Game # 51 – Navy 14, Army 2
1951: Game # 52 – Navy 42, Army 7
1952: Game # 53 – Navy 7, Army 0
1953: Game # 54 – Army 20, Navy 7

None of the above games coincide with the year or the final score of the episode game.

The radio announcer's voice is that of Hy Averback, who directed several *M*A*S*H* episodes, including 3 in the first season: "Requiem For A Lightweight," "The Moose" and "I Hate A Mystery." Hy Averback's voice will be heard again in the O.R. over the speaker on the wall in a future episode.

In Chapter 3, Henry's diploma is seen in its usual spot on the wall. A few seconds before the heater chimney falls, the diploma is not there.

Henry's wife's name is Mildred. This will change in future episodes. Mildred is also the name of Larry Gelbart's cousin.

As we've seen Klinger earlier in "Dear Dad" wearing regulation fatigues, this is another rare appearance of Klinger wearing the suit and hat he was drafted in.

As the show progresses, so do Klinger's attempts at getting out of the army. Aside from wearing women's clothing, in this episode, while at the draft board, he ate the eye chart, licked the doctor's ear and jammed the doctor's letter opener in his heel. He's also wearing a stuffed bra in the tag.

Radar is smoking a cigar and drinking brandy in the office with Henry. This will become significant later in the series.

Radar also wishes he could wink, but Nurse Hardy goes with him to "check out" the supply shed anyway. This will also become significant later in the series.

Sticky Wicket – 3/4/1973

Season 1 / Episode 21 / Production 21 – J321

Columbia House VHS Tape . . . . *Operation Overload (Catalog # 3669)*
Fox DVD. . . . . *Season 1, Disc 3*

Alan Alda, Wayne Rogers, McLean Stevenson,
Loretta Swit, Larry Linville, Gary Burghoff

Produced by Gene Reynolds
Executive Script Consultant: Larry Gelbart
Teleplay By Laurence Marks & Larry Gelbart
Story By Richard Baer
Directed by Don Weis

John Orchard. . . . . .Ugly John
Lynette Mettey . . . . .Lieutenant Nancy Griffin
Wayne Bryan. . . . . Private Thompson
Copyright 1973 – 20th Century Fox Film Corporation

Non-Credited Appearances. . . . . .Roy Goldman, Dennis Troy, Gwen Farrell,
Marcia Gelman, Sheila Lauritsen, Ralph Grosh, Bonnie Jones

Chapters

1: *Main Titles*	6: *Going Buggy – 12:24*
2: *Surgically Incompetent – 0:47*	7: *No Privacy – 16:49*
3: *A Disruptive Influence – 4:28*	8: *Something Missed – 20:42*
4: *The Private's Problem – 7:32*	9: *Home Again – 24:11*
5: *Doctor Screw-Up – 10:30*	10: *End Titles – 24:56*

Closing Stills

1: *Radar with potatoes on his face – Mess Tent*
2: *Hawkeye*
3: *Henry and Hawkeye*
4: *Hawkeye gets Margaret*

Synopsis: When Hawkeye's patient develops a fever and abdominal pain in post-op, he doesn't know why. Frank takes this opportunity to taunt him about it in the mess tent, but soon regrets it when he's manhandled. Frustrated, Hawkeye now moves out of the Swamp to be alone when, in the middle of the night, he thinks he might know what the problem is and wakes Margaret to assist, then finds Frank hiding in her closet. During the operation, his hunch pays off and even Frank admits, "Anybody could've missed that." With his patient on the mend, Hawkeye returns to the Swamp and has a Martini with Trapper.

Authors' Notes: There are no PA announcements in this episode.
Hawkeye won't "officially" move out of the swamp again until the episode "Picture This," in Season 10.
The name "Blake" is seen inside both of Henry's boots.
Trapper mentions the movie *Bonzo Goes To College* from 1952. According to Hawkeye in "I Hate A Mystery," it's 1951.
In Chapter 6, the top of Hawkeye's shorts can be seen just as he enters the shower.
There's a Martini by Radar when he's playing poker in the Swamp, presumably his.

Major Fred C. Dobbs – 3/11/1973

Season 1 / Episode 22 / Production 20 – J320

Columbia House VHS Tape . . . . .Hawkeye Vs Frank (Catalog # 3771)
Fox DVD. . . . . Season 1, Disc 3

Alan Alda, Wayne Rogers, McLean Stevenson,
Loretta Swit, Larry Linville, Gary Burghoff

Produced by Gene Reynolds
Executive Script Consultant: Larry Gelbart
Written by Sid Dorfman
Directed by Don Weis

Harvey J. Goldenberg . . . . Captain Kaplan
Odessa Cleveland . . . . Lieutenant Ginger Bayliss

Copyright 1973 – 20th Century Fox Film Corporation

Non-Credited Appearances. . . . . Marcia Gelman, Gwen Farrell

Chapters

1: Main Titles	6: Going Too Far – 12:19
2: Ginger's Bad Day – 0:49	7: Gullible for Gold – 14:27
3: The Last Straw – 3:12	8: Frank's Final Decision – 19:51
4: Frank's Farewell – 8:07	9: Making Amends – 24:08
5: The Big Broadcast – 10:10	10: End Titles – 24:57

Closing Stills

1: Trapper and Hawkeye
2: Frank waking Radar
3: Henry and Frank
4: Hawkeye hugs Frank in scrub room

Synopsis: When Hawkeye and Trapper play one too many practical jokes on Frank, he demands a transfer and Henry approves it. However, it doesn't prevent them from taping a private conversation between Frank and Margaret and broadcasting it over the PA. Now, Margaret, after being publicly humiliated, also wants a transfer, and the doctors have to pull double duty until replacements can be found. But Hawkeye hatches a plan that plays to Frank's greed and love of money by making him believe there's gold in a nearby field.

Commentary by Harvey J. Goldenberg: "I was actually hired, and unhired, without ever getting a script for a part in which the character cross-dresses while trying to get out of the service. He appears in the mess hall in full drag. When he is stared at, he points to his pearls (or something) and says something like "What else would you wear with basic black?" As we know, the incident was expanded and Max Klinger was born and Jamie Farr became a *M*A*S*H* favorite.

"To pay me back for unhiring me, I was given the role of the dentist Captain Kaplan. In this episode, Trapper John plants dental gold in the field, and convinces Major Burns that the area was loaded with gold. Wayne Rogers was a very nice guy. I ran into him a couple of times after he left the show and he still remembered my name. My scene was shot on the 20th Century Fox lot where the *M*A*S*H* set was."

Commentary by Larry Gelbart: "From the Prop Department." (Responding to the question where would the doctors have gotten spray paint to make a gold jeep in Korea.)

It wasn't my voice on the PA. In the early days it was an actor named James Lydon. Todd Sussman did a few."

PA Announcement by Sal Viscuso

Authors' Notes: Though both Larry Gelbart and Wayne Rogers have cited this episode as poor in previous accounts, author Mark O'Neill finds the scene with Hawkeye and Trapper listening to their favorite radio soap opera utterly hysterical.

Hawkeye's favorite soap opera, *Just Plain MacArthur*, heard in the Swamp, stars "Nurse Dribble" and Dr. Manure" and is actually a private conversation between Frank and Margaret. (This may be Hawkeye's favorite soap opera, but as far as Alan Alda is concerned, this episode doesn't work.)

Margaret again uses hydrogen peroxide on her roots.

A host of practical jokes were played on Frank in this episode, including "The Princess and the Pea Treatment." *(For a complete list of jokes played on Frank, see "Prank Frank Season 1" on Page 131.)*

The sign on Margaret's tent door is in block lettering and has her name only. In previous episodes, the sign on her door was in a free-hand style and had, "Knock before entering" underneath.

The frames on Radar's glasses, prospecting tools, part of the horse's harness, the PA speaker, an area of small rocks in a nearby field and an entire jeep were all painted gold.

The title of this episode is a reference to the Humphrey Bogart character in the 1948 film, *The Treasure of Sierra Madre,* an adaptation of the 1927 novel by B. Traven.

Harvey J. Goldenberg will return again as the dentist, Captain Kaplan in the Season 1 finale, "Showtime."

PHOTO COURTESY HARVEY J. GOLDENBERG

Harvey J. Goldenberg — aka Captain Kaplan

Ceasefire – 3/18/1973

Season 1 / Episode 23 / Production 23 – J323

Columbia House Vhs Tape . . . . *Going Home (Catalog # 3741)*
Fox DVD. . . . . *Season 1, Disc 3*

Alan Alda, Wayne Rogers, McLean Stevenson,
Loretta Swit, Larry Linville, Gary Burghoff

Produced by Gene Reynolds
Executive Script Consultant: Larry Gelbart
Teleplay By Laurence Marks & Larry Gelbart
Story By Robert Klane
Directed by Earl Bellamy

Herb Voland . . . . General Crandall Clayton
Jamie Farr . . . . Corporal Klinger
William Christopher . . . . Father Mulcahy
Patrick Adiarte . . . . Ho Jon
Lynette Mettey . . . . Lieutenant Nancy Griffin
Marcia Strassman . . . . Lieutenant Margie Cutler
Bonnie Jones . . . . Barbara
Odessa Cleveland . . . . Lieutenant Ginger Bayliss
Bruce Kimmel . . . . Private Gilbert

Copyright 1973 – 20th Century Fox Film Corporation

Non-Credited Appearances. . . . . Roy Goldman, Dennis Troy

Chapters

1: *Main Titles*	6: *Cease Fire Sale – 17:52*
2: *A Cease Fire? – 2:42*	7: *Unhappy Hot Lips – 18:56*
3: *Radar's Scrapbook – 8:05*	8: *The Cease Fire Party – 20:28*
4: *No Cease Fire Yet! – 10:23*	9: *Back in Business – 23:40*
5: *Promises – 12:42*	10: *End Titles – 24:57*

Closing Stills

1: *All in the office – ceasefire!*
2: *Ceasefire party on 9 compound*
3: *Ceasefire party in the Mess Tent*
4: *Hawkeye and Trapper in empty Swamp – no walls*

Synopsis: After General Clayton calls the 4077 to let them know a ceasefire's been arranged, a celebration ensues on the compound. Hawkeye offers the Swamp to Ho Jon, Klinger sells his clothes and Radar wants people to sign his scrapbook. Henry can't wait to get home so he can trip over his kid's roller skates while complaining about his taxes, and "loving every minute of it," while Margaret, a little drunk, is upset that she can't go home with Frank, who is also drunk. But Trapper isn't celebrating much since the only way he'll believe the war is over is when he's home refusing his first house call. Clayton arrives for a final drink with his "favorite MASH unit" and in the mess tent, Hawkeye pays homage to Clayton with a slide show of less than flattering pictures of Clayton, several of which are with Margaret. Everyone is having a good time in the mess tent when Radar hands the General a message. It seems Trapper was right; there is no ceasefire and the PA announces incoming wounded.

Commentary by Larry Gelbart: "Like every actor who found himself doing the series, Voland was disciplined, cooperative and a pleasure to work with."

PA Announcements by Sal Viscuso

Authors' Notes: Although Hawkeye mentions that he was the pickup sticks champion of Southern Maine, ("The Ringbanger") he clearly makes a reference to being from Vermont in this episode.

Margaret, drunk, loves Frank's thin lips and the bristle where he shaves his earlobes.

In "Yankee Doodle Doctor," Clayton pronounces his name as, "Crandall." Hawkeye, in this episode, pronounces it, "Brandle."

Radar is working the slide projector showing 12 photos of Clayton alone and with Margaret:

1: *Standing in a jeep saluting*
2: *Getting off the jeep saluting*
3: *Henry giving a lecture with Clayton asleep behind him*
4: *Exits the officer's latrine adjusting his belt with his right hand and his jacket over left arm*
5: *In front of the officer's latrine still adjusting his belt with his right hand and jacket over left arm*
6: *In Margaret's tent with Margaret on his lap while kissing her left cheek. Margaret has a big smile*
7: *Similar to picture #6*
8: *In Margaret's tent with Margaret on his lap – his left arm around her neck – right arm around her waist*
9: *In Margaret's tent with Margaret on his lap and both are in full-pucker*
10: *In Margaret's tent on his lap and both arms around her waist – kisses right cheek – Margaret laughing*
11: *In a jeep holding her around with her head on his chest. Both have eyes closed and smiling*
12: *Standing behind 2 55-gallon drums holding Margaret around while she's touching his chin*

Showtime – 3/25/1973

Season 1 / Episode 24 / Production 23 – J324

Columbia House VHS Tape . . . . *Leisure Time (Catalog # 10995)*
Fox DVD . . . . *Season 1, Disc 3*

Alan Alda, Wayne Rogers, McLean Stevenson,
Loretta Swit, Larry Linville, Gary Burghoff

Produced by Gene Reynolds
Teleplay By Robert Klane & Larry Gelbart
Story By Larry Gelbart
Directed by Jackie Cooper

Joey Forman . . . . Jackie Flash
William Christopher . . . . Father Mulcahy
Harvey J. Goldenberg . . . . Captain Kaplan
Stanley Clay . . . . Driver
Sheila Lauritsen . . . . Nurse
Oksun Kim . . . . Korean Woman *(Mother)*

The Miller Sisters: . . . . Marilyn King
Jean Turrell
Joan Lucksinger

Copyright 1973 – 20th Century Fox Film Corporation

Non-Credited Appearances . . . . .Dennis Troy, Roy Goldman, Gwen Farrell

Chapters

1: *Main Titles*	6: *Bad Jokes – 13:25*
2: *The Miller Sisters – 0:49*	7: *The Band – 18:26*
3: *The Dentist – 5:31*	8: *Farewell, Dentist – 19:11*
4: *Doctor vs. Priest – 7:06*	9: *A Baby for the Colonel – 20:41*
5: *Henry's Expecting – 9:37*	10: *End Titles – 24:20*

Closing Stills

1 *Jackie Flash*
2: *The Miller Sisters*
3: *Frank and Hawkeye*
4: *Water dumped on Hawkeye (Practical joke by Frank)*
5: *Radar gives Henry a baby*

Synopsis: The USO (United Service Organization) has brought their show to the 4077th, a welcome respite that nearly everyone is enjoying. Although the emcee, Jackie Flash, tells corny jokes, the Miller Sisters sing some of the hits of the day in beautiful harmonies. But not everyone is enjoying the show. Henry is worried about his wife, who is about to give birth for the third time, and Trapper has a difficult surgery in the O.R. Father Mulcahy expresses his concern over whether or not he's doing any good at the 4077th since his results are "far less tangible" than that of the doctors and Radar sits in on drums with the USO band, even taking a solo.

Commentary by Harvey J. Goldenberg: "For my second episode, a few weeks later, Gene Reynolds had me come in. He said 'I'm not going to insult you by asking you to read.' That is how I came to be featured in my second and last episode, where I was the same dentist, Captain Kaplan. But now, I was getting out of the service. Jackie Cooper was the director. When I first read the part, I thought the character was more introverted. But Jackie suggested that it would set an edge in the scenes if I were more paranoid. I had a great monologue, which was delivered after Hawkeye throws a football to me (I'm a Jewish prince…what do I know about a pigskin?). I dropped it the first time Alan threw it to me. Jackie said, 'Catch it, we're losing light.' So, I caught it (I was afraid not to). Of course, that scene was cut from the show. But it was a goodie. The second episode was shot on both the soundstage and at the ranch." *(Mr. Goldenberg has his own web site: http:// www.geocities.com/hollywood/set/5657.)*

Commentary by Larry Gelbart: "Some scripts (which were usually the result of a first and second draft by the assigned writer), were then lightly dusted, jokes and business inserted, some even as we filmed."

Authors' Notes: There are no PA announcements in this episode.
This episode is one of the few where Frank plays practical jokes on Hawkeye:

1: *When Hawkeye checks to see why nothing is coming out of the still, it suddenly sprays in his face.*
2: *Frank ties a rope to the cot legs and when Hawkeye enters the Swamp, his foot hits the rope and a bucket of water is dumped on his head.*
3: *Hawkeye enters the right shower stall (looking at the screen) and no water comes out. When he reaches over and pulls the chain in the left stall, it works, but when he moves into the left stall, water now comes out of the right shower stall, and not the left.*

Hawkeye gets even when Frank is on his way to the Officer's Latrine. After Frank enters, Hawkeye signals Dennis to cut the latrine's support ropes and there's Frank sitting there reading Stars & Stripes.

The song "Stars and Stripes Forever" is heard. This was Written by John Philip Sousa and, by an Act of Congress, is the National March of the United States.

PHOTO COURTESY JEAN TURRELL-WRIGHT

Jean Turrell-Wright appears in the Season 1 finale, "Show Time."

The songs The Miller Sisters sang were pre-recorded in the studio and were lip-synched on the show.

The cast is shown on-screen with their names underneath in the following order: *William Christopher, Gary Burghoff, Larry Linville, Loretta Swit, McLean Stevenson, Wayne Rogers, Alan Alda.*

Jean Turrell-Wright, one of the Miller Sisters, (the one on the right) studied with vocal coach, Tena Rone of Hollywood and toured with the Ray Conniff Singers, Jimmy Joyce Singers, Decormier Folk Singers, and the Roger Wagner Chorale. Jean, Joan Lucksinger, and Marilyn King (far left and middle), were contracted by Jimmy Joyce to do the *M*A*S*H* episode. Jean also had the honor to sing with the Ray Conniff Singers at The White House for President Nixon.

She enjoyed her time working on the show, and instead of a poor quality VHS tape, she now enjoys the episode on DVD. Jean is a retired music educator and is the Director of the Capistrano Valley Church of Religious Science Celebration Choir and the mother of two children.

Appendix – Season 1

Character Profiles

Hawkeye

Episode 1: Parents.
    1: Dean Lodge — Head of his Alma Mater.
    3: Transmission mechanic before the war *(sarcastic)*.
    3: Knows a girl back home like Margaret — her name is "Rover."
    3: Said he was on the boxing team at school, but has a bad shoulder *(sarcastic)*.
    4: Appointed Chief Surgeon.
    4: Was working in a hospital when called up.
    5: Refers to a sister.
    5: Said his father wished he had a Sister.
    10: Let Ho Jon keep $309.68 in poker winnings.
    10: The year is 1951.
    10: Frank became a doctor to meet girls *(sarcastic)*.
    10: Sent General Barker brownies with a laxative filling.
    12: Vermont.
    16: Pickup Sticks Champion of southern Maine (first reference of being from Maine).
    17: Tommy Gillis — one of his best friends; has known him more than 15 years.
    17: First time he cries in Korea is when Tommy dies on an operating table.
    17: Milk monitor during the depression.
    17: "Ode To A Pretty Teacher" — Poem written.
    17: Refers to taking Radar's appendix out.
    18: Father sent the tuxedo.
    18: Mother and Sister.
    19: Father sent the long johns.
    22: Dentist in Detroit *(maybe sarcastic)*.
    23: Reference to -.
    24: Quote by professor in medical school — "G-d cures the patient, but the doctor takes the fee."

Trapper

Episode 1: Only time seen in a red MD robe.
    1: Only time hair is parted on the side.
    1: Married.
    3: On school boxing team and "very good."
    3: Weighs 175 pounds as "Kid Doctor."
    4: Wrote on the school walls as opposed to the school paper.
    5: Only time seen in a blue terrycloth robe — yellow the rest of the way.

23: First autopsy, colleagues put a kidney under his cap.

24: Started out as an architect, but couldn't handle the math.

Henry

Episode 3: Brother is a warden.

8: Wife with a fistful of credit cards and a going practice back home.

8: Radar keeps a duplicate set of master keys in the company safe.

8: Radar keeps the duty roster in the top left file cabinet.

9: From Bloomington, Illinois.

9: Family doctor had a touring car with Isinglass curtains.

9: Awarded the Special Citation of Merit, 4th Class.

16: Likes boneless sardines, chunky peanut butter, cheese balls and smoked oysters.

16: Drunk.

19: Hawkeye & Trapper perform an appendectomy on him.

20: Wife's name is Mildred.

20: Team manager for Illinois State football.

20: Taped tank Washington's wrong leg.

20: Tank shoots out his porch light once a year and is now a judge.

21: Wears an eye mask to sleep.

21: The name, "Blake" is written inside each boot.

21: Wife is still Mildred.

24: Wife in labor and has the best obstetrician in Bloomington, Marv Handleman.

24: Newborn son stats — 7 pounds, 2 ounces and 21 inches.

24: Wife is still Mildred.

Margaret

Episode 1: Served under General Hammond at Fort Benning.

4: First time seen using hydrogen peroxide on her roots.

7: Her psychiatrist friend, Phil Sherman, is stationed at the 423rd EVAC.

10: The hair brushes Ho Jon took were given to her by her father.

16: Left handed, according to Hawkeye.

17: "I'm In the Mood For Love" gives her goose bumps.

22: Hydrogen peroxide on her roots again.

23: Loves Frank's thin lips and his bristle when Frank shaves his lobes.

23: Drunk.

Frank

Episode 2: Margaret's lobes "drive him wild."

3: Frank W. Burns.

3: Serial number is RA98672412.

4: Wrote on the school paper.

4: From Indiana, as per Trapper.

4: Was in practice for 3 years before called up.

4: $35,000 house and 2 cars.

4: Likes Margaret to call him, "Tiger."

4: Old Spice cologne seen by his bunk.

10: Became a doctor because it was, "the wish of my dear mother."

11: Blood type is AB negative.

11: Paranoid because everyone's against him.

11: Cannot hold beer.

11: Tricked into peeing in a bucket.

15: If Margaret is seeing Tuttle, he'll put his head under a jeep.

17: "Pennsylvania 6, 5000" gives him goose bumps.

17: Voted "Most Graceful" at Veloz & Yolanda.

17: The last time his back went out was V-J Day in Times Square when a big sailor hugged him.

17: Franklin D. Burns.

18: Drunk.

18: Nobody ever called him, "pal or buddy in his whole rotten life."

18: His brother called him, "Ferret Face."

19: His minister lives right up the street from him.

19: When he gets nervous chilblains, his finger crack open.

22: Belongs to a country club.

22: Has a 30-foot yacht.

22: Became a doctor for money and married for money, according to Hawkeye.

22: Cancels his transfer when he thinks there's gold near the camp.

23: He's supposed to keep his inner ear dry.

Radar

Episode 2: Black market connections.

6: From Ottumwa, Iowa.

10: Bear makes first appearance.

11: The war gives him an appetite.

14: Rushing makes him nervous and can't pee.

14: Was engaged to Linda Sue — She's going to marry Elroy Fimple.

14: Holtzman's Department Store, assumed to be in Iowa.

15: Knows a guy who has pictures of Frank and Margaret.

16: Has a friend at Walter Reed.

18: Henry passed him for his high school diploma from the AAA High School Diploma Co. of Delavan, IN.

18: Above is the proudest moment of his life.

20: Wishes he could wink.

21: Won $803 playing poker.

23: Mother wears a size 12 dress.

Radar drinking and smoking cigars

(This will be significant as the series progresses)

Episode 3: Martini and cigar *(not lit)*.

4: Brandy and cigar.

5: Martini.

15: Martini *(two)*.

20: Brandy.

21: Martini.

24: Cigar

Klinger

Episode 12: Wears a red bandana his mother sent. If he doesn't wear it, she thinks something will happen to him.

20: Wearing the suit he was drafted in.

20: Ate the eye chart at the draft board.

20: Licked the doctor's ear at the draft board.

20: Jammed the doctor's letter opener in his heel at the draft board

Father Mulcahy

Episode 3: Trained boys for boxing back home.

18: Back went bad in Jesuit school from "all that kneeling."

Seen, Heard, Mentioned or Referenced – Season 1

Movies

Episode 1: *The Mummy* (1932) Hawkeye makes a reference.

   4: The latest War Department film on the dangers of V.D.

   6: *Yankee Doodle Doctor* filmed and seen by Hawkeye and Trapper.

  10: *Les Miserable* (1935) Mentioned over the PA.

  11: War Department film on "How to Lead A Good Clean Life" mentioned over the PA.

  11: *Dracula* (1931) Hawkeye does a Bela Lugosi impersonation from this movie.

  12: Hawkeye mentions Daffy Duck whose first appearance was in the animated short *Porky's Duck Hunt* (1937).

  14: Medical movie on the newest methods of treating cardiogenic shock and slides on the newest drugs available.

  17: Trapper is watching a Deborah Paget movie in the mess tent, as per Hawkeye; her first notable movie was *Cry of the City* (1948).

  19: Trapper refers to *The Mummy* (1932).

  19: Hawkeye mentions *Duck Soup* (1933).

  21: Trapper mentions *Bride of the Gorilla* (1951).

  21: Trapper mentions *Bonzo Goes to College* (1952).

  21: Radar mentions *Love Life of a Gorilla* (1937).

  21: Radar mentions *Bedtime for Bonzo* (1951).

  22: "Major Fred C. Dobbs" is a reference to the movie *The Treasure of the Sierra Madre* (1948).

  22: *Greed* (1924) Mentioned over the PA.

  22: "The Major was A Miner" *(not real)* Mentioned over the PA.

Songs

Episode 1: "My Blue Heaven" (1927) *(Male Japanese voice heard)* Words by George Whiting, music by Walter Donaldson.

   1: "Happy Days Are Here Again" (1929) *(Female Japanese voice heard)* Words by Jack Yellin, music by Milton Ager.

   1: "Brahms' Lullaby" *(Heard)* Written by Johannes Brahms (May 7, 1833-April 3, 1897).

   1: "Shoeshine Boy" *(Male Japanese voice heard)* From the movie *Shoeshine Boy* (1943).

   1: "Chattanooga Choo-Choo" *(Male Japanese voice heard)* Words by Mack Gordon, music by Harry Warren. From the 1941 movie *Sun Valley Serenade*.

   1: "The Japanese Farewell Song" *(Words heard over the PA: "I will always be yours for eternity" by female Japanese voice.)* Written by Morgan, Yoshida, Hashigawa. (Note: this song was written in 1955.)

   2: "Chattanooga Choo-Choo" *(Male Japanese voice heard on radio)* See Episode 1 for details.

   2: "My Blue Heaven" *(Male Japanese voice heard)* See Episode 1 for details.

   4: "Pomp and Circumstance" *(Heard)* Written by Sir Edward Elgar and premiered in Liverpool in 1901.

   6: "I'm In the Mood for Love" (1935) *(Instrumental heard)* Words by Dorothy Fields, music by Jimmy McHugh.

   6: "Yankee Doodle" *(Hawkeye and Trapper sing: "Stuck a feather in his nurse and called her macaroni")* Pre-Revolutionary War song sung by the British mocking American soldiers

6: "Chattanooga Choo-Choo" *(Male Japanese voice heard)* See Episode 1 for details.

7: "My Blue Heaven" *(Hawkeye hums)* See Episode 1 for details.

7: "My Blue Heaven" *(Male Japanese voice heard, in Margaret's tent)* See Episode 1 for details.

7: "My Blue Heaven" *(Hawkeye and Trapper singing)* See "Episode 1 for details.

9: "Cocktails for Two" *(Hawkeye sings)* Words by Arthur Johnston, music by Sam Coslow from the 1934 movie, *Murder at the Vanities.*

9: "Thanks for the Memories" *(Hawkeye mentions)* Words by Leo Robin, music by Ralph Rainger from the movie, *The Big Broadcast of 1938.*

9: "Reveille" *(Bugle over the PA)* First use in the military was in 1812 as a drum call to signify that soldiers should rise for the day.

9: "If I Knew You Were Coming I'd Have Baked A Cake" *(Sung by two Japanese women)* Written by Eileen Barton in 1950.

10: "I'm In the Mood for Love" *(Instrumental heard in Margaret's tent)* See Episode 6 for details.

10: "Someone to Watch Over Me" *(Instrumental heard over PA)* Words by Ira Gershwin, music by George Gershwin. From the 1926 musical, "Oh, Kay."

11: "Happy Days Are Here Again" *(Female Japanese voice heard)* See Episode 1 for details.

12: "Hark, The Herald Angel Sings" *(Instrumental)* Words by Charles Wesley, brother of John Wesley, founder of the Methodist Church in 1739. Music added by Felix Mendelssohn in 1840

12: "I'm Confessin' That I Love You" *(Mentioned over the PA)* Written by Doc Daugherty, Al J. Neiberg and Ellis Reynolds in 1930.

12: "Winter Wonderland" *(Instrumental)* Words by Richard B. Smith, music by Felix Bernard, published in 1934.

12: "The First Noel" *(Instrumental)* Unknown in origin, thought to be English dating back to the 16th Century

12: "Good King Wenchelaus" *(Instrumental)* Words by John Mason Neal circa 1849, music first published in 1582.

12: "Joy to the World" *(Instrumental)* Words by Isaac Watts, music by Lowell Mason, first recorded in 1954. Arranged from an older melody believed to have originated from George Frideric Handel (February 23, 1685-April 14, 1759).

12: "Away In A Manger" *(Instrumental)* Written before 1861.

12: "Jingle Bells" *(Instrumental)* Originally written for Thanksgiving by Minister James Pierpont for kids celebrating his Boston Sunday School Thanksgiving. It was sung again for Christmas and it stuck.

12: Hawkeye mentions "Some Enchanted Evening" From the 1949 Rodgers & Hammerstein musical, "South Pacific"

13: "For He's A Jolly Good Fellow" *(Sung at Edwina's birthday party with "She" for "He")* British/American Traditional. Second most popular song in English behind "Happy Birthday" (according to Guinness).

15: "Pomp and Circumstance" *(Instrumental)* See Episode 4 for details.

16: "Home On the Range" *(Henry sings, "where the dear and the antelope play...")* Arranged by David Guion (1892-1981), often credited as composer, words originally written by Dr. Brewster M. Higley in the 1870's, music added by Daniel E. Kelly, Higley's friend. Original words are *not* identical to the newer arrangement. *(Note: "Home On the Range" became the state song of Kansas in 1947.)*

17: "I'm In the Mood for Love" *(Instrumental)* See Episode 6 for details.

17: "Pennsylvania 6, 5000" *(Mentioned by Frank)* Recorded by Glen Miller in 1940.

18: "I Got A Gal In Kalamazoo" *(Frank sings, "A-B-C-D-E-F-G-H-I, I got a gal in Kalamazoo...")* Words by Mack Gordon, music by Harry Warren. From the 1942 movie, *Orchestra Wives.*

18: "One for My Baby" (And One for the Road) *(Frank sings, "There's no one in the place except you and me...")* Words by Johnny Mercer, music by Harold Arlen from the 1943 musical, "The Sky's The Limit."

18: "My Blue Heaven" *(Hawkeye & His Swinging Surgeons, Margaret and Hawkeye sing)* See Episode 1 for details.

19: "In the Cool, Cool, Cool of the Evening" *(Hawkeye sings, "in the cool, cool, cool of the evening, when the singin' fills the air, and in the shank of the night, when the doin's all right, you can tell them I'll be there, you can tell them I'll be there...")* Words by Johnny Mercer, music by Hoagy Carmicheal from the 1951 movie, *Here Comes The Groom;* Academy award for Best Original Song.

19: "I've Got My Love To Keep Me Warm" *(Hawkeye sings "The snow is snowing, the wind is blowing but I can weather the storm...")* Words and Music written by Irving Berlin, 1936.

20: "Auld Lange Syne" *(Margaret sings in her tent)* Written as a poem by Robert Byrns (1759-1796).

23: "Happy Days Are Here Again" *(Japanese female voice, in English)* See Episode 1 for details.

23: "The Star Spangled Banner" *(mentioned).*

23: "Auld Lang Syne" *(Sung in the mess tent)* See Episode 20 for details.

24: "Give Me the Simple Life" *(The Miller Sisters sing, "A cottage small is all I'm after, not one that's spacious and wide...")* Words by Harry Ruby (October 29, 1895-February 23, 1974), music by Rube Bloom (April. 24, 1902-March 30, 1976). From the 1950 movie *Father of the Bride.*

24: "Why Don't We Do This More Often?" *(The Miller Sisters sing, "Why don't we do this more often, just what we're doin' tonight...?")* Words by Charles Newman, music by Allie Wrobel, published in 1941.

24: "Again" *(The Miller Sisters sing, "Again, this couldn't happen again, this is that once in a lifetime, this is time thrill divine...")* Words by Dorcas Cochran, music by Lionel newman from the 1948 movie, *Road House.*

24: "I Had the Craziest Dream" *(The Miller Sisters sing, "I had the craziest dream last night, yes I did...")* Words by Mack Gordon, music by Harry Warren. From the 1942 movie, *Springtime In The Rockies.*

24: "You Make Me Feel So Young" *(The Miller Sisters sing, "You make me feel so young, you make me feel there are songs to be sung...")* Words by Mack Gordon, music by Josef Myrow, 1946.

24: "Stars and Stripes Forever" *(Instrumental)* Written by John Philip Sousa (November 6, 1854-March 6, 1932) in 1896. By an Act of Congress, "Stars and Stripes Forever" is the National March of the United States.

Prank Frank – Season 1

Episode 1: Trapper and Hawkeye put a duffle bag over his head, and push him out of the Swamp *(seen)*.
Sedated and bandaged over head and face in Post-Op *(seen)*.

7: Hawkeye tied his big toes to the cot legs and yelled "fire!" *(mentioned)*.

7: Hawkeye put all four limbs in plaster and hung Frank from the ceiling with traction ropes. Frank thought he had four broken limbs *(mentioned)*.

11: Hawkeye and Trapper siphon a pint of blood while Frank's asleep *(seen)*.

11: Frank is tricked into urinating in a bucket *(seen, partially)*.

11: Trapper handcuffs Frank to Margaret in the scrub room *(seen)*.

14: Hawkeye sits next to Frank for movie in the mess tent. Frank thinks it's Margaret and "walks" his fingers up Hawkeye's thigh *(seen)*.

14: Hawkeye and Trapper sew Frank into his blanket *(mentioned)*.

14: Chloroform in his cologne: "A cologne overdose" *(seen)*.

14: Hawkeye and Trapper in Margaret's bed *(seen)*.

15: Hawkeye and Trapper glued Frank's Bible together *(mentioned)*.

15: Hawkeye and Trapper drew fangs on Frank's picture of Senator McCarthy *(mentioned)*.

16: Hawkeye and Trapper put a pair of gold high-heels by Frank's cot to imply that he wears them *(seen)*.

16: Radar delivers Frank's laundry of negligees and bras to imply that he wears these items *(seen)*.

16: Frank's patient is wheeled into the OR: it's Hawkeye, wanting the "Dick Haymes look" *(seen)*.

21: Hawkeye finds Frank hiding in Margaret's locker/closet in her tent *(seen)*.

22: A cast with a hook is placed on Frank's right arm and hits his head swatting a fly *(seen)*.

22: Hawkeye and Trapper nail five cots on top of each other — Frank is sleeping 12 feet off the floor. Known as the "Princess and the Pea Treatment" *(seen)*.

22: Hawkeye and Trapper stuffed Frank's ears with hamburger and a dog wakes him by licking his ears *(seen)*.

22: Frank holds flowers behind his back, unaware that Radar's horse is eating them *(seen)*.

22: Hawkeye and Trapper put cream cheese in his house slippers *(mentioned)*.

22: Hawkeye and Trapper secretly recorded a private conversation between Frank and Margaret and broadcast it over the PA *(seen)*.

24: Frank is in the officer's latrine reading *Stars & Stripes* when Hawkeye has Dennis cut the support ropes *(seen)*.

Appearances - Season 1

Adiarte, Patrick .... Episode 1, 5, 8, 9, 10, 11, 23 *(Ho Jon)*
Booke, Sorrell .... Episode 3, 4 *(General Barker)*
Bowman, Gail .... Episode 18 *(Nurse)*
Brown, Timothy .... Episode 1, 4, 5, 9, 10, 11 *(Captain Spearchucker Jones)*
Brownell, Barbara .... Episode 5, 14 *(Lieutenant Jones)*
Bryan, Wayne .... Episode 20 *(Private Thompson)*
Bush, Billy Green .... Episode 8 *(Cowboy John Hodges)*
Callahan, James .... Episode 17 *(Corporal Tommy Gillis)*
Christopher, William .... Episode 3, 8, 9, 10, 12, 15, 17, 18, 19, 20, 23, 24
(Father Mulcahy)
Chung, Byron .... Episode 11 *(P.O.W.)*
Cleveland, Odessa .... Episode 1, 2, 3, 4, 7, 9, 10, 11, 12, 18, 22, 23
(Lieutenant Ginger Bayliss)
Clay, Stanley .... Episode 24 *(Driver)*
Corey, Joseph .... Episode 8 *(Goldstein)*
Danks, Indira .... Episode 14 *(Lieutenant O'Brien)*
Deen, Lizabeth .... Episode 12 *(Becky)*
Farr, Jamie .... Episode 4, 12, 18, 19, 20, 23 *(Corporal Klinger)*
Fimple, Dennis .... Episode 15 *(Sergeant "Sparky" Pryor)*
Flanders, Ed .... Episode 6 *(Lieutenant William Duane Bricker)*
Forman, Joey .... Episode 24 *(Jackie Flash)*
Goldenberg, Harvey J. .... Episode 22, 24 *(Captain Kaplan)*
Golonka, Arlene .... Episode 13 *(Lieutenant Edwina Ferguson)*
Gooden, Bob .... Episode 4, 9, 11 *(Boone)*
Harper, Jerry .... Episode 14 *(Sergeant)*
Henteloff, Alex .... Episode 18 *(Captain Adam Casey (Sergeant Schwartz)*
Hicks, Chuck .... Episode 17 *(Patient #2)*
Howard, Ronny .... Episode 17 *(Private Wendell/Walter Petersen)*
Ito, Robert .... Episode 2 *(Lin)*
Jenkins, Paul .... Episode 5 *(Sergeant Baker)*
Johnson, John C. .... Episode 2 *(Truck driver)*
Jones, Bonnie .... Episode 10, 12, 23 *(Lieutenant Barbara Bannerman)*
Jue, Craig .... Episode 5 *(Benny)*
Kaat, Bill .... Episode 12 *(P.F.C.)*
Kim, Oksun .... Episode 24 *(Korean Woman, Mother)*
Kimmel, Bruce .... Episode 23 *(Private Gilbert)*
King, Kathleen .... Episode 19 *(Nurse Beddoes)*
King, Marilyn .... Episode 24 *(Miller Sister)*
Kirby, Jr. B. *(Bruno)* .... Episode 1 *(Boone)*
Kramer, Bert .... Episode 6 *(Sergeant Martin)*
Lauritsen, Sheila .... Episode 20, 24 *(Nurse Hardy)*
Lee, Virginia .... Episode 5 *(Young Hi)*
Lerner, Fred .... Episode 17 *(Patient #1)*
Lucksinger, Joan .... Episode 24 *(Miller Sister)*
Manson, Alan .... Episode 20 *(Colonel Hersh)*
Margolin, Stuart .... Episode 7 *(Captain Philip G. Sherman)*
Meiklejohn, Linda .... Episode 1, 4, 5, 9, 10, 13, 16 *(Lieutenant Leslie Scorch)*
Metty, Lynette .... Episode 17, 20, 23 *(Lieutenant Nancy Griffin)*
Miller, Laura .... Episode 1 *(Knocko)*
Mitchell, Bobbie .... Episode 20 *(Nurse Mason)*
Morgan, George .... Episode 1 *(Father John P. Mulcahy)*

Nielson, Leslie...Episode 16 *(Colonel Buzz Brighton)*
Orchard, John................................. Episode 1, 3, 4, 5, 8, 9, 20, 21 *(Ugly John)*
Perry, Joseph...Episode 19 *(The Cook)*
Peters, Kelly Jean............................... Episode 14 *(Lieutenant Louise Anderson)*
Philipp, Karen .... Episode 1, 11 *(Lieutenant Dish)*
Pleet, Jean..Episode 9 *(Nurse)*
Powell, Jean .... Episode 8 *(Lieutenant Baker)*
Redd, Mary Robin .... Episode 15 *(Sister Theresa)*
Riley, Jack...Episode 4 *(Captain Kaplan)*
Robello, Mike..Episode 8 *(The Cook)*
Sikking, James .... Episode 15 *(Finance Officer)*
Soo, Jack.. Episode 2 *(Charlie Lee)*
Sakuro, Kasuko..Episode 9 *(Cho-Cho)*
Sparks, Tom.. Episode 6 *(Corpsman)*
Strassman, Marcia....................... Episode 3, 6, 7, 13, 14, 23 *(Lieutenant Margie Cutler)*
Svanoe, Bill ....Episode 9 *(Aide)*
Toy, Noel .... Episode 9 *(Mama San)*
Turrell, Jean...Episode 24 *(Miller Sister)*
Tuttle, Jonathon S. .... Episode 15 *(Himself)*
Van Orman, Gary... Episode 12 *(Corporal)*
Voland, Herb...............................Episode 6, 15, 23 *(General Crandall Clayton)*
Wood, G. (George)................................ Episode 1, 2, 9 *(General Hamilton Hammond)*
Young, Buck .... Episode 12 *(M.P.)*
Zee, John A.....................................Episode 20 *(Naval Commander Sturner)*

Broadcast/Production Order – Season 1

Broadcast

1: Pilot *(9/17/1972)*
2: To Market, To Market *(9/24/1972)*
3: Requiem For A Lightweight *(10/1/1972)*
4: Chief Surgeon, Who? *(10/8/1972)*
5: The Moose *(10/15/1972)*
6: Yankee Doodle Doctor *(10/22/1972)*
7: Bananas, Crackers & Nuts *(11/5/1972)*
8: Cowboy *(11/12/1972)*
9: Henry, Please Come Home *(11/19/1972)*
10: I Hate A Mystery *(11/26/1972)*
11: Germ Warfare *(12/10/1972)*
12: Dear Dad *(12/17/1972)*
13: Edwina *(12/24/1972)*
14: Love Story *(1/7/1973)*
15: Tuttle *(1/14/1973)*
16: The Ringbanger *(1/21/1973)*
17: Sometimes You Hear the Bullet *(1/28/1973)*
18: Dear Dad, Again *(2/4/1973)*

19: The Longjohn Flap *(2/18/1973)*
20: The Army-Navy Game *(2/25/1973)*
21: Sticky Wicket *(3/4/1973)*
22: Major Fred C. Dobbs *(3/11/1973)*
23: Ceasefire *(3/18/1973)*
24: Showtime *(3/25/1973)*

Production

1: *(Z9522)* Pilot
2: *(J302)* Henry, Please Come Home
3: *(J303)* To Market, To Market
4: *(J304)* Germ Warfare
5: *(J305)* The Moose
6: *(J306)* I Hate A Mystery
7: *(J307)* Chief Surgeon, Who?
8: *(J308)* Requiem For A Lightweight
9: *(J309)* Cowboy
10: *(J310)* Yankee Doodle Doctor
11: *(J311)* Bananas, Crackers & Nuts
12: *(J312)* Edwina
13: *(J313)* Dear Dad
14: *(J314)* Love Story
15: *(J315)* Tuttle
16: *(J316)* The Ringbanger
17: *(J317)* Dear Dad, Again
18: *(J318)* Sometimes You Hear the Bullet
19: *(J319)* The Longjohn Flap
20: *(J320)* Major Fred C. Dobbs
21: *(J321)* Sticky Wicket
22: *(J322)* The Army-Navy Game
23: *(J323)* Ceasefire
24: *(J324)* Showtime

Season 2

Among many *M*A*S*H* fans, Season 2 sets the standard for excellence. After a rocky first season in the ratings, viewers had tuned in when, about halfway into the season, CBS placed *M*A*S*H* after *All in the Family*. Season 2 starts out at the peak of television excellence, and then, somehow, manages to ascend even higher. "Divided We Stand" was written by Larry Gelbart as a way to re-introduce the characters to new viewers. It manages to do so with classic *M*A*S*H* humor. If it's one thing that Season 2 demonstrates, it's that no matter how outrageously funny the plot or dialogue was, nothing ever looked or sounded contrived. In keeping with the trend of Season 1, Season 2 perfected the seamless blend of comedy and drama. The comedy, in this season, seems to gush forth as though the show was really a Master's course in comedy writing. And yet, realism was omnipresent and the horrors of war were not trivialized or made to play second fiddle to the comedy. This season introduces the viewer to Colonel Flagg and Psychiatrist Sydney Freedman. Trapper almost exacts revenge on an enemy patient whose actions caused the death of one of Trapper's patients, and Hawkeye nearly becomes unglued in a war-induced spell of insomnia. Highlights from the season include Henry's sex lectures, infamous staff meetings, Hot Lips speaking for Frank and Radar continuing to think for Henry. Notable episodes from Season 2 include "Divided We Stand," "5 O'Clock Charlie," "Crisis," "Deal Me Out," "For Want of a Boot" and "Operation Noselift." Background music was never used better than in the hilarious opening of the classic, "The Incubator."

Divided We Stand – 9/15/1973

Season 2 / Episode 25 / Production 25 – K401

Columbia House VHS Tape . . . . *Cracking Up (Catalog # 3745)*
Fox DVD . . . . *Season 2, Disc 1*

Alan Alda, Wayne Rogers, McLean Stevenson,
Loretta Swit, Larry Linville, Gary Burghoff

Produced by Gene Reynolds and Larry Gelbart
Script Consultant: Laurence Marks
Written by Larry Gelbart
Directed by Jackie Cooper

Herb Voland . . . . .General Clayton
Anthony Holland . . . . .Captain Hildebrand
Jamie Farr . . . . Corporal Klinger
Linda Meiklejohn . . . . Leslie
Odessa Cleveland . . . . Ginger
Bobbie Mitchell. . . . . .Nurse Marshall
Leslie Evans . . . . .Nurse Bryan
Copyright 1973 – 20th Century Fox Film Corporation

Non-Credited Appearances. . . . . Kellye Nakahara, Roy Goldman, Gwen Farrell,
Marcia Gelman

Chapters

1: *Main Titles*	6: *One Big Happy Family – 13:44*
2: *Adverse Effects – 0:49*	7: *The Party's Over – 18:10*
3: *Standing Room Only – 4:43*	8: *Screwing Up In Reverse – 21:29*
4: *Discreet Observations – 6:12*	9: *The Cast of Characters – 24:39*
5: *Midnight Meetings – 10:08*	10: *End Titles – 25:25*

Closing Stills

1: *Hawkeye taps Hildebrand w/ skeleton in Henry's off.*
2: *Henry talking to Hawkeye & Trapper in the shower*
3: *Margaret complains to Hildebrand in Henry's office*
4: *Radar startles Trapper awake in the Swamp*

Synopsis: After receiving negative reports about the 4077, General Clayton becomes concerned that the unit might be suffering adverse effects doing the work they do close to the front line. Clayton sends Captain Hildebrand, a psychiatrist, to observe the members of the 4077 and his report back will weigh heavily on Clayton's decision whether or not to break them up. Hildebrand explains to Henry why he's there and informs him that he is to be the only staff member to know the real reason for him being there. Henry goes into a mild panic and tells the rest of the staff anyway in the hopes that they will behave themselves while Hildebrand is there.

Commentary by Larry Gelbart: "The episode was the first show of the 2nd season. The idea was to make the script a 2nd Pilot, i.e., introduce the characters and the background. This is understandable for viewers who might be seeing the show for the first time. The 1st season we had very low ratings and so was an opportunity — and a necessity — in educating 1st time viewers as to what we were all about. Anthony Holland, a very fine actor, played Dr. Hildebrand (named for a doctor I used to see in London). Holland took his life a number of years ago."

Commentary by Wayne Rogers: "I have not the vaguest idea of what Mr. Alda and I talked about in the voice-over scene. However, we often discussed things that would enhance the mood of the upcoming scene, such that it was preparation for something that would follow."

PA Announcements by Jimmy Lydon

Authors' Notes: After surgery, General Clayton is looking for Captain Hildebrand. The direction that he is facing, coming out of the hospital, and the direction Hawkeye is facing as he holds open the door of the Swamp and says, "Mon General," do not match up. The two men would not be able to see each other from their prospective locations.

When talking to Capt. Hildebrand in his office, we hear Henry say, "Oh, of course," but his lips don't move.

This is the first episode where you can see out of Henry's office windows. The first thing seen is a corrugated building. This will greatly vary in future episodes, in the same episode and sometimes the view will change mid-scene.

In Chapter 2, as the camera zooms in from a long shot of the Ranch compound, a light-colored "every day" van can be seen driving on a dirt road in the distance.

Action is seen outside of the CO's window...a rarity, as Radar peeks in.

A microphone shadow can be seen in the upper left in General Clayton's office.

Trapper is seen reading, *New Feature* magazine with MacArthur on the cover and a Seagram 7 ad on the back.

Captain Hildebrand says the 4077th is three miles from the front. This varies, but not much.

Anthony Holland, born on March 3, 1928 in Brooklyn, NY, sadly took his own life on July 9, 1988 in his Manhattan apartment. He had been suffering from AIDS, according to his cousin, Jessica Holland (July 12, 1988, *New York Times*).

5 O'Clock Charlie – 9/22/1973

Season 2 / Episode 26 / Production 27 – K403

Columbia House VHS Tape . . . . *Enemy Fire (Catalog # 3746)*
Fox DVD . . . . *Season 2, Disc 1*

Alan Alda, Wayne Rogers, McLean Stevenson,
Loretta Swit, Larry Linville, Gary Burghoff

Produced by Gene Reynolds and Larry Gelbart
Script Consultant: Laurence Marks
Teleplay by Larry Gelbart & Laurence Marks and Keith Walker
Story by Keith Walker
Directed by Norman Tokar

Herb Voland . . . . .General Clayton
Corey Fisher . . . . Captain Phil Cardoza
William Christopher. . . . . Father Mulcahy
Odessa Cleveland . . . . Ginger
Lloyd Kino . . . . Soldier
Sarah Fankboner . . . . Nurse Klein
Gail Bowman . . . . Nurse Powell
Deborah Newman. . . . . .Nurse Richards

Copyright 1973 – 20th Century Fox Film Corporation

Non-Credited Appearances. . . . . Jeff Maxwell, Kellye Nakahara, Dennis Troy,
Roy Goldman, Gwen Farrell, Marcia Gelman

Chapters

1: *Main Titles*	6: *An Important Mission – 14:41*
2: *Charlie's Coming – 0:49*	7: *Get Rid of the Dump – 17:40*
3: *The Astigmatic Bomber – 4:38*	8: *Frank's Folly – 21:09*
4: *A Gun Or A Nug? – 8:34*	9: *Missing Charlie – 24:34*
5: *The General's Visit – 11:12*	10: *End Titles – 25:25*

Closing Stills

1: *Radar taking Mulcahy's bet*
2: *Hawkeye & Trapper in lounge chairs watch Charlie*
3: *Trapper as McArthur with Frank*
4: *Hawkeye, Trapper, Henry & Clayton behind big rock*

Synopsis: 5 O'Clock Charlie, a somewhat spastic enemy bomber who can't fly in a straight line, sputters overhead in his single-engine propeller airplane while lobbing grenades in an effort to hit the ammo dump close to the hospital. Frank insists that General Clayton send an anti-aircraft gun and when Clayton arrives to see for himself if they need it, Charlie blows up Clayton's jeep. Now that Frank has his anti-aircraft gun, all he has to do now is get his three-man South Korean platoon to operate it.

Commentary by Larry Gelbart: "Laurence Marks and I first met when we were both on the writing staff of a radio show called *Duffy's Tavern*. That was 1946. We repeated that experience on the Jack Paar radio show in 1947. We then became partners and worked as a team for Bob Hope from 1948 until 1952. In syndication, it's called 2 O'Clock Charlie."

PA Announcements by Todd Sussman

Authors' Notes: Frank mentions the Gary Cooper movie, *The Court-Martial of Billy Mitchell.* This movie is from 1955 — two years after the Korean War ended.

Radar's Report – 9/29/1973

Season 2 / Episode 27 / Production 26 – K402

Columbia House VHS Tape . . . . Welcome To M*A*S*H (Catalog # 3569)
Fox DVD . . . . Season 2, Disc 1

Alan Alda, Wayne Rogers, McLean Stevenson,
Loretta Swit, Larry Linville, Gary Burghoff

Produced by Gene Reynolds and Larry Gelbart
Script Consultant: Laurence Marks
Teleplay by Laurence Marks
Story by Sheldon Keller
Directed by Jackie Cooper

Allan Arbus . . . . Major Milton Freedman *(First Appearance)*
Joan Van Ark . . . . Nurse Erika Johnson
Jamie Farr . . . . Corporal Max Klinger
William Christopher . . . . Father Mulcahy
Derrick Shimatsu . . . . Chinese Prisoner
Copyright 1973 – 20th Century Fox Film Corporation

Non-Credited Appearances . . . . Jeff Maxwell, Kellye Nakahara, Dennis Troy,
Roy Goldman, Gwen Farrell

Chapters

1: *Main Titles*	6: *The Klinger Problem – 10:51*
2: *The Activity Report - 0:47*	7: *Trapper's Patient – 18:28*
3: *Panic in the OR – 3:52*	8: *I'm Just Crazy – 20:44*
4: *Who Bit Who? – 8:40*	9: *The Wedding's Off – 21:29*
5: *Love At First Blood – 9:36*	10: *End Titles – 25:23*

Closing Stills

1: *Erika moves stethoscope for Hawkeye*
2: *Radar typing his report*
3: *Frank bites Klinger's neck*
4: *Trapper stands over POW in private tent*

Synopsis: Included in Radar's weekly activity and personnel report is the unusually heavy influx of wounded and a Chinese P.O.W. The frightened P.O.W. jumps off the operating table knocking down an I.V. of blood resulting in major complications for Trapper's patient, while grabbing a scalpel and cutting Nurse Erika Johnson on the arm. Klinger, after hearing the commotion in O.R., aims his rifle at the P.O.W., but not before he cuts the strap on his $39 dress, which he fully intends to be reimbursed for by North Korea. After Hawkeye takes personal care of Nurse Johnson, he falls for her and has plans to get married. But when Trapper learns that his patient died as a result of the P.O.W.'s actions, Hawkeye finds him alone with the man and stops his friend from doing something he'll later regret.

Commentary by Larry Gelbart: "Something went wrong with the processing of the film and so we added the voiceover line." (on the scene with Alan Alda and Joan Van Ark when the lights flicker. *See authors' notes below*).

Commentary by Joan Van Ark: "Loretta Swit was the 'hostess,' the warm, welcoming one. I already knew Linville. Also, classy Alan Alda was friendly. Alda, basically, directed

Joan Van Ark appears in "Radar's Report" in Season 2.

me because the director and I didn't seem to connect very well. I couldn't understand what he wanted, and couldn't seem to please him. We did rehearse, and overall it was somewhat tense with little laughter. You knew you were working on a TV masterpiece, something special with special people. It doesn't get any better than Larry Gelbart or Gene Reynolds." *(Joan Van Ark's web site is http://www.joanvanark.com.)*

PA Announcements by Jimmy Lydon

Authors' Notes: When Radar tells Trapper his patient is in trouble, Trapper runs off… but to the side of the mess tent, not at all in the direction of the hospital building.

This marks the debut of Allan Arbus as Dr. Milton Freedman, and the only time his name will be "Milton." His name will be Sidney Freedman for the remainder of his appearances.

When Nurse Erika Johnson's arm is cut in Chapter 3, she's standing in the O.R. with her nose out from her mask.

Klinger wears a "Miss Hi Rise" bra, 36-B cup.

The voice-over Mr. Gelbart refers to takes place in Chapter 5. As Hawkeye and Erika are together in her cot, the lights begin to flicker. This was the result of a power failure on the set and completely un-scripted. Since there was not enough time to re-shoot the scene, the flickering lights were covered up with a PA announcement about the generator acting up again. It should be noted here that, although the power failure was real and unexpected, Alan Alda and Joan Van Ark did not miss a beat. They kept going without interruption because the director, Jackie Cooper, did not say *Cut!*

The sinks in the scrub room are in the middle opposite each other. In earlier episodes, they were side by side.

This episode is another rarity in that it has a laugh track in the operating room when Henry grabs a syringe by the needle at the end of the scene and begins counting backwards from 99 *(see Larry Gelbart's commentary)*.

Commentary by Larry Gelbart: "We did put a laugh there. There was no surgery going on at that moment. It was the very last beat of the scene. Mac's performance was (by design) comic. It cried out for a laugh."

For the Good of the Outfit – 10/6/1973

Season 2 / Episode 28 / Production 28 – K404

Columbia House VHS Tape . . . .*Friendly Fire (Catalog # 3743)*
Fox DVD . . . . *Season 2, Disc 1*

Alan Alda, Wayne Rogers, McLean Stevenson,
Loretta Swit, Larry Linville, Gary Burghoff

Produced by Gene Reynolds and Larry Gelbart
Script Consultant: Laurence Marks
Written by Jerry Mayer
Directed by Jackie Cooper

Herb Voland . . . . .General Clayton
Frank Aletter. . . . . Major Stoner
Odessa Cleveland . . . . Ginger
Leslie Evans . . . . Nurse Mason
Gwen Farrell . . . . .Nurse Butler

Copyright 1973 – 20th Century Fox Film Corporation

Non-Credited Appearances. . . . . Jeff Maxwell, Kellye Nakahara, Dennis Troy,
Marcia Gelman, Ralph Grosh

Chapters

1: *Main Titles*	6: *Hawkeye's Letter – 15:16*
2: *Clobbered by the Good Guys – 0:47*	7: *The General's Advice – 18:36*
3: *A Report to Seoul – 4:23*	8: *A Re-Evaluation – 22:07*
4: *A Classified Matter – 7:33*	9: *A Letter from Dad – 24:15*
5: *The Official Story – 12:55*	10: *End Titles – 25:25*

Closing Stills

1: *Radar & Stoner by Henry's tent door*
2: *Henry washes golf balls while Hawkeye talks*
3: *Trapper reads Stars & Stripes in Mess Tent*
4: *Frank & Margaret by Henry's office window*

Synopsis: It's just another routine O.R. session until Trapper and Hawkeye realize that all the wounded are Korean locals. Margaret confirms it when she reveals that a local village, Tai-Dong, was shelled causing Hawkeye to take a closer look at the shrapnel he's removing and discovers that it might have been from friendly fire. Trapper investigates and learns that the only artillery unit anywhere near the village was the 348th, and the shrapnel is American. Saving shrapnel in bottles as evidence and armed with x-rays, Hawkeye and Trapper file a report in an attempt to get the army to take responsibility. When Major Stoner arrives to investigate, he promises that "Heads will roll," and leaves with the evidence. Weeks later, Hawkeye can't get Stoner on the phone and learns that he's been transferred to Honolulu. General Clayton comes to camp to try and convince the doctors to leave the matter alone and with the evidence gone, as well as the only person that had it, it seems they have no choice until help arrives from an unexpected source.

Commentary by Larry Gelbart: "After reading and rehearsing funny lines and material, any laughter exhibited onscreen is done for effect, not necessarily because the actor is having such a good time. My then young son, Adam, built a model Huey, which I hung in Henry Blake's office. You can see it in several episodes. We took it down when someone pointed out its presence was anachronistic. My daughter, Becky, then also young, did all the children's artwork on Henry's walls. A lot of the series served as a home movie for me."

PA Announcement by Todd Sussman

Authors' Notes: In the scrub room, the sinks are side by side on the right wall, not in the middle of the room as in previous episodes.

Henry claims he just got the doll on his desk, but this doll is clearly seen in nearly every episode before this one.

Hawkeye gets a letter from his father dated, May 24, 1951. In the previous episode, "Radar's Report," the report is dated "17 October – 22 October, inclusive, 1951."

"Radar's Report" is episode # 27 and was the 2nd episode produced for the 2nd season. "For the Good of the Outfit" is episode # 28 and the 4th episode produced for the 2nd season.

In Chapter 7, a rare view from the compound looking in to the office windows shows Henry looking out in anticipation of General Clayton's arrival.

The view from Henry's office windows changes in this episode from a corrugated building, as in earlier episodes of the 2nd season, to trees, shrubs and mountains.

Dr. Pierce and Mr. Hyde – 10/13/1973

Season 2 / Episode 29 / Production 29 – K405

Columbia House VHS Tape. . . . . *Cracking Up (Catalog # 3745)*
Fox DVD . . . . *Season 2, Disc 1*

Alan Alda, Wayne Rogers, McLean Stevenson,
Loretta Swit, Larry Linville, Gary Burghoff

Produced by Gene Reynolds and Larry Gelbart
Script Consultant: Laurence Marks
Written by Alan Alda and Robert Klane
Directed by Jackie Cooper

Herb Voland . . . . .General Clayton
Buck Young. . . . . .Chopper Pilot O'Brien
Copyright 1973 – 20th Century Fox Film Corporation

Non-Credited Appearances. . . . . Kellye Nakahara, Dennis Troy, Roy Goldman,
Marcia Gelman, Gwen Farrell

Chapters

1: *Main Titles*	6: *The Telegram – 15:08*
2: *Hawkeye is Tired – 0:48*	7: *Taking Pictures – 18:46*
3: *A M*A*S*H Taxi – 4:59*	8: *The General – 23:01*
4: *Wartime Observation – 7:14*	9: *Asleep At Last – 24:27*
5: *Back to Work – 13:37*	10: *End Titles – 25:23*

Closing Stills
1: *Henry & Radar in Radar's office (Madder 'n hell)*
2: *Hawkeye, Trapper, Radar in Swamp (Spiked drink)*
3: *Margaret & Frank in R compound (Hawk's pictures)*
4: *Hawkeye singing in Radar's office*

Synopsis: Hawkeye's exhaustion begins to catch up with him when he demands his next patient after the OR session is over. As soon as he gets into his bunk, he hears choppers and heads for OR, even though he's operated for 20 straight hours and begins to exhibit behavior that, even by Hawkeye's standards, is bizarre. His behavior later borders on psychotic when he lurks around the compound in the rain taking notes. He wakes Trapper in the middle of the night to tell him his theory: There's a war going on and he needs to find out who started it and get them to call it off, then gets Radar to send a telegram to President Truman. After a failed attempt to sedate Hawkeye, Trapper knows the perfect way to do it… with a Martini, but not before Hawkeye chains the latrine, with General Clayton inside, to an ambulance.

Commentary by Larry Gelbart: "We always tried to get to the ranch for at least one day of shooting."

PA Announcements by Radar

Authors' Notes: In Chapter 2, the Swamp at the Ranch has the dartboard. In Chapter 3, the Swamp on both sets, the Ranch and Stage 9 have no dartboard, but in Chapter 7, the Swamp on Stage 9 has it.
The sinks in the scrub room are side by side, but are now on the left wall.

Kim – 10/20/1973

Season 2 / Episode 30 / Production 31 – K407

Columbia House VHS Tape . . . . *Fatherhood (Catalog # 3772)*
Fox DVD . . . . *Season 2, Disc 1*

Alan Alda, Wayne Rogers, McLean Stevenson,
Loretta Swit, Larry Linville, Gary Burghoff

Produced by Gene Reynolds and Larry Gelbart
Script Consultant: Laurence Marks
Written by Marc Mandel and Larry Gelbart & Laurence Marks
Directed by William Wiard

Jamie Farr . . . . Corporal Klinger
William Christopher . . . . Father Mulcahy
Leslie Evans . . . . Nurse Mitchell
Edgar Miller . . . . Kim
Momo Yashima . . . . Kim's Mother
Maggie Roswell . . . . Sister Theresa

Copyright 1973 – 20th Century Fox Film Corporation

Non-Credited Appearances. . . . . Jeff Maxwell, Kellye Nakahara, Dennis Troy,
Roy Goldman, Gwen Farrell, Robert Gruber

Chapters

1: *Main Titles*
2: *A Wounded Child – 0:48*
3: *Reading to the Patients – 3:30*
4: *Calling the Orphanage – 5:33*
5: *Adoption – 8:58*
6: *Playtime – 9:54*
7: *The Letter – 13:45*
8: *A Minefield – 16:22*
9: *Mom – 22:48*
10: *End Titles – 25:23*

Closing Stills

1: *Trapper & Kim / Cointrick in the Swamp*
2: *Radar & Kim sleeping*
3: *Margaret reads "The Three Bears" to Kim*
4: *Close-up of Kim*

Synopsis: When Radar is unable to find out anything about a 5-year-old Korean boy Hawkeye removed a bit of shrapnel from, Henry has no choice but to send him to Sister Theresa's orphanage. Hating the idea so much, Trapper wants to adopt the boy and his wife and daughters are in complete agreement. But when Frank and Margaret watch the boy while on a picnic, he winds up in the middle of the minefield. Trapper, with the help of a chopper, rescues the boy and is very disappointed when the boy's mother arrives to take him back.

Authors' Notes: There are no PA announcements in this episode.

It was obviously very overcast for the scenes of the boy in the minefield. After he's rescued, it's suddenly sunny, without a cloud in the blue sky.

Jeff Maxwell was a cook in Chapter 2. In Chapter 3, he has a head wound in post-op.

In Chapter 4, while Henry is by the office windows, the view shows trees and mountains, and a building out of the right window. The shot switches to Hawkeye and Trapper, but when it switches back to Henry, the view out of the window has changed, mid-scene, to all trees.

In Chapter 5, The Swamp has the dartboard, but later in the same chapter, it's missing. The same thing occurs in Chapter 6, but the other way around. The Swamp is missing the dartboard, then it shows it, and the original view out of the office windows returns to trees and mountains.

In the Swamp in Chapter 6, Hawkeye reads the numbers from Nurse Mitchell's dog tags as 35591715. A few seconds later, he reads the numbers again, but this time it reads 39591715.

Maggie Roswell is the second actress to play the part of Sister Theresa, but is better known for her voice acting on *The Simpsons* as Maude Flanders, Helen Lovejoy, Miss Hoover and Luann Van Houten, among others.

L.I.P. (Local Indigenous Personnel) – 10/27/1973

Season 2 / Episode 31 / Production 30 – K406

Columbia House VHS Tape . . . . *Fatherhood (Catalog # 3772)*
Fox DVD . . . . *Season 2, Disc 1*

Alan Alda, Wayne Rogers, McLean Stevenson,
Loretta Swit, Larry Linville, Gary Burghoff

Produced by Gene Reynolds and Larry Gelbart
Script Consultant: Laurence Marks
Written by Carl Kleinschmitt and Larry Gelbart & Laurence Marks
Story by Carl Kleinschmitt
Directed by William Wiard

Corrine Camacho . . . . Lieutenant Regina Hoffman
Burt Young . . . . Lieutenant Willis
Jamie Farr . . . . Corporal Klinger
William Christopher . . . . Father Mulcahy
Jerry Zaks . . . . Corporal Phil Walker
Odessa Cleveland . . . . Ginger
Copyright 1973 – 20th Century Fox Film Corporation

Non-Credited Appearances . . . . Jeff Maxwell, Kellye Nakahara, Dennis Troy,
Roy Goldman, Ralph Grosh, Marcia Gelman

Chapters

1: *Main Titles*	6: *Lieutenant Willis – 12:31*
2: *At the Movies – 0:49*	7: *Blackmail – 19:03*
3: *A Young Patient – 3:51*	8: *Plural at Last – 21:44*
4: *Local Indigenous Personnel – 5:50*	9: *A Wedding – 24:51*
5: *Business as Usual – 9:35*	10: *End Titles – 25:25*

Closing Stills

1: *Regina w/ Hawkeye kissing her neck*
2: *Willis wakes after passing out*
3: *Margaret cries in Henry's office*
4: *Klinger catches bouquet*

Synopsis: Hawkeye tells Corporal Phil Walker that his baby has a touch of colic, but the bigger problem is Walker himself. He's being shipped home in a couple of weeks and wants to marry the Korean woman holding his son and bring them back to the States. Since going through normal channels can take more than a year, Walker asks Hawkeye to try and expedite the process. Lieutenant Willis, CID, arrives to investigate Walker and wants to begin immediately, even though Hawkeye is getting ready for a date, or he'll leave. Not left with much of a choice, Hawkeye agrees. Willis sees nothing important enough to bypass procedures, but does see the importance of a 4th Martini, and passes out before Hawkeye can fill his glass. Trapper sees this as an opportunity for a setup and with help from Radar, some lipstick and a brassiere, a picture "suitable for framing" takes shape.

Commentary by Larry Gelbart: "I didn't pay much attention to the pressure to 'lighten' the show. I loved it dark — and dirty. Moral, to be sure — but dirty, too — in an innocent way."

PA Announcement by Jimmy Lydon

Authors' Notes: The movie *Flying Leathernecks* starred John Wayne, but not Ward Bond and Maureen O'Hara.

The cover of the book Hawkeye is reading, *Badman's Roost,* falls off.

Hawkeye mentions Kraftt-Ebbing. Richard Kraftt-Ebbing (8/4/1840-12/22/1902) was a German psychiatrist who wrote *Psychopathia Sexualis* in 1886.

Burt Young went on to co-star in the *Rocky* movies, as Paulie.

The Trial of Henry Blake – 11/3/1973

Season 2 / Episode 32 / Production 32 – K408

Columbia House VHS Tape . . . . *Frank's In Charge (Catalog # 3744)*
Fox DVD . . . . *Season 2, Disc 1*

Alan Alda, Wayne Rogers, McLean Stevenson,
Loretta Swit, Larry Linville, Gary Burghoff

Produced by Gene Reynolds and Larry Gelbart
Script Consultant: Laurence Marks
Written by McLean Stevenson
Directed by Don Weis

Hope Summers . . . . Meg Cratty
Robert F. Simon . . . . General Mitchell
Jamie Farr . . . . Corporal Klinger
Jack Aaron . . . . Major Murphy
Bobbie Mitchell . . . . Nurse Marshall
Roy Goldman . . . . M.P.

Copyright 1973 – 20th Century Fox Film Corporation

Non-Credited Appearances . . . . Jeff Maxwell, Kellye Nakahara, Dennis Troy,
Gwen Farrell, Ralph Grosh, Marcia Gelman

Chapters

1: Main Titles	6: Under Arrest – 12:05
2: A Hearing – 0:49	7: Meg Cratty – 18:18
3: Gurney Races – 3:04	8: The Decision – 21:36
4: Wing Tips – 5:57	9: Back at the 4077th – 24:13
5: Klinger Flies – 9:32	10: End Titles – 25:25

Closing Stills

1: Henry & General Mitchell in Jeep
2: Margaret massaging Frank with hand vibrator
3: Radar & Hawkeye in the Mess Tent
4: Klinger set to glide out of camp

Synopsis: Acting on charges filed by Frank and Margaret, General Mitchell has convened a hearing to determine Henry's fitness to command, beginning with gurney races and betting that took place at the 4077th and Henry's participation in the event, followed with Henry allowing an enlisted man to sell wing tip shoes in camp and having a noncom transvestite and his unsuccessful attempt at hang gliding home. The most serious charges are falsifying records and lending comfort and aid to the enemy, leaving General Mitchell with no alternative but to place Henry under arrest. Meg Cratty, an American nurse who helps the hill people, regardless of where they come from, tells the panel of all the good that Henry has done for her and especially newborn babies who rarely survive the first few weeks, and the General dismisses the case. But before that can happen, he needs to have Frank and Margaret drop the charges, which at first, Frank refuses to do, until he reads a letter that Hawkeye and Trapper will send to Mrs. Burns if he doesn't.

Commentary by Larry Gelbart: "Actors submitted whatever ideas they might have had much like free lance writers did (and only free lancers were employed in my time). They did not proceed to script until the idea had gone through the process of constructive criticism. All the scripts, to be honest, received the same sort of revision or polish as was deemed necessary. I remember one or two story ideas suggested by cast members that didn't get to the script stage — at least during the first four seasons. That script went past the story stage and was turned into a script. But it was not written by a cast member, but a professional writer, Stanley Ralph Ross (in reference to an un-filmed plot where two nurses plan to convince Hawkeye that each of them is pregnant, as revenge).

Commentary by Jeff Maxwell: "Igor reacting to Major Burns was never less than a moment of pure acting joy. I question if there would have ever been a Private Igor without the talent of Larry Linville. Gratefully, I will always 'turn them over at night' and forever, to you, Mr. Linville, fire the ceremonial salute. That was a good episode for Igor. I have a very special autograph from McLean Stevenson. It says, 'Then turn 'em over at night.'"

PA Announcements by Todd Sussman

Authors' Notes: The PA announcement for a ten-mile hike is the second time it was used, with the exception of the word "people" instead of "men" the first time.

Jeff Maxwell was used as Alan Alda's stand-in for several seasons, in preparation for camera shots.

This episode features what many believe to be Klinger's most outrageous escape attempt by hang gliding out of camp. Slow motion photography is used for the second time, as Klinger's superimposed body was clearly filmed in slow motion.

In Chapter 4, the Swamp is seen first without the dartboard, then with it.

In Chapter 6, there is no dartboard in the Swamp.

Hope Summers, who played "Meg Cratty" in this episode, had an extensive list of television credits. Ms. Summers appeared in such shows as *The Rifleman, Wagon Train, Divorce Court, Hazel, Gunsmoke, The Dick Van Dyke Show, Bewitched, Hawaii Five-0, Starsky & Hutch, Welcome Back Kotter* and several others. She's probably best known for her role on *The Andy Griffith Show* as Clara Edwards, Aunt Bea's neighbor. Ms. Summers also appeared in *Rosemary's Baby*. She passed away in 1979 and the age of 77.

The role of "Meg Cratty" will appear again in Season 4's episode "The Kids," and will be played by actress Ann Doran.

Dear Dad, Three – 11/10/1973

Season 2 / Episode 33 / Production 33 – K409

Columbia House VHS Tape . . . . *Dear Dad (Catalog # 10993)*
Fox DVD . . . . *Season 2, Disc 2*

Alan Alda, Wayne Rogers, McLean Stevenson,
Loretta Swit, Larry Linville, Gary Burghoff

Produced by Gene Reynolds and Larry Gelbart
Script Consultant: Laurence Marks
Written by Larry Gelbart & Laurence Marks
Directed by Don Weis

Mills Watson . . . . Sergeant Condon
Jamie Farr . . . . Corporal Klinger
William Christopher . . . . Father Mulcahy
Odessa Cleveland . . . . Ginger
Bobbie Mitchell . . . . Nurse Gilbert
Kathleen Hughes . . . . Lorraine Blake
Arthur Abelson . . . . Milt Jaffe
Louise Vienna . . . . Sylvia Jaffe
Sivi Aberg . . . . Anna Lindstrom

Copyright 1973 – 20th Century Fox Film Corporation

Non-Credited Appearances . . . . Kellye Nakahara, Dennis Troy, Roy Goldman,
Sheila Lauretsen, Gwen Farrell, Marcia Gelman

Chapters

1: *Main Titles*	6: *Home Movies – 8:51*
2: *Dear Dad – 0:48*	7: *Common Practices – 14:37*
3: *In Surgery – 1:59*	8: *Staff Meeting – 17:50*
4: *A Live Grenade – 3:57*	9: *The Wrong Blood – 22:28*
5: *Happy Hour – 6:21*	10: *End Titles – 25:23*

Closing Stills

1: *Condon in Post-Op*
2: *Nurse Gilbert & Radar*
3: *Henry smiling at staff meeting*
4: *Frank & Margaret at staff meeting*
5: *Hawkeye & Trapper at staff meeting*

Synopsis: In the third of three Dear Dad episodes, Hawkeye brings his father up to date on the goings-on at the 4077th, with boredom still being the biggest enemy; only this enemy has Trapper and Frank playing gin rummy together. The O.R. becomes deadly when a patient is brought to the scrub room with a live grenade shot into his body, a patient in post-op wonders if he's been given "the wrong color blood" and Henry gets a home movie of his daughter's birthday party. When things settle down and Hawkeye finishes his letter, he lets his father know that the "Happy Hour" is alive and well.

Commentary by Larry Gelbart: "While the actors were meticulous about sticking to the script, there were certainly bits of business they were free to improvise, or the director of any given episode was free to come up with. Much of this had to be cleared to insure that, whatever the piece of business, it did not interfere or compete with the written material."

Authors' Notes: There are no PA announcements in this episode.

When Radar tells Henry that a patient is in the scrub room, Henry turns and tells Hawkeye that the patient is in pre-op.

Radar claims he doesn't know if he's a virgin or not, but in Season 1's episode, "Love Story," he was engaged. This would suggest that, whether he is or isn't, he'd at least know the difference.

In Chapter 6, the scenery changes out of Henry's office windows from trees and shrubs to different trees mid-scene.

Henry receives a home movie of his daughter Molly's 6th birthday party. This is the first episode to feature a home movie, and the first time Henry's wife is "Lorraine." Mrs. Blake will remain "Lorraine" for the remainder of Henry's time at the 4077th.

The Sniper – 11/17/1973

Season 2 / Episode 34 / Production 34 – K410

Columbia House VHS Tape . . . . .Enemy Fire (Catalog # 3746)
Fox DVD. . . . . Season 2, Disc 2

Alan Alda, Wayne Rogers, McLean Stevenson,
Loretta Swit, Larry Linville, Gary Burghoff

Produced by Gene Reynolds and Larry Gelbart
Script Consultant: Laurence Marks
Written by Richard M. Powell
Directed by Jackie Cooper

Teri Garr . . . . Lieutenant Suzanne Marquette
Dennis Troy. . . . . Ambulance Driver
Marcia Gelman . . . . Nurse

Copyright 1973 – 20th Century Fox Film Corporation

Non-Credited Appearances. . . . . .Jeff Maxwell, Kelley Nakahara, Roy Goldman,
Gwen Farrell, Ralph Grosh, Robert Gruber

Chapters

1:	Main Titles	6:	Tension in the Dark – 14:16
2:	Frank's Gun – 0:48	7:	Sniper Hunt – 17:07
3:	The Sniper – 4:36	8:	Rescued – 20:59
4:	Pinned Down – 8:42	9:	MacArthur's Return – 24:18
5:	Surrender? – 11:30	10:	End Titles – 25:24

Closing Stills

1: *Hawkeye shaving in the Swamp*
2: *Trapper in his robe washing socks*
3: *Henry & Radar hugging in the shower*
4: *Frank holding a pillow in Post-Op*
5: *Hawkeye peeking out the door at the sniper*

Synopsis: On a picnic near camp with a nurse, a bullet hits a wine bottle by Hawkeye's foot and Hawkeye thinks it's Frank's fault since he's out taking target practice. While confronting Frank and Margaret, another shot is fired, not by Frank, but a sniper and they all run back to camp. With everyone in post-op taking cover, Frank assumes command as Henry is pinned in the showers with Radar. The situation then becomes critical when the sniper shoots at an ambulance arriving with wounded, hitting the driver in the arm. Henry and Radar finally make it to post-op and learn of Hawkeye's plan to get the wounded off the ambulance: surrender. With a white flag in hand, Trapper walks out with Hawkeye and the wounded are taken inside just before the sniper fires at Trapper and his flag. As Henry is on the phone trying to get help, a chopper arrives with a sharpshooter and wounds the sniper who then raises a white flag of his own. Rejecting Frank's suggestion of revenge, Hawkeye provides a house call and after surgery, learns the sniper is just a teenager who was cut off from his unit and thought the 4077th was MacArthur's headquarters.

Commentary by Larry Gelbart: "We did not show the briefest of flashes of Radar's behind because we thought it was what viewers were dying to see, but because we thought the idea was funny — and that war strips you naked and reduces you to almost infantile helplessness."

Commentary by Gary Burghoff: "Anything can happen when Jackie Cooper directs. In 'The Sniper,' my towel was rigged so it would come off right at the moment I entered the shower tent. I knew what Jackie intended, by having the towel come off, but it was just meant to be fun."

Commentary by Gene Reynolds: "I really liked it, but had to fight for it. It starts out funny...the Henry and Radar bit. I was very proud of that episode. Once it was being filmed, the actors kind of took it over and did something different in shooting. I had to go into the editing room to bring the episode back to how I really wanted it." (On "The Sniper" being his favorite episode)

Commentary by Larry Gelbart: "That was full backal nudity." (on Radar's dropping of the towel) "No one gave Radar's rear cleavage a second thought. Now, if we'd shot a brief(less) butt shot of Hot Lips..."

Authors' Notes: There are no PA announcements in this episode.
The Swamp in Chapter 2 has no dartboard.
In Chapter 9, the dartboard in the Swamp is on a table next to Frank's bunk.
Actress Teri Garr, who played Lieutenant Suzanne Marquette in this episode, is from Lakewood, Ohio and made her film debut as an extra in the 1963 film *A Swingin' Affair*. Miss Garr appeared in many Elvis Presley movies as un-credited dancers, and had a cameo in the Monkees movie, *Head.* She had significant roles in *Young Frankenstein, Oh, God! Close Encounters of the Third Kind, Mr. Mom* and was nominated for an Academy Award for the role of Sandy Lester, Dustin Hoffman's actress friend, in *Tootsie.* As early as 1968, Miss Garr appeared in the *Star Trek* episode, "Assignment Earth," and in the late 1970's and early 1980's, hosted *Saturday Night Live* three times. Garr also had a recurring role in the television sitcom *Friends,* as Phoebe's mother.
In October 2002, Teri Garr announced her battle with Multiple Sclerosis and has become the National Ambassador for the National Multiple Sclerosis Society. She was honored as the Society's Ambassador of the Year for her commitment to M.S awareness, an honor given only four times since the Society was founded. Miss Garr suffered a brain aneurysm on December 21, 2006. Her 13-year-old daughter, after not being able to wake her, called for help. Garr's publicist, Heidi Schaeffer, said she expected Miss Garr to make a full recovery.
The authors of this book would like to convey our best wishes to Teri Garr, and we hope all of her future endeavors are healthy and successful.
We would also like to note that the movies, *Oh, God!* and *Tootsie* were written by a very smart and clever writer...Larry Gelbart.

Carry On, Hawkeye – 11/24/1973

Season 2 / Episode 35 / Production 35 – K411

Columbia House VHS Tape . . . . *Operation Overload (Catalog # 3669)*
Fox DVD . . . . *Season 2, Disc 2*

Alan Alda, Wayne Rogers, McLean Stevenson,
Loretta Swit, Larry Linville, Gary Burghoff

Produced by Gene Reynolds and Larry Gelbart
Script Consultant: Laurence Marks
Teleplay by Bernard Dilbert and Larry Gelbart & Laurence Marks
Directed by Jackie Cooper

Lynnette Mettey . . . . Nurse Sheila Anderson
William Christopher . . . . Father Mulcahy
Marcia Gelman . . . . .Nurse Jacobs
Gwen Farrell . . . . .Nurse Wilson

Copyright 1973 – 20th Century Fox Film Corporation

Non-Credited Appearances . . . . .Jeff Maxwell, Kellye Nakahara, Roy Goldman,
Sheila Lauretsen

Chapters

1: Main Titles	6: Mr. & Mrs. 4077th – 12:06
2: The Flu Epidemic – 0:48	7: Back on Their Feet – 14:54
3: Emergency Help – 3:24	8: Working with the Flu – 19:31
4: The Ranking Surgeon – 4:42	9: Hawkeye's Award – 24:33
5: Hawkeye in Charge – 8:24	10: End Titles – 25:23

Closing Stills

1: Trapper in bed with the flu
2: Henry slides off his chair
3: Margaret smiles at Hawkeye in the office
4: Radar on the phone calling for help
5: Hawkeye in bed wit the flu

Synopsis: The Korean winter not only brings bone-numbing cold, it also brings a flu epidemic that the 4077th cannot escape, and Trapper is but the first to take ill. Henry and Frank quickly follow leaving Hawkeye to handle all the surgery with help unavailable since the epidemic is wide spread. Choppers arrive with wounded and Hawkeye is left with no choice but to have Father Mulcahy scrub and assist Nurse Anderson while another nurse assists Margaret. Things go from bad to worse when, after getting a flu shot that the army thinks might work, Hawkeye acknowledges its success when he tells Margaret that he has the flu. Once again, only this time with chills and a fever, Hawkeye has no choice but to operate.

Commentary by Gary Burghoff: "I always admired Jackie's work. A lot of directors are resigned to the fact that you can't get the good shot. But Jackie did it. He'd shoot it like a movie. I once suggested to another director, not Jackie, that we could get a great dramatic shot in one instance. But, he said, 'No, that would be feature,' meaning the kind of shot you do in a feature film. And my heart just sank."

PA Announcements by Todd Sussman

Authors' Notes: In Chapter 4, the scene out of Henry's office windows is now a corrugated building with small windows.

No dartboard in the Swamp.

Radar's two friends are Charlie and Harry (calls them for help getting replacement doctors).

When Hawkeye injects Margaret with a flu shot, the liquid can be heard hitting the floor.

The wall clock in post-op says the time is 3:20 and minutes later, it's still 3:20.

Two nurses in the operating room are not wearing masks.

The sinks in the scrub room are in the original position of side by side and in the middle of the room.

The Incubator – 12/1/1973

Season 2 / Episode 36 / Production 36 – K412

Columbia House VHS Tape . . . . *Up In Arms (Catalog # 21032)*
Fox DVD . . . . *Season 2, Disc 2*

Alan Alda, Wayne Rogers, McLean Stevenson,
Loretta Swit, Larry Linville, Gary Burghoff

Produced by Gene Reynolds and Larry Gelbart
Script Consultant: Laurence Marks
Written by Larry Gelbart & Laurence Marks
Directed by Jackie Cooper

Eldon Quick . . . . Captain Sloan
Robert F. Simon . . . . General Maynard M Mitchell
Logan Ramsey . . . . Colonel Lambert
Ted Gehring . . . . Major Morris
Sarah Fankboner . . . . Nurse Owens
Helen Funai . . . . Betty Lou
John Alvin . . . . Mr. Bowman
Jerry Harper . . . . Mr. Phillips
Copyright 1973 – 20th Century Fox Film Corporation

Non-Credited Appearances . . . . Roy Goldman, Ralph Grosh

Chapters

1: *Main Titles*	6: *No Incubator – 15:40*
2: *Hung Over – 0:47*	7: *A Real Bargain – 17:29*
3: *The Need for an Incubator – 5:29*	8: *Troublemakers – 20:04*
4: *An Unnecessary Luxury – 10:04*	9: *A Suitable Punishment – 22:59*
5: *Jackpot – 14:19*	10: *End Titles – 25:23*

Closing Stills

1: *General Mitchell at press conference*
2: *Hawkeye hung over in the Swamp*
3: *Hawkeye hung over in the Swamp*
4: *Henry listening to Captain Sloan*
5: *Radar unveils new incubator*

Synopsis: After a patient develops a fever and doesn't respond to penicillin, the doctors take a blood sample, but because the 4077th does not have an incubator, it will take 72 hours to get the results back from Tokyo. A request is submitted to get one, but Captain Sloan from Quartermaster denies the request as it's considered a luxury. Radar locates three incubators at the 728th EVAC, but the major in charge won't part with any and suggests Hawkeye and Trapper see his CO, who is currently in a Tokyo bathhouse. Colonel Lambert is willing to give them an incubator for $1,000, but since he likes Hawkeye, he cuts the price to $627.50, cost. Not to be denied, the doctors now move up to General Mitchell, who is holding a press conference and when they ask the General about incubators, explaining that they grow germs, it causes a ruckus when the reporters ask Mitchell if the US is involved in germ warfare.

Commentary by Larry Gelbart: "About 'The Incubator.' It was written in one overnight session by Laurence Marks and me. Sometimes it works out that the more the pressure, the better the result. Marks and I also wrote 'Deal Me Out,' but not under the same time restrictions. My only regret about the two episodes is that we can't go back and write them all over again, and have them come just the same way. Originally, I was going to play the supply sergeant. I decided against it for a variety of reasons. We then hired Vic Tayback for the role. I can't remember why, but we weren't happy about the way the scene turned out, so we hired another actor and re-shot it with him playing the part that Tayback had and that I hadn't. Someone obviously screwed up when putting the final credits together."

Commentary by Eldon Quick: "By the time I made my appearance on the *M*A*S*H* set, it was the best set to work on in Hollywood. I had appeared in a number of situation comedies before *M*A*S*H*, and had learned it was a mean world out there. Comics or comedic actors are a competitive bunch, and a new guy on the set was fair game for all to attack. Since I'm not a quick wit, with one-liners to devastate all who test me, I had learned to keep a low profile and just do my job. So, I approached my first day's work prepared for shots from all sides. Just the opposite was true. A new comer was instantly welcomed into the group as a professional ready to be part of a team. It was a relaxed, but disciplined set. On the read through, you read the lines exactly as written, no added ahs or uhs, or brilliant ad-libs, just the words. Then, after the reading, one could make suggestions. One could say, 'I think the line could work better this way,' or 'What if I said this, here.' Larry and Gene would take notes, and off they would go into producer land."

"A note about 'The Incubator,' the first episode I was in. The scene was originally written for Larry as Major Burns. But since the speeches were all numbers and initials and very difficult to memorize, Larry requested that they give the scene to someone else (lucky for me). Without knowing that, I attempted to create a character all 'by the book,' 'polished brass,' 'chicken shit,' not unlike certain elements of the Major Burns character."

Authors' Notes: There are no PA announcements in this episode.

To many fans, this episode features the best opening scene of *M*A*S*H*, where the camera pans through the aftermath of a wild party in the Swamp, with accompanying background music. This episode is also considered by many to be one of the best of the "early" seasons.

A can of Budweiser is seen in Chapter 2.

According to Hawkeye, the war has been running for two years, although the letter from his father in "For the Good of the Outfit" states the date as May 24, 1951.

The scene out of Henry's office windows has changed to a partial corrugated building in the left window and small trees in the right.

Colonel Lambert claims he can get a B-52 with a week's notice (crew is extra, of course). Although the B-52's maiden flight was on April 15, 1952, it wasn't introduced until February 1955.

Hawkeye makes a reference to a song, "All Kinds of Weather," which was written in 1958, five years after the war ended.

Eldon Quick will return as the by-the-book Captain Sloan again is Season 3's "Payday," and will return again in Season 4's "The Late Captain Pierce" as Captain Pratt. Mr. Quick was also a magazine editor in an episode of *The Monkees* and played Chronos in the final episode of *Buck Rogers in the 25th Century*. Aside from being a fan-favorite on *M*A*S*H*, Mr. Quick has committed Homer's *The Iliad* to memory.

Logan C. Ramsey Jr. appeared in the television shows *The Edge of Night, Mission: Impossible, Hawaii Five-O, Mork & Mindy, Charlie's Angels, Knight Rider, Night Court* and was in the original series *Star Trek* episode "Bread and Circuses," as Claudius Marcus. The son of Admiral Logan C. Ramsey Sr., the Naval aviator who raised the alarm for the attack on Pearl Harbor, and also served as a Naval aviator aboard the USS Block Island. He married actress Anne Ramsey, who played Ma in *The Goonies*, in 1954. Mr. Ramsey suffered a fatal heart attack on June 26, 2000.

Deal Me Out – 12/8/1973

Season 2 / Episode 37 / Production 37 – K413

Columbia House VHS Tape. . . . . *Card Tricks (Catalog # 3748)*
Fox DVD . . . .*Season 2, Disc 2*

Alan Alda, Wayne Rogers, McLean Stevenson,
Loretta Swit, Larry Linville, Gary Burghoff

Produced by Gene Reynolds and Larry Gelbart
Script Consultant: Laurence Marks
Written by Larry Gelbart & Laurence Marks
Directed by Gene Reynolds

John Ritter. . . . . .Private Carter
Edward Winter . . . . Captain Halloran
Allan Arbus . . . . .Major Sidney Freedman
Pat Morita. . . . . Captain Sam Pak
Jamie Farr . . . . Corporal Klinger
Jerry Fujikawa . . . . .Whiplash Hwang
Tom Dever . . . . Lieutenant Rogers
Gwen Farrell . . . . Nurse
Copyright 1973 – 20th Century Fox Film Corporation

Non-Credited Appearances. . . . . Kellye Nakahara, Dennis Troy, Roy Goldman

Chapters

1: *Main Titles*	6: *Combat Fatigue – 12:05*
2: *Visiting Officers – 0:48*	7: *A Court-Martial Offense – 15:46*
3: *The "Conference" – 3:58*	8: *Whiplash Hwang – 19:31*
4: *A Korean Thump – 7:01*	9: *Carter Goes Crazy – 20:53*
5: *The C.I.D. Man – 9:45*	10: *End Titles – 25:24*

Closing Stills

1: *Sidney & Sam arrive early for the "conference"*
2: *Halloran & Klinger at the poker game (Hey, up close)*
3: *Radar tells Henry about accident*
4: *Carter has a gun on Frank in the shower*
5: *Henry & Hawkeye at the poker game*

Synopsis: Sidney Freedman and Sam Pak arrive for a conference set to start at 1800 hours, the assembled guests convene in the Swamp and a marathon poker game is underway. Henry is called away from the game when Radar returns to camp early because he ran over a Korean national, and Sam Pak knows who it is: "Whiplash Wang," a Korean who stages phony accidents to try and get some money out of it. Meanwhile, Frank's patient is prepped and ready, but learns that the wounded man is from CID and refuses to operate until another man from CID shows up for security reasons, but Hawkeye and Trapper, going against regulations, saves the man's life. When the CID man finally arrives, he learns of the operation and wants Hawkeye and Trapper arrested. Since the man gave away no secrets while under anesthesia, Captain Halloran from CID joins the poker game instead. Now Frank has another problem to deal with when a patient he angered earlier holds a gun on him in the shower.

Commentary by Larry Gelbart: "In his stand-up comic days, Morita billed himself as 'The Hip Nip.' Ed Winter was a marvelous actor. I for one, made no secret of my admiration of his work. And all of the intelligence and devotion he brought to it. Not sure how quickly that one got written. Shows with more than one storyline were relatively easier to write. Doing short bits and then writing the connective tissue was a great way to work. Remember, though, that in addition to writing there were countless other production chores going on at the same time. It's not as though one had a clear day to do nothing but simply write. B-girls were young women employed by nightclubs and other places that served alcohol to attach themselves to male patrons and encourage them to buy drinks from the bar (the B in B-girls standing for bar). The B-girls kept drinking right along with the customer; only the women's' drinks would be watered down.

Commentary by Wayne Rogers: "The Colonel Flagg character came out of a story idea that I submitted to Larry Gelbart, sometime in the first season. And while we never used the story, the character was so rich with possibilities that, as you know, he appeared several times. Once again, not unlike Frank Burns, Flagg could be used as an antagonist in the structural sense of the word."

PA Announcement by Todd Sussman

Authors' Notes: This is one time when a scene edit can be heard as opposed to seen. When Radar enters the showers to talk to Hawkeye and Trapper, the sound of the water changes when his glasses "fog" over.

Frank suddenly wears a shower cap that he did not wear in previous episodes.

This is Edward Winter's first appearance on *M*A*S*H* as Captain Halloran, CID. He'll return in future episodes as, Colonel Sam Flagg, CIA, CIC, CID, and any other identification that was required by the over-the-top intelligence officer, including Captain Louise Klein. Some have suggested that as Halloran, he was using one if his infamous ID's, as he mentions in a future episode to Sidney Freedman that they had once played cards together. Mr. Winter also had a recurring role on the ABC sitcom, *Soap*, and was the corrupt senator in the movie, *Porky's II: The Next Day*.

The two-time Tony Award nominee died from complications resulting from Parkinson's disease on March 8, 2001 in Woodland Hills, California at the age of 64.

John Ritter, best known for his role of Jack Tripper on *Three's Company*, had appeared in the Charles Bronson film *The Stone Killer* with Norman Fell, Jack Tripper's landlord on *Three's Company*. On September 11, 2003, Ritter, while rehearsing scenes for an episode of *8 Simple Rules For Dating My Teenage Daughter* (Henry Winkler was to guest-star in this episode) had collapsed and was taken to the hospital across the street from the studio. Mr. Ritter died less than an hour later at the hospital, which happens to be the same hospital he was born in, from an aortic dissection caused by a previously undiagnosed congenital heart defect. He was 54.

Pat Morita had an extensive film and television background and is probably best known as Arnold on *Happy Days* and Mr. Miyagi in the *Karate Kid* movies, which he was nominated for the Academy Award for Best Supporting Actor in 1984. After developing spinal tuberculosis as a yong child, he was told he'd never walk again, but after a surgeon fused four vertabre in his spine, at the age of 11, he learned to walk again. After the surgery he was taken directly to the Gila River internment camp in Arizona, where his family had been sent to be detained for the duration of World War II. It's interesting to note that Pat Morita had worked for an aerospace company that designed and manufactured rocket engines, including those for the US Navy's UGM-27 Polaris. Morita died on November 24, 2005 at his home in Las Vegas. He was 73.

Hot Lips and Empty Arms – 12/15/1973

Season 2 / Episode 38 / Production 38 – K414

Columbia House VHS Tape . . . . *Hot Lips (Catalog # 3749)*
Fox DVD . . . . *Season 2, Disc 2*

Alan Alda, Wayne Rogers, McLean Stevenson,
Loretta Swit, Larry Linville, Gary Burghoff

Produced by Gene Reynolds and Larry Gelbart
Script Consultant: Laurence Marks
Written by Linda Bloodworth & Mary Kay Place
Directed by Jackie Cooper

Odessa Cleveland . . . . Ginger
Sheila Lauritsen . . . . .Nurse Watson
Kellye Nakahara . . . . .Nurse Yamato

Copyright 1973 – 20th Century Fox Film Corporation

Non-Credited Appearances. . . . . .Dennis Troy, Roy Goldman, Gwen Farrell

Chapters

1: Main Titles	6: To A Brand New Life – 14:02
2: Mail Call – 0:48	7: A Farewell Drink – 16:44
3: Margaret's Regrets – 4:12	8: Sobering Up – 19:38
4: A Transfer Request – 7:45	9: Together Again – 24:10
5: Toast to Margaret – 11:33	10: End Titles – 25:24

Closing Stills

1: Margaret in her tent after shower
2: Hawkeye & Trapper laughing at drunk Margaret
3: Henry in his office smiling (Radar signs his name)
4: Radar gives Henry funny look in the office
5: Frank & "Bimbo" in the Swamp

Synopsis: When Margaret gets a letter from an old friend, it causes her to question choices she's made such as turning down a doctor her friend married who now lives with her children in an expensive home with a swimming pool and a two-car garage and complains about marrying the army instead. Angry and frustrated with "rotten living conditions and insolent doctors," she sees Henry about a transfer. Hawkeye and Trapper try to smooth things over when they bring a bottle of champagne to her tent, but it won't prevent her from sending a negative report to General Mitchell, but has some of the so-called champagne anyway. Later in the Swamp, and a little tipsy from drinking, she returns a few items to Frank and has another drink from the still, then heads to Henry's office to hand in her final report, only this time, she has some Rye instead of gin. While Henry waits in the compound with Hawkeye and Trapper for wounded to arrive, Margaret, now drunk, stumbles up to them and offers to drive a jeep to get the wounded. But Henry shows some compassion and has Hawkeye and Trapper try to sober her up before someone sees her and it goes on her record.

Commentary by Gene Reynolds: "We wanted to do a show for Loretta. Well, someone had sent me a wonderful Mary Tyler Moore script. I brought the writers in and had them meet Loretta. I don't know why I wanted them to meet her, but they did. I love the idea of dilemma. They were terrific writers."

Authors' Notes: In Chapter 7, there is no dartboard in the Swamp.

While trying to sober up Margaret in the shower, she turns to hug Trapper, but Trapper's shirt is already wet before that happens.

Margaret says Henry looks just like her father before he died. However, in the Season 7 episode, "The Party," Margaret gets a letter from her parents telling her they got together for the party, and her father appears in Season 9's episode, "Father's Day." Margaret also gets letters from her father in the series finale, "Goodbye, Farewell and Amen."

Another scenery change can be seen out of Henry's office windows: this time, a partial building with swinging doors.

On the Stage 9 compound, Henry wants Hawkeye and Trapper to try to sober up a drunken Margaret (played beautifully by Loretta Swit) by taking her to the showers, and Henry laughs. However, it's actually McLean Stevenson laughing, not Henry, as is also noted by Larry Gelbart.

Officers Only – 12/22/1973

Season 2 / Episode 39 / Production 39 – K415

Columbia House VHS Tape. . . . .*Career Advancement (Catalog # 10994)*
Fox DVD . . . .*Season 2, Disc 2*

Alan Alda, Wayne Rogers, McLean Stevenson,
Loretta Swit, Larry Linville, Gary Burghoff

Produced by Gene Reynolds and Larry Gelbart
Script Consultant: Laurence Marks
Written by Ed Jurist
Directed by Jackie Cooper

Robert F. Simon . . . . .General Maynard M. Mitchell
Jamie Farr . . . . Corporal Klinger
Odessa Cleveland . . . . Ginger
Clyde Kusatsu . . . . Kwang Duk
Robert Weaver. . . . . Private Gary Mitchell
Sheila Lauritsen . . . . .Nurse Watson
Ralph Grosh . . . . General's Aid *(Listed as "Captain's Aid" in closing credits)*
Copyright 1973 – 20th Century Fox Film Corporation

Non-Credited Appearances. . . . . Jeff Maxwell, Kellye Nakahara, Dennis Troy,
Roy Goldman, Gwen Farrell, Robert Gruber

Chapters

1:	*Main Titles*	6:	*The Officer's Club – 11:16*
2:	*A Chest Case – 0:48*	7:	*No Discrimination – 12:34*
3:	*The General's Son – 3:04*	8:	*The Petition – 16:10*
4:	*Three Days in Tokyo – 8:47*	9:	*Baptizing the Bar – 20:23*
5:	*A Little Out of Line – 9:39*	10:	*End Titles – 25:16*

Closing Stills

1: *Henry & Mitchell talk to Pvt. Mitchell at Officer's Club door*
2: *Radar hangs "Officers Only" sign*
3: *Hawkeye & Trapper in Mess Tent (Enlisted only)*
4: *Frank & Margaret in Officer's Club*
5: *Henry lights pregnant Klinger's cigar in Henry's tent*

Synopsis: To show his gratitude for operating on his son, a paratrooper with the 5th Airborne, General Mitchell arrives with a case of 12-year old Scotch for Henry, and arranges three days and nights in Tokyo for Hawkeye and Trapper. When they return from Tokyo, they're surprised to see a new structure in camp: an Officer's Club and even more surprised that Frank is responsible for it being there. Frank is also responsible for restricting entrance to officers only, leaving the enlisted personnel less than happy. But when General Mitchell's son, a private, wants to come in, Hawkeye reminds the General that, after all, it's for officers only, but cleverly comes up with a plan to bend the rules allowing family in, thus paving the way for Hawkeye's extended family to enter the club.

Commentary by Larry Gelbart: "It was Alda not wearing the glasses and the nose thing and not pretending to be Groucho that he would often seem to sound like Groucho to me. A certain percentage of the material I wrote for Alda was unavoidably Marxian, Groucho rhythm, style, sound and attitude, his general M.O. (his 'Modus Night at the

Operandi') being practically part of my DNA. Mr Quang was the real name of a real man who served in a real MASH unit."

PA Announcement by Todd Sussman

Authors' Notes: In the scrub room, the sinks are in the middle of the room, but they're facing each other this time.

Klinger is pregnant this time.

Henry is reading *Special Nurse* magazine.

A mistake in the closing credits lists Ralph Grosh as "Captain's Aid." It should be "General's Aid."

Robert F. Simon, who played the part of General Maynard M. Mitchell in "The Trial of Henry Blake" and again in "The Incubator," will play the part for the third and last time in "Officer's Only." Mr. Simon had an extensive list of television and movie credits, spanning 35 years from 1950 to 1985. He appeared in *The Philco Television Playhouse, Alfred Hitchcock Presents, The Court-Martial of Billy Mitchell, The Benny Goodman Story* and *The 20th Century Fox Hour,* among others, including *Quincy, M.E.* and 6 episodes of *Bewitched.* Born on December 2, 1908, Robert F. Simon suffered a fatal heart attack on November 29, 1992.

Clyde Kusatsu also has quite an extensive list of credits to his name, appearing in some of televisions most popular shows such as *All In the Family, Taxi, Quincy, M.E., Alice, Boston Legal, E.R.,* and 16 episodes of *The Young and the Restless* between 2006 and 2007. He's also one of several actors to appear in both *M*A*S*H* and *Star Trek: The Next Generation.* Mr. Kutsatsu will return in the following episode, "Henry In Love," also as Kwang Duk, the bartender.

Henry in Love – 1/5/1974

Season 2 / Episode 40 / Production 40 – K416

Columbia House VHS Tape . . . . *Love And War (Catalog # 10996)*
Fox DVD . . . . *Season 2, Disc 2*

Alan Alda, Wayne Rogers, McLean Stevenson,
Loretta Swit, Larry Linville, Gary Burghoff

Produced by Gene Reynolds and Larry Gelbart
Script Consultant: Laurence Marks
Written by Larry Gelbart & Laurence Marks
Directed by Don Weis

Katherine Bauman . . . . Nancy Sue Parker
Sheila Lauritsen . . . . Lieutenant Sheila Sturner
Odessa Cleveland . . . . Ginger
Clyde Kusatsu . . . . Kwang Duk
Gwen Farrell . . . . Nurse

Copyright 1973 – 20th Century Fox Film Corporation

Non-Credited Appearances . . . . Kellye Nakahara, Dennis Troy, Roy Goldman,
Robert Gruber (Bob Deutch)

Chapters

1: *Main Titles*
2: *Officiousness – 0:49*
3: *Henry's Return – 4:56*
4: *In Love – 6:08*
5: *Henry's Hair – 9:33*

6: *Nancy Sue Arrives – 12:26*
7: *At the Club – 15:38*
8: *Making A Pass – 19:52*
9: *Saying Good-Bye – 24:33*
10: *End Titles – 25:24*

Closing Stills

1: *Henry & Nancy enter Officer's Club*
2: *Henry checks hair dye in mirror*
3: *Frank & Margaret at table in Officer's Club*
4: *Hawkeye holds up Henry's 3 picture desk photo set*
5: *Radar*

Synopsis: Henry, age 44, has fallen in love with Miss Nancy Sue Parker, a civilian clerk-typist with the Air Force who will be 21 in August. Hawkeye and Trapper acknowledge Henry's "fling," and that should be the end of it, but Henry insists it's the real thing and she's coming to visit the 4077th. Hawkeye escorts Nancy back to her tent from the Officer's Club after Henry and Trapper are called away for emergency surgery, where she gives Hawkeye a sensual kiss. After telling Trapper what happened, they head for the office where Henry is on the phone with his wife, to keep him from ruining his marriage.

PA Announcement by Todd Sussman

Authors' Notes: The usual view of the CO's office was from that opposite of the wall with the window on it. In this episode, we see Henry against the backdrop of "the 4th wall," opposite the window.

The view out of Henry's window shows trees only, no buildings.

This is the only time Margaret has a diary.

Radar tells Frank that he doesn't smoke. Up to this point in the series, Radar has smoked cigars in Season 1 episodes, "Requiem For A Lightweight," "Chief Surgeon,

Who?" and "Showtime." So far in Season 2, he's had cigars in "The Trial of Henry Blake" and "Hot Lips and Empty Arms."

This is the only time a Captain Cosgrove will be mentioned as a chopper pilot (*unseen*).

Henry is 44 and Lorraine is 42.

"Nancy Sue Parker" was from Independence, Ohio and was a cheerleader, as was the actress who played her, Katherine Bauman (sometimes spelled Baumann). Miss Bauman was Miss Ohio in 1969 and Miss America Runner-up in 1970. She's appeared in other television shows, such as *CHiPS, Trapper John, M.D., Knight Rider, McCloud* and several others. Today, Katherine Bauman is a successful jewelry designer in Beverly Hills.

For Want of A Boot – 1/12/1974

Season 2 / Episode 41 / Production 41 – K417

Columbia House VHS Tape. . . . . *Prize Possessions (Catalog # 3773)*
Fox DVD . . . . *Season 2, Disc 3*

Alan Alda, Wayne Rogers, McLean Stevenson,
Loretta Swit, Larry Linville, Gary Burghoff

Produced by Gene Reynolds and Larry Gelbart
Script Consultant: Laurence Marks
Written by Sheldon Keller
Directed by Don Weis

Michael Lerner . . . . Captain Bernie Futterman
Johnny Haymer . . . . Sergeant Zale *(First Appearance)*
Jamie Farr . . . . Corporal Klinger
Patricia Stevens . . . . Nurse Mitchell
Sheila Lauritsen . . . . Sheila
Suzanne Zenor . . . . Nurse Murphy
Copyright 1974 – 20th Century Fox Film Corporation

Non-Credited Appearances. . . . . Jeff Maxwell, Kellye Nakahara, Dennis Troy,
Roy Goldman, Robert Gruber

Chapters

1: Main Titles	6: Radar is Lonely – 12:57
2: Winter Weather – 0:49	7: Frank's Birthday – 16:55
3: Hole-y Boot – 1:42	8: Everything Falls Apart – 22:06
4: The Dentist – 4:35	9: A New Boot? – 24:52
5: Margaret's Vendetta – 9:02	10: End Titles – 25:23

Closing Stills

1: Hawkeye shows Trapper hole in boot
2: Frank holding two small, pink hot water bottles
3: Trapper & Henry at Frank's birthday party
4: Margaret in her tent with Hawkeye & Trapper
5: Radar – "Lonely"

Synopsis: Waiting three months for new boots, Hawkeye goes to see Zale, the supply sergeant. Zale, less than sympathetic, has been waiting a long time for the dentist to fill a cavity. Zale will, however, get the boots for Hawkeye if Hawkeye gets the dentist for Zale and a long, fragile string of favors begins. Some of the deals include a surprise birthday party with presents for Frank, fixing Radar up with a nurse and signatures on Klinger's "crazy papers" in return for a hair dryer.

Commentary by Larry Gelbart: "I'm delighted that so much of what was done so long ago can still continue to give people pleasure."

PA Announcement by Todd Sussman

Authors' Notes: A page falls out of Sergeant Zale's book as he's putting it back. He puts it back anyway with the page on the table.
Radar wears his white paratrooper scarf again.
Nurse Murphy is reading, "Feminine View" magazine.

The progression of Hawkeye's deals for new boots is as follows:

Zale
Futterman
Henry
Margaret
Radar
Nurse Murphy
Klinger
Frank

Captain Bernie Futterman is the third dentist so far at the 4077.

This is the first appearance of Johnny Haymer as Sergeant Zelmo Zale. Johnny Haymer was born on January 19, 1920 and appeared in the Woody Allen movie *Annie Hall*. Mr. Haymer was also a server in the original McDonalds ad, "You Deserve a Break Today" and did the voices of, Swindle, Vortex, Highbrow and Calibus in *The Transformers*. He also appeared in the next to last episode of *Star Trek*, the original series in the episode, "All Our Yesterdays," and returned to *M*A*S*H* as Sergeant Zale in several future episodes, up to "Goodbye, Radar, Part 2." Mr. Haymer died of cancer in Los Angeles on November 18, 1989.

Michael Lerner, an Academy Award Nominee, was born in Brooklyn, NY and grew up in Bensonhurst and Red Hook. He appeared in the television shows *The Brady Bunch*, *The Odd Couple* and an episode of *The Rockford Files*. He made his film debut in the 1970 film *Alex in Wonderland* and also had a role in *The Candidate*, *St. Ives* and *The Postman Always Rings Twice*. More recently, Mr. Lerner has appeared in the movie, *Elf* and on the television show *Law and Order: Special Victims Unit*.

Patricia Stevens appears in *M*A*S*H* as various nurses for several episodes, but is probably better known as the voice of Velma Dinkley on the Saturday morning cartoon *Scooby-Doo*.

Suzanne Zenor began acting in 1970 and appeared in the movie *Moonshine War*. She was in the 1972 Woody Allen film *Play It Again, Sam*, and appeared in several television shows, including *McMillan & Wife*, *Love American Style* and *Barnaby Jones*. Miss Zenor did the original pilot for *Three's Company* alongside John Ritter, but is best known for her role on *Days of Our Lives* from 1977-80.

Operation Noselift – 1/19/1974

Season 2 / Episode 42 / Production 42 – K418

Columbia House VHS Tape . . . . *Not A Pretty Sight (Catalog # 21036)*
Fox DVD . . . . *Season 2, Disc 3*

Alan Alda, Wayne Rogers, McLean Stevenson,
Loretta Swit, Larry Linville, Gary Burghoff

Produced by Gene Reynolds and Larry Gelbart
Script Consultant: Laurence Marks
Teleplay by Erik Tarloff
Story by Paul Richards and Erik Tarloff
Directed by Hy Averback

Stuart Margolin . . . . Major Stanley "Stosh" Robbins
Todd Sussman . . . . Private Daniel Baker
William Christopher . . . . Father Mulcahy
Patricia Stevens . . . . Nurse Mitchell
Lou Elias . . . . M.P. Sergeant
Bobbie Mitchell . . . . Nurse Lyons
Copyright 1974 – 20th Century Fox Film Corporation

Non-Credited Appearances . . . . Jeff Maxwell, Kellye Nakahara, Dennis Troy,
Roy Goldman, Sheila Lauritsen, Gwen Farrell, Robert Gruber

Chapters

1: Main Titles
2: Blake Writes A Reply – 0:48
3: Baker's Return – 3:10
4: Baker's Problem – 5:02
5: A Plastic Surgeon – 8:37
6: The Jowls of A Goddess – 13:36
7: Picking A Nose – 15:06
8: Secret Surgery – 17:51
9: Deception – 22:30
10: End Titles – 25:25

Closing Stills

1: Robbins tells Margaret about her jowls
2: Henry talks to Baker after M.P. returns him
3: Hawkeye & Trapper smiling
4: Frank looks at Radar's nose (Radar on the phone)
5: Trapper holds Margaret in Supply Room

Synopsis: Private Daniel Baker, a GI with a nose big enough to qualify for it's own serial number, keeps running away to other hospitals for a nose job, but the doctors won't operate unless he wounded. Baker expresses his concerns about life after the army, especially with women, something Hawkeye fully understands, and he, along with Trapper agree to help him. Hawkeye enlists the help of his friend, Major Stanley "Stosh" Robbins, a well-known plastic surgeon in Hollywood who happens to be stationed at Tokyo General. Robbins at first claims he's too busy, but after promising him a date with a nurse nicknamed, "The Barracuda," Robbins agrees. Everything is set in O.R., but Robbins is missing, until Hawkeye finds him groping Margaret in the supply room thinking she's The Barracuda.

Commentary by Erik Tarloff: "Larry Gelbart was the most brilliant writer I had ever worked with. It was always exciting to see how fast his mind worked, and with what unerring accuracy he went straight to the right development or the most interesting attitude or the perfect joke. Also, how quickly and completely he grasped what other writers were trying to accomplish. He was a good listener as well as a good talker, which is rare in someone so talented."

PA Announcement by Sal Viscuso

Authors' Notes: Henry mentions the movie *The Blob*. However, it wasn't made until 1958, five years after the war.

Sometimes Henry's office chair is wood, sometimes metal. For this episode, it's metal.

Only trees and mountains are seen from the office windows and stay this way for the entire episode.

The scrub room sinks are in the middle of the room, side by side.

It should be noted that there were four different arrangements for these sinks. The one mentioned here, on the right wall side by side, on the left wall and facing each other in the middle.

Private Daniel Baker's serial number is RA 6941327.

As Hawkeye tries to keep Frank and Hot Lips out of the O.R., they are suddenly summoned elsewhere by the PA announcer. When the scene quickly cuts to a long shot of Private Baker (Todd Sussman) running towards the same hospital building door Frank and Hot Lips were just standing at, they are nowhere in sight. For this to have been real, the two would have had to literally sprint to their destinations.

Another episode where background music enhanced the action, as Hawkeye and Trapper walk amongst everyone with bandages on their noses, to hide who had the plastic surgery from the on-looking Hot Lips and Frank.

Todd Sussman has a formidable list of television credits, appearing in shows such as *Room 222, Eight Is Enough, The Waltons* and *Barney Miller*. Aside from being the unseen PA announcer in several *M*A*S*H* episodes, other well-known voice-over commercials include Mitsubishi Motors, Greyhound and Bull's Eye Bar-B-Cue Sauce, as well as the popular Sonicare tooth fairy.

This is the only time there is a camp sheepdog.

The Chosan People – 1/26/1974

Season 2 / Episode 43 / Production 43 – K419

Columbia House VHS Tape . . . . *Fatherhood (Catalog # 3772)*
Fox DVD . . . . *Season 2, Disc 3*

Alan Alda, Wayne Rogers, McLean Stevenson,
Loretta Swit, Larry Linville, Gary Burghoff

Produced by Gene Reynolds and Larry Gelbart
Script Consultant: Laurence Marks
Teleplay by Laurence Marks & Sheldon Keller & Larry Gelbart
Story by Gerry Renert & Jeff Wilhelm
Directed by Jackie Cooper

Pat Morita . . . . Captain Sam Pak
William Christopher . . . . Father Mulcahy
Dennis Robertson . . . . Lieutenant Michael Harper
Clare Nono . . . . Choon Hi
Jerry Fujikawa . . . . The Korean Father
Jay Jay Jue . . . . The Korean Boy
Bobbie Mitchell . . . . Nurse Lyons
Copyright 1974 – 20th Century Fox Film Corporation

Non-Credited Appearances . . . . Jeff Maxwell, Kellye Nakahara, Dennis Troy,
Roy Goldman, Robert Gruber

Chapters

1: Main Titles
2: The Korean Observer – 0:48
3: The Rightful Owners – 3:01
4: A Pregnant Pause – 8:29
5: Daddy Radar – 11:55
6: The Paternity Test – 15:03
7: Lunch with the Family – 16:35
8: The Test Results – 21:00
9: Relocated – 23:18
10: End Titles – 25:23

Closing Stills

1: Hawkeye & Sam in the compound with Korean family
2: Radar hit with an egg
3: Henry sees an ox in his tent
4: Close-up of Choon Hi's baby
5: Trapper & Frank by refugee truck

Synopsis: Henry soon discovers the ox that wandered into his tent belongs to a Korean family living in the middle of the compound. Sam Pak talks to the father and learns that the 4077th used to be his farm and Henry has three days to get off his land. After hanging up with Civilian Affairs, Henry notices a Korean woman standing in his office holding a baby and accuses the least likely person of being the father: Radar. Sam explains that the father was probably an American GI who got her pregnant and left her, then was ostracized by her family. When Civilian Affairs sends a truck to relocate the Korean family living in the compound, the woman leaves with them and has a family again.

Commentary by Larry Gelbart: "Chosan was the name of ancient Korea. The chief purpose of that piece of business was to do something humorous. Detesting the bugler is an age-old Army tradition (in Irving Berlin's song, "Oh, How I Hate to Get Up in the Morning," one lyric says, "Some day I'm going to murder the bugler"). Perhaps there is something Freudian about Radar getting hit with a raw egg and then being accused of impregnating a girl. But that is a more than 30-year-old afterthought" (on Radar getting hit with an egg in the episode's opener).

Commentary by Jeff Maxwell: "I don't remember the episode name ("The Chosan People") but one of the story lines had everybody in camp thinking that Radar had fathered a baby with a local Korean woman. My first six words on *M*A*S*H* were to Radar. We stood in the chow line and I said, 'You son of a gun, you.' The only other thing I remember was that Jackie Cooper directed."

Authors' Notes: There are no PA announcements in this episode.

Once again, action is seen outside of Henry's window. Rarely did we see anyone out there.

According to Henry, Civilian Affairs personnel earn $640 a month. Hawkeye says in a letter to his father that surgeons earn $413.50 a month and Margaret tells Frank that she (as a Major and a nurse) earns $400.00 a month. This means that Civilian Affairs personnel earn $226.50 a month more than a surgeon and $240 a month more than a major who is a surgical nurse?

Radar and Trapper have blood type B.

Henry, Mulcahy and Sam Pak are eating a local Korean dish outside. Oddly, Henry and Mulcahy are using chopsticks while Sam uses a fork.

When the truck horn is heard inside, the sound of the horn changes when the scene switches to outside.

Jerry Fujikawa, whose birth name is Hatsuo Fujikawa, was born on February 18, 1912, and appeared in many television shows, including seven appearances on *M*A*S*H*, perhaps most notably as the shady doctor in Season 3's "Love and Marriage." Mr. Fujikawa died on April 30, 1983 in Los Angeles.

As You Were – 2/2/1974

Season 2 / Episode 44 / Production 44 – K420

Columbia House VHS Tape . . . . Leisure Time (Catalog # 10995)
Fox DVD . . . . Season 2, Disc 3

Alan Alda, Wayne Rogers, McLean Stevenson,
Loretta Swit, Larry Linville, Gary Burghoff

Produced by Gene Reynolds and Larry Gelbart
Script Consultant: Laurence Marks
Teleplay by Larry Gelbart & Laurence Marks
Story by Gene Reynolds
Directed by Hy Averback

Jamie Farr . . . . Corporal Klinger
William Christopher . . . . Father Mulcahy
Patricia Stevens . . . . Nurse Baker
Bobbie Mitchell . . . . Nurse Murphy
Kelley Nakahara . . . . Nurse Able

Copyright 1974 – 20th Century Fox Film Corporation

Non-Credited Appearances . . . . Jeff Maxwell, Dennis Troy, Roy Goldman,
Robert Gruber

Chapters

1:	Main Titles	6:	Frank's Emergency – 17:37
2:	Nothing to Do – 0:48	7:	Taking A Break – 21:24
3:	Henry's Lecture – 5:17	8:	A Hot Mayday – 22:24
4:	Frank's Hernia – 9:53	9:	Back to Normal – 24:30
5:	Back in Business – 13:03	10:	End Titles – 25:23

Closing Stills

1: Hawkeye helps Frank in Post-Op with his hernia
2: Henry giving a lecture
3: Hawkeye & Trapper laughing at Henry's lecture
4: Margaret telling Frank to let Hawk & Trap operate
5: Trapper on cot in Swamp

Synopsis: With a lull in the action, Henry uses the time to give a VD lecture in the mess tent while Frank discusses a medical condition with Margaret that's needed attention for some time. Frank has a hernia and Margaret recommends that he ask Hawkeye and Trapper to operate now that it's slow and reluctantly, Frank heads for the Swamp with Margaret. Wearing gorilla costumes they received in the mail, and after acting like a couple of crazed apes, Hawkeye and Trapper agree to operate. But just before the procedure begins, the war picks up, the O.R. is soon in full swing again and Frank has to wait for his surgery. But Frank's hernia becomes strangulated and with no tables available, Hawkeye puts him in traction and gives him an injection for the pain. Klinger brings in a Korean woman in labor and Frank, who is feeling no pain from the earlier injection, is finally brought in while Henry delivers the baby. The shelling intensifies, the baby is delivered and Hawkeye takes care of Frank's hernia. When the session is over and the shelling stops, Hawkeye and Trapper are at the officer's club…in their gorilla suits.

Commentary by Larry Gelbart: "Alda and Rogers wore the suits. Too hard to find stunt gorillas. That piece of business (Frank lining up the condiments) was inspired by my own Army experience. I was drafted at 18, right after WWII, served one year and 11 days. When I was in basic training at then-Camp Polk in Louisiana, our Mess Sergeant was a fanatic about lining up the ketchup, mustard, A-1, etc., in exactly the way we showed it on the show."

PA Announcements by Todd Sussman

Authors' Notes: Radar plays piano in this episode and is heard as the opening scene begins. While the music is playing, it appears that there are four people on a platform practicing a line-dance. This same clip is seen again in Chapter 9.

The order in which Frank lines up the mess tent condiments are as follows: *ketchup, mustard, relish, mayo, oil & vinegar, salt & pepper, sweet & sour gherkin.*

Oddly, the tent-windows behind Frank are lopsided.

Another ploy by Klinger to get out of the army is a letter to General Mitchell and threatens to send a photo to Mrs. Mitchell telling her that her husband has been seeing him on the side if he doesn't get a discharge.

Radar is 19 years old.

Scrub room sinks are in the middle facing each other.

Crisis – 2/9/1974

Season 2 / Episode 45 / Production 45 – K421

Columbia House VHS Tape . . . . *Enemy Fire (Catalog # 3746)*
Fox DVD . . . . *Season 2, Disc 3*

Alan Alda, Wayne Rogers, McLean Stevenson,
Loretta Swit, Larry Linville, Gary Burghoff

Produced by Gene Reynolds and Larry Gelbart
Script Consultant: Laurence Marks
Teleplay by Larry Gelbart & Laurence Marks
Directed by Don Weis

Jamie Farr . . . . Corporal Klinger
William Christopher . . . . Father Mulcahy

Copyright 1974 – 20th Century Fox Film Corporation

Non-Credited Appearances . . . . Jeff Maxwell, Kellye Nakahara, Dennis Troy,
Roy Goldman, Gwen Farrell

Chapters

1:	Main Titles	6:	On Full Alert – 16:30
2:	Cut Off – 0:48	7:	Running out of Supplies – 17:09
3:	Living Dangerously – 5:56	8:	Nighttime Nastiness – 19:49
4:	Priorities – 8:02	9:	The Army Comes Through – 23:30
5:	Bunk Buddies – 11:29	10:	End Titles – 25:22

Closing Stills

1: Klinger enters Henry's tent with makeup case
2: Mulcahy – "What am I saying?"
3: Hawkeye and Trapper lying under Frank's hammock
4: Margaret and the ham
5: Henry – "A real big empty"

Synopsis: When the supply line is cut, Henry reads a partial list of items they won't be getting for a while. Included are some foods, winter clothing, fuel oil and toilet paper. To make supplies on hand last, he puts the senior staff members in charge of different departments, and appoints Radar as Housing Officer. Radar sets up extra cots in the Swamp to conserve heat, but it's Henry who might have the hardest time of all when he discovers that someone stole the legs and draws from his desk to burn the wood. But sleep won't come as the PA announces wounded on the way. In OR, Radar makes the announcement everyone's been waiting for: A supply truck is in the compound with everything they need, including oil, foodstuffs, warm clothing and firewood, which comes a little too late for Henry.

Commentary by Larry Gelbart: "It was one of those scripts that was just a joy to develop, to write and to help come to life. The final result, I think is a testament to how much fun we had making it. We had a particularly good time writing this one. Sometimes you get on a roll and I think we had a pretty good one going throughout the second season, given the odd clinker here and there."

PA Announcements by Todd Sussman

Authors' Notes: According to Gelbart, the stateroom scene in the Marx Brother's movie, *A Night at the Opera,* influenced the scenes in the tents where cots were set up to conserve heat.

Radar's bear appears in this episode.

The last scene of this episode (The tag) where Henry is talking on the phone from "a real, big empty" is one of the most popular "Henry" scenes.

George – 2/16/1974

Season 2 / Episode 46 / Production 46 – K422

Columbia House VHS Tape . . . . *Hawkeye vs Frank (Catalog # 3771)*
Fox DVD . . . .*Season 2, Disc 3*

Alan Alda, Wayne Rogers, McLean Stevenson,
Loretta Swit, Larry Linville, Gary Burghoff

Produced by Gene Reynolds and Larry Gelbart
Script Consultant: Laurence Marks
Written by Regier and Markowitz
Directed by Gene Reynolds

Richard Ely . . . . Private George Weston
William Christopher . . . . Father Mulcahy
Patricia Stevens . . . . Nurse Stevens
Bobbie Mitchell . . . . .Nurse Mitchell
George Simmons . . . . Simmons

Copyright 1974 – 20th Century Fox Film Corporation

Non-Credited Appearances . . . . Jeff Maxwell, Kellye Nakahara, Dennis Troy,
Roy Goldman, Gwen Farrell

Chapters

1: *Main Titles*
2: *Another Day in the OR – 0:48*
3: *In the Recovery Room – 4:14*
4: *A Soldier's Secret – 7:34*
5: *Terminal Righteousness – 9:40*

6: *Private Weston's Perversion – 13:30*
7: *Frank's Campaign – 15:43*
8: *Foiling Frank – 20:20*
9: *A Peerless Life – 24:48*
10: *End Titles – 25:23*

Closing Stills

1: *Weston laughing in Post-Op*
2: *Hawkeye having a "Glass of checkers" in the Swamp*
3: *Trapper plays "Martini checkers" in the Swamp*
4: *Radar examines Henry's ear*
5: *Frank licks envelope in the Swamp*

Synopsis: Private George Weston is recovering in post-op when Frank realizes that the private has been wounded several times in combat, also realizing his current bruises are not consistent with those received in combat. However, Frank won't report Weston for fighting within his unit because of the private's service record. Weston later confides in Hawkeye that he and his buddies got drunk on leave and after he mentioned a homosexual incident that happened a couple of years ago, they beat him up. When Frank finds out about Weston, he writes a letter to Division to get Weston a dishonorable discharge. To prevent Frank from sending his report, Hawkeye and Trapper stage a fake fight between them and get Frank to admit to something in his past that if word got out, Frank could suffer serious repercussions.

Commentary by Larry Gelbart: "Fox was not interested in content. But CBS was extremely nervous about this episode. The subject was more to be avoided than confronted in those days. The network demanded certain changes and it was a challenge to place them while maintaining the integrity of the idea."

PA Announcements by Todd Sussman

Authors' Notes: Magazines seen in Margaret's tent are *Feminine View* (seen in an earlier episode, though not in Margaret's tent) and *Beauty Secrets.*

The book *War and Peace* is seen in the Swamp.

Richard Ely, sometimes billed as Richard K Weber, appeared in about ten different television shows between the 1960's and the 1980's, including 15 episodes of *The Young Rebels* in 1970-71. He played the part of Jeremy Larkin.

Mail Call – 2/23/1974

Season 2 / Episode 47 / Production 47 – K423

Columbia House VHS Tape . . . . News from Home (Catalog # 10992)
Fox DVD . . . . Season 2, Disc 3

Alan Alda, Wayne Rogers, McLean Stevenson,
Loretta Swit, Larry Linville, Gary Burghoff

Produced by Gene Reynolds and Larry Gelbart
Script Consultant: Laurence Marks
Written by Larry Gelbart & Laurence Marks
Directed by Alan Alda

Jamie Farr . . . . Corporal Klinger
William Christopher . . . . Father Mulcahy

Copyright 1974 – 20th Century Fox Film Corporation

Non-Credited Appearances . . . . Jeff Maxwell, Kellye Nakahara, Dennis Troy,
Roy Goldman, Gwen Farrell

Chapters

1: *Main Titles*	6: *Time Zone Turmoil – 12:42*
2: *Mail from Home – 0:48*	7: *Radar's Pen-Pal – 15:42*
3: *A Profitable War – 3:47*	8: *Leaving the War – 22:00*
4: *Klinger's Letter – 8:17*	9: *Forgiving Frank – 24:41*
5: *A Stock Tip – 11:00*	10: *End Titles – 25:22*

Closing Stills

1: *Klinger in Henry's office*
2: *Mulcahy & Trapper in the Officer's Club*
3: *Frank reads his mail in the Swamp*
4: *Hawkeye puts pimentos in olives in the Swamp*
5: *Radar in his office*

Synopsis: An event with great anticipation is mail call. A few words from home can alleviate the unpleasant business of war for a short while, but can also have an adverse effect as well. Trapper becomes angry that his daughters are growing up without him while Hawkeye gets a sweater his sister made that's too big. Henry thinks his wife sent him a sour cream and chocolate cake but what she really sent was a box full of bank stubs and canceled checks so he can balance her checkbook. Since the war started, Frank's stock portfolio has earned him a nice profit, which makes Frank very happy. But Hawkeye sets Frank up by hiding a phony letter from his father with a stock tip that's sure to make him wealthy, and Frank takes the bait. He contacts his broker to sell his entire portfolio and invest the money in Hawkeye's fictitious stock tip.

Commentary by Larry Gelbart: "Major Frank Burns was called 'Ferret Face.' Why? It's an insulting reference to his appearance; because he 'has no chin,' he resembles a ferret. Actually, Larry Linville supplied us with the insult. 'Ferret Face' was what his brother used to call him."

Authors' Notes: There are no PA announcements in this episode.
Trapper's daughters, Becky and Cathy, were named after Larry Gelbart's daughters.
Hawkeye's sister is alive and well in this episode as she sent him a sweater "with a guest room."

Klinger's attempt at a discharge is in the form of another letter, this time sent by his mother, to tell him his father is dying.

This is not the first time Klinger has tried writing his way out of the army. Henry has kept a record of previous written attempts:

Father dying last year, mother dying last year
Mother and Father dying
Mother, Father and older Sister dying
Mother dying and older Sister pregnant
Older Sister dying and Mother pregnant
Younger Sister pregnant and older Sister dying
Half of the family dying, the other half pregnant.

Margaret earns $400 a month.

The bit about "Pioneer Aviation" and Margaret screaming the supposedly confidential information on the compound remains a fan favorite.

A Smattering of Intelligence – 3/2/1974

Season 2 / Episode 48 / Production 48 – K424

Columbia House VHS Tape . . . . *American Flagg (Catalog # 13109)*
Fox DVD . . . . *Season 2, Disc 3*

Alan Alda, Wayne Rogers, McLean Stevenson,
Loretta Swit, Larry Linville, Gary Burghoff

Produced by Gene Reynolds and Larry Gelbart
Script Consultant: Laurence Marks
Written by Larry Gelbart & Laurence Marks
Directed by Larry Gelbart
Edward Winter . . . . .Colonel Sam Flagg
Bill Fletcher. . . . . .Captain Vinny Pratt
Copyright 1974 – 20th Century Fox Film Corporation

Non-Credited Appearances. . . . . .Jeff Maxwell, Kellye Nakahara, Roy Goldman,
Gwen Farrell

Chapters

1: *Main Titles*	6: *A Secret Message – 13:01*
2: *Colonel Flagg – 0:48*	7: *Frank's File – 19:23*
3: *The C.I.A. Man – 3:00*	8: *Comrade Burns – 22:04*
4: *A Friend from G-2 – 7:22*	9: *Intelligence Report – 24:49*
5: *Playing Spy – 11:23*	10: *End Titles – 25:22*

Closing Stills

1: *Flagg crashes x-ray machine on his arm*
2: *Hawkeye in the Swamp with cowboy hat*
3: *Trapper in the Swamp*
4: *Margaret, Frank & Flagg in the Officer's Club*
5: *Radar removes his glasses while "sleeping"*

Synopsis: Colonel Flagg arrives at the 4077th to investigate security leaks and orders Henry to forget the name Flagg, but allows him to make a report using any of his other ID's, including "Captain Louise Klein." But Flagg is not the only intelligence man to show up. An old friend of Trapper's is waiting for him in the Swamp. Captain Vinny Pratt, G-2 Intelligence, is there because his organization monitored a call made earlier by Flagg. Pratt's job is to find out why Flagg infiltrated the 4077th and stop him. Hawkeye and Trapper help the intelligence men find their security leaks by switching Frank's file with one that makes Frank appear as a Communist to Flagg, and another to make it appear Frank is a Fascist to Pratt, and both men now want to arrest Frank at the same time.

Commentary by Larry Gelbart: "The co-author of this episode was Laurence Marks. I believe we introduced Col. Flagg in 'Deal Me Out.' This was the first of the half dozen or so episodes I directed. I cannot tell you what a great help Gene Reynolds was; first, encouraging me to do it all, then being a tremendous help, explaining the process as I went through it. I truly couldn't, and wouldn't, do it without him. It's nice to know that the episode has a different feel to it. The best part of directing was the ability to keep shaping the episode, to take advantage of the extended period to refine it and improve what had already been written and rehearsed."

Authors' Notes: There are no PA announcements in this episode.

The scene looking out of Henry's office window in Chapter 2 shows a partial building in the right window with trees and mountains through both windows. This changes in Chapter 4 and again in Chapter 7.

Flagg's ID's in this episode are: *Major Brooks, Lieutenant Carter, Ensign Troy,* and *Captain Louise Klein* — which he needs for next week in Tokyo.

Joint Report from Flagg and Pratt: Surveillance report from G2 and the CIA combined as each cast member is shown on-screen at the end of the episode. Captain Benjamin Franklin Pierce *(on screen still photo in gorilla costume),* Captain John McIntyre *(on screen still photo in gorilla costume),* Lieutenant Colonel Henry Blake *(on screen still photo standing behind lingerie in his tent),* Major Margaret Houlihan and Major Frank Burns *(on screen still photo, Margaret washing Frank's hair in her tent)* and Corporal Radar O'Reilly *(on screen still photo with mirror by slot machine).*

This being the last episode of Season 2, this was done to remind viewers of the characters on the show, and an attempt to keep viewer's interest for Season 3. It worked.

Bill Fletcher's acting career began in 1951 and appeared in *The Jack Benny Program, Daniel Boone,* three episodes of *Bonanza,* three episodes of *McCloud,* two episodes of *Cannon,* as well as appearances in *Baretta* and *The Dukes of Hazzard.*

Appendix – Season 2

Character Profiles

Hawkeye

Episode 25: Ear to nurse's naval in med school — he could hear the ocean
Grandfather Sparky Pierce did 6 months at New Hampshire License Place Academy. Sparky said in the Academy, "There are some who do and some who don't."

33: Earns $413.50 a month in the army.

35: Spent Saturday mornings and afternoons in dark theaters. (Could've easily been a mushroom instead of a doctor).
Awarded toilet paper scroll signed by all at the 4077 (Will always think of Frank when he sees it).

36: Together with Trapper got 4 people in a sleeping bag *(mentioned)*.

38: Friend Charlie Abrams receptionist in an adult movie *(seen by Hawkeye)*.
All night binges with Trapper *(mentioned)*.
Secret nurse ceremonies with Trapper *(mentioned)*.
Plants microphones in sleeping bags *(mentioned)*.
Switches names on latrines *(mentioned)*.
With Trapper, held a "Come As Your Favorite Nude Pilgrim Party" *(mentioned)*.

39: With Trapper, received a suite at The Imperial Hotel *(mentioned)*.
Extended "family": Cousin Fred, Brother-In-Law Leroy, Cousin Phil, Ed, 2nd cousin on Mother's side, Mother's cousin Bill, Cousin's Brother's Mother Sam.

41: Shoe store in Vermont. Shoe size is 10½ C.

42: Did residency with Major Stanley "Stosh" Robbins.

44: Did a year at Bellevue.
Gorilla costumes from The Peerless Costume Company in Philadelphia.

45: In charge of maintenance and general services & supplies.

47: SISTER sent a "sweater with a guestroom."
Great Grandfather Tombstone Pierce sold whiskey and hors d'oevres to Indians.

Trapper

Episode 25: New Feature Magazine — MacArthur on the cover — Seagram 7 ad on the back.

29: 170 Pounds *(Lost 5 pounds since Episode 3)*.

30: Kids: Cathy 7, Becky, wife Louise.

31: Gives Hawkeye haircut in the Swamp.

36: Together with Hawkeye got 4 people in a sleeping bag *(mentioned)*.

38: All night binges with Hawkeye *(mentioned)*.
   Secret nurse ceremonies with Hawkeye *(mentioned)*.
   Plants microphones in sleeping bags *(mentioned)*.
   Switches names on latrines *(mentioned)*.
   With Hawkeye, held a "Come As Your Favorite Nude Pilgrim Party"
   (mentioned).
39: With Hawkeye, received a suite at The Imperial Hotel *(mentioned)*.
   #32 basketball jersey.
42: Broke Henry's doll and stuffed it in a card file.
43: Blood type B.
45: Heating and electrical officer.
46: 6' 3" tall.
47: Cookies and pictures of his daughters in mail call.
48: #32 basketball jersey

Henry

Episode 30: Took a course in map reading.
   Has a 3" finger.
31: Can see the movie, "The Thing That Ate the Bronx" every night.
32: Announces gurney races.
   Can't wear wing tip shoes because of high arches.
33: Ordered by a general to give a coffee enema — asked about cream & sugar
   and was on a plane 12 hours later for Korea.
   Home movie of his 6 year old daughter Molly's birthday party and a clip of
   his neighbors, Milt & Sylvia Jaffe — Milt Jaffe is a gynecologist & Sylvia
   Jaffe is "loaded for bear."
   Lorraine was Succotash Queen at Illinois, Normal & met her at a
   freshman mixer.
   She was with Buzz Wilensky, the captain of the football team.
   Henry begged her for a date after she looked at him — proposed on first
   date "right there on the ice."
   Buzz Wilensky is the biggest cement contractor in the mid-west.
35: If he were home with the flu, Lorraine would be taking care of him leaning
   over the bed with curlers, cold cream and chipped fingernails.
   His kids would be playing ball on the side of the house.
   The dog would be having an accident by the foot of the bed — he's glad
   he's in Korea.
36: Likes his steaks rare, sprinkles sugar and pours Brandy on them.
38: Postcard from his parents on a 2nd honeymoon in Niagara Falls.
   Orders adult films from The Tabasco Film Company, Box 245, Havana,
   Cuba.
   Lorraine is slightly pigeon-toed and has $2000 worth of bridgework of
   which he owes $1500.
39: Gets a case of 12 year old Scotch from General Mitchell.
   Reads "Special Nurse" magazine.
   Was drunk and wearing a lampshade 2 ½ hours after the Officer's Club
   opened.
40: 44 years old — half deaf — brushes his hair with a towel.
   Dyes his hair and it "bleeds" after sweating from jogging.
   Does 8 pushups.
   Lorraine is 42 years old and $68 overdrawn.
   Son Andrew.
42: Was King Neptune at the Mardis Gras Celebration at the 4077.

His costume covered his body completely from the waist down, including his pelvic region.

Wore a rhinestone in his belly button.

Took over 6 months to housebreak his dog during a newspaper strike.

Avoids church religiously.

44: BLT on wheat toast, no mayo, chocolate shake.

45: Bought a lot of war bonds.

47: $236 veterinarian bill for his 15-year-old cat.

48: Was at the Happy Hour Motel in Elkhart, Indiana in June, 1948.

Signed in as Mr. Carl Williams and daughter.

Signature near the smudged license plate number.

Was with a woman named Linda Collins in Room 312.

Electric blanket controller was a microphone and doorknob was a camera.

Was with a rent-a-car girl in Houston before arriving at the AMA convention in 1949.

By the time he got to the AMA, they were folding up the chairs

Margaret

Episode 29: Peroxide.

38: Friend Tricia Spalding — did their training together.

Tricia married a doctor Margaret turned down and has two children.

Lives in a $45,000 house with 2 car garage and a pool.

Margaret wants a transfer.

Returns a picture of her and Frank in Osaka.

Returns a Mother's Day card.

Returns, "Bimbo," a black & white spotted stuffed dog.

Wants back from Frank her leather-bound copy of The Army Officer's Guide.

Wants back her cuticle scissors and tweezers.

Wants back her Doris Day scrapbook.

Father was a drunk / Father died.

Margaret is drunk and said she could've gone for Trapper.

After forced shower, she wears Trapper's yellow robe.

40: Keeps a diary in which she enters a passage about her "scrumptious Major F.B. and his growth as a commander.

41: Gave Frank her father's riding crop for his birthday.

Her mother gave riding crop to her father on their wedding night.

45: In charge of the nurses.

46: Pancreas under her pillow.

47: Earns $400 a month

Frank

Episode 25: Specialty is post-op infections.

26: Gunnery experience in the ROTC.

27: Specialty is post-op infections. *(In Season 5, Episode 104, his specialty will change to feet).*

29: Gives orientation lecture every Friday afternoon.

30: Plans his week around Thursday nights for "discussion" with Margaret.

31: Always plucks a hair and puts it on his letters to see if anyone touched them.

Trapper read and copied his letter to his wife (11 major operations).

Has a blood pressure situation.

32: Meets Margaret behind the lard cans.

33: Became a doctor to clear up his face.
Major Frank Marion Burns.
34: "Optic adjustment to darkness is subnormal."
Took twice as long to become a doctor.
Flunked out of 2 medical schools.
Would've been a male nurse but couldn't make hospital corners.
During his internship, the local undertaker sent him Christmas presents
and calendars.
35: With a fever, he calls Margaret "Louise" (his wife).
With a fever, he calls Margaret "Nancy" (his receptionist).
Nancy was the best receptionist he ever had.
37: Doesn't like to be around when rules are broken.
"Intelligence is something i try to avoid."
Sees almost every war picture that comes out — feels it's his duty.
38: Neighborhood is not restricted as there's a Catholic right across the street
from him.
$2,000 richer as his investments are paying off.
"Anglo Chemical" is up 47 ½ thanks to Napalm - Frank bought at $39.
"United Foundry" is up as well.
Has meetings with Margaret behind the delousing tent.
Has meetings with Margaret in laundry trucks.
Reads *The Wall Street Journal.*
39: Drinks "Shirley Temples."
40: Has 3 daughters.
41: Puts a nurse on report for giving him the surgical instrument he asked for.
Birthday card from Louise.
Birthday present from Margaret — riding crop.
Birthday present from x-ray — lead-lined jockey shorts.
Birthday present — medical student's specimen stein from Old Heidelberg.
Birthday cake is yellow and white with 4 blue candles, 2 pink and 2 green.
Mother sent 30 birthday invitations just to get 4 kids to come.
Got "Thank you" notes from people he said he'd never see again.
42: Sends weekly anonymous reports to General Mitchell.
Anniversary call to Louise got through a month late.
44: Lines up ketchup, mustard, relish, mayo, oil & vinegar, salt & pepper and
sweet & sour gherkins, in a row.
Fred is a friend from school.
Family had a maid when he was a kid.
45: In charge of distribution and possible rationing of food.
Wife uses Crème de Menthe on her corns.
Has hunting socks to keep warm.
Hyperthyroid.
46: Paid $400 for first-year medical exams.
47: Wife gets ½ of everything if they divorce.
Stockbroker: Henderson, Landers and Flynn, Prescott Building, Wall
Street, New York.
Stockbroker telephone number: Canal 9-7000.
Offers to kiss Margaret's feet for forgiveness.
48: Had the idea of putting the 4077 on pontoons.
Has a complete list of everyone in camp who's ever been subversive or
promoted ahead of "certain doctors" by showing off and saving more lives.
Attended the Russian Ballet last month.

Radar

Episode 25: Bear.

    27: Bear.

    29: Has a preacher back home who whistled while he preached.

        Martini.

    30: Bear.

        Files the minefield map under "B" for boom.

        Has some of Trapper's Martini.

    32: Cigar.

        Style Right Shoe Company of Storm Lake, Iowa (selling wing-tip shoes).

        Wing tip shoes cost $8.95 — Arch supports additional $1.95.

    33: Doesn't know if he's a virgin or not *(was engaged in Season 1)*.

        Last monthly staff meeting was 6 months ago.

        Vote took place for officer's yearly reunion after the war is over — motion failed when it didn't get 1vote.

    34: Bear.

        Everything in his body turns to liquid if he doesn't eat regularly — shoes are full of water.

    36: Friend at the 331 EVAC got a 20 x 40 inflatable pool.

        Trades a bar-b-cue for an incubator.

    37: Likes "The Purple Dragon" in Dai Wank.

        "The Purple Dragon" is an empty Lockheed packing crate with a jukebox and "B" girls on roller skates.

        Wears a white paratrooper scarf.

    38: Sends away for things just to get mail.

        Got a packet of oregano and a house painter's color chart in the mail.

        Brandy.

        Cigar.

    39: Hawkeye and Trapper got him drunk the 1st time and taught him to drive a jeep — both on same night.

    40: Plays bugle.

        Tells Frank he doesn't smoke *(Had a cigar in Episode 38 and 3 in Season 1, one not lit)*.

    41: White paratrooper scarf — had a date at 8:00.

    43: Plays bugle — hit with a raw egg.

        Blood type B.

        Met Choon Hi on September 15th.

        Wanted to get a tattoo, but the artist printed "mother" so much that he ran out of ink.

    44: Plays piano.

        19 years old.

        Tony Rizzo — friend from Division H.Q.

    45: Housing Officer.

        Wears boots to bed, "just in case."

    46: Gives Henry his monthly examination.

    47: Sent 25 cents for a pen pal, Mary Jo Carpenter from Port Salut, Montana.

    48: Bear.

        Cigarette smoke signal — coughs but smoked cigars in earlier episodes.

Klinger

Episode 31: Catches bouquet at wedding.

    32: Hang glides out of camp — Big red bird with fuzzy pink feet.

    37: Ran into Grand Central Station to avoid the draft — trapped in a pay-toilet.

Cost the army $4 in nickels to get him out.

Had to be jabbed with a coat hanger to get him to cough at the draft board.

    41: Has gotten 2 proposals and a hurt letter from a peeping Tom.

Needs 4 signatures on his "crazy papers." *(This will change in a future episode to two signatures.)*

    44: Wearing an exact copy of the dress Rita Hayworth wore in Gilda.

At least close as he was sewing from memory and only saw the movie once.

Will send picture to General Mitchell's wife if he doesn't give him a discharge.

    45: Uses Crème de Menthe cold cream.

    47: Letter from mother — Father dying *(ploy)*.

Previous letters in his file — Father dying last year, Mother dying last year, Mother and father dying, Mother, father and older sister dying, Mother dying and older sister pregnant, Older sister dying and mother pregnant, Younger sister pregnant and older sister dying, Half the family dying, the other half pregnant.

Father Mulcahy

Episode 45: In charge of morale.

Blue plaid robe and Loyola sweatshirt.

Seen, Heard, Mentioned or Referenced – Season 2

Movies

Episode 26: Frank mentions Gary Cooper in the role of Billy Mitchell in *The Court-Martial of Billy Mitchell* (1955).

26: Frank mentions Gary Cooper in the title role in *Sergeant York* (1941).

26: Frank mentions Gary Cooper in the role of Lou Gehrig in *The Pride of the Yankees* (1942).

27: Hawkeye mentions Dr. Hackenbush from Marx Brothers' movie *A Day At the Races* (1937).

29: Hawkeye calls Frank Sleepy & Dopey, from the movie, *Snow White and the Seven Dwarfs* (1937).

29: Hawkeye says "Slowly I turn…" from the Three Stooges short, *Gents Without Cents* (1944).

31: PA announces *Flying Leathernecks* (1951) with John Wayne, Ward Bond and Maureen O'Hara. *(Note: Ward Bond and Maureen O'Hara were not in this movie.)*

31: Radar mentions *Bonzo Goes to College* (1952).

31: Radar mentions The Thing That Ate the Bronx *(not real)*.

31: Radar mentions Bonzo Runs for President *(not real)*.

33: Henry's home movie.

35: Henry mentions *Double Indemnity* (1944).

37: Training film on trench foot, mentioned.

38: Unidentified adult movie in Henry's office seen by Henry, Hawkeye and Trapper.

38: *Paulina Paris and Her Pelican*, mentioned.

38: *Francine LaFlame and Her Tassels In the Air*, mentioned.

38: Radar mentions *Flash Gordon* (1936)

39: Animated VD cartoon *Hansel and Regretel* mentioned in PA announcement.

42: Henry mentions *The Thing*, also known as *The Thing from Another Planet* (1951).

42: Henry mentions *The Blob* (1958).

44: PA announces a midnight movie, no name given.

44: *Gilda* (1944), mentioned.

45: PA announces tonight's movie will be burned, no name given

46: PA announces another training film on trench foot

46: Hawkeye calls Radar "Tinker Bell," a reference to *Peter Pan* (1924).

Songs

Episode 25: "Reveille" *(Heard over the PA)* See Episode 9 (page 129) for details.

25: "Hi Lily, Hi Lo" *(Female Korean voice heard over PA)* from the 1953 musical "Lili." Words by Bronislav Kaper, music by Helen Deutch.

26: "Chattanooga Choo-Choo" *(Male Korean voice heard over PA)* Words by Mack Gordon, music by Harry Warren. From the 1941 movie *Sun Valley Serenade.*

26: "Call to Post" *(on bugle.)*

26: "Wild Blue Yonder" Written by Robert Crawford in 1939. The official US Air Force Song.

27: "Tokyo Shoe-Shine Boy"*(Female Japanese voice heard)* Released by Teruko Akatsuki in 1951.

27, 28: "As Time Goes By" *(Heard on the radio)* Written by Herman Hupfeld, from the 1942 movie *Casablanca.*

28: "Pack Up Your Troubles" *(Hawkeye makes a reference)* Words by George Henry Powell, music by Felix Powell, from 1915.

29: "I'll Be Home for Christmas" *(Hawkeye sings)* Written by Kim Gannon, Walter Kent & Buck Ram in 1943.

29: "Der Fuehrer's Face" *(Hawkeye sings)* Written by Oliver Wallace, from the 1942 Disney animated short *Der Fuehrer's Face.*

30: "You Made Me Love You (I Didn't Want to Do It)" *(Hawkeye mentions)* The Cole Porter arrangement; words by Joseph McArthy, music by Jimmy Monaco, from 1913.

31: "Charge" *(on bugle heard in a movie)* Civil War bugle call.

32: "Happy Days Are Here Again" *(Heard over the PA)* See Episode 1 (page 128) for details.

32: "Call to Post" Civil War call.

33: "Makin' Whoopee" *(Hawkeye sings "So don't forget folks, that's what you get folks, for makin' whoopee...")* Words by Gus Kahn, music by Walter Donaldson, 1928.

34: "Happy Days Are Here Again" *(Heard over the PA)* See Episode 1 (page 128) for details.

36: "All Kinds of Weather" *(Hawkeye makes a reference)* Written by Red Garland in 1958.

37: "The Good Ship Lollipop" *(Hawkeye mentions)* Words by Sidney Claire, music by Richard A. Whiting. From the 1934 movie *Bright Eyes.*

40: "Pomp and Circumstance" *(Heard over the PA)* See Episode 4 (page 86) for details.

40: "You Make Me Feel So Young" *(Mentioned and later heard)* See Episode 24 (page 130) for details.

40: "Buckle Down Winsocki" *(Instrumental version heard on jukebox)* Words by Ralph Blaine, music by Hugh Martin. From the 1941 musical *Best Foot Forward.*

41: "Can't Help Lovin' That Man of Mine" *(Hawkeye says)* Words by Oscar Hammerstein, music by Jerome Kern. From the 1936 movie *Showboat.*

43: "Reveille" *(Radar on bugle, heard twice in this episode. Radar is later hit with an egg)* See Episode 9 (page 129) for details.

44: "You'll Never Know" *(Klinger sings "You'll never know just how much I miss you...")* Words by Mack Gordon, music by Harry Warren (1943).

45: "Comrades" *(Mulcahy sings "Comrade, comrade, ever since we were boys, sharing each other's sorrows, sharing each other's joys...")* Written and composed by Felix McLennon in 1837.

45: "On, On, On, The Boys Are Marching" *(Hawkeye sings, "The boys are marching...")* Written by George Frederick Root in 1865

46: "I've Got You Under My Skin" *(Trapper sings "I've got you under my skin...")* Written by Cole Porter in 1936.

46: "Too Ra Loo Ra Loo Ral" *(Hawkeye mentions)* Written by J.R. Shannon and copyright 1913 by Warner Brothers.

48: "Vinny Prat" *(In response to "Pretty gung ho," Hawkeye sings "...And I don't care...")* Written circa 1846, first credited vocals from the Virginia Minstrels.

Prank Frank – Season 2

Episode 25: "Who rewrote these commandments?" *(seen by Frank)*.
Appendix in one boot, tonsils in the other *(seen by Frank)*.
Hawkeye and Trapper nail shut Margaret's tent door from the outside with Frank inside *(seen)*.

26: Sidearm replaced with a stapler *(seen)*.
Sidearm replaced with a water gun *(seen)*.
Sidearm replaced with a toilet plunger *(seen)*.
Sidearm replaced with a "Bang" gun *(seen)*.

28: Peanut butter in his stethoscope *(mentioned)*.
Ether in his aftershave *(mentioned)*.
"Dear Frank, Dad was not your father, Love Mom" on his mother's picture *(seen by Frank)*.

29: Sedative injection meant for Hawkeye *(seen)*.

32: "Dear Mrs. Burns, since you're so proud of your husband as an officer, it is sad to report that he is frequently out of uniform, and maybe you should know with who" (Hawkeye and Trapper will send this to Mrs. Burns if charges against Henry aren't dropped).

33: Trapper unscrewed his clusters at the last monthly staff meeting *(mentioned)*.

34: Hawkeye and Trapper dress Frank to look like MacArthur *(seen)*.

39: Hawkeye and Trapper empty Martinis in Frank's "Shirley Temple" drinks, Frank faints *(seen)*.

41: Meatloaf in his pajamas *(mentioned)*.
Hawkeye and Trapper put an extra number on his dog tags *(mentioned)*.
Woke with nail polish and mascara *(mentioned)*.
Hawkeye and Trapper glued his head to his pillow *(mentioned)*.

42: Hawkeye and Trapper successfully keep Frank and Margaret away from OR so a nose job can be performed on Private Baker.

44: Hawkeye and Trapper nailed him inside a big crate *(seen)*.
Oatmeal in his gas mask *(mentioned)*.
Hawkeye and Trapper stapled a whole roll of his toilet paper *(mentioned)*.

48: Hawkeye and Trapper replaced Frank's file with two fake files, one for Flagg and one for Vinny Pratt.
In Flagg's file: Frank is a Communist with 17 left wing causes and charities contributed to.
In Pratt's file: Frank is a Fascist and engages in radical right wing activities: usher at a Bund meeting in 1939, pledging $25 to a Martin Borman telethon in Argentina, and running a linen laundry for the KKK. Flagg and Pratt both want to arrest Frank at the same time.

Appearances – Season 2

Aaron, Jack ....Episode 32 *(Major Murphy)*
Abelson, Arthur ....Episode 33 *(Milt Jaffe)*
Aberg, Sivi .... Episode 33 *(Anna Lindstrom)*
Aletter, Frank ....Episode 28 *(Major Stoner)*
Alvin, John .... Episode 36 *(Mr. Bowman)*
Arbus, Allan .... Episode 27 *(Major Milton Freedman)*
Arbus, Allan ....Episode 37 *(Major Sidney Freedman)*
Bauman, Katherine ....Episode 40 *(Nancy Sue Parker)*
Bowman, Gail ....Episode 26 *(Nurse Powell)*
Camacho, Corrine..Episode 31 *(Lieutenant Regina Hoffman)*
Christopher, William............................ Episode 26, 27, 30, 33, 35, 42, 43, 44, 45, 46, 47
(Father Mulcahy)
Cleveland, Odessa.............Episode 25, 26, 28, 31, 38, 39, 40 *(Lieutenant Ginger Bayliss)*
Dever, Tom .... Episode 37 *(Lieutenant Rogers)*
Elias, Lou.. Episode 42 *(M.P. Sergeant)*
Ely, Richard ....Episode 46 *(Private George Weston)*
Evans, Leslie ....Episode 25 *(Nurse Bryan)*
Evans, Leslie ....Episode 28 *(Nurse Mason)*
Evans, Leslie ....Episode 30 *(Nurse Mitchell)*
Fankboner, Sarah ....Episode 26 *(Nurse Klein)*
Fankboner, Sarah ....Episode 36 *(Nurse Owens)*
Farr, Jamie...............Episode 25, 27, 30, 31, 33, 37, 39, 41, 44, 45, 47 *(Corporal Klinger)*
Farrell, Gwen ....Episode 28 *(Nurse Butler)*
Farrell, Gwen ....Episode 35 *(Nurse Wilson)*
Farrell, Gwen .... Episode 37, 40 *(Nurse)*
Fisher, Corey.. Episode 26 *(Captain Phil Cardoza)*
Fletcher, Bill .... Episode 48 *(Captain Vinny Pratt)*
Fujikawa, Jerry..Episode 37 *(Whiplash Wang)*
Fujikawa, Jerry.. Episode 43 *(The Korean Father)*
Funai, Helen .... Episode 36 *(Betty Lou)*
Garr, Terry.. Episode 34 *(Lieutenant Suzanne Marquette)*
Gelman, Marcia .... Episode 34 *(Nurse)*
Gelman, Marcia .... Episode 35 *(Nurse Jacobs)*
Gehring, Ted..Episode 36 *(Major Morris)*
Goldman, Roy.. Episode 32 *(M.P.)*
Grosh, Ralph..Episode 39 *(General's Aid)*
Harper, Jerry..Episode 36 *(Mr. Phillips)*
Haymer, Johnny..Episode 41 *(Sergeant Zale)*
Holland, Anthony.. Episode 25 *(Captain Hildebrand)*
Hughes, Kathleen .... Episode 33 *(Lorraine Blake)*
Jue, Jay Jay..Episode 43 *(The Korean Boy)*
Kino, Lloyd .... Episode 26 *(Korean Soldier)*
Kusatsu, Clyde .... Episode 39, 40 *(Kwang Duk)*
Lauritsen, Sheila .... Episode 38, 39 *(Nurse Watson)*
Lauritsen, Sheila .... Episode 40 *(Lieutenant Sheila Sturner)*
Lauritsen, Sheila ....Episode 41 *(Sheila)*
Lerner, Michael .... Episode 41 *(Captain Bernie Futterman)*
Margolin, Stuart..Episode 42 *(Major Stanley "Stosh" Robbins)*
Meiklejohn, Linda .... Episode 25 *(Lieutenant Leslie Scorch)*
Mettey, Lynette..Episode 35 *(Lieutenant Sheila Anderson)*
Miller, Edgar.. Episode 30 *(Kim)*

Broadcast/Production Order – Season 2

Broadcast	*Production*
25: Divided We Stand *(9/15/1973)*	25: *(K401)* Divided We Stand
26: 5 O'Clock Charlie *(9/22/1973)*	26: *(K402)* Radar's Report
27: Radar's Report *(9/29/1973)*	27: *(K403)* 5 O'Clock Charlie
28: For The Good Of The Outfit *(10/6/1973)*	28: *(K404)* For The Good Of The Outfit
29: Dr. Pierce and Mr. Hyde *(10/13/1973)*	29: *(K405)* Dr. Pierce And Mr. Hyde
30: Kim *(10/20/1973)*	30: *(K406)* L.I.P.
31: L.I.P. *(10/27/1973)*	31: *(K407)* Kim
32: The Trial Of Henry Blake *(11/3/1973)*	32: *(K408)* The Trial Of Henry Blake
33: Dear Dad, Three *(11/10/1973)*	33: *(K409)* Dear Dad, Three
34: The Sniper *(11/17/1973)*	34: *(K410)* The Sniper
35: Carry On, Hawkeye *(11/24/1973)*	35: *(K411)* Carry On, Hawkeye
36: The Incubator *(12/1/1973)*	36: *(K412)* The Incubator
37: Deal Me Out *(12/8/1973)*	37: *(K413)* Deal Me Out
38: Hot Lips And Empty Arms *(12/15/1973)*	38: *(K414)* Hot Lips And Empty Arms
39: Officers Only *(12/22/1973)*	39: *(K415)* Officers Only
40: Henry In Love *(1/5/1974)*	40: *(K416)* Henry In Love
41: For Want Of A Boot *(1/12/1974)*	41: *(K417)* For Want Of A Boot
42: Operation Noselift *(1/19/1974)*	42: *(K418)* Operation Noselift
43: The Chosan People *(1/26/1974)*	43: *(K419)* The Chosan People
44: As You Were *(2/2/1974)*	44: *(K420)* As You Were
45: Crisis *(2/9/1974)*	45: *(K421)* Crisis
46: George *(2/16/1974)*	46: *(K422)* George
47: Mail Call *(2/23/1974)*	47: *(K423)* Mail Call
48: A Smattering Of Intelligence *(3/2/1974)*	48: *(K424)* A Smattering Of Intelligence

Season 3

Season 3 of *M*A*S*H* is every bit as funny and genius in its blend of comedy and drama as Season 2. But, between seasons 2 and 3, Larry Gelbart and Gene Reynolds visited Korea. Their experience affected them, and it intensified their awareness of the horrors of war. Whether or not this affected what the viewers saw on the screen in this season is open to opinion. Nevertheless, there seems to be a few more twists and turns in the season. And, although almost imperceptible and indefinable, the mood seems a tad darker. McLean Stevenson was unhappy with working conditions on the show, and Wayne Rogers felt his character wasn't being used to his potential. Subsequently, both Stevenson and Rogers left after this season. The knowledge of their impending departures is likely another factor contributing to any perceived minor atmosphere change in Season 3. But, the perfect blend of top-notch comedy and drama continued, and made for a marriage of entertainment bliss. Flagg returned and the audience was introduced to Richard Lee Sung's recurring character, in this case, Kim Luck ("This is me!"). Highlight episodes from this season include "Alcoholics Unanimous," "Iron Guts Kelly," "Private Charles Lamb," "Springtime" and "There's Nothing Like a Nurse." Harry Morgan appeared in the classic, "The General Flipped at Dawn," letting the viewer see both Morgan and Stevenson together. And "Aid Station" offered a bit of unintentional foreshadowing, as Hawkeye, Hot Lips and Klinger go off to an aid station together. Alda, Swit and Farr (along with Christopher) would be the only remaining cast from the first season troupe by the end of its eleven year run. In "Abyssinia Henry," McLean Stevenson's final episode, the character of Henry Blake is killed in a plane crash. This took *M*A*S*H* in a decidedly more serious direction for all seasons to come.

The General Flipped at Dawn – 9/10/1974

Season 3 / Episode 49 / Production 56 – B308

Columbia House VHS Tape . . . . *Army Brass (Catalog # 3742)*
Fox DVD . . . . *Season 3, Disc 1*

Alan Alda, Wayne Rogers, McLean Stevenson,
Loretta Swit, Larry Linville, Gary Burghoff

Produced by Gene Reynolds and Larry Gelbart
Written by Jim Fritzell & Everett Greenbaum
Directed by Larry Gelbart

Harry Morgan . . . . Major General Bartford Hamilton Steele
Jamie Farr . . . . Corporal Klinger
William Christopher . . . . Father Mulcahy
Lynnette Mettey . . . . Nurse Baker
Theodore Wilson . . . . Warrant Officer Martin H. Williams
Brad Trumbull . . . . Colonel Atkins
Dennis Erdman . . . . Harrison

Copyright 1974 – 20th Century Fox Film Corporation

Non-Credited Appearances . . . . Kellye Nakahara, Dennis Troy, Roy Goldman

Chapters

1: *Main Titles*	6: *A Date – 15:19*
2: *Seeing Colonel Blake – 0:49*	7: *A Three-Star Loony – 17:48*
3: *About General Steele – 2:22*	8: *A Court-Martial – 22:50*
4: *General Steele Arrives – 9:07*	9: *A Promotion – 24:35*
5: *General Wacko – 12:11*	10: *End Titles – 25:30*

Closing Stills

1: *Steele arrives in Jeep (Close-up)*
2: *Hawkeye writes "article" in supply*
3: *Trapper in the Officer's Club*
4: *Henry and his new fatigues in his tent*
5: *Frank trimming his nose hair*

Synopsis: General Bartford Hamilton Steele, a no-nonsense, by-the-book 62-year-old two-star general, has sent word that he will headquarter at the 4077th for a week. The General exhibits eccentric behavior when the unit falls out for inspection but his eccentricities become dangerous when he wants to relocate the unit closer to the front lines, against Henry's objections. After Steele selects a new home for the 4077th, he wants to "observe" the move in a chopper, but Hawkeye has other plans and orders the pilot to take off with a patient who needs the chopper more than the General does.

Commentary by Larry Gelbart: "Gary definitely had a hard time not breaking up when Harry, as General Steele, asked him his name and Radar replied, 'Corporal O'Reilly, sir,' and Steele barked, "No talking in the ranks!" It was impossible for budget reasons to ever shoot an entire show on location. The location was the Fox Ranch in the Malibu Hills. It was where a great deal of the *Planet of the Apes* pics were shot. The situation (with General Steele) was based on a real one that Everett Greenbaum witnessed during his days as a Navy pilot in WW2."

Commentary by Gary Burghoff: "There was a scene that was unbearably funny to do. Harry, as Steele, is inspecting the troops and I can see him coming. Harry asks me a question and then yells, 'NO TALKING IN RANKS!' I knew it was coming and I'd start to go. I think we did it like 18 times. See, behind Harry was McLean. And I'd see that silly expression on McLean's face. But Morgan was secure, as an actor, so he'd be ok if you'd go (break up). I think that was the decisive moment when Gelbart and Reynolds saw the incredible chemistry with Morgan. I think you probably see me biting my lip in one of those long shots when Harry Morgan is inspecting us."

PA Announcements by Todd Sussman

Authors' Notes: General Steele would soon become Colonel Potter. This is the only time we see McLean Stevenson and Harry Morgan together.

Hawkeye tells an ambulance driver that Lenox Hill Hospital in New York City is located at "71st and 3rd," but it's actually located on E. 77th Street between Lexington Avenue and Park Avenue.

Theodore Wilson, who played Warrant Officer Martin H. Williams, the chopper pilot, is probably best known for his role on CBS's *Good Times* as Sweet Daddy Williams. Mr. Wilson died on July 21, 1991 of heart related complications (even though he had bypass surgery a few years earlier), and not from AIDS, as rumored.

Rainbow Bridge – 9/17/1974

Season 3 / Episode 50 / Production 49 – B301

Columbia House VHS Tape . . . . *Bending The Rules (Catalog # 3740)*
Fox DVD . . . . *Season 3, Disc 1*

Alan Alda, Wayne Rogers, McLean Stevenson,
Loretta Swit, Larry Linville, Gary Burghoff

Produced by Gene Reynolds and Larry Gelbart
Written by Larry Gelbart & Laurence Marks
Directed by Hy Averback

Louden Wainwright, III . . . . Captain Calvin Spalding
Mako. . . . . Dr. Lin Tam
Jamie Farr . . . . Corporal Klinger
William Christopher. . . . . Father Mulcahy

Copyright 1974 – 20th Century Fox Film Corporation

Non-Credited Appearances. . . . . Jeff Maxwell, Kellye Nakahara, Bobbie Mitchell,
Dennis Troy, Gwen Farrell

Chapters

1: Main Titles	6: Going to Rainbow Bridge – 16:38
2: Going to Tokyo – 0:49	7: The Meeting – 19:29
3: War Casualties – 5:55	8: Almost Trouble – 21:52
4: An Offer – 10:08	9: No Tokyo – 23:36
5: A Gun – 14:35	10: End Titles – 25:30

Closing Stills

1: Dr Tam smiles at Frank's gun
2: Klinger buffing Hawkeye's nails
3: Henry in the Mess Tent (You decide)
4: Frank puts the safety on his gun
5: Radar

Synopsis: When the Chinese send a message to the 4077th to come and get nine wounded GI's who need more attention than they can provide, the message is greeted with skepticism by most of the staff, as the location is deep within Chinese territory. Even Hawkeye suggests the possibility of a trap, but Trapper thinks they should go since they give the Chinese a break with their wounded. Included in the message are instructions for the pickup, including no weapons, but Margaret talks Frank into hiding a pistol in his waistband, which puts the mission in jeopardy with the Chinese keeping the wounded right where they are.

Commentary by Larry Gelbart: "Loved Loudon Wainwright's songs, so we gave it a shot. I wish we had done more episodes with him as Captain Spalding (of course, named for Groucho Marx's captain of the very same name) but tight shooting schedules made it impossible. I have been to Korea three times. Once, during the Korean 'police action,' going there with the American entertainer/icon, Bob Hope, as one of his writers. The second time, I went there with Gene Reynolds after M*A*S*H's second season for additional, first hand research. Finally, a few years ago, at the invitation of the USO to be present at the closing down of the 43rd Medical Unit, and the host of the real life 4077 (the 8055). Larry Linville also accepted the invitation, as did David Ogden Stiers. Each trip was, for different reasons, memorable and each has been and continues to be cherished."

Authors' Notes: Footage of the bus coming to a stop was used in "Love and Marriage," and would be used again in "The Bus."

In Chapter 2, the Swamp has no dartboard, and later in the same scene, it's still not there.

The clip of Cowboy landing the chopper and Radar riding the side of an ambulance and jumping off from the Season 1 episode, "Cowboy," is seen again.

The US flag is now joined by the UN and the South Korean flags on the Ranch set.

In 36 hours, the 4077th handled 473 cases.

In Chapter 4, Henry says Rainbow Bridge, the pickup point, is 50 miles inside China. He later says its 20 miles from their border.

The Swamp in Chapter 9 is still missing the dartboard.

Mako, born Makoto Iwamatsu, had quite an extensive background in television and theater, appearing in *Magnum, P.I., Hawaii Five-0, Mannix, Quincy, M.E.,* and eight episodes of *McHale's Navy,* among many others. Nominated for Best Supporting Actor by the Academy Awards and the Golden Globes for the 1966 film, *The Sand Pebbles,* Mako also has an extensive list of voice roles, including the voice in the video game, Wrath Unleashed. With a star on Hollywood's Walk of Fame, Mako will return to *M*A*S*H* for 3 more episodes. Mako passed away on July 21, 2006 from esophageal cancer at the age of 73.

Loudon Wainwright III composed and performed the songs in this episode and has 22 albums to his credit. Bob Dylan inspired the Grammy-nominated artist musically when he saw him at the Newport Folk Festival in 1962, and has released 22 albums, the first in 1970.

Officer of the Day – 9/24/1974

Season 3 / Episode 51 / Production 55 – B307

Columbia House VHS Tape . . . . *American Flagg (Catalog # 13109)*
Fox DVD . . . . *Season 3, Disc 1*

Alan Alda, Wayne Rogers, McLean Stevenson,
Loretta Swit, Larry Linville, Gary Burghoff

Produced by Gene Reynolds and Larry Gelbart
Written by Laurence Marks
Directed by Hy Averback

Edward Winter . . . . .Colonel Sam Flagg
Jamie Farr . . . . Corporal Klinger
Jerry Fujikawa . . . . Sang Yu
Tad Horino . . . . 1st Korean
Richard Lee Sung . . . . .2nd Korean
Jeff Maxwell. . . . . .Igor
Dennis Troy. . . . . .Carter

Copyright 1974 – 20th Century Fox Film Corporation

Non-Credited Appearances. .Kellye Nakahara, Roy Goldman

Chapters

1: *Main Titles*	6: *The Colonel Wants to Watch – 14:33*
2: *Reveille – 0:47*	7: *He Can't Be Moved – 18:25*
3: *The Officer of the Day – 4:52*	8: *Release the Prisoner – 21:03*
4: *Colonel Flagg – 10:06*	9: *The Pinstripe Suit – 24:23*
5: *A Kim Lucky Day – 13:41*	10: *End Titles – 25:31*

Closing Stills

1: *Flagg cocks his gin in the Mess Tent*
2: *Hawkeye points to O.D. armband*
3: *Frank, Margaret & Hawkeye in the Mess Tent*
4: *Radar covers up in front of Hawkeye*
5: *Trapper in his pinstripe suit*

Synopsis: As Officer of the Day, one of the first orders Hawkeye gives is to send all the troops home, and promptly goes to sleep in the office. Radar reminds him that sleep is not part of the job, and a Korean farmer is in need of medical attention. Things are about to get worse for Hawkeye when he discovers the person honking a horn incessantly is Colonel Flagg. Flagg has a wounded prisoner with him; a wound inflicted by Flagg and now wants the doctors to treat him so he can take the prisoner to Seoul to be executed.

Commentary by Larry Gelbart: "'Nutsy Fagin' was (in my politically incorrect youth) a reference to someone who had a screw loose, who wasn't all there."

Commentary by Burt Metcalfe: "Richard Lee Sung was funny. He wasn't really a trained actor, and so he was often funny in spite of himself. Sometimes, he didn't even know he was being funny."

Commentary by Richard Lee Sung: "The cast was a wonderful cast. They were professionals and really great human beings...all of them. That's why they worked so well

Jeff Maxwell as Private Igor Straminsky.

together. And when I joined them, they went hysterical with me over the 'Kim Luck' thing. The crew and everyone went hysterical over the scene and my one line, 'This is me.' It was my first experience where the crew was applauding and having a heck of a time. So, it was just a wonderful moment for me."

Commentary by Jeff Maxwell: "Dennis Troy sometimes used a wig, sometimes grew a mustache and sometimes stuck one on. These disguises allowed him the opportunity to perform double-duty work in the same episode as background in the camp and as a driver for incoming vehicles. He was also often called upon to do stunts."

Author's Notes: There are no PA announcements in this episode.

This was the first of several appearances by Richard Lee Sung, one of the most popular guest stars of the entire series.

Radar tucks his bear in wearing short sleeves, but a close-up reveals the arms doing the tucking are in long sleeves.

This is the only time a cot was ever setup in the CO's office.

A rarity: an ambulance is seen pulling away from camp, at night on the Ranch set.

Iron Guts Kelly – 10/1/1974

Season 3 / Episode 52 / Production 52 – B304

Columbia House VHS Tape . . . . *Army Brass (Catalog # 3742)*
Fox DVD . . . . *Season 3, Disc 1*

Alan Alda, Wayne Rogers, McLean Stevenson,
Loretta Swit, Larry Linville, Gary Burghoff

Produced by Gene Reynolds and Larry Gelbart
Written by Larry Gelbart & Sid Dorfman
Directed by Don Weis

James Gregory . . . . General "Iron Guts" Kelly
Keene Curtis . . . . Colonel Wortman
Bobbie Mitchell. . . . . Nurse Able
Jeff Maxwell. . . . . G.I.
Dennis Troy. . . . . 2nd G.I.
Alberta Jay . . . . Anesthetist
Copyright 1974 – 20th Century Fox Film Corporation

Non-Credited Appearances. . . . . .Byron Chung, Gwen Farrell

Chapters

1: *Main Titles*
2: *General Kelly Arrives – 0:48*
3: *At the Officer's Club – 5:31*
4: *A Nighttime Emergency – 9:11*
5: *The General on the Move – 12:15*
6: *A Blaze of Glory – 14:10*
7: *Looking for Action – 15:52*
8: *The General's Demise – 21:18*
9: *The Press Release – 24:45*
10: *End Titles – 25:31*

Closing Stills

1: *Wortman and Kelly*
2: *Henry learns Kelly died*
3: *Frank & Margaret meet Kelly in the Officer's Club*
4: *Hawkeye in Margaret's tent (Kelly dead)*
5: *Trapper/reality - fantasy*

Synopsis: General Robert "Iron Guts" Kelly visits the 4077th, a tribute to their efficiency. A frantic Margaret wakes Hawkeye and Trapper in the middle of the night as something has gone horribly wrong and they discover the General, dead, in Margaret's tent. Colonel Wortman, the General's aid wants to make sure the headlines say he died in combat and Hawkeye and Trapper put the General's body in an ambulance, only to be ordered away from camp by Frank, not knowing the General's body is inside with a few local Korean "business" women.

Commentary by Larry Gelbart: "Night is, perforce, the best time for drama and the time when a laugh is most welcome, helping us forget the fear we all feel in the dark. The episode was based on the experiences of Red Saunders, one-time UCLA football coach and the actor, John Garfield, both of whom met their Maker while making someone else."

Authors' Notes: There are no PA announcements in this episode.
   Colonel Wortman, the General's aide, correctly introduces the General as "Lieutenant General Iron Guts Kelly," but in Chapter 8 calls him "Major General."
   In Chapter 7, in Margaret's tent, she says to Frank, "Did he what?" It's clearly a different shot that was edited in, as her hair isn't messy as it was just prior to that and the lamp in the background is in a slightly different location before the cut.

James Gregory is probably best known as Barney Miller's captain in the show of the same name, and another actor who appeared in *M*A*S*H* as well as *Star Trek,* as Doctor Tristan Adams, director of a penal colony in "Dagger of the Mind." Mr. Gregory had also appeared on Broadway in roughly 25 productions as well as television, and died of natural causes in Arizona in 2002. He was 91.

Keene Curtis, a 1971 Tony Award winner for Best Featured Actor in the musical *The Rothschilds,* appeared in many television shows, including a recurring role in *Cheers.* Also to Mr. Curtis' credits are appearances in *Hawaii Five-0, Sanford and Son, Three's Company, Benson* and *Newhart.* He died of Alzheimer's disease at the age of 79 in Bountiful, Utah.

O.R. – 10/8/1974

Season 3 / Episode 53 / Production 54 – B306

Columbia House VHS Tape . . . . Operation Overload (Catalog # 3669)
Fox DVD . . . . .Season 3, Disc 1

Alan Alda, Wayne Rogers, McLean Stevenson,
Loretta Swit, Larry Linville, Gary Burghoff

Produced by Gene Reynolds and Larry Gelbart
Written by Larry Gelbart & Laurence Marks
Directed by Gene Reynolds

Allan Arbus . . . . .Major Sidney Freedman
Jamie Farr . . . . Corporal Klinger
William Christopher . . . . Father Mulcahy
Bobbie Mitchell . . . . .Nurse Able
Odessa Cleveland . . . . Ginger
Bobby Herbeck . . . . Patient
Jeanne Schulherr . . . . .Anesthetist
Orlando Dole . . . . .Ethiopian Soldier

Copyright 1974 – 20th Century Fox Film Corporation

Non-Credited Appearances . . . . Jeff Maxwell, Dennis Troy, Roy Goldman

Chapters

1: Main Titles	6: No Pulse – 9:49
2: Get Ready – 0:50	7: Getting Shot At – 12:10
3: A Short Break – 3:49	8: Major Freedman – 17:31
4: Arthritis – 5:48	9: Fire! – 23:34
5: "Blood and Sand" – 7:06	10: End Titles – 25:30

Closing Stills

1: Freedman & Klinger in O.R.
2: Hawkeye & Henry on break
3: Trapper on break
4: Radar in break room
5: Frank and his missing brush in O.R.

Synopsis: A long and busy O.R. session is underway where hard decisions are made, new procedures are tried and 30 to 40 wounded are still waiting. During a break, Henry admits that, as unpleasant as the place is, he's able to do more "doctoring" than he ever could back home, and back in O.R., Hawkeye is left with no choice but to perform an untried procedure to save his patient, leaving Hawkeye physically and emotionally drained. When Sidney Freedman shows up for the weekly poker game, Trapper has him scrub for surgery instead. Although it's been a while since Freedman has practiced this type of medicine, Hawkeye is impressed. Now it's Henry who has no choice when he orders regular sewing thread be used since they ran out of silk. And to top it off, a small fire breaks out on the wall behind Trapper.

Commentary by Larry Gelbart: "It saved money not having to provide scenery or extras or any sort of action that one would see if the windows were clean" (LG, on why the windows in the O.R. were always too dirty to see out of). It was Gene Reynolds who hired Dr. Walter Dishell, who proved an invaluable asset to the show as a medical advisor. He was not only a help in medical matters, but had a great theatrical flair."

Author's Notes: No laugh track was used in this episode, as most of the scenes were in the O.R.

The break room just outside O.R. with the double glass doors is seen, and not too often.

As in earlier episodes, and as will be the case for the series' run, Trapper's voice can be heard in O.R. scenes saying, "Okay, cut that." However, in this episode, it can be heard 24 times, sometimes while the camera is on him talking.

Jeanne Schuhlherr, the anesthetist in this episode, will appear again in Episode 58, "There is Nothing Like A Nurse," as Frank's wife, Mrs. Louise Burns, and again in Episode 69, "Big Mac," as an un-credited nurse.

Springtime – 10/15/1974

Season 3 / Episode 54 / Production 51 – B303

Columbia House VHS Tape . . . . *Love And War (Catalog # 10996)*
Fox DVD . . . . *Season 3, Disc 1*

Alan Alda, Wayne Rogers, McLean Stevenson,
Loretta Swit, Larry Linville, Gary Burghoff

Produced by Gene Reynolds and Larry Gelbart
Written by Linda Bloodworth & Mary Kay Place
Directed by Don Weis

Alex Karras . . . . Corporal Lyle Wesson
Jamie Farr . . . . Corporal Klinger
William Christopher . . . . Father Mulcahy
Mary Kay Place . . . . Lieutenant Louise Simmons
Greg Mabrey . . . . Pasco
Jeff Maxwell . . . . Server (Igor)
Roy Goldman . . . . Corpsman
Copyright 1974 – 20th Century Fox Film Corporation

Non-Credited Appearances . . . . Kellye Nakahara, Dennis Troy, Patricia Stevens,
Gwen Farrell

Chapters

1: Main Titles
2: A Day in Spring – 0:48
3: Love in Bloom – 4:26
4: A Grateful Patient – 9:51
5: Advice – 11:37
6: Release the Doctor – 15:39
7: A Visit – 17:49
8: Radio Wedding – 19:58
9: Radar Has A Girlfriend – 24:22
10: End Titles – 25:31

Closing Stills

1: Lyle in post-op
2: Klinger reads letter in field
3: Hawkeye in his tuxedo
4: Frank & Margaret stop wedding
5: Radar "slaked"

Synopsis: A beautiful spring day greets the staff as they exit O.R. and the only thing to do now is figure out how to spend it. While most of the staff engages in outdoor activities, Father Mulcahy tries to comfort a GI who will not let go of a cat, and needs Hawkeye to help him. When the GI has Hawkeye in a headlock, Corporal Lyle Wesson, a very large man who Hawkeye operated on, releases the GI's hold and insists on repaying Hawkeye for saving his life. Meanwhile, Klinger, dressed like Scarlet O'Hara, reads poetry under a tree when Radar delivers a special delivery letter for him. Klinger's high school sweetheart has agreed to marry him, but since Henry won't allow him to go home for a quick wedding, he arranges for them to marry over a short-wave radio with Father Mulcahy officiating and Radar, after reading the poetry book that Klinger had, discovers what "slaking" is with Louise Simmons.

Commentary by Jeff Maxwell: "Mr. Karras wasn't quite as big or mean as I anticipated him being, but big enough to allow the intimidation to register. Part of me was thinking that he didn't seem so tough. I'm sure the football field offered a different set of impressions. I always allowed myself to be a little nervous on the set. I believed unsettled but controlled terror was a legitimate emotion to always be stirring in Igor."

Authors' Notes: There are no PA announcements in this episode.

The DVD lists Chapter 2 starting 2:26.

The view from Henry's office window this time shows a partial building and trees from the right window.

In Chapter 4, another rarity as the scene inside the mess tent was filmed at the Ranch set, not Stage 9 and even rarer is hearing Trapper's famous, "Okay, cut that" in the mess tent.

A movie, "The First Born of Godzilla" is mentioned. However, *Godzilla* was not released in the US until 1954. It's possible that while on leave in Tokyo, someone saw it.

The 4077's radio call letters are KN5YVJ.

A 6' 2", 255 pound defensive tackle for the Detroit Lions from 1958 to 1962 and again from 1964 to 1970, Alex Karras was also a four-time Pro Bowl selection (the Pro Bowl, played after the regular season, is the NFL's equivalent of the All-Star Game). Mr. Karras went on to star in his own show, *Webster* for 6 years, playing a retired football player, George Papadapolis, the father of an adopted African-American son, Webster, and starred alongside his real-life wife, Susan Clark. It's worth noting that Alex Karras had a small but a very memorable role as Mongo in the Mel Brooks film *Blazing Saddles*, where he knocked out a horse with one punch.

Mary Kay Place co-wrote this episode and two other *M*A*S*H* episodes with Linda Bloodworth: "Hot Lips and Empty Arms" from Season 2 and "Mad Dogs and Servicemen" from Season 3. Place appeared in 13 episodes of *Mary Hartman, Mary Hartman*. Also a host of *Saturday Night Live*, she's appeared in *The Mary Tyler Moore Show, All in the Family* and was a guest on the *Tonight Show Starring Johnny Carson*.

Check-Up – 10/22/1974

Season 3 / Episode 55 / Production 60 – B312

Columbia House VHS Tape . . . . *Staff Infections (Catalog # 3769)*
Fox DVD . . . . *Season 3, Disc 1*

Alan Alda, Wayne Rogers, McLean Stevenson,
Loretta Swit, Larry Linville, Gary Burghoff

Produced by Gene Reynolds and Larry Gelbart
Written by Laurence Marks
Directed by Don Weis

Jamie Farr . . . . Corporal Klinger
Copyright 1974 – 20th Century Fox Film Corporation

Non-Credited Appearances . . . . Jeff Maxwell, Kellye Nakahara, Dennis Troy,
Roy Goldman, Patricia Stevens, Gwen Farrell

Chapters

1: *Main Titles*	6: *Trapper's Diagnosis – 12:06*
2: *Physicals – 0:50*	7: *A Going-Away Party – 17:32*
3: *Hawkeye & Hot Lips – 4:11*	8: *Presents – 21:43*
4: *Radar's Check-Up – 6:20*	9: *The Patient – 24:41*
5: *Trapper Refuses – 9:31*	10: *End Titles – 25:31*

Closing Stills

1: *Hawkeye examines Klinger (Mess Tent)*
2: *Trapper in the Swamp*
3: *Hawkeye thanking Trapper in the Swamp*
4: *Radar in his office*
5: *Margaret with Frank drunk at Trapper's party*

Synopsis: Everyone at the 4077th has to undergo a physical, and nobody is happier than Hawkeye, since he's scheduled to give Margaret hers. On the opposite end, Trapper is not happy about his upcoming checkup because the place is "medically medieval," but worse, Frank is scheduled to do it. Trapper, in obvious discomfort tells Hawkeye that he might have an ulcer. Hawkeye thinks this is Trapper's ticket home, but just before his farewell party, Trapper learns otherwise.

Commentary by Larry Gelbart: "When I asked him that question, his answer was, 'Just jealousy' (on Robert Altman's negativity with regard to the series).

PA Announcement by Henry

Authors' Notes: "I Got a Gal in Kalamazoo," sung by Radar over the PA, was written by Harry Warren and Mack Gordon in 1942. This song, which has appeared in *M*A*S*H* previously, is also in 2 Fox movies, *Orchestra Wives* (1942) and *Kiss Them for Me* (1957).

A movie, "Godzilla and the Bobby-Soxer," is mentioned. However, *Godzilla* was not released in the U.S. until 1954. It's possible that while on leave in Tokyo, someone saw it.

Klinger has two degrees of temperature because, as Trapper put it, "He's not a well woman."

Tries to touch up his x-rays.

20 minutes to live – blood pressure is 200 over 310.

The scenery seen out of Henry's office windows now is trees and shrubs through both windows and nothing else, but changes later to taller trees.

Margaret is drunk in this episode and again confesses to being attracted to "Captain Trapper John-Intyre."

Life with Father – 10/29/1974

Season 3 / Episode 56 / Production 50 – B302

Columbia House VHS Tape . . . . *News From Home (Catalog # 10992)*
Fox DVD . . . . *Season 3, Disc 1*

Alan Alda, Wayne Rogers, McLean Stevenson,
Loretta Swit, Larry Linville, Gary Burghoff

Produced by Gene Reynolds and Larry Gelbart
Written by Everett Greenbaum & Jim Fritzell
Directed by Hy Averback

William Christopher . . . . Father Mulcahy
Sachiko Penny Lee . . . . Chim Sah
Patricia Stevens . . . . Nurse
Copyright 1974 – 20th Century Fox Film Corporation

Non-Credited Appearances . . . . Jeff Maxwell, Kellye Nakahara, Dennis Troy, Gwen Farrell

Chapters

1: *Main Titles*	6: *Wife Worries – 10:32*
2: *The Anesthetist – 0:48*	7: *Mrs. Blake – 17:12*
3: *Mail Call – 2:29*	8: *A Ceremonial Phone Call – 20:15*
4: *A Bris – 4:23*	9: *Celebration – 23:53*
5: *A Lip-Lock in X-ray – 8:31*	10: *End Titles – 25:01*

Closing Stills

1: *Hawkeye in the Mess Tent*
2: *Trapper in O.R.*
3: *Henry on the phone with Lorraine*
4: *Radar relaying the ceremony*
5: *Mulcahy holding the baby*

Synopsis: When a young Korean mother holding her baby approaches Frank and Margaret, she asks for a "labbi," leaving Frank to think she wants to sell her baby and won't let Margaret talk to her. When the Korean woman shows Hawkeye and Trapper a letter, they realize that the baby is the son of a Jewish Corporal and she needs a Rabbi to perform the traditional Hebrew ceremony called a "bris." Father Mulcahy has learned that his sister, a nun, wants to leave the order to raise a family of her own and Mulcahy is confused and distressed over the idea. But when he officiates the Hebrew ceremony and sees how happy the Korean mother is, he better understands his sister's desire to raise a family.

Commentary by Larry Gelbart: "I tried, whenever possible, to pack an episode with a multiplicity of events. There are people who still try to convince me that M*A*S*H was an hour show."

Authors' Notes: There are no PA announcements in this episode.
   In some of the previous episodes of the third season, the sinks in the scrub room were side by side. In this episode, they're facing each other in the middle of the room.
   This is the second episode to have a horse. It was supposed to be a Shetland pony, but it appears to be a full-grown horse.
   Henry's adult movies, Yvonne, Renee and Loretta in "What the Parrot Saw" and Renee, Loretta and the Parrot in "What Yvonne Saw," were to be screened at midnight in the generator shed. We have yet to see a generator shed.

Alcoholics Unanimous – 11/12/1974

Season 3 / Episode 57 / Production 62 – B314

Columbia House VHS Tape . . . . *Frank's In Charge (Catalog # 3744)*
Fox DVD . . . .*Season 3, Disc 2*

Alan Alda, Wayne Rogers, McLean Stevenson,
Loretta Swit, Larry Linville, Gary Burghoff

Produced by Gene Reynolds and Larry Gelbart
Written by Everett Greenbaum & Jim Fritzell
Directed by Hy Averback

Jamie Farr . . . . Corporal Klinger
William Christopher. . . . . Father Mulcahy
Bobbie Mitchell. . . . . Nurse Baker

Copyright 1974 – 20th Century Fox Film Corporation

Non-Credited Appearances. . . . . Jeff Maxwell, Kellye Nakahara, Dennis Troy,
Roy Goldman, Gwen Farrell

Chapters

1: *Main Titles*	6: *A Dry Compound – 12:45*
2: *A Rainy Night – 0:47*	7: *A Lecture – 15:24*
3: *No Still Allowed – 3:27*	8: *A Large Audience – 19:43*
4: *Sunday Services – 6:15*	9: *Moderation – 24:43*
5: *Houlihan's Stash – 10:58*	10: *End Titles – 25:27*

Closing Stills

1: *Klinger helps Mulcahy with his collar*
2: *Hawkeye drunk in the Swamp*
3: *Trapper gets water instead of sound*
4: *Margaret busted in supply*
5: *Radar taking the still apart*

Synopsis: While Hawkeye and Trapper are watching a movie, Frank orders Radar to dismantle the still, then has him nail shut the Officer's Club, declaring the 4077th dry. While the doctors search the supply room at night for something to drink, they're surprised when Margaret comes in with a flashlight and refills her flask from a beaker of Brandy hidden in a file cabinet. Caught in the act, Margaret joins Hawkeye and Trapper in the Swamp where the three of them get drunk. Incensed, Frank threatens to "severely discipline" anyone caught with booze, including Margaret. But during Father Mulcahy's sermon on "the evil of drink," a melee breaks out causing Frank to get hit in the stomach and take a drink from Margaret's flask filled with Brandy. Hawkeye now declares prohibition repealed.

PA Announcements by Todd Sussman

Authors' Notes: This is Father Frank Toste's favorite episode. Father Toste was the technical advisor for the Father Mulcahy character, and can be seen sitting on the end of a bench listening to Father Mulcahy's sermon on the original print, but he's cut off when the episode airs and again on the DVD.
The sign on Margaret's tent door is in block letters instead of the usual free-hand style.
The sinks in the scrub room are on the front (camera) wall side by side.
One of the very few times Father Mulcahy displays the effects of alcohol.
Hawkeye and Trapper have their second fight.

There is Nothing Like A Nurse – 11/19/1974
Season 3 / Episode 58 / Production 57 – B309

Columbia House VHS Tape . . . . *The Unexpected (Catalog # 22050)*
Fox DVD . . . . *Season 3, Disc 2*

Alan Alda, Wayne Rogers, McLean Stevenson,
Loretta Swit, Larry Linville, Gary Burghoff

Produced by Gene Reynolds and Larry Gelbart
Written by Larry Gelbart
Directed by Hy Averback

Jamie Farr . . . . Corporal Klinger
Loudon Wainwright III . . . . Captain Calvin Spalding
William Christopher . . . . Father Mulcahy
Bobbie Mitchell . . . . Nurse Able
Jeanne Schulherr . . . . Mrs. Louise Burns
Leland Sun . . . . Mr. Kwang
Copyright 1974 – 20th Century Fox Film Corporation

Non-Credited Appearances . . . . Jeff Maxwell, Kellye Nakahara, Dennis Troy,
Roy Goldman, Gwen Farrell

Chapters

1: *Main Titles*
2: *Houlihan's Complaint – 0:48*
3: *Saying Goodbye – 3:54*
4: *Ready to Roll – 9:15*
5: *The Lonely Officer's Club – 10:38*
6: *"I Wonder if They Miss Us" – 12:55*
7: *Let the Enemy Come – 14:14*
8: *Home Movies – 19:26*
9: *Air Raid – 22:37*
10: *End Titles – 25:28*

Closing Stills

1: *Klinger, Trapper & Hawkeye in Officer's Club*
2: *Spalding plays "I Wonder If They Miss Us" in Officer's Club*
3: *Henry in his office*
4: *Margaret in Henry's office yapping at him*
5: *Frank at Henry's desk on the phone with Margaret*

Synopsis: Under the threat of a Chinese attack, the nurses, along with all the wounded that can be moved, are shipped out to the 44th Field Hospital while the doctors and corpsmen remain behind due to heavy incoming casualties. Radar informs everyone that the 4077th can expect a Chinese paratroop drop, but this does nothing to slow the influx of wounded arriving by chopper, bus and ambulance and the remaining corpsmen are ordered to help out in OR by assisting the surgeons, which is easier said than done. During a lull, the staff watches a home movie of Frank's wedding, except Frank who has fallen in a foxhole and is kept there when Trapper parks a Jeep over him. Radar's warning of an enemy paratroop drop becomes a reality when an air-raid siren is heard, but the threat is put to rest when he discovers it's 5 O'Clock Charlie.

Commentary by Loudon Wainwright: "It was fun at the time (playing Capt. Calvin Spalding), and I've enjoyed hearing the words 'I saw you on *M*A*S*H* last night,' for the last 30 something years."

Commentary by Larry Gelbart: "Frank's home movies were filmed on the Fox lot, just outside the Old Writers Building, which housed my office. It was formerly a school house, where child actors such as Shirley Temple and, yes, Jackie Cooper, attended classes when they were filming. There existed a number of small cottages that served as offices of one kind or another. They had just the right period look for Frank's wedding picture sequence, so the crew moved from the sound stage, just a few hundred yards away from this on-lot location, and we shot what was some of my favorite footage of the series. Such stuff was an opportunity to get away from the endlessly military look of the show. It also let us realistically include black and white film sequences, a favorite look of mine, from the days of my youth when most movies I saw were shot that way. Damn, I enjoyed making those."

PA Announcements by Todd Sussman

Authors' Notes: Margaret's serial number is 53084499
Mrs. Frank Burns is seen in Frank's home movie of his wedding.
Henry's orange mug says HANK on one side and has the letter "I" (Illinois, Normal) on the other. In Chapter 8, it's holding pens but earlier in this episode, it had coffee.
Original songs sung and composed by Loudon Wainwright III.

Adam's Rib – 11/26/1974

Season 3 / Episode 59 / Production 64 – B316

Columbia House VHS Tape . . . . *Prize Possessions (Catalog # 3773)*
Fox DVD . . . . *Season 3, Disc 2*

Alan Alda, Wayne Rogers, McLean Stevenson,
Loretta Swit, Larry Linville, Gary Burghoff

Produced by Gene Reynolds and Larry Gelbart
Written by Laurence Marks
Directed by Gene Reynolds

Jamie Farr . . . . Corporal Klinger
Joseph Stern . . . . Master Sergeant Tarola
Basil Hoffman . . . . Major Pfiefer
Jeff Maxwell . . . . .Igor
Copyright 1974 – 20th Century Fox Film Corporation

Non-Credited Appearances . . . . .Dennis Troy, Roy Goldman, Gwen Farrell

Chapters

1: Main Titles	*6: Adam's Ribs – 12:20*
2: Boredom – 0:48	*7: Pick-Up and Delivery – 13:12*
3: A Lunch-Time Protest – 2:05	*8: The Ribs Arrive – 19:04*
4: Rib Memories – 5:04	*9: Kindred Spirits – 22:59*
5: Calling Chicago – 7:17	*10: End Titles – 24:54*

Closing Stills

1: Hawkeye stares at skeleton
2: Trapper smiling in Henry's office
3: Radar looks at Hawkeye on the phone
4: Henry in his office (angry at Hawkeye)
5: Radar asleep holding his bear

Synopsis: Unfortunately for Hawkeye, and for the eleventh straight day, Igor offers him liver or fish, and Hawkeye, unable to contain himself, causes a riot in the mess tent. Now in Henry's office, it dawns on Hawkeye that what he wants are ribs. And not just any ribs, he wants Adam's Ribs. Only one problem…Adam's Ribs is in Chicago and Hawkeye is in Korea. After some careful planning, including Trapper's call to an old girlfriend in Chicago and a rib & sauce payoff to a sergeant in Seoul, the ribs finally make it to the 4077th. Unfortunately, they don't make it to Hawkeye.

Commentary by Larry Gelbart: "The take-out restaurant dates back to the Ming Dynasty. The name and location of the place was sheer fiction on my part. There was no such place, to the best of my knowledge. It just seemed a logical name; also, my then-baby son was named Adam, and I'm from Chicago — the place with the big shoulders. The $225,000 budget was for everything from the actors' salaries down to the rivers of liver. Dreck is Yiddish for excrement. Smelling his food was Alda's idea."

Commentary by Jeff Maxwell: "'Adam's Ribs' is a favorite. Being a part of the famous 'We want something else!' scene was definitely a highlight of my *M*A*S*H* days. All the episodes with me in them were some of my other favorites. It was a great time. I truly appreciated every minute of everyday that I spent in a room with that many deliciously talented people. Take one may have been cut just prior to Alan slinging the food. Take two was the entire rage, including the food slinging. There was a bit of tension due to all the gears needing to mesh at just the right time. Not too much laughing until it was all over. I remember being quite impressed with Alan's ability to go through the emotional and physical moves so effortlessly. Out of the mouths of others, that rage may not have been so memorable. I was also impressed with the crew's ability to capture the scene perfectly. And Roy and I were pretty cute."

PA Announcements by Todd Sussman

Authors' Notes: As in every episode filmed at the Ranch location, the steps leading to the chopper pads were made with railroad ties.

As this episode opens after the credits, it appears there are four people on a platform practicing a line-dance. This is the same clip seen in Season 2, Episode 44, "As You Were," in Chapters 2 and 9.

Hawkeye has parents in this episode.

In Chapter 3 during "We want something else!" the wide shot in the mess tent shows Klinger with a handbag on his left arm, but in the close-up, there's no handbag on either arm.

Henry met his wife at the Dearborn Street Station in this episode, but in Season 2, Episode 33, "Dear Dad Three," he said he met her at a freshman mixer.

Radar's bear appears in this episode.

Klinger needs three signatures for his "crazy papers." In Season 2, Episode 41, "For Want of a Boot," he needed four signatures, and in Season 7, Episode 160, he'll need only two signatures.

A Full, Rich Day – 12/3/1974

Season 3 / Episode 60 / Production 59 – B311

Columbia House VHS Tape . . . . *Friendly Fire (Catalog # 3743)*
Fox DVD . . . . *Season 3, Disc 2*

Alan Alda, Wayne Rogers, McLean Stevenson,
Loretta Swit, Larry Linville, Gary Burghoff

Produced by Gene Reynolds and Larry Gelbart
Written by John D. Hess
Directed by Gene Reynolds

William Watson . . . . Lieutenant Smith
Jamie Farr . . . . Corporal Klinger
Curt Lowens . . . . Colonel Blanche
Michael Keller . . . . Lieutenant Le Clerq
Kellye Nakahara . . . . Nurse Able
Sirri Murad . . . . The Turkish Soldier
Copyright 1974 – 20th Century Fox Film Corporation

Non-Credited Appearances . . . . Jeff Maxwell, Dennis Troy, Roy Goldman,
Gwen Farrell

Chapters

1: Main Titles	6: A Crazy Day – 14:50
2: A Tape Recorder – 0:48	7: Walking Wounded – 20:24
3: A Busload – 2:37	8: The Luxembourg Lieutenant – 21:45
4: The Wounded Sergeant – 4:37	9: Saying Hello – 24:14
5: The Mad Turk – 10:28	10: End Titles – 25:27

Closing Stills

1: *Lieutenant Smith listens to Hawkeye outside Pre-Op*
2: *The "Mad Turk" in the kitchen*
3: *Hawkeye in the kitchen with the "Mad Turk"*
4: *Henry grabs sedative injection in his hand*
5: *Trapper saying "Hello" on tape to Hawkeye's father*

Synopsis: For the first time, Hawkeye tape-records a letter to his father, describing what he calls, "A full, rich day." The bus brings in wounded, including a Turkish G.I. who's been wounded in the shoulder and loaded with sedatives, but wants nothing more than to get back to the fighting, cutting his way out from in between two stretchers, and Lieutenant Smith pulls up in a jeep with his wounded sergeant and "orders" Frank to take care of him immediately. When Frank tells the lieutenant that his friend will be taken care of in "due course," Smith uses his rifle to persuade Frank that "due course" means right now. Colonel Blanche, the commander of the Luxembourg contingent to the UN Forces comes to the 4077th to see his wounded lieutenant, but Radar informs him that the man has died and they cannot find him. Henry holds a ceremony to honor the fallen Luxembourg lieutenant when, during the National Anthem of Luxembourg, the lieutenant seems to have made a miraculous recovery.

Commentary by Larry Gelbart: "While complaints against Army food probably go back to the Roman Legions (i.e., 'I saved my battalion. I shot the cook'), the doctors at the 4077th would have had a different life and eating style in their civilian lives than the average fighting man and therefore tended to be a bit more critical."

PA Announcements by Todd Sussman

Authors' Notes: The name "Hawkeye" comes from The Last of the Mohicans, according to Hawkeye, the only book his father ever read. This will become a point of contention later in the series when it's established that his father is a doctor.

The mud splatter on Lieutenant Smith's face is different the second time we see him.

This is another of the very rare instances when a laugh track is heard in the O.R. As Larry Gelbart explains this, there is no surgery going on, and it's the "last beat" of the scene when Henry grabs a syringe from the wounded Turk, counts backwards from 99 and it "cried out" for it.

Sirri Murad, the Turkish Soldier, will appear again on *M*A*S*H* in Season 8's "Captains Outrageous."

Mad Dogs and Servicemen – 12/10/1974
Season 3 / Episode 61 / Production 65 – B317

Columbia House VHS Tape . . . . *Staff Infections (Catalog # 3769)*
Fox DVD . . . . *Season 3, Disc 2*

Alan Alda, Wayne Rogers, McLean Stevenson,
Loretta Swit, Larry Linville, Gary Burghoff

Produced by Gene Reynolds and Larry Gelbart
Written by Linda Bloodworth & Mary Kay Place
Directed by Hy Averback

Michael O'keefe . . . . Corporal Travis
Shizuko Hoshi . . . . Rosie
Bobbie Mitchell . . . . Nurse Baker
Arthur Song . . . . Korean Man
Jeff Maxwell . . . . Igor
Copyright 1974 – 20th Century Fox Film Corporation

Non-Credited Appearances . . . . Kellye Nakahara, Roy Goldman, Gwen Farrell

Chapters

1: *Main Titles*	6: *Rabies Shots – 12:35*
2: *Radar's Menagerie – 0:48*	7: *Trapper's Talk Therapy – 18:24*
3: *He's Not Wounded – 3:13*	8: *Radar's Dog – 21:56*
4: *Hawkeye's Cure – 6:06*	9: *Recovery – 23:42*
5: *Looking for the Dog – 9:30*	10: *End Titles – 25:29*

Closing Stills
1: *Hawkeye talks to Travis in Post-Op*
2: *Trapper talks to Travis in Post-Op*
3: *Henry talks to Hawkeye & Trapper in his office*
4: *Margaret with Radar in Post-Op*
5: *Margaret takes Radar's temperature in Post-Op*

Synopsis: After Radar gets a scratch on his hand from a dog, Hawkeye wants the dog tested for rabies. Henry sets out with Radar in search of the dog, and when they cannot find him, Radar begins a series of painful rabies injections. Corporal Travis, who has no apparent injuries, can't move his legs. After speaking to Sidney Freedman, Hawkeye tries a new therapy that Sidney has been having good results with. Hawkeye comes down hard on the corporal, and leaves orders that he's not to have a bedpan or food. If he wants to eat, he'll have to walk to the mess tent. But Travis still refuses to talk about the tanks, until Trapper gives it a try with a softer approach. While Frank and Margaret demand Travis be shipped out, he suddenly walks into Henry's office, much to Hawkeye's delight, and Henry brings Radar good news about the dog.

Commentary by Michael O'Keefe: "My time on M*A*S*H was very valuable to me. I was only 19 years old, and to get on a show with the kind of success M*A*S*H had was quite a coup. I appeared twice, interestingly enough in similar parts and, frankly, didn't like my first performance but liked my second one."

Authors' Notes: There are no PA announcements in this episode.
Radar's little zoo on the compound includes a skunk, raccoon, rabbit and possum, plus the turtle in the shower with Henry.

We've seen the tailor at the 4077th, and in Chapter 5, for the first time, we see where he's located. The sign "Tailor" is right next to the sign that says "Goldie's" (to the left of Rosie's).

In Chapter 6, the view from Henry's office windows changes from trees to trees and mountains.

Wanda Nell McCandless wrote a letter to Radar and mentions two songs that need attention:

1: *"The Wayward Wind,"* words by Herb Newman, Music by Stan Lebowksi and recorded by Gogi Grant in 1956, three years after the war ended.
2: *"Pretty Thing"* written by Bo Diddley in 1957, four years after the war ended.

In Chapter 7, Trapper, after telling Corporal Travis that he interned in Boston, mentioned Ted Williams being drafted and on his way to Korea, then mentions: "Ted Williams had 531 at-bats and a batting average of 318 last year." *Note: Trapper's statistics for Ted Williams are correct for the year 1951. At midnight, May 1, 1952, Ted Williams reported to Willow Grove, Pennsylvania for active duty as a Marine captain. He was a fighter pilot. This bit of information places M*A*S*H's third season in 1951 (or at least, this episode).*

Henry makes a reference to "Godzilla," but as previously noted, *Godzilla* was not released in the United States until 1954.

After Radar's rabies injections are cut off, he says, "I'm gonna live past 18." In Season 2's episode, "As You Were," he says he's 19.

When Trapper tells a patient in Post-Op that he interned in Boston when he wasn't trying to sneak into the ball park, most people are led to believe that Boston is Trapper's home town. However, home towns are not usually referred to in this fashion.

Private Charles Lamb – 12/31/1974

Season 3 / Episode 62 / Production 58 – B310

Columbia House VHS Tape.................. *Going Home (Catalog # 3741)*
Fox DVD .... *Season 3, Disc 2*

Alan Alda, Wayne Rogers, McLean Stevenson,
Loretta Swit, Larry Linville, Gary Burghoff

Produced by Gene Reynolds and Larry Gelbart
Written by Sid Dorfman
Directed by Hy Averback

Titos Vandis .... Colonel Andropolis
Ted Eccles.. Private Chapman

Copyright 1974 – 20th Century Fox Film Corporation

Non-Credited Appearances........... Jeff Maxwell, Kellye Nakahara, Dennis Troy,
Roy Goldman, Gwen Farrell

Chapters

1: Main Titles	6: The Greek Goods – 9:16
2: A Vegetarian – 0:48	7: A Festival Lamb – 11:55
3: Dear Dad – 3:05	8: Where's the Meat? – 20:17
4: Colonel Andropolis – 4:58	9: A Greek Festival – 22:11
5: A Self-Inflicted Wound- 7:23	10: End Titles – 25:29

Closing Stills

1: Colonel Andropolis salutes Henry
2: Chapman in Post-Op
3: Hat party by Henry
4: Radar talking to "Private" Charles Lamb
5: Close-up of "Private" Charles Lamb

Synopsis: Colonel Andropolis of the Greek Army wants to show his gratitude for the treatment his men received at the 4077 and invites the camp to share in celebrating Greek Easter. Andropolis is having Greek delicacies airlifted in, and Henry cancels a training film on the history of athlete's foot for the promise of a tub filled with the Greek liquor ouzo. Included in the delicacies is the main course…a lamb, but Radar has a plan to save the lamb and tricks Henry into giving it a discharge.

Commentary by Larry Gelbart: "The Prop people on the show, who took great pride in providing whatever the script called for, and always did so in the most loving and skillful fashion. The Spam lamb was indeed made of Spam. We were, when we were lucky, several minutes over what the show's length had to be in terms of airtime. Sometimes we couldn't trim as much as we wanted because the show would have been short of that time. We would often cut anyway, making us short, but we shoot pick up scenes to make up for the lost, not so precious minutes."

Commentary by Gary Burghoff: "I didn't use a mirror, out of camera range, to see when McLean stuck his head around the corner behind me. McLean and I just had perfect timing, together." (He's referring to the scene where Radar appears very calm at his desk, until Henry goes in his office. Radar lets his guard down then, but instantly assumes his calm demeanor again when Henry peeks around the corner, behind him.)

PA Announcements by Todd Sussman

Authors' Notes: As Henry asks Hawkeye what that is in front of him, and as Hawkeye replies "a spam lamb," look closely. In the shot of Henry and the Spam Lamb, we see Hawkeye's shadow and the shadow's mouth thereof, responding with the words "spam lamb," before they cut to a close up and we actually see and hear Hawkeye say it.

The ouzo is Metaxa. The company started with Spyros Metaxas in 1888.

Radar has 16 cats back home. This changes in the next episode, "Bombed."

The scenery again changes out of Henry's office windows from trees to fewer trees and more mountains, and will change again to having a partial building through the right window.

Titos Vandis was born in Salonika, Greece (now Thessalomki, Greece) in 1917, and before coming to Hollywood in the 1960's, was a long-time actor on the Greek stage. He has over 100 credits to his name, appearing in *The Mary Tyler Moore Show, Kojak, Trapper John, M.D., The Odd Couple* and *Newhart,* among many others. In the James Bond film of 1964, *Goldfinger,* Mr. Vandis tested for the title role and was in the running before the part went to the German actor, Gert Frobe. Titos Vandis died on February 23, 2003 in Athens, Greece, at the age of 86.

Bombed – 1/7/1975

Season 3 / Episode 63 / Production 68 – B320

Columbia House VHS Tape . . . . *Friendly Fire (Catalog # 3743)*
Fox DVD . . . . *Season 3, Disc 2*

Alan Alda, Wayne Rogers, McLean Stevenson,
Loretta Swit, Larry Linville, Gary Burghoff

Produced by Gene Reynolds and Larry Gelbart
Written by Jim Fritzell & Everett Geeenbaum
Directed by Hy Averback

Jamie Farr . . . . Corporal Klinger
William Christopher . . . . Father Mulcahy
Louisa Moritz . . . . Nurse Sanchez
Edward Marshall . . . . Delboss

Non-Credited Appearances . . . . Jeff Maxwell, Kellye Nakahara, Roy Goldman,
George Simmons

Chapters

1: Main Titles	6: Trapper is Trapped – 11:05
2: Being Bombed – 0:47	7: Frank is Jealous – 18:31
3: The Latrine – 4:47	8: A Letter from Home – 22:44
4: An Explosive Situation – 7:12	9: Frank's Proposal – 24:31
5: Friendly Fire – 9:28	10: End Titles – 25:28

Closing Stills

1: Mulcahy after coming out of bombed latrine
2: Hawkeye in the "R" compound
3: Margaret crying in supply with Trapper
4: Frank in the Mess Tent
5: Radar in his office on P.A. (Watch out!)

Synopsis: A Red Cross painted on the roof of a field hospital in a war zone does not ensure safety as the camp comes under heavy shelling and heavy casualties. Non-medical personnel take cover under the mess tent tables, while Radar, on the phone with I-Corps takes cover under Henry's desk as the office windows blow out, but I-Corps insists that since there are no enemy units near them, they cannot be under fire. When the latrine takes a hit with Henry and Mulcahy inside, Henry sustains a broken arm while Mulcahy, dazed, thinks Klinger is his mother and the possibility of an explosion inside O.R. becomes a very real threat when a booby-trapped patient is brought in with a wire across his chest connected to a grenade.

Commentary by Larry Gelbart: "Somewhere around the end of the second or the start of the third year, we decided to cut down on the amount of drinking, especially in The Swamp. Don Newcombe, former Dodger pitcher and spokesman for alcohol abstinence, made a strong pitch about not letting such popular characters be seen imbibing either to celebrate or to drown their sorrows. While it is true that an awful lot of drinking goes on in the military, Newcombe's point was well-taken. While our characters obviously did not go on the wagon, we had them stop climbing on to it a bit less frequently. As one who has seen close up and personal the awful human toll that alcohol can and does extract from its abusers, I have never doubted that we made the right choice, but it was sure fun writing dry martini jokes."

PA Announcements by Todd Sussman
PA Announcement by Radar
(Reads a letter from his Mother. Mrs. O'Reilly tells Radar that they don't have a cat anymore, but in the previous episode, "Private Charles Lamb," Radar said he has 16 cats back home.

PA Broadcast into the O.R. introducing The Bob Hope Show
(The show's announcer is Hy Averback, the director of this and several other episodes.)

PA Radio Broadcast into the O.R. of Seoul City Sue
(Seoul City Sue tells them of their cheating wives and girlfriends back home.)

Authors' Notes: A rare and brief shot of the interior of the mess tent on the Ranch set.

In Chapter 2, Kellye fixes Nurse Sanchez's mask, but it comes off a second time, exposing her nose.

When a shell explodes on the Ranch set in Chapter 2, a tent catches fire.

When Nurse Sanchez is seen leaving O.R. in Chapter 4, her nose is out of her mask again, but when the shot changes to see her entering the break room, her mask is in place.

In Chapter 6, the scene inside the Swamp was filmed on the Ranch set as evidenced by an exploding shell on the compound.

Bulletin Board – 1/14/1975

Season 3 / Episode 64 / Production 71 – B323

Columbia House VHS Tape . . . . *Welcome To M*A*S*H (Catalog # 3569)*

Fox DVD . . . . *Season 3, Disc 2*

Alan Alda, Wayne Rogers, McLean Stevenson,
Loretta Swit, Larry Linville, Gary Burghoff

Produced by Gene Reynolds and Larry Gelbart
Written by Larry Gelbart & Simon Muntner
Directed by Alan Alda

Jamie Farr . . . . Corporal Klinger
William Christopher . . . . Father Mulcahy
Patricia Stevens . . . . Nurse Brown
Kellye Nakahara . . . . .Nurse Charlie
Johnny Haymer . . . . Sergeant Zale

Copyright 1974 – 20th Century Fox Film Corporation

Non-Credited Appearances. . . . . Jeff Maxwell, Dennis Troy, Roy Goldman,
Gwen Farrell, Robert Gruber

Chapters

1: Main Titles	6: A Charity Event – 14:34
2: A Lecture – 0:49	7: A Disagreement – 19:30
3: Major Houlihan's Request – 4:56	8: Games – 21:31
4: A Letter to Home – 7:21	9: Back to Work – 24:04
5: At the Movies – 11:03	10: End Titles – 24:59

Closing Stills

1: Klinger in the "Kissing Booth"
2: Hawkeye & Trapper at the movie
3: Henry giving a lecture
4: Frank shouting
5: Radar at the movie (Shirley Temple)

Synopsis: The bulletin board is where general news and camp business is posted, such as Henry's upcoming sex lecture and a notice for bonds through the army's payroll savings plan. Margaret's younger sister, a captain, is getting married and wants Frank to lend her $240, but Frank is less than receptive to the idea of lending money, even to Margaret while Trapper, in a letter to his daughter, expresses his regrets at not being at her birthday party and tries to explain why he's in Korea. Posted to the bulletin board is a notice for the "First Annual Polly Adler Birthday Cookout, Picnic and Barbecue," with all proceeds going to Sister Theresa's Korean Orphan's Fund. But Frank, knowing Margaret is angry with him, gives in and offers to lend her the money, at 5% interest.

Commentary by Larry Gelbart: "Most of the shows I participated were done in a pleasant, constructive atmosphere. No Degrees of Separation Department: Roy Goldman's future father-in-law was my clarinet teacher when I was a kid growing up in Chicago."

PA Announcements by Todd Sussman

Authors' Notes: Polly Adler ran the most notorious brothel in New York City in the 1920's and 1930's.

Henry's lecture is "US Army's Contribution to Birth Control."

Frank is the only one to sign up for bonds, and pulls Mulcahy into the mud.

In Chapter 8, Radar says, "Choppers," but his lips don't move.

The Consultant – 1/21/1975

Season 3 / Episode 65 / Production 66 – B318

Columbia House VHS Tape . . . . *Career Advancement (Catalog # 10994)*
Fox DVD . . . . *Season 3, Disc 3*

Alan Alda, Wayne Rogers, McLean Stevenson,
Loretta Swit, Larry Linville, Gary Burghoff

Produced by Gene Reynolds and Larry Gelbart
Teleplay by Robert Klane
Story by Larry Gelbart
Directed by Gene Reynolds

Robert Alda . . . . .Major Anthony Borelli
William Christopher . . . . Father Mulcahy
Joseph Maher . . . . .Major Taylor
Tad Horino . . . . Bartender

Copyright 1974 – 20th Century Fox Film Corporation

Non-Credited Appearances . . . . Jeff Maxwell, Kellye Nakahara, Dennis Troy,
Roy Goldman, Gwen Farrell, Ralph Grosh

Chapters

1: *Main Titles*	6: *A New Technique – 12:43*
2: *Going to Japan – 0:48*	7: *Going for an Artery – 16:56*
3: *At A Bar – 3:52*	8: *The Doctor is Soused – 19:09*
4: *The M*A*S*H Pool – 7:21*	9: *Saying Goodbye – 23:44*
5: *Doctor Borelli – 9:31*	10: *End Titles – 24:58*

Closing Stills

1: *Borelli soused in the Swamp*
2: *Hawkeye sees Borelli soused*
3: *Henry listens to Borelli's new surgery in the Swamp*
4: *Frank & Margaret in the Mess Tent*
5: *Radar calling for an artery*

Synopsis: Hawkeye and Trapper are expected at Tokyo General for a surgical clinic, but they stop at a bar on the Ginza instead where they meet Doctor Anthony Borelli, an honorary army major who's in Japan as a civilian medical consultant from San Francisco. The doctors invite him to visit a MASH unit or an aid station, but Borelli politely declines as he's already served in WW I and II. Borelli surprises everyone when he makes an unannounced visit to the 4077, and he brings with him a new surgical procedure that could save a man's leg, but when everything is ready in O.R., Borelli, the only doctor there who has experience with the new surgical procedure is in the Swamp unfit to operate.

Commentary by Larry Gelbart: "Robert Alda appeared as Dr. Borelli during the third season. I'm not sure who originated the idea for his appearance, a lot of details like that being buried in the sands of time. But it was obviously a good one."

PA Announcements by Todd Sussman

Author's Notes: Robert Alda, a well known actor in his own right and Alan's father, will appear again in Season 8's, "Lend a Hand," along with Alan's step-brother, Anthony Alda.

The serial number of the jeep Radar drives to the chopper pad is 16930382, but arrives in a jeep numbered 11172419

When Trapper asks Radar where he learned to drive, Radar tells him, "the bumper cars." But in Episode 39, Season 2 "Officers Only," it was established that Hawkeye and Trapper taught him how to drive.

In Chapter 6, after stopping by a tree for Trapper, he gets back into the jeep. Hawkeye says, "You're kidding," and Trapper replies, "Would I kid you?" But, their mouths do not move.

The sinks in the scrub room in this episode are in the middle of the room facing each other.

House Arrest – 2/4/1975

Season 3 / Episode 66 / Production 63 – B315

Columbia House VHS Tape . . . . Hot Lips (Catalog # 3749)
Fox DVD . . . . Season 3, Disc 3

Alan Alda, Wayne Rogers, McLean Stevenson,
Loretta Swit, Larry Linville, Gary Burghoff

Produced by Gene Reynolds and Larry Gelbart
Written by Jim Fritzell & Everett Greenbaum
Directed by Hy Averback

Mary Wickes . . . . Colonel Reese
Jamie Farr . . . . Corporal Klinger
William Christopher . . . . Father Mulcahy
Bobbie Mitchell . . . . Nurse Baker
Jeff Maxwell . . . . Igor
Dennis Troy . . . . M.P.
Kellye Nakahara . . . . Nurse

Copyright 1974 – 20th Century Fox Film Corporation

Non-Credited Appearances . . . . Roy Goldman, Gwen Farrell, George Simmons

Chapters

1: Main Titles
2: A Court-Martial Offense – 0:50
3: Colonel Reese – 5:07
4: Trapper's Testimony – 8:12
5: A Prisoner of War – 9:49
6: Movie Night – 15:08
7: No More Little Guy – 18:12
8: Comfort from the Colonel – 19:43
9: Frank's House Arrest – 24:49
10: End Titles – 25:31

Closing Stills

1: Colonel Reese in a red robe
2: Klinger helps Radar with elevator shoes
3: Trapper & Hawkeye in the Scrub Room
4: Margaret & Frank in the Scrub Room
5: "Tall" Radar smiling with Hawkeye

Synopsis: Margaret, nervous about the impending visit of Colonel Reese, the most decorated nurse in the Army, makes mistakes assisting Hawkeye in OR and when he reprimands her in the scrub room, Frank defends her honor by snapping a towel on Hawkeye's rear end. Not to be outdone, Hawkeye returns the favor by punching Frank in the face, and Hawkeye is placed under house arrest. Colonel Reese arrives and, alone in Margaret's tent with Frank, she makes a play for him, giving him blackberry brandy and visions of "Colonel Burns" and Walter Reed Hospital. But when Margaret comes in and sees them embracing, the Colonel immediately starts yelling, "Rape," and now, Margaret drops the charges against Hawkeye and Frank is placed under house arrest and wonders what he's going to tell his wife.

Commentary by Larry Gelbart: "As was the case with so many actors of Mary Wickes' age and experience, she was an absolute joy to work with. Solid as a performer, a terrific companion for the two or three days she spent with us. Prepared, co-operative, creative, and any other positive attributes you can think of. In hindsight, we would have been wise to use her more often. By himself, Gary Burghoff is 5 feet 7. Standing on someone else, he can be up to 12 feet tall. 'Keed' for "kid" (a term Frank uses), is just like from the time when Henry said 'Abyssinia' for 'I'll be seeing you.'"

Commentary by Gene Reynolds: "Mary Wickes was a favorite of two wonderful writers. She'd be massaging her gums and then say, 'My gums are singing.' Those two writers from 'House Arrest' wrote great stuff. Great whimsy, very light, silly stuff."

PA Announcements by Todd Sussman

Authors' Notes: In this episode, Frank is seen wearing a bathrobe that was usually worn by Henry. In "I Hate A Mystery" from Season 1, Frank was seen in a plaid robe. Trapper alone had three different bathrobes, starting with the Pilot, in which he wore a red M.D. robe (the only time he was ever seen in that robe), and in "The Moose" from Season 1, he was seen in a blue robe. However, it's the yellow bathrobe he's best known for wearing. Hawkeye always wore the red M.D. robe, but the other members of the 4077th, including Margaret, had different robes from time to time.

Mary Wickes was born Mary Isabella Wickenhauser on June 13, 1910 in St. Louis, MO. She had an impressive list of credits to her name that spanned the better part of 60 years. Some of the television shows Miss Wickes appeared in besides *M*A*S*H* were *I Love Lucy, The Lucy Show, Alfred Hitchcock Presents, My Three Sons, Bonanza,* and *F-Troop.* Yet, the part that the co-author of this book, Eddie, remembers best was her recurring role in *Dennis the Menace* as Miss Esther Cathcart. Mary Wickes also appeared in over 200 stage productions, 27 of which were on Broadway. For years, Mary Wickes was a volunteer at the Hospital of Good Samaritan in Los Angeles. Mary Wickes suffered from several ailments including renal failure, massive gastrointestinal bleeding, severe hypotension, ischemic cardiomyopathy, anemia and breast cancer. Before she died at the age of 85 on October 22, 1995, the never-married actress left a $2 million bequest in memory of her parents for the Isabella and Frank Wickenhauser Memorial Library Fund for Television, Film and Theater Arts.

Aid Station – 2/11/1975

Season 3 / Episode 67 / Production 70 – B322

Columbia House VHS Tape . . . . *Hot Lips (Catalog # 3749)*
Fox DVD . . . . *Season 3, Disc 3*

Alan Alda, Wayne Rogers, McLean Stevenson,
Loretta Swit, Larry Linville, Gary Burghoff

Produced by Gene Reynolds and Larry Gelbart
Written by Larry Gelbart & Simon Muntner
Directed by William Jurgensen

Jamie Farr . . . . Corporal Klinger
William Christopher . . . . Father Mulcahy
Copyright 1974 – 20th Century Fox Film Corporation

Non-Credited Appearances . . . . Jeff Maxwell, Kellye Nakahara, Tom Dever

Chapters

1: *Main Titles*
2: *Emergency at the Front – 0:50*
3: *Preparing to Go – 5:02*
4: *The Aid Station – 10:13*
5: *Primitive Conditions – 12:15*

6: *Bedtime – 15:35*
7: *Exhausted – 18:29*
8: *Ready for the Army – 21:18*
9: *Mutual Respect – 22:35*
10: *End Titles – 25:03*

Closing Stills

1: *Radar in Klinger's tent*
2: *Mulcahy in Henry's office*
3: *Trapper in the Swamp*
4: *Margaret toasts Hawkeye w/ coffee in the Mess Tent*
5: *Hawkeye toasts Margaret*

Synopsis: "I" Company aid station has sustained shelling and their surgeon has been killed. The 4077th is to send a surgeon, scrub nurse and a corpsman until replacements arrive. Margaret volunteers, Hawkeye draws the short sausage and Father Mulcahy picks Klinger from the personnel cards and when they get to the aid station, they hardly recognize it as such since the Red Cross was blown off along with the roof. Klinger makes radio contact with Radar while shells explode close by and after an initial walk-through, Hawkeye sets up shop and operates while the shelling continues. It's nightfall, the shelling has stopped and the wounded have been taken care of. Klinger is fast asleep from exhaustion while Hawkeye and Margaret finish their C-rations, wondering about snipers. In the mess tent with everyone back and accounted for, the usual complaints are made about cold coffee and flavorless food, but Hawkeye and Margaret silently toast each other for a job well done and are glad to be back, cold coffee and all.

Commentary by Larry Gelbart: "That extra later died of a staph infection" (on the mistake noted that Henry goes from one patient to another without getting new gloves).

PA Announcement by Todd Sussman

Author's Notes: Once again, we see a view of the "fourth wall" (with Hawkeye), the one from which the camera did the filming from.

Tom Dever, the actor who played Lieutenant Rogers, the CID man from Season 2's Episode 37, "Deal Me Out," (and who will appear again in Season 4's "Welcome to

Korea") is not credited for his appearance in this episode. Although he had a minor speaking role here, he introduces himself to Hawkeye as "Dever," using his real name.

This is not the only time Margaret has had to perform surgery. She did it in Season 2's "Carry On, Hawkeye."

Henry has a bottle of J & B Scotch in his liquor cabinet.

In Chapter 7, for the second time, a rare view from the compound looking in to the office windows shows Henry looking out in anticipation of Hawkeye, Margaret and Klinger returning from the Aid Station.

In Chapter 9, Trapper wraps a tea bag string around a nail on a support post in the Swamp. When he turns away, the string unravels and the tea bag falls off.

Love and Marriage – 2/18/1975

Season 3 / Episode 68 / Production 69 – B321

Columbia House VHS Tape . . . . *Love And War (Catalog # 10996)*
Fox DVD . . . . *Season 3, Disc 3*

Alan Alda, Wayne Rogers, McLean Stevenson,
Loretta Swit, Larry Linville, Gary Burghoff

Produced by Gene Reynolds and Larry Gelbart
Written by Arthur Julian
Directed by Lee Philips

Johnny Haymer . . . . Sergeant Zale
Soon-Taik Oh . . . . Mr. Kwang
(Soon-Tek Oh was occasionally credited as Soon-Taik and is not an error)
William Christopher . . . . Father Mulcahy
Dennis Dugan . . . . Private Danny McShane
Jerry Fujikawa . . . . Dr. Pak
Pat Li . . . . Soong Hi
Jeanne Joe . . . . Mrs. Kwang
Robert Gruber . . . . Sergeant
Roy Goldman . . . . Orderly
Copyright 1974 – 20th Century Fox Film Corporation

Non-Credited Appearances . . . . Kellye Nakahara, Dennis Troy

Chapters

1: Main Titles	6: Dr. Pak's Proposition – 14:17
2: Tension, Insults & Bickering – 0:48	7: Desertion Charges – 16:11
3: Mr. Kwang's Problem – 3:01	8: McShane's Deal – 19:00
4: McShane's Bride – 7:32	9: A Birth on the Bus – 21:14
5: A Fake Pass – 12:44	10: End Titles – 25:00

Closing Stills

1: Mr. Kwang in the Swamp
2: McShane
3: Hawkeye playing poker in the Swamp
4: Radar about to pass out on the bus
5: Henry playing poker in the Swamp

Synopsis: Mr. Kwang was a student at the University of Seoul when war broke out and was officially drafted when he was tossed into the back of a South Korean military truck, and has never had the chance to say goodbye to his wife. Radar tricks Henry into signing a three-day pass for Mr. Kwang, who wants to get to his village to see his wife who is pregnant with their first child, but is harassed by Frank and brought up on charges of desertion. Meanwhile, the doctors are performing pre-marital exams for GI's marrying Korean locals, but Trapper discovers that Private Danny McShane is getting $1000 to marry a Korean woman, arranged by a phony Dr. Pak to enable the girls to "work for friends" of his back in the States.

Commentary by Larry Gelbart: "There was never any intention of demeaning a people whose freedom the United States sought to protect. When we learned he was available to us, we employed the services of Soon Tek Oh, a brilliant Korean actor. It was virtually impossible to hire any other Korean actors in the 70's."

PA Announcement by Todd Sussman

Authors' Notes: Dennis Dugan, who played Private Danny McShane in this episode, will later play Colonel Potter's son-in-law in season 11's "Strange Bedfellows."

Hawkeye mentions *The Student Prince,* an operetta from 1924, and a musical movie from 1957.

Soon-Tek Oh was occasionally credited as Soon-Taik.

Mr. Kwang's son is Radar Benjamin Franklin Trapper John Henry Kwang.

Big Mac – 2/25/1975

Season 3 / Episode 69 / Production 61 – B313

Columbia House VHS Tape . . . . *Army Brass (Catalog # 3742)*
Fox DVD . . . . *Season 3, Disc 3*

Alan Alda, Wayne Rogers, McLean Stevenson,
Loretta Swit, Larry Linville, Gary Burghoff

Produced by Gene Reynolds and Larry Gelbart
Written by Laurence Marks
Directed by Don Weis

Loudon Wainwright, III . . . . Captain Calvin Spalding
Graham Jarvis . . . . Colonel Whiteman
Jamie Farr . . . . Corporal Klinger
Copyright 1974 – 20th Century Fox Film Corporation

Non-Credited Appearances. . . . . Kellye Nakahara, Jeff Maxwell, Dennis Troy,
Roy Goldman, Gwen Farrell

Chapters

1: *Main Titles*	6: *Klinger's Big Chance – 14:03*
2: *Big Mac is Coming – 0:48*	7: *The General's Tent – 17:20*
3: *The General's Schedule – 5:06*	8: *The Rehearsal – 19:25*
4: *"De-shambilizing" – 9:30*	9: *MacArthur's Visit – 23:42*
5: *Dirty Books – 12:34*	10: *End Titles – 25:28*

Closing Stills

1: *Spalding singing "It's Not Corrigidor"*
2: *Trapper & Hawkeye with Whiteman in the Mess Tent*
3: *Henry in his office*
4: *Frank & Margaret in the V.I.P. tent*
5: *Klinger in a pink dress in Henry's office*

Synopsis: In recognition of the 4077th having the most impressive record of any medical unit in Korea, Henry promises that on the 19th of the month, the 4077th will be ready for a visit by General Douglas MacArthur. Colonel Whiteman, the General's administrative aid arrives in camp to brief the unit on proper protocols with a strict timetable for the General's impending visit. Frank and Margaret, impressed with the way Radar decorated the VIP tent, now treat it as a place of worship, while Frank later burns literary classics by Norman Mailer because it "has that word in it." But during a camp rehearsal, the PA unexpectedly announces that MacArthur has entered Checkpoint 1 and will be there in a matter of seconds and the whole camp comes to attention. MacArthur does indeed arrive and returns the salute, but keeps going straight through camp without ever stopping.

Commentary by Larry Gelbart: "Here's a possible scenario: Klinger, quite by chance, commits an incredible act of bravery; maybe someone else's act of bravery. He is decorated for it, even though he tries to avoid getting the recognition. In doing whatever it was he did, he receives a medal or two. One of them is a Purple Heart for wounds he sustained. He goes home with a medical discharge. He goes home a hero" (if Jamie Farr had decided to leave the show during his tenure).

PA Announcement by Todd Sussman

Authors' Notes: This is the third and final appearance of Loudon Wainwright III, who composed and performed the original songs in this episode.

As previously mentioned, the audio of Trapper in O.R. saying, "Okay, cut that," is heard as well in this episode no less than five times in the O.R. in Chapter 2.

The tailor's sign appears again next to Goldie's sign.

According to Henry, the 4077th is four miles from the front. This varies throughout the series between three and four miles.

This episode might be the only time Hawkeye takes a drink from a flask, but it's vodka, not gin, since they were only rehearsing for MacArthur's visit.

One of the more memorable outfits worn by Klinger, dressed as The Statue of Liberty, complete with sparklers shooting out from where the torch would be.

Payday – 3/4/1975

Season 3 / Episode 70 / Production 53 – B305

Columbia House VHS Tape . . . . *Card Tricks (Catalog # 3748)*
Fox DVD . . . . *Season 3, Disc 3*

Alan Alda, Wayne Rogers, McLean Stevenson,
Loretta Swit, Larry Linville, Gary Burghoff

Produced by Gene Reynolds and Larry Gelbart
Written by Regier & Markowitz
Directed by Hy Averback

Johnny Haymer . . . . Sergeant Zale
Eldon Quick . . . . Captain Sloan
Jack Soo. . . . . Kim Chun Quoc
Jamie Farr . . . . Corporal Klinger
William Christopher. . . . . Father Mulcahy
Pat Marshall . . . . Lieutenant Nelson
Jeff Maxwell. . . . . .Igor

Copyright 1974 – 20th Century Fox Film Corporation

Non-Credited Appearances. . . . . Bobbie Mitchell, Dennis Troy, Roy Goldman,
Gwen Farrell

Chapters

1: *Main Titles*	6: *Klinger's Proposition – 12:29*
2: *It's Payday – 0:48*	7: *Real Pearls – 14:41*
3: *Leftover Money – 6:07*	8: *The Man from ACFIN – 21:07*
4: *Tiffany on Wheels – 7:39*	9: *Trapper's Big Payoff – 22:47*
5: *Three Thousand Dollars – 10:27*	10: *End Titles – 25:28*

Closing Stills

1: *Quoc in Margaret's tent*
2: *Trapper winning a big poker hand*
3: *Margaret in the shower*
4: *Klinger salutes Hawkeye*
5: *Radar in the Swamp*

Synopsis: One of the most anticipated events at the 4077th is payday and it's Hawkeye's turn as Pay Officer. Radar tells him exactly what he's supposed to do, making sure he understands that he's responsible for the money distributed. Hawkeye realizes he has $10 left over and gives it to Radar as he complains that being in Korea has cost him $3,000 in his civilian practice. On Hawkeye's behalf and unbeknownst to him, Radar, after sending the right amount of forms, gives Hawkeye an envelope with $3,000 inside and Hawkeye turns it over to Father Mulcahy for the orphans. Trapper lost all his money playing poker, and when Hawkeye refuses to lend him more, he steals Hawkeye's watch and wins a huge poker pot. But when Captain Sloan from Accounting and Finance arrives to arrest Hawkeye for the $3,000 he received, Hawkeye pays the Captain back with Trapper's winnings and keeps the $8 left over as a watch-rental fee.

Commentary by Eldon Quick: "During blocking rehearsals, the cast not involved would sit or stand around and chat, tell jokes reminisce, or maybe work on some bit of business, or timing of a gag. Everybody was approachable. Everybody was at ease. Mac was quick to take off with some bit of improvised comedic stuff, using something said or done as a

PHOTO COURTESY ELDON QUICK

Eldon Quick appears in "The Incubator" (Season 2) and "Payday" (Season 3).

springboard. He was a major comedic talent, up there with Jonathan Winters and maybe Robin Williams. He should have had his own show, if only a suitable format could have been found for him."

Commentary by Eddie: When speaking with Pat Marshall, I asked if she wanted to do more episodes of *M*A*S*H,* but she was content with the one she did and opted to be with her family.

PA Announcements by Todd Sussman

Authors' Notes: Pat Marshall, who played Lieutenant Nelson, is Mrs. Larry Gelbart.

In future episodes, a Red Cross sign can be clearly seen in the Officer's Club. On the left side, if you look carefully, it reads: "Pat and Larry Marshall."

Private Frank Daily's serial number is 56709546 and, according to the Private, his pay is $75.33.

According to Klinger, his serial number is 36-24-36, and his pay is $159 a month. This was calculated on the bribe he made to Henry by offering him $477, three month's pay.

Hawkeye has a "warm bed in Maine."

This is the second and final appearance of Jack Soo.

Henry's pay is $831.75, but after federal and unemployment taxes, he's left with $43 to play poker with.

The shower schedule: *Males: 1600 to 1630, Nurses: 1630 to 1700.*

White Gold – 3/11/1975

Season 3 / Episode 71 / Production 67 – B319

Columbia House VHS Tape . . . . American Flagg (Catalog # 13109)
Fox DVD . . . . Season 3, Disc 3

Alan Alda, Wayne Rogers, McLean Stevenson,
Loretta Swit, Larry Linville, Gary Burghoff

Produced by Gene Reynolds and Larry Gelbart
Written by Larry Gelbart & Simon Muntner
Directed by Hy Averback

Edward Winter . . . . .Colonel Sam Flagg
Jamie Farr . . . . Corporal Klinger
Hilly Hicks . . . . Corporal Perkins
William Christopher. . . . . Father Mulcahy
Stafford Repp . . . . .Sergeant Clay
Danil Torppe . . . . Morris
Michael A. Salcido . . . . .Rodriguez

Copyright 1974 – 20th Century Fox Film Corporation

Non-Credited Appearances. . . . . .Jeff Maxwell, Kellye Nakahara, Gwen Farrell,
Dennis Troy, Roy Goldman, Robert Gruber

Chapters

1: Main Titles
2: The Penicillin Thieves – 0:48
3: Corporal Perkins – 5:28
4: Flagg's New Assignment – 6:55
5: Take A Powder – 11:20
6: Something's Fishy – 15:17
7: Caught in the Act – 17:30
8: The Penicillin Problem – 20:12
9: Flagg's Operation – 22:34
10: End Titles – 24:58

Closing Stills

1: Flagg in V.I.P tent (Take a powder)
2: Corporal Johnson in Henry's office
3: Hawkeye & Margaret help Trapper with Flagg
4: Trapper laughing in the Swamp
5: Radar in Henry's office

Synopsis: When a penicillin thief is caught and sustains bruised ribs in the struggle, he refuses to say anything other than he was not stealing the medicine to sell on the Black Market, that his reasons are his own. With the theft of penicillin getting out of hand, Colonel Flagg, disguised as Rabbi Captain Goldberg, shows up to question the thief, Corporal Perkins. Alone with Perkins, Flagg, in an unusual move, allows him to leave and then trashes the tent, but Hawkeye doesn't believe Perkins did all that damage and wants to know what Flagg is up to. When Klinger tells them that someone is in supply again, Hawkeye and Trapper discover that it's not Perkins, but Flagg himself who later tells them that his people need the penicillin to use as barter to buy information from the North and has every intention of leaving the 4077th with the drug, but Hawkeye has other plans.

Commentary by Burt Metcalfe: "Ed Winter was one of the proudest pieces of casting I ever did. Here was an example of where we only brought one actor in. I met him through his friend, Bert Convy, who was a friend of mine. There was something about his face. He had sort of a comic book face. I don't want to sound like I'm taking full credit.

Naturally, at the outset I had no idea how he'd perform. A few weeks or months later, Larry Gelbart conceived of this Colonel Flagg character, and I thought of Ed. I was just overjoyed at how well he did."

Author's Notes: There are no PA announcements in this episode.

Some of the best use of background music on *M*A*S*H* was utilized in the beginning of this episode, as well as when Col. Flagg makes it look like there was a fight in a tent. In the opening scene, we get a rare camera dolly from the perspective of looking out to the Swamp and compound from behind the various other tents.

The sign over supply reads, "4077th SUPPLY." Other times it says, "SUPPLY ROOM."

When Colonel Flagg trashes the tent to make it appear there was a fight, he breaks a telephone over his head. Other than an occasional extension into the OR and the compound directly outside the office, this is only one of two times a telephone was seen anywhere other than the CO's office. The next time a telephone will be seen outside the CO's office will be in Season 8's "Too Many Cooks" where Klinger will be on a telephone in the Mess Tent.

According to Klinger, last week's password was "Bull Feathers."

In a much-talked about event, in Chapter 9, Hawkeye spikes Flagg's coffee, resulting in an unnecessary appendectomy to keep Flagg from taking the penicillin. In a future episode, but under different circumstances, Hawkeye repeats this and performs another unnecessary appendectomy. The difference between these two events is Trapper didn't mind, even covering for Hawkeye by telling Igor that what Hawkeye put in the coffee was vitamins, while BJ held a completely different perspective and wanted no part in what is clearly a flagrant violation of the Hippocratic Oath. These two appendectomies continue to be a point of contention among fans.

Abyssinia, Henry – 3/18/1975

Season 3 / Episode 72 / Production 72 – B324

Columbia House VHS Tape . . . . *Going Home (Catalog # 3741)*
Fox DVD . . . . *Season 3, Disc 3*

Alan Alda, Wayne Rogers, McLean Stevenson,
Loretta Swit, Larry Linville, Gary Burghoff

Produced by Gene Reynolds and Larry Gelbart
Written by Everett Greenbaum & Jim Fritzell
Directed by Larry Gelbart

Jamie Farr . . . . Corporal Klinger
William Christopher . . . . Father Mulcahy
Copyright 1975 – 20th Century Fox Film Corporation

Non-Credited Appearances . . . . Kellye Nakahara, Jeff Maxwell, Gwen Farrell,
Virginia Lee

Chapters

1: Main Titles
2: Going Home – 0:48
3: Frank's Destiny – 4:45
4: A Call Home – 5:58
5: Getting Gushy – 8:18
6: The Goodbye Party – 11:28
7: A Jolly Good Fellow – 17:28
8: Shot Down – 22:39
9: Farewell, Henry – 23:53
10: End Titles – 24:58

Closing Stills

1: Henry zipping Klinger (Up, Sir)
2: Hawkeye at Henry's party
3: Trapper at Henry's party
4: Margaret & Frank in Henry's office
5: Radar saluting Henry

Synopsis: Henry finally gets the news he's been waiting for: he's being discharged from the army and calls Lorraine to tell her he should be home in about three days. He and Radar exchange small mementos of their time together in Korea, but when Henry gives him his father's thermometer, Radar quickly realizes it's not oral. Hawkeye, Trapper and Radar throw him a farewell party complete with Korean food, plenty of booze, and give him a brand new suit and silk tie, all handmade in Korea. Henry leaves his tent for the last time wearing his new suit, to cheers and applause, then says goodbye to his friends. He tells Frank that the 4077th is now his, but when Hawkeye whispers something in Henry's ear, Henry gives Margaret a long goodbye kiss, and heads for the chopper pad. When his chopper lands with wounded, he immediately begins doing triage, new suit and all, and Hawkeye fires him. But when he gets on the chopper, he sees Radar standing on the pad saluting, and Henry goes to hug him goodbye. The war continues in Henry's absence and the O.R. is busy when Radar comes in, visibly shaken, without a mask, and seems to not hear Trapper tell him to put one on. He tells the staff that he has a message and after taking a deep breath, delivers a message no one expected, and no one wanted to hear.

Commentary by Larry Gelbart: "The first take had a technical flaw. The instrument never dropped on the first take. It was unplanned, happening only by chance on the second take. (On the instrument that fell and broke the silence in the O.R. after Henry's death is announced) Alda was not a member of the staff. He was a member of the actors' ensemble. He was also, by that time, clearly the star of the series. On that basis, he and he alone was told of Henry's death in the episode. Not a single other actor. Not a single member of the crew. Not even the typing pool. There was no rehearsal of the dialogue. Gary B. had the only spoken lines and he needed no rehearsing. It was a deliberate foreshadowing (commenting about a dual shot of Henry and the skeleton in his office). 'Toity' is slang for toilet. It's a bit of coy baby talk. Please understand that Rogers never asked, nor did the producers ever promise, that his role would be bolstered to be equal to Alda's. Rogers had other issues.

"Stevenson's representative asked if Mac couldn't return to the series (rescued at sea and all that). We didn't spend a lot of time thinking the idea over. With Stevenson definitely gone at the end of Season 3, plotting began on what would have been the first episode of Season 4, 'Change of Command.' The work was done during the hiatus between [seasons] 3 and 4. During that period, we sweated out the Rogers situation - would he leave the show, wouldn't he, etc. When it became clear that he was leaving, we began casting for another actor and preparing the script for 'Welcome to Korea,' without a whole lot of time to get it ready."

Commentary by Jeff Maxwell: "I was there on the test day and saw all the potential BJ's (James Cromwell, Sam Elliott, Alan Fudge, Mike Farrell). I have a fuzzy memory of a fifth contestant, but it may just be fuzz. A screen test is a tough day. It can be, and was on stage 9, a life-changing moment. None of those actors wanted to walk away from that experience with nothing but the experience. All but one did. I remember being so impressed, awed maybe, with Alan's stamina, dedication and willingness to be there for each actor. A huge part was up for grabs, one that could make or break the chemistry of a hit TV show. It was certainly not a day to mail in a performance, and Alan sure didn't. One by one, he opened up to each man allowing whatever chemistry there was between them to show up. He repeated each scene with equal energy and attention. It was a very cool thing for a young, slightly goofy, but ravenously interested actor/comic to witness. In all honesty, I thought each actor gave a credible performance and could've played the role. Cromwell was literally head and shoulders above the crowd. His height forced Alan to play the scene with his head tilted to an uncomfortable angle. I remember thinking how terrific Cromwell was and how painful it would be for Alan to play the next umpteen years looking up at his comrade. Mike was likable guy. He looked good and had a physical presence some of the others didn't. It must have been his Marine training. Though I thought there was more stuff going on between Alan and Cromwell, Mike and Alan seem very compatible. And so it went."

PA Announcements by Todd Sussman

Authors' Notes: The O.R. scene in Chapter 8 is the last time we see Trapper (not counting his shadow and arm in the opening credits, as described in another chapter). One reason there was never a "goodbye" episode for Trapper was because Wayne Rogers didn't decide to leave the series until after the third season had been completed.

Trapper will continue to be heard in O.R. scenes saying, "Okay, cut that."

This episode marks the last time Jamie Farr will be credited in the closing credits.

The view from Henry's office windows now shows big trees with big branches. This changes in Chapter 5 to different trees and mountains and changes again mid-scene to show a building.

Radar claims that a drink makes his eyes red and he falls down. However, it didn't seem to bother him when, prior to this statement, he's had seven Martinis, three Brandies and either a Scotch or bourbon. After Henry describes Lorraine and her short "nighties" to Radar, he reconsiders and wants a drink and he's drunk at Henry's party at Rosie's.

Frank tells Margaret that he wishes he'd taken ROTC in school. In Season 2, Episode 26, "5 O'clock Charlie," he has gunnery experience in the ROTC.

After Radar delivers the sad news, a surgical instrument falls to the floor. This could be the best-known "accident" to be purposely left in.

Many people have commented about the "point" system used in this episode as being inaccurate and not in effect during the Korean War. It was proposed and began at the beginning of the Korean War by psychiatrist (and WWII vet) Albert Glass to "protect soldiers from becoming psychiatric casualties." After obtaining 36 points, the soldier could go home no matter what the progress of the war: infantrymen = 4 points per month; artillerymen = 3 points per month; rear-echelon = 2 points per month. In WWII, the psychiatric casualties were 23%. When Glass took over in the Korean War, the psychiatric casualties dropped to 6%. *Thanks to Lynnita Brown and her web site, www.koreanwar-educator.org, for her help in acquiring this information.*

Appendix – Season 3

Character Profiles

Hawkeye

Episode 49: Making a seashell necklace for his Sister.
Reads, "Joy of Nudity" magazine.

50: Dai Ichi Hotel in Tokyo asked that he and Trapper not come back — too loud.
Mother gave him a pen and pencil set for graduation
Falls asleep with a Martini in his hand.

51: Post grad specialty was "Blindfold & last cigarette 102" *(sarcastic).*

52: Didn't know if he wanted to be a doctor or a fireman when he was younger *(in Episode 4, all he ever wanted to be was a doctor).*
Took a cadaver to a football game in med school — was more fun than his date.

53: The two things he'll miss the most are Radar and dysentery.
Never wears underwear in surgery because the blood stains right through.

54: Likes tying knots in varicose veins — did postmortem an hour before patient was ready *(sarcastic).*

55: Wears the tuxedo his grandfather was buried in at Klinger's wedding ceremony.
Gives Margaret her physical.
Makes a pact to never stop drinking.

56: Occupant, MASH 4077 — Picture of barnyard animals find10 hidden presidents and win Shetland pony.
Coolidge near horse's tail; Teddy Roosevelt in a tree; finds Millard Fillmore.
James Buchanan under a haystack; Ulysses Grant's nose looks like a big red apple.
Wants to name the horse, "Prince" or "Norman."
Rides white horse and Trapper jumps on the back.
Lieutenant Forbes is a dermatologist with pimples.

58: Has seen every picture of every female in camp.

59: Parents
Liver or fish for eleven straight days.
Speaks to Bernard Resnick at the Dearborn Street Station.
Adam's Ribs phone number is Dearborn 5-2750.
Party for Mother out on parole *(sarcastic).*
Ate 12 banana sandwiches and slept in the toilet for a week.
Rides in chopper's rumble seat to get the ribs.
Tape records first letter to his father.

"Hawkeye" is from Last of the Mohicans" — only book his father ever read *(Note: It hasn't been established yet that his father is a doctor).*

60: Wrote to MacArthur suggesting the war be called a draw
MacArthur sent him an autographed photo of him wading ashore in the Philippines.

62: He couldn't stop sneezing because of a girl's angora sweater.

63: Packs nudist magazines for evacuation
Reading a serial from nudist magazine called, "The Sun Burnt Fool" about a woman who smuggles 10 pounds of pistachio ice cream out of a nudist camp.
Cuts Trapper's hair.

65: Loved a girl in San Francisco once, "no, twice."
Has light blue bathing trunks, sneakers *(from where?)* and "Groucho glasses."
Operates on the same G.I he operated on twice before.

66: Punches Frank in the left eye.
Cook made him a steak for dinner when he heard Hawkeye punched Frank.
Harriet Mackey was a friend of Hawkeye's in junior high school — "Gene Tierney in a training bra."

67: Marks his bottle of after shave — doesn't drink it, just gargles with it.
Has his will in his locker — Leaving everything to the Benjamin Franklin Pierce Memorial Brothel.
Admits to Margaret that she's his favorite officer in the whole army — will deny it if mentioned.

69: His two favorite words from a nurse are "Yes, doctor."

70: Has a warm bed in MAINE.
Has lost almost $3,000 of his civilian practice because of the war.
Besides being pay officer, he's also the rodent officer, rumor officer and termite officer on Arbor Day.

Trapper

Episode 50: Dai Ichi Hotel asked him and Hawkeye not to come back — too loud.
Only goes out with women who don't know he's married
Russian "burp" gun shoots 30 rounds a second.

51: Wants 2" cuff on tailored pants.
2 pair of pants and a vest from his tailor is $12.
Pinstripe suit of all-time — horizontal stripes.

53: Drunk in the Officer's Club — tried to eat the cherries in the slot machines, and left with a nurse over.
shoulder — according to Hawkeye.

54: Is Klinger's wedding photographer.

55: Has a duodenal ulcer — 1.2 centimeters — to report to Tokyo for 3 weeks of therapy, planned diet and tranquilizers but not sent home — can stay at the 4077 for treatment.
4077 *gave* him the ulcer.
Trapper's gifts: *From the nurses:* Pair of all-weather pajamas, tops only — bottoms a week after he's home
From the enlisted men: Matched pair of cockroaches — bronzed and suitable as cuff links
From the hospital staff: An album for "Quiet evenings after the day's surgery has been botched" — "Sonia Henning Sings Figure Eights for You."

56: Letter from his 5-year-old daughter.

Captain Forrest — brain surgeon who fell down a lot

Wants to name the horse "Lightening" or "Buck."

57: Has his wife's car keys because she's a lousy driver.

58: Has a picture of his mother — mentioned.

59: Three-night stand in Chicago with Mildred Feeney.

Mildred Feeney calls him, "Big John."

60: Tape records a message to Hawkeye's father — "Your son's no good."

62: Neighbor puts a lamb on a rack every Easter — bastes it with lots of lemon and tons of butter.

63: 10 years in medical school / Ran naked in the subway

Has hemorrhoids — old football injury from spending a lot of time on the bench.

Elected "Crumb Boy" on graham cracker day.

Didn't study medicine in his own state, according to Frank.

64: Daughter Becky is 7 years old — Writes her a birthday letter and explains why he and the others are there, as well as a brief description of his tent-mates.

Is "Punch" the puppet in a puppet show.

65: Has dark blue swim trunks and blue swim fins *(from where?)*.

71: Penicillin on the black market is "50 bucks a pop"

Henry

Episode 49: Mother's canary had bronchitis — dies when it fell off its perch and "smashed" it's bill.

50: Uses the name, "Orville Carver" when ordering Japanese "prints."

Gives $34 to Hawkeye and Trapper to get them in Tokyo.

6' 3" according to Hawkeye.

51: In Tokyo attending a series of medical conferences.

Chews Wrigley's Juicy Fruit gum (from Radar).

53: Performed two thoracotomies, a bowel resection, a splenectomy & used "a half mile of silk."

Dropped instruments 3 times in surgery — Hawkeye diagnosis the onset of arthritis.

4077 gives him an opportunity to do more "doctoring" than back home.

Has a great practice back home and there's nobody in Bloomington he hasn't seen naked.

1 extra brandy and has to leave an I.O.U on his wife's pillow.

Mother's name was Margaret *(was?) (In Episode 38, parents were on a second honeymoon).*

Package of sewing thread Lorraine sent is under his bed next to the milk bottle.

54: 4 A.M. in camp = 6 P.M. in Des Moines — Ham operator in Des Moines is BS2XYZ.

BS2XYZ will call Lavern collect at chapel in Toledo, patch her into radio, Klinger will hear Lavern.

Lavern's folks will hear on extension phone.

4077's call letters are KN5YVJ.

55: Gets his physicals from Radar.

56: Gets adult films from The Tabasco Film Company, Box 245, Havana, Cuba.

Films received are, "Yvonne, Renee, & Loretta in What the Parrot Saw," and "Renee, Loretta & the Parrot in What Yvonne Saw."

Letter from Lorraine giving him permission to "fool around."

Screening of the "parrot" movies at midnight in the generator shed

Cost $1,000 to join country club plus $150 a month in green fees.

Country club doesn't allow Catholics.

Used to collect butterflies, but never caught any — caught a sick moth once eating father's blue serge.

Slammed closet door on moth

Never cried as a kid — a sin to cry in Bloomington.

Father walked 5 miles into the woods to scream after a tractor tipped over on him.

Lyle Pendergrast always kissing Lorraine's hand — got moustache caught in her ring and his eyes watered.

Loraine took up tennis and wears those short, little skirts — "gorgeous legs" after varicose vein surgery.

Sailor followed her 4 blocks and she was wearing orthopedic shoes.

Lorraine is a "little flirty" especially after a couple of Scotch & 7 Up.

Henry was in the latrine when it caught fire, but "nothing important got burned, just a little singed."

Al Franklin, tall with a 12 handicap, drives a yellow "Jag" — took Lorraine to the Pumpkin Dance at the club.

Al Franklin is an orthodontist — Lorraine mentions the movie, "Brief Encounter."

58: Drinks Bromo Seltzer for a hangover.

59: Knows the Dearborn Street Station because it was the first place his mother let him go to the men's room alone.

Dearborn Station phone number is, Dearborn 5-7500.

Met his wife there at the Dearborn Street Station *(In Episode 33, he met his wife at a freshman mixer at Illinois, Normal)*.

60: Can't put his dog near papers.

If he gets the wrong shot, he turns blue and curls up into a ball.

Meets his first, "Luxembourger."

Wants Hawkeye's father to call Lorraine to send him new shorts.

62: Usually waits until noon to have a drink.

Gave a medical discharge to a lamb.

63: Usually sits on the far side of the latrine by the "picture window."

63: Lorraine sent stateside toilet paper for their anniversary.

Has a broken left arm and is worried about his back swing.

63: First time in 6 months he got a toothbrush that's just right — not too hard and not too soft.

Has teeth like Turhan Bey.

Cousin Floyd emotionally attached to a goat.

There's a "Harry" at the country club, but Lorraine wouldn't "Horse around" with a busboy.

Another "Harry" at the club who repairs golf carts, "Dirty nails and always digging one finger in his ear."

65: Has a light blue shower cap he wore in the pool.

66: Orders glazed fruit for Christmas.

Cries during a Gene Tierney movie.

67: Biggest decisions back home is whether or not to have his own bowling ball made and does he get the cat fixed.

Has a bottle of J&B Scotch in his liquor cabinet.

68: Signature has a fat "K" and a skinny "A" according to Radar.

69: Big Mac's visit is the biggest thing that's ever happened to him since he did his first strangulated hernia.

Hometown newspaper is, "The Daily Bloomington Pantograph."

Tonsillectomy just went from $50 to $75 a "tonse."
70: Once spent a week in Radar's hometown.
Makes $831.75 a month.
71: Got new "Picassos from Bloomington" in the mail.
Will not allow anyone to be tortured at the 4077.
72: Got all his points and is being discharged
"Lorraine has the most fantastic body in downstate Illinois" — 36-24-34 with alabaster skin.
Wears "little, short, flimsy nighties"
Every Wednesday Lorraine gets together with Ella, Bea, Marie & Olive and goes to the "Old Red Barn" on Route 26 for lunch. They have two Dai Quire's, a watercress sandwich and Olive tells of her hysterectomy. They stay a couple of hours; kill an hour on the way back feeling yarn at the knit shop. Can't call Lorraine at 4:00 P.M. because Olive gets carsick. 4:30 P.M. is better. 5:00 P.M. is no good because Andrew has a trombone lesson. He's learning to play Ravel's Bolero. He'll call Lorraine at 5:30 P.M.
On the phone with Lorraine — she wants to re-cover the furniture — he only cares about the bed.
Lost weight in Korea — now a 34 waist — wants his brown double-breasted suit cleaned.
Mother-In-Law wore his suit to a party dressed as Conrad Nagel.
Talks to his daughter, "Janie-Poo."
Found a picture of him and Radar after he took out Radar's appendix *(see below) (In Episode 17, Hawkeye refers to taking out Radar's appendix).*
Gave Radar his father's thermometer — not oral.
Given a new suit and silk tie all handmade in Seoul

Margaret
Episode 50: Father gave her mother a small handgun on wedding night. Inscription on gun: *"To my little shot from her big shot — your loving husband, Lt. Col. Alvin F. Houlihan, Regular Army."*
51: Has a secret pocket on her garter belt, according to Hawkeye.
54: Gets excited when Frank flares his nostrils.
55: Reads "Beauty Secrets" magazine.
55: Drunk — confesses to "Captain Trapper John Intyre" she watches him play football in his swim trunks.
Drunk — tells Trapper that she's stuck with "Needle Nose."
56: Wanted to bite Frank in chow line.
57: Father gave mother a flask on wedding night. Inscription on flask: *"To my buttercup, from Alvin. The best things in life are worth waiting for. Bottoms up."*
Margaret keeps brandy in the flask
Has a large beaker of brandy hidden in a file cabinet in supply.
58: Serial number off foot locker — 53084499.
63: Ran naked in the snow every morning where she was raised.
Calls Trapper "John."
She and Frank both listen to Montovani, both trim the crust on their bread
Both hold hands while saying the Pledge of Allegiance.
64: Younger Sister, a Captain, is getting married.
Wants to borrow $240 from Frank as "Key Money" for sister's apartment.
Her father left her money but her mother drank it.
Half her salary goes toward bail for her mother, the other half for drying her out.
When her mother is sober, she's a klepto.

Mother caught in a store last week stuffing a radio up her jumper.

66: Made three mistakes on one operation working with Hawkeye.

67: An army brat — father was a colonel and mother was a nurse — she was conceived on maneuvers.

Thrills to the sight of a precise parade.

Could faint from looking down at her own brass.

69: Father served under MacArthur in the Calvary.

Father and MacArthur fought the Huks together in the Philippines.

Has an autographed photo of MacArthur on the mantle: *"Best wishes to my friend, 'Howitzer' Al Houlihan. Knock 'em dead, fella."*

MacArthur and her father exchanged shrunken tribesman heads that Christmas.

71: Her intellectual life would stagnate without Frank.

Frank

Episode 53: Has a tortoise-shell scrub brush with his initials in gold leaf sent by his "lovely mother."

Scrub brush is missing…again.

Nearly removed a man's only kidney — Trapper saved him.

Comes from a very strict family and wasn't allowed to talk at meals — couldn't even hum.

If anyone hummed they got a punch in the throat — became a snitch to talk to someone.

Will squeal on anyone — caught his best friend smoking in the bathroom but didn't report him.

He snitched on himself for not snitching on his friend.

54: Gets excited when Margaret says, "excited."

55: Polished Margaret's toenails.

Always gets stuck with, "Turn your head and cough."

Garbage officer.

Can play, "America the Beautiful" on the spoons.

56: Margaret's off-duty tee drives him crazy.

57: Has two warts on his back, according to Margaret.

Could've had an appointment to West Point, but his congressman is a Lithuanian.

58: Saves his haircuts for his mother — she glues them into flower shapes and puts them under glass.

Tells Margaret that the only thing that keeps him going are the letters from his wife.

60: Thinks the tape recorder microphone will squirt water in his face.

61: "Anybody that needs psychiatry is sick in the head."

A doctor should base his fee on 5 % of the patient's yearly income.

62: Knows a Greek back home — owns an ice cream parlor.

63: Blames shaking hands *(nervous in OR)* on a sinus condition.

Complains that enlisted get free uniforms while officers have to pay for theirs.

Uncle in Texarkana emotionally attached to a mule.

Proposes to Margaret when he thinks Trapper made time with her while the camp was under fire.

He and Margaret both listen to Montovani, both trim the crust on their bread, both hold hands saying the Pledge of Allegiance.

Belongs to The American Legion.

64: Only one to sign up for the Payroll Savings Plan for bonds.

Declares a patient froze to death, but had hypothermia, as per Trapper *(again)*.

Buys orange balloon for Margaret, but she pops it with a pin.

Agrees to lend her $240, but wants her to sign an I.O.U and 5% interest.

Has his shower cap and a chenille robe in Margaret's tent — told to pick them up.

66: Snaps a towel on Hawkeye's butt.

Will break out if he doesn't spend some time with Margaret.

Needs tweezers for a hair in his mole.

"Cursed with perfection"

As a child, always sorted his marbles according to size and degree of perfection: "Nibs, aggies, purees and shooters."

"A swell boy" with pressed corduroy knickers with matching stocking and sweater set.

Wife Louise has no sense of order — gets into his drawer and mixes up his marbles.

"Rough and Ready" is his after-shave.

Gets "C"-rations for dinner as a "jumper" under house arrest.

67: Flosses — 14 choruses of "G-d Bless America."

Slept with one of Margaret's boots under his pillow.

Wrote her the longest love-letter of his life — took up almost a whole role of toilet paper.

68: Officer of the Day — shot out the light in the Swamp.

69: Has been practicing surgery for 12 years.

Prepares a souvenir book with pictures and a complete history of the 4077th.

A picture of Frank in the latrine was placed in the above souvenir book for MacArthur.

70: Keeps money in a money belt.

Wants to be buried in Margaret's black sweater.

71: Reads *Readers Digest (seen)*.

Smokes a pipe *(only time)*.

If he were a woman, he'd find Colonel Flagg attractive.

72: Wishes he had taken ROTC in school *(in Episode 26, he had Gunnery experience in ROTC)*.

President of the Stamp Club — needed someone to lick stamps — he had the biggest tongue.

Radar

Episode 50: Would like to be a doctor, but doesn't like being around sick people that much.

51: His bear used to belong to his Brother.

Brother was 4 F and a box boy at a supermarket.

52: Files furniture polish under "P."

53: Donated blood twice — second time he fell asleep in the mess tent and someone siphoned him.

54: Received his annual issue of *Archie Comics*.

Last year the camp was 2,986 square feet — today it's 2,863 square feet — needs to find where it shrunk

Got "slaked" — Hawkeye and Trapper notice his voice is deeper and his skin cleared up.

55: Has either Scotch or bourbon.

4077th gave him the runs.

Parents never took off their clothes — "The skin was the devil's slipcover."
Has a tattoo of an anchor, tried to a Red Cross, but it was $1.50 (the anchor was 50 cents).

56: Can reach Commander Cornfield for the Bris ceremony by code for the next 4 hours.
Commander Cornfield is on the USS Essex off of Inchon.
Captain Epstein was rotated to temple Beth-El in Buffalo.
Called the 121st and spoke to Corporal Sweeny.
Radar translates Morse code for ceremony.
Margaret looks like Radar's older Sister — older sister is 37.

59: Ordered turkey to be marked "urgent" and received 5000 athletic supporters instead.
Can eat mess tent food because his mouth is tone-deaf.
Klinger looks like his dead aunt.
Doesn't know how good sex is *(in Episode 14, he is Engaged to Linda Sue)*.
The way Linda Sue and Elroy were behaving on his record would seem to imply he's had sex.

60: Has a Turkish to English dictionary put out by the UN.
Snores a tape-recorded message to Hawkeye's father.

61: His turtle was in the shower with Henry.
Has a zoo on the compound — skunk, raccoon, rabbit, and possum with dog tags for each.
"P" on dog tags means possum and they're grouped according to family.
Brought a field mouse to Henry to fit for glasses.
Pen Pal Wanda Nell McAndless, a 17 year-old girl from Catoosa, Oklahoma. She got Radar's name from a Red Cross lady off a list of American soldiers she could make happy with a letter.

61: Gets car sick when he reads in bed.
Has the key to the bottom of Henry's liquor cabinet
Says, "I'm gonna live past 18." *(in Episode 44, he's 19)*.

62: Has a raccoon, rabbit and a skunk — Doesn't know if skunk is a boy or girl.
"Deficiency of malnutrition" *(sarcastic?)*.
Vegetarian — "won't touch popcorn" *(sarcastic? Has been seen eating all kinds of meats)*.
Has 16 cats back home — Draft board found a fur ball in his throat.

62: Loves lamb, but not with peas and carrots — sends the lamb to Iowa
Has a 20 year-old turtle that he raised from a "pup."

63: Letter from his mother that he reads over the PA.

65: Tells Trapper that he learned to drive at the bumper cars *(in Episode 39, it was established that Hawkeye and Trapper taught him how to drive)*.

66: Had Klinger lengthen his pants by 3" due to chafing.
Has a glass pistol filled with candy
Has 18 months left in service, according to Henry.
Elevated shoes from O'Brien and Brophy's because he's always last to be picked for the team, looks girls straight in the throat and never sees over the crowd.
Only parade he's ever seen was the one he was in.
Everyone's always making fun of him.

67: Has two mounds of mashed potatoes for breakfast.
Short wave radio name is, "Snow White."
Likes to sleep with a night-light.

68: Ate one of Hawkeye's poker chips.
Wants to be an officer in his next life.

Missed school the year they taught about child birth.

Was sent to the movies when the cat had kittens.

72: Tells Henry that a drink makes his eyes red and he falls down *(drinks several Martinis in Seasons 1 and 2).*

After Henry describes Lorraine, he wants a drink.

The States are a day ahead plus 14 hours.

Spells F-R-A-J-I-L-E with one "J."

Father didn't have him till he was 63 and died the first time they played peek-a-boo.

Made a key chain for Henry with a Winchester fob: *"To Colonel HB from Corp. O'R, Korea, 1952."*

Was going to get Henry a bamboo flute, but they only had 3-holers.

Took Henry's measurements by tracing him in his sleep.

Klinger

Episode 49: Dying to get into a size 9.

51: Uses Flame d'Amour nail polish — A symphony in coordination.

53: Found $20,000 on a business girl.

Broke right heel on a pair of $14.95 shoes.

54: Wants to marry Lavern — dating since high school.

55: *Ploy:* 2 degrees of temperature.

Ploy: Touches up his x-ray.

Ploy: 20 minutes to live — blood pressure is 200 over 310.

57: Only one to attend Mulcahy's Sunday service.

Really an atheist but the service gives him a chance to wear his white gloves.

Dresses not working — may have to reenlist to prove he's crazy.

59: Looks like Radar's dead aunt, according to Radar.

Uncle in Chicago will kill anybody for $100.

Gets his lingerie from Chicago.

Needs 3 signatures for his "crazy papers" *(in Episode 41, he needs four signatures).*

67: Got his mink coat for his interview with "That shrink" at H.Q. Seoul.

"Shrink's" coat was a white fox, full-length and only wore it on leaves.

Short wave radio name is, "Grumpy."

Mother was mugged bringing him home from the hospital.

70: Serial number is 36-24-36.

Ploy: Offers Henry $477, plus $250 more in a locker at Grand Central Station, plus 25 cents for the key.

Makes $159 a month *(Offered Henry $477, which would be three months pay).*

71: Last week's pass word was "Bull Feathers."

Father Mulcahy

Episode 56: Sister Kathy is a nun — Sister Maria Angelica.

Went through indoctrination with Captain Epstein — "Eppy" — Jewish Chaplain with the 109th.

"Eppy" is a water skier and a paratrooper — "A bit meshuga, actually" — Conservative, not Orthodox.

Sister is a teacher and loves children — might want one of her own.

Gives his blessing for sister to leave the order and raise a family.

57: Does Protestant service at 11:00 AM.

His best subjects are "Turning the other cheek" and "The prodigal son."

Bottle of Scotch was a gift from a Marine for a successful confession.

Was on a troop ship and asked to give a lecture on "the sex thing."

63: As kids, sister learned to make apple pie from crabapples and used brown sugar — ate the whole pie before dinner.

First time he heard his mother swear was when she said, "What the hell's going on here."

Seen, Heard, Mentioned or Referenced – Season 3

Movies

Episode 50: Trapper says "We're off to see the wizard," a reference to *The Wizard of Oz* (1939).

Hawkeye says "Mutiny on the Bus," a reference to *Mutiny On the Bounty* (1935).

53: The soundtrack from *Blood and Sand* is piped into the O.R. (with Tyrone Power and Rita Hayworth, from 1941).

Hawkeye makes a reference to *The Barber of Seville*, first shown in 1904.

54: Henry mentions the movie *Gone with the Wind* (1939).

Radar mentions "The First Born of Godzilla" *(Not real)*.

55: Henry mentions "Godzilla and the Bobby-Soxer" *(Not real)*.

Henry mentions "Ma & Pa Kettle Have A Baby" *(Not real)*.

The Bells of Saint Mary (1945) is mentioned.

Trapper mentions *The Garden of Allah*, a 1936 movie, (also a novel and a hotel and villa in California).

56: Henry gets the movies, "Yvonne, Renee and Loretta in What The parrot Saw" and "Renee, Loretta and the Parrot in What Yvonne saw"

The movie *Brief Encounter* (1945) is mentioned

The episode title, "Life with Father" was originally a book by Clarence Day Jr. from 1936, a 1939 Broadway play, and a 1947 movie and TV series.

57: *Tin Pan Alley* (1940) is seen in the mess tent.

Mulcahy describes a Protestant movie about two sailors, one from Cleveland and one from a rural area. The one from Cleveland wrote to his high school sweetheart, a young girl with a megaphone on her chest. The one from the rural area got mixed up with a lady in a trailer with three other ladies plus a man with a whip. The man with the whip "Broke his wristwatch and everything."

59: Hawkeye refers to "Tillie & Mac" from the 1927 & 1941 movies *Tillie the Toiler*, based on a popular newspaper comic strip.

60: Hawkeye mentions "Dracula." Dracula's first appearance was in *Terror of Dracula* in 1922.

61: Henry makes a reference to *Godzilla*, first seen in 1954.

62: "The History of Athlete's Foot," mentioned by Henry.

63: *Gone with the Wind* (1939), mentioned.

Unidentified black & white WW II-era movie in the mess tent

The Yearling (1946), mentioned.

64: *The Littlest Rebel* (1935) seen in the mess tent, with Shirley Temple.

"Twelve Ways to Infiltrate A Nazi Bunker," mentioned *(Not real)*

Holdover movie from last week *(no name given)* mentioned over the PA.

65: *Madame Butterfly* (1932) is mentioned.

66: *Leave Her to Heaven* (1945) with Gene Tierney, Cornel Wilde and Vincent Price, seen in the mess tent.

Jiminy Cricket (1925), mentioned.

67: Klinger's radio name is "Grumpy" and Radar's name is "Snow White," from the Disney animated film from 1937.

67: Henry mentions a Sherlock Holmes movie that nobody went to, but not the title. The first Holmes film was a short in 1908.

68: Hawkeye mentions *The Student Prince*, a musical from 1957.

Hawkeye mentions "Judge Hardy." The first of the long-running series of Andy Hardy films is *You're Only Young Once* (1937).

Trapper mentions *The Good Earth* (1937)

Trapper mentions *Huck Finn* (1920)

Trapper mentions *Broadway Rose* (1922)

70: A new hygiene film, mentioned.

71: The title of this episode, "White Gold," is also a 1927 movie.

Songs

Episode 49: "I Love A Parade" *(General Steele sings)* Words by Ted Koehler, music by Harold Arlen. Seen in the 1932 Merry Melodies short of the same name. "Mississippi Mud" *(General Steele sings)* Written by James Cavanaugh and Harry Barris in 1928.

50: "North Korean Blues" Written and performed by Loudon Wainwright III.

51: "Retreat" *(Radar plays on the bugle, off-key).*

53: "Tramp, Tramp, Tramp (The Boys Are Marching) *(Hawkeye sings "…The boys are marching")* from the 1926 movie, *Tramp, Tramp, Tramp The Boys Are Marching.*

54: "The Wedding March" *(Hawkeye and Trapper hum)* Written by Felix Mendelssohn in 1842 as incidental music for "A Midsummer's Night Dream."

55: "I Got A Gal in Kalamazoo" *(Radar sings, over the PA)* Written by Harry Warren and Mack Gordon in 1942; from two Fox movies, *Orchestra Wives* (1942) and *Kiss Them For Me* (1957).
"America the Beautiful" *(Frank mentions he can play it on the spoons.)* Written by Katherine Lee Bates (1859-1929) This song was joined in 1910 with music from "Materna" written in 1882 by Samuel A. Ward.
"Cheek to Cheek" *(Jazzy instrumental heard on Margaret's record player)* Written by Irving Berlin, from the 1935 movie *Top Hat.*

56: "The Star Spangled Banner" *(Mentioned)* Written in 1814 By Francis Scott Key.
"Hava Nagila" *(Instrumental)* A traditional Hebrew folk song of uncertain origins whose title means "Let Us Rejoice," circa 1918.
"Kyrie Eleison" *(Mulcahy hums)* Part of the introductory rights of the Roman Catholic mass and a song which the faithful praise the Lord and implore His mercy.

57: "America I Love You" *(heard from the movie, seen in the Mess Tent)* from the 1940 movie *Tin Pan Alley.* Words by Edgar Leslie, music by Archie Gottler, from 1915.
"All Things Bright and Beautiful" *(Hawkeye and Trapper sing, "from page 216 of the Green Book")* Words by Cecil Francis Alexander in 1848, origins of the music are uncertain, but it could have been a monk.
"I Wish There Was A Radio Way Up In Heaven" *(Hawkeye sings)* Words by Joseph Manuel & Henry White, music by Willy White, from 1922.
"Taint No Sin to Take Off Your Skin and Dance around in Your Bones," *(Hawkeye sings "Come on in, take off your skin, and rattle around in your bones…")* Words by Edgar Leslie, music by Walter Donaldson, from 1929.

58: "When I Die" *(Sung by Captain Spalding, Hawkeye and Trapper)* Written by Loudon Wainwright III.
"Here Comes the Bride" See Episode 54 for details.
"Happy Days Are Here Again" *(Female Korean voice heard, over the PA)* See Episode 1 (page 128) for details.
"I Wonder If They Miss Us" Performed by Loudon Wainwright III

60: "Ons Heemecht" (Our Motherland) The National Anthem of Luxembourg, words by Michel Lentz, music by Jean-Antoine Zinnen First performed in 1864

61: "The Wayward Wind" (Mentioned in a pen-pal letter to Radar) Words by Herb Newman, music by Stan Lebowski, recorded by Gogi Grant in 1956.
"Pretty Thing, Diddy Wah Diddy" Written and performed by Bo Diddley in 1957.

62: "Come Home Father" *(Frank sings "Father dear Father come home with me now...")* Written by Henry Clay Work in 1864.
Traditional Greek music played live in the mess tent

63: "Chattanooga Choo-Choo" *(Big band arrangement, heard on the PA)* See Episode 1 (page 128) for details.

66: "Fools Rush In (Where Angels Fear to Tread)" *(Hawkeye sings "Fools rush in where angels fear to tread...")* Words by Johnny Mercer, music by Rube Bloom, from 1940. Originally a quote from "An Essay on Criticism" by Alexander Pope (1688-1744).
"Back in the Saddle Again" *(Sung by Colonel Reese)* Written by Gene Autry, from the 1941 movie of the same name.

64: "God Bless America" *(Frank hums)* Written by Irving Berlin in 1939.

67: "The Caissons Go Rolling Along" *(Sung by Hawkeye, Margaret and Klinger)* Written by Major Edmund L. Gruber in 1907 (he later became a brigadier general).

69: "Big Mac" Composed and performed by Loudon Wainwright III.
"Stars and Stripes Forever" See Episode 24 (page 130) for details.
"Big Mac Is Comin'" Composed and performed by Loudon Wainwright III.

71: Henry whistles a traditional Navy tune. McLean Stevenson served in the Navy.

72: "In A Little Spanish Town" *(Mentioned)* Words by Lewis & Young, music by Mabel Wayne, 1926.
"O Shepherd, Guide Thy Flock" *(Mulcahy hums)* Traditional Christian hymn.
"On Wisconsin" *(All sing)* Words by Carl Beck, music by W. T. Purdy from 1909. The Official State Song of Wisconsin
"Avalon" *(Mentioned)* Written by Richard Rose, Al Jolson and B. G. DeSylva, recorded in 1937. From the 1937 short *Auld Lang Syne*.
"America the Beautiful" *(Korean girls hum)* See Episode 55 for details.
"Sleepy Lagoon" *(Radar on bugle; played "Reveille" but it was really Sleep Lagoon fast)* Written by Eric Coats, from the 1943 movie of the same name.
"For He's A Jolly Good Fellow" *(Camp hums)* See Episode 13 (page 129) for details.

Prank Frank – Season 3

Episode 52: Had to give Colonel Wortman a pillow case count and the history of urology.
Sat on one of General Kelly's stars on Margaret's cot *(seen)*.

53: Tortoise shell scrub brush with his initials in gold leaf, given to him by his "lovely mother" is missing from the scrub room — again.
Hawkeye squirts a syringe in his face *(seen)*.

55: Gets stuck with "Turn your head and cough" for pre-marital physicals.
Garbage Officer.

56: Frank takes out the roll of film with pictures of circumcision and Trapper exposes the whole role *(seen)*.

57: Frank declares the 4077 dry, but Hawkeye, Margaret and Trapper get drunk behind his back *(seen)*.
Hawkeye and Trapper tell Frank where the booze came from:
Hawkeye: "11 string beans, 1 onion, ½ radish and 4 'banamas'"
Trapper: "Mix it all up and let it soak for 6 weeks — days."
Hawkeye: "Find the tallest tree and hang the stuff in an 'emina' bag and let it lay for 18 weeks — days."
After Frank leaves the Swamp, Margaret asks "Who was that?"

58: Radar uses Frank and Margaret's secret knock at Margaret's tent *(seen)*.
Hawkeye and Trapper filled his foxhole with peas and carrots *(mentioned)*.
Hawkeye and Trapper put a whoopee cushion in his helmet liner *(mentioned)*.
Frank chases Hawkeye and Trapper after listening in on his call to Margaret, then falls into his foxhole *(seen)*.
Trapper parks a jeep over the foxhole with Frank in it and he can't get out.
Hawkeye, Trapper, Henry, Radar, Mulcahy and Klinger watch Frank's wedding movie behind his back.
Frank gets his face stuck to a fly strip in his wedding movie.
Hawkeye gives Margaret a long kiss goodbye…while Frank watches.

61: Hawkeye and Trapper throw magazines at Frank in the Swamp.

62: Drunk and dancing, he leans to his side and falls down.
Hawkeye and Trapper won't back Frank against charges of impersonating a priest.

63: Trapper makes Frank think something went on between him and Margaret.

64: Margaret sticks a pin in his balloon.

66: Hawkeye punches Frank in the left eye after Frank snaps a towel on Hawkeye's butt.
When Colonel Reese yells "Rape!" and accuses Frank, he is placed under house arrest, even though the charges are not true.
He gets C-rations for dinner while Hawkeye got steak when he was under house arrest. (The cook made steak for Hawkeye when he heard Hawkeye punched Frank.)

68: Caught eavesdropping by Henry's office door.

69: Hawkeye calls Frank "Dr. Hitler" because he's burning books (literary classics).
Picture of Frank in the latrine placed in his souvenir book for MacArthur.

70: Described by peddler Kim Chun Quoc as "Fertilizer Face"

71: "I think they're fooling around with my coffee again."
Can't open Margaret's snaps.

Appearances - Season 3

Alda, Robert... Episode 65 *(Major Anthony Borelli)*
Arbus, Allan ....Episode 53 *(Major Sidney Freedman)*
Christopher, William.................... Episode 49, 50, 53, 54, 56, 57, 58, 63, 64, 65, 66, 67, 68, 70, 71, 72 *(Father Mulcahy)*
Cleveland, Odessa................................. Episode 53 *(Lieutenant Ginger Bayliss)*
Curtis, Keene .... Episode 52 *(Colonel Wortman)*
Dole, Orlando.. Episode 53 *(Ethiopian Soldier)*
Dugan, Dennis...Episode 68 *(Private Danny McShane)*
Eccles, Ted .... Episode 62 *(Private Chapman)*
Erdman, Dennis..Episode 49 *(Harrison)*
Farr, Jamie....................... Episode 49, 50, 51, 53, 54, 55, 57, 58, 59, 60, 63, 64, 66, 67, 69, 70, 71, 72 *(Corporal Klinger)*
Fujikawa, Jerry... Episode 51 *(Sang Yu)*
Fujikawa, Jerry.. Episode 68 *(Dr. Pak)*
Goldman, Roy.. Episode 54 *(Corpsman)*
Goldman, Roy... Episode 68 *(Orderly)*
Gregory, James........................... Episode 52 *(General "Iron Guts" Kelly)*
Gruber, Robert...Episode 68 *(Sergeant)*
Haymer, Johnny...Episode 64, 68, 70 *(Sergeant Zale)*
Herbeck, Bobby ....Episode 53 *(Patient)*
Hicks, Hilly.................... Episode 71 *(Corporal Perkins (Corporal Johnson)*
Hoffman, Basil.. Episode 59 *(Major Pfiefer)*
Horino, Tad .... Episode 51 *(1st Korean)*
Horino, Tad ....Episode 65 *(Bartender)*
Hoshi, Shizuko ....Episode 61 *(Rosie)*
Jarvis, Graham ....Episode 69 *(Colonel Whiteman)*
Jay, Alberta.. Episode 52 *(Anesthetist)*
Joe, Jeanne..Episode 68 *(Mrs. Kwang)*
Karras, Alex..Episode 54 *(Corporal Lyle Wesson)*
Keller, Michael.. Episode 60 *(Lieutenant Le Clerq)*
Li, Pat..Episode 68 *(Soong Hi)*
Lowens, Curt ....Episode 60 *(Colonel Blanche)*
Mabrey, Greg..Episode 54 *(Pasco)*
Maher, Joseph ....Episode 65 *(Major Taylor)*
Mako... Episode 50 *(Dr. Lin Tam)*
Marshall, Edward..Episode 63 *(Delboss)*
Marshall, Pat .... Episode 70 *(Lieutenant Nelson)*
Maxwell, Jeff ....Episode 51, 59, 61, 66, 70 *(Igor)*
Maxwell, Jeff ....Episode 52 *(G.I.)*
Maxwell, Jeff .... Episode 54 *(Server)*
Mettey, Lynette... Episode 49 *(Nurse Baker)*
Mitchell, Bobbie .... Episode 52, 53, 58 *(Nurse Able)*
Mitchell, Bobbie .... Episode 57, 61, 66 *(Nurse Baker)*
Morgan, Harry............................. Episode 49 *(Major General Bartford Hamilton Steele)*
Moritz, Louisa ....Episode 63 *(Nurse Sanchez)*
Murad, Sirri .... Episode 60 *(The Turkish Soldier)*
Nakahara, Kellye .... Episode 60 *(Nurse Able)*
Nakahara, Kellye ....Episode 64 *(Nurse Charlie)*
Nakahara, Kellye .... Episode 66 *(Nurse)*
Oh, Soon-Taik .... Episode 68 *(Mr. Kwang)*
O'Keefe, Michael ....Episode 61 *(Corporal Travis)*

Broadcast/Production Order – Season 3

Broadcast

49: The General Flipped At Dawn *(9/10/1974)*

50: Rainbow Bridge *(9/17/1974)*

51: Officer Of The Day *(9/24/1974)*

52: Iron Guts Kelly *(10/1/1974)*

53: O.R. *(10/8/1974)*

54: Springtime *(10/15/1974)*

55: Check-Up *(10/22/1974)*

56: Life With Father *(10/29/1974)*

57: Alcoholics Unanimous *(11/12/1974)*

58: There Is Nothing Like A Nurse *(11/19/1974)*

59: Adam's Rib *(11/26/1974)*

60: A Full, Rich Day *(12/3/1974)*

61: Maddogs And Servicemen *(12/10/1974)*

62: Private Charles Lamb *(12/31/1974)*

63: Bombed *(1/7/1975)*

64: Bulletin Board *(1/14/1975)*

65: The Consultant *(1/21/1975)*

66: House Arrest *(2/4/1975)*

67: Aid Station *(2/11/1975)*

68: Love And Marriage *(2/18/1975)*

69: Big Mac *(2/25/1975)*

70: Payday *(3/4/1975)*

71: White Gold *(3/11/1975)*

72: Abyssinia, Henry *(3/18/1975)*

Production

49: (B301) Rainbow Bridge

50: (B302) Life With Father

51: (B303) Springtime

52: (B304) Iron Guts Kelly

53: (B305) Payday

54: (B306) O.R.

55: (B307) Officer Of The Day

56: (B308) The General Flipped At Dawn

57: (B309) There Is Nothing Like A Nurse

58: (B310) Private Charles Lamb

59: (B311) A Full, Rich Day

60: (B312) Check-Up

61: (B313) Big Mac

62: (B314) Alcoholics Unanimous

63: (B315) House Arrest

64: (B316) Adam's Rib

65: (B317) Maddogs And Servicemen

66: (B318) The Consultant

67: (B319) White Gold

68: (B320) Bombed

69: (B321) Love And Marriage

70: (B322) Aid Station

71: (B323) Bulletin Board

72: (B324) Abyssinia, Henry

Season 4

With the departure of McLean Stevenson, (and the way in which his character was written out) after Season 3, Season 4 was bound to be different. Over the hiatus, Wayne Rogers decided to leave. Two main, popular characters were gone, and two very different ones were about to replace them. A military base offers the perfect setting for the arrival and departures of characters. So, these changes fit right in. Harry Morgan was brought in as Colonel Sherman Potter. Unlike Blake, Potter was regular army. He was also seasoned, and not one to be fooled with. Yet, Morgan brought his own, unmistakable humor to the role. Mike Farrell was brought in to replace Wayne Rogers. It could be said that Wayne Rogers' personality suited him as more of a comedic actor who could do drama, whereas Mike Farrell's personality suited him as more of a dramatic actor who could do comedy. With the change of characters came a change in the dynamics at the 4077th. With Potter handily in charge, Hot Lips and Frank could no longer pose as much of a threat as authority figures. Similarly, Hawkeye and BJ were a different team than Hawkeye and Trapper. Where it had been Hawkeye and Trapper versus Hot Lips and Frank, the character changes marked the beginning of everyone venturing off on their own. Margaret began to be more serious, and Frank became sillier. It may have taken Alda a few episodes to completely adapt to his new tent mate. At times, it seems as though Hawkeye attempts to bounce jokes off of or react to BJ in the manner he did with Trapper. But, Rogers and Farrell had totally different personalities, so the character of BJ responds differently. Jamie Farr's name was added to the credits, and along with William Christopher, was utilized more. But, despite all the changes, Gelbart and Reynolds were still running the show. So, it had the same feel to it. Adding to the more serious feel of Season 4 was a particularly dramatic scene in which BJ tends to his first wounded soldiers. There are funny episodes, like "Hey Doc," and poignant, yet funny ones, like "Dear Mildred." (Watch for the classic return of Richard Lee Sung, as the sculptor of the wooden bust of Potter) "Quo Vadis, Captain Chandler?" is one of the most riveting and unusual episodes of *M*A*S*H*, as a soldier believes he's Jesus Christ. Larry Gelbart, the creator of *M*A*S*H* and genius behind it all, decided to leave after the fourth season. His final episode was a classic, "The Interview." Gelbart's departure would bring the biggest change to the show.

Welcome to Korea – 9/12/1975
Season 4 / Episode 73 and Episode 74
Production 76 and Production 78 – G504 / G506

Columbia House VHS Tape . . . . *New Staff (Catalog # 10997)*
Fox DVD . . . . *Season 4, Disc 1*

Alan Alda, Mike Farrell, Harry Morgan
Loretta Swit, Larry Linville, Gary Burghoff, Jamie Farr
(This cast will remain in place until next season.)

Produced by Gene Reynolds and Larry Gelbart
Written by Everett Greenbaum & Jim Fritzell and Larry Gelbart
Directed by Gene Reynolds

William Christopher . . . . Father Mulcahy
Tom Dever . . . . M.P. Lieutenant
Robert Karnes . . . . The Colonel
Ted Ziegler . . . . Sergeant Dale
Reid Cruickshanks . . . . Staff Sergeant
Nat Jones . . . . G.I.

Copyright 1975 – 20th Century Fox Film Corporation

Non-Credited Appearances . . . . Jeff Maxwell, Roy Goldman

Chapters

1:	*Main Titles*	11:	*A.W.O.L. – 27:48*
2:	*Frank in Charge – 0:49*	12:	*Back to the 4077th – 29:04*
3:	*Back from Tokyo – 5:57*	13:	*The Minefield – 31:34*
4:	*Trapper's Gone-7:11*	14:	*A Flat Tire – 35:00*
5:	*Hunnicutt's Papers – 11:14*	15:	*Guerillas – 36:31*
6:	*Off to Kimpo- 12:58*	16:	*Mortar Attack – 39:02*
7:	*Ten Minutes Late – 16:33*	17:	*First Day at School – 41:57*
8:	*B.J. – 17:46*	18:	*Rest Stop – 43:59*
9:	*The Officer's Club – 20:17*	19:	*The Jeep Thief – 47:45*
10:	*The General's Jeep – 26:33*	20:	*End Titles – 49:51*

Closing Stills

1: *Radar, the Corporal Captain*
2: *Korean girls looking for mines*
3: *B.J. & Hawkeye tend to wounded soldier*
4: *Frank in Jeep with the M.P's*
5: *Hawkeye & B.J. on the way to the showers*

Synopsis: In the fourth season opener, and the first hour-long episode, Hawkeye returns from leave only to find out that Trapper has gone home and is disappointed that he didn't leave a note. Radar gets permission to go to Kimpo to pickup Trapper's replacement and, going against Frank's orders, Hawkeye goes with him hoping to see Trapper before he takes off, but he's too late: he left 10 minutes ago, while Radar meets Trapper's replacement, Captain BJ Hunnicutt. With nothing left to do in Kimpo, Hawkeye and Radar decide to go back to camp, then realize their jeep was stolen. In the meantime, Hawkeye heads for the Transient Officer's Club at the airfield, but this is not like the officer's club at the 4077th and Radar is reluctant to go inside. Borrowing some of Hunnicutt's captain's bars, Hawkeye promotes Radar to the new rank of "Corporal-Captain," which makes Radar nervous when a full-bird colonel comes over to investigate someone wearing corporal's

The road traveled and seen in many episodes.

strips and captain's bars. After stealing a general's jeep, they head back to the 4077th and on the way, BJ is rudely introduced to war when a platoon comes under fire and he begins to treat the wounded. Hawkeye helps BJ back to his feet and they continue on, but stop at Rosie's first, making BJ's introduction to Frank and Margaret a memorable one.

Commentary by Larry Gelbart: "We found some of the M*A*S*H movie locations and they served as Kimpo. As I recall, the reference to The Last of the Mohicans as the only book Hawkeye's father ever read came from the original novel, a book I must have read a dozen times. For the record, my own father and mother, being teen-age immigrants who were put to work the day they stepped off the boat rather than being allowed an education, never read as much as one book between them. That fact made it quite credible, to me, at least, that someone could have a parent much like Hawkeye's dad. Jerry Colonna was a big band trombonist, with a huge, handlebar moustache. The reference to him was because of his long association with Bob Hope, who of course, entertained during the Korean conflict. Colonna was also a terrific guy and it was nice to be able to give him a bit of posthumous recognition. The scoring for that episode was done by Pete Rugolo. One of the top big band arrangers in the swing era, he was responsible for the late Stan Kenton's most memorable orchestrations. In 'Welcome to Korea,' Pete recreated the sounds of many of the bands of that era — Glenn Miller, Benny Goodman, etc.

"The implication was that Radar acted so reflexively, he brushed his fear to one side to save the girls — amazing even himself in a cooler moment of hindsight. BJ was named after the show's Director of Photography Bill Jurgensen, called by his initials by everyone connected with the series. It was just our salute to a very fine craftsman."

PA Announcement by unknown at MATS in Kimpo
PA Announcement by Todd Sussman

Authors' Notes: Jamie Farr has been added to the opening credits starting with this, the fourth season. William Christopher will be added to the opening credits next season.

The series' first hour-long episode is actually two episodes: 73 and 74, and were the 76th and 78th episodes produced. The first half has the production code G504; the second has the production code G506. This will hold true for the remaining hour-long episodes and will only be explained here, as this was the first.

Shower times are seen again, and they remain, *MEN 1600-1630 hours / WOMEN 1630-1700 hours.*

In Chapter 3, the view from Potter's windows shows a building with windows through the left window and trees and mountains through the right.

In Chapter 4, the view changes mid-scene to trees out the left window and buildings out the right, and changes back again mid-scene to the original view from Chapter 3.

The jeep used to get BJ has the serial number, 18210717, but it's not the same jeep they arrive back at camp with since it became one of the jeeps at the MP checkpoint.

A note about vehicles and their serial numbers: In "Welcome to Korea," Hawkeye reaches a checkpoint on the way to Kimpo with Radar. One of the jeep's serial numbers is 2A401. This is also the same jeep that Hawkeye steals from the General and the same jeep Potter first arrives in. The same jeeps are used for various transport purposes throughout the series. An example of this is in the episode, "The Late Captain Pierce." The 4077th's bus has the serial number, 18210715. This does not change since there was only one bus. It's also the same bus and serial number used in "Rainbow Bridge" and the same bus and serial number that Lieutenant Detmuller from Quartermaster Corps, Morgue Detail uses in "The Late Captain Pierce" to pickup bodies.

Another example of this is in the episode "Hey, Doc." Lieutenant Chivers, the British officer that needed attention on his foot, arrives in jeep number 20963388 to bring the Scotch for Hawkeye and BJ as payment. This is also Potter's jeep.

In Chapter 8, there's a boom shadow on Radar's back-left shoulder.

In Chapter 9, Hawkeye tells BJ that there are 16 UN countries fighting in Korea. There were 17.

The sign indicating the tailor that was present in two episodes in Season 3 is not there in this episode.

In Chapter 18, a fight breaks out in Rosie's. Two men fall through a paper window, although it's made to sound like they went through glass.

In the early years of *M*A*S*H* (1973 to 1975), Alan Alda also worked on writing scripts for a TV show he created with actress Nina Merson called *We'll Get By.* Alda and Merson had appeared in a play called *The King of Hearts.* However, the show only lasted from March 14 to May 30, 1975 and aired on Friday at 8:30 to 9:00 PM on CBS.

Change of Command – 9/19/1975

Season 4 / Episode 75 / Production 73 – G501

Columbia House VHS Tape . . . . *New Staff (Catalog # 10997)*
Fox DVD . . . . *Season 4, Disc 1*

Alan Alda, Mike Farrell, Harry Morgan
Loretta Swit, Larry Linville, Gary Burghoff, Jamie Farr

Produced by Gene Reynolds and Larry Gelbart
Written by Jim Fritzell & Everett Greenbaum
Directed by Gene Reynolds
William Christopher . . . . Father Mulcahy
Copyright 1975 – 20th Century Fox Film Corporation

Non-Credited Appearances . . . . Jeff Maxwell, Kellye Nakahara

Chapters

1: Main Titles	6: Colorful Officers – 11:51
2: A Dream Come True – 0:49	7: Klinger's Problem – 14:48
3: The New C.O. – 2:08	8: Potter's First Day – 15:49
4: Frank's Bad News – 4:26	9: One of the Boys – 21:44
5: Colonel Potter – 8:33	10: End Titles – 24:56

Closing Stills

1: Potter in his office
2: Hawkeye
3: B.J.
4: Margaret & Frank
5: Radar delivers mail

Synopsis: When Radar informs Frank that he's been replaced, Frank takes the news surprisingly well, then throws a temper tantrum in Margaret's tent. Colonel Potter arrives, sets up his office and now wants to see his officers, but Frank, upset at not getting command, has ran away. Since Potter hasn't been in an operating room for 2 years, Hawkeye wants Margaret to keep an eye on him in OR, but Potter handles the OR well. When the session is over, Potter wants a drink, and Hawkeye knows just where he can get one. Frank finally reports for duty, just in time to hear Potter compliment Klinger on his new outfit.

Commentary by Larry Gelbart: "Once we agreed we wanted Harry Morgan, the process of creating a character for him started. I had a good friend named Dr. Sherman. I gave his name to Potter. The T in Sherman T. Potter was inspired (if one single letter can have such a lofty pedigree) by the fact that the S in Harry S. Truman was put there only because the late president thought he ought to have a middle initial even though he did not in fact have a middle name. We were, when we were lucky, several minutes over what the show's length had to be in terms of airtime. Sometimes we couldn't trim as much as we wanted because the show would have been short of that time. We would often cut anyway, making us short, but we shoot 'pick up' scenes to make up for the lost, not so precious minutes. Very often the new material would be a new Radar at the desk scene, since those were the easiest for time and budget constraints."

PA Announcements by Todd Sussman
PA Announcement by Radar

Authors' Notes: The view out of Potter's office windows shows a building only – no trees anywhere, but this will change in Chapter 6 to show trees and mountains out the right window.

The Swamp in Chapter 3 has no dartboard.

In Chapter 4, Frank calls Igor "Sergeant."

Potterism: "Horse hockey"

In Chapter 7, the Swamp still has no dartboard.

The scrub room sinks are in the middle of the room, side by side.

The picture of Mrs. Potter is actually Mrs. Harry Morgan. He asked if this can be used, and the producers had no objections (according to Larry Gelbart).

It Happened One Night – 9/26/1975

Season 4 / Episode 76 / Production 74 – G502

Columbia House VHS Tape . . . . *On The Move (Catalog # 10998)*
Fox DVD . . . . *Season 4, Disc 1*

Alan Alda, Mike Farrell, Harry Morgan
Loretta Swit, Larry Linville, Gary Burghoff, Jamie Farr

Produced by Gene Reynolds and Larry Gelbart
Teleplay by Larry Gelbart & Simon Muntner
Directed by Gene Reynolds

Christopher Allport . . . . Abbott
Darren O'Connor . . . . Private Jenkins
Copyright 1975 – 20th Century Fox Film Corporation

Non-Credited Appearances . . . . Roy Goldman, Gwen Farrell

Chapters

1: *Main Titles*
2: *Cold and Dark – 0:49*
3: *The Night Shift – 5:38*
4: *Margaret's Note – 8:14*
5: *The Shelling – 9:33*
6: *Just A Scratch – 13:31*
7: *Patient Problems – 17:13*
8: *Shell Shock – 21:23*
9: *Margaret's Surprise – 23:51*
10: *End Titles – 24:56*

Closing Stills

1: *Hawkeye in Post-Op*
2: *B.J. in Post-Op*
3: *Margaret in bed with a book*
4: *Klinger in helmet and mink coat*
5: *Radar*

Synopsis: It's midnight and a bone-chilling 2 degrees below zero when Radar wakes Hawkeye and Margaret for post-op duty. Frank reports that Edwards, BJ's patient, hasn't been any trouble until Margaret notices his blood pressure is 85 over 50, a Chinese POW is a "crafty devil," despite having 13 broken bones, and a GI is in danger of pulling out IV tubes when the shelling starts. After Edwards receives three more units of blood and the last unit of B+ is administered, there's still no improvement and BJ realizes he has to operate on the man again, this time successfully.

Commentary by Larry Gelbart: "Simon Munter was a solid, decent guy. He was brought to my attention by another such man, his cousin, Hy Averback."

PA Announcement by Todd Sussman

Authors' Notes: In Chapter 2, not only is part of the Swamp out of focus, it's also missing the dartboard.

Margaret is seen reading *A Kindled Flame* (written by Margaret Pedler in 1931), which she was reading in Season 3.

Margaret's tent, for this episode, has wooden walls. Even though it's very cold, the tents usually had canvas over the screens that could be seen moving around with the wind blowing.

When Klinger thinks he's dying from a gunshot wound that Hawkeye can barely find, he says his goodbyes to Harry and Frieda. Harry and Frieda were not only Jonathon Tuttle's parents from Season 1, they're also the names of Larry Gelbart's parents.

There's another Colonel Potter, but this Colonel was the PX C.O. who just retired and shipped home a temple to open as a drive-in.

Klinger's blood type is B-positive.

The Late Captain Pierce – 10/3/1975

Season 4 / Episode 77 / Production 79 – G507

Columbia House VHS Tape . . . . *Benjamin Franklin Pierce (Catalog # 11002)*
Fox DVD . . . . *Season 4, Disc 1*

Alan Alda, Mike Farrell, Harry Morgan
Loretta Swit, Larry Linville, Gary Burghoff, Jamie Farr

Produced by Gene Reynolds and Larry Gelbart
Written by Glen Charles & Les Charles
Directed by Alan Alda

Eldon Quick . . . . Captain Pratt
Richard Masur. . . . . Lieutenant "Digger" Detmuller
Sherry Steffens . . . . .Nurse Able
Kellye Nakahara . . . . Nurse Baker

Copyright 1975 – 20th Century Fox Film Corporation

Non-Credited Appearances. . . . . Jeff Maxwell, Dennis Troy

Chapters

1:	Main Titles	6:	No Mail, No Money – 14:25
2:	Phone Call from the States – 0:49	7:	An Un-Person – 18:26
3:	The Man from the Morgue – 5:24	8:	Dead Serious – 20:18
4:	Dead Dead – 9:07	9:	Don't Cry, Dad – 23:46
5:	Hawkeye's Wake – 12:25	10:	End Titles – 24:56

Closing Stills

1: *Digger*
2: *Klinger*
3: *Potter*
4: *B.J.*
5: *Hawkeye on the phone with his father*

Synopsis: Nobody can understand why Hawkeye's father calls and insists on talking only to BJ, but when Lieutenant Detmuller from Quartermaster Corps, Morgue Detail shows up, he shows Hawkeye a copy of a death certificate made out in his name. Worse is the original copy has been sent to the next of kin, Mr. Pierce, who now thinks his son is dead, and due to General Eisenhower's impending visit to Korea, new strict security measures ban all calls, in or out. Expressing his dire concern over his father mourning him, and since he's "dead," he packs his duffle bag and gets on Detmuller's bus to go home. But when the bus gets to Rosie's, choppers are heard and Hawkeye heads for the O.R., after which, he finally talks to his father and would like his allowance sent.

Commentary by Eldon Quick: "Alan was always ready to run lines or explore possibilities in a scene. Loretta was, often, just one of the boys. Larry was building his own kit built glider (not a model, but a real one for a human pilot). Since I was very interested in flying and aircraft, I enjoyed talking to him about that. Perhaps the most fun, was with Bill and Jamie recalling favorite scenes from past segments."

PA Announcement by Todd Sussman

Authors' Notes: This is the first episode without Gary Burghoff. Subsequently, he began appearing in only about 15 episodes per season.

The serial number on the bus, 18210715, was usually seen in bold print, but in this episode, it's faded.

Hawkeye's serial number is US 19905607. He'll have a different serial number later in the series.

The sinks in the scrub room are on the front (camera) wall side by side.

BJ's serial number is 39729966. (*Note:* BJ's serial number, which is actually Larry Gelbart's real army number, is the same as Tuttle's from Season 1.)

Across the side from Rosie's is another establishment rarely seen, "Hollywood Tails."

Richard Masur, who played the part of Lieutenant Detmuller, has appeared in over 80 movies and had recurring roles on the television shows *Rhoda* (from 1974 to 1978) and *One Day At A Time* (between 1975 and 1976). In January 2006, he began another recurring role on the soap opera *All My Children*. Mr. Masur, born in 1948, has also served two terms as the President of The Screen Actor's Guild (SAG).

Hey, Doc – 10/10/1975

Season 4 / Episode 78 / Production 82 – G510

Columbia House VHS Tape . . . . *Doctor's Orders (Catalog # 11003)*
Fox DVD . . . . *Season 4, Disc 1*

Alan Alda, Mike Farrell, Harry Morgan
Loretta Swit, Larry Linville, Gary Burghoff, Jamie Farr

Produced by Gene Reynolds and Larry Gelbart
Written by Rick Mittleman
Directed by William Jurgensen

Frank Marth . . . . .Colonel Griswald
Bruce Kirby . . . . Sergeant Kimble
William Christopher . . . . Father Mulcahy
Ted Hamilton . . . . Lieutenant Chivers

Copyright 1975 – 20th Century Fox Film Corporation

Non-Credited Appearances . . . . Kellye Nakahara, Jeff Maxwell, Dennis Troy,
Roy Goldman

Chapters

1: *Main Titles*
2: *Kimble's Condition – 0:48*
3: *Sniper Trouble – 3:54*
4: *The Offending Digit – 5:09*
5: *A Delicate Disease – 8:07*
6: *A Fake Profile – 13:13*
7: *Another Sniper Attack – 16:08*
8: *The Tank Expert – 20:25*
9: *Blackmail – 23:59*
10: *End Titles – 24:56*

Closing Stills

1: *Hawkeye injects Griswald*
2: *Lieutenant Chivers*
3: *Potter & Radar*
4: *Margaret helps Frank after tank ride*
5: *Klinger in the shower*

Synopsis: When a tank commander shows up at the 4077th to visit one of his men, he needs a favor from Hawkeye that, if seen on his record, could have certain ramifications. In return for Hawkeye's discretion, the colonel offers his assistance if and when needed, but when the camp comes under sniper fire, the colonel is too busy for Hawkeye. After Hawkeye threatens the colonel with the possibility of his private records being seen, he sends a tank to scare off the sniper, and Frank scares the camp when he operates the tank.

Commentary by Larry Gelbart: "As you probably know, lighting plays a major role in cinematography, and so both men (Dominick Palmer, William Jurgensen) were responsible for the look of the show. Unfortunately, the network standardized the lighting of every show they transmitted, so that, all too often, this extra effort to create a certain mood was for naught."

PA Announcement by Todd Sussman

Authors' Notes: The Swamp in Chapter 2 has no dartboard.
A rare shower scene with Radar in the right stall and Klinger in the left.
Father Mulcahy is wearing a bathrobe that was usually worn by Henry.

As previously noted, Lieutenant Chivers arrives in a jeep with the serial number 20963388, which is also Potter's jeep.

A barber's tent, which is rarely seen, can be seen in this episode on the Ranch set. (In previous episodes, we've seen Trapper cutting Hawkeye's hair and in the background, we've also seen Kellye giving Jeff Maxwell a haircut.)

In Chapter 7, there's a building with a door seen through Potter's office windows.

Also in Chapter 7, the captioning on the DVD lists Radar as the PA announcer, when it's actually Todd Sussman.

The Swamp in Chapter 8 is still missing the dartboard, but even more rare is the interior of the Swamp on the Ranch set.

Chapter 8 has one of the more memorable scenes when Potter puts a bullet into his jeep after Frank flattens it with the tank.

Frank trained for a week in a tank at Fort Benning, but you'd never know it as he nearly destroys the entire camp with it. Fort Benning is also where we see Margaret in a nurse's uniform with General Hammond in the Pilot episode.

The Bus – 10/17/1975

Season 4 / Episode 79 / Production 84 – G512

Columbia House VHS Tape . . . . *Damaged Goods (Catalog # 11004)*
Fox DVD . . . . *Season 4, Disc 1*

Alan Alda, Mike Farrell, Harry Morgan
Loretta Swit, Larry Linville, Gary Burghoff, Jamie Farr

Produced by Gene Reynolds and Larry Gelbart
Written by John D. Hess
Directed by Gene Reynolds

Soon-Teck Oh . . . . .North Korean Soldier
(No extras were used in this episode.)

Copyright 1975 – 20th Century Fox Film Corporation

Chapters

1: *Main Titles*	6: *Worried About Radar – 15:13*
2: *Lost – 0:47*	7: *The Wounded Prisoner – 16:36*
3: *The Broken Bus – 6:22*	8: *Radar's Return – 20:17*
4: *The Walkie Talkie – 8:46*	9: *A Korean Mechanic – 21:55*
5: *Stories of Romance – 12:22*	10: *End Titles – 24:54*

Closing Stills

1: *North Korean soldier on the bus*
2: *Frank*
3: *B.J. on the bus*
4: *Potter smiling on the bus*
5: *Radar on the bus nervous*

Synopsis: While Radar drives the doctors back to camp from a 38th Parallel Medical Society meeting, they become lost in the woods, but when Potter orders the bus back to where it started for new directions, it won't start. The situation is compounded realizing they have no food, no water, no blankets and no communications. They also realize the 4077th is 20 miles away, and they might be in enemy territory. After an unsuccessful attempt at repairing the bus, and in the middle of the night, help arrives from the least likely source.

Commentary by Gene Reynolds: "The Bus was fun in the wilds of the Fox ranch. It rained like hell. Very exciting."

Authors' Notes: There are no PA announcements in this episode.
There is no laugh track in this episode.
The entire episode takes place in or just outside the bus.
In Chapter 2, Hawkeye writes the name "Kilroy" on the bus window. This is the first of three times we'll see the name on the window, and all three are slightly different. The second time is in Chapter 5 and the third time is in Chapter 9.

Dear Mildred – 10/24/1975

Season 4 / Episode 80 / Production 77 – G505

Columbia House VHS Tape . . . . Dear Someone (Catalog # 11001)
Fox DVD . . . . Season 4, Disc 1

Alan Alda, Mike Farrell, Harry Morgan
Loretta Swit, Larry Linville, Gary Burghoff, Jamie Farr

Produced by Gene Reynolds and Larry Gelbart
Written by Everett Greenbaum & Jim Fritzell
Directed by Alan Alda

William Christopher . . . . Father Mulcahy
Richard Lee Sung . . . . Cho Man Chin
Buck Young . . . . Dan
Patricia Stevens . . . . Nurse Able
Barbara Christopher *(Mrs. William Christopher)* . . . . Nurse O'Connor
Copyright 1975 – 20th Century Fox Film Corporation

Non-Credited Appearances . . . . Jeff Maxwell, Kellye Nakahara, Dennis Troy,
Roy Goldman

Chapters

1: Main Titles	6: An Anniversary Present – 15:01
2: A Letter to Mildred – 0:50	7: My First Horsectomy – 17:46
3: Potter Problems – 5:31	8: A Dandy Likeness – 20:29
4: The Singing Chaplain – 8:39	9: Radar's Gift – 23:11
5: Radar's Roundup – 11:29	10: End Titles – 24:56

Closing Stills

1: Mulcahy & O'Connor sing a duet
2: Hawkeye & B.J. watch the duet
3: Frank & Margaret watch the duet
4: Potter in his office
5: Radar brings Potter a horse

Synopsis: In a letter to his wife, Colonel Potter acknowledges the fact that their anniversary will again be spent away from each other and that he's still trying to get used to his new command. Radar too, is trying to adjust to a new CO and he's having a difficult time of it. But after Radar helps an injured horse, he gives it to Potter for his anniversary, leaving the Colonel speechless and deeply moved by the gesture.

Commentary by Richard Lee Sung: "It was a shock when we were doing 'Dear Mildred,' and Alan Alda came up to me. I think it was the second day of filming and he said to me 'You know, I couldn't sleep last night, and decided you should forget the accent. Portray this man as lost in the war, and well educated. He's a businessman. Just play him as a human being.' I was so shocked. They usually want a certain image, and for Alan Alda to tell me that was a shock. No one had ever done that in Hollywood, in all the years I'd worked. I haven't worked that much because I have to wait for Asian roles. *Kung Fu* and *M*A*S*H* was where all the Asian American actors got to work. So, that was a story I really wanted to tell. I wish the whole world knew how wonderful Alan Alda is...how caring, in trying to make things right."

PA Announcements by Todd Sussman

Authors' Notes: "Mildred" is the name of Larry Gelbart's cousin.

Radar tells Potter that he doesn't smoke. Between Seasons 1 and 2, Radar has had five cigars.

Nurse O'Connor, the woman Father Mulcahy performs a duet with, is actually Barbara Christopher, William Christopher's wife.

At least four different horses were used for this episode.

Radar mentions that Henry used to let him keep "Black Beauty," a hamster. In Season 3, Radar had a skunk, raccoon, rabbit, opossum and a turtle that Henry knew about.

Radar gives horse #3 to Potter for his anniversary, but its horse #4 that Potter rides in the tag.

The Kids – 10/31/1975

Season 4 / Episode 81 / Production 83 – G511

Columbia House VHS Tape . . . . *War Is Hell (Catalog # 13112)*
Fox DVD . . . . *Season 4, Disc 1*

Alan Alda, Mike Farrell, Harry Morgan
Loretta Swit, Larry Linville, Gary Burghoff, Jamie Farr

Produced by Gene Reynolds and Larry Gelbart
Written by Jim Fritzell & Everett Greenbaum
Directed by Alan Alda

William Christopher . . . . Father Mulcahy
Ann Doran . . . . Meg Cratty
Mitchell Sakamoto . . . . Slicky Boy
Haunani Minn . . . . Sung Lee
Kellye Nakahara . . . . Nurse Kellye
Chrisleen Sun . . . . Korean Girl
Darrin Lee . . . . Korean Boy
Copyright 1975 – 20th Century Fox Film Corporation

Non-Credited Appearances . . . . Roy Goldman, Dennis Troy, Jeff Maxwell

Chapters

1: *Main Titles*
2: *Message from Nurse Cratty – 0:49*
3: *Frank's Purple Heart – 2:52*
4: *Cratty's Kids – 5:05*
5: *Bedtime Stories – 8:02*
6: *The Pregnant Problem – 12:48*
7: *A Rough Delivery – 14:40*
8: *The Missing Medal – 21:07*
9: *Going Home – 23:19*
10: *End Titles – 24:29*

Closing Stills

1: *Hawkeye curling his tongue*
2: *B.J. in the Swamp*
3: *Potter reading to the kids*
4: *Korean boy*
5: *Korean baby*

Synopsis: When an orphanage run by Meg Cratty is being shelled, she sends a message to the 4077th and shortly after arrives with the kids. Everyone, except Frank who claims they took a roll of his best toilet paper last year, warmly welcomes them. The orphans, including a boy who lost his leg picking up shells to sell for brass, are cleaned, fed, and given medical checkups. Everyone helps take care of these children until it's safe to return to the orphanage 30 miles north of the 4077th.

Commentary by Larry Gelbart: "I decided I would leave the series about midway through the fourth season. As soon as I was certain, I informed all of the *M*A*S*H* family. They were sad, I was sad, but I knew I had to move on."

PA Announcement by Todd Sussman

Authors' Notes: Frank was wounded when snipers infiltrated the 4077th. He was awarded the Purple Heart for a shell fragment in the eye when he got nervous cracking open a boiled egg.

Hawkeye implies that he had a sister when he mentions driving his nephew to his grandmother's.

Ann Doran, whose career spanned seven decades, is the second actress to play Meg Cratty. Ann Lee Doran appeared in more than 500 movies and 1,000 television shows. A career that began in 1922 included parts in *The Adventures of Superman, I Love Lucy, Burns and Allen, Leave It To Beaver* and more recent appearances in *Cagney & Lacy, Trapper John M.D.* and *Hunter.* Ann Doran died on September 19, 2000 in California, from natural causes.

Quo Vadis, Captain Chandler? – 11/7/1975

Season 4 / Episode 82 / Production 85 – G513

Columbia House VHS Tape . . . . *Outside Reporting (Catalog # 11006)*
Fox DVD . . . . *Season 4, Disc 2*

Alan Alda, Mike Farrell, Harry Morgan
Loretta Swit, Larry Linville, Gary Burghoff, Jamie Farr

Produced by Gene Reynolds and Larry Gelbart
Written by Burt Prelutsky
Directed by Larry Gelbart

Alan Fudge . . . . Captain Arnold T. Chandler
William Christopher . . . . Father Mulcahy
Edward Winter . . . . .Colonel Sam Flagg
Allan Arbus . . . . .Major Sidney Freedman
Copyright 1975 – 20th Century Fox Film Corporation

Non-Credited Appearances. . . . . Kellye Nakahara, Dennis Troy, Gwen Farrell,
Roy Goldman

Chapters

1: Main Titles	6: Comrade Freedman – 12:19
2: The New Patient – 0:49	7: Sidney's Analysis – 15:35
3: Captain Christ – 3:49	8: The Diagnosis – 19:47
4: Flagg's Investigation – 7:48	9: Bless this Bear – 22:15
5: Arnold T. Chandler – 9:16	10: End Titles – 24:57

Closing Stills

1: Flagg in Potter's office
2: Freedman in Post-Op
3: Chandler in Post-Op
4: Radar
5: B.J. & Hawkeye in Post-Op

Synopsis: When a wounded GI arrives with an apparent head injury, he gives his name as Jesus Christ. His real name however is Arnold T. Chandler, a bombardier who has flown 57 missions before his plane was shot down 4 days ago. Colonel Flagg informs the staff that Chandler's psychological test shows "no susceptibility to battle psychosis," and wants him back in his plane or he'll charge him with dereliction of duty. Sid Freedman acknowledges Chandler isn't Christ, but also acknowledges he isn't Chandler right now either and needs his kind of help, not Flagg's.

Commentary by Burt Prelutsky: "The reaction I got when I submitted 'Quo Vadis, Captain Chandler?' (Season 4) was very positive. Obviously. I mean, Larry Gelbart did decide to direct it. And it did lead to my having the opportunity to write seven more episodes (and even to an invitation to join the writing staff). A bit of *M*A*S*H* trivia: It was me who named Radar, 'Walter.'"

PA Announcements by Todd Sussman

Authors' Notes: No laugh track was used in this episode due to the sensitive nature of the material.
Potterism: "Horse Hockey!"

Jamie Farr and M*A*S*H *writer Burt Prelutsky.*

Sidney Freedman's middle name is Theodore.

Colonel Flagg mentions that he played poker with Freedman once. This is an assumed reference to "Deal Me Out" from Season 2, when Flagg was Captain Halloran.

Frank is now wearing the bathrobe that was usually worn by Henry.

In Chapter 8, the view out of Potter's office windows changes mid-scene from trees to a building out the right window.

Radar's first name is revealed for the first time in this episode: Walter.

Dear Peggy – 11/11/1975

Season 4 / Episode 83 / Production 81 – G509

Columbia House VHS Tape . . . . *Dear Someone (Catalog # 11001)*
Fox DVD . . . . *Season 4, Disc 2*

Alan Alda, Mike Farrell, Harry Morgan
Loretta Swit, Larry Linville, Gary Burghoff, Jamie Farr

Produced by Gene Reynolds and Larry Gelbart
Written by Jim Fritzell & Everett Greenbaum
Directed by Burt Metcalfe

Ned Beatty . . . . Colonel Maurice Hollister
William Christopher . . . . Father Mulcahy

Copyright 1975 – 20th Century Fox Film Corporation

Non-Credited Appearances . . . . Kellye Nakahara, Dennis Troy, Bobbie Mitchell,
Jeff Maxwell, Roy Goldman, Robert Gruber

Chapters

1: *Main Titles*	6: *Which One is Nuts? – 10:34*
2: *Another Thrilling Night – 0:50*	7: *The Division Chaplain – 12:54*
3: *Frank's Foul-Up – 3:07*	8: *English Lessons – 17:09*
4: *Klinger's Dream – 5:03*	9: *Father Mulcahy's Letter – 21:32*
5: *One of A Kind – 7:49*	10: *End Titles – 24:56*

Closing Stills

1: *Hollister & Mulcahy after service*
2: *Hawkeye in the Officer's Club*
3: *B.J. in Post-Op*
4: *Potter in his office*
5: *Klinger in Post-Op*

Synopsis: In a letter to his wife Peggy, BJ describes how boring it is when they're not working, and how he sometimes has to help out as an anesthesiologist when they are working. He also tells her of Hawkeye trying to set a world record by stuffing 16 people into a jeep and how Father Mulcahy is being run "ragged" by the Divisional Chaplain, Colonel Hollister, who insists that Mulcahy write a positive letter to a GI's family, without him knowing if the man will live or die.

Commentary by Burt Metcalfe: "Ned Beatty was in the first episode I'd ever directed. It was terrific for me, as a director, to have such a great actor. As a director, you're only a virgin once."

Commentary by William Christopher: "He (Ned Beatty) was great. He was a very large presence. Mulcahy was blown away by the guy, and this is how Ned Beatty was. At that time, I didn't know who he was, even though he was established. I was busy working. The best role in the episode happened to be mine, and I was delighted. Ned made it very easy for me."

PA Announcement by Todd Sussman

Authors' Notes: The jeep Hawkeye uses to set a world-record in has a canopy, which is rarely seen.

In Chapter 6, Potter's office windows show a windowless structure and changes mid-scene to a structure with windows. This changes again in Chapter 8.

Potterism: "Kindness don't feed the bulldogs."

Father Mulcahy mentions "Palisades Amusement Park" in New Jersey. The park opened in 1898 and closed, sadly, on September 12, 1971.

Ned Beatty's 40-year career includes appearances on *CSI, Murder She Wrote, The Streets of San Francisco, The Rockford Files* and a recurring role on *Roseanne.* Nominated for Best Actor in a Supporting Role for the 1976 movie, *Network,* Mr. Beatty is also well known for his role as Otis in the *Superman* movies.

Of Moose and Men – 11/21/1975

Season 4 / Episode 84 / Production 75 – G503

Columbia House VHS Tape . . . . *The Unexpected (Catalog # 22050)*
Fox DVD . . . . *Season 4, Disc 2*

Alan Alda, Mike Farrell, Harry Morgan
Loretta Swit, Larry Linville, Gary Burghoff, Jamie Farr

Produced by Gene Reynolds and Larry Gelbart
Written by Jay Folb
Directed by John Erman

Tim O'Connor . . . . Colonel Spiker
Johnny Haymer . . . . Sergeant Zale

Copyright 1975 – 20th Century Fox Film Corporation

Non-Credited Appearances . . . . Kellye Nakahara, Sarah Fankboner, Dennis Troy,
Jeff Maxwell

Chapters

1: *Main Titles*
2: *Military Discourtesy – 0:50*
3: *Zale's Letter – 2:55*
4: *Two for Pre-Op – 4:49*
5: *Dear Hillda – 7:45*

6: *The Oddball Surgeon – 14:20*
7: *Off the Hook – 17:43*
8: *Zale's Moose – 20:18*
9: *Frank's Bomb – 22:16*
10: *End Titles – 24:56*

Closing Stills

1: *Colonel Spiker in Post-Op*
2: *Potter in Post-Op*
3: *B.J. in the Mess Tent*
4: *Frank*
5: *Hawkeye on beach chair in the compound (R)*

Synopsis: When Hawkeye splashes mud on Colonel Spiker at a checkpoint, he further angers the Colonel with insolence and drives off. But after Spiker is wounded and brought to the 4077th, he still wants to press charges on Hawkeye, even after he saves the Colonel's life, until Potter steps in and convinces Spiker otherwise. Meanwhile, Sergeant Zale, who has his own "moose" with a hut just outside of camp, gets a letter from his wife apologizing for having an affair, and breaks his hand after punching a heater in anger.

Commentary by Larry Gelbart: "All the tents ware made of government issued canvas. The Swamp was rigged so that the canvas could be rolled up and we were able to see what was going on in the immediate vicinity through the mosquito netting. Hot Lips' tent was supplied with wooden walls, as a result of going to Korea and seeing that certain nurse's quarters had been given this treatment. Potter and Henry's tent was used only for that purpose (with perhaps a few exceptions). Enough of this past tents talk."

PA Announcement by Todd Sussman

Authors' Notes: The serial number of the jeep Hawkeye drives and splashes mud on Colonel Spiker is 20963388, the same jeep Colonel Hollister from the previous episode arrives in and the same jeep Potter put a bullet into.
Colonel Potter is one-fourth Cherokee Indian.
Potterisms: "Jumpin' Jodhpurs," "Sufferin' saddle soap"

According to Sergeant Zale, the 4077th is three miles from the front (sometimes it's four miles).

Tim O'Connor, one of several actors to appear in both *M*A*S*H* and *Star Trek*, has an extensive list of credits to his 60-year career, appearing in *The FBI, Mannix, Hawaii Five-0, Trapper John, M.D.,* and a recurring role as Elliot Carson on *Peyton Place.* Tim O'Connor will return to *M*A*S*H* in Season 9's, "Operation Friendship," as Captain Norman Traeger, M.D.

Soldier of the Month – 11/28/1975

Season 4 / Episode 85 / Production 86 – G514

Columbia House VHS Tape . . . . War Ailments (Catalog # 13111)
Fox DVD . . . . Season 4, Disc 2

Alan Alda, Mike Farrell, Harry Morgan
Loretta Swit, Larry Linville, Gary Burghoff, Jamie Farr

Produced by Gene Reynolds and Larry Gelbart
Written by Linda Bloodworth
Directed by Gene Reynolds

William Christopher . . . . Father Mulcahy
Johnny Haymer . . . . Sergeant Zale

Copyright 1975 – 20th Century Fox Film Corporation

Non-Credited Appearances . . . . Jeff Maxwell, Kellye Nakahara, Roy Goldman

Chapters

1: Main Titles
2: Rats and Morale – 0:50
3: Renal Failure – 5:21
4: Hemorrhagic Fever – 6:39
5: The Rat Hunter – 8:38

6: Frank's Fever – 11:29
7: The Contest – 14:26
8: Frank's Will – 19:10
9: Soldier of the Month – 21:00
10: End Titles – 24:57

Closing Stills

1: Mulcahy
2: Hawkeye in Post-Op
3: B.J. in Post-Op
4: Margaret in Post-Op
5: Frank in the Mess Tent

Synopsis: A lucky enlisted GI will get six days in Tokyo as the winner of The Soldier of the Month contest. Candidates will be judged on dress and deportment, with the finalists to be given an oral quiz on historical knowledge, and Klinger is finally in a dress uniform with answers to the questions written on various body parts. By order of HQ, the judge will be the second in command, Frank Burns. But Frank is the Rat Control Officer and comes down with the same mysterious illness as patients in post-op causing acute renal shutdown and high fever, which the doctors have not yet identified.

Commentary by Larry Gelbart: "Potter's paintings were not the work of Gary Burghoff. They were done by studio artisans."

Commentary by Jeff Maxwell: "I worked in many non-acting jobs at Twentieth-Century Fox (print shop, mail dept., casting) before landing the BIG one. To amuse my co-workers and relieve the stress and boredom of printing thousands of pages of scripts, I used to chain one leg to a patio umbrella and leap out at tour busses running through the studio. This prank made the day almost tolerable and gave me the nickname of 'Igor.' Years later, simply to amuse my co-workers and relieve the stress of television production, I revived the character of Igor, the tour-bus hunchback, by clowning around on the set of *M*A*S*H*. I was immediately nicknamed "Igor" by my pal (and one of the funniest people of the face of the Earth) Roy Goldman. From that day forward, I was known as Igor on Stage 9. It was common practice for the real names of the 'mini-*M*A*S*H*.' cast (Goldman, Gwen, Kelly, Fuffendorker, etc.) to be used in scenes."

Authors' Notes: There are no PA announcements in this episode.

In this episode, Frank claims to have studied medicine for seven years. In Season 2's "The Sniper," he states that it took him twice as long to become a doctor. In Season 4's "Hey, Doc," Hawkeye and BJ were in medical school for 8 years, while Trapper, in Season 3's "Bombed," said he was in medical school for 10 years.

The combination to the company safe is 42-36-42, Mrs. Potter's measurements.

In Chapter 6, Hawkeye states, when he sees an orderly sleeping on a chair, "Albert Anastasia's doorman." Albert Anastasia was killed in the Park Sheraton Hotel's barbershop on October 25, 1957. This was more than four years after the Korean War ended.

The Gun – 12/2/1975

Season 4 / Episode 86 / Production 89 – G517

Columbia House VHS Tape . . . . Frank Burned (Catalog # 13110)
Fox DVD . . . . Season 4, Disc 2

Alan Alda, Mike Farrell, Harry Morgan
Loretta Swit, Larry Linville, Gary Burghoff, Jamie Farr

Produced by Gene Reynolds and Larry Gelbart
Written by Larry Gelbart & Gene Reynolds
Directed by Burt Metcalfe

Warren Stevens . . . . Colonel Chaffey
William Christopher . . . . Father Mulcahy

Copyright 1975 – 20th Century Fox Film Corporation

Non-Credited Appearances . . . . Dennis Troy, Kellye Nakahara, Roy Goldman,
Jeff Maxwell

Chapters

1: Main Titles	6: Radar's Problem – 10:55
2: Road Accident – 0:51	7: A Born Liar – 14:04
3: More Injured – 5:42	8: The Man Responsible – 19:46
4: The Colonel's Colt – 6:57	9: Get Rid of that Gun – 23:18
5: Frank's New Gun – 9:17	10: End Titles – 24:57

Closing Stills

1: Chaffey in Post-Op
2: B.J. & Hawkeye corner Frank in O.R.
3: Potter in Post-Op
4: Frank & Margaret in Margaret's tent
5: Radar in the Officer's Club

Synopsis: When Colonel Chaffey arrives at the 4077th with a broken ankle and a possible skull fracture, he also arrives with an 1884 chrome Colt .45 sidearm with bone grips. Just before Radar puts it in the gun bin, Frank checks it for balance, but Frank can't resist the temptation and later, while Radar is asleep, he takes the keys, and then takes the gun. Radar is ultimately responsible for the guns in the bin, and faces 15 years in the stockade, and Colonel Chaffey demands to know who's responsible for his missing Colt. Radar, now drunk after one beer, confronts Chaffey about his gun when a shot rings out, proving he didn't take it. Frank returns the gun to the gun bin, anonymously, but not before shooting himself in the foot while cleaning it.

Commentary by Larry Gelbart: "Every *M*A*S*H* script I ever had anything to do with resides at the UCLA Theatre Arts Library. Giving a writer an assignment usually included giving him (it usually was a him) a story idea, and scene breakdown of that idea as well. Five scenes in the first act, five in the second, and what the tag was to contain. Some writers came in with ideas, and we would work out the breakdown together, but more often it worked the way I first described. Many ideas did come from the research; others were pulled from the air. I did whatever rewriting and polishing was required."

PA Announcements by Todd Sussman

Authors' Notes: Radar has a pony back home. First and last time this is mentioned.

Radar has a sister and when she borrows his bike, the chain slips off.

Radar attended Ottumwa Central High School that had 400 kids.

Radar also gets drunk on less than one can of beer. Several martinis and Henry's brandy didn't seem to faze him in earlier episodes.

Potter claims to have confiscated "a ton of moonshine equipment." What about the still in the Swamp?

Potter has an army-green robe. He also had a dark red and gray striped robe as well.

Mail Call Again – 12/9/1975

Season 4 / Episode 87 / Production 90 – G518

Columbia House VHS Tape . . . . Infidelity (Catalog # 11000)
Fox DVD . . . . Season 4, Disc 2

Alan Alda, Mike Farrell, Harry Morgan
Loretta Swit, Larry Linville, Gary Burghoff, Jamie Farr
Produced by Gene Reynolds and Larry Gelbart
Written by Jim Fritzell & Everett Greenbaum
Directed by George Tyne
William Christopher . . . . Father Mulcahy
Copyright 1975 – 20th Century Fox Film Corporation

Non-Credited Appearances . . . . Kellye Nakahara, Jeff Maxwell

Chapters

1: Main Titles
2: Mail Call – 0:51
3: Frank's Letter – 5:08
4: Phoning Home – 9:07
5: Klinger's Tragedy – 12:29

6: Louise on the Line – 15:56
7: Frank's New Nightie – 19:16
8: Home Movies – 20:09
9: Colonel Grandpa – 23:37
10: End Titles – 24:58

Closing Stills

1: Hawkeye in the Swamp
2: B.J. reading mail in the Swamp
3: Potter in the office
4: Radar
5: Klinger in black dress in Potter's office

Synopsis: Letters and news from home is usually a welcome event at the 4077th and Colonel Potter may be the happiest when he learns he's going to be a grandfather. Margaret receives a negligee from Frederick's of Hollywood, but it loses its effect when Frank learns his wife wants a divorce. Father Mulcahy's sister, a nun who coaches girl's basketball at Saint Mary's, is on a winning streak while BJ gets three letters from Peg, plus one from his dog. Klinger tries again for a discharge claiming his mother wrote him that his 2 brothers died in a boiler explosion, and Hawkeye gets a copy of *The Crab Apple Cove Courier,* bringing him up to date on all the news back home, including a man who leaves his farm to a donkey. But it's Radar's home movie of "Dinner at Ottumwa, Iowa" that may have the biggest impact.

Commentary by Gary Burghoff: "Larry Gelbart and I did it with total glee (Gary playing Radar's mom). When they made me up, I looked like my paternal grandmother. You know when Radar's mom serves that salad with the marshmallows in it, and someone asks Radar what it's called and he says 'that salad with the marshmallows in it'? That's what I always knew it as in my family. I think it's called 'Ambrosia.'"

Authors' Notes: There are no PA announcements in this episode.
In this episode, Potter's son is a dentist, and married to Janine. In Season 11's "Strange Bedfellows," Potter has a daughter named Evie, and his son-in-law is a traveling salesman.
Father Mulcahy's given name is, "Francis." In The Pilot episode, his name was John P. Mulcahy.
Hawkeye's hometown newspaper is *The Crabapple Cove Courier.*

Klinger ploys:

All black mourning attire, including a black veil and a letter from his mother in the mail.

Family tragedy: 2 older brothers, Maurice and Hakim died in an explosion of the boiler at the Toledo Harmonica Company: Hakim would bathe him and Maurice would nurse him — in the US illegally and lived under the front porch and were fed through the cracks.

Letter in Klinger's handwriting as he translated his mother's Lebanese, but burned the letter as part of a religious ceremony when 2 brothers die in a harmonica factory or a camel race.

Selective Service Act: Subsection 31–B, paragraph 6, small a, tragedy-wise. As sole remaining son, he's entitled to an immediate discharge.

Calls Potter, "Sherm" because he was hit with a wave of "civilianism."

Klinger's Personal record states he has no brothers.

In Chapter 7, a microphone can be seen above and to the left of Frank on Stage 9.

Radar's home movie, taken by his Uncle Ed, "Sunday Dinner at Ottumwa, Iowa," lets us see his family, starting with his mother and his dog Ranger, Uncle David, Cousin Millie, Uncle Bill, Aunt Emily, and Cousin Jimmy.

Potter's granddaughter is Sherry Pershing Potter, born on the 23rd, and weighing 8½ pounds.

The Price of Tomato Juice – 12/16/1975

Season 4 / Episode 88 / Production 91 – G519

Columbia House VHS Tape . . . . *Spoils Of War (Catalog # 11007)*
Fox DVD . . . . *Season 4, Disc 2*

Alan Alda, Mike Farrell, Harry Morgan
Loretta Swit, Larry Linville, Gary Burghoff, Jamie Farr

Produced by Gene Reynolds and Larry Gelbart
Written by Larry Gelbart & Gene Reynolds
Directed by Gene Reynolds

William Christopher . . . . Father Mulcahy

Copyright 1975 – 20th Century Fox Film Corporation

Non-Credited Appearances . . . . Kellye Nakahara, Dennis Troy, Jeff Maxwell,
Roy Goldman

Chapters

1: *Main Titles*
2: *The Colonel's Juice – 0:49*
3: *A Favor for the Colonel – 4:53*
4: *A Pass for Klinger – 7:09*
5: *A Date with General Barker – 10:27*

6: *Frank's Last Snivel – 14:12*
7: *Love Notes – 18:08*
8: *Frank Who? – 21:04*
9: *A Fly in the Juice – 23:11*
10: *End Titles – 24:57*

Closing Stills

1: *Frank in the shower*
2: *Hawkeye & B.J. in the Mess Tent*
3: *Potter in the Mess Tent*
4: *Margaret & Frank*
5: *Radar with tomato juice in the Mess Tent*

Synopsis: Radar wants to get tomato juice for Colonel Potter, but he has to go through the requisition officer first: Frank Burns. At first, Frank refuses to requisition the juice, then gets into an argument with Margaret when she tells him she's going to Seoul to meet with General Barker and storms out of her tent straight to the Officer's Club and gets drunk. With some help from Hawkeye and BJ, Frank now thinks Margaret is staying and in his inebriated state, happily signs Radar's requisition, but it's all for nothing when Potter refuses the tomato juice.

Commentary by Larry Gelbart: "I did, indeed, fall into a number of self-created clichés: too many easy jokes about Radar's height (or lack of it); Klinger's costumes becoming predictable. My one consolation: they were my clichés, and not someone else's."

Commentary by Jeff Maxwell: "I did not accidentally say my last name in 'The Price of Tomato Juice,' Maxwell was written in the script. And, that's how and why the name Igor eventually made its way into the show. Straminsky was a later addition. Though it sounds like something I would have made up, I didn't. Some M*A*S*H writer had the good thought that Igor Staminsky made more sense than Igor Maxwell. I liked it because it gave me the chance to make the Igor character more of a Straminsky than a Maxwell. In truth, Igor, Igor Maxwell and Igor Straminsky were all written into M*A*S*H by the same folks who gave Radar's bear its name."

Authors' Notes: There are no PA announcements in this episode.

Radar's little brother died.

Potterism: "Oysters ice cakes."

As mentioned by Jeff Maxwell, when he gave his name to Frank as "Maxwell," it was not a mistake. That's how it was written in.

Father Mulcahy is now wearing the bathrobe usually worn by Henry. Mulcahy had a blue plaid robe in Season 2's "Crisis."

Dear Ma – 12/23/1975

Season 4 / Episode 89 / Production 87 – G515

Columbia House VHS Tape . . . . *Dear Someone (Catalog # 11001)*
Fox DVD . . . .*Season 4, Disc 2*

Alan Alda, Mike Farrell, Harry Morgan
Loretta Swit, Larry Linville, Gary Burghoff, Jamie Farr

Produced by Gene Reynolds and Larry Gelbart
Written by Everett Greenbaum & Jim Fritzell
Directed by Alan Alda

William Christopher . . . . Father Mulcahy
Redmond Gleeson . . . . Sergeant Callan
John Fujioka . . . . General Park
Byron Chung . . . . Korean Soldier
Lynn Marie Stewart . . . . Nurse Fox
Gwen Farrell . . . . Nurse Able
Copyright 1975 – 20th Century Fox Film Corporation

Non-Credited Appearances . . . . Kellye Nakahara, Roy Goldman, Dennis Troy,
Jeff Maxwell

Chapters

1: Main Titles
2: Dear Ma – 0:49
3: Foot Inspection – 2:02
4: Margaret's Exam – 6:14
5: A Commie in the Camp – 9:03

6: Frank and the General – 13:44
7: Klinger's Letter – 14:58
8: One in the Bucket – 18:05
9: Frank's Secret – 23:22
10: End Titles – 24:57

Closing Stills

1: Mulcahy has feet inspected in his tent
2: Radar in Margaret's tent
3: Potter is ticklish
4: Klinger in his tent
5: Hawkeye

Synopsis: In a letter to his mother, Radar describes some of his duties and responsibilities at the 4077th. Writing slow because his mother can't read fast, he tells her of helping patients EVAC to other hospitals or to their units, assisting Hawkeye administer the monthly foot inspection and going to local villages once a month to help treat the sick and old. And even though his mother might hear bad news about the war, he wants her to know that he's okay.

Commentary by Larry Gelbart: "When I was 15 years old, I had a screen test at Fox (believe it or not) for a role in a movie called, *Junior Miss.* As a result, not being able to attend my regular high school classes that day, I had to spend a few hours in the schoolroom (what was later to become The Old Writers Building). One of my classmates that day was Carl 'Alfalfa' Switzer, one of the old 'Our Gang.' Just a few years later, he was shot and killed when he tried to collect $50 that someone owed him. I never got the acting part — which is not quite as bad as getting a bullet in your stomach, but I did get to spend four years in the Old Writers Building once I became an old writer myself. But revenge is sweet. As I've said before, I've been using the pencils I stole from 20th Century Fox right on into the 21st Century."

PA Announcements by Todd Sussman

Authors' Notes: Hawkeye is reading the same magazine from an earlier episode, Fun, with a bikini-clad woman on the cover.

Klinger Ploy: Wearing a floral headband / pink housecoat / pink slippers / Writing a letter to President Eisenhower about his mental condition with a photo of him wearing black boots and a garter belt.

Potterisms: "Buffalo Chips," "Pig Feathers."

Radar tells his mother that he's happy about finally getting a pet, a guinea pig he named, "Dopey." He had a mini zoo in Season 3's "Mad Dogs and Servicemen," consisting of a skunk, raccoon, rabbit, opossum and the turtle that took a shower with Henry.

Der Tag – 1/6/1976

Season 4 / Episode 90 / Production 94 – G522

Columbia House VHS Tape . . . . *Frank Burned (Catalog # 13110)*
Fox DVD . . . .*Season 4, Disc 3*

Alan Alda, Mike Farrell, Harry Morgan
Loretta Swit, Larry Linville, Gary Burghoff, Jamie Farr

Produced by Gene Reynolds and Larry Gelbart
Written by Everett Greenbaum & Jim Fritzell
Directed by Gene Reynolds

William Christopher. . . . . Father Mulcahy
Joe Morton . . . . Captain Nick Saunders
Copyright 1976 – 20th Century Fox Film Corporation

Non-Credited Appearances. . . . . Kellye Nakahara, Jeff Maxwell, Roy Goldman

Chapters

1: Main Titles	6: Off to the Front – 13:57
2: Three in the Morning – 0:50	7: Where's Major Burns? – 15:14
3: A Problem with Frank – 3:09	8: Volunteers – 17:48
4: Poker Buddies – 5:13	9: Hated Again – 20:19
5: The Party Guy – 9:54	10: End Titles – 24:28

Closing Stills

1: Klinger & Mulcahy at card game in the Swamp
2: Frank & Hawkeye at card game in the Swamp
3: B.J. & Potter at card game in the Swamp
4: Margaret on the phone to Frank
5: Radar at card game in the Swamp

Synopsis: If Frank was difficult to get along with before, he's downright impossible now since Margaret went to Tokyo. As a favor to Colonel Potter, Hawkeye and BJ act friendly to him, even inviting him to sit in a poker game where Frank promptly gets drunk and worse, wins nearly $200. Asleep, Hawkeye and BJ hang a toe-tag on his foot and later, when Frank leaves the latrine, he stumbles right into the open-back of an ambulance headed straight for the front.

Commentary by Larry Gelbart: "The Nazis used 'Der Tag' as some sort of militaristic slogan (it was pronounced der tahg, of course). The play on words in the episode's title was a pun on the word 'tag' (with its English pronunciation). Der Tag, in English, means The Day."

PA Announcement by Todd Sussman

Authors' Notes: The PA announcement mentions Ralph Kiner hitting his 47th home run. During the years 1950 to 1953, Ralph Kiner, who played for the Pittsburgh Pirates from 1946 to 1953, hit 47 home runs only in 1950. The only time he hit more homes runs than 47 was in 1949, when he hit 54. That puts this episode in September 1950, even though Hawkeye said he lived with Trapper for more than a year.

The PA announcement also states there is a laundry room, but it's never been seen.

Chapter 8 now shows the "4077 SUPPLY" and crates from Potter's office windows.

Hawkeye and BJ went to get Frank at the aid station in jeep number 18210717, but returned in jeep number 20963388.

Hawkeye – 1/13/1976

Season 4 / Episode 91 / Production 92 – G520
Columbia House VHS Tape.......*Benjamin Franklin Pierce (Catalog # 11002)*
Fox DVD ....*Season 4, Disc 3*

Alan Alda *(No other cast members appear in this episode.)*

Produced by Gene Reynolds and Larry Gelbart
Written by Larry Gelbart & Simon Muntner
Directed by Larry Gelbart

Philip Ahn... The Father
Shizuko Hoshie... The Mother
June Kim .... The Pregnant Woman
Susan Sakimoto..The Oldest Child
Jeff Osaka .... Younger Child
Jayleen Sun .... Younger Child

Copyright 1976 – 20th Century Fox Film Corporation

Chapters

1: *Main Titles*
2: *Hawkeye's Accident – 0:50*
3: *A Concussion – 3:56*
4: *Whitefish – 7:31*
5: *Presents – 10:40*

6: *Childhood Memories – 12:25*
7: *Dinner and A Show – 15:33*
8: *Rescued – 23:07*
9: *Thank-You Gifts – 23:59*
10: *End Titles – 24:57*

Closing Stills

1: *The father*
2: *Hawkeye*
3: *The mother and the pregnant woman*
4: *The kids*
5: *Hawkeye*

Synopsis: Driving back to camp from an aid station, Hawkeye swerves to miss Korean children playing in the road and flips over in his Jeep. The children help him into the family hut, and he realizes he has serious injuries but is afraid to go to sleep with a concussion. To help stay awake, he talks to the family, nearly non-stop, even though they do not understand English and they help care for him. After Radar brings him back to camp, he returns with gifts for the family, including instructions on how to contact him when an older pregnant daughter is ready to give birth, and tobacco for the father instead of him having to smoke manure.

Commentary by Larry Gelbart: "The reason for doing it was because it represented a terrific writing and acting challenge, and by Season 4, the challenges were getting tougher and tougher. Alda was very helpful in terms of the script, as well. It was not his idea, but he contributed several bits and ideas to the script. While there's many an episode in the first four seasons that I think were complete or partial misses, I can't say I feel that way about this one."

Authors' Notes: Alan Alda is the only cast member to appear in this episode and there were no PA announcements.

Hawkeye claims that the Pierce's have been in Maine since 1680, although he stated earlier in the series that he was from Vermont.

He also states that he has no siblings, but earlier in the series, he made mention of a sister several times.

While talking to the Korean family, Hawkeye said, "they know what causes pregnancy." That is the second time that line was said. Radar said that in Season 1's "Showtime."

In Chapter 7, Hawkeye sings, "There's No Vinism Like Chauvinism," which is taken from, "There's No Business Like Show Business," a song from the movie of the same name in 1954, after the Korean War ended.

Philip Ahn, the actor who played the Korean father in this episode, was born on March 29, 1905 as Phi Lip Ahn. It is believed that Mr. Ahn is the first American citizen born in the United States of Korean parents. His career spanned 50 years with appearances on *Mannix, Hawaii Five-0, Sanford & Son*, two episodes of *Police Woman* between 1976 and 1977 and 30 episodes of Kung Fu. Philip Ahn will return later in *M*A*S*H* in Season 5's "Excocism" and Season 6's "Change Day." Philip Ahn died on February 28, 1978.

Some 38th Parallels – 1/20/1976

Season 4 / Episode 92 / Production 93 – G521

Columbia House VHS Tape . . . . *Spoils Of War (Catalog # 11007)*
Fox DVD . . . . *Season 4, Disc 3*

Alan Alda, Mike Farrell, Harry Morgan
Loretta Swit, Larry Linville, Gary Burghoff, Jamie Farr

Produced by Gene Reynolds and Larry Gelbart
Written by Regier & Markowitz
Directed by Burt Metcalfe

William Christopher . . . . Father Mulcahy
Kevin Hagen . . . . Colonel Coner
George O'Hanlon, Jr.. . . . . Private Gerald Phelan
Lynette Mettey . . . . Nurse Able

Copyright 1976 – 20th Century Fox Film Corporation

Non-Credited Appearances. . . . . Kellye Nakahara, Dennis Troy, Roy Goldman,
Richard Lee Sung, Tad Horino

Chapters

1: *Main Titles*	6: *Radar's Patient – 13:07*
2: *Trash Thieves – 0:50*	7: *The Big Garbage Sale – 15:46*
3: *Radar the Hero – 3:44*	8: *Dead the Next Second – 17:27*
4: *The Dysfunctional Doctor – 7:44*	9: *An Appropriate Aloha – 22:05*
5: *Colonel Coner – 11:58*	10: *End Titles – 24:27*

Closing Stills

1: *Mulcahy in O.R.*
2: *Colonel Coner in the Mess Tent*
3: *Hawkeye & Nurse Able*
4: *Frank*
5: *Radar*

Synopsis: Colonel Coner's unit retrieves mortally wounded GI's, some of whom get killed themselves. When one of Coner's men dies in post-op, the Colonel barely remembers who he is, but Private Phelan's death has a profound impact on Radar, while Frank holds an auction for local villagers to buy the 4077th's garbage. Surprisingly, Hawkeye has a profound impact on the auction.

Commentary by Kevin Hagen: "As my jeep was pulling away, a load of garbage was spilled on my head. It didn't look real. So, a real load of garbage was used after several attempts. Of all the shows I did, M*A*S*H and Little House on the Prairie were the best prepared and the most fun to work on."

Authors' Notes: There are no PA announcements in this episode
The yellow sign seen in the break room to the left of the O.R. doors is not always there. Sometimes, there's a different sign.
Klinger is in regulation fatigues on KP.
Richard Lee Sung is in this episode, although he's not listed in the credits.
Potter states the fastest amputation took 33 seconds by Dr. R. Liston in 1801 without an anesthetic. His assistant lost three fingers in the process. *Note:* Dr. Robert Liston (1794-1847) is said to have been able to perform an amputation and stitch up the back in

28 seconds. Additionally, a source records that Dr. Robert Liston, "The fastest saw in the west," in one 2½ minute operation, amputated the leg of his patient, who later died from gangrene, sliced the fingers off his assistant, who later died of blood-poisoning, and slashed through the coat-tails of a spectator, who dropped dead from fright. This was the only operation in surgical history to have a 300% mortality rate (according to *Wikipedia*).

In Chapter 8, Hawkeye and Potter are talking on the Ranch set and it's very windy. Hawkeye's hair and shirt, as well as the tents are flapping around in the wind. This changes mid-scene to a perfectly calm day with no wind and nothing flapping around, including Hawkeye's hair.

Kevin Hagen, whose acting career spanned five decades with appearances on *Bonanza, The Man From U.N.C.L.E., The Dukes of Hazzard* and 113 episodes of *Little House On The Prairie* will return to *M*A*S*H* in Season 7's "Peace On Us." Mr. Hagen, born on April 3, 1928, passed away from esophageal cancer on July 9, 2005 in Grants Pass, Oregon.

The Novocaine Mutiny – 1/27/1976

Season 4 / Episode 93 / Production 95 – G523

Columbia House VHS Tape . . . . *Frank Burned (Catalog # 13110)*
Fox DVD . . . . *Season 4, Disc 3*

Alan Alda, Mike Farrell, Harry Morgan
Loretta Swit, Larry Linville, Gary Burghoff, Jamie Farr

Produced by Gene Reynolds and Larry Gelbart
Written by Burt Prelutsky
Directed by Harry Morgan

William Christopher . . . . Father Mulcahy
Ned Wilson . . . . Colonel Carmichael
Johnny Haymer . . . . Sergeant Zale

Copyright 1976 – 20th Century Fox Film Corporation

Non-Credited Appearances . . . . Kellye Nakahara, Jeff Maxwell, Dennis Troy, Patricia Stevens

Chapters

1: *Main Titles*	6: *The Search – 12:23*
2: *Court-Martial – 0:50*	7: *Frank's Version – 17:34*
3: *The Accused – 3:32*	8: *The Real Story – 20:32*
4: *The Temporary Commander – 4:48*	9: *The Verdict – 22:26*
5: *Poker Problems – 8:07*	10: *End Titles – 24:57*

Closing Stills

1: *Zale & Mulcahy*
2: *Colonel Carmichael*
3: *Hawkeye testifies*
4: *Frank at the proceedings*
5: *Radar testifies*

Synopsis: After Frank files a charge of mutiny on Hawkeye, a hearing takes place in Seoul and if Hawkeye is found guilty, he could be hanged. To prove his case, Frank gives a detailed account of incidents that took place in O.R., which makes him out to be Albert Schweitzer and Mother Theresa, even finishing a prayer in Latin. But when Colonel Carmichael hears testimony from the other witnesses, he clears Hawkeye of the charges and suggests that Frank, if not drafted as a doctor, would've been assigned as a pastry chef.

Commentary by Burt Prelutsky: "I did not do any rewriting on the script to deal with Loretta Swit's absence in 'The Novocaine Mutiny,' so I must have been told before I started that she would not be available."

Authors' Notes: There are no PA announcements in this episode.

A rarely seen hook for "Simmons" to hang garments before surgery is seen in the change room.

Frank finds *Spider-Man* and *The Avengers* comic books in Radar's office. Spider-Man didn't get his own comic until March 1963 and the first *Avengers* comic book was in September 1963, both ten years after the Korean War ended.

Frank's blood type is B, except is Season 1's "Germ Warfare," when it was AB-negative.

Smilin' Jack – 2/3/1976

Season 4 / Episode 94 / Production 80 – G508

Columbia House VHS Tape . . . . *War Ailments (Catalog # 13111)*
Fox DVD . . . . *Season 4, Disc 3*

Alan Alda, Mike Farrell, Harry Morgan
Loretta Swit, Larry Linville, Gary Burghoff, Jamie Farr

Produced by Gene Reynolds and Larry Gelbart
Written by Larry Gelbart & Simon Muntner
Directed by Charles Dubin

Robert Hogan . . . . .Lieutenant "Smilin'" Jack Mitchell
Dennis Kort. . . . . Corporal Howard Owens

Copyright 1975 – 20th Century Fox Film Corporation

Non-Credited Appearances. . . . . Dennis Troy, Kellye Nakahara, Roy Goldman,
Robert Gruber

Chapters

1: *Main Titles*	6: *Diabetes – 13:09*
2: *Another Casualty – 0:50*	7: *The Reluctant Hero – 14:45*
3: *Number 839 – 3:31*	8: *Jack's Last Ride – 19:28*
4: *Two Purple Hearts – 5:45*	9: *The Worst War – 23:57*
5: *Smilin' Jack – 8:23*	10: *End Titles – 24:56*

Closing Stills

1: *Potter & Smilin' Jack in the office*
2: *Hawkeye in the Officer's Club*
3: *B.J.*
4: *Frank & Margaret*
5: *Radar*

Synopsis: Lieutenant "Smilin'" Jack Mitchell, a front-runner for Chopper Pilot of the Year, takes pictures of the wounded he flies in because when he does, they live. He just brought #839 to the 4077th, which puts him only 3 behind Dangerous Dan who has 842. But when the doctors give him an examination, they learn he has diabetes. Going against orders, he flies one more mission and returns with #843 to take the lead, and Potter, not happy, grounds him permanently, just in time to see Dangerous Dan land with # 844.

Commentary by Larry Gelbart: "We worked together only once ('Smilin' Jack,' Season 4). He did the bulk of his work after I was no longer with the series. A lovely man and a very good director" (on Charles S. Dubin).

"After the second season of the series, Gene Reynolds and I went to spend some time with the 8055th, still stationed in South Korea. The 8055th was the real unit that served as the model for the fictional 4077th. We recorded 22 hours of tape (audio) with the unit's personnel — doctors, nurses, orderlies, etc. One of the people interviewed was a chopper pilot named Dan Sullivan. A very colorful guy, we created a character for the series based on his experiences. We added a twist by having our fictional chopper pilot fall victim to diabetes. This was purely a creative invention. Sullivan never had that condition. Sometime after the episode aired, Dan — the real Dan — became afflicted with diabetes. It was a bizarre case of life being imitated by art only to have art then be imitated in life. I only mention all of this now because I was recently written by a friend of Sullivan's (ah, the wondrous Web) telling me of his illness (of which I had been unaware) and saying that a group of friends were gathering this week to honor him — and would I care to write a few words to him, as well. Of course, I was happy to."

PA Announcements by Todd Sussman

Authors' Notes: Potter penned a letter of apology to Major General Handley Wacker, 8th Army, I-Corps, for Hawkeye showing up for the unit inspection wearing only an athletic supporter.

Radar spells s-u-p-p-o-r-t-e-r with one 'p.'

Of the three wars Potter's been in, the worst was all of 'em.

Not only the name of this episode, "Smilin' Jack," a comic strip created by Zack Mosely, appeared in the *Chicago Tribune* on October 1, 1933 and ended on April 1, 1973. It was the longest running aviation comic strip. Mr. Mosely was a 27-year-old aviation enthusiast when he created the strip.

The More I See You – 2/10/1976

Season 4 / Episode 95 / Production 96 – G524

Columbia House VHS Tape . . . . *Infidelity (Catalog # 11000)*
Fox DVD . . . . *Season 4, Disc 3*

Alan Alda, Mike Farrell, Harry Morgan
Loretta Swit, Larry Linville, Gary Burghoff, Jamie Farr

Produced by Gene Reynolds and Larry Gelbart
Written by Larry Gelbart & Gene Reynolds
Directed by Gene Reynolds

Blythe Danner . . . . Lieutenant Carlye Breslin Walton
William Christopher . . . . Father Mulcahy
Mary Jo Catlett . . . . .Lieutenant Becky Anderson
Copyright 1976 – 20th Century Fox Film Corporation

Non-Credited Appearances . . . . .Kellye Nakahara

Chapters

1: *Main Titles*	6: *The Master Complicator – 12:53*
2: *Hawkeye's Ex – 0:51*	7: *B.J.'s Opinion – 17:53*
3: *The Welcome Wagon – 4:58*	8: *Carlye's Transfer – 19:44*
4: *Old Friends – 7:13*	9: *She's Gone Again – 23:21*
5: *Radar's Hobby – 11:44*	10: *End Titles – 24:31*

Closing Stills

1: *Carlye*
2: *B.J.*
3: *Hawkeye in the Swamp*
4: *Potter painting outdoors*
5: *Radar posing for Potter / Impersonations*

Synopsis: Of the five MASH units and three EVAC hospitals in Korea, Hawkeye, in a mild panic, can't believe that a new nurse, Lieutenant Carlye Breslin, has been stationed at the 4077th. Hawkeye and Carlye had lived together for a year and a half in Boston, and the only reason he didn't ask her to marry him was he was in residency at the time. It took Hawkeye a long time to get over her, and now that she's in camp, he learns that she's married, but Hawkeye can't help the way he feels about her. Carlye, not wanting to take a back seat to his work again, has put in for a transfer, granting Hawkeye one last request: to tell people that he left her.

Commentary by Larry Gelbart: "Half way through writing the script for this episode, the whole idea suggesting itself merely by remembering the song of the same title, as sung by Alice Faye in an old Fox movie, the idea of Blythe Danner popped up and from that moment no one else would do. Only problem was, she didn't do half hour shows and we didn't yet have a script to show her. Gene Reynolds got her on the phone and we both made a very strong pitch to her, promising the part would be worthy of her talent. She took a chance, not seeing a word on paper. She was divine on the show. It's still a personal favorite of mine. End of Memorygram. As I recall that was written as a deliberate spoonerism that was meant to show how thrown Hawkeye was having Carlye pop up in his life after so long an absence (on Alda seeming to stumble over some lines).

"I must confess that although I worked with Benny Golson on the series, I had absolutely no idea that he wrote 'Again.' It was a song that meant a great deal to me personally, and so I would work it into the series whenever and wherever I could. To discover that Golson wrote it is an unexpected cherry on top. Blythe Danner is the mother of Gwyneth Paltrow."

Authors' Notes: There are no PA announcements in this episode.

"Becky," as in Lieutenant Becky Anderson, is the name of Larry Gelbart's daughter.

The blue robe with red trim Carlye hangs in her tent is Margaret's.

Radar mentions a song written by Harry Warren on his honeymoon night in 1901. Since Harry Warren was born in 1893, that would have rendered him eight years old on his honeymoon.

Deluge – 2/17/1976

Season 4 / Episode 96 / Production 88 – G516

Columbia House VHS Tape . . . . *Command Center Chaos (Catalog # 21037)*
Fox DVD . . . . *Season 4, Disc 3*

Alan Alda, Mike Farrell, Harry Morgan
Loretta Swit, Larry Linville, Gary Burghoff, Jamie Farr

Produced by Gene Reynolds and Larry Gelbart
Written by Larry Gelbart & Simon Muntner
Directed by William Jurgensen

William Christopher . . . . Father Mulcahy
Kario Salem . . . . .The Youngster
Anthony Palmer . . . . The Sergeant
Lois Foraker . . . . .Nurse Able
Albert Hall . . . . .Corporal
Tom Ruben . . . . P.F.C.
Lynn Marie Stewart . . . . Nurse Plummer

Copyright 1976 – 20th Century Fox Film Corporation

Non-Credited Appearances . . . . Dennis Troy, Kellye Nakahara, Roy Goldman,
Sarah Fankboner, Jeff Maxwell

Chapters

1: *Main Titles*
2: *The Police Action – 0:51*
3: *A Promise to God – 5:40*
4: *Phosphorus Burns – 7:03*
5: *One Sponge Short – 10:18*

6: *Deluge – 11:49*
7: *Plasma Problems – 15:06*
8: *A Drastic Situation – 17:26*
9: *Something's Burning – 21:31*
10: *End Titles – 24:31*

Closing Stills

1: *Mulcahy*
2: *Hawkeye*
3: *B.J.*
4: *Margaret*
5: *Potter in the shower*

Synopsis: The 4077th is inundated with casualties, including those from the South Korean Army, a GI with phosphorus burns who's treated in the kitchen sink, a plasma shortage as well as a shortage of surgical gloves and a fire in the laundry bin outside O.R. Interspersed with newsreel footage of Winston Churchill praising the American Army, President Truman speaking at the University of Wyoming and light-hearted news back home, the PA announces that China has attacked the UN lines with 300,000 men. Despite working in adverse field conditions, the 4077th is awarded The Meritorious Unit Commendation by order of the Secretary of the Army, but nobody seems very concerned about it, just fatigued

Commentary by Larry Gelbart: "Although we used snippets of newsreel footage in several shows, 'Deluge' was the first episode we used such material as the glue for a show. In fact, it was only after we shot the episode and found that we really didn't have enough for the 24 minutes and 20 seconds that the show ran that we decided the only way to bulk it up (shooting more original material would have been impossible) was to buy archival footage (none of that stuff is ever free) and splice it between our own filmed sequences." Commentary by Gene Reynolds: "I'd always wanted to do a show where the whole thing took place in the O.R. or whatever."

PA Announcements by Todd Sussman

Authors' Notes: The barber's tent is seen again on the Ranch set.

The ambulance arriving at the chopper pad with Radar jumping off is the same clip from Season 1's "Cowboy," and Cowboy can be seen landing the chopper.

In Episode 91, "Some 38th Parallels," it's been noted that a yellow sign that says, "We Deliver," can be seen in the break room next to the O.R. doors. It's not in the break room in this episode.

Once again, Frank is wearing the bathrobe usually worn by Henry. This is the third robe worn by Frank (blue plaid, red plaid and the one in this episode).

The Interview – 2/24/1976

Season 4 / Episode 97 / Production 97 – G525

Alan Alda, Mike Farrell, Harry Morgan
Loretta Swit, Larry Linville, Gary Burghoff, Jamie Farr

Produced by Gene Reynolds and Larry Gelbart
Written by Larry Gelbart
Directed by Larry Gelbart *(his last episode with* M*A*S*H)

(This episode is in black and white without a laugh track)

William Christopher. . . . . Father Mulcahy
Clete Roberts . . . . The Interviewer

Non-Credited Appearances. . . . . Dennis Troy, Jeff Maxwell

Chapters

1: *Main Titles*
2: *A Look at the 4077th – 0:49*
3: *Boredom – 4:21*
4: *An Unequal Balance – 6:51*
5: *Fear – 7:46*

6: *Feeling Changed – 11:18*
7: *Heroes – 15:23*
8: *What I Miss Most – 18:10*
9: *When the War's Over... – 19:09*
10: *End Titles – 25:03*

Closing Stills

1: *Mulcahy*
2: *Clete Roberts / Interviewer*
3: *B.J.*
4: *Potter*
5: *Frank*
6: *Radar*
7: *Klinger*
8: *Hawkeye*

Synopsis: One of the most critically acclaimed episodes of the series, "The Interview," filmed in black and white and without a laugh track features Clete Roberts interviewing the staff of the 4077th. Inspired by Edward R. Murrow's field interviews of troops during the Korean War, the cast, in a rare display, ad-libs their responses as their characters would. Written and directed by Larry Gelbart, "The Interview," a Humanitas Prize-winning episode, marks the end of Gelbart's four-year run on *M*A*S*H*, which many consider to be the show's best years.

Commentary by Larry Gelbart: "'The Interview' script is a mixture of written portions and others that were improvised (for the first and only time in the life of the series), some of those improvised in rehearsal, some as the cameras were rolling. As is generally known, Loretta Swit was appearing in a play in NY when we shot this episode. She had been given permission to go to NY to appear in a play and so she was not on hand when we filmed 'The Interview.' I wish we had been able to include her. 'The Interview' was not simply a matter of filming improvised lines from the actors. It was far more complicated than that and did, indeed, require the writing of certain speeches for them. They pitched similar proposals. I had always been trying to do as much as possible. I wouldn't have known how to do anything less than too much" (on why he refused similar offers, like those made to Reynolds, to stay on as creative consultant).

Commentary by Gene Reynolds: "I saw something that Edward R. Murrow had done and I said to Gelbart, 'That's a show for us.' It came to the end of the season and they wanted one more episode. I said to Gelbart, 'Hey, remember that idea for a show I had?' We lined them all up (the cast) and had them answer some questions, in character. They'd been on the show for four years and sure as hell knew their characters."

Authors' Notes: There are no PA announcements in this episode.

This is one of Alan Alda's episodes "that worked." He is not alone in that opinion as "The Interview" remains a fan favorite.

The closing stills are all in color with the exception of #2.

All the closing stills, except # 2, are of the staff being interviewed.

When asked if this experience has changed him, Father Mulcahy speaks one of most poignant lines in the series' 11-year run. Amazingly, this little speech by Mulcahy is, in most cases, cut in syndication.

This is the last episode that William Christopher will be listed in the closing credits. Starting with Season 5, he will become part of the main cast and his name will appear in the opening credits for the remainder of the series.

This episode, as noted, marks the end of Larry Gelbart's time with *M*A*S*H*, as he felt it was time to move on to work on other projects. While doing research for this book, the authors were surprised, and yet not surprised, at the praise Mr. Gelbart has received and continues to receive, not only from other writers before and after his departure, but the cast as well. Mike Farrell summed it up nicely when he said that he felt cheated he was only able to work with Gelbart for one season. Larry Gelbart could not have left on a higher note than "The Interview."

After WWII and Korea, serving as a war correspondent, Clete Roberts became a well-known Southern Californian newscaster for over 30 years, as well as some acting in movies and TV dramas. Roberts, born in Portland, Oregon, on February 1, 1912, died in Los Angeles on September 30, 1984. The Associated Press Television and Radio Association of California, Nevada and Hawaii, established a $1500 scholarship in his memory.

The Interviews

Fans have often wondered how Henry Blake, Margaret Houlihan and Trapper John would have responded to the interviewer in "The Interview." 30 years later, Larry Gelbart has returned to his *M*A*S*H* days to satisfy the curiosity with newly-written interviews, most of which have never been seen before; featuring the three missing cast members from the original episode. As an added bonus, Larry has included an interview with Colonel Flagg. Once again, we are unable to adequately express our gratitude for Larry's continuing efforts and contributions to help make this book what it is.

Henry Blake

Reporter: Do you have a minute, Colonel Blake?

Henry: God only knows how that happened.

Reporter: Being in charge of a MASH unit must keep you on your toes.

Henry: If I took my boots off, all you'd see'd be ten little stubs. This job's enough to make a one-armed paperhanger seem ambidextrous.

Reporter: I'm struck by the fact that everyone I've talked to seems to have retained their sense of humor.

Henry: Around here? Around here laughter's just crying without the tears.

Reporter: It must get pretty grim at times.

Henry: The truth is, there's only one thing that saves our sanity.

Reporter: Mail from home? Your faith?

Henry: The latrine.

Reporter: That's the last answer I —

Henry: The latrine's the one place anyone can be alone. Where you can read a book, where you can take a minute to remember that there's more to life than just dying. It's the one place where no one's asking you to sew someone's leg back on or you find yourself working on a kid that should be going to the prom instead of going into shock.

Reporter: You're married?

Henry: I was born that way.

Reporter: In what town, if I may ask?

Henry: Bloomington. The one in Illinois, not in Indiana — unless that's changed, too, since I went away.

Reporter: Is that where your family is?

Henry: That's where I left them.

Reporter: Would you like to say hello on television?

Henry: Be better if this was hug-and-kissovision, but, yeah, can I?

Reporter: Go right ahead.

Henry: (To camera) Lorraine? Hi, honey. Hi, kids. I got your report cards this morning and I had Radar go out and post 'em on the compound bulletin board so everybody can see why I'm so proud of you both. Especially how you're doing in math. You must get those brains from your mom. Got to be. Old as I am, I still don't know how many tens to give someone for a five-dollar bill. (To Reporter) Thanks.

Reporter: Is that it?

Henry: That's it. (To camera) Except I'm counting the days till we're back together again.

Reporter: You have any idea when that will be?

Henry: I try not to have too many ideas. There's always someone who ranks you who's sure you'll agree that he's got a better one. Anyway, you tend to lose all sense of time when you're this far away from normal. It's kinda like somebody broke one hand off my clock.

Reporter: When you do finally get home —

Henry: From your lips, right?

Reporter: — what are you going to tell your children is the biggest lesson being over here has taught you?

Henry: To always try to work things out, I guess. Whatever those things might happen to be. You don't make your point killing the other guy. Even if you do, it's kinda wasted if the other guy's not around to get the message.

Reporter: And that you'll see them as soon as possible?

Henry: That goes without saying, which is why I say it all the time.

Reporter: It's just that business is just too good around here, right?

Henry: Let's just say it takes a whole lot longer to take a bullet out of a belly than it does putting one into one. Did that sound too preachy?

Reporter: It sounded just fine, Colonel.

Henry: Henry. I'm much more a "Henry" than I'll ever be a colonel.

Reporter: Thank you, *Henry.* I think you put things excellently.

Henry: That's why I'm over here getting eight hundred bucks a month.

Trapper John McIntyre

Reporter: Captain John McIntyre is a surgeon attached here at the 4077. What they call a chest cutter, is that right, Captain?

Trapper John: Right. I look inside 'em for any souvenirs our troops might be trying to smuggle home as souvenirs.

Reporter: And removing them forthwith.

Trapper John: I don't get into a lot of fights from any patients who want to hold on to them.

Reporter: A lot of them are very young, is that true?

Trapper John: Too young to be doing what they're doing. Our job's giving 'em a chance to get old.

Reporter: You have a most unusual nickname, I'm told. "Trapper John," is that correct?

Trapper John: It's a hangover from college.

Reporter: Would you tell us how you got it?

Trapper John: The hangover?

Reporter: The nickname.

Trapper John: Nope.

Reporter: Too personal?

Trapper John: Sorry.

Reporter: Didn't mean to pry.

Trapper John: I'll tell you the college, if you like.

Reporter: But not how you —

Trapper John: It happened a long time ago. Happened B.M., you could say. Before Marriage.

Reporter: Well, we certainly wouldn't want to get you into any trouble back home.

Trapper John: Let me clue you in on something: I wouldn't mind being in trouble back home one bit. I wouldn't mind anything if I could be doing it back home.

Reporter: It's not easy being this far away.

Trapper John: You know what's easy? Hating being this far away. Hating just being a picture on the mantle that my two little girls say goodnight to.

Reporter: General Sherman was right, huh? About war being hell?

Trapper John: If generals hate war so much, how come they can never wait to get into the next one?

Reporter: I understand you tried to adopt what you thought was a Korean orphan some time back.

Trapper John: I thought I could make us both a little less miserable about what was going on here. Happily, the kid's mother was still alive.

Reporter: That would have been a lovely gesture.

Trapper John: I'm not big on gestures. Unless there's some kind of payoff.

Reporter: Would you like to say hello to your own children right now?

Trapper John: Not really. Not as just one more picture in our living room. It's enough they're seeing me. That's a big enough kick for all of us.

Reporter: Do you feel this experience has in any way helped you as a doctor?

Trapper John: Let me ask you a question: just how many people you figure're going to be carried into my office someday with a chunk of shrapnel sticking out of their heads? I don't know where you live pal, but where I come from very few folks ever step on a landmine in the middle of trying to cross the street.

Reporter: Would you say there's been any positive aspect of any of this for you at all?

Trapper John: Of course, there is. You see people at their best around here — see them coping with the results of what some people can do when they're at their worst.

Reporter: The doctors, you mean?

Trapper John: The doctors, the nurses, the orderlies — Koreans mostly. Every day kind of bleeds into the next around here — in every sense of the word — the routine gets to be fairly unmemorable. But I have the feeling that years from now I'm gonna remember each and every one of them. And the face that goes with each one. *(A pause, then to the camera)* Hi, sweetheart. Hi, Becky. Hi, Cathy.

Colonel Flagg

Reporter: As you might imagine, an army field hospital sees an awful lot of traffic in any 24-hour period. A certain percentage of those comings and goings have nothing to do with the medical personnel stationed here with the 4077. We spoke with one such officer on the strict condition that he be allowed to be interviewed only if he could respond to our questions with his back to the camera. Why this was so would soon become apparent — even if his identity did not. May I at least call you by your rank, sir?

Flagg: I'd prefer you didn't.

Reporter: It's all right to say that you're an officer, though?

Flagg: It's all right to say anything you like. One of the things our country is fighting for over here is the right for anyone and everyone to say anything at all they like. Likewise, it's my right not to say whatever it is I don't want to say.

Reporter: Fair enough.

Flagg: It's also my duty to report anyone to the proper authorities for saying something that they thought it was all right to.

Reporter: I'm not sure I follow.

Flagg: I'm not sure you realize just how much you do.

Reporter: When you say "the proper authorities," can you be a bit more specific?

Flagg: About what?

Reporter: About just who "the proper authorities" might be?

Flagg: If you're not doing anything wrong, you'll probably never have any occasion to find that out.

Reporter: And what would qualify as doing something wrong?

Flagg: Anything, anybody that questions what we're doing over here — any questions about our leadership.

Reporter: In short, anything that questions anything at all.

Flagg: Anything having to do with the war.

Reporter: Technically, this isn't a war.

Flagg: Then technically no one's dying, right?

Reporter: And just how does all that concern you, if I may ask?

Flagg: It's my job to see that everyone in this effort is all on the same team. That everyone on our side has the right amount of blue and white to go along with however red they might be.

Reporter: You're from army intelligence?

Flagg: You setting up your own punchline? Save it. I've heard them all.

Reporter: Basically speaking, what it is, is you're spying on people.

Flagg: Spying's a crass word. I think of what I'm doing as monitoring their patriotism.

Reporter: And this is all in the cause of freedom?

Flagg: The price of freedom includes giving up however much of it is required so that you can hold onto the rest.

Reporter: Do you ever listen to whatever it is you're saying?

Flagg: I don't have that kind of time, really.

Reporter: I think I'm beginning to understand why it is you won't face the camera, sir.

Flagg: Who I am is not important. The more people know about me, the harder it is to find out about them.

Reporter: Does that include getting all the dirt you can on the surgeons at this MASH unit? The medical officers?

Flagg: (Scoffs) Officers. There're enough bleeding hearts around here to fill up a bucket a minute.

Reporter: You don't think that they do their job well?

Flagg: Saving lives? The odd limb? I'll give 'em that.

Reporter: I'm sure they'd appreciate it.

Flagg: You going to need much more time, fella?

Reporter: You have to get back to work?

Flagg: Vigilance is not piecework, friend. It's not a hobby either.

Reporter: I'll let you go then. And I do thank you for your time.

Flagg: You mind if I ask you a few questions?

Reporter: Turnabout's fair play. Shoot.

Flagg: Not now. Before you go. I did a little research when I heard you were coming here and there's a couple of organizations you belong to that I'd like to know a little more about.

Reporter: Anytime you say. I'm not leaving until tomorrow.

Flagg: Let's hope you do.

Igor

Reporter: I wonder if I might have a minute of your time?

Igor: Anyone can have my minutes, sir.

Reporter: What're you serving for dinner tonight?

Igor: You really don't want to know.

Margaret Houlihan

The Interviewer: Major Margaret Houlihan is in charge of the nursing staff at the 4077th. Major Houlihan.

Margaret: Present and accounted for.

The Interviewer: I'm told you're not the first member of your family officer to serve in the armed forces, is that true?

Margaret: Brass runs in the Houlihan family, sir. My father fought in World War One and Two. He'd have volunteered if there'd been a Three. Or even a four.

The Interviewer: He was a man of action, I take it.

Margaret: He fathered seven children, sir.

The Interviewer: He was a member of the cavalry, was he not?

Margaret: He never hesitated to go with the whip.

The Interviewer: What is it that gets you down the most, around here Major?

Margaret: Whenever we lose a patient. Whenever I think I could have, should have done something more. When I feel I should have anticipated a complication — or I overlooked something that was right in front of my eyes all the time, and I was thinking about something other than what I should have been thinking about.

The Interviewer: Like missing being home?

Margaret: This is home, sir. This place. This war. These men. Their sacrifices.

The Interviewer: Do I hear a tear in your voice?

Margaret: There's no time for tears around here. I'll cry when it's over.

The Interviewer: It must be a great responsibility, caring for so many casualties.

Margaret: We just take them one or two, or sometimes twenty at a time. The big trick is not to think of the patients as just numbers — as just so many statistics that go into a report that winds up in somebody's filing cabinet under "out of sight, out of mind." You've got to remember to take a peek at the odd dog tag from time to time to remind yourself that that dangling leg or exposed gut you're helping put back together belongs to somebody's dad or son or brother or boyfriend — that all that blood and pus soiling your linen is coming out of someone who's got a name attached to him.

The Interviewer: You seem — if I may so, Major — you seem near exhaustion.

Margaret: What I am mostly, is tired of being tired. It's a special responsibility, a grind, really, knowing that your hand might be the first one a patient's felt since he left home. Possibly the last hand some of them will ever know.

The Interviewer: Something even the best surgeon can't give them.

Margaret: It's nothing you can learn.

The Interviewer: It's essentially a man's world, wouldn't you say, this business of war?

Margaret: Getting into them seems to be.

The Interviewer: What about leave? You ever get any?

Margaret: Just enough to make you realize you don't get nearly as the number you need. There're just so many senses you can afford to lose, you know.

The Interviewer: Humor apparently not being one of them.

Margaret: Some of what happens around here would be tragic if it weren't so funny; sometimes it's so tragic, it's funny.

The Interviewer: What do you think will happen when the U.S. leaves?

Margaret: The truth? I think I'll be a little old nurse by the time we ever get out of here.

The Interviewer: Here's hoping it's sooner than that.

Margaret: I'm not a spokeswoman or anything, but may I just tell how grateful we all are for this attention you're paying to the job we're doing. You get the feeling sometimes that, aside from our families, we've kind of dropped off the planet, that we've been kind of disinvited to the party — like everyone back home is busy living their real lives and for us to give them a call when we get back to town.

The Interviewer: You make an excellent spokeswoman.

Margaret: I clean a pretty mean bedpan, too.

The Interviewer: Can you tell me what you miss most?

Margaret: Being over here?

The Interviewer: There must be something.

Margaret: Being selfish, I guess. Being able to cry over a chipped nail. Or a run in my stockings. Or just stockings. Anything to pamper myself. Soaking in a tub. I haven't seen a bubble in a year.

The Interviewer: How about your family?

Margaret: We write. We talk. Being apart, we're closer than we've ever been.

The Interviewer: Anyone at home you'd like to say hello to, to send a message? They'll see it.

Margaret: Hi, everyone. I'm a bit behind on the mail, but everything's great here, the war to one side, that is. Please send the recipe for your Toll House cookies, Mom. We just can't get enough of them even though the nursing staff has put on about a hundred pounds collectively.

The Interviewer: Thanks for talking with us, Major.

Margaret: Any time. I'm always here.

Appendix – Season 4

Character Profiles

Hawkeye

Episode 73 and 74: Brings Frank a gift from Tokyo — a MacArthur doll — wind him up and he returns from anywhere.

Let Radar develop the nurse's chest x-rays.

Stayed up all night with Radar when his earthworm farm was wiped out.

Had a live chicken flown in by chopper — said it was a rare bird... it could tap dance *(in his file)*.

A year ago, Provost Marshall said he stole a steam shovel — "Couldn't get a cab" *(in his file)*.

Father crazy about Indians / Grandfather sold them whiskey and hors d'ovuvres.

77: Serial number — US 19905607.

Father notified of Hawkeye's death.

On the phone with his father — Orville threw a no-hitter.

78: Has an uncle in Suffolk — a sheep farmer that never married — lifelong Anglophile.

England is the only place he knows of where "a boy can grow up to be the Queen."

79: Accused a French gynecologist of not taking his work seriously.

80: Only pet he ever had was a stuffed owl.

81: Worked in a resort hotel to help his way through pre-med school — earned $10 per week and all the "pride he could swallow."

Gave Klinger jockey shorts on Mother's Day.

New aging process for good gin — lets it sit a full 20 minutes.

Hasn't delivered a kid since he drove his Nephew to his grandmother's.

83: Klinger's egg reminds him of Nedick's in Grand Central Station.

Read in *Life* magazine that students at Cal Tech stuffed 15 people into a Volkswagen.

Teaches English to Korean locals — "Frank Burns eats worms."

Chess move from Vienna, 1906: "The Lapinsky Move" — Learned it from Mrs. Lapinsky, tall woman with hairy legs — always carried a bag of strudel. Caught 'hairy leg' from her.

84: Operated on 40 civilians — bus blew up.

86: Studied the violin until he got beat up by the teacher.

87: Crabapple Cove Courier — Hometown newspaper.

89: Stretch Pulaski — tallest Pole Hawkeye knows.

Reads *Fun* magazine with bikini-clad woman on cover.

91: Makes $400 per month *(In Episode 12, he makes $413.50 per month).*

Spent untold hours with "Lefty" — Sol & Sol's daughter and waitress.
Only child *(has a nephew in Episode 80 and a mother & sister in previous episodes).*
Eloise McKay — girl he knew in 8th grade let him touch her slip in a box behind science building.
Samuel Sacks — Smartest doctor he ever knew and head of his medical school.
Mrs. Tomassino — geometry teacher Hawkeye hated — stood over him with a yardstick — looked like she had 3 nostrils.
Used to have a practice back in Boston before drafted.
Strippers Margie Heart and Polly O'Day *(mentioned).*
Ann Corio, a real stripper *(mentioned).*

92: Impotent — never happened before.
Knew a woman who collected clippings of mine shafts accidents.
Was in the back of a fruit truck on a pile of rotting peaches with a copy of Fanny Hill — went over a bump and it was heaven.

93: White civilian boxer shorts.

94: Uncle spent time at Bellevue — caught in subway with mirrors on top of shoes.

95: Surgical residency in Boston.
Lived with Carlye Breslin for a year and a half in a small flat.
Painted their flat "hunter green."
Didn't ask for marriage as he was in residency — the best medical learning experience outside the 4077th he could have.

97: Brought dictionary from home — has all the books in it.
Most difficult thing to adjust to is everything is painted green.
Loved Hemingway.
Misses pistachio ice cream — banana pancakes and the smell of bacon frying.
Wrote a "heartfelt" letter to Bess Truman and wants to know why she hasn't written back

B.J.

Episode 73 Was in residency in Sausalito two months ago.
and 74: Went to Stanford Medical School — Tau Phi Epsilon Fraternity.
In the top ten every time he graduated.
Has a house in Mill Valley.
Wife Peggy was 8 months pregnant.
Five weeks training at Fort Sam Houston with "some idiot shooting live ammo" over their heads.
Was with Peggy at "The Top of the Mark," her first night out since having the baby.
Baby sitter, Norma Jean is 16 years old, gave him the message to report to Travis in two days to ship out.
Comes from three generations of doctors.
28 years old.
First time he meets Frank: "What say, Ferret face?" and grabs Margaret's leg as he falls (drunk).

79: Has a compass…back home in San Francisco.

80: Knows about horses because he stepped in manure once.
Lasso'd his little Sister because she owed him a nickel.

81: Has a fear of heights.
Peg is 5'1."

Likes bubble gum.

83: Writing his third letter home this week (the only way to keep his sanity). Peggy sent her first overseas package: cake in a tin packed in newspapers, chocolate bar melted onto the jockey shorts.

Chess move from Heidelberg, 1910 — "Zuckertort's Attack" *(according to Hawkeye).*

86: Father wouldn't allow him any toys that looked like guns — miserable until he discovered dolls.

87: Three letters from Peggy — one from Waggles, his dog.

95: High school drama teacher was Gerald Rasmussen (terrible actor).

97: Did three amputations before he had his first breakfast at the 4077. Daughter — Erin.

Colonel Potter

Episode 73 Takes command of the 4077 on September 19, 1952 at 1600 hours —
and 74: Regular Army.

75: Saddle goes in his office — box goes in his office — the rest in his tent *(belongings when he arrives).*

Has his saddle from his Calvary days in the "Great War" — WW I.

Was 15 years old in WW I — lied about his age — Had big thighs for a boy.

Knew a private who pretended he was a mare and carried a colt in his arms for weeks.

Another man said he was a daisy and insisted on being watered every morning.

Methodist — Hates to sing alone — two or three other Methodists in camp.

Has 18 months left and would appreciate everyone "Keeping their noses clean."

Picture of horse, "Lillie Bell" (bottom row, 2nd from right).

Picture of horse, "Royal King" (bottom row, 3rd from right).

Picture of horse, "Opel's Pride" — a filly Potter bought in 1947.

Picture of horse, "Sylvia Bee" — Opel's Pride's sister (bottom row, 3rd from right as is Royal King).

Picture of Mrs. Potter always goes on the right side of his desk — never starts a day without saluting her.

Mrs. Potter has 5 sisters and "Not a bum in the lot."

Has a "Good Conduct Medal with a clasp" — only an enlisted man can get one — not MacArthur or Bradley.

Mostly administration — hasn't been in an OR for 2 years *(according to Radar).*

Had a still on Guam in WW II — it blew up — that's how he got his Purple Heart — friends call him "Stud."

76: Has an American Indian blanket.

Another Colonel Potter — PX Colonel — Just retired — Shipped a temple home to open as a drive-in.

Friends with General Nate Morrison and his wife, Violet — could use one of her legs as an umbrella stand.

78: After Frank crushes his jeep, he shoots one bullet into it.

79: Was lost in the Argonne Forrest during WW I — couldn't find his outfit — no food for 3 days.

Taken prisoner — had his head shaved and "beaten to a pulp"

WW I, after Chateau Thierry, was temporarily blinded by gas — spent over a month in a French hospital with bandaged eyes — taken care of by a nurse named Colette — saw her for the first time after the bandages came off and pretended to still be blind.

80: Married for 27 years.

Mildred sent him talcum powder — took a long walk — no chafing.

Mildred had a corn removed.

Mildred's cousin Natalie said, "War is hell."

Opens beer cans with a surgical hammer and chisel.

A slip on horse manure is "A tiptoe through the tulips."

Rides the horse Radar gave him for his anniversary to the chopper pad — incoming wounded

81: Reads the kids a story: "Field stripping, cleaning and routine maintenance of Garand rifles — section 22."

82: Will be in command of the 4077 for another 17 months, 2 weeks and 6 days.

84: One-fourth Cherokee Indian.

85: Has a bottle of liquor in the company safe — combination 42-36-42 — Wife's measurements.

86: Uncle Claude collected fancy guns — prized piece went off while cleaning it — severed his foot and kept going across the room and killed the cat — buried "Tabby" in one shoe box and Claude's toe in another.

87: Letter from Dr. Norman Chase from Cleveland — proctologist — "Good 'ol Squint."

Letter from his son the dentist — specializes in gums — lots of pyorrhea — daughter-in-law Jeanine a week late – son says girl.

Son was born at City general in 1926 — Mrs. P went into labor when she heard Valentino died.

Jeanine at City general — Baby born on the 23rd, 8 ½ pounds, girl — Sherry Pershing Potter

88: Last time he had tomato juice was at Camp Dix — house on base — peacetime — did odd hot appendix and taught dirty words to their mynah bird.

Klinger was AWOL 4 time this month.

Allergic to tomato juice.

89: Learned about foot care from Truman in WW I — good feet run in family except Uncle Ben, two extra toes — little leather side-cars on Ben's shoes.

Wife gets premonition something happens to Potter.

Wife listens to the crazy gypsy that runs fruit stand.

Wife having root canal — no vertical hold on the TV — and the scales came off her guppy.

Calls her "Mother."

90: Letter to General Harrison Hardcastle, Letterman General Hospital, S.F. — daughter Amanda sells McCall's subscriptions — Potter takes two years.

Was stationed at Fort Leavenworth — four-year subscription to Mrs. Hardcastle's cupcakes.

92: Notes on Equestrian Etiquette are in his "in" basket under his toenail clippers.

Made the semi-finals at fort Dix in 1925 in horseshoes — Aced out a 300 pound supply sergeant.

Grandpa Roy whistles moose calls.

Mrs. Potter needlepoint's migratory fowl as a hobby.

Impotent in WWI — got over it in WW II.

94: Duncan McShane — 1st pilot Potter ever knew from WW I — pulled pin — wind blew back grenade.

95: He, Churchill and Eisenhower all paint, according to Potter.
96: Knew a general in the army who ordered all horses corked before parades.
Sister-In-Law Rose swallowed a dried apricot at bridge club — 10 minutes
later drank water.
Apricot expanded to original size — rushed to hospital — Potter did
"Apricotectomy."
97: Got into the Calvary as a kid — excited by the glamour of it — then went
into medicine.
Greatest hero is Abraham Lincoln, "The most interesting American that
ever lived."
Misses his wife, son, daughter-in-law and his new baby grandchild who he
hasn't seen yet.
Also misses people his own age for companionship.
Won't say hello on camera because he doesn't think it's dignified.

Margaret

Episode 75: Has a yellow pillow on her bed that says, "Aloha Hawaii."
10 years — spotless record.
"Major Frank Burns" — "Just friends, sir."
76: Reading a book, "Kindled Flame" *(written by Margaret Pedler in 1931)*.
Sends Frank a love-note: *"I'm dying to keep you warm."* Frank tears it into
little pieces — has saved everything Frank has ever written her.
85: Hits Frank right in the chin with an uppercut after being willed his clothes.
86: Father had a Colt just like the one Frank has under his shirt.
87: Black nightie w/ purple trim in mail from Frederick's of Hollywood.
88: Served under General Barker at Fort Ord — once asked by Barker to
spank him, according to Frank.
Knows 2 General Barkers.
89: Wee bit of fungus, two bunions, one corn, ankles a bit swollen, according to
Hawkeye .
90: Went to a medical conference in Tokyo — stayed at The Hollywood Hotel.
Fred — physical therapist likes to stay underwater.
Captain Parish — Gave a talk on earwax problems in the military.
Doctor Nyler — gave a talk on peristaltic rhythm — nearly won Nobel
Prize for dysentery.
Also a talk on suppositories — "The Bullet of Health."
Sardine sandwich on plane back from Tokyo.
Brought Frank a box of glazed plums.
Went to see a play at The Kabuki — English — Geisha Girl.
Fred understands Japanese — has the most beautiful Samurai sword with
picture in wallet.
96: Born in an army hospital.
Father assigned to Forts Benning, Ord, Dix and Kilmer.
At five years old had a crying fit because they wouldn't let her get a crew
cut.

Frank

Episode 73 Wants everyone to stand at attention when he enters and exits a movie.
and 74: Tau Phi Epsilon blackballed him because they insisted on double-breasted
tuxedos and he didn't have one. He dyed his brown suit, but it ran when he
danced.
Perspires a lot — family thing on his mother's side. Has father's face and
mother's glands.

Knew a Doctor Hunnicutt who was killed in an explosion at the goiter clinic.

Has a Korean college graduate who does nothing but keep his boots shined at all times — pays him 3 cigarettes a day, "But it's worth it."

Has nothing against the UN, except that it's full of foreigners

Episode 75: Boyhood dream to have his own command.

Service station back home having a free buffet to open their new lube rack with punch and Greasy the Clown.

Calls his wife "Mommy."

Personal papers from his tenure in command to be donated to his college library after the war.

Personal papers not only benefit humanity, they're also tax deductible.

From Frank Burns, Commanding Officer to Sergeant Zale, supply: an order to glue cracked bedpans.

To the Mess Sergeant: Hereafter, you will drain the oil from tuna fish.

Reprimanded Hawkeye and BJ for setting fire to the latrine (BJ said it was a weenie roast).

77: Voluntary calisthenics program isn't working out — "People volunteer better by force."

78: Likes to play, "shoe salesman."

Sick of hearing about the wounded.

Trained for a week in a tank at Fort Benning *(The same place we saw Margaret in a nurse's uniform with General Hammond in the Pilot episode).*

After starting the tank, he runs over the nurse's shower, the Swamp and crushes Potter's jeep.

79: Rigged the toilet seats at camp to rise to attention, only for inspections.

Took automotive shop in high school *(implied).*

Sophomore year he met a little brunette Jewish girl named Helen Rappaport — "Smart as a whip."

Was on opposite side of the class debate — "Should Father Coughlin be our next president?"

Helen talked very fast and won the debate — offered to drive Frank home and "ran out of gas."

Frank wanted to save himself for "Miss Right."

He and Louise did not approve of "That sort of happiness before marriage."

80: Camera setting for Potter's picture — F4 and 1/100.

Spit-shines Margaret's shoes.

81: The kids took a roll of his best toilet paper.

Wounded last month when snipers infiltrated. He got nervous cracking open a boiled egg and was awarded the Purple Heart for a shell fragment in the eye.

Has had two Judo lessons.

82: All Burns men crack their knuckles.

Always prays for chocolate pudding.

83: Loves it at the 4077th.

Regular churchgoer — "Great place to kill an hour."

Teaches English to the locals: "Better dead than red," "Get us out of the UN," "Don't contaminate our drinking water with fluoridation."

85: Rat and Rumor Control Officer.

Faints after taking rats out to the trash.

RAT TRAP — Rat enters — sees himself in mirror — thinks it's another rat — device swings down and taps him — turns to see who wants him — WHAMO! Steel knob comes down and cracks him "right in the skull."

Delirious from fever: Thinks he swallowed his lips — wouldn't mind being a doctor if he didn't have to be around sick people — Mother used to smack him when he got sick and smacked him when he got well, too — nobody ever wanted to talk to him except his high school janitor who used to show him pictures of heavyweight champions and was the last to like him — wants Louise and Margaret to be friends — After he's gone, they can both work on the Frank Burns Memorial together — wants Margaret to look for him on the "other side" but ignore him if he's with Louise.

Makes his will to Mulcahy: *The car, house and all the money buried in the back yard goes to the only woman who ever cared and understood him... Louise.* (Louise will have to thaw out the map because it's inside some ground chuck in the basement freezer — savings account number is in the same bottle as his appendix — all profits from his prescription kickbacks go to his children and are recorded in the RED ledger, not the BLUE one he shows to the government.)

To Major Margaret Houlihan: friend, comrade, his "little soldier" he leaves all his clothes.

86: Shot himself in the left foot while cleaning the Colt — has a low threshold for pain — hemorrhoid could put him in a coma — stealing is worse than lying — did both — he ought to know.

87: Wife wants divorce — Chuck passed through the 4077 — meets Louise — tells her about Margaret.

Wife worships ground he walks on — Mother said so.

Parents never divorced — he'd have done better from a broken home — lost all interest in women when he met Louise.

$45 for Margaret's nightie from Frederick's of Hollywood.

88: Wife has a schnauzer.

89: Thinks judo is a religion.

Discussed trench foot with Margaret, got silly and polished his toenails red

90: Once killed a gopher with a stick.

Got a new Andre Kostelanetz record, "Two Alone."

Made Klinger cry when he told him his platform shoes made him look like a tramp, according to Potter.

Has a "snapper" purse that says "no to pickpockets."

Reads *National Geographic* magazine.

Marines stole *The Jolson Story* and won't give it back.

93: Could've eaten off mother's floors.

Blood type B.

97: Wife and children are his strength — after the war, he might write a book on his experiences in Korea.

Possibly go into politics after the war.

"Marriage is the headstone of American society."

Radar

Episode 73: Only oversleeps in the morning / Wears uniform to bed because the
and 74: blankets itch.

Files his bugle under "B" — Files his clipboard under "K."

Brushes his teeth after breakfast, otherwise he can taste the food.

Dropped his watch in the latrine and really doesn't want it back.

Never had a mouthful of cotton because they were vegetarians.

Trapper ran naked through the mess tent "With no clothes on" when he learned he was going home.

Rats ate his dry uniform.

Frank is always feeling Radar's toothbrush to see if it's wet — wakes him at night to inspect him in his shorts.

Runs into a minefield after a mine goes off to save a Korean girl who was checking the field.

Drove his mother's car, but she always changed the tires.

Left his gum in another jeep with a picture-card of Rosalind Russell.

Chews Chiclets for nerves

75: Frank makes him shave and bathe — afraid Frank will hit him when he tells him a new CO is coming.

Good with hamsters, not horses

78: Lent Klinger money against next month last month.

Read that MacArthur doesn't sweat at all

80: Tells Potter he doesn't smoke *(had three cigars in Season 1, 2 in Season 2)*.

Wants a '46 Chevy before finding a girl to settle down with.

Cleaning the office is one of his "best things."

Recommends Frank set his camera for Potter's photo at 2.8 and 1/125 *(rejected by Frank)*.

Not comfortable with Potter — can't dunk his Zwiebacks in Bosco.

Spent 15 summers with his aunt and always came home with "hyperaciditiy."

Henry was like a father to him — taught him everything about life and women.

Henry let him keep "Black Beauty" — a hamster *(in Episode 61, he had a mini-zoo)*.

82: First name is Walter.

83: Doesn't do The Peabody while dancing.

Faints when VD films are shown.

84: Plays "Battleship" with Sparky over the phone.

Likes his ice cream mushy "The mushier, the better."

Likes Chinese food and walking in the rain.

85: Wins the Soldier of the Month contest — 6 days in Tokyo — broke his toothbrush — will get new one in Tokyo — knows how to protect himself from the girls in Tokyo as he studied karate.

Brought back from Tokyo by MP — charged with "drunk and disorderly."

Tried to drink the ink in a tattoo parlor.

Swam 50 laps in an eight-foot bathhouse tub.

Calls Potter "Sherm."

86: Margaret's leg reminds him of his pony back home except pony's hair is brown.

Keys to Potter's office and oats for the horse and his bike back in Iowa — key to gun bin.

Every time his Sister borrows the bike, the chain slips off.

Sleeps and showers with the keys.

Drunk on one beer but he's okay because knows when to throw up *(Martinis didn't make him drunk?)*.

400 kids in his high school — Ottumwa Central.

25 "bucks" in photo booth and 16 hours for pics when he got his corporal stripes.

Keeps bear in a box under his bed.

87: Uncle Ed made the home-movie, "Sunday Dinner At Ottumwa, Iowa."

Ranger, Radar's dog — they grew up together.

Radar's sled *(seen)*.

Uncle David — Does "Binoculars" with corn cobs, salt & pepper shakers and rolls of toilet paper.

Cousin Millie — Runs a charm school and a gas station.

Uncle Bill (dark suit) — Wanted to be a clergyman but couldn't find a good corner.

Aunt Emily.

Cousin Jimmy — Just started wearing glasses like Radar's.

Radar's Mother — Makes a good chocolate cake *(seen on table)*.

87: Continued — Food: Chocolate cake, milk, fruit salad with those little marshmallows, chicken, peas.

Buns Mother made.

Saying Grace: *"Thank you for the world so sweet, thank you for the food we eat, thank you for the birds that sing, thank you G-d for everything."*

All go into the house to listen to the radio — BJ: Jack Benny, Potter: Fred Allen, Mulcahy: Bishop Sheen.

88: Little brother died.

89: Keeps grape Nehi in a crate marked, "Human Blood" — Keeps pretzels in heater.

Uncle Ed went off the wagon on hunting trip — hopes he can play pump organ without those toes.

Helped Hawkeye with foot inspection.

Potter is like what Pop would've been if he hadn't died *(used to be angry about it)*.

Klinger looks a little like Aunt Jean before electrolysis.

Long thin telescope peeks into Margaret's tent *(Frank is there)*.

Potter likes coffee real strong — Potterism: *"It grows hair on your saddle horns."*

Only souvenir he has so far is a small ivory Jesus for his mother's car.

Ate grasshoppers and rice but sauce made him sick — thinks it's Mexican.

Pet guinea pig in his office — sent away for it — named Dopey.

Aunt Dorothy got premonitions when truss got warm

90: Learning to dance my mail

92: Hamster back home.

Visited Mount Rushmore when the army was cleaning out his nose.

Called for the time in Kansas City and listened for over an hour

93: Gets his intuition from his Uncle Ernest.

Ernest knew he was going to die a week before it happened — moved next to undertaker so he wouldn't have so far to travel.

Spells cretin C-R-I-T-E-N.

His guinea pig in the office bites Frank

94: Likes *National Geographic* for the African pictures — hears a twig — thinks Uncle Ed will catch him.

Best thing is fear *(aside from cleaning the office)*.

97: Only went as far as high school.

Hardest thing to get used to are the toilet seats — splinters and slivers.

Grows earthworms — puts them in a ditch he dug behind OR and filled it with "ash & stuff" from the latrines — they double in 60 days — he must have 160 to 180,000 worms and will give most of them to local farmers and race the rest.

Has #6 cockroach in a jar — numbers 1-5 died, or #6 ate them.

Puts #6 in a track with the worms and races them.

Fixing up a '41 Chevy he swapped with a neighbor for a pregnant sow.

Eleanor Roosevelt's car stalled at the train crossing in Ottumwa.

Doesn't have a TV — nearest TV is at Grange Hall in Mooseville, 50 miles away.

Mooseville is two hours away by car, or one hour by foot.

Says hello to "Mom & Uncle Ed"

Klinger

Episode 75: Wears a Warner Bra and plays with dolls *(ploy)*.

Last wish is to be buried in his mother's wedding gown.

In regulation fatigues complete with hat *(rare)*.

Wherever uniform touches him, he has a rash — rash okay "downstairs," because he's wearing a half-slip.

Business girls don't like him because they're jealous of his clothes.

Very careful about "tiny livestock"

76: Mink coat.

Sent a photo of himself in a garter belt to MacArthur — MacArthur sent one back of himself smoking a pipe.

Allergic to tetanus — "Blows up like a balloon."

Thinks he has what Bette Davis had in the movie *Mr. Skeffington* (he says *"Mrs. Skeffington"*).

Blood type B positive.

77: Knows when Frank gets a letter from his wife — he can smell the disinfectant.

81: Was an atheist, but gave it up for Lent.

82: Dressed like Moses *(ploy)*.

83: In a dream he was holding a piece of paper that said, "Klinger's nuts," signed by Potter and was waving goodbye to everybody.

Clipped a curl of chest hair for Margaret to keep in her watch *(dream)*.

Margaret kissed him "right on the mouth" *(dream)*.

In San Francisco — big parade with four bands & people carrying a banner that says, "Klinger's nuts" *(dream)*.

In Toledo with loved ones *(dream)* — owns a delicatessen with 8 tables. and individual relish jars *(dream)*.

Margaret is the waitress and still has his chest hair in her watch, pinned on a see-through blouse *(dream)*.

Won a real egg in a poker game *(real)*.

Ploy: Was caught 7 miles down the road by a stream with an inflatable Naval raft — was going to take the stream to the Inchon River to the Sea of Japan to the Golden Gate.

Developed an x-ray in 87 seconds.

85: Uses Louise Burns' fruitcake for rattrap bait.

Wearing the correct underwear for a person of his sex and gender for the first time since he's been in the service

87: *Ploy:* All black mourning attire, including a black veil and a letter from his mother in the mail.

Family tragedy — two older brothers, Maurice and Hakim died in an explosion of the boiler at the Toledo Harmonica Company — Hakim would bathe him and Maurice would nurse him — in the US illegally and lived under the front porch and were fed through the cracks.

Letter in Klinger's handwriting as he translated his mother's Lebanese, but burned the letter as part of a religious ceremony when two brothers die in a harmonica factory or a camel race.

Selective Service Act — Subsection 31-B, paragraph 6, small a, tragedy-wise — As sole remaining son, he's entitled to an immediate discharge.

Personal record states he has no brothers and made up the whole story.

89: Wrote to General Ridgeway saying he loves him asked to be his husband — aid wrote back General Ridgeway happily married.

Mother had premonition about Pearl Harbor but not until December 9.

92: Amos — father stole a violin & stuck it in his crib — started sucking on the bridge.

95: Always looks a little blue due to his heavy beard.

Started shaving at 12 — Sister started shaving at 10.

96: *Ploy:* Told draft board his religion is Aztec.

Told draft board "Bring me a virgin — I'll cut her heart out."

Said, "Ahh" when they checked his ears.

When asked to stick his tongue out, he pulled his pants down.

Kissed the psychiatrist on the mouth.

Was told: "Keep this up and we'll make you an officer."

Archie Jagloff — kid from neighborhood who fell into a sewer — a little jerky after Jagloff grew up and became a Nazi — Army turned him down because of flat feet from goose steppin' in his basement.

97: Wants VD to break up the boredom.

Lavern went to Toledo Waite High School on the Hungarian side of town.

Tony Paco's is also on the Hungarian side of town — has the "Greatest Hungarian hot dogs."

Paco's hot dogs with chili peppers cost 35 cents.

Also has a cold beer — Stroh's Bohemian.

Misses El Verso Cigars *(real cigars from Havana).*

Father's nickname is Butch — Sister is Yvonne.

Says hello to "all the guys at Leo's Grill and J&J's Sweet Shop.

Father Mulcahy

Episode 73 His watch was given to him by his Bishop.

and 74: Frank wants him to write a sermon on "Strength through Obedience."

Handles all denominations.

80: Has dysentery.

81: Boxed before the Jesuits as a featherweight — was wanted for Willie Pep's stable.

87: Given name is, Francis.

Mail from his sister — Sister Angelica — coaches girl's basketball at St. Mary's. *St. Mary's: 42, Visitors: 28. St. Mary's: 56, Visitors: 39.*

Beat Our Lady of Perpetual Sorrow.

Wins Potter's baby pool.

89: Sister has an overbite — bit him on his on his toe when they were kids — kids used to call her, "beaver" and they told her it was because she was a good swimmer.

96: Worked his way through Divinity School as a "B" girl in San Diego *(joking).*

"Doesn't pack 'em in" for services.

Doesn't mind being the only priest — he has a corner on the market.

Wants to be warm, clean and maybe run the CYO.

Seen, Heard, Mentioned or Referenced – Season 4

Movies

Episode 73: Hawkeye mentions "Play it again, Sam" from *Casablanca* (1942).

and 74: Hawkeye mentions "Follow the yellow brick road" from *The Wizard of Oz* (1939).

76: Klinger mentions, "Mrs. Skeffington" from the Bette Davis movie *Mr. Skeffington* (1944).

80: "Lassie" mentioned, Lassie Come Home (1943).
Custer's Last Stand (1936) seen.

83: Annie Get Your Gun (1950) mentioned.
"Trench Foot Through the Ages" VD film mentioned,
"The Bleeding Gum Story" Hygiene film mentioned.

84: "Fresh Earth" with Luise Rainer and Paul Muni, mentioned by B.J. *(This is a mistake; Luise Rainer and Paul Muni were in the 1937 movie* The Good Earth*).*

85: *The Shadow* (1937) mentioned.

86: *Gone with the Wind* (1939) mentioned.
Kansas City Confidential (1952) mentioned in PA announcement.

87: Jiminy Cricket (1925) mentioned.
"How to Make Vaseline at Home" mentioned *(not real).*
"How to Make Vaseline In Combat" mentioned *(not real).*
"Sunday Dinner at Ottumwa Iowa" – Radar's home movie seen.
The Shadow (1937) mentioned by Klinger.

88: *King Kong* (1933) mentioned.

89: B.J. mentions Ashley Wilkes, a reference to *Gone with the Wind* (1939).

90: Hawkeye calls Frank, "Mr. Ravenal," a gambler from the 1936 movie *Showboat.*
The Jolson Story (1946) mentioned by Frank.
"Of Ice and Lice" A Sonja Henie hygiene film mentioned *(not real).*

91: Hawkeye sings "I'm a Yankee Doodle Dandy" from the movie of the same name (from 1942).
The Lost Horizon (1937) mentioned by Hawkeye.
The Ox Bow Incident (1943) mentioned by Hawkeye.
A Yank at Oxford (1938) mentioned by Hawkeye.
"The Wizard of Ox" mentioned by Hawkeye (*The Wizard of Oz,* 1939).
"Cow Green Was My Valley" mentioned by Hawkeye (*How Green Was My Valley,* 1941).
Lassie mentioned by Hawkeye. The original *Lassie* film appeared in 1943.

92: "Clean as A Whistle" VD film mentioned *(not real).*
"Buy You A Drink, Sailor" VD film mentioned *(not real).*
Unidentified movie in the mess tent

96: *Fox Movie Tone News* seen throughout this episode, copyright 1950 20th Century-Fox Film Corporation.

97: "VD is the Enemy" VD film mentioned.
"Don't Let This Happen to You" VD film mentioned.

Songs

Episode 73: Radar plays Assembly on the bugle

and 74: "Follow the Yellow Brick Road" (mentioned by Hawkeye) a song from the 1939 movie, *The Wizard of Oz.*

75: "Baa, Baa, Black Sheep" *(Igor says, "Yes, sir yes, sir. Three bags full…")* from the children's song. Written by unknown and copyright unknown, the earliest publication date for the rhyme or song is 1744.

"There's A Long, Long Trail A-Winding" *("Down that long, long trail with you..." sung by Hawkeye, BJ and Potter)* a WWI-era song. Words by Stoddard King, music by Alonzo "Zo" Elliott, from 1915.

77: "For He's A Jolly Good Fellow" *(sung by BJ, at first, "For he was a jolly good fellow...")* See Episode 13 (page 129) for details.

78: "The Lambert Walk" *(Hawkeye mentions)* from the 1937 musical *Me and My Gal.*

80: "Tiptoe Through the Tulips *(Potter mentions)* Written in 1929 by Al Dubin & Joe Burke.

81: Korean girl plays Mozart on the piano.
"Bye-Lo, baby" *(Radar sings)* Words and music by Ray Perkins, 1919.

82: "The More I See You" *(Klinger sings)* Words by Mack Gordon, music by Harry Warren, 1945.

83: "Harrigan, That's Me" *(Hawkeye sings)* From the Broadway show *Fifty Miles From Boston* by George M. Cohan, 1908.

87: "Afraid to Come Home in the Dark"*(Potter sings)* Words by Harry Williams, music by Egbert Van Alstyne, 1907.
The theme song from "The Shadow" *(Radar hums)* The series premiered as a radio show in 1937. The character itself, a mysterious narrator, first appeared on July 31, 1930 on a Street & Smith radio program, *The Detective Story Hour.*
"Let Me Call You Sweetheart" *(All sing)* Words by Beth Slater Whitson, music by Leo Friedman, 1910.

88: "Serenade in Blue"*(Klinger sings)* Words by Mack Gordon, music by Harry Warren, 1942.
"The Wedding March" *(Margaret hums)* Written by Felix Mendelssohn in 1842 as incidental music for *A Midsummer's Night Dream.*

90: "Swanee" *(Klinger sings "Swanee, how I love ya...")* From the 1939 movie *Swanee River.*

91: "It's Magic" *(Hawkeye sings)* Words by Sammy Cahn, music by Julie Styne, 1948.
"Halo Everybody, Halo" *(Hawkeye sings)* an ad for Halo Shampoo, first heard July 4, 1944 on the CBS radio show *Theater of Romance.*
"The Minute Waltz" *(Hawkeye mentions)* Written by Chopin (1810-1849).
"I'm a Yankee Doodle Dandy" *(Hawkeye sings)* from the 1942 movie of the same name. (Hawkeye also sings "Yankee Doodle Herring.")
"I Can't Dance, My Head Hurts."*(Hawkeye sings)* Origins unknown.
Hawkeye sings bits of two songs from the Broadway musical "South Pacific" (which ran from 1949-54).
Hawkeye sings "You're mine, I'm yours, we're ours" *(not real).*
"There's No Business Like Show Business" *(Hawkeye sings "There's no 'vinism like chauvinism...")* from the movie *There's No Business Like Show Business* (1954).

92: "Carmen" *(Nurse Able whistles)* Composed by George Bizet, first performed in Paris on March 3, 1875.

96: "Ah, Sweet Mystery of Life At Last I Found You," *("Ah, sweet Syngman Rhee of life at last I found you.")* From "Naughty Marietta," an operetta written by Victor Herbert (1859-1924), words by Rida Johnson Young (1869-1926), music by Victor Herbert.
"The Tennessee Waltz" heard in *Fox Movietone News* Footage at dance marathon. "The Charleston" is also heard, written by Redd Stewart (1920s) and recorded by Pee Wee King in 1947.

Prank Frank – Season 4

Episode 73 and 74: Can of Danish ham missing from his office, a gift from his insurance man *(mentioned)*.

Trapper sedated him and shaved "every bit of hair" off his body *(mentioned)*.

Arrested for stealing a general's jeep *(seen)*.

75: Fell down, filthy — a dog chased him and bit his duffle bag (in Margaret's tent) *(seen and mentioned)*.

Reports for duty with a black and blue mark over his left eye *(seen)*.

77: While asleep, Klinger throws snow on Frank's bare feet *(seen)*.

B.J., after shaking a pen, gets a big ink splatter on Frank's pay sheet *(seen)*.

Hawkeye throws him around the mess tent (he's dead) and shoves carrots down his shirt (Frank hates carrots).

79: Implying he took automotive shop in high school, Radar starts the bus engine and Frank falls off the bumper after getting a shock *(seen)*.

Potter tricked him into admitting that he was sending anonymous letters about Radar selling tickets to the hole in the nurse's shower (he felt it was his duty) *(seen)*.

Falls asleep while guarding a prisoner *(seen)*.

The prisoner, with help from Hawkeye and B.J., talks into a walkie-talkie making Frank think he's talking to the enemy *(seen)*.

80: After haggling over a $6.00 charge, Cho Man Chin haggles back with a price of $7.50; Frank accepts *(seen)*.

81: The kids took a roll of his best toilet paper last year *(mentioned)*.

Gives a Korean boy 25 cents. The boy bets double or nothing, Frank loses *(seen)*.

Chasing a Korean boy into the shower thinking he has Frank's Purple Heart, the boy turns the water on in Frank's face. Says he wants to give Korea back to the Indians *(seen)*.

82: Hawkeye and B.J. stuck a turtle in his shorts *(mentioned)*.

83: Hawkeye sewed up his fly *(mentioned)*.

Hawkeye teaches Korean locals to say, "Frank Burns eats worms" and "You tell 'em, Ferret Face" *(both seen)*.

84: Stops on the road to take a picture of a sign that says "Don't stop here — you're under direct enemy vision" and gets shot at *(seen)*.

Radar mocks him behind his back *(seen)*.

Sees locals digging and thinks it's a bomb. Uses a metal detector to search the area and finds Kimchee, pickled cabbage that the Koreans ferment in jars in the ground. *(seen)*.

Hawkeye and B.J. blow up rubber gloves and pop them while Frank's sleeping. He wakes and shoots his cigarette-lighter gun *(seen)*.

85: Hawkeye and B.J. sewed up all the legs on Frank's jockey shorts *(mentioned)*.

86: Last time Frank was alone with Hawkeye and B.J., they whitewashed his behind *(mentioned)*.

87: After listening in on Frank's call to his wife, Margaret throws a chair at him *(seen)*.

88: Hawkeye and B.J. stuffed lard in his gun belt *(mentioned)*.

Hawkeye and B.J. keep writing nasty things on his shorts.

Hawkeye swats him with a towel. Frank asks, "Did you get it?" Hawkeye replies, "Get what?" *(seen)*.

Last month, Potter said Frank's brain had a Charlie horse *(dialog)*.

Potter said, "Kick him in the shins, give Frank a headache" *(dialog)*.

Radar makes Margaret think Frank is proposing, and then gives Frank a note thinking it's from Margaret.

Frank is drunk and signs the requisition to get tomato juice for Colonel Potter *(seen)*.

89: Tied his bootlace to a table leg in Margaret's tent *(seen)*.

Tackles a Korean general. thinking he's the enemy. Apologizes when the Korean general bends his wrist, bringing him to his knees *(seen)*.

Hawkeye glued his boots to two bedpans *(mentioned)*.

Asks a corpsman to throw a football to him. He drops it, then screams for not letting him know the ball was on its way *(seen)*.

During a foot inspection, it's discovered that he has red toenail polish. He was discussing trench foot with Margaret and "Got a little silly" *(seen)*.

90: While drunk, Hawkeye and B.J. put a toe tag on Frank's toe: "Emotionally exhausted and morally bankrupt" *(seen)*.

Leaving the latrine still drunk and with the tag, he stumbles into the back of an ambulance and winds up at a front-line aid station...sound asleep *(partially seen)*.

92: Wishes Korean locals "Chang-Yo" which means, "prostitute" (he meant to say "prosperity").

93: Under his framed photo of Senator McCarthy, Hawkeye wrote in big letters, "Know your enema."

In the real version of events, a nurse opens a door into Frank, knocking him out.

94: Awards a Purple Heart to a wounded GI in post-op and sticks the man with the pin.

Appearances – Season 4

Ahn, Philip .... Episode 91 *(The Father)*
Allport, Christopher .... Episode 76 *(Abbott)*
Arbus, Allan .... Episode 82 *(Major Sidney Freedman)*
Beaty, Ned .... Episode 83 *(Colonel Maurice Hollister)*
Catlett, Mary Jo .... Episode 95 *(Lieutenant Becky Anderson)*
Christopher, Barbara *(Mrs. William Christopher)* .... Episode 80 *(Nurse O'Connor)*
Christopher, William .... Episode 73, 74, 78, 80, 81, 82, 83, 85, 86, 87, 88, 89,
90, 92, 93, 95, 96, 97 *(Father Mulcahy)*
Chung, Byron .... Episode 89 *(Korean Soldier)*
Cruickshanks, Reid .... Episode 73, 74 *(Staff Sergeant)*
Danner, Blythe .... Episode 95 *(Lieutenant Carlye Breslin Walton)*
Dever, Tom .... Episode 73, 74 *(M.P. Lieutenant)*
Doran, Ann .... Episode 81 *(Meg Cratty)*
Farrell, Gwen .... Episode 89 *(Nurse Able)*
Foraker, Lois .... Episode 96 *(Nurse Able)*
Fudge, Alan .... Episode 82 *(Captain Arnold T. Chandler)*
Fujioka, John .... Episode 89 *(General Park)*
Gleeson, Redmond .... Episode 89 *(Sergeant Callan)*
Hagen, Kevin .... Episode 92 *(Colonel Coner)*
Hall, Albert .... Episode 96 *(Corporal)*
Hamilton, Ted .... Episode 78 *(Lieutenant Chivers)*
Haymer, Johnny .... Episode 84, 85, 93 *(Sergeant Zale)*
Hogan, Robert .... Episode 94 *(Lieutenant "Smilin" Jack Mitchell)*
Hoshie, Shizuko .... Episode 91 *(The Mother)*
Jayleen, Sun .... Episode 91 *(Younger Child)*
Jones, Nat .... Episode 73, 74 *(G.I.)*
Karnes, Robert .... Episode 73, 74 *(The Colonel)*
Kim, June .... Episode 91 *(The Pregnant Woman)*
Kirby, Bruce .... Episode 78 *(Sergeant Kimble)*
Kort, Dennis .... Episode 94 *(Corporal Howard Owens)*
Lee, Darrin .... Episode 81 *(Korean Boy)*
Marth, Frank .... Episode 78 *(Colonel Griswald)*
Masur, Richard .... Episode 77 *(Lieutenant "Digger" Detmuller)*
Mettey, Lynette .... Episode 92 *(Nurse Able)*
Minn, Haunani .... Episode 81 *(Sung Lee)*
Morton, Joe .... Episode 90 *(Captain Nick Saunders)*
Nakahara, Kellye .... Episode 77 *(Nurse Baker)*
Nakahara, Kellye .... Episode 81 *(Nurse Kellye)*
O'Connor, Darren .... Episode 75 *(Private Jenkins)*
O'Connor, Tim .... Episode 84 *(Colonel Spiker)*
O'Hanlon, George Jr. .... Episode 92 *(Private Gerald Phelan)*
Osaka, Jeff .... Episode 91 *(Younger Child)*
Palmer, Anthony .... Episode 96 *(The Sergeant)*
Quick, Eldon .... Episode 77 *(Captain Pratt)*
Roberts, Clete .... Episode 97 *(The Interviewer)*
Ruben, Tom .... Episode 96 *(P.F.C.)*
Sakamoto, Mitchell .... Episode 81 *(Slicky Boy)*
Sakimoto, Susan .... Episode 91 *(The Oldest Child)*
Salem, Kario .... Episode 96 *(The Youngster)*
Steffens, Sherry .... Episode 77 *(Nurse Able)*
Stevens, Patricia .... Episode 80 *(Nurse Able)*

Broadcast/Production Order – Season 4

Broadcast	Production
73: Welcome To Korea, Part 1 *(9/12/1975)*	73: *(G501)* Change of Command
74: Welcome To Korea, Part 2 *(9/12/1975)*	74: *(G502)* It Happened One Night
75: Change of Command *(9/19/1975)*	75: *(G503)* Of Moose And Men
76: It Happened One Night *(9/26/1975)*	76: *(G504)* Welcome To Korea, Part 1
77: The Late Captain Pierce *(10/3/1975)*	77: *(G505)* Dear Mildred
78: Hey, Doc *(10/10/1975)*	78: *(G506)* Welcome To Korea, Part 2
79: The Bus *(10/17/1975)*	79: *(G507)* The Late Captain Pierce
80: Dear Mildred *(10/24/1975)*	80: *(G508)* Smilin' Jack
81: The Kids *(10/31/1975)*	81: *(G509)* Dear Peggy
82: Quo Vadis, Captain Chandler? *(11/7/1975)*	82: *(G510)* Hey, Doc
83: Dear Peggy *(11/11/1975)*	83: *(G511)* The Kids
84: Of Moose And Men *(11/21/1975)*	84: *(G512)* The Bus
85: Soldier Of The Month *(11/28/1975)*	85: *(G513)* Quo Vadis, Captain Chandler?
86: The Gun *(12/2/1975)*	86: *(G514)* Soldier Of The Month
87: Mail Call Again *(12/9/1975)*	87: *(G515)* Dear Ma
88: The Price Of Tomato Juice *(12/16/1975)*	88: *(G516)* Deluge
89: Dear Ma *(12/23/1975)*	89: *(G517)* The Gun
90: Der Tag *(1/6/1976)*	90: *(G518)* Mail Call Again
91: Hawkeye *(1/13/1976)*	91: *(G519)* The Price Of Tomato Juice
92: Some 38th Parallels *(1/20/1976)*	92: *(G520)* Hawkeye
93: The Novocaine Mutiny *(1/27/1976)*	93: *(G521)* Some 38th Parallels
94: Smilin' Jack *(2/3/1976)*	94: *(G522)* Der Tag
95: The More I See You *(2/10/1976)*	95: *(G523)* The Novocaine Mutiny
96: Deluge *(2/17/1976)*	96: *(G524)* The More I See You
97: The Interview *(2/24/1976)*	97: *(G525)* The Interview

Season 5

Despite the monumental loss of Gelbart at the helm, and the departures of Stevenson and Rogers two seasons earlier, Season 5 of *M*A*S*H* retains much of the feel of the early seasons. This is, most likely, due to the continued presence of producer Gene Reynolds. Reynolds, with Gelbart, had shaped the show. He knew what made *M*A*S*H* work, when to be funny and, by all accounts, was the guy in charge. The season begins with "Bug Out." It's a solid, funny episode and, though the dialogue is a little more rhythmic and a little less Gelbart (obviously), it kicks the season off to a very nice start. Early on in Season 5, the character of Frank starts to be written more and more as a caricature. Larry Linville played the character splendidly, but even he would later admit that his character was solely being used as a punch line to a joke. Potter was, clearly, the authority figure and the producers decided to marry off Margaret. This took away any of Frank's potential authority, as well as his tag team partner. Linville decided to leave after this season. The producers could have taken the character of Frank in a different direction, as he has a scene where he gets a particularly good dig in against Margaret, and enjoys a subsequent laugh with Hawkeye and BJ. Alas, the tone of that scene was never further developed. With Potter more serious than Blake, BJ less cantankerous than Trapper, Margaret losing interest in Frank and Gelbart gone, the fifth season of *M*A*S*H* adapts to its new members, and new dynamics. Despite the loss of Gelbart, the comedy remains superb. Margaret's bragging about her husband-to-be, Donald Penobscott, in the O.R. doesn't seem in keeping with her character, however. Among the high points of this season are episodes such as "Bug Out," "Dear Sigmund," "38 Across," and "Margaret's Marriage." The latter was the last episode Linville appeared in. He opted not to return for a farewell episode, feeling he had taken his character as far as he could go. William Christopher's name was added to the opening credits. Season 5 was also the last for Gene Reynolds, the original producer. He also felt he had done his best for *M*A*S*H*, and went on to produce *Lou Grant*. This signaled another big change in the show, as Reynolds was a powerful and creative presence.

Bug Out - 9/21/1976
Season 5 / Episode 98 and Episode 99
Production 98 and Production 99 - U801 / U802
Columbia House VHS Tape . . . . *On The Move (Catalog # 10998)*
Fox DVD . . . . *Season 5, Disc 1*

Alan Alda, Mike Farrell, Harry Morgan
Loretta Swit, Larry Linville, Gary Burghoff, Jamie Farr, William Christopher
(This cast will remain in place until next season.)

Executive Producer - Gene Reynolds
Produced by Allan Katz & Don Reo and Burt Metcalfe
Story Consultant - Jay Folb
Written by Jim Fritzell & Everett Greenbaum
Directed by Gene Reynolds

Richard Lee Sung	Cho Man Chin
Francis Fong	Rosie
Don Eitner	Captain Stevens
Barry Cahill	Barry The Chopper Pilot
Eileen Saki	Korean Woman at New Site
James Cough	Enlisted Man

Copyright 1976 - 20th Century Fox Film Corporation

Non-Credited Appearances. . . . . Jeff Maxwell (Salkowitz), Kellye Nakahara, Dennis Troy, Roy Goldman

Chapters

1:	Main Titles	11:	On the Move - 26:57
2:	A New Latrine - 0:53	12:	Fear and Waiting - 28:10
3:	"Bug Out" - 3:05	13:	Rosie's Farewell - 32:10
4:	Rumors - 5:13	14:	The New Site - 34:11
5:	Back Surgery - 9:26	15:	Negotiations - 39:00
6:	Not Moving! - 10:13	16:	Under Fire - 41:53
7:	Moving! - 14:22	17:	Saying Goodbye - 44:29
8:	Packing Up - 15:08	18:	Coming Home - 46:32
9:	Location Scouting - 22:14	19:	Back to the Beginning - 49:02
10:	Staying Behind - 23:29	20:	End Titles - 49:27

Closing Stills

1: Hawkeye at Rosie's
2: B.J.
3: Potter helps Klinger after giving away clothes
4: Margaret & Frank
5: Radar

Synopsis: When word gets around that the 4077th is going to bug out, Potter, in an attempt to put an end to rumors, calls his friend, General Hamilton. The General, a 30-year friend of Potter's assures him that the 4077th is staying put. While addressing the unit, Radar brings the Colonel a message he took over the phone, and Potter announces that the 4077th is bugging out in three hours. Meanwhile, Hawkeye has performed delicate back surgery on a G.I. with multiple fractures, and the patient cannot be moved for 24 hours, resulting in the camp leaving them behind with Margaret and Radar. From a chopper, Potter selects a new location that already has a structure in place, but it's occupied by local "business" women, who happen to know "Binky" Hamilton. The women agree to vacate the building, but it's up to Klinger to seal the deal. Back at what used to be the 4077th and what is now enemy territory, the patient is doing okay, but Hawkeye, Margaret and Radar aren't when they hear vehicles approaching, thinking that the enemy has arrived.

Commentary by Jeff Maxwell: "Gene Reynolds impressed me so much when I watched him direct. He mouthed every word every character spoke, and understood the scenes with the wisdom and intensity only an actor who had been acting since he was a kid could. 'Kid' could? Didn't he fight Mayweather?"

Authors' Notes: There are no PA announcements in this episode.

This is the second hour-long episode of the series.

Potterisms: "Horse hockey," "Hell's bells," "Crock of beans," "Bull cookies," "Scuttlebutt is as common as cooties in your skivvies," "Skeezix" (to Frank) and "Land-O-Goshen."

In Chapter 4, Father Mulcahy and Colonel Potter are in the shower. Mulcahy pulls the lever for water, but the lever breaks off and he continues to shower anyway.

In the same chapter, a chopper landing blows the sign down. This clip will be seen in other episodes as well.

Potter's office in Chapter 6 has frosted windows, therefore, no view outside. This changes in "Margaret's Engagement."

The Swamp in Chapter 8 has no dartboard.

Radar's black goat is named, "Pokey" and his rabbit is named, "Scruffy."

Klinger calls the Montgomery Ward Catalog, "Monkey Ward," a common nickname for the company at the time.

Margaret's Engagement – 9/28/1976

Season 5 / Episode 100 / Production 100 – U803

Columbia House VHS Tape . . . . *Margaret (Catalog # 11008)*
Fox DVD . . . . *Season 5, Disc 1*

Alan Alda, Mike Farrell, Harry Morgan
Loretta Swit, Larry Linville, Gary Burghoff, Jamie Farr, William Christopher

Executive Producer – Gene Reynolds
Produced by Allan Katz & Don Reo and Burt Metcalfe
Story Consultant – Jay Folb
Written by Gary Markowitz
Directed by Alan Alda
Non-Credited Appearances. . . . . Kellye Nakahara, Dennis Troy
Copyright 1976 – 20th Century Fox Film Corporation

Chapters

1: *Main Titles*	6: *Margaret's Insensitivity – 13:36*
2: *A Call from Tokyo – 0:55*	7: *One Last Kiss? – 15:40*
3: *Hot Lips' News – 5:00*	8: *Burns – The Non-Hero – 19:31*
4: *A Medical Report – 9:53*	9: *Talking to Mom – 20:57*
5: *Frank Finds Out – 11:27*	10: *End Titles – 23:59*

Closing Stills

1: *Margaret in Potter's office*
2: *Frank wearing camouflage w/rifle in Potter's office*
3: *B.J. & Hawkeye in Margaret's tent*
4: *Potter in his office*
5: *Radar in his office*

Synopsis: When Margaret returns from a medical follow-up in Tokyo, she brings with her an update on a patient operated on by Frank, who developed peritonitis and required emergency surgery in Tokyo as a result of improper procedure. Potter informs Frank that if this happens again, it goes on his record, and as far as Frank is concerned, that's the good news. After the briefing is over, Margaret shows him the small diamond ring she's wearing and lets him know that she's engaged. Surprisingly, Frank takes the news well, even congratulating her and proceeds to rip the mess tent doors off their hinges. Making things worse for Frank is Margaret's relentless boasting of her fiancé, Lieutenant Colonel Donald Penobscott. An unlikely ally comes to Frank's defense but it might not be enough as Frank, who left camp without telling anyone, returns with a Korean family he's holding as prisoners for interrogation because he thinks they're a band of enemy guerrillas, and Potter lets him know that he's headed straight for a Section 8.

Commentary by Larry Gelbart: "Having Hot Lips marry was the one suggestion I made when I left the series."

PA Announcement by Sal Viscuso

Authors' Notes: In the previous episode, "Bug Out," the windows in Potter's office were frosted over and provided no view outside. This changes in Chapter 2 of this episode: Potter's office windows provide a view of a corrugated building with windows on both sides.

Out of Sight, Out of Mind – 10/5/1976

Season 5 / Episode 101 / Production 103 – U806

Columbia House VHS Tape . . . . *Damaged Goods (Catalog # 11004)*
Fox DVD . . . . *Season 5, Disc 1*

Alan Alda, Mike Farrell, Harry Morgan
Loretta Swit, Larry Linville, Gary Burghoff, Jamie Farr, William Christopher

Executive Producer – Gene Reynolds
Produced by Allan Katz & Don Reo and Burt Metcalfe
Story Consultant – Jay Folb
Written by Ken Levine & David Isaacs
Directed by Gene Reynolds

Tom Sullivan . . . . Lieutenant Tom S. Straw
Judy Farrell . . . . Nurse Able
Enid Kent . . . . Nurse Bigelow
Bobbie Mitchell. . . . . Lieutenant Gage
Dudley Knight . . . . Major James Overman
Kellye Nakahara . . . . Nurse Kellye

Copyright 1976 – 20th Century Fox Film Corporation

Non-Credited Appearances. . . . . Jeff Maxwell, Gwen Farrell, Dennis Troy,
Roy Goldman

Chapters

1:	Main Titles	6:	*The Blind Visiting the Blind* – 14:33
2:	*Night Baseball* – 0:53	7:	*Hawkeye's Point of View* – 16:01
3:	*An Accident* – 2:10	8:	*Scamming the Scammer* – 20:30
4:	*Recuperation* – 7:17	9:	*The Big Day* – 21:54
5:	*A Betting Scam* – 12:05	10:	*End Titles* – 24:26

Closing Stills

1: Tom Straw bandaged in Post-Op
2: Hawkeye – "Five, right?"
3: B.J. in Post-Op
4: Potter in his office
5: Frank writing a note

Synopsis: When the nurses ask Hawkeye to help them relight their heater, it explodes in his face, followed by a blood-curdling scream. Major Overman, an ophthalmologist with the 121st EVAC arrives to examine Hawkeye and after bandaging his eyes, tells him it'll be a few days to determine if he'll get his sight back. Even though he can't see, he still makes rounds in post-op, where he meets another man who was blinded when a grenade went off 10 feet in front of him, and is still a better doctor than Frank when he finds a bandage too tight because Frank didn't loosen it since he was on a break. Recognizing Margaret by the scent of her perfume, and also helping BJ in surgery by, "Catching a whiff of bowel," being blind does not prevent him from paying Frank back for a bet he made on a baseball game, already knowing how the game ended. Late getting to the 4077th because he couldn't get a chopper, Major Overman gently removes Hawkeye's bandages and the news couldn't be better.

Commentary by Ken Levine: "This was our first *M*A*S*H*. David and I joined the agency that represented Gene Reynolds. He read a script of ours and liked it well enough to invite us in to pitch stories for *M*A*S*H*. Not wanting to take any chances, we came in with 50 stories. Two of them were combined for this episode (Hawkeye being temporarily blinded, and Frank's baseball broadcast scam). That story came directly from a friend who worked at AFVN in Korea. There's a speech in which Hawkeye talks about what it's like to be blind. It took us three days to write that speech."

Commentary by Enid Kent Sperber: I got the job on *M*A*S*H*, as I recall, because my mother knew Gene Reynolds and Burt Metcalfe. My mother was actress Irene Tedrow and had known Gene since he was a child actor in radio. 'Out of Sight, Out of Mind' was memorable particularly because of Tom Sullivan, the blind actor who was the guest star. One of the things he was noted for was having dived into a swimming pool to rescue his young daughter. Alan (Alda) and Mike (Farrell) were having a conversation with him when he bragged that he could 'see'! 'What do you mean?' they said. 'Hold up fingers to my face and I will tell you how many fingers you are holding up,' he challenged. Mike held up three fingers and without missing a beat, Tom said, 'three.' 'How did you do that?' they wanted to know. He explained that since he was totally blind his other senses had been heightened and he was able to 'see' Mike's fingers by body heat.

PA Announcement by Sal Viscuso

Authors' Notes: Enid Kent makes her *M*A*S*H* debut as Nurse Bigelow in this episode.

This is Judy Farrell's first appearance on *M*A*S*H* and was, at the time, Mrs. Mike Farrell.

In Chapter 4, Goldie's, which is usually seen to the left of Rosie's, is not there, but the "Hollywood Tailor" is.

Potter's office windows now show a tent, mountains and trees out of both windows in Chapter 5.

Tom Sullivan, who played the blind patient in post-op, was born prematurely and needed oxygen treatment. The treatment saved his life, but caused blindness, a condition known as retinopathy of prematurity. However, being blind has never stopped Mr. Sullivan from enjoying sky diving, bungee jumping, skiing, and golf, and once saved his infant daughter from drowning in his pool by listening for air bubbles. A singer, composer and an actor, Tom Sullivan is also a motivational speaker. His autobiography inspired the movie *If You Could See What I Hear.*

Lieutenant Radar O'Reilly – 10/12/1976

Season 5 / Episode 102 / Production 102 – U805

Columbia House VHS Tape . . . . *Radar (Catalog # 13110)*
Fox DVD . . . . *Season 5, Disc 1*

Alan Alda, Mike Farrell, Harry Morgan
Loretta Swit, Larry Linville, Gary Burghoff, Jamie Farr, William Christopher

Executive Producer – Gene Reynolds
Produced by Allan Katz & Don Reo and Burt Metcalfe
Story Consultant – Jay Folb
Written by Everett Greenbaum & Jim Fritzell
Directed by Alan Rafkin

Johnny Haymer . . . . Sergeant Zale
Sandy Kenyon . . . . Master Sergeant Woodruff
Lynn Marie Stewart . . . . Nurse Baker
Jeff Maxwell. . . . . Igor
Raymond Chao . . . . Korean Boy on Guard Duty
Copyright 1976 – 20th Century Fox Film Corporation

Non-Credited Appearances. . . . . Kellye Nakahara

Chapters

1: Main Titles	6: Showing His Bars – 12:26
2: Poker Face – 0:55	7: Questioning Authority – 15:15
3: Poker Debt – 3:46	8: Advice – 20:55
4: Mail Call – 4:55	9: Back to Normal – 22:37
5: Lieutenant O'Reilly – 7:31	10: End Titles – 23:59

Closing Stills

1: Radar reads about his promotion
2: Hawkeye
3: B.J.
4: Margaret in her tent
5: Klinger

Synopsis: Sergeant Woodruff owes Hawkeye $85 playing poker and owes BJ $35 from last week, and can't pay either debt since he has obligations, and also plays poker at HQ. However, he's in charge of the I-Corps mimeograph setup and offers to run orders through making Hawkeye a major, but BJ has a better idea…Lieutenant Radar O'Reilly. When Radar delivers the mail, he begins to read a message from I-Corps, but stammers over a passage that Potter has to finish: Radar has been promoted to 2nd Lieutenant for "efficiency, punctuality and bugling over and above the call of duty," and now Radar can use the officer's latrine while reading *National Geographic*. He soon realizes that being an officer is not what he thought it would be when Zale and Igor become angry with him, and Klinger wants to be addressed as "Corporal."

Commentary by Jeff Maxwell: "To my knowledge, the food was prepared in the studio commissary. It was actually quite tasty and very enjoyable to munch on between, during and after shots. I especially liked the tater-tots and the bacon. As I recall, all the creamed dishes were creamed by the prop folks — not the commissary. As a result, nobody ever pilfered the creamed turnips, peas, corn or weenies."

PA Announcement by Sal Viscuso
PA Announcement by Radar
PA Announcement by Klinger

Authors' Notes: Radar's serial number is 3911810, but will change later in the series.

In previous episodes, the nurses shared tents, but in this one, Nurse Baker has her own.

The Nurses – 10/19/1976

Season 5 / Episode 103 / Production 106 – U809

Columbia House VHS Tape . . . . *Up In Arms (Catalog # 21032)*
Fox DVD . . . . *Season 5, Disc 1*

Alan Alda, Mike Farrell, Harry Morgan
Loretta Swit, Larry Linville, Gary Burghoff, Jamie Farr, William Christopher

Executive Producer – Gene Reynolds
Produced by Allan Katz & Don Reo and Burt Metcalfe
Story Consultant – Jay Folb
Written by Linda Bloodworth
Directed by Joan Darling

Linda Kelsey . . . . .Nurse Mickey Baker
Mary Jo Catlett . . . . .Nurse Mary Jo Walsh
Carol Lawson Locatell . . . . .Nurse Gaynor
Patricia Sturgis . . . . .Nurse Preston
Gregory Harrison . . . . .Lieutenant Tony Baker
Copyright 1976 – 20th Century Fox Film Corporation

Non-Credited Appearances. . . . . Roy Goldman, Dennis Troy

Chapters

1: Main Titles	6: Swapping Tents – 14:21
2: The Reds are Up – 0:56	7: Together at Last – 17:20
3: The Major is Mean – 3:37	8: The Major Breaks Down – 19:43
4: Baker's Husband – 5:45	9: Making Fudge – 23:34
5: A Quarantine Husband – 8:51	10: End Titles – 24:31

Closing Stills

1: Nurses in their tent
2: Margaret in the nurse's tent
3: Hawkeye
4: Potter
5: Radar

Synopsis: Lieutenant Tony Baker arrives at the 4077th with a 24-hour pass to surprise his wife, Nurse Mickey Baker, who he hasn't seen in two months; nor has the recently married couple had a honeymoon. But getting to spend time with her is going to be difficult since Margaret has confined the nurse to her quarters after putting her on report for cooking in her tent. Hawkeye and BJ hatch a plan that forces Margaret into the uncomfortable position of having to sleep in the nurse's quarters after having words with them, while they use her tent to "quarantine" a patient, who happens to be Tony Baker. Nurse Baker sneaks out that night to be with her husband, only to get caught sneaking back to her bunk by Margaret, who the nurse thought was fast asleep.

Commentary by Gene Reynolds: "You had to have a sense of when to be sentimental."

Authors' Notes: There are no PA announcements in this episode.
The Brooklyn Dodgers vs The Cincinnati Reds baseball game is on Armed Forces Radio in Chapter 2. The pitcher for the Brooklyn Dodgers is Don Newcombe, who signed with the Dodgers in 1946 and it's stated that he's going for his 16th win. Don Newcombe's record for 1950 was 19-11 and for 1951 it was 20-9. Mr. Newcombe was sworn into the

army on February 26, 1952, well before the 1952 baseball season started, and did not return to the game until April 14, 1954. This puts this episode either in 1950 or 1951.

In Chapter 3, Margaret states that it's against regulations to cook in tents. In Season 2's "Crisis," Margaret had a hot plate in her tent.

In Chapter 5, BJ tells Potter that the quarantined patient has either typhoid or schistosomiasis, which is a real illness caused by parasitic worms and is not found in the US.

Chapter 8 contains what could be Loretta Swit's most memorable performance when she tells the nurses about "a lousy cup of coffee."

Actress Linda Kelsey, who played Nurse Mickey Baker, has appeared in several television shows spanning over 30 years, including *St. Elsewhere, Matlock, Quincy, M.E.* and *Murder, She Wrote.* Kelsey also had a starring role in the short-lived *Day by Day,* which ran from 1988-89, airing 25 episodes. But Linda Kelsey is probably best known for her role as Billie Newman on *Lou Grant,* which earned her five Emmy nominations for best supporting actress for five years running from 1978-82.

Gregory Harrison's 40-year career includes recurring roles in *Falcon's Crest, Ed, Reunion, Joey, Judging Amy* and the lead in *Logan's Run.* Harrison is well known for his role as "Gonzo" Gates in *Trapper John, M.D.,* as well as more recent appearances on *Law & Order: S.V.U.*

The Abduction of Margaret Houlihan – 10/26/1976

Season 5 / Episode 104 / Production 105 – U808

Columbia House VHS Tape . . . . *Margaret (Catalog # 11008)*
Fox DVD . . . . *Season 5, Disc 1*

Alan Alda, Mike Farrell, Harry Morgan
Loretta Swit, Larry Linville, Gary Burghoff, Jamie Farr, William Christopher

Executive Producer – Gene Reynolds
Produced by Allan Katz & Don Reo and Burt Metcalfe
Story Consultant – Jay Folb
Teleplay by Allan Katz & Don Reo
Story by Gene Reynolds
Directed by Gene Reynolds

Edward Winter . . . . Colonel Flagg
Lynn Marie Stewart . . . . Nurse Baker
Susan Bredhoff . . . . Nurse Able
June Kim . . . . Korean Woman
Le Quynh . . . . Korean Husband
Susan Sakimoto . . . . Korean Girl
Jon Yune . . . . Korean Translator
Jay Fenichel . . . . Patient

Copyright 1976 – 20th Century Fox Film Corporation

Non-Credited Appearances . . . . Dennis Troy, Roy Goldman,
Kellye Nakahara *(giving a haircut opposite the Swamp)*

Chapters

1: *Main Titles*	6: *Colonel Flagg – 11:48*
2: *Night Duty – 0:56*	7: *Birth Instructions – 16:19*
3: *Where's Margaret – 3:17*	8: *Colonel Flagg's Opinion – 18:35*
4: *An Accident – 6:53*	9: *Margaret and Child – 20:52*
5: *A Birth – 9:28*	10: *End Titles – 23:59*

Closing Stills

1: *Flagg in Potter's office*
2: *B.J. & Hawkeye in the Swamp*
3: *Potter*
4: *Frank in the Swamp*
5: *Radar giving birth*

Synopsis: When Klinger escorts Margaret to her tent in the middle of the night, a young Korean girl shows up requesting help for her mother who's about to give birth. Margaret goes with the girl and Klinger goes to sleep without telling anyone that Margaret left camp. When she's discovered missing and after a thorough search of the camp, realizing the possibility that Margaret might have been captured by the Chinese, Potter informs Intelligence of the situation and the 4077th's favorite intelligence officer shows up to investigate: Colonel Flagg.

Authors' Notes: There are no PA announcements in this episode.
    Hawkeye's robe in Chapter 3 is not the usual red "MD" robe, as the color seems darker and there's no "MD" on it.

The view from Potter's windows in Chapter 3 now shows a corrugated building, but this changes in Chapter 9 when a tent is seen through the office windows instead of the building.

Hawkeye claims to have lost his virginity 20 years ago.

Dear Sigmund – 11/9/1976

Season 5 / Episode 105 / Production 107 – U810

Columbia House VHS Tape . . . . *Outside Reporting (Catalog # 11006)*
Fox DVD . . . . *Season 5, Disc 1*

Alan Alda, Mike Farrell, Harry Morgan
Loretta Swit, Larry Linville, Gary Burghoff, Jamie Farr, William Christopher

Executive Producer – Gene Reynolds
Produced by Allan Katz & Don Reo and Burt Metcalfe
Story Consultant – Jay Folb
Written by Alan Alda
Directed by Alan Alda

Allan Arbus . . . . .Major Sidney Freedman
Charles Frank . . . . Captain Hathaway
Bart Braverman . . . . .Private Habib
Sal Viscuso . . . . Patient John
J. Andrew Kenny . . . . Patient
Jennifer Davis . . . . Nurse

Copyright 1976 – 20th Century Fox Film Corporation

Non-Credited Appearances. . . . . Kellye Nakahara, Jeff Maxwell, Dennis Troy,
Roy Goldman, Robert Gruber

Chapters

1: Main Titles	6: Pain – 15:20
2: M*A*S*H Madness – 0:55	7: Radar – 19:13
3: A Downed Pilot – 6:31	8: B.J. – 21:21
4: Freedman's Letter – 8:12	9: Back to Work – 23:19
5: An Accident – 10:38	10: End Titles – 24:30

Closing Stills

1: Sidney in the Swamp
2: Hawkeye in the Swamp
3: B.J.
4: Klinger & Margaret play poker
5: Radar laughs at Potter and black eye rings

Synopsis: Business is good for a psychiatrist in a war zone with longer winter nights and colder weather, fear and anxiety reaching its peak. But where does a psychiatrist turn when he seeks help? The 4077th. Sidney Freedman, finding comfort in the unit's ability to cope, likens the 4077th to a "kind of spa." Each member having their own way of dealing with the pressures associated with the type of work they do, and where they do it, inspires Sidney to write a letter that he's been putting off. Unfortunately for Sidney, he hides the letter in the one place it's sure to be found... under his pillow and that's exactly where Hawkeye and BJ find his letter to Sigmund Freud.

Authors' Notes: There are no PA announcements in this episode.

Sal Viscuso, the voice of many PA announcements, makes his first appearance on *M*A*S*H* in this episode as Patient John in post-op.

Klinger wants to win back earrings he sold so the holes in his lobes don't close up. In reality, Jamie Farr never had pierced ears.

This is the first episode we hear the name of Potter's horse as "Sophie."

BJ reveals that he's an expert practical joker, as a future episode will attest to.

Klinger refers to wearing earrings the size of Hula Hoops if they would get him out of the army. This would be quite a feat since the Hula Hoop first came out in 1957, four years after the Korean War ended.

Although Klinger seems to know about the Hula Hoop in this Season 5 episode, this perception will change in Season 11's "Who Knew?" when he behaves as if he just invented them.

A prank pulled on Frank has eggs in his helmet. In some episodes, the staff complains about powdered eggs, while in others, an egg won in a poker game is a grand prize. Then there are episodes when Radar gets hit with a real egg and other episodes where real eggs are plentiful.

In Season 4's Episode 91, "Some 38th Parallels," there's a yellow sign next to the O.R. doors in the break room that says, "WE DELIVER (with minimum purchase) DRINKS NOT INCLUDED IN MINIMUM." In this episode, that sign is replaced with a Red Cross sign.

Mulcahy's War – 11/16/1976

Season 5 / Episode 106 / Production 109 – U812

Columbia House VHS Tape . . . . *Father Mulcahy (Catalog # 19500)*
Fox DVD . . . . *Season 5, Disc 1*

Alan Alda, Mike Farrell, Harry Morgan
Loretta Swit, Larry Linville, Gary Burghoff, Jamie Farr, William Christopher

Executive Producer – Gene Reynolds
Produced by Allan Katz & Don Reo and Burt Metcalfe
Story Consultant – Jay Folb
Written by Richard Cogan
Directed by George Tyne

Brian Byers . . . . Private Danny Fitzsimons
Ric Mancini. . . . . Sergeant Hodkey
Richard Foronjy. . . . . Sergeant

Copyright 1976 – 20th Century Fox Film Corporation

Non-Credited Appearances. . . . . Jeff Maxwell, Kellye Nakahara, Dennis Troy,
Roy Goldman

Chapters

1: *Main Titles*
2: *Shot in the Foot – 0:55*
3: *A Dog Soldier – 3:16*
4: *Visiting the Sick – 7:05*
5: *Going to the Front – 10:31*

6: *A Bad Situation – 16:23*
7: *Operating Under Fire – 18:12*
8: *Back to Camp – 21:30*
9: *A New Point of View – 22:52*
10: *End Titles – 24:15*

Closing Stills

1: *Mulcahy by wounded G.I. on the Jeep*
2: *Radar by wounded G.I. on the Jeep*
3: *Potter in the Officer's Club*
4: *Hawkeye in the Mess Tent*

Synopsis: Father Mulcahy and Private Danny Fitzsimmons have something in common: they're both from Philadelphia and both know Father Marty "Boom Boom" Gallagher. "Boom Boom" is Fitzsimmons' Pastor and Father Mulcahy studied with him in the Seminary. But when the private learns that Mulcahy has never been to the front, he has nothing further to discuss with him. Confessing to Colonel Potter that he feels useless, Mulcahy is still denied permission to go to the front, but takes things into his own hands and going against orders, he hitches a ride with Radar to pickup a wounded G.I at a front-line aid station. On the way back, the patient's tongue swells and blocks his airway, requiring an emergency tracheotomy, but the only people with him are Radar and Father Mulcahy, who has no choice but to operate as Hawkeye guides him over the radio.

Commentary by William Christopher: "This was sort of a favorite. In this one, I think we attempted to show that even Father Mulcahy didn't think he could do something as brave as he did (cutting into a man's throat to help him breathe). And, he felt inadequate. We all have certain resources. When you're under pressure, you use them."

Authors' Notes: There are no PA announcements in this episode.

Frank's specialty in this episode is feet. In Season 2's "5 O'Clock Charlie," his specialty was post-op infections.

A rarity in that a Corporal is a German shepherd (that could conceivably outrank Frank one day), which requires surgery resulting from tripping a landmine that saved his sergeant's life.

The Korean Surgeon – 11/23/1976

Season 5 / Episode 107 / Production 111 – U814

Columbia House VHS Tape . . . . *Enemies Are People Too (Catalog # 21033)*
Fox DVD . . . . *Season 5, Disc 2*

Alan Alda, Mike Farrell, Harry Morgan
Loretta Swit, Larry Linville, Gary Burghoff, Jamie Farr, William Christopher

Executive Producer – Gene Reynolds
Produced by Allan Katz & Don Reo and Burt Metcalfe
Story Consultant – Jay Folb
Written by Bill Idelson
Directed by Gene Reynolds

Soon-Teck Oh . . . . Doctor Syn Paik
Robert Ito . . . . North Korean (Driver)
Larry Hama . . . . North Korean (Passenger)
Copyright 1976 – 20th Century Fox Film Corporation

Non-Credited Appearances . . . . Roy Goldman, Kellye Nakahara, Dennis Troy

Chapters

1: *Main Titles*
2: *A Busload of Wounded – 0:54*
3: *A Request – 3:10*
4: *Post-Op Trauma – 4:43*
5: *Another Surgeon – 7:59*
6: *Margaret is Suspicious – 12:09*
7: *Imposters – 14:08*
8: *Burns Goes for A Ride – 16:31*
9: *Rejected – 20:40*
10: *End Titles – 24:29*

Closing Stills

1: *Syn Paik / The Korean surgeon*
2: *Hawkeye*
3: *Potter in his office*
4: *Suspicious Margaret in Potter's office*
5: *Frank tossed out of North Korean's Jeep*

Synopsis: When the bus arrives with wounded, one of them turns out to be a surgeon. The only problem is he's North Korean who attended the University of Chicago and trained at Cooks County Hospital. The prospect of being sent to a POW camp, treating foot fungus and diarrhea, is less than appealing to Doctor Syn Paik, and expresses a desire to work with Hawkeye and BJ. With help from Radar, they're able to get a set of orders, dog tags, and a uniform. Dr. Paik then shaves his beard and everything is set, even impressing an unsuspecting Colonel Potter in OR, but Margaret is convinced she met him before and becomes suspicious, especially when Dr. Paik recognizes North Korean infiltrators disguised as South Koreans requesting supplies.

Commentary by Larry Hama: "On the set, Mr. Linville and Mr. Ito were so laid back and friendly that it put me at ease immediately. Those guys were very serious about the craft, but never pretentious. Light-hearted, but well prepared and ready to go as soon as the camera was rolling. It's almost impossible to convey how thrilling and satisfying it is to be part of such a well-oiled and precise machine like that even for the brief amount of time I was there."

Authors' Notes: There are no PA announcements in this episode.

Frank is wearing the robe usually worn by Henry.

The jeep at the MP checkpoint has serial number 18210717. This jeep is seen in a great number of episodes.

Hawkeye, Get Your Gun – 11/30/1976

Season 5 / Episode 108 / Production 110 – U813

Columbia House VHS Tape . . . . Doctor's Orders (Catalog # 11003)
Fox DVD . . . . Season 5, Disc 2

Alan Alda, Mike Farrell, Harry Morgan
Loretta Swit, Larry Linville, Gary Burghoff, Jamie Farr, William Christopher

Executive Producer – Gene Reynolds
Produced by Allan Katz & Don Reo and Burt Metcalfe
Story Consultant – Jay Folb
Teleplay by Jay Folb
Story by Gene Reynolds & Jay Folb
Directed by William Jurgensen

Mako . . . . Major Choi
Richard Doyle . . . . Mp
Thomas Botosan . . . . Sergeant
Carmine Scelza . . . . G.I. (Server)
Phyllis Katz . . . . Nurse Able
Jae Woo Lee . . . . Korean Guard

Copyright 1976 – 20th Century Fox Film Corporation

Non-Credited Appearances . . . . Jeff Maxwell, Kellye Nakahara, Dennis Troy,
Roy Goldman, Gwen Farrell

Chapters

1: Main Titles
2: Klinger, The Secretary – 0:55
3: Zoltan – 3:03
4: In the Cards – 4:42
5: Packing – 8:46

6: Under Fire – 10:35
7: The Korean Army Hospital – 12:08
8: On the Road – 16:49
9: The Fighting's Over – 22:26
10: End Titles – 24:30

Closing Stills

1: Major Choi
2: Hawkeye after session
3: Potter after session
4: Frank in the Mess Tent
5: Klinger / Zoltan

A call comes in from Korean Army Hospital 426 requesting supplies and surgeons, the surgeons to be determined by drawing the two low cards. Hawkeye draws a 3, Potter draws a deuce, and the jeep is loaded and ready. Dodging exploding shells on the way, Potter and Hawkeye arrive at KAH 426, which is just a big tent with conditions less than stellar for surgery. Major Choi orders his men to unload the jeep, and explains that they do the best they can with what they have, which isn't much. The long session is over and Major Choi thanks the doctors for their efforts and supplies, then acknowledges "Old Ferret Face" since he worked on a few of his men, and luckily, they survived. On the way back, Potter is thrilled when he discovers that Klinger didn't fill the canteen with water, but with liquor instead and he and Hawkeye promptly get drunk just before the shelling starts again and they have to ditch the jeep and take cover in a bunker.

Commentary by Jeff Maxwell: "George Simmons was a career extra. A good guy, friendly but hard working and very disciplined, he served many years on Stage 9 as an extra. It was my understanding he was also a licensed nurse. Though Dr. Walter Dishell was the official medical advisor, *M*A*S*H* regularly called upon George's nursing skills to help guarantee that general medical procedures were portrayed accurately. He bore a decent resemblance to the television Superman, George Reeves. George told me that he often doubled for Mr. Reeves when shooting many of Superman's stock flying scenes; a time consuming process the star wasn't crazy about. Roy Goldman and I kidded him relentlessly about the Superman connection, and only once did he try to stab us with a scalpel. In my earliest days with the show, George was helpful to me in learning the ropes of a television set."

Authors' Notes: There are no PA announcements in this episode.

Klinger gets a package address as 4770 MASH.

Klinger is Zoltan, King of the Gypsies (ploy).

Potterism: "Who the Sam Hill are you?"

In Chapter 8, when Potter and Hawkeye jump into the bunker, there is one sandbag missing where they jump in.

The jeep Hawkeye and Potter drove in to KAH 426 had no visible serial number, but the jeep they drove from KAH 426 is 18210717, which happens to be the same jeep at the MP checkpoint.

The Colonel's Horse – 12/7/1976

Season 5 / Episode 109 / Production 108 – U811

Columbia House VHS Tape . . . . *Not Released by Columbia House*
Fox DVD . . . . *Season 5, Disc 2*

Alan Alda, Mike Farrell, Harry Morgan
Loretta Swit, Larry Linville, Gary Burghoff, Jamie Farr, William Christopher

Executive Producer – Gene Reynolds
Produced by Allan Katz & Don Reo and Burt Metcalfe
Story Consultant – Jay Folb
Written by Jim Fritzell & Everett Greenbaum
Story by Gene Reynolds & Jay Folb
Directed by Burt Metcalfe

Copyright 1976 – 20th Century Fox Film Corporation

Non-Credited Appearances . . . . Kellye Nakahara, Roy Goldman, Gwen Farrell,
Dennis Troy, Robert Gruber

Chapters

1: *Main Titles*	6: *A Sick Horse – 10:02*
2: *Going to Tokyo – 0:54*	7: *Watering the Horse – 16:05*
3: *Margaret is Sick – 4:09*	8: *The Colonel Returns – 19:20*
4: *Klinger is Depressed – 7:01*	9: *Margaret's Appendectomy – 21:32*
5: *A Tent Call – 8:47*	10: *End Titles – 23:56*

Closing Stills

1: *Hawkeye*
2: *BJ in the Swamp*
3: *Potter*
4: *Margaret*
5: *Frank in the Swamp*
6: *Klinger / 9 compound*
7: *Radar / R compound*

Synopsis: Mildred Potter has arranged a flight to Japan, and Colonel Potter is going to meet her, but refuses Hawkeye's request to pick up his nudist magazines, as he'll be in uniform. However, Mrs. Potter will get them because, as the Colonel says, "She's a good sport." Before the Colonel leaves, he instructs Radar on the care of his horse, Sophie. He also informs Hawkeye that if Margaret's appendix flares up, she wants him to perform an appendectomy, not Frank. Shortly after Potter leaves, Radar finds Sophie down, and Margaret finds that she can no longer tolerate the pain of a hot appendix.

Commentary by Gary Burghoff: "For one scene, when Potter's horse was supposed to be laying down, they were going to tranquilize this 14-year-old horse. I told Burt I wouldn't do the scene. See, they could have gotten a 'lay down horse,' one specifically trained to lay down. But they didn't. Well, someone among the extras called Actors and Others for Animals, secretly. And, they were on the phone saying, 'We support Gary.' And so, they postponed filming it."

PA Announcements by Sal Viscuso

Authors' Notes: Radar is angry enough in Chapter 6 to say, "Hell!"

Also in Chapter 6, Hawkeye sings, "M-O-U-S-E" from *The Mickey Mouse Club:* however, the first five episodes of The Mickey Mouse Club were shown from October 3-7, 1955, more than two years after The Korean War ended.

Klinger in Chapter 8 sings, "I'm puttin' on my top hat, I'm puttin' on my wide tie, I'm puttin' on my tails" and this is how it's seen on the DVD captioning. The correct lyrics for this song, "Top Hat, White Tie and Tails," written by Irving Berlin in 1935 are: "Oh, I'm puttin' on my top hat, tying up my white tie, brushing off my tails" (from the 1935 movie, *Top Hat*).

Exorcism – 12/14/1976

Season 5 / Episode 110 / Production 112 – U815

Columbia House VHS Tape . . . . Ego's, Exorcisms, Etc (Catalog # 22051)
Fox DVD . . . . Season 5, Disc 2

Alan Alda, Mike Farrell, Harry Morgan
Loretta Swit, Larry Linville, Gary Burghoff, Jamie Farr, William Christopher

Executive Producer – Gene Reynolds
Produced by Allan Katz & Don Reo and Burt Metcalfe
Story Consultant – Jay Folb
Teleplay by Jay Folb
Story by Gene Reynolds & Jay Folb
Directed by Alan Alda

Philip Ahn . . . . The Korean Grandfather
Virginia Ann Lee . . . . Kyong Ja
James Canning . . . . Corporal Marsh
Copyright 1976 – 20th Century Fox Film Corporation

Non-Credited Appearances . . . . Kellye Nakahara, Johnny Yune, Roy Goldman,
Dennis Troy, Robert Gruber

Chapters

1: Main Titles	6: Burns Complains – 14:10
2: A Spirit Post – 0:55	7: The Exorcism – 17:04
3: Bad Luck – 2:52	8: Back to Normal – 21:02
4: Evil Spirits – 6:26	9: Hawkeye's Magic – 23:20
5: Fear of Evil Spirits – 10:22	10: End Titles – 24:29

Closing Stills

1: Kyong Ja & Hawkeye
2: B.J.
3: Potter in his office
4: Frank in the Swamp
5: Radar and the Spirit Post

Synopsis: Mr. Yee, a local peddler, is trying to negotiate the price of a lighter with Colonel Potter, but when Radar moves a spirit post, a man on a bicycle crashes into Mr. Yee's cart and Potter's new lighter won't light. The bad luck continues in O.R. when an oxygen gauge stops working, Potter injures himself with a surgical instrument and the PA, along with the light over Frank's table, both break down, and it's Friday the 13th. Kyong Ja, a young Korean woman brings her grandfather to the 4077th after he jumped in front of an ambulance to scare away evil spirits. The grandfather, believing evil spirits were following him, had hoped the driver would understand and stop in time, but it was too late. Complicating matters further, the grandfather needs surgery but insists a local priestess be called to exorcise the evil spirits from the camp, or he'll leave, refusing any medical treatment.

PA Announcement by Sal Viscuso

Authors' Notes: Potterisms: "Jumpin' Jehosphat," "Hell's Bells"
Corporal Marsh is loaded into the back of an ambulance in Chapter 8 on the Stage 9 compound, but the ambulance leaves on the Ranch compound.

Hawk's Nightmare – 12/21/1976
Season 5 / Episode 111 / Production 101 – U804

Columbia House VHS Tape . . . . .Benjamin Franklin Pierce (Catalog # 11002)
Fox DVD . . . . .Season 5, Disc 2

Alan Alda, Mike Farrell, Harry Morgan
Loretta Swit, Larry Linville, Gary Burghoff, Jamie Farr, William Christopher

Executive Producer – Gene Reynolds
Produced by Allan Katz & Don Reo and Burt Metcalfe
Story Consultant – Jay Folb
Written by Burt Prelutsky
Directed by Burt Metcalfe

Allan Arbus . . . . .Major Sidney Freedman
Sean Roche . . . . .Private Timothy Burke
Patricia Stevens . . . . Nurse
Copyright 1976 – 20th Century Fox Film Corporation

Non-Credited Appearances. . . . . .Kellye Nakahara, Jeff Maxwell, Roy Goldman

Chapters

1:	Main Titles	6:	Dream Talk – 11:04
2:	Baby Soldiers – 0:52	7:	Staying Up – 12:42
3:	Crazy with Fatigue – 1:49	8:	Another Dream – 15:28
4:	Reminiscences – 6:50	9:	Talking it Out – 18:23
5:	Sleepwalking – 7:57	10:	End Titles – 23:57

Closing Stills

1: Sidney
2: Hawkeye
3: B.J.
4: Potter in the Mess Tent
5: Klinger & Radar

Synopsis: Hawkeye doesn't believe he's playing basketball in his sleep, until Klinger mentions Clarence Vanderhaven, the new principal of Hawkeye's school. But his sleep-walking takes a turn for the worse when he has nightmares of his childhood friends having horrific accidents. He calls his old friends, only to find out they're fine; one of them thinking he still owes him $37 and while Radar makes a call for Hawkeye, Potter quietly has him make a second call to Sidney Freedman.

Commentary by Burt Prelutsky: "I don't believe 'Hawk's Nightmare' was my idea. And in as much as I wasn't on the staff, I don't know whose notion it was. I liked it, though, and I liked the end result."

Authors' Notes: There are no PA announcements in this episode.
In Chapter 9, Hawkeye calls the States and everybody is watching Milton Berle.
Milton Berle was on Tuesday nights on NBC from June 1948 to June 1956. He was on at other times as well, but this concerns the M*A*S*H timeline.

The Most Unforgettable Characters – 1/4/1977
Season 5 / Episode 112 / Production 115 – U818

Columbia House VHS Tape . . . . *Not Released by Columbia House*

Fox DVD . . . . *Season 5, Disc 2*

Alan Alda, Mike Farrell, Harry Morgan
Loretta Swit, Larry Linville, Gary Burghoff, Jamie Farr, William Christopher

Executive Producer – Gene Reynolds
Produced by Allan Katz & Don Reo and Burt Metcalfe
Story Consultant – Jay Folb
Written by Ken Levine & David Isaacs
Directed by Burt Metcalfe

Copyright 1977 – 20th Century Fox Film Corporation

Non-Credited Appearances. . . . . Jeff Maxwell, Kellye Nakahara, Roy Goldman,
Robert Gruber, Dennis Troy, Gwen Farrell

Chapters

1: *Main Titles*	6: *Rewarding Klinger – 12:54*
2: *The Duty Log – 0:54*	7: *A Romantic Interlude – 16:17*
3: *An Anecdote – 4:08*	8: *A Burning Threat – 17:16*
4: *Frank's Birthday – 7:05*	9: *Radar Changes His Mind – 22:36*
5: *A Birthday Present – 10:26*	10: *End Titles – 24:29*

Closing Stills
1: *B.J. & Hawkeye having martinis*
2: *Radar admires his writing*
3: *Potter in his office*
4: *Frank in the Mess Tent*
5: *Klinger in Potter's office*

Synopsis: Responding to an ad on the back of a Superman comic, Radar enrolls in a creative writing course run by very famous writers: Ethel Hemmingway, Jerry Steinbeck and Eunice O'Neill and in only ten weeks, he'll be "respected by a crowd." But filling out the staff duty log under the guidelines of his creative writing course nearly makes Potter sick when he sees the report and explains that military logs have to be in military jargon. Radar continues applying his creative writing to more reports, but Colonel Potter has had enough. He convinces Radar, after a little yelling and ripping a report from the typewriter, that to be a good writer, just be yourself. Radar decides that, instead of writing, magic might be his calling, and performs a magic trick that Frank won't soon forget.

Commentary by Ken Levine: "We were thrilled, after turning in 'Out of Sight/Out of Mind,' that Gene gave us another assignment so quickly. Most of this story had been worked out by the staff before we were assigned it. My favorite moment was when Frank's yo-yo string breaks, and it rolls away from him while he just stares at it."

Authors' Notes: There are no PA announcements in this episode.
The clip of Cowboy landing his chopper is seen in Chapter 2.
The shower tent in Chapter 8 does not have the designated times posted as in earlier episodes.

38 Across – 1/11/1977

Season 5 / Episode 113 / Production 118 – U821

Columbia House VHS Tape.........*Enemies Are People Too (Catalog # 21033)*
Fox DVD ....*Season 5, Disc 2*

Alan Alda, Mike Farrell, Harry Morgan
Loretta Swit, Larry Linville, Gary Burghoff, Jamie Farr, William Christopher

Executive Producer – Gene Reynolds
Produced by Allan Katz & Don Reo and Burt Metcalfe
Story Consultant – Jay Folb
Written by Jim Fritzell & Everett Greenbaum
Directed by Burt Metcalfe

Dick O'Neill .... Admiral Cox
Oliver Clark ....Lieutenant Tippy Brooks
Ron Kolman .... Corporal Shapiro
Mo Mo Yashima ....Korean Mother
Bill Shinkai .... Soo Ling *(Chinese Patient)*
Rex Knowels ....American Patient
Gwen Farrell ....Anesthetist
Copyright 1977 – 20th Century Fox Film Corporation

Non-Credited Appearances........... Kellye Nakahara, Jeff Maxwell, Dennis Troy,
Roy Goldman

Chapters

1: *Main Titles*	6: *The Emergency – 13:38*
2: *Killing Time – 0:52*	7: *A Waste of Time – 16:37*
3: *The Crossword Puzzle – 3:38*	8: *A Real Emergency – 18:47*
4: *One More Word – 6:24*	9: *The Magic Word – 22:20*
5: *Eating A Jeep – 9:15*	10: *End Titles – 23:55*

Closing Stills

1: *The Admiral in the Mess Tent*
2: *Hawkeye knitting in the Swamp*
3: *B.J. & baby in the Mess Tent*
4: *Frank and his toy in the Mess Tent*
5: *Klinger eats a Jeep*

Synopsis: Hawkeye attempts to finish a Times crossword puzzle, something he has never been able to do, until he runs into the fifth clue, 38 across, five letters and begins with "V." The clue is, "Yiddish for bedbug" and he doesn't know the word. Hawkeye contacts a college friend of his, a "crossword freak" who does double-crostic puzzles in ink, Tippy Brooks, a doctor aboard the Essex in Pusan Harbor. Hawkeye leaves word for Brooks that it's an emergency and Hawkeye needs to speak with him as soon as possible. Radar has gotten word that Brooks, along with his admiral after learning there's an emergency, is on his way to the 4077th not realizing the emergency is a crossword puzzle clue.

PA Announcement over the radio by Seoul City Sue

Authors' Notes: The crossword puzzle clue for 1 down: four letters is "Young Fellow" and the word is "Chap." The puzzle clue for 1 across: four letters is "Member of the Company," starts with "C" and the word is "Cast." However, a close-up of the crossword puzzle in Chapter 3 shows 1 down and 1 across as having 5 letters and is blank.

Potter's office windows in Chapter 5 show a corrugated building through the left window, but a later view has a wooden building with windows.

Klinger's nose is out of his mask in O.R. in Chapter 8.

Long-time actor Dick O'Neill's 50-year career began after he returned from his service in the Navy in the late 50's. His lengthy list of credits include appearances on *M*A*S*H* spin-offs *House Calls* and *Trapper John, M.D.* Mr. O'Neill was also on the television shows *Good Times, Sanford and Son, Baretta, Kojak* and recurring roles included Art Leonard, Tim Taylor's high-school teacher, in *Home Improvement.* Dick O'Neill will return in Season 7's "BJ Papa-San" and Season 10's "Sons and Bowlers." Dick O'Neill passed away November 17, 1998 at the age of 70.

Oliver Clark, born Richard Mardirosian in Buffalo, NY, in 1939, has entered his 40th years as an actor. Mr. Clark has appeared in *Mary Hartman, Mary Hartman, The Rockford Files, Trapper John, M.D.* and has had recurring roles on *The Bob Newhart Show* and *St. Elsewhere.* Oliver Clark will make another appearance on *M*A*S*H* in Season 6's "Mail Call, Three" as Ben Pierce, a "very funny fellow."

Ping Pong – 1/18/1977

Season 5 / Episode 114 / Production 114 – U817

Columbia House VHS Tape . . . .*Enemies Are People Too (Catalog # 21033)*
Fox DVD . . . .*Season 5, Disc 2*

Alan Alda, Mike Farrell, Harry Morgan
Loretta Swit, Larry Linville, Gary Burghoff, Jamie Farr, William Christopher

Executive Producer – Gene Reynolds
Produced by Allan Katz & Don Reo and Burt Metcalfe
Story Consultant – Jay Folb
Written by Sid Dorfman
Directed by William Jurgensen

Richard Narita.	Cho Lin
Frank Maxwell	Lieutenant Colonel Harold Becket
Sachiko Penny Lee	Soony
Robert Phalen	Sergeant Blanchard
Enid Kent	Nurse Able

Copyright 1977 – 20th Century Fox Film Corporation

Non-Credited Appearances. . . . . .Jeff Maxwell, Roy Goldman, Kellye Nakahara,
Dennis Troy, Gwen Farrell

Chapters

1: Main Titles	6: Colonel Becket – 9:37
2: Ping-Pong – 0:54	7: Incompetence – 15:49
3: A Poor Loser – 2:42	8: Potter Steps In – 20:03
4: Cho Lin's Fiancée – 4:38	9: The Wedding – 21:32
5: A Job Interview – 7:35	10: End Titles – 24:14

Closing Stills

1: Cho Lin
2: Soony
3: Mulcahy & Potter at the wedding ceremony
4: Margaret (Crying) & Frank at the wedding ceremony
5: Hawkeye & Klinger at the wedding ceremony

Synopsis: Cho Lin represents the 4077th in a ping-pong game against the 8063rd and wins the tournament, but needs $40 more to buy an engagement ring for his fiancée, Soony. Hawkeye and BJ lend him the money, but two days after he leaves for Seoul to buy the ring, Soony thinks he's not coming back. Cho does come back with shrapnel in his shoulder after he was tossed into the back of a South Korean Army truck, given an hour's worth of training and sent to the front. Meanwhile, an old friend of Potter's, who hasn't seen fighting in years, is put in command of a front-line unit so he can earn his Combat Infantry Badge and retire as a full-bird colonel. But when it's learned that his actions caused most of his men to wind up at the 4077th, and needing only five more days to get his badge, Potter denies his request and sends him back down instead.

PA Announcement by Sal Viscuso

Authors' Notes: A new sign has been added in the supply room in Chapter 5: "Free speech doesn't mean careless talk"

Frank mentions, "The Marshall Plan." George C. Marshall, US Secretary of State, called for assistance in restoring the economic infrastructure of Europe in post-WWII and the eventual restoration of European agricultural and industrial productivity. Also prevented famine and political chaos and won the Nobel Prize for "The Marshall Plan."

Colonel Potter has 16 months, 3 weeks and 4 days before he can barbecue on his patio in Nebraska (chapter 6).

In Chapter 9, Frank, aside from Klinger, is the only one not in a dress uniform.

End Run – 1/25/1977

Season 5 / Episode 115 / Production 113 – U816

Columbia House VHS Tape . . . . *War Is Hell (Catalog # 13112)*
Fox DVD . . . . *Season 5, Disc 3*

Alan Alda, Mike Farrell, Harry Morgan
Loretta Swit, Larry Linville, Gary Burghoff, Jamie Farr, William Christopher

Executive Producer – Gene Reynolds
Produced by Allan Katz & Don Reo and Burt Metcalfe
Story Consultant – Jay Folb
Written by John D. Hess
Directed by Harry Morgan

Henry Brown . . . . Sergeant Billy Tyler
Johnny Haymer . . . . Sergeant Zale
James Lough . . . . .PFC Felix Kornhause
Tom Tarpey . . . . Battalion Surgeon
Peter D. Greene . . . . .Medic
Greg Mabrey . . . . Wounded Soldier
Copyright 1977 – 20th Century Fox Film Corporation

Non-Credited Appearances . . . . Roy Goldman, Kellye Nakahara, Robert Gruber,
Dennis Troy, Gwen Farrell

Chapters

1:	*Main Titles*	
2:	*Fighting – 0:54*	
3:	*A Football Star – 3:57*	
4:	*Food Fighting – 8:01*	
5:	*A Phantom Leg – 10:44*	

6:	*In Training – 15:35*	
7:	*A Death Wish – 17:11*	
8:	*The Boxing Match – 20:07*	
9:	*Billy Lives – 22:25*	
10:	*End Titles – 24:27*	

Closing Stills

1: *Billy Tyler leaves the 4077th*
2: *Hawkeye in Post-Op*
3: *B.J. in the Swamp*
4: *Radar in Post-Op*
5: *Klinger*

Synopsis: Sergeant Billy Tyler, an All-American running back from Iowa who tied the Big Ten rushing record for a single season is brought to the 4077th with a serious leg wound. Tyler, who played a whole quarter against Michigan with a sprained ankle, tells the doctors that if they can't save his leg, not to bother saving him. After surgery, Hawkeye tells Billy that they couldn't save the leg, but Billy doesn't believe him since he feels, what Hawkeye calls, a "phantom pain." Now Billy is asking for another way out… with pills, until Radar makes him realize there's a better way. Meanwhile, to prove his manhood, Frank arranges a boxing match between Zale and Klinger, but it's Frank who loses the fight.

Authors' Notes: There are no PA announcements in this episode.
    When a fight breaks out at Rosie's in Chapter 2, a corpsman goes through the window and glass is heard breaking, but the windows seem to be made out of paper.
    In Chapter 5, Radar has a Martini, and acts as if he's never had one before when he gasps. As noted, he's had several Martinis early on in the series.

Father Mulcahy, the timekeeper for the boxing match between Klinger and Zale, uses a bedpan as the bell and when he strikes it with a retractor, chips of paint come off the bedpan.

Frank, as the referee for the boxing match is wearing a sweatshirt and pants with what appears to be modern-day white sneakers. This is the only time Frank was dressed this way, including the sneakers.

Another rarity is Margaret wearing a regulation fatigue cap.

Hanky Panky - 2/1/1977

Season 5 / Episode 116 / Production 119 – U822

Columbia House VHS Tape . . . . *Infidelity (Catalog # 11000)*
Fox DVD . . . . *Season 5, Disc 3*

Alan Alda, Mike Farrell, Harry Morgan
Loretta Swit, Larry Linville, Gary Burghoff, Jamie Farr, William Christopher

Executive Producer – Gene Reynolds
Produced by Allan Katz & Don Reo and Burt Metcalfe
Story Consultant – Jay Folb
Written by Gene Reynolds
Directed by Gene Reynolds
Ann Sweeny. . . . . .Lieutenant Carrie Donovan
Copyright 1977 – 20th Century Fox Film Corporation

Non-Credited Appearances. . . . . .Kellye Nakahara, Gwen Farrell, Dennis Troy

Chapters

1: *Main Titles*
2: *Singing in the O.R. – 0:52*
3: *Bad News in the Mail – 4:20*
4: *Calling Colonel Penobscott – 8:26*
5: *A Sympathetic Ear – 10:39*

6: *The Morning After – 11:46*
7: *Off the Fidelity Wagon – 15:15*
8: *An Attack of the Guilts – 19:37*
9: *The Colonel's Condition – 23:18*
10: *End Titles – 24:24*

Closing Stills

1: *Carrie in Post-Op*
2: *B.J.*
3: *Margaret & Hawkeye in the Mess Tent*
4: *Radar*

Synopsis: Mail call brings a mixed bag as Potter gets a letter from his wife, Frank gets a "wonderful" letter from his old Sunday school teacher and BJ gets three from Peg. Margaret, however, hasn't received a letter from Donald in four days, and Lieutenant Carrie Donovan gets a "Dear Jane" from her husband back in the States. After Carrie tells BJ that her marriage is in trouble, they find themselves embraced in a kiss, and BJ winds up staying with her through the night. Now back in the Swamp, guilt has caught up with BJ and to alleviate it, he starts writing a letter to Peg to tell her what happened, but Hawkeye realizes that just because BJ stumbled a bit doesn't mean he has to make Peg miserable over it and tears the letter up before BJ ruins his own marriage.

Authors' Notes: There are no PA announcements in this episode.
There are hooks in the change room for personnel we've never seen: Frazier and Aidman.
Potterism: "Buffalo Bagels"
Klinger claims to be the Toledo Strangler (ploy).

Hepatitis – 2/8/1977
Season 5 / Episode 117 / Production 120 – U823
Columbia House VHS Tape . . . . *War Ailments (Catalog # 13111)*
Fox DVD . . . . *Season 5, Disc 3*

Alan Alda, Mike Farrell, Harry Morgan
Loretta Swit, Larry Linville, Gary Burghoff, Jamie Farr, William Christopher

Executive Producer – Gene Reynolds
Produced by Allan Katz & Don Reo and Burt Metcalfe
Story Consultant – Jay Folb
Written by Alan Alda
Directed by Alan Alda

Copyright 1977 – 20th Century Fox Film Corporation

Non-Credited Appearances. . . . . Roy Goldman, Kellye Nakahara, Dennis Troy
(Gwen Farrell is Nurse Baker but is not credited as she spoke no lines.)

Chapters
1: *Main Titles*	6: *Gastrectomy – 11:04*
2: *Mail Delivery – 0:54*	7: *Quarantined – 13:14*
3: *Hepatitis – 3:44*	8: *Stomach Surgery – 16:54*
4: *Frank the Hypochondriac – 5:28*	9: *Seeing Colonel Potter – 21:26*
5: *Respect – 7:32*	10: *End Titles – 24:14*

Closing Stills
1: *Hawkeye*
2: *B.J. in the Swamp*
3: *Potter in his office*
4: *Frank in the Swamp*
5: *Radar on his bunk*
6: *Klinger in the kitchen*
7: *Mulcahy in bed with hepatitis*

Synopsis: When Hawkeye gets the Crabapple Cove Courier, he reads yet another story on "incredibly average" Vernon Parsons. Parsons, described by Hawkeye as a "dunce" he went through medical school with, has just been given a $100,000 grant from Boston Hospital for a two-year study of infectious diseases in mice, and it's giving Hawkeye a pain in his back that's making him walk bent over. Father Mulcahy isn't feeling too good either, when in the mess tent he admits he's feeling a little arthritic. A quick check of his eyes and tongue reveals hepatitis. Potter orders Hawkeye, bad back notwithstanding, to check everyone in camp and give everyone a shot of gamma globulin.

PA Announcement by Sal Viscuso

Authors' Notes: The chopper pad in Chapter 6 is of the same clip in an earlier episode of the chopper's blades blowing down signs.

The General's Practitioner – 2/15/1977
Season 5 / Episode 118 / Production 104 – U807

Columbia House VHS Tape . . . . *Doctor's Orders (Catalog # 11003)*
Fox DVD . . . . *Season 5, Disc 3*

Alan Alda, Mike Farrell, Harry Morgan
Loretta Swit, Larry Linville, Gary Burghoff, Jamie Farr, William Christopher

Executive Producer – Gene Reynolds
Produced by Allan Katz & Don Reo and Burt Metcalfe
Story Consultant – Jay Folb
Written by Burt Prelutsky
Directed by Alan Rafkin

Larry Wilcox. . . . . Corporal Mulligan
Edward Binns . . . . General Theodore A. Korshak
Leonard Stone. . . . . Colonel Bidwell
Susie Elene . . . . Mai Ping
Copyright 1977 – 20th Century Fox Film Corporation

Non-Credited Appearances. . . Kellye Nakahara, Roy Goldman *(Orderly & Anesthetist),*
Gwen Farrell, Dennis Troy, Jeff Maxwell

Chapters

1: *Main Titles*	6: *Mulligan's Request – 7:32*
2: *Patriotism – 0:54*	7: *The Family Man – 10:06*
3: *Colonel Bidwell – 1:53*	8: *The General – 14:46*
4: *An Emergency – 4:05*	9: *Hawkeye's Prognosis – 21:00*
5: *Operating Room Etiquette – 5:46*	10: *End Titles – 23:59*

Closing Stills

1: *General Korshak*
2: *Hawkeye in the Swamp*
3: *Radar and baby*
4: *Potter in the Swamp*
5: *B.J. and baby*

Synopsis: General Theodore A. Korshak, I-Corps Commander, has sent Colonel Bidwell to the 4077th to find the best doctor to be his personal physician. Hawkeye's insolence and flippant attitude, especially towards generals, who he feels the only medical attention they need, are daily high colonics, does nothing to change the colonel's mind. General Korshak, "The Tamer of the Tiger Tank," has come to see his new personal physician: this general does not take no for an answer. Meanwhile, Corporal Mulligan, after getting enough points, is being shipped home, but before he leaves, he wants Radar to look after Mai Ping and their infant son. Mulligan makes it to Seoul, but comes back as he couldn't leave Korea without them.

Authors' Notes: There are no PA announcements in this episode.
Colonel Bidwell, I-Corps Operation Officer, arrives at the 4077th in jeep # 18210717, a jeep seen in nearly every episode.
In this episode there is a bowl of real eggs. In other episodes, it's powdered eggs.
The view from Potter's office windows in Chapter 8 is first a corrugated building, and then later, it's a tent.
Potter now has 14 months and 11 days until retirement.

Although the tailor's sign can be seen next to "Goldie's" in previous episodes, it's not there in this one.

The jeep Colonel Bidwell arrived and left camp with, 18210717, is the same jeep General Korshak leaves in.

Potter's office windows in Chapter 9 now show a wooden structure not there earlier.

Actor Larry Wilcox has appeared in *The Streets of San Francisco, The Partridge Family, Hawaii Five-0, McGyver, Cannon,* and is probably best known as Officer Jon Baker in *CHiPS.*

Movie Tonight – 2/22/1977

Season 5 / Episode 119 / Production 121 – U824

Columbia House VHS Tape . . . . *Doctor's Orders (Catalog # 11003)*
Fox DVD . . . . *Season 5, Disc 3*

Alan Alda, Mike Farrell, Harry Morgan
Loretta Swit, Larry Linville, Gary Burghoff, Jamie Farr, William Christopher

Executive Producer – Gene Reynolds
Produced by Allan Katz & Don Reo and Burt Metcalfe
Story Consultant – Jay Folb
Written by Gene Reynolds / Don Reo / Allan Katz / Jay Folb
Directed by Burt Metcalfe

Enid Kent . . . . Nurse Bigelow
Judy Farrell . . . . Nurse Able
Jeffrey Kramer . . . . Driver
Carmine Scelza . . . . Corpsman

Copyright 1977 – 20th Century Fox Film Corporation

Non-Credited Appearances. . . . . .Jeff Maxwell, Gwen Farrell, Kellye Nakahara,
Dennis Troy, Roy Goldman

Chapters

1:	Main Titles	6:	A Sing-Along – 11:51
2:	Cleaning Detail – 0:52	7:	The Pianist – 14:27
3:	Good News – 3:58	8:	A Solo – 19:30
4:	Going Out – 6:27	9:	Back to Work – 23:21
5:	"My Darling Clementine" – 9:42	10:	End Titles – 24:28

Closing Stills

1: The nurses at the movie
2: B.J. at the movie
3: Potter at the movie
4: Margaret in her tent
5: Frank
6: Radar does impersonations at the movie
7: Klinger at the movie
8: Mulcahy playing the piano at the movie

Synopsis: Colonel Potter's favorite movie has horses, cowboys, and horses, the three ingredients that make My Darling Clementine his favorite, and it'll be seen after supper. Unfortunately for everyone, the film breaks and while Klinger attempts to splice it back together, Potter orders a sing-along, and everyone in the mess tent starts singing what might be the most popular song on *M*A*S*H*: "Gee Mom, I Wanna Go Home." The nurses, who were invited to a party at I-Corps, hear what's going on, and they refuse the car that was sent for them, instead, joining the crowd in the mess tent, as does the driver.

PA Announcement by Radar and Colonel Potter

Authors' Notes: In Chapter 7, Radar does a John Wayne impersonation from the movie, *McLintock,* which came out in 1963, ten years after the Korean War ended.
In Chapter 8, Margaret sings, "When love comes in and takes you for a spin, ooh, la la." The song, written by Cole Porter, is from the Broadway show *Can-Can,* which debuted

at The Schubert Theater on May 7, 1953 and ran until June 25, 1955. It's unlikely that this song or show was known to anyone in Korea at the time.

Souvenirs – 3/1/1977
Season 5 / Episode 120 / Production 116 – U819
Columbia House VHS Tape . . . . Spoils Of War (Catalog # 11007)
Fox DVD . . . . Season 5, Disc 3

Alan Alda, Mike Farrell, Harry Morgan
Loretta Swit, Larry Linville, Gary Burghoff, Jamie Farr, William Christopher

Executive Producer – Gene Reynolds
Produced by Allan Katz & Don Reo and Burt Metcalfe
Story Consultant – Jay Folb
Teleplay by Burt Prelutsky
Story by Burt Prelutsky and Reinhold Weege
Directed by Joshua Shelly
Michael Bell . . . . Lieutenant Stratton (Chopper Pilot)
Brian Dennehy . . . . M.P. Ernie Connors
Scott Mulhern . . . . Andy Cooper
June Kim . . . . Korean Woman
Crandal Jue . . . . Korean Boy
Alvin Kim . . . . Korean Boy
Copyright 1977 – 20th Century Fox Film Corporation

Non-Credited Appearances . . . . Gwen Farrell, Roy Goldman, Kellye Nakahara

Chapters

1: Main Titles
2: The Souvenir Epidemic – 0:52
3: Klinger's Stand – 7:09
4: Black Market Bargain – 8:48
5: Supply & Demand – 10:25
6: Frank's Vase – 14:30
7: Going for the Record – 18:02
8: So Long, Stratton – 20:10
9: A New Record – 22:48
10: End Titles – 24:28

Closing Stills

1: Stratton
2: B.J. & Hawkeye
3: Margaret
4: Frank
5: Klinger sitting on the pole

Synopsis: The enemy leaves booby-trapped pistols, bayonets and helmets lying around, but UN troops are not their only victim as Korean children search the grounds for material to sell, helping to support their families, including the Korean boy who was searching a minefield for brass and who is now on Hawkeye's table. Lieutenant Stratton buys this material to make souvenirs, to sell without any regard for his young suppliers, creating an intolerable situation. Stratton has for sale a necklace made from 100-hand-grenade safety pins, aluminum watchbands and bracelets from a MIG and had earrings made for Klinger from .45 caliber shells, but Klinger refuses to do business with Stratton. Later in the Officer's Club, Margaret, in a drunken fit of rage, punches Stratton right in the mouth.

Commentary by Burt Prelutsky: "Sometimes credits can be misleading. Weege had apparently written a script they didn't shoot, but Gene Reynolds had liked the idea of Klinger's trying to set a flagpole sitting record as a minor story element. He asked me if I would be kind enough to share the story credit with Weege, whom I had never met. I figured I owed it to Gene and the show to go along with it, although I personally didn't care for the bit. It just seemed stupid, and not at all funny, to me. It also didn't seem like something Klinger would decide to do. Staging a fashion show, maybe. But freezing his butt off sitting halfway up a flagpole? Nah."

Authors' Notes: There are no PA announcements in this episode.

Something new has been added to the scenery outside Potter's office windows: 55-gallon drums and crates in the distance from the right window and a building in the distance from the left.

Potterism: "Creeping crud."

Klinger mentions "Shipwreck Kelly" in Chapter 5. Alvin "Shipwreck" Kelly (1885-1952) was a world-record flagpole sitter who sat for seven weeks in Atlantic City's Steel Pier in the 1920s.

Chapter 6, Frank's serial number on his footlocker is 5683698. In Season 1, Episode 3, "Requiem for A Lightweight," Frank's serial number seen on his duffle bag is RA98672412.

Frank's address is 2845 Elm Street, Fort Wayne, Indiana.

Hawkeye makes a big deal out of a "real egg," when in previous episodes of this season, real eggs seem to be abundant.

Frank has a ring inscribed with, "To Louise, Love, Frank B."

Brian Dennehy, who played M.P. Ernie Connors in this episode, has an extensive list of credits and has appeared in *Lou Grant, Kojak, Knots Landing, Cagney & Lacey* and *Hunter.* The five-time Emmy nominee and Golden Globe winner for *Death of A Salesman* is also well known for his role in *Rambo: First Blood* as Sheriff Will Teasle, and is one of Eddie's favorite actors.

Post-Op – 3/8/1977

Season 5 / Episode 121 / Production 122 – U825

Columbia House VHS Tape . . . . *War Is Hell (Catalog # 13112)*
Fox DVD . . . . *Season 5, Disc 3*

Alan Alda, Mike Farrell, Harry Morgan
Loretta Swit, Larry Linville, Gary Burghoff, Jamie Farr, William Christopher

Executive Producer – Gene Reynolds
Produced by Allan Katz & Don Reo and Burt Metcalfe
Story Consultant – Jay Folb
Teleplay by Ken Levine & David Isaacs
Story by Gene Reynolds & Jay Folb
Directed by Gene Reynolds

Hilly Hicks . . . . Corporal Jerris Moody
Andy Romano . . . . Sergeant Justiss
Sal Viscuso . . . . Sergeant Raymond Mcgill
Richard Beauchamp . . . . Corporal Robelo
Alan McRea . . . . Corporal Nessen
Gary Springer . . . . Private Garvin
Andrew Bloch . . . . Private Gordon
John-Anthony Bailey. . . . . Private Whitney
Daniel Zippe . . . . Private Corey
Zitto Kazann . . . . Sergeant Attias

Copyright 1977 – 20th Century Fox Film Corporation

Non-Credited Appearances. . . . . Robert Gruber, Roy Goldman, Jeff Maxwell,
Kellye Nakahara, Gwen Farrell, Dennis Troy

Chapters

1: *Main Titles*
2: *Out of Blood – 0:55*
3: *Incoming Wounded – 2:21*
4: *Marathon Surgery – 3:47*
5: *In Post-Op – 6:27*

6: *Racism – 12:22*
7: *Going Home – 14:14*
8: *Flirting – 18:47*
9: *Blood Drive – 20:48*
10: *End Titles – 24:15*

Closing Stills

1: *Hawkeye & Corporal Moody*
2: *B.J.*
3: *Potter in Post-Op*
4: *Margaret in Post-Op*
5: *Klinger in Post-Op*

Synopsis: After surgery, the people in post-op present a different set of problems, some more difficult than others as BJ now has to tell his patient that he had to amputate his leg. Herb, a G.I who laid out mines, forgot that they bobby-trapped a few in case the enemy cut any wires. Frank has a patient who is unconscious and can't find anything wrong with him until Colonel Potter suspects a snakebite. Klinger helps a fellow corporal regain his "manhood" by making a moustache out of his own hair and a G.I with a foot wound tries to pick up Margaret. Meanwhile, Hawkeye patches up Corporal Moody, a medic who's been to the 4077th previously, after he encounters racism and another patient doesn't want to be sent home as he's making a lot of money in Korea selling liquor and has the only Polaroid camera in his sector, selling photos for $2 a piece.

Commentary by Ken Levine: "CBS ordered another show at the last moment and this was it. Taken from interviews with doctors and *M*A*S*H* participants, this episode was pieced together and assigned to us."

PA Announcement by Sal Viscuso
PA Announcement by Colonel Potter

Authors' Notes: Hilly Hicks, who plays Corporal Jerris Moody in this episode makes his second appearance on *M*A*S*H*, with a reference to his first appearance in Season 3's "White Gold." Although he plays a medic in both episodes, his name in "White Gold" was Corporal Perkins / Johnson.

There is usually a wall clock in post-op, but the clock in this episode, Chapter 4, is not the same as the clock seen previously. Aside from the regular time, this clock also shows the "hundred-hour" time as well.

This episode tells of Frank and a "kid" who came in with a rash that he spotted first, calling it, "Burns's Blight," the "catchiest name since diarrhea."

Potterism: "Dry as a hump-less camel in the sunshine" (from the PA announcement).

Sergeant Attias, of the Turkish Brigade, has arrived with his men to give blood in exchange for the 4077th saving the life of his captain. The only thing wrong here is the sergeant is wearing corporal stripes.

Dracula drawn on a sign is seen over the entrance to the mess tent that says, "Blood Drive."

Margaret's Marriage – 3/15/1977

Season 5 / Episode 122 / Production 117 – U820

Columbia House VHS Tape . . . .*Margaret (Catalog # 11008)*
Fox DVD . . . .*Season 5, Disc 3*

Alan Alda, Mike Farrell, Harry Morgan
Loretta Swit, Larry Linville, Gary Burghoff, Jamie Farr, William Christopher

Executive Producer – Gene Reynolds
Produced by Allan Katz & Don Reo and Burt Metcalfe
Story Consultant – Jay Folb
Written by Everett Greenbaum & Jim Fritzell
Directed by Gene Reynolds

Beeson Carroll. . . . . .Lieutenant Colonel Donald Penobscott
Judy Farrell . . . . .Nurse Able
Patricia Stevens . . . . Nurse Baker
Lynn Marie Stewart . . . . Nurse Clark
Kellye Nakahara . . . . .Nurse Kellye

Copyright 1977 – 20th Century Fox Film Corporation

Non-Credited Appearances. . . . . Gwen Farrell, Jeff Maxwell, Robert Gruber,
Roy Goldman

Chapters

1: *Main Titles*	6: *The Smoker – 10:57*
2: *Time to Get Married – 0:54*	7: *Wedding Day – 15:25*
3: *Margaret's Fiancée – 3:41*	8: *The Bride Goes to Work – 18:45*
4: *The Best Man – 7:36*	9: *Goodbye, Margaret – 20:34*
5: *The Wedding Shower – 9:41*	10: *End Titles – 24:00*

Closing Stills

1: *Donald arrives*
2: *Donald & Hawkeye*
3: *Margaret*
4: *B.J. in the Swamp*
5: *Potter gives the bride away*
6: *Radar*
7: *Klinger cries at the wedding in the Mess Tent*
8: *Mulcahy*
9: *Frank watches Margaret & Donald fly away*

Synopsis: After Frank pushes the issue, Lieutenant Colonel Donald Penobscott is finally coming to the 4077th to marry Margaret, and Frank's request for a two-week furlough is denied. Donald arrives and wants to talk to Frank, but he has to catch him first as Frank starts to run away and in an odd twist, Donald wants him to be his best man. BJ and Hawkeye make Donald a bachelor party and when Donald, drunk, passes out, they play what is perhaps one of the cruelest practical jokes by putting Donald in a full body cast, chest to toes and make him think he broke his legs. Everyone is in place and the wedding ceremony begins, with Donald still in a body cast, but becomes rushed when wounded start arriving. Margaret begins triage in her wedding gown and Donald, who insists on seeing Margaret work, is wheeled on a hand truck to the windows of the OR doors. The session is over and everyone is at the chopper pad to see Margaret and Donald off on their honeymoon. Just before the chopper leaves with Margaret inside and

Donald, still in the body cast on the side stretcher, Hawkeye and BJ try to tell her that the cast isn't real, but she can't hear them. The chopper leaves and after everyone has left the pad, Frank, by himself, watches the chopper in the distance and simply says, "Goodbye, Margaret."

Commentary by Larry Gelbart: "There was so much more to Larry Linville than what he got to show as Frank Burns. I regret not having developed the character further. I doubt that I would have tried to talk him into not leaving. I'm afraid I helped painting Larry's Frank Burns into a corner, not making him more complex, not more dimensional. I couldn't promise him that if he stayed, his character would be written differently. I think he was smart to go when he did. Had I written his manner of departure, I would have tried to surprise him, myself, and, of course, the audience." (Gelbart had left the season before.)

Commentary by Jeff Maxwell: "The prop department had a number of prop casts that could be easily removed from the body part they were 'protecting.' I'm certain that that particular cast was custom made for the episode and, as I remember it, Beeson was able to step in and out of the device as needed."

Authors' Notes: There are no PA announcements in this episode.

The shower tent on the Ranch compound has no sign indicating shower times as in previous episodes on the Ranch set.

Just a reminder that Trapper can still be heard in O.R. scenes, as in this episode, saying, "Okay, cut that."

Beeson Carroll, a.k.a. Lieutenant Colonel Donald Penobscott, has around 40 credits to his name with appearances on *Matt Helm, Good Times, Maude, Barnaby Jones, Miami Vice* and *Hill Street Blues.*

This is Larry Linville's last episode on *M*A*S*H.* According to Mr. Linville, he had taken the Frank Burns character as far as it could go. More than 30 years later, Major Frank "Ferret Face" Burns remains a fan favorite character that people love to hate. Still a topic of discussion, this is a testament to Linville's ability to pull himself out of reality and step into a role completely opposite the man and for five years, his portrayal of Major Burns was nearly flawless. Goodbye, Ferret Face, we salute you.

Appendix – Season 5

Character Profiles

Hawkeye

Episode 98 and 99: Could have worked in Uncle John's car lot for $50 a week and "all the Studebakers you can eat."

Was never a Boy Scout, but always prepared.

Gives Rosie blue medicine for her gums.

Steps on BJ's racing cockroach, Blue Velvet.

Bar tab at Rosie's is $51.55.

100: Had to explain why he had sand in his tuxedo pants on his prom night.

101: Nurse's heater explodes in his face and is blinded.

Radar reads a letter from his father: Sandy Falcon asked about Hawkeye and is still "sweet on him."

She used to dip Hawkeye's "pigtails" in the ink well.

So obnoxious that she was voted most likely to marry out of her species.

Recognizes Margaret by her perfume: "Moon Over Fort Dix" *(real perfume is "Forbidden Furlough").*

Recognizes food on the chow line: spinach and meatloaf.

Crabapple Cove Lobster Festival: two days and two nights — 3,000 people do nothing but "gorge themselves on the biggest, reddest, juiciest lobsters." Lobster boats start coming in at sunset.

Took three baskets and a "little home-wrecker named Sharon" down to a deserted cove one year.

They used to call Sharon, "Sharon share alike."

Was at the cove with Sharon for four days, and never got to the lobster.

Will tell Potter the story about two priests and a mule later.

Hit some golf balls earlier.

Spent two hours listening to the rain and how it sounds like steak being barbecued.

Never spent a more conscious day in his life.

Knows Nurse Bigelow by "touch."

102: "If it weren't for that leprechaun *(meaning Radar)*, the 4077th would be a license plate."

Wants to be "Dr. Pierce with a liquor store in front and surgery in the back."

Sews socks.

RJ Harlidge — Nudist of the Year.

104: Uses Frank's shirt as a basketball.

Lost his virginity 20 years ago.

Saw Colonel Flagg when he was a showgirl — he was the only one carrying a machine gun.

105: Bets with BJ that Margaret is wearing boxer shorts and wins $1.50 from BJ.

Makes rounds in post-op in a tuxedo, safari hat and funny glasses *(not Groucho)* and blue swim fins.

106: Instructs Mulcahy over the radio how to perform a tracheotomy.

Scared stiff the first time he operated and there were no bombs going off.

107: Bribes Radar with the nurse's annual physical in exchange for getting a North Korean surgeon to the 4077.

Made a going-away cake for the North Korean surgeon in the mess tent.

108: In a certain light, Potter looks like Greer Garson.

109: Little newspaper stand across from Goldstein's on the Ginza — wants this month's editions of *"Nudist Frolics," "Naked Health," and "Bare Back News"* — Just wants the volleyball scores.

Went to a "skin farm" once but didn't have the nerve to put down his ukulele.

When Margaret is angry, she looks like Victor Mature.

Delivered Radar's guinea pig triplets — *"Manny, Moe and Jack."*

Gave Radar's chicken an aspirin when it got hysterical.

Dropped the thermometer in the corral — temperature of the manure is 62 degrees.

Sophie's heart rate is 50.

With BJ, they belted Frank when he wanted to cook Radar's rabbit for Easter.

Pony rides in Atlantic City would cost $7.50.

Father has a Chevy.

Prefers working with curved blades, according to Margaret.

110: Spent a Friday the 13th in a haunted house with a friend.

Never more frightened — his friend's husband materialized out of nowhere.

111: Sleepwalking his way to a root beer float.

Plays imaginary basketball with imaginary new tennis shoes.

Calls Klinger "Scooter."

New principal at school is Clarence Vanderhaven.

Father won't allow him to get a BB gun.

Geography was never a strong subject for him.

A stream with fish ran behind his house in Crab Apple Cove.

People in Crab Apple Cove never change — they're always off-white.

The greatest man he ever knew is his father, who was born in Crab Apple Cove.

Father never wanted to live anywhere else.

Hasn't seen his father in two years.

Sleepwalking, he plays Hopscotch, then marbles on the compound.

Calls Radar, "Stinky" and/or "Dexter."

Wakes from a nightmare screaming for Toby to watch out for the trees.

Saw Toby riding a sled down Hermitage Hill too fast headed for the trees.

He, Toby and Dickey Barber were the "Three Musketeers" when they were around 11 or 12 years old.

Toby Wilder was his best friend from childhood.

Toby Wilder has children and thinks Hawkeye owes him $37 — Hawkeye paid him back years ago.

Dickey Barber was another friend from his childhood.
The only green vegetables he gets are Martini olives.
11,000 miles from home.
Crab Apple Cove first settles in 1684 and has a population of 3,976.
Had another nightmare that Dickey Barber was hurt in an explosion — calls and Dickey is fine.
Afraid to go to sleep.
Calls the States and everyone is watching Milton Berle.
Plays imaginary basketball with Sidney Freedman.

112: Darns socks

113: Reading the *Times* — Senator McCarthy claims Communists have infiltrated the military.
With BJ, they don't like Frank because "he's a lousy doctor and a rotten person."
Never been able to finish a *Times* crossword puzzle.
Had a friend in college that used to make tomato soup out of ketchup and hot water.
His friend, Tippy Brooks, is a "crossword freak" who does double-crostic puzzles in ink.
Tippy Brooks is a doctor aboard the USS Essex in Pusan Harbor.

114: Chips in with BJ $20 for Cho to buy his ring.

115: "I know I'm Dr. Pierce, but I wanna be G-d."

116: Is the "Porfirio Rubirosa" of Ouijongbu *(A Dominican diplomat, sportsman and playboy).*

117: Crab Apple Cove Courier in the mail.
Wanted this month's "Journal from the Institute of Applied Nudism."
Back pain that goes right through to his lung.
Exercises by wrestling periodically with the nurses.
Vernon Parsons — "A dunce" he went through medical school with and "incredibly average."
Parsons got a $100,000 grant from Boston Hospital for a 2-year study of infectious disease in mice.
Saw a movie with a guy's nodes that got so big they took over Minneapolis.
Wants to send Parsons a letter stating he was caught cheating on an exam.
Thought he had pleurisy causing back pain, than maybe a disc.

118: War is the world's favorite spectator sport.
"Don't let the bastard win" *(death).*
Without leadership, he'd be in the back seat of a '46 DeSoto "schnuggling" with Wanda Lamperski.
Had the mumps, measles and colic as a child.

119: Brought BJ a hand-picked shirt from Seoul with one sleeve longer than the other *(light green).*

120: Cracks a real egg.

122: Used to play water polo but the horse drowned.
With BJ, he put Donald Penobscott in a body cast.

B.J.

Episode 98 and 99: Spelled "Connecticut" in a spelling bee and won a wax pistol full of grape juice.

102: In charge of spleens and small intestine.

104: Accidentally shot in the leg by Frank *(not serious).*

105: Loses $1.50 to Hawkeye on a bet that Margaret wears boxer shorts.
Is the practical joker — *Frank sits on bench with sawed through legs.*
Potter with black rings around his eyes from binoculars.
Eggs in Frank's helmet.
Margaret opens a can of coiled snakes.
Frank falls into water-filled foxhole.
Empty water and gas cans tied to the back of Sidney's jeep.

109: Owes Hawkeye $3,427 playing darts and wants to pay on Diner's Club.
Father in law is Floyd Hayden & lives in Quapaw, Oklahoma for 50 years.
Floyd knows all about horses, cows, pigs etc, and still thinks they're fighting the Germans.

110: Aunt once spoke to the spirit of Sigmund Freud.
Koreans were printing with movable type in 1403 *(fact).*

112: Puts on a fake fight with Hawkeye for Frank's birthday

113: Paper-trained a cockroach.
Louis Helper went to high school with BJ and was expelled for burrowing into the girl's washroom.

114: Used a pair of 1949 sweat socks and a matching garter belt in the last batch from the still.
Chips in $20 with Hawkeye so Cho can get his engagement ring.

116: BJ kisses Lieutenant Carrie Donovan — spends the night and wants to write a letter to Peg to tell her.
Nearly stops talking to Carrie because the last time they talked, they didn't.

117: Gets a surgical journal in the mail.
While scrubbing, he studies a surgical procedure from a book that Kellye is holding open for him.
Now operates from the book as Kellye holds it open for him *(successfully, then gets drunk).*

118: 8,000 miles from home.
Having a family is better than being a doctor or an officer.

119: Received a Dutch apple crumb cake from Peg *(awful, according to Hawkeye).*

120: Daughter saying complete sentences at two years old.

121: The nurse's shower is the end zone for football.

122: With Hawkeye, they put Donald in a body cast just before he marries Margaret. *(When she found out, she punched a hole through her tent.)*

Colonel Potter

Episode 98 *Rumor:* The Radio City Rockets were supposed to play at the 4077th.
and 99: Got an Italian "sissy" who played Valencia with his armpits.
Sent General Irving R. "Binky" Hamilton a case of Preparation-H.
General Hamilton is watching them wash his jeep.
Mrs. Potter plays bingo with the Catholics — last month won talcum powder and a carton of Wings *(Cigarettes).*
Bought wild boar tusks from Cho Man Chin and they turned out to be plastic.
His unit in WW II got word that Nazis dressed as Eskimos had overrun Seattle — half the unit believed it and began hoarding canned salmon.
Has known Bink Hamilton going on 30 years.
Is the Godfather of Sherman Potter Hamilton, 15 years old and can name 24 of the 48 states.

Sherman Potter Hamilton already has an appointment to West Point.
Mrs. Potter is looking forward to meeting Hawkeye.
On horse leading convoy to new M*A*S*H site *(and later, back to the old site)*.
Loves chipped beef on toast after church.
Always liked Klinger's blue chiffon dress.
Finest act of bravery he ever witnessed was Klinger trading his clothes for the schoolhouse.

100: Four squirts of goat's milk and three sugar cubes *(Radar puts these in his coffee)*.
Has an aunt who got a black & blue mark at a little league game when a foul ball hit her in the shoulder — blood clot went to her brain and the next day she keeled over in her bean salad.
Dressed as Santa Clause last Christmas.

102: Has a wart on his head.
Gets a letter from his five year old granddaughter — granddaughter made toast at three.
Has a friend who was a plumber one-day and in charge of the Panama Canal the next.
40 years in the army.
Gets cranky when he lances a boil *(according to Radar)*.

105: Cleans Sophie's hooves.
Was pranked with black circles from binoculars around his eyes.
Has a granddaughter back home around eight years old *(in Episode 100, his granddaughter is five years old)*.
The lousiest duty he has to perform is writing parents, informing them their son has died.
In OR, he's standing in a basin of water.

106: Has heard of Father Marty "Boom-Boom" Gallagher — famous for poker games he organized when German artillery took a break.
Saw a picture of Calvin Coolidge in a war bonnet, "but that doesn't make him an Indian."

107: Frank is as good a doctor as the next man, "provided the next man is Lou Costello."

108: Has worked around the clock in OR.
This is the episode where he does a painting of Hawkeye holding a drink with feet on the desk.
Started surgery in 1932.
By his own admission, he couldn't hit a bullet with the side of a barn.

109: Going to Tokyo — Mildred got a flight to Japan.
Sophie sometimes favors the right-front hoof and likes to be groomed every other day.
Can put horseshoes on a mosquito, but can't get rid of his gas.
Horseshoes made by a Korean blacksmith — "Hopalong Wang."
Instructs Radar to give Sophie salt and water for regular irrigation.
Wants his book: *How to Sweat With Closed Pores* by Dr. Hugo Schlecter, dermatologist.
Won't get Hawkeye's nudist magazines because he'll be in uniform — Mildred will because "she's a good sport."
Mildred bought a 10-speed bike.
Will arrange a discharge for Klinger because "Depression is a ticket home" *(not serious)*.

Picked up red material for Klinger and wants him to sing "Top Hat" for the wounded in a red dress.

110: Paid $3.00 for a lighter.

Was in a "Parisian house of instant happiness" in WW I.

The horseshoe Radar hangs comes from Potter's cousin Elmer.

113: Dinner special tonight is Egyptian Sauerkraut — part of their UN contribution — sent back the camels.

"Seoul City Sue" lies as much as his sister in law Bertha.

114: Bet $3.00 on the ping-pong game.

Old friends with Lieutenant Harold Beckett — they were in Camp Grant together *(in Illinois)*.

Beckett was quartered in Washington buying vegetables, fruit and meat for the troops — was married to a woman who looked like "Man-O-War" but it didn't last — needed 30 days on the front line for his Combat Infantry Badge and needs 5 more to retire a full colonel — hasn't seen action in 25 years and is at the front only for the badge but due to his actions, Potter is sending him back down.

Has 16 months, 3 weeks and 4 days left before he can barbecue on his patio in Nebraska.

Wishes "Mother" could be there to see him give away the bride — Mother loves to cry.

Doesn't want to play horseshoes with Klinger anymore because he doesn't want to be beaten 5 times by someone in a skirt

117: Ate turnips in WW I for breakfast every day for a month — tongue smelled like Arthur Murray's Footbath.

When he was an enlisted man, he was short — not like he is now. Thought he would look taller if he could knock a few of the big guys on their backs.

"Fig Newton's and Scotch — great if you dunk 'em."

118: 14 months and 11 days till retirement *(in Episode 112, he has 16 months, 3 weeks and 4 days)*.

Hawkeye hates generals more than watered gin and earaches put together, according to Potter.

Hawkeye drinks in groups of 1 or more, according to Potter.

119: The three things that make a movie great are horses, cowboys and horses. Favorite movie is *My Darling Clementine*.

120: Has a nephew who's a sucker for souvenirs — takes trips so he can cover his car with decals of where he's been — now the "nitwit" can't see where he's going.

Reading *Stars & Stripes* — A private from the 8063rd set a new pole-sitting record: 94 hours — 18 minutes.

Potter held the Camp Grant record by swallowing 22 goldfish and was "sick as a dog" for a week.

Drake, the Commanding Officer at the 8063rd swallowed 23 goldfish to break the record.

Gave Klinger a 3-day pass to Tokyo for breaking the flagpole sitting record.

121: Accidentally put a stitch in his glove.

Will excuse blood donors from his hygiene lectures for a month.

Was a bachelor at Camp Grant for two years.

Mentions the "Dew Drop Inn and Tavern" at the southeast corner of Broadway and Lawrence.

GI in post-op tells him there's a bank on that corner since around 1900.

Used to take the "L" *(elevated)* train at Diversy and catch the Chicago White Sox at Comiskey Park.
GI tells him he means the Chicago Cubs at Wrigley Field.
Potter's favorite tavern was "The Shamrock" at State & Dearborn.
GI tells him that State & Dearborn never meet as they run parallel.
GI has never been to Detroit so Potter will talk to him about Detroit tomorrow.

122: Gives the bride away *(Margaret).*

Margaret

Episode 100: Was at the Zen Bar and Grill in Tokyo — Got engaged.
Donald sleeps on a bare piece of wood — is a "West Pointer" — calls her his "Little Plebe."
Full name — Lieutenant Colonel Donald Penobscott.
Has photo of Donald with a girl — maybe his "cousin."
Couldn't love anyone who didn't outrank her.
Donald paid for the shower curtain out of his own pocket and it wasn't even their fault it ripped.
Donald has, "dancer's legs and a cute little behind and medals all over his chest — all man."
Donald finished 203rd in a class of 600.
Able to pursue an army career with Donald and have a home, children and a washer & dryer.
Donald has enormous arms and a tattoo of a Sherman Tank on his right bicep.
When he flexes his muscle, the tank gets bigger and bigger.

101: Perfume is "Forbidden Furlough."
Hawkeye recognized Margaret's perfume as "Moon Over Fort Dix."

102: Received a leather whip from Donald in the mail.

103: Loves children.

105: Buys earring from Klinger for $2.50.
Donald celebrated his birthday last night without Margaret and "they" had a good time.
Brought a cherry tree branch back from Tokyo.

109: Appendix acting up — chronic, not hot and wants Hawkeye to operate if necessary.

111: Her perfume, "Forbidden Furlough" cost $8.00 an ounce.
Frank tells her she "smells like a French hooker."

112: Donald is the most romantic man she ever met.
In Seoul, a 250-pound man brushed her leg — she screamed — Donald ready to punch the man in the mouth — the man's seeing-eye dog bit Donald in the leg.

114: Donald is not cheap, he's conservative.

115: Frank's father made a joke — Frank.

116: Hasn't received a letter from Donald in four days.
Donald has made 126 paratrooper jumps.
Donald hurt himself doing a rope climb on the obstacle course — was operated on for a double-hernia.
Donald will be out of action for 8 weeks, according to Potter.

117: Received a "strange letter" from Donald's mother.

120: Gave Frank a ruby ring on their 1st anniversary — a "precious family heirloom" and wants to give it to Donald.
Drunk, she punches Lieutenant Stratton right in the mouth and goes

flying onto a table in the Officer's Club.
Finds the ring she wanted back from Frank in his footlocker.
Frank had the ring inscribed with *"To Louise, Love, Frank B."*
Margaret wants either $15.00 or 15 teeth from Frank

122: Engaged for eight months.
Donald is a Methodist.
To get married — Permission from the CO / Form # 1027A / Overseas nuptials in a combat zone / Form 1136 / Embassy Registration Form L1101 / All typed in triplicate / Blood test *(BJ)*.
According to Donald, he was 227th in a class of 396. *(According to Margaret, in Episode 100, he was 203rd in a class of 600).*
Throws the bouquet and Frank catches it — Frank throws it to Kellye

Frank

Episode 98 Always says, "Buy American."
and 99: Nostrils flare when he's in charge.
Has a black bra and a Hare Kari knife in his footlocker.
Used to sing after, "Amen" in his church.

100: Doesn't exteriorize patients he's working on.
Bible came from an expensive curio shop at the Indianapolis Speedway.
Was a Boy Scout, then Scoutmaster.
"Doctors are trained to ignore people's pain."
Offers Radar a job after the war and to look him up in Fort Wayne.
Has a nephew who owns a chain of pet mortuaries.
Has covers on his sofas.
Tells his mother that nobody likes him… as usual.
Had a friend who pretended to like him the way his father used to

101: Didn't loosen a patient's bandage because he was on a break

104: Accidentally shoots BJ in the leg *(not serious)*.
When he was a kid, his "Daddy" used to take him to the pony rides.
Is the prime suspect in Margaret's disappearance, as per Colonel Flagg.
Flagg has films of Frank and Margaret.
Reads Reader's Digest.

105: Doesn't intend to be more than 6 paces from a good hole if somebody yells, "air raid."
Getting signals from his wife — she "needs a man, a whole man" and she's not behaving like herself.
Got together with her "lady" friends and went to Indianapolis, "Just to look around" — Cost $55.
Wife is stuffing envelopes for the Republican Club and maybe ringing doorbells.
Becoming "sexy and provocative."
Got a letter with a picture of her in slacks walking away from the camera.
Believes in the sanctity of marriage no matter how ugly or disgusting it gets.
Will kill her before he divorces her.
Should've known better than to tell something personal to a psychiatrist.

106: Specialty is feet *(In Episode 27, his specialty was post-op infections).*

107: Nobody double-dares him and gets away with it.
If Albert Schweitzer were a good doctor, he'd be in Beverly Hills helping the wealthy.
Is "sort of" the Albert Schweitzer of Korea.

Was a Boy Scout.

Rode a two-wheeler at 13.

Taught his rabbit how to smile.

Worked his way through medical school by selling burial plots door to door

108: Is 20 years younger than Potter.

Is known by Major Choi at KAH 426 as "Ferret Face" — worked on a few of his men and they survived.

109: Had chili for dinner last night.

110: After shave lotion a gift from a friend — cracks his mirror.

Margaret squirts saline solution in his face *(accidentally)*.

111: Tells Margaret she smells like a French hooker.

From Fort Wayne.

Had a Popeye night-light when he was a kid, but his father took it away. Father said it was dark 12 out of 24 hours and wouldn't put up with a son who was a coward half the time.

112: A "Sickly kid" named Timmy lived on his block and sat on his porch in a wheelchair and waved at passersby. Timmy lost control of his wheelchair — rolled down the stairs and across the lawn into Frank's father's car. He scratched the paint a little, but it was okay because Timmy's folks had money.

Always has tapioca pudding on his birthday.

Tells a sleeping patient in post-op that his birthday used to be the most important day of his life and used to have parties in his honor with cards and gifts. *(In an earlier episode, his mother "would send out 30 invitations just to get 4 kids to show up").*

Tries to take the sleeping patient's Purple Heart, but Hawkeye and BJ enter and he leaves it alone..

Plays with a yo-yo — the string breaks off.

Hawkeye and BJ stage a fake fight for a birthday present and Frank loved it.

Got his watch from a whiplash patient and it's worth $14.

113: Has pimples because his pores won't close.

Gets a toy from a former receptionist where he has to put little balls in holes and took three days to complete it before Hawkeye slapped his back and knocked all the balls loose

113: Continued — Won a white Bible at his church for organ playing.

Was 122nd in a class of 200.

114: Bet on the 8063rd in a ping pong match because he got 3 to 1 odds.

Is the only one not in a dress uniform at Cho's wedding.

115: Refuses to operate on a foreigner.

116: Got a "wonderful" letter from his old Sunday school teacher.

Gives Margaret a gift: A Japanese umbrella made in Texas.

117: Gets *Popular Mechanics* in the mail.

Gets shortness of breath and heart palpitations.

Has a lump under his sternum that's not supposed to be there — feels like a marble *(An immie, not aggie)*.

Thinks his arms are getting longer and swollen nodes getting bigger.

118: Wants to be a general's personal physician — has a thriving practice in Fort Wayne.

Frank's qualifications to be a general's personal physician:

Dropped his bubble gum in a patient *(according to Hawkeye)*.

Sneezed and performed an accidental appendectomy *(according to*

Hawkeye).
Threw up in post-op 12 times *(according to Hawkeye)*.
Did a hysterectomy on a male sergeant *(according to Hawkeye)*.
Fainted in OR 27 times *(according to BJ)*.
Overslept 48 times *(according to BJ)*.

119: Used to play "war games" with Margaret — Margaret would hide under the covers and pretend it was a tent, then Frank would be a bomb and fall on her.
"Penobscott" is a "stupid name."
Is the garbage officer.
Sings Late — "Ol' Hawkeye and Ol' BJ, they think they're pretty smart — I'd like to take a scalpel and stab them in the heart"

120: Has souvenirs from every place he's been.
Corporal Thomas Hinton was dealing in Korean antiques on the Black Market and Frank's name was on a list of customers given to the MPs.
Bought an 800-year-old vase of the Koyou Dynasty for $27.75.
Serial number on footlocker — "Maj. F. Burns — 5683698.
In Season 1, *Episode3*, his name was "Major Frank W. Burns and his serial number was RA98672412.
His address is 2845 Elm Street.
Has been hiding the ring Margaret wanted back in his footlocker.
Frank had the ring inscribed: *"To Louise, Love, Frank B."* and Margaret wants $15 or 15 teeth.

121: In OR for 18 hours — has not donated blood as part of his strategy — "One of us should always have a full tank."
Talking to a wounded GI in post-op — Louise has changed and only sends cookies couple times a month.
Is positive she's been fooling around.
Hired a "private dick" to follow her to PTA meeting and church functions and came up with nothing.
Thinks the private dick he hired is one of her "caballeros" too.
Hired a second cop to follow the first, but he wanted expenses paid.
A kid came in with a rash — he spotted it first and called it "Burns Blight" because it was the catchiest name since diarrhea.

122: A Presbyterian *(according to Hawkeye)*.
Penobscott's Best Man.

Radar

Episode 98   Never been to New Jersey.
and 99: Warms a Spam sandwich under his armpit for Potter *(refused)*.
Hot rice dish at Rosie's is called, "hot rice."
Plays "Assembly" poorly on his bugle.
Goat's name is "Pokey" — rabbit's name is "Scruffy."
"Scruffy" gets carrots and "Pokey" gets the rest of the lettuce.
Recognizes BJ's racing cockroach as "Blue Velvet" because it has a limp.
Has a grape Nehi at Rosie's that was bottled in 1951 and still has its fizz.
Used to go down to Main Street & watch them undress the window dummies at the dry goods store every Saturday night.
Jeep won't start and he can't fix it because nothing is where it is on his mother's Nash.
Scruffy and "The Twins" has a baby.

100: Got penicillin from the Black Market at the regular price.
Death gives him a rash.

101: "General Walter O'Reilly — three stars and real mad" *(trying to get an ophthalmologist for Hawkeye).*
Wants to be one of the 1st six guys on chow line because they're serving fried shrimp.
Requisitions 300 rubber gloves — they're almost out because they were used for balloons New Year's Eve.

102: Pays for his mother's electrolysis.
Supply folks mostly Presbyterian but sent Biblical bookmarks.
Nurse Baker has a towel around Radar's neck and he can kiss her if he wants to, but doesn't because he thinks she's getting strep throat.
Put milk on his cereal at four years old.
Serial number — 3911810.
(Fake) Promotion due to "Efficiency, punctuality and bugling over and above the call of duty."
Broke out in hives when he made corporal.
Uncle Howard was a notary public and a dance instructor.
Will be able to use the officer's latrine and read *National Geographic.*
Calls Potter, "Sherm."
Klinger made a choker out of his typewriter ribbon.
Wants to be a corporal again — nobody likes him anymore.

103: Somebody broke into the snowflake paperweight his mother sent him for his birthday because of the heat.
Calls Margaret's garter a "slingshot."

104: Never had cheerleaders in school.
"Nudidity" makes him breathe funny.
Birth lectures make him gag.

105: Uncle dreamt he was dancing with a whale — when he woke, their cow had eaten his pants.
Ordered 500 hams.
Flies kites with local orphans.

106: Doesn't know if Fordham has a football team because he's been in post-op all morning.
Had a test in school and Leonard Gerst wanted to cheat off him.
Knew Leonard's mother would beat him up if he flunked the test.
He let Leonard cheat off him, plus Leonard gave him $3.00.
Car sick from watching Mulcahy operate.

107: His camera is rusty from taking nurse's shower pictures for Hawkeye.
Sparky won't be able to tell time on a Chinese watch with Chinese numbers.

109: Potter's horse, Sophie, smiled at him.
Mother says, "Better to hold the phone than to get a kidney stone."
Says, "hell!"
Sparky can't use after-shave lotion because it irritates his pimples.
Chewed a whole pack of gum with a bag of potato chips.
Sparky will need a year to watch the film, "Ecstasy" due to a woman running naked through the woods.

110: The PA won't be fixed till tomorrow because the electrician is resting at Rosie's.
Electrician was fixing wires and it shot him through the wall.
Protestant.
Won a horseshoe from Igor — said it came from Man-O-War.

112: Accepted to the Famous Las Vegas Writer's School, "Serving the creative community since 1950."

Replied to an ad on the back cover of a *Superman* comic, next to an ad for x-ray glasses.

School said he has "extraordinary potential" after sending a sample of his writing.

School cost $50.00 plus $5.00 for student activity fee.

School run by very famous writers: "Ethel Hemmingway, Jerry Steinbeck," Eunice O'Neill.

In 10 weeks, he'll be "respected by a crowd."

First assignment is to relate an amusing anecdote.

Second assignment is to describe a beautiful scene outside his window *(he's in the Swamp)*.

Page 5 of his writer's book says: "More and more, a man is judged by how good he expresses himself."

Has to write about a romantic interlude.

Has nephews.

Gave up writing and is now, "Amazing Radaro" and performs a magic trick.

Puts Frank's watch in a cloth — Frank grabs the cloth and a hammer and smashes his own watch.

113: Checks his bread for maggots.

Radioman 1st Class Stevens, Radar knows by voice only — oatmeal cookie caught fire in ashtray — lost the cookie but saved the raisins.

Uses Hawkeye and BJ as antennae for his radio.

Can see through dirty glasses because he knows where everything is.

Swamp smells like dirty socks.

3rd hole in the latrine pinches.

114: Ping Pong scorekeeper.

Boris, a guy back home, used to wear dresses like Klinger but he wasn't in the army.

Boris would walk down the street with a cotton dress carrying an umbrella — Uncle Ed called him a sissy.

Boris "flattened" Uncle Ed.

Beats Potter at Ping Pong by a score of 21 to 18.

Spots Potter 18 points.

115: Brings *Life* magazine for Billy with article on last year's Iowa-Minnesota game with a picture of Billy getting tackled in the 1st quarter.

Listened to the game on Armed Forces Radio.

Treats Hawkeye to a drink at Rosie's *(mentioned, not seen)*.

116: While dreaming, he grabs Margaret and calls out, "Betty" and kisses her.

Has lipstick mark from Margaret.

Dreamt he was dancing with Margaret and Betty Grable woke him up.

117: Likes sausage because they have extra grease.

Feels different when the guys start joking with business girls at Rosie's — he gets sleepy.

Would like to "bust out & drink & tell lies to strange girls & come back to camp the next morning without sleep and throw up all day — at least once.

118: Wears his white paratrooper scarf.

Only his mother calls him "Walter."

Gets antsy if he doesn't see Lee Chin every day *(Baby he was asked to watch with Mai Ping)*.

119: Hurt his tooth eating peas.

Makes him woozy to look at his food tray when throwing away food.

122: Cook baked a wedding cake with chocolate frosting and Radar licked the spoon *(Potter wanted to).*

First wedding was Uncle Ernie's — had potato salad, pecan pie, punch, turkey, Jell-O, tongue sandwiches, chopped liver — threw up all over the flower girl.

Leaves the Swamp to throw up and passes out on the Stage 9 compound

Klinger

Episode 98 and 99: Gets a box of El Redondo cigars — Havana cigars made by Puerto Ricans in Newark, New Jersey.

Cigars are "eight bucks a box and limited."

Gets one box a year — the rest go to Milton Berle, Nelson Rockefeller and Bishop Sheen.

"A good cigar is like a beautiful girl with a great body who also knows the American League box scores."

Not army — delicatessen.

Has brocade from the Spiegel Catalog from Chicago / Will never give up the "Klinger Collection."

Has $300 invested in clothes.

Blue chiffon from "Murdoch's of Toledo" — pearls won't go with anything else.

Confirmation dress on rack is a "Chubby" with real fake fur.

Fought his way through "snipers" for the month-end sale at "Wang's of Seoul."

Took threee years of alterations, sewing and staying up all night studying the "Monkey Ward" *(Montgomery Ward)* catalog.

Exchanges all the clothes for the new M*A*S*H building.

101: Makes Frank want to throw up.

Brings Hawkeye a duck-call instead of a Howitzer in case he needs anything.

102: Holds up stockings with band aids — stings and pulls clumps of hair off his legs.

Gives Potter a haircut.

Family rents — doesn't own the house.

Has to take earring off to answer the phone.

Wishes he could hear through his nose.

Is Lebanese — "Full of the juices of life."

104: Usually doesn't let guys undo his bra on a first date.

Wears a yellow shower cap.

In his family, every baby had a nose like a hawk.

105: Paid $7.50 for earrings at the Tokyo PX.

Wants to win them back so the holes in his lobes don't close up again.

Would wear Hula-Hoops if they would get him out of the army.

In Arabic, he tells Potter: "My olive has no pit and there is no yoke in my egg."

In Arabic, he tells Potter: "Grandfather, may your pomegranates grow as big as the Queen's fanny."

In Arabic, he tells Potter: Father, give me your cheese from the windowsill."

In Arabic, he tells Potter: "May the fleas of a thousand camels nest in your armpits."

106: Won't shoot himself in the foot to get out because he'll ruin a perfectly good pair of nylons.

107: If anything happens to him, he wants to be buried in his blue chiffon.
108: Is "Zoltan, King of the Gypsies" — stolen by Lebanese and brought up
as their own *(ploy).*
Not in the army, not even an American citizen — has a signed
confession from the culprits *(ploy).*
Elected King of the whole tribe with an urgent request to return to his
throne *(ploy).*
Now knows why the sound of violins "set his blood on fire" and why he's
attracted to storefront windows *(ploy).*
The smell of paprika makes him face towards Budapest.
Has an urge to roam.
Working on a plan to turn the motor pool into a gypsy caravan.
Tells the future with cards *(Draws an ace-high straight).*
109: Wants material from Goldstein's on the Ginza — four yards because he's
putting in pleats.
Red and blue material okay, no aquamarine because it matches his skin
and nobody would know he's there
110: Came from a long line of short-nosed people *(In Episode 102 he says "In
his family, every baby had a nose like a hawk").*
Grandfather spit in the eye of the village witch — big noses ever since.
111: Hawkeye will get lockjaw if woken during sleepwalking.
112: Vito, Klinger's friend, met his wife through a mail order catalog — Vito
is a mailman.
Pours "gas" over himself *(ploy).*
Wants to be kept in a blue jar because that's his best color.
Wants his ashes sprinkled over Toledo.
Calls Potter, "Sherm."
Pours real gas over himself *(Potter ordered it to replace the water the first
time).*
Covered in gas, runs into the nurse's showers
113: Takes nuts and bolts off jeep with "squeaky seats," eats them with 30
weight motor oil *(Salt & Pepper).*
Second course is a windshield wiper blade.
Has a blue wig, according to Potter.
Has eaten two bolts, a horn button, wiper and a condenser — Now has a
stomach ache.
In bed in post-op, he kisses Admiral Cox on the cheek but usually
doesn't kiss on the 1st date *(ploy).*
114: Learned to throw horseshoes in Toledo for self-defense.
116: *(Ploy)* Is the Toledo Strangler — struck 8 times — "The Terror of Toledo."
Kills only women motorcycle cops.
Wants to be extradited back to Toledo for a "lengthy trial by jury."
The sirens on the motorcycles drive him "bananas."
Potter reads the "Strangler" article — last murder took place two weeks ago.
117: Drew KP for 30 straight days for punching out Zale — Zale insulted the
Toledo Mudhens.
Won't drop his pants for examination because the last time he did, they
put him in the army.
Laverne keeps writing that, "When you get angry, count to ten and ask
St. Anthony for help."
Once counted to eight. never made it to St. Anthony.
If he has hepatitis, he's going to kiss Zale right on the mouth.
118: Wants to see the "Commies" run Newark *(New Jersey).*

In 2 weeks, the Commies will wind up in the trunk of a Buick.

119: Operates movie projector.

120: "Section 8 Time" — Sitting on top of a flagpole with lingerie hanging and a helmet holding fruit.

Afraid of high places but he's desperate.

Loves pancakes with maple syrup.

On the flagpole for 48 hours, according to Potter.

Has 46 hours and 19 minutes to go for the MASH flagpole-sitting record.

Or he can swallow 24 goldfish — the first 18 are easy, according to Potter

122: To Margaret: "May your life be an oasis surrounded by waving palms, warm breezes and spit-free camels."

Shower gift for Margaret is a wedding gown — If he had a daughter, he'd want her to wear it.

Uncle Zak used that wedding gown to get out of WW I.

To Donald: "May your house be filled with children and your garage filled with camels."

Has to shave his back because he'll be wearing a morning frock.

If he cries, he has three hankies in his purse — he cries

Father Mulcahy

Episode 98 and 99: Blesses all new construction, including new latrines and the new M*A*S*H location.

Wears a light blue shower cap

102: Out $16.00 playing poker.

Was sent Ritz Crackers instead of Communion wafers.

105: Dreamt he was a Cardinal in Rome and the Pope had a bad cold.

Had to sleep with his brothers when he was a boy *(Brothers?)*

106: Was in the Seminary in Philadelphia and studied with Father Marty "Boom-Boom" Gallagher.

Gallagher used to tell stories about the war.

Has never been to the front — not allowed — feels useless but Potter won't let him go — he's a priest, not a soldier.

Was excited by Boom-Boom's stories of being at the front — wants to go to offer comfort.

Against orders, he goes with Radar to a front-line aid station to bring back a GI in need of surgery.

A wise priest once said, "No matter how well you bluff, eventually, you have to put your cards on the table.

Has a "Tom Mix" pocketknife.

Says, "Grace" because he couldn't think of any other prayer before performing an emergency tracheotomy.

109: Once did a prayer for a Great Dane with peritonitis.

110: His Bishop at the Seminary was Bishop O'Hara.

O'Hara always said, "That's the way the ball bounces."

Koreans practice almost every religion known to man, including Shamanism.

112: Reads *Sport* magazine with orange cover as seen in earlier episodes.

Most unforgettable character is his sister, Sister Theresa, who did her Benedictine in San Diego.

Sister Theresa teaches at the Seminary and plays guard on the basketball team.

Sister Theresa can slam-dunk while wearing a heavy Crucifix.

115: Is the timekeeper for Klinger vs. Zale boxing match.

117: Feels arthritic — tongue is yellow — has hepatitis.

119: Returns to camp with Potter's favorite movie *My Darling Clementine.*

Order of Mulcahy sound-alike contest: Hawkeye, Klinger, Margaret. Radar, Potter and Mulcahy.

All boo when Mulcahy impersonates himself.

122: Has been to one other "stag smoker" — a nun jumped out of an angel-food cake.

After his first time in OR, he couldn't eat liver for a year.

Seen, Heard, Mentioned or Referenced – Season 5

Movies

Episode 102: "One Ticket to Broadway" with Lyle Bennett, Mitzi Price, Leonard W. Grossman and "Teddy, the Wonder Lizard" *(not real).* (Note: There is a movie from 1951, *Two Tickets to Broadway.*)
"Two Lizards to Broadway" *(not real).*

104: *Gone with the Wind* (1939) mentioned.

108: *Mrs. Miniver* (1942) mentioned.

109: *King Kong* (1933) mentioned.
Gilda (1946) mentioned.
Ecstasy (1933) mentioned (Spelled "Extase").

119: *My Darling Clementine* (1946) seen.

Songs

Episode 98: "I love to go swimmin' with bow-legged women and swim between their
and 99: legs…" *(Potter sings in the shower)* No info found.
"Mississippi Mud" *(Hawkeye says the line "Time to beat your feet on the Mississippi mud…")* See Episode 49 (page 258) for details.
"Assembly" Military call to rise.
"Shuffle Off to Buffalo," *(Klinger sings "You go home & pack your panties, I'll go home & pack my scanties and away we'll go…")* Words by Al Dubin, music by Harry Warren, from *42nd Street* (1933).
"Pack Up Your Troubles" *(Hawkeye says the line "Pack up my troubles in my old kit bag…")* Written by George Henry Powell and Felix Powell, from 1912.

100: "Back in the Saddle Again" (Frank "clucks") Written by Gene Autry, from the 1939 movie, *Ravin' Tumbleweed.*

101: "Three Blind Mice" *(Frank whistles)* Written by John W. Ivimey in 1926, from the movie short *Three Blind Mice.*
"I'll See You in My Dreams" *(Hawkeye sings "I'll hear you in my dreams…")* Words by Gus Kahn, music by Isham Jones, 1924.

102: "You Ought to Be in Pictures" *(Klinger sings)* Written by Little Jack Little in 1934.

104: "You're the Top" *(Klinger sings "I'm on top, I'm the Tower of Pisa…")* by Cole Porter, 1934.
"Let's Call the Whole Thing Off" *(Hawkeye sings)* Written by Ira Gershwin (1937).
"Smoke Gets in Your Eyes" *(Hawkeye sings "They asked me how I knew her brassiere was blue…")* Song is by The Platters, from 1958.
"A Pretty Girl is Like A Melody" *(Hawkeye sings)* Written by Irving Berlin in 1919.

108: "Play Gypsy, Dance Gypsy" *(Said by Klinger)* Written by Emmerich Kalman (October 24, 1882-October 30, 1952).

109: "Chinatown, My Chinatown" *(Potter sings)* Written by William Jerome & Jean Schwartz in 1910.
"Mickey Mouse Club March" *(Hawkeye sings "M-O-U-S-E")* From *The Mickey Mouse Club* (1955). (Note: the first five episodes were shown on television October 3-7, 1955.)
"Top Hat, White Tie and Tails" *(Klinger sings "I'm puttin' on my top hat, tying up my wide tie, I'm puttin' on my tails…")* Written by Irving Berlin for the 1935 movie *Top Hat.* (The correct lyrics are "Oh, I'm puttin' on my top hat, tying up my white tie, brushing off up my tails.")

112: "My Funny Valentine" *(Hawkeye sings "Don't change a hair for me…" B.J. sings "Not if you care for me…")* From the song written by Richard Rogers and Lorenz Hart between 1936 and 1940.

"Happy Days Are Here Again" *(Frank hums)* See Episode 1 (page 128) for details.

116: "I Only Have Eyes For You" *(Hawkeye sings "Are the stars out tonight? I don't know if it's cloudy or bright…")* Written by Al Dubin & Harry Warren, 1933.

"I'm Late" *(Hawkeye sings "No time to say hello, goodbye. I'm late, I'm late I'm late…")* From *Alice in Wonderland* (1951), written by Sammy Fain & Bob Hilliard.

117: "I Get A Kick Out of You" *(B.J. sings "I get no kick from champagne…")* by Cole Porter from the 1934 movie *Anything Goes.*

119: "Nobody Knows the Troubles I've Seen" *(Klinger sings)* Traditional lyrics and music by Harry T. Burleigh (1866-1949).

"Git Along Little Doggy" *(B.J. sings "Get along little doggy…")* Gene Autry (1937).

"My Darling Clementine" Song heard from the 1946 movie of the same name.

"Gee, Mom, I Wanna Go Home" (WWII) *(All sing in the mess tent when the movie breaks).*

120: "Chela Luna" Traditional Italian.

122: "Stormy Weather" *("Don't know why there's no sun up in the sky, stormy weather…" B.J. starts, all join in O.R.)* By Harold Arlen, written in 1933.

"Here Comes the Bride" *(Radar intentionally off-key on piano)* Wedding march by Felix Mendelssohn from *A Midsummer's Night Dream.* See Episode 88 (page 333) for details.

Prank Frank – Season 5

Episode 98 and 99: Frank gets knocked into the new latrine ditch he had several corpsmen dig *(seen)*.

100: Boy Scouts set his pants on fire and told him it was a drill *(mentioned)*.
Hiding in a bush, a corpsman empties his coffee cup on him *(seen)*.

101: Hawkeye screams, "GOOD NIGHT!" into Frank's ear while he's asleep *(seen)*.
Earlier in the episode, only Frank listens to a baseball game on Armed Forces Radio (knowing that it would be repeated later), and then took bets on the game. Hawkeye, B.J., Klinger and Radar fake the repeat broadcast, making Frank lose and everyone in camp after him to be paid *(seen)*.

102: Radar salutes Frank and drops Frank's package as a result *(seen)*.

104: Hawkeye uses Frank's shirt for a basketball *(seen)*.

105: With a tray of food, Frank sits on the end seat in the mess tent after someone sawed through the legs *(seen)*.
Eggs in his helmet *(seen)*.
B.J. fills Frank's foxhole with water, then has Sidney yell, "AIR RAID!" Frank runs from the Swamp and falls into the water-filled hole *(seen)*.

106: Corporal Cupcake, a German shepherd who was operated on growls and snaps at Frank *(seen)*.

107: Unknowingly leaves camp with North Korean infiltrators. They throw him out of the jeep because he's driving them crazy *(seen)*.

109: Hawkeye and B.J. belted Frank when he wanted to cook Radar's rabbit for Easter *(mentioned)*.
As Frank leaves Potter's office, Potter crosses his eyes and sticks his tongue out at him *(seen)*.
Earlier in the same episode, Hawkeye did the same thing Potter did to Frank *(mentioned)*.
Margaret needs an appendectomy and throws Frank out of OR *(seen)*.

110: Frank's radio isn't working. Hawkeye bets him $10, then makes the radio work. B.J. was plugging and unplugging the radio *(seen)*.

112: Frank takes Igor's tapioca pudding and likes the raisins. Igor tells him they're flies, not raisins *(seen)*.
Tries to take a sleeping patient's Purple Heart, but Hawkeye and B.J. come in *(seen)*.
Thinking he knows how the magic trick Radar is about to perform with his watch works, he grabs the cloth, smashes it with a hammer and destroys his own watch *(seen)*.

113: Hawkeye locked Frank in the nurse's latrine last Friday *(mentioned)*.
Hawkeye gave Frank a chocolate-coated lizard *(mentioned)*.
After taking three days to finish a game putting little balls into holes, Hawkeye slaps him in the back knocking all the little balls out *(seen)*.

115: After setting up a boxing match between Zale and Klinger, Hawkeye has the fighters both punch Frank at the same time instead, knocking him out *(seen)*.

120: Frank bought an 800-year-old celadon vase of the Koyou Dynasty for $27.75 (knowing the vase is considered priceless), and packs it up to send it home. Hawkeye and B.J. switch the vase with a bedpan. *(seen)*.

121: Hawkeye and B.J. force Frank to the front of the blood-donor line, in spite of his screaming *(seen)*.

Appearances – Season 5

Ahn, Philip...Episode 110 *(The Korean Grandfather)*
Arbus, Allan...Episode 105, 111 *(Major Sidney Freedman)*
Bailey, John-Anthony... Episode 121 *(Private Whitney)*
Beauchamp, Richard..Episode 121 *(Corporal Robelo)*
Bell, Michael...................................... Episode 120 *(Lieutenant Stratton, Chopper Pilot)*
Botosan, Thomas...Episode 108 *(Sergeant)*
Binns, Edward...Episode 118 *(General Theodore A. Korshak)*
Bloch, Andrew... Episode 121 *(Private Gordon)*
Braverman, Bart..Episode 105 *(Private Habib)*
Bredhoff, Susan.. Episode 104 *(Nurse Able)*
Brown, Henry .... Episode 115 *(Sergeant Billy Taylor)*
Byers, Brian...Episode 106 *(Private Danny Fitzsimons)*
Cahill, Barry.. Episode 98 & 99 *(Barry the Chopper Pilot)*
Canning, James...Episode 110 *(Corporal Marsh)*
Catlett, Mary Jo ....Episode 103 *(Nurse Mary Jo Walsh)*
Carroll, Beeson............................... Episode 122 *(Lieutenant Colonel Donald Penobscott)*
Chao, Raymond...Episode 102 *(Korean Boy On Guard Duty)*
Clark, Oliver .... Episode 113 *(Lieutenant Tippy Brooks)*
Cough, James...Episode 98 & 99 *(Enlisted Man)*
Davis, Jennifer.. Episode 105 *(Nurse)*
Dennehy, Brian.. Episode 120 *(M.P. Ernie Connors)*
Doyle, Richard .... Episode 108 *(M.P.)*
Eitner, Don.. Episode 98 & 99 *(Captain Stevens)*
Elene, Susie..Episode 118 *(Mai Ping)*
Farrell, Gwen .... Episode 113 *(Anesthetist)*
Farrell, Gwen .... Episode 117 *(Nurse Baker, Uncredited)*
Farrell, Judy...Episode 101, 119, 122 *(Nurse Able)*
Fenichel, Jay..Episode 104 *(Patient)*
Fong, Francis...Episode 98 & 99 *(Rosie)*
Foronjy, Richard ....Episode 106 *(Sergeant)*
Frank, Charles.. Episode 105 *(Captain Hathaway)*
Greene, Peter D. .... Episode 115 *(Medic)*
Hama, Larry...Episode 107 *(North Korean, Passenger)*
Harrison, Gregory...Episode 103 *(Lieutenant Tony Baker)*
Haymer, Johnny..Episode 102, 115 *(Sergeant Zale)*
Hicks, Hilly.. Episode 121 *(Corporal Jerris Moody)*
Ito, Robert.. Episode 107 *(North Korean (Driver))*
Jue, Crandal.. Episode 120 *(Korean Boy)*
Katz, Phyllis .... Episode 108 *(Nurse Able)*
Kazann, Zitto..Episode 121 *(Sergeant Attias)*
Kelsey, Linda... Episode 103 *(Nurse Mickey Baker)*
Kenny, Andrew J...Episode 105 *(Patient)*
Kent, Enid..Episode 101, 119 *(Nurse Bigelow)*
Kent, Enid.. Episode 114 *(Nurse Able)*
Kenyon, Sandy .... Episode 102 *(Sergeant Woodruff)*
Kim, Alvin...Episode 120 *(Korean boy)*
Kim, June ....Episode 104, 120 *(Korean Woman)*
Knight, Dudley .... Episode 101 *(Major James Overman)*
Knowels, Rex.. Episode 113 *(American Patient)*
Kolman, Ron...Episode 113 *(Corporal Shapiro)*
Kramer, Jeffrey... Episode 119 *(Driver)*

Lee, Sachiko Penny..Episode 114 *(Soony)*
Lee, Jae Woo..Episode 108 *(Korean Guard)*
Lee, Virginia Ann..Episode 110 *(Kyong Ja)*
Locatell, Carol Lawson..Episode 103 *(Nurse Gaynor)*
Lough, James...Episode 115 *(P.F.C. Felix Kornhause)*
Mabrey, Greg..Episode 115 *(Wounded Soldier)*
Mako..Episode 108 *(Major Choi)*
Mancini, Ric...Episode 106 *(Sergeant Hodkey)*
Maxwell, Frank..............................Episode 114 *(Lieutenant Colonel Harold Becket)*
Maxwell, Jeff..Episode 102 *(Igor)*
McRea, Alan..Episode 121 *(Corporal Nessen)*
Mitchell, Bobbie...Episode 101 *(Nurse Gage)*
Mulhern, Scott...Episode 120 *(Andy Cooper)*
Nakahara, Kellye...................................Episode 101, 122 *(Nurse Kellye)*
Narita, Richard....................................Episode 114 *(Cho Lin)*
Oh, Soon-Teck...Episode 107 *(Doctor Syn Paik)*
O'Neill, Dick...Episode 113 *(Admiral Cox)*
Phalen, Robert...Episode 114 *(Sergeant Blanchard)*
Quynh, Le...Episode 104 *(Korean Husband)*
Roche, Sean..Episode 111 *(Private Timothy Burke)*
Romano, Andy..Episode 121 *(Sergeant Justiss)*
Saki, Eileen.....................Episode 98 & 99 *(Korean Woman at the New Site)*
Sakimoto, Susan...Episode 104 *(Korean Girl)*
Scelza, Carmine...Episode 108 *(G.I. (Server))*
Scelza, Carmine...Episode 119 *(Corpsman)*
Shinkai, Bill........................Episode 113 *(Soo Ling (Chinese Patient))*
Springer, Gary..Episode 121 *(Private Garvin)*
Stevens, Patricia...Episode 111 *(Nurse)*
Stevens, Patricia...Episode 122 *(Nurse Baker)*
Stewart, Lynn Marie.........................Episode 102, 104 *(Nurse Baker)*
Stewart, Lynn Marie.........................Episode 122 *(Nurse Clark)*
Stone, Leonard..Episode 118 *(Colonel Bidwell)*
Sturgis, Patricia..Episode 103 *(Nurse Preston)*
Sweeny, Ann........................Episode 116 *(Lieutenant Carrie Donovan)*
Sullivan, Tom........................Episode 101 *(Lieutenant Tom S. Straw)*
Sung, Richard Lee.........................Episode 98 & 99 *(Cho Man Chin)*
Tarpey, Tom........................Episode 115 *(Battalion Surgeon)*
Viscuso, Sal..Episode 105 *(Patient John)*
Viscuso, Sal.........................Episode 121 *(Sergeant Raymond McGill)*
Wilcox, Larry........................Episode 118 *(Corporal Mulligan)*
Winter, Edward........................Episode 104 *(Colonel Flagg)*
Yashima, Mo Mo........................Episode 113 *(Korean Mother)*
Yune, Jon........................Episode 104 *(Korean Translator)*
Zippe, Daniel........................Episode 121 *(Private Corey)*

Broadcast/Production Order – Season 5

Broadcast	Production
98: Bug Out, Part 1 (9/21/1976)	98: (U801) Bug Out, Part 1
99: Bug Out, Part 2 (9/21/1976)	99: (U802) Bug Out, Part 2
100: Margaret's Engagement (9/28/1976)	100: (U803) Margaret's Engagement
101: Out of Sight, Out of Mind (10/5/1976)	101: (U804) Hawk's Nightmare
102: Lt. Radar O'Reilly (10/12/1976)	102: (U805) Lt. Radar O'Reilly
103: The Nurses (10/19/1976)	103: (U806) Out of Sight, Out of Mind
104: The Abduction of Margaret Houlihan (10/26/1976)	104: (U807) The General's Practitioner
105: Dear Sigmund (11/9/1976)	105: (U808) The Abduction of Margaret Houlihan
106: Mulcahy's War (11/16/1976)	106: (U809) The Nurses
107: The Korean Surgeon (11/23/1976)	107: (U810) Dear Sigmund
108: Hawkeye Get Your Gun (11/30/1976)	108: (U811) The Colonel's Horse
109: The Colonel's Horse (12/7/1976)	109: (U812) Mulcahy's War
110: Exorcism (12/14/1976)	110: (U813) Hawkeye Get Your Gun
111: Hawk's Nightmare (12/21/1976)	111: (U814) The Korean Surgeon
112: Unforgettable Characters (1/4/1977)	112: (U815) Exorcism
113: 38 Across (1/11/1977)	113: (U816) End Run
114: Ping Pong (1/18/1977)	114: (U817) Ping Pong
115: End Run (1/25/1977)	115: (U818) Forgettable Characters
116: Hanky Panky (2/1/1977)	116: (U819) Souvenirs
117: Hepatitis (2/8/1977)	117: (U820) Margaret's Marriage
118: The General's Practitioner (2/15/1977)	118: (U821) 38 Across
119: Movie Tonight (2/22/1977)	119: (U822) Hanky Panky
120: Souvenirs (3/1/1977)	120: (U823) Hepatitis
121: Post-Op (3/8/1977)	121: (U824) Movie Tonight
122: Margaret's Marriage (3/15/1977)	122: (U825) Post-Op

Season 6

With the departure of three main characters and the two creators/producers, it's a wonder that M*A*S*H survived for a sixth season. But, survive it did. Burt Metcalfe, who had been with the show since the beginning, first as casting director, then as associate producer, took over for Gene Reynolds as producer. This provided a sense of continuity for the show, and a guiding force for the writers. Also, and increasingly, Alda began having more of a voice in the kind of show M*A*S*H became. Season 6 begins with "Fade Out/Fade In," an episode dealing with the departure of Frank Burns and the arrival of Major Charles Emerson Winchester, III wonderfully played by David Ogden Stiers. Despite all of the M*A*S*H departures, "Fade Out/Fade In" has some of the feel of the early seasons, but a unique freshness all of its own. The producers needed a foil for Hawkeye and BJ, but once again, it was wisely decided not to try to copy a departing character with a new one. Indeed, neither Charles nor Margaret posed much of a military threat to Hawkeye and BJ, and that dynamic of the show "faded out." But, Stiers brought a tremendous amount of humor to the show in his portrayal of the uppity Charles. The trend towards more drama continues, but the sixth season of M*A*S*H is high quality in its own right and, in spite of losing key personnel, it survived. Notable episodes from this season include "Fade Out / Fade In," "The Light That Failed," "Temporary Duty," and "Change Day." Beginning with this season, each episode of M*A*S*H ended with a freeze frame. It had only been used once before, in Season 1's "Germ Warfare."

Fade Out / Fade In – 9/20/1977

Season 6 / Episode 123 and Episode 124
Production 123 and Production 124 – Y101 / Y102
Columbia House VHS Tape. . . . . *The Reluctant Recruit (Catalog # 13113)*
Fox DVD . . . . *Season 6, Disc 1*

Alan Alda, Mike Farrell, Harry Morgan
Loretta Swit, David Ogden Stiers, Gary Burghoff, Jamie Farr, William Christopher
(New Cast Will Remain In Place Until Season 8)

Produced by Burt Metcalfe
Executive Story Consultant – Jay Folb
Written by Jim Fritzell & Everett Greenbaum
Directed by Hy Averback

Story Editors – Ken Levine & David Isaacs
Program Consultant – Ronny Graham
Creative Consultants – Gene Reynolds / Alan Alda

Rick Hurst.	Captain/Private Schaeffer
Raymond Singer	Doctor Berman
Robert Symonds	Colonel Baldwin
Tom Stovall.	The Sergeant
William Flatley . . . . M.P. Sergeant Williams/ "I" Corps Military Police
James Lough	Driver
Joseph Burns	Patient
Kimiko Hiroshige	Korean Woman

Copyright 1977 – 20th Century Fox Film Corporation

Chapters

1: *Main Titles / Frank's Late*	11: *Here's to Frank – 22:59*
2: *Clobbered – 4:17*	12: *No Frank Burns – 25:08*
3: *Back from the Honeymoon – 7:58*	13: *A Different Problem – 28:53*
4: *An Incident in Seoul – 8:45*	14: *Ready to Roll – 31:28*
5: *Damn Cribbage – 9:53*	15: *Another Loony – 34:39*
6: *Mrs. Penobscott – 11:56*	16: *Last Call – 36:30*
7: *Enemy Fire – 13:15*	17: *The Winchester Spirit – 38:25*
8: *A Doctor, A Lawyer – 14:53*	18: *Why Me? – 40:20*
9: *Burns Again? – 17:08*	19: *Rush Hour – 42:51*
10: *Charles's Initiation – 17:44*	20: *Breaking Him In / End Titles – 45:55*

Closing Stills

1: *Freeze – Charles in the Swamp (Please, Mozart)*
2: *Hawkeye in the Swamp*
3: *B.J. in the Swamp*
4: *Potter on R compound*
5: *Margaret*
6: *Charles after O.R. session*
7: *Radar sees Charles's arrival*
8: *Klinger in Potter's office*
9: *Mulcahy*

Synopsis: "A lousy surgeon and a pain in the butt" is how Colonel Potter describes Frank Burns, but also describes him as always being on time, except now. Hawkeye and

BJ arranged R&R for Frank after Margaret's wedding, but an I-Corps M.P. calls to let the unit know that Frank was involved in an incident in Seoul, and while drunk, accosted a blonde WAC thinking she was Margaret and ran off before he was apprehended. Making matters worse, wounded begin arriving and the 4077 is short a surgeon. Potter calls Tokyo General Hospital where Colonel Baldwin who, at first, can't spare anyone, but after losing a game of cribbage to a snooty major, he loans the major to the 4077th for the next 48 hours, assuring him that a MASH unit is just like Tokyo General, except for artillery and snakes. Major Charles Emerson Winchester, III, a highly skilled and highly educated surgeon from society's "upper crust" arrives. A Harvard Medical School graduate working at Massachusetts General and demonstrating new surgical techniques in Tokyo is just in time to perform a delicate operation that the rest of the staff doesn't have much experience with and performs it successfully. Potter, after getting negative updates on Frank's bizarre behavior, finally gets a call letting him know that Frank Burns is being held for a psychiatric evaluation, then transferred out of the 4077, making the staff happy, but makes Major Charles Emerson Winchester III miserable and angry when Potter arranges for the Major to be a permanent resident.

Commentary by Ken Levine: "David and I came aboard the staff as story editors this season. When the head writer, Jay Folb, left in late October, we just assumed his responsibilities."

Commentary by Rick Hurst: "It was a joy and a privilege to be in the episode 'Fade Out / Fade In,' and even more flattering to be included in the retrospective 'Our Finest Hour.' The cast was extremely warm and supportive of guest stars, and I think that's why some of our best work was done in this show. One reason *M*A*S*H* will always be special for me is because, shortly after appearing in the show, I became friends with McLean. We were constant golfing buddies here in L.A., and saw each other at countless charity tournaments around the country. He was a wonderfully gifted person, and I'm proud to have been his friend. Mostly, my gratitude at having been on *M*A*S*H* comes from having been selected to participate in such a unique show. Seldom, in our industry, does such a strong political view provide the platform for weekly entertainment. The original film, *M*A*S*H*, was an anti-war statement and I feel truly honored to have been associated with a program that so fervently and consistently sought to instill that sentiment in each and every episode in its long and exalted run."

PA Announcements by Sal Viscuso

Authors' Notes: The third hour-long episode of the series.
Beginning with season 6, episodes of *M*A*S*H* ended with a freeze frame and accompanying music.
Guest star Rick Hurst would soon go on to play Deputy Cletus Hogg on *The Dukes of Hazzard.*
Potterism: "Road apples."
The cigar Radar smokes makes him sick, as opposed to the several he smoked, mostly in Seasons 1 and 2.
The barber's tent has been seen in previous episodes with a barber pole, but the pole is not there this time.
In Chapter 7, Charles and the jeep's driver talk, but the distance shots, and when they get out of the jeep, there's no mouth movement.
Radar gives his middle name for the first time in Chapter 10 as "Eugene."
Also in Chapter 10, Hawkeye mentions the actress, Anita Ekberg. Her first two movies were *The Mississippi Gambler* and *Take Me to Town,* both from 1953 and both unaccredited appearances. How did Hawkeye know about her?

Fallen Idol – 9/27/1977

Season 6 / Episode 125 / Production 126 – Y104

Columbia House VHS Tape . . . . To Err Is Human (Catalog # 13116)
Fox DVD . . . . Season 6, Disc 1

Alan Alda, Mike Farrell, Harry Morgan
Loretta Swit, David Ogden Stiers, Gary Burghoff, Jamie Farr, William Christopher

Produced by Burt Metcalfe
Executive Story Consultant – Jay Folb
Written by Alan Alda
Directed by Alan Alda

Story Editors – Ken Levine & David Isaacs
Program Consultant – Ronny Graham
Creative Consultants – Gene Reynolds / Alan Alda

Francis Fong . . . . Rosie
Patricia Stevens . . . . Nurse Baker
Robin Riker. . . . . Nurse Perry
Larry Gelman . . . . G.I. #1
Michael Talbot . . . . G.I. #2
Copyright 1977 – 20th Century Fox Film Corporation

Non-Credited Appearances. . . . . Kellye Nakahara, Gwen Farrell, Dennis Troy

Chapters

1: *Main Titles / Mail Call*
2: *Sound Advice – 1:39*
3: *Guilt and Shame – 4:59*
4: *Indisposed – 8:01*
5: *The Riot Act – 10:24*

6: *Hero Worship – 11:48*
7: *Outrage – 14:59*
8: *Eye to Eye – 17:35*
9: *Making Up – 20:09*
10: *Purple Heart / End Titles – 22:49*

Closing Stills

1: *Freeze – Radar & Hawkeye after pinning medal*
2: *Hawkeye*
3: *B.J.*
4: *Potter in his office*
5: *Radar*
6: *Margaret*
7: *Charles*
8: *Klinger*
9: *Mulcahy*
10: *Radar in bed in Post-Op*

Synopsis: After taking Hawkeye's advice to go to the Pink Pagoda in Seoul to "let nature take it's course," the last thing anyone expected when wounded arrive is Radar among the casualties, wounded from mortar fire. Hawkeye immediately blames himself and operates on Radar, then gets drunk. Asleep only two hours before wounded arrive again, Charles insists Hawkeye get up and pull his weight in O.R., where Hawkeye needs to be relieved so he can go outside and be sick, something Hawkeye has never done before, something Colonel Potter is not happy about, and something Radar cannot accept, which causes an angry rift between them.

PA Announcement by Sal Viscuso

Authors' Notes: In Chapter 3, Hawkeye says Judy Garland, the Tin Man and Radar are all from Iowa. Actually, Judy Garland is from Grand Rapids, Michigan, not Iowa.

Hawkeye jokingly mentions that the song, "Somewhere Over the Rainbow," is the "national anthem of Iowa." It should be noted that the official state song of Iowa is "Song of Iowa," set to the music of "O, Tannenbaum." The Iowa Legislature adopted this song as the official state song in 1911.

Last Laugh – 10/4/1977

Season 6 / Episode 126 / Production 125 – Y103

Columbia House VHS Tape . . . . .Beej (Catalog # 19501)
Fox DVD . . . . .Season 6, Disc 1

Alan Alda, Mike Farrell, Harry Morgan
Loretta Swit, David Ogden Stiers, Gary Burghoff, Jamie Farr, William Christopher

Produced by Burt Metcalfe
Executive Story Consultant – Jay Folb
Written by Everett Greenbaum & Jim Fritzell
Directed by Don Weis

Story Editors – Ken Levine & David Isaacs
Program Consultant – Ronny Graham
Creative Consultants – Gene Reynolds / Alan Alda
James Cromwell. . . . . .Captain Leo Bardonaro
Robert Karnes . . . . .Major General Fred Fox
John Ashton . . . . M.P.
Copyright 1977 – 20th Century Fox Film Corporation

Non-Credited Appearances. . . . . Roy Goldman, Kellye Nakahara, Gwen Farrell,
Jeff Maxwell

Chapters

1: *Main Titles*	6: *Permission Denied – 13:43*
2: *Bad News – 0:57*	7: *Temper Tantrum – 15:52*
3: *Credentials – 3:59*	8: *The Brass – 17:04*
4: *Practical Joker – 6:18*	9: *Last Laugh – 20:54*
5: *Arrest Order – 9:48*	10: *R & R / End Titles – 23:11*

Closing Stills

1: *Freeze – B.J., Hawkeye, Potter in Potter's office*
2: *Bardonaro in the Swamp*
3: *General Fox*
4: *Hawkeye in the Swamp*
5: *Potter in his office*
6: *Margaret returns in Potter's office*

Synopsis: The Provost Marshall is sending someone to investigate BJ claiming he's an imposter, not a doctor, but when Potter mentions the name, "General Leo Bardonaro," BJ recognizes it as an old friend from Stanford who lives for practical jokes. The jokes goes too far when a real general sends MPs to the 4077th with an arrest order for BJ accusing him of throwing a wild party in a hotel in Seoul with loud music, girls, and barbecuing steaks on the balcony causing the room next door, the general's room, to fill with smoke forcing the general and his secretary into the hallway naked. BJ proves that it wasn't him, and eventually gets the last laugh on his friend Leo.

Authors' Notes: There are no PA announcements in this episode.
In Chapter 8, Hawkeye says, "Always trust your car to the man who wears a star." This line is from a commercial for Texaco gas that ran in the 1950s.
James Cromwell, who stands at nearly 6' 6", is a well-known actor who has appeared in *All in the Family* as "Stretch Cunningham." Mr. Cromwell has also appeared in

four episodes of *E.R.*, 27 episodes of *Six Feet Under* and to date, eight episodes of the highly rated *24* on Fox. The Emmy and Oscar nominee was born in L.A., but raised in Manhattan.

Robert Karnes makes his second appearance on *M*A*S*H*, the first in the Season 4 opener, "Welcome to Korea" as the intimidating colonel in the Transient Officer's Club who did not like the idea of Radar's new rank, "Corporal Captain."

War of Nerves – 10/11/1977
Season 6 / Episode 127 / Production 128 – Y106
Columbia House VHS Tape . . . . *Paging Dr. Freedman (Catalog # 19503)*
Fox DVD . . . . *Season 6, Disc 1*

Alan Alda, Mike Farrell, Harry Morgan
Loretta Swit, David Ogden Stiers, Gary Burghoff, Jamie Farr, William Christopher

Produced by Burt Metcalfe
Executive Story Consultant – Jay Folb
Written by Alan Alda
Directed by Alan Alda

Story Editors – Ken Levine & David Isaacs
Program Consultant – Ronny Graham
Creative Consultants – Gene Reynolds / Alan Alda
Allan Arbus . . . . .Major Sidney Freedman
Michael O'keefe . . . . Tom
Peter Riegert . . . . .Igor
Copyright 1977 – 20th Century Fox Film Corporation

Non-Credited Appearances. . . . . Johnny Haymer, Kellye Nakahara, Gwen Farrell,
Dennis Troy, Roy Goldman

Chapters

1:	*Main Titles / Wounded Shrink – 0:54*	6: *Klinger's Reasons – 12:42*
2:	*Battle of the Noses – 2:08*	7: *Firebugs – 15:18*
3:	*Lunatic Asylum – 3:47*	8: *Radar's Teddy – 16:38*
4:	*On the Couch – 6:56*	9: *House Call – 18:09*
5:	*Hot and Cold – 10:56*	10: *Burn, Baby, Burn / End Titles – 21:13*

Closing Stills

1: *Freeze – Radar finds his bugle*
2: *Freedman*
3: *Potter*
4: *B.J. & Hawkeye in the Mess Tent*
5: *Radar & Klinger*
6: *Margaret & Charles*
7: *Mulcahy*

Synopsis: The unit is on edge, bickering with each other as the wounded keep coming, but nobody expects to find Sidney among them. Doing therapy in a foxhole, Sidney suffered a minor head wound, but Potter's glad to see him. Margaret insists Charles touched his nose during surgery and makes him scrub again and Hawkeye makes BJ smell his food, making it impossible for BJ to eat. After Potter orders all the Chinese uniforms burned due to infestation, Zale and Igor begin to get on each other's nerves and Sidney sees the members of the 4077th one on one, making each one feel better. The only one who doesn't feel better is Sidney himself when the GI he was helping in the field refuses to forgive him for sending him back to the front.

Commentary by Michael O'Keefe: "The second episode I appeared in was directed by Alan Alda. He was considerate, insightful, and patient with me. I will always be grateful

PHOTO CREDIT MARK MURRAY

Michael O'Keefe appeared in "Mad Dogs and Servicemen" in Season 3 and "War of Nerves" in Season 6.

for that. All of the other actors were great, and I have only fond memories of going to 20th Century Fox studios and their ranch in the hills near Malibu where the outside set was."

PA Announcement by Sal Viscuso

Authors' Notes: This is the first episode where Peter Riegert, instead of Jeff Maxwell, played Igor, and will play Igor again in another episode, "Change Day," also in Season 6.

Potterism: "Unit running as smoothly as a pig on stilts."

In Chapter 3, BJ makes a reference to *The Music Man.* This Meredith Willson musical ran on Broadway from December 19, 1957 to April 15, 1961 at The Majestic Theater and The Broadway Theater. The movie followed in 1962.

The V.I.P. tent in Chapter 4 seems to be Margaret's tent as the walls are plywood, and this was seen only in Margaret's tent. Also in this tent is a black and white picture that used to hang next to Henry's diploma in his office.

The bonfire in Chapter 10 was filmed at night on the Ranch set.

The Winchester Tapes – 10/18/1977

Season 6 / Episode 128 / Production 129 – Y107

Columbia House VHS Tape . . . . *The Reluctant Recruit (Catalog # 13113)*
Fox DVD . . . . *Season 6, Disc 1*

Alan Alda, Mike Farrell, Harry Morgan
Loretta Swit, David Ogden Stiers, Gary Burghoff, Jamie Farr, William Christopher

Produced by Burt Metcalfe
Executive Story Consultant – Jay Folb
Written by Everett Greenbaum & Jim Fritzell
Directed by Burt Metcalfe

Story Editors – Ken Levine & David Isaacs
Program Consultant – Ronny Graham
Creative Consultants – Gene Reynolds / Alan Alda

Thomas Carter . . . . Patient Mccloud
Kimiko Hiroshige . . . . Korean Laundry Woman
Copyright 1977 – 20th Century Fox Film Corporation

Non-Credited Appearances. . . . . Roy Goldman, Dennis Troy, Kellye Nakahara

Chapters

1: Main Titles / Letter Home	*6: Hanky Panky? – 12:54*
2: Three-Day Pass – 2:22	*7: Thwarted Again – 14:55*
3: Poseur – 5:31	*8: Loss and Gain – 16:24*
4: Tomorrow – 7:48	*9: Too Much – 21:48*
5: Stymied – 10:58	*10: Done / End Titles – 22:49*

Closing Stills

1: Freeze – Charles. "Get me the hell out of here!"
2: B.J. & Charles in the Swamp
3: Charles & Mulcahy
4: Potter paints in his office with Radar
5: Klinger & Hawkeye in the Mess Tent
6: Charles checks Margaret's eye in the Scrub Room

Synopsis: In a tape-recorded letter home, Charles is less than flattering in his descriptions of life at the 4077th, calling Potter "bandy-legged" and Mulcahy a "cock-eyed optimist." But the one person he cannot afford to annoy is Radar, as his telephone is his only link to the outside world. Surprisingly, he acknowledges BJ as an excellent surgeon, even though he's from, and studied in, California, but together with Hawkeye is more than even Charles can bear. As desperate as he is for deodorant so he doesn't offend himself, the only thing he wants more is for his father to talk to someone of influence and get him out of there.

PA Announcement by Colonel Potter
PA Announcement by Sal Viscuso

Authors' Notes: The tape recorder Charles uses for his letter is a Webcor Model 210, manufactured by the Webster-Chicago Company in 1952.

According to Radar in Chapter 4, the 4077th's departure lounge is the dead tree by the latrine, and the unit has its own cockroach collection that takes an hour to see.

Klinger, in Chapter 5, mentions S&H Green Stamps. S&H Green Stamps started in 1896 and became the most successful loyalty program in history.

In Chapter 7, B.J. has to operate on Corporal Graham again. This is the second time B.J. had to operate on a patient a second time, the first in Season 4's "It Happened One Night," when he had to operate again on Edwards.

The Light that Failed – 10/25/1977

Season 6 / Episode 129 / Production 130 – Y108

Columbia House VHS Tape . . . . To Err Is Human (Catalog # 13116)
Fox DVD . . . . Season 6, Disc 1

Alan Alda, Mike Farrell, Harry Morgan
Loretta Swit, David Ogden Stiers, Gary Burghoff, Jamie Farr, William Christopher

Produced by Burt Metcalfe
Executive Story Consultant – Jay Folb
Written by Burt Prelutsky
Directed by Charles Dubin

Story Editors – Ken Levine & David Isaacs
Program Consultant – Ronny Graham
Creative Consultants – Gene Reynolds / Alan Alda

Enid Kent . . . . Nurse Bigelow
Philip Baker Hall . . . . .Sergeant Hacker (Supply Truck Driver)
Gary Erwin . . . . Corporal Dobson (Post-Op Patient)
Copyright 1977 – 20th Century Fox Film Corporation

Non-Credited Appearances. . . . . Kellye Nakahara, Gwen Farrell, Roy Goldman

Chapters

1: Main Titles / The Wrong Stuff
2: Slow Reader – 5:28
3: By Candlelight – 7:23
4: Whodunit – 10:14
5: Major Disaster – 11:29
6: The Usual Suspects – 14:11
7: Big Lox – 16:30
8: Author, Author – 18:35
9: The Right Stuff – 21:24
10: Attached / End Titles – 22:50

Closing Stills

1: Freeze – Charles & Hawkeye in Post-Op
2: Charles
3: Margaret
4: Mulcahy in the Mess Tent
5: B.J. on the phone
6: Hawkeye in Potter's office

Synopsis: Operating under adverse conditions is hard enough, but the task becomes even more difficult when light bulbs become scarce along with surgical silk, rubber gloves and gel foam, but things seem to brighten up when a supply truck rolls in. Only problem is it's winter and the truck has salt tablets, mosquito netting, but no light bulbs. The truck also has, in a canvas bag, a book, The Rooster Crowed at Midnight, a mystery by Abigail Porterfield, and everyone is itching to read it. Meanwhile in post-op, Charles injects a patient with what he thinks is morphine, but when the man passes out and nearly stops breathing, Hawkeye discovers the medicine was curare, a paralyzing agent and Charles refuses to thank Hawkeye for saving the man's life and worse, refuses to accept responsibility but rather, blames it on poor lighting.

Commentary by Burt Prelutsky: "By the sixth season, it seemed like there were six or seven guys in the room (instead of just Gelbart)…which struck me as four or five too many."

PA Announcements by Sal Viscuso
PA Announcement by Colonel Potter

Authors' Notes: Potterism: "Mule fritters"

Hawkeye mentions Mischa Auer. Auer (1905-1967) was an actor.

Klinger mentions, "Bozo." Bozo the Clown started as a sing-along in 1946 on Capitol Records.

It should be noted that the book, *The Rooster Crowed at Midnight,* by Abigail Porterfield is not a real book, although there have been many who thought it was.

In Love and War – 11/1/1977

Season 6 / Episode 130 / Production 134 – Y112
Columbia House VHS Tape . . . . *Warhawk (Catalog # 13118)*
Fox DVD . . . . *Season 6, Disc 1*

Alan Alda, Mike Farrell, Harry Morgan
Loretta Swit, David Ogden Stiers, Gary Burghoff, Jamie Farr, William Christopher

Produced by Burt Metcalfe
Executive Story Consultant – Jay Folb
Written by Alan Alda
Directed by Alan Alda

Story Editors – Ken Levine & David Isaacs
Program Consultant – Ronny Graham
Creative Consultants – Gene Reynolds / Alan Alda
Kieu Chinh . . . . Kyung Soon
Susan Krebs. . . . . Nurse Bobbie Gleason
Enid Kent . . . . Nurse Peggy Bigelow
Copyright 1977 – 20th Century Fox Film Corporation

Non-Credited Appearances. . . . . Kellye Nakahara, Roy Goldman, Gwen Farrell

Chapters

1: *Main Titles / ASAP*	6: *Creepy – 14:25*
2: *Old Donald – 3:57*	7: *A Death in the Family – 15:26*
3: *Parlez-Vous? – 5:01*	8: *Far Away – 17:01*
4: *Dinner Invitation – 7:52*	9: *Moving On – 17:54*
5: *Arrows to the Heart – 10:14*	10: *No Words / End Titles – 20:59*

Closing Stills

1: *Freeze – Margaret & Hawkeye in the Swamp*
2: *Kyung Soon*
3: *Hawkeye*
4: *Kyung Soon at her home*
5: *Hawkeye at Kyung Soon's home*
6: *Kyung Soon & Hawkeye kissing*

Synopsis: During triage on the compound, the last thing Hawkeye expected to see is a new Chrysler sedan with a fashionably dressed woman driving. After the woman talks to Potter, he instructs Hawkeye to take care of the child in the car suffering from a dislocated clavicle, then orders Hawkeye to drive back with the woman to see about her mother. At first, Hawkeye resents the idea of this woman pulling into camp and getting priority, but comes to realize his first impression might not have been the correct impression. Meanwhile, Nurse Gleason tells Margaret of a date she had with a lieutenant colonel and the more she tells, the more Margaret realizes it was Donald.

Authors' Notes: There are no PA announcements in this episode.
    The car Kyung Soon drives appears to be a 1951 Plymouth Cranbrook four-door sedan.
    Potter's office in Chapter 8 shows a rare view of the compound doorway into Radar's office, and at night, a corrugated building is seen through the right window.

Kieu Chinh (born 1937 in Vietnam) is a legendary actress best known for her role in The Joy Luck Club. Kieu Chinh began her acting career in Vietnam with a starring role in 1957. She soon became one of Vietnam's best-known personalities. In the 1960s, in addition to Vietnamese films, she also appeared in several American productions. Kieu Chinh also produced a war epic *Nguoi Tinh Khong Chan Dung* (Faceless Lover, 1970), which later would be remastered and shown in the U.S. at the 2003 Vietnamese International Film Festival. In 1975, while Kieu Chinh was on the set in Singapore, the North Vietnam army overran Saigon. Kieu Chinh left for the U.S. where she resumed her acting career in this *(M*A*S*H)* episode, loosely based on her life story. Kieu Chinh subsequently acted in feature films as well as TV-movies. Her best-known role was as Suyuan, one of the women in Wayne Wang's *The Joy Luck Club* (1993). In 2005, Kieu Chinh starred in *Journey from the Fall*, an epic feature film tracing a Vietnamese family through the aftermath of the fall of Saigon, the re-education camp, the boat people experience, and the difficulties of settling in the U.S. Together with journalist Terry Anderson, Kieu Chinh co-founded the Vietnam Children's Fund, which has built schools in Vietnam attended by more than 12,000 students. In 1996, a documentary based on her life, *Kieu Chinh: A Journey Home* by Patrick Perez, won an Emmy. Chinh is a naturalized U.S. citizen. *(Used with permission from Kevin Johnson, University of California, Davis – lawprofessors.typepad.com)*

Change Day – 11/8/1977
Season 6 / Episode 131 / Production 135 – Y113
Columbia House VHS Tape . . . . Charles (Catalog # 13117)
Fox DVD . . . . Season 6, Disc 1

Alan Alda, Mike Farrell, Harry Morgan
Loretta Swit, David Ogden Stiers, Gary Burghoff, Jamie Farr, William Christopher

Produced by Burt Metcalfe
Executive Story Consultant – Jay Folb
Written by Laurence Marks
Directed by Don Weis

Story Editors – Ken Levine & David Isaacs
Program Consultant – Ronny Graham
Creative Consultants – Gene Reynolds / Alan Alda
Philip Ahn. . . . . Mr. Kim
Johnny Haymer . . . . Sergeant Zale
Tom Dever . . . . Corporal Boone
Glenn Ash. . . . . .Sergeant Maxwell
Peter Riegert . . . . .Igor
Copyright 1977 – 20th Century Fox Film Corporation

Non-Credited Appearances. . . . . Kellye Nakahara, Jeff Maxwell, Dennis Troy,
Roy Goldman, Gwen Farrell, Richard Lee Sung, Kimiko Hiroshige

Chapters
1: Main Titles / Razzle Dazzle   6: Thou Shalt Not Steal – 12:35
2: One Thin Dime – 3:53   7: One Scam, One Exam – 16:06
3: Robber Baron – 6:01   8: Roadblocks – 18:26
4: Old Nose and Guts – 7:42   9: Highway Robbery – 20:09
5: Eat Those Words – 10:56   10: Atonement / End Titles – 22:59

Closing Stills
1: Freeze – Mulcahy in Post-Op   4: Hawkeye
2: Mr. Kim in the Swamp   5: Klinger testing for West Point
3: Charles   6: Mulcahy in Post-Op

(A misprint in the DVD Guide lists the air date as 11/8/1997.)

Synopsis: As the camp prepares to exchange blue scrip for red, Charles prepares to
make a nice profit by buying all the old scrip from local villagers and paying them 10
cents on the dollar. After collecting $95, he gives the locals a 10-dollar bill. But when the
tailor, who Charles still owes for a jacket and pants he made, enlists the help of Hawkeye
and BJ, they turn the tables on Charles and offer him 10 cents on the dollar when he's
locked out of camp with a bundle of old scrip.

PA Announcement by Colonel Potter
PA Announcements by Sal Viscuso
PA Announcement by Father Mulcahy

Authors' Notes: This is the second episode in which Peter Riegert played Igor.

In Chapter 3, B.J. mentions, "Hart, Schaffner & 'Kim'" — a reference to "Hart, Schaffner & Marx," who have been making men's clothing for over 100 years, and who have twice turned their plants over to the U.S. government for uniform production.

Orders from H.Q. to give an entrance exam to West Point for Klinger, but since he couldn't even spell his name right, he now expects to be a midshipman at Annapolis "very soon" (ploys).

Images – 11/15/1977

Season 6 / Episode 132 / Production 127 – Y105

Columbia House VHS Tape . . . . Radar (Catalog # 13114)
Fox DVD . . . . Season 6, Disc 2

Alan Alda, Mike Farrell, Harry Morgan
Loretta Swit, David Ogden Stiers, Gary Burghoff, Jamie Farr, William Christopher

Produced by Burt Metcalfe
Executive Story Consultant – Jay Folb
Written by Burt Prelutsky
Directed by Burt Metcalfe

Story Editors – Ken Levine & David Isaacs
Program Consultant – Ronny Graham
Creative Consultants – Gene Reynolds / Alan Alda

Susan Blanchard . . . . Nurse Sandra Cooper
John Durren . . . . Sergeant Rimmerman
Larry Block . . . . Corporal Eddie Hendrix
Judy Farrell . . . . Nurse Able
Enid Kent . . . . Nurse Bigelow
Rebecca Taylor . . . . Nurse Campbell
Carmine Scelza . . . . G.I.
Joseph Hardin . . . . Patient

Copyright 1977 – 20th Century Fox Film Corporation

Non-Credited Appearances. . . . . Kellye Nakahara, Gwen Farrell, Roy Goldman

Chapters

1: Main Titles / Falling Apart
2: Give Her A Break – 4:08
3: Good as Rembrandt – 7:12
4: Sacked – 8:46
5: Baptism of Fire – 11:04

6: Freedom of Expression – 12:09
7: Dirty Needles – 15:25
8: Puppy Love – 17:38
9: Drop 'Em – 20:58
10: Body Building / End Titles – 22:29

Closing Stills

1: Freeze – Potter after lifting weights
2: Nurse Cooper in Post-Op
3: B.J. in the Mess Tent
4: Hawkeye in the Mess Tent
5: Potter in Radar's office
6: Radar (Drop 'em)
7: Margaret

Synopsis: A wounded corporal arrives with tattoos, and when he tells Radar that the women won't leave him alone with a tattoo, that's all the convincing Radar needs. After chow, he's going to get one at Rosie's because he's tired of being a "nobody," and wants to be the object of "respect, fear and sex." Thinking that guys with tattoos always drink beer and don't pal around with guys like him, he gets his tattoo but won't let anyone see it, which is why it's on his butt. But Potter orders him to drop his pants, revealing a tiny Teddy bear tattoo that isn't quite as permanent as first thought.

Commentary by Burt Prelutsky: "I was still writing a humor column for the *L.A. Times* and I had interviewed a tattoo artist, and a lot of the jokes in the episode about tattoos came directly from the piece I wrote. I just put them in Hawkeye's or B.J.'s mouth."

Authors' Notes: There are no PA announcements in this episode.

In Chapter 1, the scrub room for the first time has only one sink on the front wall. This appears to be a scrub and change room together.

According to Margaret, the 4077th saves lives 98% of the time.

In Chapter 3, Radar is thinking of getting a tattoo. In Season 3, Episode 55, Radar got a tattoo of an anchor. He tried to get a Red Cross, but it was $1.50 while an anchor was 50 cents.

In Chapter 5, Potter says he was married in 1913 and is still married 38 years later. This places this episode in 1951.

Hawkeye is reading *New Feature* magazine with MacArthur on the cover in Chapter 6. This is the same magazine Trapper was reading in Season 2, Episode 25.

There is a microphone and boom shadow from right to left above Klinger at Rosie's in Chapter 7.

Potterism: "I'll be hornswoggled" (upon seeing Radar's drawn-on tattoo).

The M*A*S*H Olympics – 11/22/1977

Season 6 / Episode 133 / Production 133 – Y111

Columbia House VHS Tape............... Not Released by Columbia House
Fox DVD ....Season 6, Disc 2

Alan Alda, Mike Farrell, Harry Morgan
Loretta Swit, David Ogden Stiers, Gary Burghoff, Jamie Farr, William Christopher

Produced by Burt Metcalfe
Executive Story Consultant – Jay Folb
Written by Ken Levine & David Isaacs
Directed by Don Weis

Story Editors – Ken Levine & David Isaacs
Program Consultant – Ronny Graham
Creative Consultants – Gene Reynolds / Alan Alda
Mike Henry........................Lieutenant Colonel Donald Penobscott
Michael McManus .... Sergeant Dobbin Ames
Copyright 1977 – 20th Century Fox Film Corporation

Non-Credited Appearances.....................Kellye Nakahara, Roy Goldman

Chapters

1: Main Titles / He Ain't Heavy
2: Food for Freedom – 2:36
3: Out of Shape – 5:16
4: Circulatory Stress – 7:44
5: Sweetening the Pot – 9:44
6: A Good, Clean Race – 11:56
7: Fight, Fight, Fight – 14:51
8: Ringer – 16:24
9: Tie Breaker – 19:51
10: The Victor / End Titles – 22:51

Closing Stills

1: Freeze – Hawk & B.J. wheel Ames to Mess Tent
2: Donald Penobscott
3: Sergeant Ames in the Mess Tent
4: Potter in Radar's office
5: B.J. in the Swamp
6: Margaret in the Mess Tent
7: Charles
8: Klinger in the Mess Tent
9: Mulcahy
10: Hawkeye in the Swamp

Synopsis: After 15 years in the army, Sergeant Ames is being kicked out because he's too fat to be a good soldier. He has ten days until his orders come through and Hawkeye and BJ offer to help him lose 20 pounds by then. When Potter realizes that Ames is not the only one who could use some help, he comes up with a plan designed to help everyone get back in shape while having some fun at the same time: "The M*A*S*H Olympics." Coinciding with the 1952 Helsinki Olympic Games, Hawkeye and BJ will each captain their own teams for the grand prize of three days of R&R. Donald Penobscott, an All-American in track and wrestling at West Point arrives just in time to take part in the last two events, but the outcome isn't exactly what Margaret had in mind.

Commentary by Ken Levine: "Not a classic."

PA Announcement by Todd Sussman
PA Announcement by Colonel Potter

Authors' Notes: Potterisms: "Whistle beak" (to Klinger); "Buffalo breath" (to Klinger); "Cow cookies"

Hawkeye refers to Donald as "Gorgeous George." Two of the better-known athletes nicknamed "Gorgeous George" were the baseball player, George Sisler, who started his career with the St. Louis Browns in 1915 and ended with the Boston Braves in 1930, and George Wagner, the professional wrestler whose career spanned 30 years from 1932 to 1962.

In Chapter 5, there is a quick boom shadow over B.J.'s head in the mess tent.

Mike Henry, the second actor to play Lieutenant Colonel Donald Penobscott, is probably best known for his Tarzan movies in the 1960s: *Tarzan and the Valley of Gold* (1966), *Tarzan and the Great River* (1967) and *Tarzan and the Jungle Boy* (1968). Mike was also a professional football player in the National Football League, playing for the Pittsburgh Steelers (1958 to 1961) and the Los Angeles Rams (1962 to 1964).

Michael McManus, the recipient of a Writer's Guild of America Award for "Commercials: A Steve Martin Special" in 1981, started his career in the 1970s, and has appeared in *Laverne & Shirley, Rhoda, Baretta, Happy Days* and *Night Court,* and along with Jeff Maxwell, was in the *Kentucky Fried Movie.*

The Grim Reaper – 11/29/1977

Season 6 / Episode 134 / Production 132 – Y110

Columbia House VHS Tape . . . . *A Bird In The Hand (Catalog # 19502)*
Fox DVD . . . . *Season 6, Disc 2*

Alan Alda, Mike Farrell, Harry Morgan
Loretta Swit, David Ogden Stiers, Gary Burghoff, Jamie Farr, William Christopher

Produced by Burt Metcalfe
Executive Story Consultant – Jay Folb
Written by Burt Prelutsky
Directed by George Tyne

Story Editors – Ken Levine & David Isaacs
Program Consultant – Ronny Graham
Creative Consultants – Gene Reynolds / Alan Alda

Charles Aidman . . . . .Colonel Bloodworth
Jerry Houser . . . . .Danker

Copyright 1977 – 20th Century Fox Film Corporation

Non-Credited Appearances. . . . . Kellye Nakahara, Roy Goldman, Dennis Troy

Chapters

1:	*Main Titles / Predictions*	
2:	*Bon Appetite – 3:26*	
3:	*Rotten Bird – 8:13*	
4:	*Bar Brawl – 11:10*	
5:	*Reamed – 12:55*	

6: *Toledo Boys – 13:42*
7: *No Way Out – 15:09*
8: *Schoolyard Spat – 16:05*
9: *The Grim Reaper – 18:35*
10: *Ample Reward / End Titles – 22:56*

Closing Stills

1: *Freeze – Klinger, B.J., Charles, Hawkeye in the Swamp*
2: *Bloodworth in Jeep – R compound*
3: *Danker in Post-Op*
4: *Klinger in Post-Op*
5: *Charles in Margaret's tent*
6: *Margaret in her tent*
7: *Potter – R compound*
8: *B.J. in Potter's office*
9: *Hawkeye in Potter's office*

Synopsis: Two people arrive at the 4077th, one wounded and the other predicts wounded. Colonel Bloodworth has built his reputation with "pinpoint accuracy" and the unit can expect 280-290 casualties in 24 hours, 20 more if it rains. After surgery, Hawkeye finds Bloodworth in the Officer's Club and gloats that the Colonel fell short of his predictions by 77, but Hawkeye might have spoken too soon and shoves the full-bird Colonel who now wants Hawkeye court-martialed. Meanwhile, a not-seriously wounded G.I. from Toledo arrives and brings Klinger to tears after giving him a book of matches from the Trianon, a dance hall Klinger frequented back home and Charles shares a special dinner with Margaret which they later regret.

PA Announcement by Todd Sussman

Authors' Notes: Potter's office windows in Chapter 1 now show a wooden structure through the right window. (Supply?)

The supply shed seen in Chapter 3 has a rounded roof, corrugated, and has two signs: "4077th Supply" on top, and another under it that says "Supply." This is not the same structure seen through Potter's windows.

In Chapter 8, Potter is reading a book, *Ride the Man Down*, and is annoyed at being interrupted during a Zane Grey gunfight. However, Luke Short, not Zane Grey, wrote *Ride the Man Down*. It's also a movie from 1952. See Season 7, Episode 166, "The Young and the Restless," for more information.

Charles Aidman's 40-year career began in 1952. He has an extensive list of credits to his name. Included are *All in the Family*, *Emergency*, *Kung Fu*, *S.W.A.T.*, *Eight is Enough*, six episodes of *Quincy, M.E.* and was the narrator for 28 episodes of *The Twilight Zone* from 1985 to 1987. Born in Frankfort, Indiana, on January 21, 1925, Mr. Aidman died of cancer in Beverly Hills, California on November 7, 1993.

Jerry Houser has appeared in several television shows, including *Barnaby Jones*, *Soap*, *One Day at A Time*, and *Matlock*, among others, but might be best-known as Oscar Seltzer in the Oscar-winning movie, *Summer of '42*. Born July 14, 1952 in Los Angeles, it's interesting to note that due to his high-pitched voice, he has constant work as a voice-over actor and has been the voice of one of the Keebler Elves since the 1980s.

Comrades in Arms / Part 1 – 12/6/1977

Season 6 / Episode 135 / Production 138 – Y116
Columbia House VHS Tape . . . . Hot Lips And Hawkeye (Catalog # 13115)
Fox DVD . . . . Season 6, Disc 2

Alan Alda, Mike Farrell, Harry Morgan
Loretta Swit, David Ogden Stiers, Gary Burghoff, Jamie Farr, William Christopher

Produced by Burt Metcalfe
Executive Story Consultant – Jay Folb
Written by Alan Alda
Directed by Burt Metcalfe and Alan Alda

Story Editors – Ken Levine & David Isaacs
Program Consultant – Ronny Graham
Creative Consultants – Gene Reynolds / Alan Alda

Copyright 1977 – 20th Century Fox Film Corporation

Chapters

1: Main Titles / Volunteers	6: MIA's – 10:20
2: Horse Trading – 3:41	7: Wounded – 11:10
3: Road Kill – 4:51	8: Opportunity Calls – 15:09
4: Behind Enemy Lines – 6:24	9: The Letter – 18:00
5: Jeep Thieves – 8:58	10: Losing It / End Titles – 22:18

Closing Stills

1: Freeze – Hawkeye & Margaret kiss in the shack
2: Margaret
3: Hawkeye
4: Charles on the phone
5: B.J. & Klinger in Radar's office
6: Potter staring at the phone
7: Hawkeye & Margaret hugging (bombs exploding)

Synopsis: Having heard about the 4077th's arterial transplants, the 8063rd has asked Potter to send their best surgeon to show them the technique. Since first learning this procedure from Dr. Borelli, Hawkeye has done dozens of them and is elected to go, and Margaret, denying him a nurse of his choice, goes with him. The trip to the 8063rd is not uneventful as they soon encounter shelling and worse, they arrive to an empty camp; the 8063rd has bugged out and they're now in enemy territory. With the North Koreans close by, their jeep breaks down and they're forced to hide in the bushes when they hear the enemy approaching. Making matters even worse, the North Koreans repair the jeep filled with supplies and drive off in it. Now on foot, they come across an abandoned hut and seek refuge inside. Hawkeye suffers a leg wound when the hut comes under fire and after Margaret treats the wound, they try to get some sleep, but they come under fire again, only this time, while embracing each other to combat fear, the embrace becomes passionate.

Authors' Notes: There are no PA announcements in this episode.
There is no sign on the shower tent indicating times for showers as in previous episodes.
The side of a corrugated building is seen through the office window in Chapter 6, and not that of a wooden structure in a previous episode.

Comrades in Arms / Part 2 – 12/13/1977

Season 6 / Episode 133 / Production 139 – Y117
Columbia House VHS Tape........ *Hot Lips And Hawkeye (Catalog # 13115)*
Fox DVD .... *Season 6, Disc 2*

Alan Alda, Mike Farrell, Harry Morgan
Loretta Swit, David Ogden Stiers, Gary Burghoff, Jamie Farr, William Christopher

Produced by Burt Metcalfe
Executive Story Consultant – Jay Folb
Written by Alan Alda
Directed by Alan Alda and Burt Metcalfe

Story Editors – Ken Levine & David Isaacs
Program Consultant – Ronny Graham
Creative Consultants – Gene Reynolds / Alan Alda

Doug Rowe.....................	Lieutenant Doug Aylesworth (Chopper Pilot)
Jon Yune	North Korean
James Saito	South Korean
Leland Sun	Korean Squad Leader

Copyright 1977 – 20th Century Fox Film Corporation

Non-Credited Appearances.......... Kellye Nakahara, Gwen Farrell, Roy Goldman, Dennis Troy

Chapters

1: Main Titles / Future Tense	6: Lover's Spat – 14:49
2: The Morning After – 3:00	7: Sustenance – 16:54
3: Scavenger – 6:19	8: Welcome Home Party – 17:55
4: Shake A Leg – 9:05	9: Dear Hank – 19:56
5: Waste Not, Want Not – 12:20	10: Who's Smiling? / End Titles – 23:16

Closing Stills

1: Freeze – Potter, Charles, Mulcahy, Hawkeye, B.J. in the Mess Tent
2: B.J. & Aylesworth in the Mess Tent
3: Mulcahy in the Mess Tent
4: Potter, Mulcahy, Klinger in the Mess Tent
5: Charles in Potter's office
6: B.J. in the Swamp
7: Potter on the radio
8: Hawkeye
9: Margaret

Synopsis: The morning following Hawkeye and Margaret's passionate kiss finds them waking in each other's arms. Margaret has taken recent events between them to a level that Hawkeye wasn't expecting, and isn't quite sure how to handle. Back at camp, BJ and Lieutenant Aylesworth, a chopper pilot, have gone against orders from I-Corps for choppers to remain on the ground in an effort to locate Hawkeye and Margaret who have now been missing for nearly two days. BJ tells Potter over the radio that he thinks he saw Margaret, but the North Koreans who repaired the jeep are now firing at the chopper and hit the antenna. Having no choice, the chopper sputters away. When the enemy finally pulls back, the 8063rd sends out a search party. During a rainy night, they find Hawkeye and Margaret, but not before getting into a major argument that carries over into the O.R., when demonstrating the arterial transplant at the 8063rd. Finally home at the 4077th, Hawkeye expresses his gratitude at being found just a little too much and Margaret, again, gives him something he wasn't expecting.

Authors' Notes: There are no PA announcements in this episode.

In Season 2, Episode 45, "Crisis," Mulcahy is wearing a blue plaid robe. In this episode, it's a brown plaid robe.

In Chapter 3, there's a microphone boom shadow mid-right in the shack when the North Korean collapses.

This is the second time the new vascular clamp designed at the 4077th is used.

The office in Chapter 7 has the same view out the window as in the previous episode.

The Merchant of Korea – 12/20/1977

Season 6 / Episode 137 / Production 140 – Y118

Columbia House VHS Tape . . . . *Not Released by Columbia House*

Fox DVD . . . . *Season 6, Disc 2*

Alan Alda, Mike Farrell, Harry Morgan
Loretta Swit, David Ogden Stiers, Gary Burghoff, Jamie Farr, William Christopher

Produced by Burt Metcalfe
Executive Story Consultant – Jay Folb
Written by Ken Levine & David Isaacs
Directed by William Jurgensen

Story Editors – Ken Levine & David Isaacs
Program Consultant – Ronny Graham
Creative Consultants – Gene Reynolds / Alan Alda

Johnny Haymer . . . . Sergeant Zelmo Zale
Copyright 1977 – 20th Century Fox Film Corporation

Non-Credited Appearances . . . . .Kellye Nakahara, Roy Goldman

Chapters

1:	*Main Titles / Indebted*	6:	*Revenge Match – 12:47*
2:	*Blackmail – 3:43*	7:	*Ante Up – 14:08*
3:	*The Well Runs Dry – 7:01*	8:	*Five Card Stud – 16:10*
4:	*Marital Spat – 9:04*	9:	*To the Cleaners – 19:41*
5:	*The Nerve – 10:45*	10:	*All Ours / End Titles – 23:00*

Closing Stills

1: *Freeze – B.J. kisses bottle of dirt*
2: *Zale tends bar in the Officer's Club*
3: *Hawkeye in the Officer's Club*
4: *B.J. in the Swamp*
5: *Potter*
6: *Margaret*
7: *Radar*
8: *Klinger in the Officer's Club*
9: *Mulcahy*
10: *Charles in the Officer's Club*

Synopsis: When Charles lends BJ $200, he takes advantage of his good deed by having BJ close a patient for him and later, while he's lying in his bunk, has BJ pour him a cup of coffee. Making matters worse, HQ in Tokyo sent part of the 4077th's pay to Guam and it will take at least a week before the officers get paid which forces Zale to cut Hawkeye off at the Officer's Club as his bar tab has gone over the $20 limit by $30. Charles steps in and pays Hawkeye's $50 bar bill, then has Hawkeye bring him a beer later that night in the Swamp. Not happy at becoming Charles's servants, Hawkeye arranges a poker game and everyone agrees to play when they learn Charles is going to be there. At first, Charles wins pot after pot, until Hawkeye discovers something Charles does when he doesn't have a good hand.

Commentary by Ken Levine: "This is one of my favorites of the *M*A*S*H* episodes we wrote. Actually, it was the first script ever with Charles in it. But it was held back in production while other subsequent scripts helped introduce the character."

PA Announcement by Sal Viscuso

Authors' Notes: Hawkeye mentions, "Marshall Fields" in Chapter 3. Marshall Fields, a bridal and department store, was founded in Chicago in 1852 and went on to become a major chain. Marshall Fields was acquired by Federated Department Stores on August 30, 2005 and on September 9, 2006, was officially renamed Macy*s on State Street. It is now one of three national Macy*s flagship stores.

The Smell of Music – 1/3/1978

Season 6 / Episode 138 / Production 137 – Y115

Columbia House VHS Tape . . . . Charles (Catalog # 13117)
Fox DVD . . . . Season 6, Disc 2

Alan Alda, Mike Farrell, Harry Morgan
Loretta Swit, David Ogden Stiers, Gary Burghoff, Jamie Farr, William Christopher

Produced by Burt Metcalfe
Executive Story Consultant – Jay Folb
Written by Jim Fritzell & Everett Greenbaum
Directed by Stuart Millar

Story Editors – Ken Levine & David Isaacs
Program Consultant – Ronny Graham
Creative Consultants – Gene Reynolds / Alan Alda

Jordan Clarke. . . . . .Saunders
Nancy Steene. . . . . Nurse
Lois Foraker . . . . .Nurse Denver
Richard Lee Sung . . . . Sang Nu
Copyright 1977 – 20th Century Fox Film Corporation

Non-Credited Appearances. . . . . .Kellye Nakahara, Roy Goldman

Chapters

1:	Main Titles / Big Plans	
2:	Unwashed Symphony – 2:45	
3:	National Pig Week – 4:40	
4:	Lucky – 9:09	
5:	Suicide is Painful – 13:00	

6:	Al Fresco – 14:30	
7:	Counterattack – 16:41	
8:	Fighting Back – 17:56	
9:	Bathed Beauties – 19:32	
10:	As Good as New / End Titles – 22:24	

Closing Stills

1: Freeze – Charles (No mouthpiece)
2: Saunders in Post-Op
3: Potter in the Swamp
4: Margaret in R compound
5: Klinger
6: Margaret in R compound
7: Hawkeye
8: B.J.
9: Charles

Synopsis: It's a battle between ears and noses when Charles refuses to stop playing his French horn and Hawkeye & BJ refuse to shower until he does. The situation becomes intolerable, to the point of everyone signing a petition forcing Hawkeye and BJ to eat at a table outside the mess tent. But Margaret comes up with a plan to put an end to all this, where the stinky doctors are hosed and soaped on the compound, and Charles loves it. However, Charles isn't in love with the other part of her plan. Meanwhile, Potter has his own problems when a patient, whose gun backfired into his face, tries to commit suicide.

PA Announcements by Sal Viscuso

Authors' Notes: Potterism: "Sufferin' sheep-dip."

In Chapter 8, there's a shadow moving across Potter's back while he's in the O.R. with Saunders.

The sign on Margaret's tent door is in block lettering, not the usual freehand style.

Richard Lee Sung is listed in the credits as "Sang Nu," but in Chapter 10, Charles calls him "Sang Mu."

.

Patient 4077 – 1/10/1978

Season 6 / Episode 139 / Production 136 – Y114

Columbia House VHS Tape . . . . Medical Advances (Catalog # 19499)
Fox DVD . . . . Season 6, Disc 2

Alan Alda, Mike Farrell, Harry Morgan
Loretta Swit, David Ogden Stiers, Gary Burghoff, Jamie Farr, William Christopher

Produced by Burt Metcalfe
Executive Story Consultant – Jay Folb
Written by Ken Levine & David Isaacs
Directed by Harry Morgan

Story Editors – Ken Levine & David Isaacs
Program Consultant – Ronny Graham
Creative Consultants – Gene Reynolds / Alan Alda

Keye Luke . . . . Mr. Shin
Johnny Haymer . . . . Sergeant Zelmo Zale
Brenda Thomson . . . . Nurse Campbell
Patricia Stevens . . . . Nurse Baker
Harry Gold . . . . Private Cohen
Copyright 1977 – 20th Century Fox Film Corporation

Non-Credited Appearances. . . . . Kellye Nakahara, Dennis Troy

Chapters

1:	Main Titles / Dreamers	6:	Guests of Honor – 12:42
2:	Little Band of Gold – 3:44	7:	Summer Clearance Sale – 14:49
3:	D.I.Y. – 5:21	8:	The Missing "N" – 17:22
4:	Leonard Da Vinci – 8:35	9:	Credit – 19:23
5:	Dud – 10:27	10:	Sold / End Titles – 22:35

Closing Stills

1: Freeze – B.J. & Hawkeye (Corkscrew)
2: Mr. Shin
3: Margaret in her tent
4: Klinger in Margaret's tent
5: Potter on phone in Radar's office
6: Mulcahy
7: Charles
8: B.J. & Hawkeye

Synopsis: A vascular clamp used for heart surgery is not designed for the smaller arteries of the leg, and the 4077th needs just such a clamp but it doesn't exist. Hawkeye and BJ attempt to make one, but fail almost before they begin and Zale, who can "fix or build anything," gives it try, but he too is met with limited success. Meanwhile, Margaret is ready to have Klinger executed after he accidentally throws away her wedding ring, but Mr. Shin, a local peddler, happens to have an exact replacement ring that Hawkeye and BJ buy and give to Klinger, thus saving his life. Mr. Shin is also a master when it comes to working with metal and the doctors have him make a new clamp for them. When wounded arrive, they have an opportunity to try their newly designed clamp and this time, it works beautifully.

Commentary by Ken Levine: "We got technical help from my father-in-law, who was a doctor."

PA Announcement by Sal Viscuso

Authors' Notes: The scrub room, seen through the change room in Chapter 2, has only one sink against the far wall. The scrub room usually has two sinks, but not always in the same location.

Charles wants to watch Hawkeye and B.J.'s attempt at making a vascular clamp while having three hard-boiled eggs for lunch. Eggs, as it relates to *M*A*S*H*, are usually in powdered form and a precious commodity, but sometimes, there seem to be plenty of the real thing.

Veteran actor Keye Luke, born on June 18, 1904 in Guangzhou, China, made his film debut in *The Painted Veil* (1934, uncredited) and had over 200 credits to his name. Doing English dubbing voice-overs for several *Godzilla* and other Japanese films, Keye Luke gained notoriety in the *Kung Fu* series, appearing in 34 episodes as Master Po. Mr. Luke also appeared in *Family Affair, Marcus Welby, M.D., Quincy, M.E., Trapper John, M.D.* and many other television shows. Keye Luke will be seen again on *M*A*S*H* in Season 7's "A Night at Rosie's" and Season 9's "Death Takes A Holiday." Mr. Luke, after suffering a stroke, passed away on January 12, 1991 in Whittier, California.

Tea and Empathy – 1/17/1978

Season 6 / Episode 140 / Production 131 – Y109

Columbia House VHS Tape . . . . *To Err Is Human (Catalog # 13116)*
Fox DVD . . . . *Season 6, Disc 3*

Alan Alda, Mike Farrell, Harry Morgan
Loretta Swit, David Ogden Stiers, Gary Burghoff, Jamie Farr, William Christopher

Produced by Burt Metcalfe
Executive Story Consultant – Jay Folb
Written by Bill Idelson
Directed by Don Weis

Story Editors – Ken Levine & David Isaacs
Program Consultant – Ronny Graham
Creative Consultants – Gene Reynolds / Alan Alda

Bernard Fox.	Major Derek Ross
Sal Viscuso	Corporal Bryant
Neil Thompson	Johnson
Neil Hunt	Enright
Chris Winfield	Whitefield
Jay Pirelli	Michaels
Chris Mulkey	Soldier

Copyright 1978 – 20th Century Fox Film Corporation

Non-Credited Appearances. . . . . Kellye Nakahara

Chapters

1:	Main Titles / Thieves	6:	The Old Schoolhouse – 12:37
2:	Molly Coddling – 4:13	7:	Detox – 14:46
3:	Black Marketeer – 6:45	8:	One to A Customer – 15:24
4:	Hooked – 8:41	9:	Colonel Blimp – 17:34
5:	Spiritual Dilemma – 10:22	10:	Faux U.S.O. / End Titles – 21:48

Closing Stills

1: *Freeze – View 9 compound from Post-Op*
2: *Major Ross*
3: *B.J.*
4: *Margaret*
5: *Charles*
6: *Mulcahy*
7: *Potter in Radar's office*
8: *Mulcahy & Klinger*
9: *Hawkeye*

Synopsis: The Gloucester Regiment, an English unit that, according to Colonel Potter never wears helmets, has arrived by ambulance with mostly head wounds. But one in the unit has an abdominal wound and was treated with tea, which ultimately leads to peritonitis, and the 4077th's supply of penicillin was stolen. Major Derek Ross, the C.O. of the Gloucester Regiment visits his men in post-op and despite their wounds, thinks his men are lounging in a luxury resort, angering Hawkeye to the point of telling the Major to leave. Hawkeye later comes to understand that the Major is actually helping his men, not hurting them. Father Mulcahy learns where there's a stash of medical supplies, including penicillin, and Klinger helps him retrieve them, while B.J. has his own problems when his patient, who was once treated at the 4077th some months back, asks for morphine one time too many. B.J. realizes he's addicted to the powerful drug, and refuses him another shot of morphine, and helps him through a miserable night of withdrawal.

Commentary by Bernard Fox: "I was only on the *M*A*S*H* set for one very busy day. As I understood it, they had already hired a very fine British actor. But it turned out he was not used to our way of working (so many set pages for the day and, one just went in, rehearsed the scene and then shot it). He was accustomed to the British system of a week's rehearsal and shooting the whole thing in one day. In effect, I did a week's work on the Friday, finished at about 7:30 PM, and then shot down to the Mayfair Music Hall in Santa Monica, where I was acting as Master of Ceremonies in the evening. As it happens, I am a huge fan, and must have seen each episode several times. I never cease to be impressed by the wonderful performances, the dedication and the energy they brought to every episode. Loretta, I thought, was particularly fine…especially in the scene where she choked on her tears on the line 'Did you ever think to offer me a lousy cup of coffee?' (Season 5, 'The Nurses'). Now that is acting. I don't remember WWI, of course (my father was in it), and as a child I do remember rusting steel helmets hanging by their chin straps full of geraniums. So, you can imagine what a grabber it is for me when Harry Morgan turns up in his WWI uniform to open the bottle of Cognac, sent to him by the last of his wartime buddies (Season 5, 'Old Soldiers'). I used to bump into Loretta on sound stages, from time to time, and she was always most friendly and gracious."

Authors' Notes: There are no PA announcements in this episode.

B.J. mentions Dempsey/Firpo in Chapter 1. Jack Dempsey and Luis Firpo fought at the Polo grounds in New York City on September 14, 1923. Dempsey won the fight after knocking out Firpo with a right cross.

In Chapter 8, Father Mulcahy mentions "Father Duffy." Father Francis P. Duffy (1871-1932) was a military chaplain.

Bernard Fox, who played Major Derek Ross in this episode, was born on May 5, 1927 in Port Talbot, West Glamorgan, Wales, U.K. and his earliest credited appearance was in four episodes of *Sixpenny Corner* as Tom Norton in 1955-56. Mr. Fox also appeared in, among many other shows, three episodes of *Make Room for Daddy* (The Danny Thomas Show), *McHale's Navy,* three episodes of *The Dick Van Dyke Show, F-Troop* (four episodes of *F-Troop* were directed by Gene Reynolds) and memorable appearances in three episodes of *The Andy Griffith Show,* as the bicycle-riding Malcolm Merriweather. Also notable are his eight appearances in *Hogan's Heroes* as Colonel Crittendon (Gene Reynolds directed 26 episodes of *Hogan's Heroes).*

Neil Thompson, the morphine-addicted Johnson, will return in Season 7's "Rally 'Round the Flagg, Boys" as Corporal Basgall, accusing Hawkeye of being a Communist sympathizer.

Your Hit Parade – 1/24/1978

Season 6 / Episode 141 / Production 146 – Y124

Columbia House VHS Tape . . . . *Not Released by Columbia House*

Fox DVD . . . . *Season 6, Disc 3*

Alan Alda, Mike Farrell, Harry Morgan
Loretta Swit, David Ogden Stiers, Gary Burghoff, Jamie Farr, William Christopher

Produced by Burt Metcalfe
Executive Story Consultant – Jay Folb
Written by Ronny Graham
Directed by George Tyne

Story Editors – Ken Levine & David Isaacs
Program Consultant – Ronny Graham
Creative Consultants – Gene Reynolds / Alan Alda

Ronny Graham . . . . Sergeant Walter Gribble
Johnny Haymer . . . . Sergeant Zale
Ken Michelman . . . . Harker
Patricia Stevens . . . . Nurse Baker
William Kux . . . . Patient

Copyright 1978 – 20th Century Fox Film Corporation

Non-Credited Appearances . . . . .Kellye Nakahara, Roy Goldman

Chapters

1:	Main Titles / What Rules?	6:	Big Daddy O'Reilly – 11:07
2:	D.J. Radar – 3:06	7:	Doris Day – 12:33
3:	Full Hotel – 4:48	8:	Blood From A Stone – 15:44
4:	Musical Memories – 7:59	9:	Good News – 20:02
5:	A Matter of Time – 9:29	10:	War Stories / End Titles – 22:52

Closing Stills

1: *Freeze – Potter, BJ, Hawkeye in Swamp play Cranko*
2: *Sergeant Gribble*
3: *B.J. in the Swamp*
4: *Potter*
5: *Margaret*
6: *Charles in the Swamp*
7: *Radar in the Swamp*
8: *Klinger*
9: *Mulcahy*
10: *Hawkeye in the Swamp*

Synopsis: When the camp gets a new shipment of records from Special Services, Potter gives permission for Radar to play them over the PA, but as soon as he starts playing them, the 4077th is overrun with wounded. The 8055th has bugged out and nobody knows where they are, and the 4077th has to handle the overflow from the 8063rd plus their own wounded. The Swamp, Officer's Club and the Mess Tent have all been transformed into post-op units while Radar becomes "Big Daddy O'Reilly," the 4077th's disc jockey.

PA Announcement by Sal Viscuso
PA Announcements by Radar

Authors' Notes: When the camp is overrun with casualties, Potter mentions "the post-ops 2, 3 and 4." They've never been seen or mentioned before this episode.

"Cranko" is played in this episode.

This, and episodes before this, Kellye is seen in the background on the Stage 9 compound giving haircuts, sometimes to Igor, other times to Roy, but on the Ranch compound, a barber's tent has been seen.

Ronald Montcrief Stringer, born August 16, 1919, is better known as Ronny Graham, who not only played Sergeant Walter Gribble, he wrote the episode. Although he appeared only once on M*A*S*H, he wrote four other episodes: Season 6's "Dr. Winchester and Mr. Hyde," along with Ken Levine and David Isaacs, and Season 7's "An Eye for A Tooth," "Commander Pierce," "C*A*V*E" with Larry Balmagia, and was a story consultant for several other episodes. Mr. Graham was a composer, songwriter, actor, comedian, director and an author, and wrote other television and Broadway shows as well. He appeared on *The Bob Crane Show, Murder, She Wrote, Chicago Hope*, and six episodes of *Chico and the Man* among others. Born in Philadelphia, Ronny Graham died on July 4, 1999 of liver disease in Los Angeles.

What's Up, Doc? – 1/30/1978

Season 6 / Episode 142 / Production 141 – Y119
Columbia House VHS Tape . . . . Radar (Catalog # 13114)
Fox DVD . . . . Season 6, Disc 3

Alan Alda, Mike Farrell, Harry Morgan
Loretta Swit, David Ogden Stiers, Gary Burghoff, Jamie Farr, William Christopher

Produced by Burt Metcalfe
Executive Story Consultant – Jay Folb
Written by Larry Balmagia
Directed by George Tyne

Story Editors – Ken Levine & David Isaacs
Program Consultant – Ronny Graham
Creative Consultants – Gene Reynolds / Alan Alda

Charles Frank . . . . Lieutenant Tom Martinson
Lois Foraker . . . . Nurse Bell
Kurt Andon. . . . . Sergeant Whitkow
Phyllis Katz. . . . . Nurse
Copyright 1978 – 20th Century Fox Film Corporation

Non-Credited Appearances. . . . . Kellye Nakahara, Roy Goldman, Dennis Troy,
Gwen Farrell

Chapters

1: Main Titles / Hot News	6: Ivy Leaguers – 13:46
2: Not Good Enough – 4:52	7: Hostage Situation – 15:39
3: Instant Family – 6:32	8: Tag Team – 18:37
4: Rabbit Test – 8:52	9: Foiled Again – 20:39
5: Major Surgery – 11:57	10: Still A Major / End Titles – 22:13

Closing Stills

1: Freeze – Radar & Margaret in Radar's office
2: Martinson with gun in Post-Op
3: Hawkeye in Potter's office
4: Mulcahy
5: Radar in Potter's office
6: Potter in his office
7: Klinger
8: B.J. in Post-Op
9: Charles in Post-Op
10: Margaret in Potter's office

Synopsis: Hawkeye senses something is bothering Margaret when she puts a nurse on report for something inconsequential. Margaret confides in Hawkeye that she might be pregnant and if she is, it means an automatic discharge and the end of her Army career. The only way to know for sure without having to go to Tokyo for tests is to use the ovaries from Radar's rabbit, which is easier said than done. When Radar realizes this means the end of Fluffy, he wants no part of it and hides her. Lieutenant Tom Martinson, an art history major from Yale, Class of '48, is simply not cut out to lead men into battle and makes his point known when he holds a gun on Charles in order to get transportation home, making matters even worse for Margaret.

Authors' Notes: There are no PA announcements in this episode.

In this episode, the scrub room in Chapter 1 has the sinks, both of them, side by side on the front (camera) wall.

In Chapter 3, Klinger has nine children and shows Potter pictures of Erin Hunnicutt and Zelda Zale. This means he would have been a father at age eleven (ploy).

Potterism: "Prouder than a stallion out to stud."

Hawkeye, in Chapter 5, mentions "Uncle Wiggly." Uncle Wiggly Longears was a series of children's books based on an engaging elderly rabbit suffering from rheumatism who used a candy-striped walking cane, written by Howard Roger Garis (April 25, 1873-November 6, 1962).

An extra in Chapter 7 is seen on the Stage 9 compound wearing the robe worn by Henry and sometimes, Frank.

Mail Call Three – 2/6/1978

Season 6 / Episode 143 / Production 143 – Y121

Columbia House VHS Tape . . . . Over Here (Catalog # 19504)
Fox DVD . . . . Season 6, Disc 3

Alan Alda, Mike Farrell, Harry Morgan
Loretta Swit, David Ogden Stiers, Gary Burghoff, Jamie Farr, William Christopher

Produced by Burt Metcalfe
Executive Story Consultant – Jay Folb
Written by Everett Greenbaum & Jim Fritzell
Directed by Charles Dubin

Story Editors – Ken Levine & David Isaacs
Program Consultant – Ronny Graham
Creative Consultants – Gene Reynolds / Alan Alda

Oliver Clark . . . . Captain Benjamin Pierce
Jack Grapes . . . . Kelsey

Copyright 1978 – 20th Century Fox Film Corporation

Non-Credited Appearances. . . . . Kellye Nakahara, Roy Goldman, Dennis Troy,
Gwen Farrell

Chapters

1:	Main Titles / Mail Call	6:	The Worst Day – 10:06
2:	Love Letters – 1:54	7:	Jealous Men – 12:57
3:	Collapsing Worlds – 4:43	8:	A.W.O.L. – 16:59
4:	One's Own Kind – 6:11	9:	The Other Captain Pierce – 18:54
5:	At the Movies – 8:02	10:	Among Family / End Titles – 21:05

Closing Stills

1: *Freeze – Mulcahy, Charles, Hawkeye, Potter, Radar, BJ*
2: *Captain Ben Pierce in the Swamp*
3: *All gathered for mail call on 9 compound*
4: *Hawkeye in the Swamp*
5: *B.J. in the Swamp*
6: *Potter in his office*
7: *Margaret in supply*
8: *Radar on the phone in his office*
9: *Klinger in his tent*
10: *Mulcahy in the Swamp*
11: *B.J., Charles, Hawkeye in the Mess Tent*

Synopsis: The mail brings good news for some, bad news for others and love letters for Hawkeye meant for a different Captain Benjamin Pierce. When Captain Pierce shows up with Hawkeye's unopened mail, he doesn't appreciate that the favor cannot be returned since Hawkeye not only read the steamy letters, but also loved them. B.J. is bothered that, while he's in Korea, Peg had to become a plumber and failed at her attempt to fix the sink, but more disturbing to B.J. is when a good friend of theirs makes a pass at Peg, who thought it was funny. Potter gets some new pictures of his grandson who can't be seen clearly in any of them while Radar has a hard time adjusting to the news that his mother has a boyfriend. 40% of Missouri's sorghum crops destroyed by hail makes Charles happy since he's invested in Canadian sorghum and Father Mulcahy gets a "short note" from his sister in the convent. But Klinger gets a letter from Lavern that causes him to go A.W.O.L.

Authors' Notes: There are no PA announcements in this episode.

The Daughters of the American Revolution (DAR) is mentioned in Chapter 4 and is a lineage-based-membership organization of women who promote historic education and patriotism while raising funds for scholarships and preserving historical properties and artifacts. The DAR has chapters in all 50 states and the District of Columbia. International chapters are located in Australia, Bahamas, Bermuda, Canada, France, Germany, Japan, Mexico, Spain and the United Kingdom. Congressional charter incorporated DAR in 1896.

In Chapter 6, Hawkeye mentions, "The Ink Spots." The Ink Spots were a singing group that started in Indianapolis in 1932.

Radar's bear squeaks when B.J. squeezes it. This did not happen very often, if at all.

Hawkeye, in Chapter 7, mentions that his father was a widower when he was 12 years old, and was interested in a "very nice woman," but didn't marry her and implied he was an only child. This contradicts earlier episodes, mostly in Seasons 1 and 2, when Hawkeye clearly had a mother and a sister.

Temporary Duty – 2/13/1978

Season 6 / Episode 144 / Production 147 – Y125

Columbia House VHS Tape . . . . *Not Released by Columbia House*

Fox DVD . . . . *Season 6, Disc 3*

Alan Alda, Mike Farrell, Harry Morgan
Loretta Swit, David Ogden Stiers, Gary Burghoff, Jamie Farr, William Christopher

Produced by Burt Metcalfe
Executive Story Consultant – Jay Folb
Written by Larry Balmagia
Directed by Burt Metcalfe

Story Editors – Ken Levine & David Isaacs
Program Consultant – Ronny Graham
Creative Consultants – Gene Reynolds / Alan Alda

George Lindsey. . . . . Captain Roy Dupree
Marcia Rodd . . . . Captain Lorraine Anderson
Enid Kent . . . . Nurse Bigelow
Copyright 1978 – 20th Century Fox Film Corporation

Non-Credited Appearances. . . . . Dennis Troy, Roy Goldman, Kellye Nakahara

Chapters

1: *Main Titles / Horse Trade*	6: *A-One Prime – 12:34*
2: *The Terrible Twins – 4:05*	7: *Another Hired Hand – 14:34*
3: *New Swamp Rat – 5:35*	8: *Open or Closed – 17:07*
4: *Getting Acquainted – 7:51*	9: *Into the Sunset – 20:20*
5: *Crib Notes – 11:20*	10: *Confession / End Titles – 23:26*

Closing Stills

1: *Freeze – B.J. & Charles hug Hawkeye*
2: *Dupree in the Swamp*
3: *Lorraine Anderson*
4: *Hawkeye & Bigelow*
5: *Margaret*
6: *B.J.*
7: *Potter*
8: *Charles*
9: *Radar*
10: *Klinger*
11: *Mulcahy*
12: *Hawkeye*

Synopsis: The 4077th and the 8063rd are to exchange a surgeon and a nurse for a week to observe each other's methods. In return for sending Hawkeye and Nurse Bigelow, the 8063rd sends Captain Roy Dupree and Captain Lorraine Anderson, a friend of Margaret's since they were at least 15 years old who haven't seen each other in three years. Charles takes a liking to Lorraine and when it carries over into O.R., Margaret becomes Major Houlihan to her long-time friend. Roy Dupree, a high-spirited cowboy is also a fine surgeon who lives to "party hearty," and can't stop laughing at Klinger. Dupree likes it so much at the 4077th, he asks Potter to make the exchange permanent, the last thing B.J. and Charles want. When Dupree, drunk, mentions that he's been riding horses before he could speak, Charles comes up with a plan to insure he returns to the 8063rd.

Commentary by George Lindsey: "I had worked with Harry Morgan on Snowball Express, and Jamie Farr had been on The Andy Griffith Show. He played a gypsy. Interesting thing about M*A*S*H. I got the script on a Saturday, and we started it on a Monday. I had a lot of words to learn on that show. I liked a scene I had with a nurse. She kind of made my character realize he'd been a jerk. The cowboy hat and boots were mine, and so was the 'SUUUUIII' pig call. I thought the idea for that during the read through. You know, we had a real doctor off to the side. I thought I was operating when I saw the show because he made me look so good. One thing I liked about that M*A*S*H, you never thought of Goober. Now, what was that character's name ... oh yeah, 'ROY DUPRIS from the 8-0-6-3, that's me.' When I finished work on M*A*S*H, I thought I'd be hired as a regular. The character was a real pain, but turned out very nice. I had such a good time because I was working with such good actors. I liked when I kept calling BJ by the wrong initials. But later on, I called him by the right ones so that, you, the viewer, knew Dupris knew his real initials all along. I'd like to end with something special. Knock Knock (this author answered 'who's there,' on the phone). Nobel (I answered, 'Nobel who?'). That's why I went Knock, Knock."

PA Announcement by Sal Viscuso

Authors' Notes: In Chapter 1, Potter's office window shows a wooden structure through the right window.

Charles nails a new, white "Boston" sign on top of the signpost. This is the first time the "Boston" sign is on top. It's been on the signpost in many previous episodes, usually near the bottom. A note about the signpost: this was especially difficult to keep track of, as there was more than one used on the show and the locations were not always in the same spot.

Potterism: "A royal pain in the saddle blanket."

Charles mentions "Hoot Gibson" in Chapter 3. Edmund Richard "Hoot" Gibson was a rodeo champ, stuntman and a movie cowboy. For 20 years, Hoot Gibson was one of the most popular Western stars in silent films.

As noted previously, Trapper can be heard through the chatter in the O.R., including this episode.

In Chapter 9, a chain-link fence is seen at the end of the Stage 9 compound with a "MOTOR POOL" sign on it.

George Lindsey birth dates conflict, with one being December 17, 1928 and the other, 1935. Either way, George Lindsey is best known for the role of Goober Pyle on The Andy Griffith Show, and later on Mayberry, R.F.D. Born in Fairfield, Alabama, he graduated from Kemper Military School and Florence State College with a Bachelor of Bioscience. Mr. Lindsey was a public high school teacher in Madison County, Alabama, before he moved to Los Angeles. After serving in the Air Force, he moved to New York City to break into show business. George Lindsey has raised over $1 million for the Alabama Special Olympics through the George Lindsey Celebrity Weekend Golf Tournament in Montgomery, Alabama, and over $50,000 for the Alabama Association of Retarded Citizens, among his other charitable works. Lindsey's autobiography, *Goober in a Nutshell*, was published in 1995.

Potter's Retirement – 2/20/1978

Season 6 / Episode 145 / Production 142 – Y120
Columbia House VHS Tape............Going Undercover (Catalog # 13119)
Fox DVD ....Season 6, Disc 3

Alan Alda, Mike Farrell, Harry Morgan
Loretta Swit, David Ogden Stiers, Gary Burghoff, Jamie Farr, William Christopher

Produced by Burt Metcalfe
Executive Story Consultant – Jay Folb
Written by Laurence Marks
Directed by William Jurgensen

Story Editors – Ken Levine & David Isaacs
Program Consultant – Ronny Graham
Creative Consultants – Gene Reynolds / Alan Alda

Peter Hobbs.. General Waldo Kent
Johnny Haymer ....Sergeant Zale
Ken White.. Corporal Denning
George Wyner..............................Corporal/Lieutenant Joe Benson
Copyright 1978 – 20th Century Fox Film Corporation

Non-Credited Appearances............ Roy Goldman, Kellye Nakahara, Enid Kent

Chapters

1: *Main Titles / Inside Job*	6: *Guessing Game – 12:11*
2: *Party Prep – 3:45*	7: *Provocateurs – 14:03*
3: *Welcome Back – 5:29*	8: *That Dirty Fink – 16:26*
4: *Request Denied – 7:52*	9: *Snitch First Class – 17:44*
5: *Derby Day Bombshell – 10:07*	10: *Decision Time / End Titles – 20:42*

Closing Stills

1: *Freeze – Potter stays / All plus cook in Potter's office*
2: *Charles*
3: *B.J.*
4: *Hawkeye*
5: *Mulcahy*
6: *Margaret*
7: *Radar*
8: *M.P. Klinger*
9: *Potter*

Synopsis: As the 4077th prepares for a Kentucky Derby Day celebration, General Waldo Kent prepares his old friend, Colonel Potter for some bad news. I-Corps has been getting negative reports about the 4077th, specifically, lack of leadership, lapses of discipline and bypassing regulations. And if this isn't bad enough, Potter becomes rattled to learn the reports are coming from within the 4077th. Returning to camp, Potter calls off the Kentucky Derby party, and then gets a letter from General Kent informing him of a surprise inspection. Addressing the unit, he tells them of the inspection, and then tells them he's going home. Stunned, Hawkeye and B.J., with help from Radar, set out to find the person responsible.

PA Announcement by Sal Viscuso

Authors' Notes: In Chapter 4, Charles has a magazine that shows the first open-heart surgery being performed successfully. In researching this event, it became increasingly difficult to get information, as there were several different types of open-heart surgery. In one instance, it was reported that the first open-heart surgery was done in 1953 when surgeons closed a hole between the upper chambers of the heart. Another reports that an African-American doctor, Dr. Daniel Hale Williams, did the first open-heart surgery on July 10, 1893 when a patient named James Cornish was rushed to Provident Hospital in Chicago with a stab wound to the heart and left a month later.

In Chapter 7, B.J. is seen wearing a white scarf wrapped around his neck. But mid-scene, the scarf is hanging down his chest, and then it's wrapped around his neck again.

Potterism: "A bunch of dust-sniffing yahoos."

In Chapter 10, after Potter wishes for peace, the scene (on the DVD) seems to lose lighting and becomes darker.

Dr. Winchester and Mr. Hyde – 2/27/1978

Season 6 / Episode 146 / Production 144 – Y122
Columbia House VHS Tape . . . . *Not Released by Columbia House*
Fox DVD . . . . *Season 6, Disc 3*

Alan Alda, Mike Farrell, Harry Morgan
Loretta Swit, David Ogden Stiers, Gary Burghoff, Jamie Farr, William Christopher

Produced by Burt Metcalfe
Executive Story Consultant – Jay Folb
Written by Ken Levine & David Isaacs and Ronny Graham
Directed by Charles Dubin

Story Editors – Ken Levine & David Isaacs
Program Consultant – Ronny Graham
Creative Consultants – Gene Reynolds / Alan Alda

Chris Murney . . . . Remy
Joe Tornatore . . . . Sergeant Solita
Ron Max . . . . Sergeant Grich
Rod Gist . . . . Chalk
Copyright 1978 – 20th Century Fox Film Corporation

Non-Credited Appearances . . . . Kellye Nakahara, Gwen Farrell, Roy Goldman,
Dennis Troy

Chapters

1: *Main Titles / Stamina*	6: *Test Run – 12:00*
2: *Speeding Up – 2:30*	7: *Night Creature – 13:26*
3: *Mouse-To-Mouse – 4:56*	8: *And the Winner Is... 15:29*
4: *Fitting In – 7:10*	9: *Falling Apart – 19:05*
5: *Superdoc – 10:54*	10: *Back to Normal / End Titles – 22:24*

Closing Stills

1: *Freeze – B.J. & Hawkeye in the Mess Tent*
2: *Charles*
3: *Hawkeye*
4: *B.J.*
5: *Mulcahy*
6: *Radar with Daisey*
7: *Klinger*
8: *Margaret*
9: *Potter*

Synopsis: Charles denies Klinger's request for something that will help him combat fatigue, but Charles can barely stay awake himself and finds he is unable to resist the temptation of the amphetamines in front of him. Later, Hawkeye is amazed that Charles has written a 27-page article for the A.M.A. in only two hours and how well he seems to be adjusting to life at the 4077th. Meanwhile, Radar challenges the Marines to race their mouse, Sluggo, who has a record of 19-0 against Radar's mouse, Daisey. Charles bets $20 on Daisey, and then comes up with a plan to guarantee a win. Immediately following the race, Charles begins suffering the adverse effects of the drugs he's been taking, as does Daisey.

Commentary by Ken Levine: "When David and I wrote scripts, we always did it together, sitting in a room. As an experiment, we decided to split this script in half, with me writing the first act, and David writing the second. We did this so each member of the partnership would feel confident that he could write on his own. Our partnership is out of mutual agreement, not dependence. The names of the four patients were the, then, California Angels infield."

PA Announcement by Sal Viscuso

Authors' Notes: As per Ken Levine, co-writer of this episode, the names of the four patients were taken from the 1977 California Angels infielders:

Remy – Jerry Remy, # 2
Solita – Tony Solaita, # 27
Grich – Bobby Grich, # 4
Chalk – Dave Chalk, # 7

Major Topper – 3/27/1978

Season 6 / Episode 147 / Production 145 – Y123

Columbia House VHS Tape . . . . *Medical Advances (Catalog # 19499)*
Fox DVD . . . . *Season 6, Disc 3*

Alan Alda, Mike Farrell, Harry Morgan
Loretta Swit, David Ogden Stiers, Gary Burghoff, Jamie Farr, William Christopher

Produced by Burt Metcalfe
Executive Story Consultant – Jay Folb
Written by Allyn Freeman
Directed by Charles Dubin
Story Editors – Ken Levine & David Isaacs
Program Consultant – Ronny Graham
Creative Consultants – Gene Reynolds / Alan Alda

Hamilton Camp . . . . Corporal "Boots" Miller
Andrew Bloch . . . . Saxton
Donald Blackwell . . . . Graham
Peter Zapp. . . . . Rifkin
Paul Linke . . . . Collins
John Kirby. . . . . Duncan
Michael Mann. . . . . .Sergeant Glassberg

Copyright 1978 – 20th Century Fox Film Corporation

Non-Credited Appearances. . . . . Kellye Nakahara, Gwen Farrell, Dennis Troy,
Roy Goldman

Chapters

1: *Main Titles / One Upmanship*	6: *Crackers – 12:29*
2: *On the Air – 4:22*	7: *Better than Drugs – 13:45*
3: *Last of the Morphine – 5:38*	8: *Looney Tunes – 17:54*
4: *Nut-To-Nut Talk – 6:59*	9: *Not-So-Tall Tales – 19:42*
5: *Little White Lies – 8:18*	10: *Thank You Note / End Titles – 22:03*

Closing Stills

1: *Freeze – Potter & Klinger in the Mess Tent*
2: *"Boots" Miller in Klinger's tent*
3: *Charles*
4: *B.J.*
5: *Hawkeye*
6: *Mulcahy*
7: *Margaret*
8: *Klinger*
9: *Radar*
10: *Potter in the Mess Tent*

Synopsis: B.J. has done about 50 lobectomies. Charles has done over 100. According to B.J., "Beer Belly Gus" chug-a-lugged a half-keg at the Petaluma Lumberjack Festival. Charles' former handyman drank all the champagne at his sister's wedding, and so goes the battle of one upmanship between Charles and everyone else, with Charles always coming out on top, even proving he had dinner with Audrey Hepburn. But with the possibility of contaminated morphine, Charles has difficulty believing that a placebo will have the desired effect on the wounded suffering from broken bones, while Klinger now has competition for a Section 8.

Authors' Notes: There are no PA announcements in this episode.

Trivia: this episode was used for the Viewmaster Reels.

Hamilton Camp was not only an actor, but a folk singer as well. Born on October 30, 1934 in England, he was evacuated to the US with his mother and sister(s) during WWII and became a child actor. Among his many television appearances are *Three's Company, Trapper John, M.D., Soap, Mork & Mindy, Star Trek: Voyager* and *Star Trek: Deep Space Nine.* Camp, who returns for another episode of *M*A*S*H* in Season 11's "The Moon is Not Blue," died of a heart attack on October 2, 2005 in Los Angeles.

Boots Miller writes to thank Potter and informs him of his new invention, "Mr. Sock."

Appendix – Season 6

Character Profiles

Hawkeye

Episode 123 His father can get an olive from the bottom of a jar with one finger.
and 124: Going through Frank's footlocker, he takes a perfect pair of shorts.
125: Received a letter from his Congressman but the mail truck threw it in Potter's corral by mistake.
Asleep only 2 hours when Charles hits him with a magazine, and is hung-over.
Needs someone to suture a mesentery while he leaves OR to be sick over an oil drum.
126: Toasts "Goldie" — a waitress at Barney's Bar & Grill.
128: Reads *Fun,* a nudist magazine.
Nurse Nancy Gilmore invites him to spend the weekend with her in Seoul at the Regency Hotel *(Nancy was formerly engaged to a Navy dentist).*
Nurses hang their underwear on the line — Hawkeye takes a sandwich and "makes a day of it," according to B.J.
129: Knew a "Penelope" — everyone called her, "Penny," but she was worth a lot more, as per Hawkeye.
If he was hurt, he'd want Potter or B.J. to work on him because they would "bust a gut" to save a life.
130: Will pick up Kyung tomorrow night at 7:00 PM for dinner at Uncle Ho's.
According to Kyung, Uncle Ho's has been bombed out for six months.
131: Lost all his money in cockroach races — track is in his bunk.
132: Reading *New Feature* magazine *(same one Trapper read in Episode 25).*
133: Had an athletic scholarship — coach's daughter paid him to leave her alone.
With B.J., in charge of calisthenics.
Yellow Blackbirds team captain.
135: Once had a "stubborn" Studebaker.
Wounded when a piece of wood imbeds itself in his leg in the shack *(with Margaret).*
136: Margaret has the whitest teeth he's ever seen.
137: Spent his last $5.00 on a subscription to *Frolicking Nudists* and saved 50 cents off the newsstand price.
Has a bar tab of $50 when it's supposed to be $20.
139: Played "Superman" in a phone booth with Betty Dinkle.
140: Gets a letter from Aunt Eloise.
Grandma Bates.
141: Last batch of records for the 4077 had "Andy Divine Sings Cole Porter."

Plays, "Double Cranko" with B.J. *(see B.J.'s Season 6 profile)*.

143: Magazine in mail call is the bonus issue of *Nudesweek* — announcing the all-star volleyball team.

Voted for "Ilsa the Magnificent" because he loves to watch her spike.

Got two letters last month for another guy named Benjamin Pierce.

One letter from Susan for Benjamin Pierce — nibbling on her shoulder blades in an avocado grove at harvest time.

Father is a widower *(In earlier episodes in Season 1, he had a mother)*.

At 12, his father got interested in a "very nice lady" who was a bookkeeper and he was "sore as hell."

Father wanted him to like her but he wouldn't and his father didn't marry her and is alone to this day.

144: 8063rd hated him — said he was dull.

145: Uncle Chang's Changri-La Hotel has bellboys that are all girls and don't carry your bags but take off their shoes and walk on your back.

Seoul is the Jersey City of the Orient.

Dresses as Colonel Sanders for the 4077th Kentucky Derby Day.

Calls Potter, "Sherman."

146: Doesn't like mice but does bet $74.50 on Radar's mouse, Daisy.

Been using Charles's talcum powder & knows where the key is to his trunk.

147: Skowhegan Seth was his old Maine fishing guide — once fell in a seven-foot brewer's vat.

Seth got out after drinking his way down to five feet.

Lenore Clement was voted Miss New England in 1949 — knew her when she was Miss Maine in 1948.

Also knew Lenore Clement when she was Miss Crabapple Cove in 1947.

Painted a swimsuit on Lenore Clement.

B.J.

Episode 123 Presbyterian, according to Klinger.

and 124: Took a perfect pair of socks from Frank's footlocker.

126: With Leo Bardonaro — Stole a cab — took it apart and put it together in the dean's office — ran meter to $800.

Not Catholic *(See episode 121)*.

Got a water-buffalo horn from a South Korean patient to use as an ash tray, according to Hawkeye.

127: Can't eat when Hawkeye makes him smell the food.

128: Peg got poison oak in the woods.

Had pajamas when he got to the 4077th.

Uses "Babalu # 5" aftershave.

Has to operate on a patient a second time *(this is the second time B.J. has had to operate twice on the same patient, the first was in Episode 76)*.

129: Finds a book inside a canvas bag on a supply truck — *The Rooster Crowed at Midnight* by Abigail Porterfield *(not a real book)*.

132: According to B.J., Peg smokes a corncob pipe, thanks to MacArthur.

133: B.J. has 2 varsity letters.

With Hawkeye, he's in charge of calisthenics.

Is the "Pink Elephants" team captain *(Olympics)*.

137: Gets a telegram from Peg informing him to send $200 to buy property in Stinson Beach.

According to B.J., Stinson Beach has trees, beach and a view of San Francisco.

In return for Charles lending B.J. $200, B.J. had to retract a liver, close Charles's patient and pour him a cup of coffee.
With Hawkeye, they each lend Charles $20.
Has a bottle of Stinson Beach dirt.
Will start building the 2nd day he's home.
138: Had powdered eggs yesterday.
141: Plays, "Double Cranko" with Hawkeye. Game is played with cards, chess and checkers pieces.
According to Hawkeye, you can't cheat at Double Cranko because there are no rules.
Used to sleepwalk — his mother put tacks on the floor.
143: B.J.'s phone number is: 555-2657.
Peg took the car to Ron's Service Station & he wants $425 to fix it.
Peg was to go to Ron's for gas & air only, and sometimes he charges for the air.
"Gene's Body Works" in San Rafael. Gene is an old friend of B.J.'s & they played football in high school.
Tell Gene Peg is B.J.'s wife and he'll give a good price.
Originally called Peg to see if she still needs him.
145: Uses green cough medicine for mint julep.
147: Dated Esther Williams' stand-in when he was in Hollywood.

Colonel Potter

Episode 123 Been smoking five cigars a day for 45 years and never picked up the
and 124: habit. Smoked his first cigar at nine years old. The cigar was 11.
Varicose veins.
Once knew a Winchester.
Had to throw a bucket of water on him and Mrs. Potter on their honeymoon.
4077th has a 98% survival rate.
Wants a "Snickers" bar but really means "Milky Way."
Wears a dental partial.
Potterism: McKenzie is *"The Chief Engineer on the Red Nose Express."*
125: Potterism: *"The most bellicose barrelful of Bull Durham."*
126: Mrs. Potter makes *"A hell of a raisin cupcake."*
Doesn't take cold showers just because he's dirty.
127: "Unit running as smoothly as a pig on stilts."
129: Potterism: *"Mule fritters!"*
130: Once had a beautiful gelding that could jump over a fence easily.
Every time the horse saw Mildred's blue Pontiac, the horse tried to jump over it.
Didn't think to paint the car a different color.
132: Entire medical career spent in the army — 30 years a doctor and never sent out a bill.
Had a friend Radar's age in WW I who got a tattoo of his girlfriend in the middle of his chest — when his friend grew chest hair, turned his girlfriend's tattoo into the bearded lady.
Mrs. Potter was a crier when they first married but settled down after a few months.
For 38 years this April, Mrs. Potter's been a "mighty fine wife."
Got married in 1913.
Likes the oatmeal cookies with stale raisins.
Potterism: "I'll be hornswoggled."

133: 1st place to go to in Manila is the "Blue Machete Café."
Potterisms: *"Whistle beak"* & *"Buffalo breath"* — both to Klinger.
Potterism: *"Cow cookies."*
134: Potterism: *"Sweet Neferiti."*
Reading *Ride the Man Down* by Luke Short.
Been "soldiering" for 30 years.
137: Going to soak his bunions.
His house came with a mother-in-law — luckily, WW I started the next day.
Part of his pay is for a "spiffy" blanket for Sophie.
Wants to send a telegram to Mildred asking for $50 or he'll lose Sophie's blanket.
Won't borrow money from Radar because he'll have to pay Radar back.
138: Potterism: *"Sufferin' Sheep-dip."*
139: When he applied for permission to get married, by the time the papers came through, his son was divorced.
Wearing his lucky bunion pads.
141: Every time he hears Sentimental Journey, it reminds him of a "very special" young lady — after Mildred.
Happened about 12 years ago when stationed at Fort Dix.
Went with "some of the boys" to New York to hear Les Brown and his Band of Renown.
Band started playing *Sentimental Journey* and he had fallen in love with Doris Day.
Never took Mildred to see a Doris Day movie, and he's seen them all.
After the 23rd time "Sentimental Journey" is played, for the first time in 12 years, he's sick and tired of Doris Day.
Loses "Double Cranko" with a pair of checkers and owes Hawkeye $17.12.
142: In WWI, he used to dress up a mule in a petticoat and charge the "fellas" a dime a dance.
Mildred knows how hard it is to get honey and sends it in an envelope — he squeezes it out.
Potterism: *"Prouder than a stallion out to stud."*
143: Got some new snapshots of his grandson, Corey.
One in a sandbox, but you can't see him because he threw sand in the lens.
Another with his "little" friends on the swings — the blur in the middle is Corey.
Mildred was the photographer.
144: Served with, Wheatley, the CO of the 8063rd in Europe — Wheatley is a stickler for regulations, especially hair length.
Used to call Wheatley, "Old Whitewalls."
Potterism: *"A royal pain in the saddle blanket."*
145: Potterism: *"A bunch of dust-sniffing yahoos."*
146: Little sister "Madge" will be 50 years old on Valentine's Day.
147: At about eight years old, he lived across the street from "Old Doc Schumacher."
Aunt Grace was visiting when she came down with a terrible Migraine and called Doc Schumacher.
Schumacher gave her a couple of sugar pills and she was completely cured.
30 minutes she was up and baking cookies.
Has to hide pills for Sophie in an old apple core.

Margaret

Episode 123 Finds a picture of herself in a bikini and an alarm clock Frank's footlocker.
and 124: Frank said a bellboy took them.
First two days of her honeymoon were perfect, and then it was like she was with an old "Auntie."
Had a "wonderful" time playing tennis, shopping and a party at General Lyle Weiskopf's.
Talked and laughed till 3:00 A.M. then Donald stopped everything.

126: Worried about Donald's morale and well being — three days in Tokyo is denied.
Donald is at HQ 2nd Army Division in Tokyo.
Trashes Radar's office when he tells her Potter ordered no calls until after 1700 hours.
Kicks Radar in the ribs and puts a bucket over his head.

127: Money is far down Margaret's list — "second, maybe even third, no — second."

130: Donald wears a Masonic pinky ring.
Donald likes to lick girl's fingernails, as per Nurse Gleason.

131: Lost $23 to Mulcahy playing poker *(He had a full house — she had a straight).*

132: The 4077 saves lives 98% of the time, according to Margaret.
Donald is in top military form — "This war's the best thing that ever happened to him."
The dog Margaret was feeding scraps to was killed when he ran in front of a jeep — she cries over it.

133: Wins the crutch race in the M*A*S*H Olympics.
Wins the "Stay up in the saddle" race on Donald's shoulders in the M*A*S*H Olympics.

134: The last time she had caviar was with General Hardcastle in West Berlin.
Ill from Charless bad pheasant.

135: Going to the 8063rd with Hawkeye.
Hates the war, destruction, the "stupidity" of the waste and the disruption of personal lives.
Takes great pride in that she can adjust to anything.
Lost and in a hut, she's afraid and kisses Hawkeye *(Long).*

136: Always thought her teeth were her week point.
Smiles at everything Hawkeye said in OR — nobody saw her smiling under her mask.
Mentions Frank Burns.
Likes that Hawkeye doesn't shower a woman with empty praise.
Likes her men neat and is going to get Hawkeye a new shirt *(doesn't like his Hawaiian shirt).*

137: Donald has a "brilliant system" — she sends her pay and he sends her an allowance of $30 a week.
By the time the war is over, they'll have saved enough to buy their off-post dream house.
Asks Donald for a week's allowance in advance — wants him to cash in bonds — hangs up on him.
Can't afford $1.50 to have her laundry done.
A little poker always relaxes her — then yells to hurry up.

139: Wedding ring is gone — was on a shelf above clothes.
Always wraps it in tissue paper and puts on the shelf in nurses' changing room *(?).*

Donald is still paying for that ring.

14 karat gold with tiny stones all around it — every 3rd stone a diamond chip.

Donald's inscription inside ring: *"Over hill, over dale, our love will never fail."*

It was sitting next to a coffee cup wrapped in tissue, Klinger accidentally threw it away.

Klinger "finds" her ring in a garbage dump, but: *"Over hill, over dale, our love will ever fail."*

Likes it better than the original because of who "found" it.

140: Loves yoga.

142: Was with Donald about six weeks ago and is pretty sure she's pregnant. Being pregnant means an automatic discharge and her career will be gone.

Uses Fluffy's ovaries to determine if she's pregnant, but only has a little gallbladder trouble.

143: Mother-in-law still addresses her with her maiden name and refuses to acknowledge her marriage.

Donald's mother writes to him constantly recommending good lawyers.

Mother-in-law still uses the phrases, "two different worlds" and "one's own kind."

Donald put Margaret up for an associate membership in DAR and his mother blackballed her.

144: Served with Captain Lorraine Anderson in Fort Benning & haven't seen each other in three years.

Two 15-year-old army brats piercing their ears.

Was with Lorraine at Gilhooly's having their "tenth nightcap" — microbiology exam in three hours.

Exam had 500 questions — crib notes in bras — instructor wouldn't let them leave after getting wise.

After an argument, she packed Lorraine's bags because she thought she'd be happier in the nurse's tent.

Loved Lorraine, then hated her because she's "as free and open" as they both used to be.

Has no friends at the 4077th.

Donald is barely a husband, more like a toy soldier she sometimes plays with and has nobody to tell that to.

146: Charles did the tiniest and neatest stitches she'd ever seen.

Frank

Episode 123 and 124: While drunk in Seoul, he accosted a blonde WAC and kept calling her Margaret.

Acted like he was shampooing her hair and begged to clip her toenails.

Frank, "boiled," saw an officer with a blonde walking and mistook them for Donald and Margaret.

The couple went into a public bathhouse, stripped and got into the water.

Frank, still in uniform jumped in the water with them, grabbed the blonde and started crying.

Then realized it wasn't Donald and Margaret, but rather General and Mrs. Kester.

Frank is being held for a psychiatric evaluation and being transferred out of the 4077th.

(All above according to Potter).

In Frank's footlocker, Margaret finds a picture of herself in a bikini and her alarm clock that Frank said the bellboy took, then she pours a beaker of gin into the footlocker.

Frank sat next to a Red Cross lady on a bus — tried to bite off her buttons *(according to Sergeant Williams)*.

He kept calling the Red Cross lady, "Margaret, Margaret" and the lady screamed, according to Sgt. Williams.

He jumped out the window when the bus stopped, according to Sergeant Williams.

Frank calls the 4077th to talk to Hawkeye for the last time.

The army cleared Frank of the charges and was assigned to a veteran's hospital in Indiana.

The army promoted him to lieutenant colonel *(according to Hawkeye)*.

Charles

Episode 123   At Tokyo General playing cribbage with Colonel Baldwin.
and 124:   Baldwin owes him $672.11 — after mistake in math, he owes $672.17.

Is now attached to a M*A*S*H unit for the next 48 hours.

The 4077th is "an inflamed boil on the buttocks of the world."

Major Charles Emerson Winchester III, Surgeon — arrives with calf gloves.

Went to Harvard Medical School.

Was working at Massachusetts General.

Demonstrating new surgical techniques in Tokyo.

Has done at least 12 ventricular aneurysms.

Whole family has gifted hands — Mother is a concert pianist.

Father knows Harry Truman — doesn't like him, but he knows him.

Hires a dollar-a-day cleaning woman.

Practically chief of thoracic surgery at Boston General.

Can hum all four parts of the Schubert String Quartet.

Can quote Spinoza from memory.

125:   Had a similar experience as Hawkeye's when he was 14 and was nearly thrown out of school.

127:   Scrubs for 7½ minutes.

Thinks Margaret is crazy about him.

Had his fill of psychiatrists at the age of nine.

128:   Tape-records a letter home — the 4077th is either too hot or too cold.

Contemplated shooting himself in the foot, but he enjoys the annual "Deb's Cotillion."

Nephew Felix is being discharged from the service due to fainting spells.

Frazier Continental down 7 points.

Doesn't work weekends.

Endearing himself to the CO responsible for him being in this "cesspool."

Potter is a "tough bandy-legged little mustang."

Meatball surgery is causing his skills to deteriorate.

Has a "tough ear" according to Potter who's painting his portrait.

Has his father's ears.

Father knows an influential general who's now a doorman at the Plaza and close to Arthur Godfrey.

Radar is a "myopic farm boy."

Needs deodorant — doesn't care about the others, but doesn't want to offend himself.

Can't afford to upset Radar because his phone is his sole contact with the outside world.

Brings Radar a case of grape Nehi to apologize, but takes it back when Radar can't place any calls.

Mother gave him the pajamas in the laundry that he rips with Hawkeye.

Wants his parents to talk to Senator Griswald because, "you paid good money for him."

Graded quite highly in liver — has no sense of humor — "Humor is the opiate of the incompetent."

A Winchester never perspires.

Perspiring when he check's Margaret's eye in the scrub room and Mulcahy comes in.

Has small pores, according to Margaret.

Describes Mulcahy as a "cock-eyed optimist who sounds like Dennis Day."

B.J. is a "relatively inoffensive chap" and "an excellent surgeon" despite being born, raised and studied in California.

"Get me the *hell* out of here."

129: "Winchesters have always had extraordinary eyesight, particularly at night."

Can see a cat before it sees him.

Gives Corporal Dobson an injection for pain himself thinking its morphine, but its curare.

Nurses being too busy never happen at Boston General.

The worst thing that could happen to Charles is if the patient dies.

Was in surgery for 14 hours.

Thinks Hawkeye is envious of his skills and expertise.

From now on his patients will have his constant and undivided attention.

130: Won't let Hawkeye have his artichoke hearts, but will let him have his wild boar goulash — can is a "bit swollen."

Cooks steak in the Swamp — only thing capable of consuming Korean food has 4 wheels and flies.

131: Buys scrip from Korean locals for 10 cents on the dollar — offers Mr. Kim, the tailor 2% to help.

Won't lend Hawkeye $400 because all his money is tied up in a financial venture.

Collects $95 from villagers in scrip and gives them a $10 bill in exchange.

Hawkeye and B.J. give Charles $40 for $400 to exchange scrip for him since he isn't allowed to enter the camp.

132: Food is disgusting — they don't even chill the salad forks.

134: Basket of food — Devonshire pheasant in a can, Beluga caviar, truffles, pate, smoked oysters, Montrachet 1947.

After sharing the food with Margaret, they both become ill from bad pheasant.

135: On the phone with General Roberts because "someone" here should be in Tokyo.

137: Lends B.J. $200 down payment to buy property in Stinson Beach in return for B.J. closing a patient.

Father once owned property like Stinson Beach in Hyannisport.

A large family moved in next-door, "nouveau riche" & played a perpetual game of touch-football on their lawn.

Naturally, the Winchesters moved out.

Drinks black coffee.

He doesn't sweat, he perspires and he doesn't perspire.

Pays Hawkeye's $50 bar tab in return for Hawkeye bringing him a beer in the Swamp at 10:00 PM.

Whistles louder when he has nothing playing poker.

138: Plays the French horn *(Not well)*.

139: Has 3 hard boiled eggs for lunch.

140: The greatest work in the whole operatic literature is Wagner's "Der Ring Des Nibelungen."

142: Harvard Class of '43.

143: Gets good news in the mail: 40% of the Missouri sorghum crop was destroyed by hail.

Heavily invested in Canadian sorghum.

Tortoise shell fountain pen missing — won it in a debate: "Should the US permit more liberal immigration?"

Took the negative view as his family has had problems with immigrants ever since they came to America.

Found fountain pen with the nib intact in the supply room.

144: Nails a new, white "Boston" sign on top of the signpost — first time on top.

Learned to be sneaky and underhanded from Hawkeye and B.J., "the sole area in which they both excel."

Saving an old bottle of Beaujolais for a special occasion; wants to share it with Lorraine Anderson for a Bon Voyage.

145: Holds Potter personally responsible for ruining his medical career.

Is at the 4077th six months to the day.

Serial number — Maj. C. E. Winchester — RA864567 *(Footlocker)*.

"Monogrammed toilet paper," white scarf, boat captain's hat.

Ogily & Cabot's Hair Sprout *("A harvest of hair in every bottle")*.

Ogily & Cabot stationary — "Charles Emerson Winchester, Boston, Paris, Palm Beach, Korea" *(according to Hawkeye)*.

Has a magazine that shows the first open-heart surgery in medical history being performed successfully.

Transfer denied.

There are no informers in the Winchester family as they do not spy, but does on occasion hire them.

Tells "Meredith" in a letter that he can't marry her without permission from "Grandma Winchester."

Keeps 12-year-old Scotch in the hair bottle.

146: Tells Klinger that people of his genetic background are far too hyperactive to take amphetamines.

Takes the amphetamines himself.

Will pull together all his notes & finally write an article for the AMA Journal — "Korea, the Surgeon's Buffet."

Took two hours to write a 27-page article.

Little Sister Honoria ran away from home and married a farmer.

Left the farmer, family ostracized her, 'of course" and went to live with — not to marry — a shoe clerk.

Bets $20 on Radar's mouse, Daisy.

Takes more amphetamines — keeps them locked in his steamer trunk.

Gives Daisy a mouse's dose of amphetamines & after getting 10-1 odds, makes it a $50 bet.

After race he's gulping air and hyperventilating — rapid pulse — pressure is 160 over 100 *(according to B.J.)*.

Never been so ashamed — going to throw up.

Hasn't spoken to anyone in three days — first time in months he has an appetite.

He's mean, obnoxious, pompous and egotistical — in other words, he's fine according to Hawkeye.

147: Has done over 100 lobectomies.

Paddy O'Gorman — former handyman and a prodigious drinker. At his sister's wedding, there was no champagne when it was time to toast the couple.

Paddy was down the isle belching & setting up the empties for his private bowling tournament.

Was in the "Hasty Pudding Shows" at Harvard for 2 years and has the reviews to prove it.

Massachusetts General in 1947, Dr. Babcock did an appendectomy without anesthesia.

Babcock hypnotized the patient with his gold watch — all in the Massachusetts Medical Record.

Dated Audrey Hepburn, but never saw any of her films — he just had dinner with her: "Charming little girl, lovely old-world manners, appetite of a bird" — Shows Hawkeye and B.J. a photo to prove it.

Climbed the Matterhorn in winter — "more sporting that way" — 80 MPH winds.

Matterhorn guide, Lars, doubled his fee and Charles fired him — led the expedition himself.

Radar

Episode 123 and 124: Cigars make him sick *(except those he smoked in earlier seasons).*

Has an Uncle Charles.

North wind odor is the cesspool, South wind odor is the latrine.

Introduces himself to Charles as "Corporal Walter Eugene O'Reilly" — first for "Eugene."

125: Not getting much out of the 4077th — Wants to be a hot lover, or even a cold one.

Uncle Ed came home from WW I, his mother could tell by the look in his eyes he wasn't a good boy in France.

Ed's mother cried for three days.

When Radar goes home, his mother will take one look and chuckle for a week.

According to Radar, he'll be the only one to leave younger than when he came.

Wounded in the left shoulder while on his way to Seoul.

Will still talk to "ordinary people" even though he has a Purple Heart.

127: Angry at Klinger for taking his bear.

Didn't go into the VIP tent to see Sidney because he didn't want anyone to think he was crazy.

128: Cleaned Potter's paint brushes with yesterday's soup — couldn't find turpentine.

The Departure Lounge is the dead tree by the latrine.

4077th cockroach collection takes an hour to see, "But it's worth it."

Pays a "buck a bottle" for Grape Nehi at Rosie's.

Promised Mulcahy not to use "those words" *(Said to Charles).*

In a taped-letter home, Charles calls Radar a "myopic farm boy."

132: Has aluminum siding on his house.

Thinking of getting a tattoo *(must've forgotten the tattoo he got of an anchor in Episode 55).*
Wants either a panther or a "Marie" tattoo — decides to get a girl.
Getting a tattoo at Rosie's after chow because he's tired of being a "nobody."
Wants to be the object of respect, fear and sex / Tattoo ought to be "Mother."
Guys with tattoos always drink beer and don't pal around with guys like him / decides to get a snake.
Tattooed his "tush" because he didn't want anyone to talk him out of it and didn't want it seen.
Got a tiny Teddy bear tattoo — didn't want anything showy.
Was afraid of dirty needles and had the artist draw it on with ink.
Will come off next time he bathes — Hawkeye now thinks it permanent.

137: Can lend B.J. a total of $16.27.

141: Won't play "Cranko" because when he loses, he likes to know why.
Doesn't think he's cut out to be talented.

142: Alcoholic drink makes his ears wider *(except for the Martinis and Brandy in earlier seasons).*
Female rabbit is, "Fluffy" / Male rabbit is, "Bongo."
Fluffy can't be pregnant because she and Bongo live in separate cages.
Refuses testing on Fluffy for fear of killing her and hides her in his mailbag.
Agrees to test after Hawkeye promises to remove her ovaries only.
Fluffy can now live in the same cage with Bongo.

143: Uncle Ed used to tickle him.
Mother wrote to him that she has a boyfriend / Mother is almost 50 and old people shouldn't get married.
Mother's boyfriend works as a teller at the Farmer's Bank for 30 years — is a third degree Mason and church elder.
They play bingo on Wednesday night at the Masonic Lodge.
Square dancing on Friday at the Pentecostal Church.
Every Sunday they go to Lockport in his Nash for snow cones.
Suggests Hawkeye's father meet his mother.

144: Would like to visit Boston's historical sites like Concord, Bunker Hill and the Red Sox.

146: Tried to join the Marines but they said his eyes weren't good enough.
Radar's mouse "Daisy" can beat the Marine's mouse "Sluggo" "any day of the week and twice in January."
Bets 50 cents on Daisy.
No water for Daisy while in training — gets cramps — maybe water after her rubdown.
Daisy ran the garbage dump this morning in 15 seconds.
Hid cheese in his office and Daisy ran to it.
Can't calm Daisy down after race — runs around and around — shadowboxes then tap-dances — acts like she's playing drums.
Raised Daisy from a "pup."

Klinger

Episode 123   Fast due to "basic delicatessen training."
and 124:   Captain Schaeffer, a lawyer with the Adjutant General Branch claims he can get Klinger a discharge.
Captain Schaeffer is really Private Schaeffer — busted twice and spent

four months is the stockade.

Won't wear basic black before 5:00 P.M.

Has a body lice appointment.

126: Has an invisible camel, "Habibi, " a "two-humper" who spits on photo of Mrs. Potter.

Two trays in the mess tent — one for Habibi who is not a carnivore, according to Potter.

Grooms Habibi, the invisible camel on the Ranch compound.

127: Looking for his "daddy" because dinner is ready, but can't find him *(ploy)*.

Afraid he's going crazy — in mirror sees a guy in earrings, pillbox hat, veil, maybe a choker of pearls.

"Would a sane man dress like this?"

Looked at a photo of Gina Lollobrigida and all he thought was,.

"How could she wear a peasant blouse with a tweed skirt?"

Goes to sleep wondering if his pleats will hold out another day.

Palms sweaty when he read cocktail length hems are going longer in the back and doesn't have the material.

Doesn't want to die and doesn't want to watch others while they do it.

Doesn't want to be told where to stand when it happens to him.

Doesn't want to be told how to do it to someone else — overall, would rather be in a hammock with a couple of girls.

Has to leave Sidney because he has nylons soaking.

Is a monument to hope in size 12 pumps, according to Sidney Freedman.

Throws the army cookbook into the bon fire.

128: Reads an article about a nudist wedding — the bride is wearing white sneakers.

Charles tells of his nephew's fainting spells, Klinger tries it, but does it backwards *(ploy)*.

Mother sent him a garlic pie.

Doesn't have pajamas, but can give Hawkeye a "lovely low-cut peignoir, chickadee red with Oriental peacocks embroidered over each breast" and cost him eight books of Green Stamps *(S&H Green Stamps are the most successful customer loyalty program in history, since 1896.)*

129: On the phone with supply — someone cut up his best petticoat to make bandages.

The part of *The Rooster Crowed at Midnight* he likes best is there's insanity in the family.

131: Uncle Gus got out of WW I as "Aunt Gussie" and is "good buddies" with a certain Congressman *(West Point exam)*.

Misspelled his name on the West Point exam — only thing correct is he "washed out."

133: Eats chipped beef to get out for being too fat *(ploy)*.

Eats a giant salami and bread — 60 pounds means homeward bound *(ploy)*.

Dressed like a Greek God — lights the 4077 Olympic flame in a bedpan on top of a tray mounted onto a pole.

Eats salami and an apple *(ploy)*.

After 10 salamis, he sick and cannot compete in the M*A*S*H Olympics — Donald takes his place.

134: Likes mustard, chili and hot peppers on Packo's Hungarian hot dogs.

Lives on Michigan & Galena.

Took basic training at LeGrange Pool Hall — never saw anyone use a cue stick on a ball.

Used to go to the Trianon *(dance hall)* and every night he dreamt he was dancing with Agnes Goams.

Would steal away to the veranda to watch the kids bust windshields.

Patient Danker is from Toledo and gives Klinger a matchbook from the Trianon.

Girls get in the Trianon for a buck or 50 cents if they look human, according to Danker.

Danker lives on Locust & Ontario.

Cries while singing, "We're Strong for Toledo — that's where the Buckeyes grow" *(song written by Danny Thomas & Dave Henrickson).*

136: Welcome home gift for Hawkeye and Margaret is a M*A*S*H compass.

139: Accidentally threw away Margaret's wedding ring *(it was wrapped in tissue sitting next to a coffee cup).*

While going through the garbage dump to find Margaret's ring, he burnt his nose.

140: Wearing "Asian Musk" — "It creeps out of the night to weave it's magic spell."

Used to dream about the schoolhouse in Toledo burning down.

Rips his best skirt after it gets stuck under a bell covering stolen supplies.

141: His Uncle Bob will get out next month from a payola scandal two years ago in Toledo.

Was in the pool hall just before his physical — put the "3" ball in a side pocket and the "4" ball in the corner.

Told "Hymie" to hold his money & he'd be back in a half-hour with "4F" printed on his chest.

Walked in talking Lebanese, eyes crossed and measles dots painted on his face — went over like a lead salami.

142: Tells Potter he has nine kids and wants a hardship discharge.

Kids are Santos *(needs shoes)* Ellen *(needs braces)* Twins Achmed & Irene *(One is swarthy, the other blonde).*

Achmed & Irene were fraternal twins.

Klinger had a moustache at three.

According to Potter, Klinger's kids are 19; meaning Klinger was a father at 11.

Potter knows Klinger's "kids" from the photos of Erin Hunnicutt and Zelda Zale.

Volunteers to be a hostage for Lieutenant Tom Martinson who wants clothing, food and transport to Ohio.

Knows enough shady people in Toledo to keep Martinson out of sunlight for years.

143: Hasn't heard from Laverne in two months — her scent hits him like a wrecking ball.

Gets camels to stand up in the desert by tickling them.

Laverne wants a divorce — took his allotment checks, built up a nice bank account and found another guy.

Knows Laverne since they were kids — she was the lookout on fruit stand heists when Klinger was 12.

Laverne promised to wait for him — he borrows $20 from Mulcahy and goes AWOL.

Has to see Laverne before she marries Morty, who makes sausage casings and has big hands.

Returns to the 4077th in regulation fatigues.

Had reservations & deluxe accommodations in the baggage compartment of a C-47.

Bumped a general's poodle to get on — Laverne had no right to do what she did while he was in Korea.

"Let her have Morty — she'll eat all that free sausage and blow up like an elephant."

Will leave the army the honorable way — with a Section 8.

According to Klinger, women in America got most of the money, stocks, bonds, etc.

Is in the mood for a banana daiquiri.

145: Wants to be transferred to the MPs because he'd do a great job escorting them back to the States.

Father Mulcahy

Episode 123
and 124: Thinks Frank and Margaret were "somewhat attached."

131: Beat Margaret in poker with a full house over Margaret's straight — money for the children's Christmas fund.

Wants to broadcast a Commandment a week after someone returns $400.

137: Agrees to play poker when he learns Charles is new to the game — will ad-lib an ending for his sermon.

After winning — gives Charles a red chip from the orphans.

138: Will be happy to burn incense around Hawkeye and B.J. when they don't shower.

Eating outside reminds him of the Via Vene in Rome when he dined alfresco.

Was in Rome for an audience with the Pope.

140: Learned from Corporal Bryant's confession that supplies are stored under a bell at the burnt out village school.

143: Short note from his sister in the convent — Our Lady of Hermosa's basketball team has a 7-foot novice.

Seen, Heard, Mentioned or Referenced - Season 6

Movies

Episode 125: Hawkeye mentions "The Tin Man," a reference to *The Wizard of Oz* (1939).

128: Radar quotes Humphrey Bogart from the movie *All Through the Night* (1942).

133: *Fox Movietone News* newsreel of the 1952 Helsinki Olympic Games seen.

135: "Abbott & Costello Meet Hitler" mentioned *(not real)*.

138: *Beauty and the Beast* (1946) mentioned.
Hail the Conquering Hero (1944) said "Fool" mentioned.

141: "Mr. Belvedere Goes to Korea" mentioned *(not real)*.

146: Klinger mentions "Mighty Mouse," whose first appearance in an animated short was *The Mouse of Tomorrow* (1942).

147: Klinger does an imitation of Porky Pig. The character's first appearance was in *I Haven't Got A Hat* (March 2, 1935).
Hawkeye mentions *Rebecca of Sunnybrook Farm* (1938).

Songs

Episode 123 Charles listens to Mozart.

and 124: "The William Tell Overture" *(Referenced by B.J.)* Written by Gioachino Rossini (February 29, 1792-November 13, 1868) from the opera, *William Tell.*

125: "Somewhere Over the Rainbow" *(Hawkeye mentions)* Words by E.Y.Harburg, music by Harold Arlen. From the 1939 movie, *The Wizard of Oz* .

126: "Mammy" *(Hawkeye mentions)* Words by Sam A. Lewis & Joe Young, music by Walter Donaldson (1926).

127: "Keep the Home Fires Burning" *(All sing)* Words by Lena Ford, music by Ivor Novelo (1915).

129: "When the Lights Go Out Again All Over the World" *(Klinger sings)* Written by Eddie Seller, Sol Marcus and Bernie Benjamin; reached # 1 in 1943.

130: Beethoven – Kyung Soon plays the only violin record she has.

132: "Lydia, the Tattooed Lady" *(Klinger sings "Lydia, oh, Lydia, have you met Lydia…")* Words by E.Y. Harburg, music by Harold Arlen from the 1939 Marx Bros movie, *At the Circus.*

133: "I Surrender, Dear" *(Hawkeye mentions)* Words by Harry Barris, music by Gordon Clifford (1931).

134: "We're Strong for Toledo" *(Klinger sings while crying "We're strong for Toledo, that's where the Buckeyes grow…")* Written by Joe Murphy in 1906.

135: "La Donna E Mobile" from Rigoletto *(B.J. sings)* Written by Giuseppe Verdi; first performed at Teatro la Fenice in Venice on March 11, 1851.
"Goober Peas" *(Hawkeye sings "Goober's peas")* Sung by Confederate soldiers during the American Civil War, the song's earliest publication date for sheet music is 1866 by A.E. Blackmar.

137: "Manana (Is Good Enough For Me)" *(heard on the radio; sung by Charles, when cleaning the Officer's Club)* Written by Peggy Lee & Dave Barbour and published in 1947; reached Billboard charts on January 23, 1948 and stayed there for 21 weeks.
"La Traviata" *(Charles whistles)* Written by Giuseppe Verdi, first performed at Teatro la Fenice on March 6, 1853.
"Rhapsody in Blue" *(B.J. says "Rhapsody in bluff")* Written by George Gershwin in 1924.

139: "Old Man River" *(Klinger sings "Tote that barge, lift that bail...")* Written by Jerome Kern, from the 1927 musical *Showboat.*

140: "Der Ring Des Nibelungen" *(Charles mentions)* Cycle of four operas written by Richard Wagner over a 26-year period (1848-74).

141: "Syncopated Clock" *(B.J. mentions "Musical Clock")* Written by Leroy Anderson in 1945, this was the theme for *The Late Late Show* on CBS in New York City for 25 years.

"Tico Tico" *(Mulcahy mentions)* Words by Ervin M. Drake, music by Zequinha, from the 1944 movie *Bathing Beauty.*

"The Cincinnati Dancing Pig" *(Radar plays)* Words by Al Lewis, music by Guy Wood in 1950.

"Sentimental Journey" *(Radar plays)* Written by Bud Green, Les Brown and Ben Homer, sung by Doris Day in 1944.

"You're the Flower of My Heart, Sweet Adeline" *(Klinger mentions "Sweet Adeline")* Words by Richard H. Gerrard, music by Harry Armstrong in 1903. Also from the 1934 film.

"The Near Future" *(Hawkeye mentions "How dry I am...")* Written by Irving Berlin in 1919.

"May the Good Lord Bless and Keep You" *(heard in the Officer's Club-turned-Post-Op)* Words and music by Meredith Willson, published in 1940.

143: "Button Up Your Overcoat" *(Hawkeye sings, with Mulcahy on piano)* written by B.G. DeSylva, Lew Brown and Ray Henderson in 1929.

144: "Back In the Saddle Again" *(Roy Dupree sings)* See Episode 66 (page 399) for details.

145: "My Old Kentucky Home" *(All sing in the mess tent "Oh, the sun shines bright on my old Kentucky home...")* Written by Stephen C. Foster in 1853, this is the official state song of Kentucky.

"Boots and Saddles" or "Call to Post" *(heard on the radio),* a call to the cavalry to mount up.

"For He's A Jolly Good Fellow" *(All sing in Potter's office)* See Episode 13 (page 129) for details.

146: "I've Got You Under My Skin" *(Hawkeye sings)* See Episode 46 (page 192) for details.

"Another Opening, Another Show" *(Hawkeye sings)* from the 1952 musical *Kiss Me, Kate* by Cole Porter.

"Swinging Down the Lane" *(Hawkeye sings "Everybody's hand in hand...")* Written by Isham Jones & Gus Kahn in 1922.

Hawkeye sings "I tied for you" – Unidentified lyric.

"Whistle While You Work" *(Charles whistles)* Words by Larry Morey, music by Frank Churchill from *Snow White* (1937).

147: "Come On-A My House" *("Boots" Miller sings)* From the off-Broadway musical *The Son,* words by Ross Badgasarian, music by William Saroyan. The song was #1 for eight weeks in 1951.

Appearances – Season 6

Ahn, Philip... Episode 131 *(Mr. Kim)*
Aidman, Charles .... Episode 134 *(Colonel Bloodworth)*
Andon, Kurt .... Episode 142 *(Sergeant Whitkow)*
Arbus, Allan .... Episode 127 *(Major Sidney Freedman)*
Ash, Glenn .... Episode 131 *(Sergeant Maxwell)*
Ashton, John .... Episode 126 *(M.P.)*
Blackwell, Donald... Episode 147 *(Graham)*
Blanchard, Susan..................................... Episode 132 *(Nurse Sandra Cooper)*
Bloch, Andrew .... Episode 147 *(Saxton)*
Block, Larry .... Episode 132 *(Corporal Eddie Hendrix)*
Burns, Joseph .... Episode 123 & 124 *(Patient)*
Camp, Hamilton................................ Episode 147 *(Corporal "Boots" Miller)*
Carter, Thomas.. Episode 128 *(Patient McCloud)*
Chinh, Kieu .... Episode 130 *(Kyung Soon)*
Clark, Oliver .... Episode 143 *(Captain Benjamin Pierce)*
Clarke, Jordan .... Episode 138 *(Saunders)*
Cromwell, James .... Episode 126 *(Captain Leo Bardonaro)*
Dever, Tom... Episode 131/ Corporal Boone)*
Durren, John .... Episode 132 *(Sergeant Rimmerman)*
Erwin, Gary .... Episode 129 *(Corporal Dobson – Post-Op Patient)*
Farrell, Judy.. Episode 132 *(Nurse Able)*
Flatley, William....... Episode 123 & 124 *(M.P. Sergeant Williams, I-Corps Military Police)*
Fong, Francis... Episode 125 *(Rosie)*
Foraker, Lois .... Episode 138 *(Nurse Denver)*
Foraker, Lois .... Episode 142 *(Nurse Bell)*
Fox, Bernard... Episode 140 *(Major Derek Ross)*
Frank, Charles............................... Episode 142 *(Lieutenant Tom Martinson)*
Gelman, Larry... Episode 125 *(G.I. #1)*
Gold, Harry.. Episode 139 *(Private Cohen)*
Gist, Rod... Episode 146 *(Chalk)*
Graham, Ronny .... Episode 141 *(Sergeant Walter Gribble)*
Grapes, Jack .... Episode 143 *(Kelsey)*
Hall, Philip Baker .... Episode 129 *(Sergeant Hacker, Supply Truck Driver)*
Hardin, Joseph .... Episode 132 *(Patient)*
Haymer, Johnny .... Episode 131, 137, 139, 141 *(Sergeant Zelmo Zale)*
Henry, Mike............................... Episode 133 *(Lieutenant Colonel Donald Penobscott)*
Hiroshige, Kimiko .... Episode 123 & 124 *(Korean Woman)*
Hiroshige, Kimiko .... Episode 128 *(Korean Laundry Woman)*
Hobbs, Peter.................................... Episode 145 *(General Waldo Kent)*
Houser, Jerry .... Episode 134 *(Danker)*
Hunt, Neil... Episode 140 *(Enright)*
Hurst, Rick................................. Episode 123 & 124 *(Captain/Private Schaeffer)*
Karnes, Robert .... Episode 126 *(Major General Fred Fox)*
Katz, Phyllis... Episode 142 *(Nurse)*
Kent, Enid................................. Episode 129, 132, 144 *(Nurse Bigelow)*
Kirby, John .... Episode 147 *(Duncan)*
Krebs, Susan................................... Episode 130 *(Nurse Bobbie Gleason)*
Kux, William... Episode 141 *(Patient)*
Lindsey, George .... Episode 144 *(Captain Roy Dupree)*
Linke, Paul .... Episode 147 *(Collins)*
Lough, James .... Episode 123 & 124 *(Driver)*

Broadcast/Production Order – Season 6

Broadcast	Production
123: Fade Out, Fade In, Part 1 *(9/20/1977)*	*123: (Y101)* Fade Out, Fade In, Part 1
124: Fade Out, Fade In, Part 2 *(9/20/1977)*	*124: (Y102)* Fade Out, Fade In, Part 2
125: Fallen Idol *(9/27/1977)*	*125: (Y103)* Last Laugh
126: Last Laugh *(10/4/1977)*	*126: (Y104)* Fallen Idol
127: War Of Nerves *(10/11/1977)*	*127: (Y105)* Images
128: The Winchester Tapes *(10/18/1977)*	*128: (Y106)* War Of Nerves
129: The Light That Failed *(10/25/1977)*	*129: (Y107)* The WincHester Tapes
130: In Love And War *(11/1/1977)*	*130: (Y108)* The Light That Failed
131: Change Day *(11/8/1977)*	*131: (Y109)* Tea And Empathy
132: Images *(11/15/1977)*	*132: (Y110)* The Grim Reaper
133: The M*A*S*H Olympics *(11/22/1977)*	*133: (Y111)* The M*A*S*H Olympics
134: The Grim Reaper *(11/29/1977)*	*134: (Y112)* In Love And War
135: Comrades In Arms, Part 1 *(12/6/1977)*	*135: (Y113)* Change Day
136: Comrades In Arms, Part 2 *(12/13/1977)*	*136: (Y114)* Patient 4077
137: The Merchant Of Korea *(12/20/1977)*	*137: (Y115)* The Smell Of Music
138: The Smell Of Music *(1/3/1978)*	*138: (Y116)* Comrades In Arms, Part 1
139: Patient 4077 *(1/10/1978)*	*139: (Y117)* Comrades In Arms, Part 2
140: Tea And Empathy *(1/17/1978)*	*140: (Y118)* The Merchant Of Korea
141: Your Hit Parade *(1/24/1978)*	*141: (Y119)* What's Up, Doc?
142: What's Up, Doc? *(1/30/1978)*	*142: (Y120)* Potter's Retirement
143: Mail Call Three *(2/6/1978)*	*143: (Y121)* Mail Call Three
144: Temporary Duty *(2/13/1978)*	*144: (Y122)* Dr. Winchester and Mr. Hyde
145: Potter's Retirement *(2/20/1978)*	*145: (Y123)* Major Topper
146: Dr. Winchester And Mr. Hyde *(2/27/1978)*	*146: (Y124)* Your Hit Parade
147: Major Topper *(3/27/1978)*	*147: (Y125)* Temporary Duty

Season 7

Seasons 1 through 3 of *M*A*S*H* have a very similar feel to them. Season 4 stands on its own, for reasons described in that season's summary; Season 5 also stands on its own. Seasons 6 and 7 are quite similar. But with every passing season of *M*A*S*H*, the show became something quite different than its earlier inception. Season 7 is certainly commendable, and the producer's attempts to strive for a fresh look are obvious. The 4077th is bugged out for "The Party," moves to a cave in "C*A*V*E," takes place entirely in Rosie's Bar in "A Night At Rosie's" and is seen from a soldier's perspective in "Point Of View." The writing remained high quality, as did the entire show. But, with Metcalfe running things and Alda having more of a say in the direction of the show, *M*A*S*H* was becoming quite different. In Season 7, Margaret's marriage ended. Gary Burghoff would announce that this would be his last regular season. By now, Burghoff was not appearing in all episodes of a given season, and was tired; he had been a grown man playing a boy for seven years. This was the last season that Klinger would continue his mad attempts to get a Section 8 discharge, and the last season audiences would see Colonel Flagg. Other notable episodes include "None Like It Hot" and "Dear Sis."

Commander Pierce – 9/18/1978

Season 7 / Episode 148 / Production 151 – T404

Columbia House VHS Tape . . . .*Warhawk (Catalog # 13118)*
Fox DVD . . . .*Season 7, Disc 1*

Alan Alda, Mike Farrell, Harry Morgan
Loretta Swit, David Ogden Stiers, Gary Burghoff, Jamie Farr, William Christopher

Produced by Burt Metcalfe
Executive Script Consultants – Ken Levine & David Isaacs
Teleplay by Ronny Graham
Story by Ronny Graham & Don Segall
Directed by Burt Metcalfe

Story Editor – Larry Balmagia
Story Consultant – Ronny Graham
Creative Consultants – Gene Reynolds / Alan Alda

James Lough . . . . Webster
Andrew Massett . . . . Corporal Hough
Enid Kent . . . . Nurse Bigelow
Jan Jorden . . . . Nurse Baker
Kellye Nakahara . . . . .Nurse Kellye
Copyright 1978 – 20th Century Fox Film Corporation

Non-Credited Appearances. . . . . Roy Goldman, Gwen Farrell

Chapters

1: *Main Titles / Seniority*
2: *New Hire – 4:36*
3: *In and Out – 6:58*
4: *Steep Learning Curve – 8:43*
5: *Butt Out! – 10:22*

6: *Insubordination – 12:41*
7: *A Tight Ship – 13:52*
8: *Top Dog – 15:14*
9: *A Pesky Bunch – 19:01*
10: *Welcome Back / End Titles – 23:10*

Closing Stills

1: *Freeze – Potter & Radar in the office*
2: *Hawkeye in Post-Op*
3: *B.J.*
4: *Potter*
5: *Margaret*
6: *Radar*
7: *Mulcahy*
8: *Klinger in Potter's office*
9: *Charles in Post-Op*

Synopsis: Before Colonel Potter leaves for Seoul, he appoints Hawkeye as interim commanding officer: he soon gets a taste of what it's like to run the 4077th, realizing it's not as easy as he might have thought. Already short a surgeon, and with heavy casualties on the way, B.J. leaves camp to get a seriously wounded G.I., forcing Hawkeye and Charles to handle the O.R. When B.J. returns with the wounded soldier, Hawkeye expresses his anger at B.J. for leaving without permission and displays a side of his character that B.J. hasn't seen before and isn't sure he wants to see again.

Commentary by Ken Levine: "David and I were the head writers. For patient names, (Season 7) we used the Dodger's roster."

Commentary by Enid Kent Sperber: "The cast of *M*A*S*H* was the friendliest cast I ever worked with in my subsequent years in television. Alan took the lead by striding up to new cast members and thrusting his hand out to introduce himself, 'I'm Alan Alda.' I have worked many shows where the stars took no notice of the day players and we remained anonymous to everyone on he set. *M*A*S*H* was more like a theatrical company. There was a concerted effort to create a community because of the nature of the program."

PA Announcements by Sal Viscuso

Authors' Notes: The closing stills for Father Mulcahy in Episodes 149, 150, 155, 156, 157, 163, 164 and 171 are all the same. Some of the remaining stills are similar.

As per Ken Levine, the patient in this episode, Corporal Hough, is named after Charlie Hough, number 49, and a pitcher with the Los Angeles Dodgers in 1978.

In Chapter 1, Potter says, "Courage, Camille." Two possible definitions for "Courage, Camille" are:

1: *A game in which two players lock hands while a third falls backward into their arms,* and

2: *As a line spoken by Bob Hope in a 1940 horror-comedy film The Ghost Breakers.*

The view out of the office windows in Chapter 2 shows a wooden building with double doors seen through the right window and trees out of the left window; however, the view changes mid-scene to show the side of a corrugated structure not there before through the right window and different trees out the left window. But this doesn't last long as it changes again to the first view.

In Chapter 5, the view out of the office windows has now changed to show the side of a corrugated structure through both windows.

Potterism: "4-0-double natural."

In Chapter 8, there's a picture on the wall in the room in Seoul. That picture used to hang in Henry Blake's office.

Also in Chapter 8, a microphone can be seen at the top of the screen when B.J. returns to the 4077th on the Ranch compound.

In Chapter 9, Potter toasts Hawkeye "to a job well done." Although Potter's lips are clearly moving, the words, "to a" are not heard. Only, "job well done" is heard.

Also in Chapter 9, the wooden structure with double doors is seen through the office windows.

Peace on Us – 9/25/1978

Season 7 / Episode 149 / Production 148 – T401

Columbia House VHS Tape . . . . .Warhawk (Catalog # 13118)
Fox DVD . . . . .Season 7, Disc 1

Alan Alda, Mike Farrell, Harry Morgan
Loretta Swit, David Ogden Stiers, Gary Burghoff, Jamie Farr, William Christopher

Produced by Burt Metcalfe
Executive Script Consultants – Ken Levine & David Isaacs
Written by Ken Levine & David Isaacs
Directed by George Tyne

Story Editor – Larry Balmagia
Story Consultant – Ronny Graham
Creative Consultants – Gene Reynolds / Alan Alda

Kevin Hagen . . . . .Major Dean Goss
Hugh Gillan . . . . General Tomlin
Michael Payne . . . . M.P. Guard
Michael Laguardia . . . . M.P. Guard
Don Cummins . . . . M.P. Guard
Rollin Moriyama . . . . Korean Delegate
Perren Page . . . . .Driver

Copyright 1978 – 20th Century Fox Film Corporation

Non-Credited Appearances. . . . . .Roy Goldman, Dennis Troy, Gwen Farrell

Chapters

1: Main Titles / Square One
2: Working Things Out – 3:02
3: A Lousy War – 4:16
4: Anti-Green – 7:50
5: Upping the Ante – 9:21

6: Reassurance – 12:11
7: Peace Delegate – 14:25
8: A Sea of Red – 17:45
9: A Shot in the Arm – 19:50
10: The Day After / End Titles – 22:54

Closing Stills

1: Freeze – Hawkeye gets out of wheelchair
2: Major Goss red hair at party
3: Hawkeye takes general's pulse at peace talks
4: B.J.
5: Potter red hair at party
6: Charles
7: Margaret on the phone
8: Radar
9: Klinger
10: Mulcahy
11: Hawkeye at the peace talks

Synopsis: Margaret's marital problems are compounded when she tries to call Donald and finds out he was transferred to a post in the States at his own request, and Hawkeye becomes incensed when the rotation points are increased from 36 to 45 because the army is having a difficult time replacing doctors. Hawkeye then takes matters into his own hands and while still in a bloodied surgical gown, takes a jeep and talks his way into the peace talks at Panmunjon to get the delegates to end the war.

Commentary by Kevin Hagen: "The men in protest against headquarters had all dyed their hair red. As I was leaving I was asked if I would like to join the party. I took my helmet off and said 'Do you think I'll fit in?' I have red hair. I was called back after the dailies. My natural red hair did not look natural compared to the dyed red hair of the protesters. After trying several methods, they wound up using Postal paint to make my natural red hair look...natural. And I got an extra day of work."

Commentary by Ken Levine: "Everyone dying their hair red was taken from research. For whatever reason, this episode never seemed realized, to me. I think we tried to do too much."

PA Announcements by Sal Viscuso

Authors' Notes: An extra in Chapter 2 enters the mess tent wearing a robe usually worn by Henry Blake.

In Chapter 6, the wooden structure seen through the office windows in the previous episode is still there, but it's larger as a result of being closer.

The Military Police jeep is serial number 18210717 – the same jeep seen in many episodes for many purposes.

During roll call in Chapter 10, everyone is assembled on the Ranch compound. But when Radar calls for Klinger, he responds from the Stage 9 compound and is the only one not seen on the Ranch set.

Mr. Hagen passed away on July 9, 2005 from esophageal cancer in Grant's Pass, Oregon. He was 77.

A note on the point system: it was proposed and began at the beginning of the Korean War by psychiatrist (and WWII vet) Albert Glass to "protect soldiers from becoming psychiatric casualties." After obtaining 36 points, the soldier could go home no matter what the progress of the war: infantrymen = 4 points per month; artillerymen = 3 points per month; rear-echelon = 2 points per month. In WWII, the psychiatric casualties were 23%. When Glass took over in the Korean War, the psychiatric casualties dropped to 6%. *Thanks to Lynnita Brown and her web site, www.koreanwar-educator.org, for her help in acquiring this information.*

Lil – 10/2/1978

Season 7 / Episode 150 / Production 153 – T406
Columbia House VHS Tape . . . . Not Released by Columbia House
Fox DVD . . . . Season 7, Disc 1

Alan Alda, Mike Farrell, Harry Morgan
Loretta Swit, David Ogden Stiers, Gary Burghoff, Jamie Farr, William Christopher

Produced by Burt Metcalfe
Executive Script Consultants – Ken Levine & David Isaacs
Written by Sheldon Bull
Directed by Burt Metcalfe

Story Editor – Larry Balmagia
Story Consultant – Ronny Graham
Creative Consultants – Gene Reynolds / Alan Alda
Carmen Mathews . . . . Colonel Lilian Rayburn
Copyright 1978 – 20th Century Fox Film Corporation

Non-Credited Appearances. . . . . Kellye Nakahara, Gwen Farrell, Roy Goldman

Chapters

1: Main Titles / Inspection	6: Blame Game – 14:28
2: Observing – 4:26	7: The Revelers Return – 16:14
3: Confidential File – 7:46	8: Crossed Signals – 18:12
4: Call Me Lil – 9:57	9: Sigh of Relief – 22:06
5: Nice Day for A Picnic – 12:42	10: Just B.J. / End Titles – 23:24

Closing Stills

1: Freeze – Hawkeye tosses letters – B.J.'s name
2: Lil
3: Potter
4: Hawkeye
5: Radar
6: Margaret
7: B.J.
8: Klinger in the Officer's Club
9: Charles in the Swamp
10: Mulcahy in Post-Op
11: Potter and Lil in Potter's tent

Synopsis: When the 8th Army head nurse arrives for a full-scale inspection of the nursing staff, Colonel Lillian Rayburn and Colonel Potter take an instant liking to each other. In spite of Radar's best efforts to keep Potter in camp and apart from Lil, they head out for a picnic, and then return hand in hand singing shows tunes. Potter, thrilled at having someone his own age for companionship realizes he might have been sending the wrong signals when Lil tries to take their relationship to another level. In the meantime, Hawkeye gives his best effort, which includes sending out nearly 30 telegrams, to find out what B.J.'s initials stand for.

PA Announcement by Sal Viscuso
Authors' Notes: The only thing to see out of the office windows is the side of a corrugated structure.

In Chapter 5, Roy is wearing a light blue and brown pattern civilian shirt. This shirt will be seen two more times in this episode worn by two other corpsmen.

Potterism: "Jim Dandy-Dee."

According to Klinger, the date is September 10.

In Chapter 3, Radar mentions that Colonel Potter took Lil to show her the laundry room. We've never seen a laundry room, but we have seen local Koreans, mostly women, come by to either pick up or deliver laundry.

Our Finest Hour – 10/9/1978

Season 7 / Episode 151 and Episode 152
Production 155 and Production 156 – T408 / T409

Columbia House VHS Tape . . . . *A Different View (Catalog # 19505)*
Fox DVD . . . . *Season 7, Disc 1*

Alan Alda, Mike Farrell, Harry Morgan
Loretta Swit, David Ogden Stiers, Gary Burghoff, Jamie Farr, William Christopher

Executive Producer – Burt Metcalfe
Produced by David Lawrence
Executive Script Consultants – Ken Levine & David Isaacs
Written by Ken Levine & David Isaacs and Larry Balmagia & Ronny Graham
and David Lawrence
Directed by Burt Metcalfe

Co-Producer – Phil Savenick
Story Editor – Larry Balmagia
Story Consultant – Ronny Graham
Creative Consultants – Gene Reynolds / Alan Alda
Special thanks to Wayne Rogers, McLean Stevenson, Larry Linville

Writers – Alan Alda, Linda Bloodworth, Linda Bloodworth & Mary Kay Place,
Glen Charles & Les Charles, Bernard Dilbert, Sid Dorfman, Jay Folb, Jim Fritzell
& Everett Greenbaum, Larry Gelbart, Larry Gelbart & Laurence Marks, Ed
Jurist, Allan Katz, Sheldon Keller, Carl Kleinschmitt, Ken Levine & David Isaacs,
Laurence Marks, Richard M. Powell Burt Prelutsky, Don Reo, Gene Reynolds,
Gene Reynolds & Jay Folb

Directors – Alan Alda, Hy Averback, Jackie Cooper, Joan Darling, Larry Gelbart,
William Jurgensen, Burt Metcalfe, Gene Reynolds, Don Weis, William Wiard

Clete Roberts . . . . Himself
Copyright 1978 – 20th Century Fox Film Corporation

*Note: This was a one-hour episode when it first aired in 1978. In syndication, it was made
into two parts. The DVD has the option of playing this as a one-hour episode or in two
half-hour episodes. The master material was damaged and Fox decided it was not good
enough for DVD release, so the syndication version was used instead.*

Chapters – Part 1

1: Main Titles	6: Longings – 7:14
2: MovieTone News – 0:56	7: Family – 11:49
3: Interviewing Captain Pierce – 2:34	8: A New Arrival – 16:19
4: Talking to Colonel Potter – 3:57	9: About Margaret – 19:25
5: Requisitions – 5:11	10: End Titles – 22:50

Closing Stills – Part 1

1: Freeze – Hawkeye from, "Carry On, Hawkeye"
2: Hawkeye (Black & White)
3: B.J. (Black & White)
4: Potter (Black & White)
5: Margaret (Black & White)

6: Charles (Black & White)
7: Radar (Black & White)
8: Klinger (Black & White)
9: Mulcahy (Black & White)

Note: The closing stills are the same for both parts 1 and 2. Only the freeze-frame is different, and only the freeze-frame in part 1 of Hawkeye is in color.

Chapters – Part 2

1:	Main Titles	6:	The Effects of War – 10:24
2:	A Brutal Climate – 1:24	7:	One Bad Day – 13:58
3:	Relaxation – 2:40	8:	The Wounded Keep Coming – 18:54
4:	Klinger's Obsession – 5:54	9:	Rules of War – 21:38
5:	Get Me Out of Here – 8:51	10:	End Titles – 22:29

Closing Stills – Part 2

1: Freeze – Clete Roberts
2: Hawkeye (Black & White)
3: B.J. (Black & White)
4: Potter (Black & White)
5: Margaret (Black & White)
6: Charles (Black & White)
7: Radar (Black & White)
8: Klinger (Black & White)
9: Mulcahy (Black & White)

Synopsis: Reprising his role as an interviewer, Clete Roberts again finds himself at the 4077th, largely in part due to the unit's efficiency. Originally broadcast as an hour-long episode, "Our Finest Hour," although similar to Season 4's "The Interview," differs in that it's interspersed with memorable color clips of past episodes with the laugh track left in. During the interviews, members of the 4077th discuss what the other members mean to them, how they feel about being there and the memories they'll take home from the experience.

Commentary by Ken Levine: "This took forever to put together. After working all day, we would travel to a production studio in Hollywood and pour through hours and hours of past episodes. Phil Savenick and Susan Walker came aboard to handle that aspect of the show. For the wrap around, we decided to retrieve Clete Roberts and 'The Interview' set up. If I had to make that decision today, I would not have gone that way. 'The Interview,' like all masterpieces, didn't need a sequel."

Authors' Notes: The only PA announcement in this episode is by Todd Sussman from Episode 45, Season 2's "Crisis."
  Non-credited appearances, compiled from past clips, contain Kellye Nakahara, Dennis troy, Roy Goldman, Jeff Maxwell and Gwen Farrell.
  Since the original master was damaged and, as per 20th Century Fox, unworthy of DVD release, "Our Finest Hour" was taken from the syndication version and as a result, there's no option to remove the laugh track.
  Although "Our Finest Hour" was filmed in black and white, all of the clips shown from previous episodes are in color, with the exception of Season 1's "Cowboy." The clip from this episode has Radar riding to the chopper pad on the running board of an ambulance and hopping off to open the rear doors, and is the only color clip shown in black and white.

As per Clete Roberts, the date is October 9, 1952. This will become significant later in the series when, celebrating New Year's Eve, Colonel Potter welcomes 1952.

In the clip from Season 3's "Officer of the Day," Radar finally closes the office doors for privacy when taking his pants off, unaware of the Korean woman behind him watching. In this episode, she says "Excuse please, mister." However, in the original "Officer of the Day" episode, she does not speak at all.

In the clip from the Pilot episode, Frank and Margaret are watching, through binoculars, Hawkeye fawn over Lieutenant Dish. In this episode, Frank calls them "animals" twice. In the original Pilot episode, he says this only once.

The Billfold Syndrome – 10/16/1978

Season 7 / Episode 153 / Production 152 – T405

Columbia House VHS Tape . . . . *Paging Dr. Freedman (Catalog # 19503)*

Fox DVD . . . . *Season 7, Disc 1*

Alan Alda, Mike Farrell, Harry Morgan
Loretta Swit, David Ogden Stiers, Gary Burghoff, Jamie Farr, William Christopher

Produced by Burt Metcalfe
Executive Script Consultants – Ken Levine & David Isaacs
Written by Ken Levine & David Isaacs
Directed by Alan Alda

Story Editor – Larry Balmagia
Story Consultant – Ronny Graham
Creative Consultants – Gene Reynolds / Alan Alda

Allan Arbus . . . . Dr. Sidney Freedman
Kevin Geer . . . . Sergeant Jerry Nielson

Copyright 1978 – 20th Century Fox Film Corporation

Non-Credited Appearances. . . . . Kellye Nakahara, Gwen Farrell, Roy Goldman

Chapters

1: *Main Titles / Do Me A Favor*	6: *It Happened One Night – 11:46*
2: *Fear and Loathing – 3:07*	7: *Psychiatric Exam – 13:33*
3: *The Silent Treatment – 5:26*	8: *The Mummy Speaks – 16:10*
4: *A Little White Scam – 9:31*	9: *Hypnosis – 18:54*
5: *Amnesia – 10:40*	10: *Heads Up / End Titles – 23:14*

Closing Stills

1: *Freeze – The Swamped collapsed from Charles*
2: *Sidney Freedman*
3: *Jerry Nielson*
4: *Hawkeye*
5: *B.J.*
6: *Potter*
7: *Margaret*
8: *Klinger in the mess tent*
9: *Radar in the office*
10: *Mulcahy on the piano (Officer's Club)*
11: *Charles in the Officer's Club*

Synopsis: Sergeant Jerry Nielson, a medic with the 5th Regimental Combat Team, makes his third trip accompanying the wounded to the 4077th, but on the bus, Hawkeye questions the way bandages were applied. The usually steady medic, who wanted to be a doctor himself and with no apparent wounds, displays signs of amnesia by asking Hawkeye if he's the person identified on his dog tags. Sidney Freedman is called to the unit where, under hypnosis, Nielson recounts the events leading to his sudden memory loss. Meanwhile, Charles receives a message from Massachusetts General Hospital to inform him that since he's in Korea, they had no choice but to appoint someone else as the chief of thoracic surgery. Charles then vows never again to talk to anyone at the 4077th, a challenge that Hawkeye and B.J. simply cannot pass up.

Commentary by Ken Levine: "Again, this was taken from research. I'm very proud of this episode. We consulted a prominent psychiatrist on the procedure of hypnotizing (how would it work, what would the doctors say, etc.) It was maybe our most dramatic episode, coupled with a lot of fun silliness. I remember Alan Alda directed and did a superb job."

PA Announcement by Sal Viscuso

Authors' Note: The same civilian shirt is seen being worn by two different corpsmen (at two different times).

None like it Hot – 10/23/1978

Season 7 / Episode 154 / Production 157 – T410

Columbia House VHS Tape . . . . Not Released by Columbia House

Fox DVD . . . . Season 7, Disc 1

Alan Alda, Mike Farrell, Harry Morgan
Loretta Swit, David Ogden Stiers, Gary Burghoff, Jamie Farr, William Christopher

Produced by Burt Metcalfe
Executive Script Consultants – Ken Levine & David Isaacs
Written by Ken Levine & David Isaacs and Johnny Bonaduce
Directed by Tony Mordente

Story Editor – Larry Balmagia
Story Consultant – Ronny Graham
Creative Consultants – Gene Reynolds / Alan Alda

Ted Gehring . . . . Sergeant Clifford Rhoden
Supply Sergeant. . . . . 222nd Combat Engineers
Johnny Haymer. . . . . Sergeant Zelmo Zale
Jeff Maxwell. . . . . .Private Igor
Jan Jorden . . . . Nurse Baker
Kellye Nakahara . . . . .Nurse Kellye
Mic Rodgers . . . . Private

Copyright 1978 – 20th Century Fox Film Corporation

Non-Credited Appearances. . . . . Dennis Troy, Roy Goldman

Chapters

1: Main Titles / Xanadu	6: A Long Queue – 12:08
2: Furball – 3:07	7: Not For Sale – 13:53
3: Sneak Preview – 4:18	8: It's About Time – 15:41
4: 24 Hours – 6:29	9: Fight Club – 17:51
5: Privacy, Please – 8:35	10: I Scream / End Titles – 19:25

Closing Stills

1: Freeze – Klinger in Margaret's tent w/ ice cream
2: Hawkeye, Sergeant Rhoden and Radar
3: Nurses in the mess tent
4: Hawkeye in the tub with a rubber duck
5: B.J.
6: Potter in the office
7: Margaret in her tent
8: Charles
9: Radar in the office
10: Mulcahy
11: Klinger in mink coat & blue wool hat

Synopsis: When Hawkeye and B.J. get a canvas bathtub from Abercrombie & Fitch, trying to keep it a secret in the 104-degree heat proves impossible. Charles threatens to tell the entire camp unless he's allowed to use it, but word gets out anyway, and before long, Igor has to stand guard over the long line of personnel waiting their turn. Proving a disruption, Potter orders Hawkeye and B.J. to get rid of the tub, and they trade it for something that will make Radar feel better after his tonsillectomy.

Commentary from stuntman, Michael Rodgers: "I was in the episode about the bathtub. And I didn't even know I had any lines. I said, 'What lines? I'm a stunt man.' So, I quickly went over them before the scene. While everyone was in line to use the bathtub, I was supposed to come back and say, 'Thanks for saving my place in line' to another guy. Well, we shot it, and I kind of blew my line. David Ogden Stiers made a point of kind of saying, 'One more time for the stuntman.' I really wished he hadn't said it. I felt so bad. He was poking fun, but was the professional actor. The set was very friendly, and it was one day's work. I ended up coordinating the fight."

Commentary by Ken Levine: "Research prompted this story. Every year, we tried to do a few just silly, funny episodes, and this was one of them."

PA Announcement by Sal Viscuso

Authors' Notes: Sergeant Clifford Rhoden was named after Los Angeles Dodger's pitcher, number 36, Rick Rhoden.

Klinger's ploy to get out of the Army in this episode is by dehydration or heat prostration, and nearly succeeds.

In Chapter 2, for the only time during *M*A*S*H's* entire run, Potter wants Radar to burn incense. Incense?

The sinks in the scrub room in Chapter 3 are side by side in the middle of the room. This is also the first time an autoclave is seen in the wall.

Sometimes, the tops of jockey shorts can be seen on Hawkeye as he gets into or out of the showers. In this episode however, when he gets out of the canvas tub in Chapter 3, what appears to be bikini underwear or Olympic-type bikini swimming trunks are seen.

The only view seen through the office windows in Chapter 4 is the side of a corrugated structure.

A microphone shadow can be seen bobbing up and down and to the left of Klinger as he's behind Potter's desk in Chapter 4.

A blue civilian shirt with a red floral pattern is seen being worn by two different corpsmen at two different times.

In Chapter 6, Roy Goldman is wearing Trapper's yellow robe, however, later in Chapter 9, a different corpsman is wearing it.

Also in Chapter 9, Sergeant Zale is wearing the robe usually worn by Henry Blake.

Chapter 9 also contains a big visual flub. While Radar is being operated on for his tonsils, a fight breaks out on the bathtub line. As Charles calls attention to the fight, everyone on line leaves his or her spot to see the fight, while others come running, including Radar holding a football.

Sergeant Rhoden arrives at the 4077th in jeep 20963388. As with the other jeeps, they have multiple uses and owners.

A strange-moving shadow is seen on the mess tent roof in Chapter 10, but there doesn't seem to be anything visible causing it and doesn't coincide with anyone's or anything's movement.

For the second time in this episode, a second Corpsman is seen wearing the robe usually worn by Henry.

It's implied that Margaret is naked in the tub when Klinger, suffering from the heat, runs into the tub-tent. Margaret runs out screaming while trying to cover up with a towel. What's odd about this is that, instead of running into her tent, she runs right into the mess tent.

Michael Rodgers worked on such shows as *The Bionic Woman, Wonder Woman, Switch, The Incredible Hulk, Hart to Hart, Baa-Baa Black Sheep* and was Mel Gibson's stunt double in the Lethal Weapon movies. He was also second unit director on *Braveheart* and *Charlie's Angels II.*

They Call the Wind Korea – 10/30/1978

Season 7 / Episode 155 / Production 154 – T407

Columbia House VHS Tape. . . . . *Local Color (Catalog # 19506)*
Fox DVD . . . . *Season 7, Disc 1*

Alan Alda, Mike Farrell, Harry Morgan
Loretta Swit, David Ogden Stiers, Gary Burghoff, Jamie Farr, William Christopher

Produced by Burt Metcalfe
Executive Script Consultants – Ken Levine & David Isaacs
Written by Ken Levine & David Isaacs
Directed by Charles Dubin

Story Editor – Larry Balmagia
Story Consultant – Ronny Graham
Creative Consultants – Gene Reynolds / Alan Alda

Enid Kent . . . . Nurse Bigelow
Paul Cavonis . . . . Sergeant Cutrifiotis
Tom Dever . . . . M.P.
Rusty Stumpf . . . . Greek Soldier

Copyright 1978 – 20th Century Fox Film Corporation

Non-Credited Appearances. . . . . Kellye Nakahara, Gwen Farrell, Roy Goldman

Chapters

1:	Main Titles / L'Artiste	6:	Where's Babette? – 12:30
2:	Two Crisis – 3:33	7:	Improvisation – 14:49
3:	Cradle Will Rock – 6:13	8:	Land of Surprises – 18:38
4:	Bad Accident – 7:42	9:	Lets Be Serious – 20:21
5:	Greek To Me – 8:43	10:	Oh, No! / End Titles – 22:16

Closing Stills

1: Freeze – Charles on the Ranch compound
2: Hawkeye and Nurse Bigelow
3: Charles
4: Klinger
5: Potter painting in his office
6: Margaret
7: Radar
8: B.J. (Red suspenders)
9: Mulcahy
10: Hawkeye in Post-Op

Synopsis: Charles' first vacation hits a snag when choppers are grounded due to a freezing windstorm heading their way from Manchuria. Klinger balks at the idea of driving him to Seoul because it would mean he'd have to drive back in the storm, but Potter gives him permission to stay overnight. Getting lost on the way, they come across an overturned truck with wounded Greek soldiers. Charles performs impromptu surgery in the back of the truck and they stay there to wait out the storm, only to discover that they didn't have to stay in the truck.

Commentary by Ken Levine: "The subplot had Radar losing his pet hamster. We used the name Babette, which was our family dog growing up. My mother named the dog, and was teased constantly for it. In the show, there is a lot of ribbing about the name. My mom called after the show and said 'Ha, ha...Very funny.'"

Commentary by Enid Kent Sperber: "David Ogden Stiers, the consummate professional, had a passion for music and conducting. He owned my recordings of the same symphonies conducted by different artists. He loved to listen to these recordings and practice conducting 'in the style of.' He loved the fact that our stage at Twentieth Century Fox was near the famous scoring stage presided over in various years by the illustrious Newman composing family. I do have fond memories of him jumping on the [skate] board and announcing to the stage manager that he was heading over to the score stage. At this point this tall lanky fellow would glide out the large open door to the sound stage and ride over to hear live music."

Authors' Notes: There are no PA announcements in this episode.

Ken Levine, in his commentary, calls Babette a hamster, but this particular rodent was a guinea pig.

Not much to see out of the office windows in Chapter 1, other than the side of a corrugated building through the left window and the same wooden structure through the right, but further away than in previous episodes.

In Chapter 1, Potter says the water towers are "swaying like Little Egypt." Little Egypt was the stage name for two popular exotic dancers of the late 1800's: Farida Mazar Spyropoulos (also performing under the stage name Fatima), and Ashea Wabe.

Jeep number 18210717 is now a military police jeep at the checkpoint in Chapter 2.

True to his word using the names of the Los Angeles Dodgers, Hawkeye checks on Private Yeager in Post-Op, named after the Dodgers catcher, Number 7, Steve Yeager.

Major Ego – 11/6/1978

Season 7 / Episode 156 / Production 159 – T412
Columbia House VHS Tape. . . . . *Egos, Exorcisms, Etc (Catalog # 22051)*
Fox DVD . . . . *Season 7, Disc 1*

Alan Alda, Mike Farrell, Harry Morgan
Loretta Swit, David Ogden Stiers, Gary Burghoff, Jamie Farr, William Christopher

Produced by Burt Metcalfe
Executive Script Consultants – Ken Levine & David Isaacs
Written by Larry Balmagia
Directed by Alan Alda

Story Editor – Larry Balmagia
Story Consultant – Ronny Graham
Creative Consultants – Gene Reynolds / Alan Alda

Greg Mullavey. . . . . Captain Tom Greenleigh
David Dean. . . . . Private Sutton
Patricia Stevens . . . . Duty Nurse
Phyllis Katz. . . . . Triage Nurse
Frank Pettinger . . . . Anesthetist
Roy Goldman . . . . Corpsman
Copyright 1978 – 20th Century Fox Film Corporation

Non-Credited Appearances. . . . . Kellye Nakahara

Chapters

1:	Main Titles	6:	Surgical Discourse – 10:53
2:	A Bad Attitude – 1:27	7:	A Medical Concern – 13:03
3:	Mail Call – 4:13	8:	Emergency Surgery – 18:27
4:	A Reporter – 5:52	9:	The Boston Bungler – 20:51
5:	Incoming Wounded – 9:05	10:	End Titles – 23:21

Closing Stills

1: Freeze – Margaret and Charles in the mess tent
2: Captain Greenleigh (Stage 9 Compound)
3: Charles in Post-Op
4: Hawkeye in the Swamp
5: B.J. in the Swamp
6: Margaret
7: Potter in the office
8: Mulcahy
9: Radar in the office
10: Klinger in the Swamp

Synopsis: After Charles performs a tricky operation, he calls the lead in to Stars & Stripes in the hopes that a favorable article about his surgical skills will land him a position in Tokyo. When a reporter with Stars & Stripes arrives, Charles becomes more interested in telling his life story than he is about a patient he operated on who might be hemorrhaging, and Hawkeye has no choice but to operate on the man, again, infuriating Charles. But when Hawkeye finds that the man was indeed hemorrhaging, Charles realizes that his recent encounter with the press nearly cost a man his life. Meanwhile, Margaret finds out that Donald has tied up their joint savings until the divorce is finalized.

Authors' Notes: In Chapter 3, the wooden structure with double doors is closer than it has been in previous episodes.

Also in Chapter 3, Margaret is seen walking past the office windows, then a corpsman in the background.

In Chapter 5, the barber's tent is clearly seen on the Ranch compound, but in previous episodes, Kellye is seen giving haircuts, usually to Igor, on the Stage 9 compound.

In Chapter 7, there's a wounded G.I. in Post-Op named Private Sutton, named after the Los Angeles Dodgers pitcher, number 20, Don Sutton, and another wounded G.I. named Martinez, named after the Los Angeles Dodgers infielder, number 23, Ted Martinez.

Private Sutton (from above) said he was wounded at Pork Chop Hill. The battle at Pork Chop Hill is one of the most famous of the Korean War and took place during the spring and summer of 1953. However, according to Clete Roberts in episodes 151 and 152, "Our Finest Hour," the date is October 9, 1952. Later in the series, during a New Year's Eve celebration, Colonel Potter will welcome the year 1952.

Two different corpsmen are seen wearing the same civilian shirt at two different times in Chapter 8.

In Chapter 9, Klinger mentions the name Darryl Zanuck. Mr. Zanuck founded Twentieth Century Pictures with Joseph Schenck and William Goetz. In 1935, they bought out Fox Studios to form Twentieth Century Fox. Mr. Zanuck was the vice-president and actively involved producing and editing.

Also in Chapter 9, Margaret sits next to Charles in the mess tent and when she taps him with her elbow, Charles' coffee spills onto the table. This appears to be accidental and not scripted.

Baby, it's Cold Outside – 11/13/1978

Season 7 / Episode 157 / Production 150 – T403

Columbia House VHS Tape............... *Not Released by Columbia House*
Fox DVD ....*Season 7, Disc 2*

Alan Alda, Mike Farrell, Harry Morgan
Loretta Swit, David Ogden Stiers, Gary Burghoff, Jamie Farr, William Christopher

Produced by Burt Metcalfe
Executive Script Consultants – Ken Levine & David Isaacs
Written by Gary David Goldberg
Directed by George Tyne

Story Editor – Larry Balmagia
Story Consultant – Ronny Graham
Creative Consultants – Gene Reynolds / Alan Alda

Jan Jorden .... Nurse Baker
Terry Willis... Driver
Teck Murdock.. Patient
David Cramer .... Patient
Copyright 1978 – 20th Century Fox Film Corporation

Non-Credited Appearances.........................Gwen Farrell, Dennis Troy

Chapters

1:	Main Titles / Arctic Blast	6:	Ah, Sonja – 14:42
2:	Freezer Section – 3:23	7:	Dear Departed – 16:16
3:	Thick and Thin – 5:53	8:	Win Some... - 19:07
4:	Say What? – 9:48	9:	...Lose Some – 20:31
5:	Touch and Go – 12:29	10:	Thief! / End Titles – 21:34

Closing Stills

1: Freeze – Margaret and Charles in the mess tent
2: Hawkeye in Post-Op
3: Klinger in Post-Op
4: B.J. in Post-Op
5: Margaret
6: Charles in heavy parka
7: Radar
8: Mulcahy in Post-Op
9: Potter in Post-Op

Synopsis: A bone-chilling wintry day in Korea gets even colder for the staff when Potter orders all the tent heaters into post-op. Charles has no problem with the biting cold since his folks sent him a heavy polar suit, and has no problem wearing it in front of the wounded in pre-op, some of which are suffering the effects of frostbite and hypothermia. The cold helps save Sergeant Davalillo's life by keeping him from bleeding to death, but he's still in danger since his body temperature barely registers on a thermometer, and when the cold sets off landmines, Klinger loses his hearing, which could send him home.

PA Announcements by Sal Viscuso

Authors' Notes: Potterism: "I'll be the son of Princess Papuli." NOTE – Although the captioning spells the word p-a-p-u-l-i, the word also appears as p-o-o-p-o-o-l-y, p-u-p-u-l-e, and p-a-p-u-l-e. Poopooly is a play on the Hawaiian word purple. Written for Carmen Joyce, a Ziegfield Follies chorus girl who arrived in Hawaii in 1924, at the age of 26, to dance in the chorus line of a show booked in the Princess Theater (according to *Wikipedia.)*

In Chapter 4, a patient in Post-Op, Sergeant Davalillo, is named after the Los Angeles Dodger outfielder, number 33, Vic Davalillo.

Point of View – 11/20/1978

Season 7 / Episode 158 / Production 162 – T415

Columbia House VHS Tape. . . . . *A Different View (Catalog # 19505)*
Fox DVD . . . . *Season 7, Disc 2*

Alan Alda, Mike Farrell, Harry Morgan
Loretta Swit, David Ogden Stiers, Gary Burghoff, Jamie Farr, William Christopher

Produced by Burt Metcalfe
Executive Script Consultants – Ken Levine & David Isaacs
Written by Ken Levine & David Isaacs
Directed by Charles Dubin

Story Editor – Larry Balmagia
Story Consultant – Ronny Graham
Creative Consultants – Gene Reynolds / Alan Alda

Hank Ross. . . . . .Ferguson
Brad Gorman . . . . Russell
Marc Baxley. . . . . The Sergeant
Jan Jorden . . . . Nurse Baker
Edward Gallardo. . . . . Medic 1
David Stafford. . . . . .The Soldier
Paul Tuerpe . . . . Medic 2
Copyright 1978 – 20th Century Fox Film Corporation

Non-Credited Appearances. . . . . Kellye Nakahara, Gwen Farrell

Chapters

1: *Main Titles*
2: *Through A Soldier's Eyes – 0:54*
3: *The Toledo Express – 3:56*
4: *The Waiting Room – 6:12*
5: *X-rays and Operations – 8:51*
6: *The Recovery Room – 10:39*
7: *A Sponge Bath and A Tour – 13:54*
8: *Potter's Problem – 17:35*
9: *The Talk of the Town – 20:49*
10: *Going Home / End Titles – 22:48*

Closing Stills

1: *Freeze – Pvt. Rich looking out back bus window*
2: *Ferguson in Post-Op*
3: *Patient Russell in Post-Op*
4: *Potter talking to Pvt. Rich*
5: *Radar talking to Pvt. Rich*
6: *B.J. talking to Pvt. Rich*
7: *Margaret talking to Pvt. Rich*
8: *Mulcahy talking to Pvt. Rich*
9: *Charles in the Swamp*
10: *Klinger talking to Pvt. Rich*
11: *Hawkeye talking to Pvt. Rich*

Synopsis: While on patrol with his unit, Private Rich sustains a shrapnel wound to his throat after coming under fire. In an Emmy-nominated episode for writing and directing, "Point of View," filmed without a laugh track, offers the unique perspective of seeing the entire process through Private Rich's eyes. Given a sense of what it was like to be wounded, strapped to the rumble seat of a chopper and being taken care of at the 4077th, we also see the staff's interaction with the wounded in a way never seen before, and the calming effect they have in reassuring Rich that he's in good hands.

Commentary by Ken Levine: "My favorite of all our episodes. I pitched this idea of doing a show from the point of view of the soldier the year before, but it was tabled. I knew it would be a gamble, either the best or worst show of the season. Finally, we went for it in the seventh season. There was an old Sam Spade movie called Lady in the Lake that used this device. We screened it, and found it seemed to work except when the lead talked. Then, it was very uncomfortable as you just watched someone staring at you. That gave us the idea to give the patient a throat injury so he couldn't talk. So much credit for the success of this episode must go to director Charles Dubin. Without the benefit of all the portable hand held cameras of today, he managed to pull off expertly a very difficult task. I must admit that, when I saw the final version, I was horrified. We watched it on a huge movie screen and when Radar leans in and his head fills the room, you gasp. But, on television, where the size is more life-like, it worked beautifully."

PA Announcement by Sal Viscuso

Authors' Notes: Alan Alda likes this episode.

For this episode, "Ferguson" was named after Joe Ferguson, number 13, a catcher with the Los Angeles Dodgers and "Russell" was named after Bill Russell, number 18, an infielder with the Dodgers.

In Chapter 6, a patient is reading *Visiting Nurse,* written by Helen Dore Boylston in 1938, a nurse herself who graduated from Massachusetts General Hospital in 1915 and served at a front-line medical unit in WWI.

In Chapter 8, the date on a letter Private Rich is writing to his folks is [Wednesday] September 12, 1951.

According to Potter, his 35th wedding anniversary was last Saturday, making his wedding date September 8, 1916; for the first time, he forgot to call Mildred on their anniversary, and he can't seem to forgive himself for it. However, it's somewhat understandable when you consider the following:

Although this episode clearly takes place on [Wednesday] September 12, 1951, in "Welcome to Korea" (Episodes 73 and 74), Potter took command of the 4077th on [Friday] September 19, 1952 and in Episode 80, he said he and Mildred have been married for 27 years. This means they were married in 1925. His son was born in 1926.

But in Episode 132, he and Mildred were married in 1913 and they will have been married for 38 years "this April." This puts Episode 132 in 1951.

Who can blame him for not remembering his anniversary?

Dear Comrade – 11/27/1978

Season 7 / Episode 159 / Production 160 – T413

Columbia House VHS Tape. . . . . Going Under Cover (Catalog # 13119)
Fox DVD . . . . Season 7, Disc 2

Alan Alda, Mike Farrell, Harry Morgan
Loretta Swit, David Ogden Stiers, Gary Burghoff, Jamie Farr, William Christopher

Produced by Burt Metcalfe
Executive Script Consultants – Ken Levine & David Isaacs
Written by Tom Reeder
Directed by Charles Dubin

Story Editor – Larry Balmagia
Story Consultant – Ronny Graham
Creative Consultants – Gene Reynolds / Alan Alda

Sab Shimono. . . . . Mr. Kwang Yong
Larry Block. . . . . Sergeant Cimoli
Robert Clotworthy . . . . .Private Welch
David Dozer . . . . Groves
James Saito . . . . Korean Soldier
Todd Davis . . . . Latimer
Laurie Bates . . . . Surgical Nurse
Dennis Troy. . . . . Corpsman 1
Wayne Long . . . . Corpsman 2
Copyright 1978 – 20th Century Fox Film Corporation

Non-Credited Appearances. . . . . Kellye Nakahara, Gwen Farrell

Chapters

1: Main Titles	6: A Delivery – 11:00
2: The Major's Aria – 0:54	7: Local Remedy – 14:39
3: Hired Help – 2:26	8: Cannon Modification – 16:40
4: Poker Night – 5:48	9: Kwang's Reward – 20:36
5: A Mysterious Rash – 8:13	10: End Titles – 23:31

Closing Stills

1: Freeze – Potter, Kwang, Charles, Hawkeye, BJ – Club
2: Kwang in Post-Op
3: Hawkeye in the Swamp
4: Potter in the compound
5: Charles in the Swamp
6: B.J. in M.P. helmet
7: Klinger in the mess tent
8: Margaret in Post-Op
9: Mulcahy in Post-Op

Synopsis: The 4077th's reputation for saving lives is well-known, even by the enemy, and Charles' newly hired Korean houseboy is there to learn how they do it. Acting under orders from the Intelligence Section of the People's Army, Kwang Yong conducts covert surveillance of the 4077th. What he learns is how undisciplined their behavior is in O.R., and when they're off-duty, even worse. Describing the Americans as "woefully unin-formed about Korea" after they're unable to identify and treat a rash that causes severe itching, it's Kwang who comes up with a local remedy to treat the rash, earning himself a Certificate of Merit.

Commentary by Sab Shimono: "I had just come from New York, and it was one of my first auditions in L.A. I hadn't really watched the show, before, but once I saw the script I knew it was a terrific part. It was a privilege to have *M*A*S*H* as one of my first jobs. I had been a page at NBC before then, and it was amazing to see someone like Woody Allen showing up for The Tonight Show and be totally nervous about it. Everyone (on *M*A*S*H)* was helpful and supportive of me. They helped loosen me up. During one take, we were all supposed to walk in and Harry Morgan pulled my shirt so I couldn't walk in (as a joke). The cast would go over the script and seemed to learn the lines right there. Not that they didn't study at home, but they would learn them right as we read the script. They fooled around right up until the director yelled 'Action.' And then, it was magic. It seemed like there was no director. Everything seemed relaxed and effortless, like butter. And the extras were all part of the family. My character was so strong, that I read they thought of making him a recurring character."

PA Announcement by Sal Viscuso

Authors' Notes: Although the names "Pierce and Hunnicutt" are heard in the PA announcement, their names are left off the captioning.

Private Welch is named after Los Angeles Dodger pitcher, Bob Welch, number 35.

Hawkeye's serial number in this episode is 0260-103. However, in Season 4's "The Late Captain Pierce," his serial number is US 19905607.

We don't see Charles in many civilian shirts, but we see him wearing one in Chapter 4.

The same wooden structure is seen through the office windows in Chapter 5.

The jeep in Chapter 6, serial number 20963388, is now Sergeant Cimoli's, as it's the jeep used to deliver Hawkeye's howitzer.

Also, the howitzer in Chapter 6 has two different tires and they also appear to be two different sizes with one being larger in circumference than the other.

Potterism: "Sweet Limburger, that's a nose breaker, that is." This is in reference to the boiled tree bark used to treat the rash on the wounded. The smell is so bad that it causes Margaret to gasp. Where is the incense Radar was burning five episodes ago in "None Like it Hot"?

In Chapter 7, Hawkeye mentions, "B.O. Plenty," a character in the Dick Tracy comic strip who first appeared in 1945.

Out of Gas – 12/4/1978

Season 7 / Episode 156 / Production 154 – T411
Columbia House VHS Tape.................... Charles (Catalog # 13117)
Fox DVD .... Season 7, Disc 2

Alan Alda, Mike Farrell, Harry Morgan
Loretta Swit, David Ogden Stiers, Gary Burghoff, Jamie Farr, William Christopher

Produced by Burt Metcalfe
Executive Script Consultants – Ken Levine & David Isaacs
Written by Tom Reeder
Directed by Mel Danski

Story Editor – Larry Balmagia
Story Consultant – Ronny Graham
Creative Consultants – Gene Reynolds / Alan Alda

Johnny Haymer..................................... Sergeant Zelmo Zale
Justin Lord .... Harkness
Byron Chung... Myung
George Clairborne .... Phelan
Copyright 1978 – 20th Century Fox Film Corporation

Non-Credited Appearances.......... Kellye Nakahara, Dennis Troy, Roy Goldman,
Gwen Farrell is Nurse Carson

Chapters

1: Main Titles / Hot Hand	6: What A Bargain – 16:02
2: Mr. Snake Oil – 3:28	7: Happy Hour – 18:07
3: A Modern War – 6:19	8: Fair's Fair – 19:16
4: Black Marketeer – 10:17	9: A Real Blessing – 20:37
5: Small Talk – 14:56	10: Oh, My Wine / End Titles – 22:01

Closing Stills

1: *Freeze – Charles, "Oh, my wine" in O.R.*
2: *Zale in Potter's office*
3: *Charles and Black Marketeers*
4: *Hawkeye in the break room*
5: *B.J. – poker in the Officer's Club*
6: *Mulcahy in Post-Op*
7: *Potter in Post-Op*
8: *Margaret*
9: *Radar*
10: *Klinger*
11: *Charles*

Synopsis: When the 4077th is forced to use ether when they run out of sodium pentothal, they're also forced to shut the heaters in O.R., because ether can explode. Using ether brings other problems as well since not all the nurses have experience using it and Margaret, after breathing in too much of it, passes out during surgery. Radar's failed attempts to locate the valuable anesthetic leaves the unit with little choice but to go through the Black Market, and surprisingly, it's Father Mulcahy who has the connections, and it's Charles' vintage wine that's offered in trade.

Authors' Notes: There are no PA announcements in this episode.

In Chapter 1, Mulcahy is wearing the robe usually worn by Henry Blake. This is the third robe Mulcahy has been seen wearing.

As in some previous episodes, the view from the office windows in Chapter 2 is still a wooden structure and there are people milling about.

In Chapter 3, Radar is on the phone trying to get sodium pentothal and speaks with Colonel Hooten. Colonel Hooten is named after the Los Angeles Dodgers pitcher, number 46, Burt Hooton. *(Note: The name Hooten, as it appears in the captioning, is spelled wrong. There is no "e" in Hooton.)*

Radar's serial number in Chapter 3 is RA 1949069. However, in Episode 102, Season 5's "Lieutenant Radar O'Reilly," his serial number was 3911810.

In the change room in Chapter 4, the names over the coat hooks are, from left to right, Potter, Hawkeye, B.J., Winchester, and Mulcahy.

Also in Chapter 4, the scrub room is seen from the change room, but this time, the sinks are against the wall, side by side. In several previous episodes, the sinks are in the middle of the room.

Colonel Potter, in Chapter 9, mentions that he's going to kick Winchester's butt from now until St. Swithin's Day (also spelled Swithun). Saint Swithin was an early English Bishop of Winchester who died on July 2, 1862.

Potterism: "What in the Sam Hill is that?"

An Eye for A Tooth – 12/11/1978

Season 7 / Episode 161 / Production 161 – T414

Columbia House VHS Tape . . . . *Father Mulcahy (Catalog # 19500)*
Fox DVD . . . . *Season 7, Disc 2*

Alan Alda, Mike Farrell, Harry Morgan
Loretta Swit, David Ogden Stiers, Gary Burghoff, Jamie Farr, William Christopher

Produced by Burt Metcalfe
Executive Script Consultants – Ken Levine & David Isaacs
Written by Ronny Graham
Directed by Charles Dubin

Story Editor – Larry Balmagia
Story Consultant – Ronny Graham
Creative Consultants – Gene Reynolds / Alan Alda
Peter Palmer . . . . Captain Toby Hill
Copyright 1978 – 20th Century Fox Film Corporation

Non-Credited Appearances. .Kellye Nakahara, Roy Goldman

Chapters

1: *Main Titles*	6: *Retaliation – 12:43*
2: *Passed Over – 0:54*	7: *Flying for A Promotion – 18:31*
3: *Capt. Hill – 3:19*	8: *Joining Forces – 19:46*
4: *Mulcahy is Irate – 8:26*	9: *Back from War – 22:10*
5: *Margaret gets Played – 10:14*	10: *End Titles – 23:31*

Closing Stills

1: *Freeze – Mulcahy – "Stop swaying"*
2: *Toby Hill*
3: *Charles in the Swamp*
4: *B.J. in the mess tent*
5: *Margaret*
6: *Potter in the office*
7: *Klinger in the mess tent*
8: *Mulcahy hit with pie in the mess tent*
9: *Hawkeye in the mess tent*

Synopsis: Captain Toby Hill has flown over 300 casualties in and out of combat, and has been promoted twice in six months, while Father Mulcahy is passed over for promotion again. Captain Hill flies with "Little Mac," a dummy the size and weight of a man, to act as a counter balance when flying with only one wounded, and when "Little Mac" is damaged, Father Mulcahy volunteers to take "Little Mac's" place in the rumble seat. "Little Mac" was damaged in a war of practical jokes that takes on a serious and dangerous tone in an attempt to get even with Charles, who's been playing both sides.

PA Announcements by Sal Viscuso

Authors' Notes: According to the PA announcement, this episode marks the first anniversary of the Officer's Club (seems like it's been there for years).
Toby Hill is wearing Trapper's yellow robe in Chapter 3.
Meanwhile in Chapter 4, Mulcahy is wearing Henry's robe.

Also in Chapter 4, the wooden structure seen through the office windows is further away than in previous episodes.

While Hawkeye and B.J. are supposed to be naked after Margaret takes their clothes out of the shower in Chapter 6, the top of Hawkeye's jockey shorts is clearly seen as he and B.J. leave the shower.

Father Mulcahy is now wearing a brown plaid robe in Chapter 6. This is the third different robe seen on the good Father. One was a blue plaid robe seen in Episode 45, Season 2's "Crisis" and Henry Blake's robe seen in this and other episodes. The brown plaid robe has also been seen in previous episodes.

Dear Sis – 12/18/1978

Season 7 / Episode 162 / Production 164 – T417

Columbia House VHS Tape . . . .*Father Mulcahy (Catalog # 19500)*
Fox DVD . . . . *Season 7, Disc 2*

Alan Alda, Mike Farrell, Harry Morgan
Loretta Swit, David Ogden Stiers, Gary Burghoff, Jamie Farr, William Christopher

Produced by Burt Metcalfe
Executive Script Consultants – Ken Levine & David Isaacs
Written and Directed by Alan Alda

Story Editor – Larry Balmagia
Story Consultant – Ronny Graham
Creative Consultants – Gene Reynolds / Alan Alda

Lawrason Driscoll . . . . .Lieutenant Forrester
Jeff Maxwell. . . . . .Igor
Patrick Driscoll . . . . Patient
W. Perren Page . . . . .Driver
Jo Ann Thompson . . . . Nurse
Copyright 1978 – 20th Century Fox Film Corporation

Non-Credited Appearances. . . . . Kellye Nakahara, Gwen Farrell, Dennis Troy,
Roy Goldman

Chapters

1: *Main Titles*
2: *Dear Sis – 0:54*
3: *An All-Purpose Blessing – 4:40*
4: *Desperate to be Useful – 7:22*
5: *Slugger Mulcahy – 10:03*
6: *Feeling Guilty – 11:08*
7: *Christmas – 14:30*
8: *Winchester's Gift – 19:01*
9: *To Father Mulcahy – 21:08*
10: *End Titles – 24:01*

Closing Stills

1: *Freeze – Snowing on Stage 9 compound*
2: *Hawkeye in Potter's office*
3: *Charles in the mess tent*
4: *Margaret in the Officer's Club*
5: *Klinger in the Officer's Club*
6: *B.J. in Potter's office*
7: *Potter in the office*
8: *Radar*
9: *Potter and Mulcahy*

Synopsis: In a letter to his sister, Father Mulcahy confesses that offering spiritual comfort doesn't seem to be enough, considering all the physical pain they deal with. No one comes to confession, much less his sermons, and wishes someone would "bend his ear" for a few minutes. Making matters worse for Mulcahy is the fact it's Christmas season and both sides try to inflict as much damage as they can before the Christmas truce. When a wounded lieutenant is brought in with the rest of the casualties, he insists only a doctor look at him and gives Margaret a difficult time of it. Mulcahy tries to make him understand that he'll be taken care of, but the lieutenant punches Mulcahy in the face. Mulcahy, who used to coach boxing for the C.Y.O., and who from time to time dons the gloves in camp, strikes the lieutenant in the jaw, knocking him over, and Mulcahy can't believe what he just did, nor can he forgive himself.

Commentary by William Christopher: "The sentimental part of 'Dear Sis' appealed to me. And I always thought they should have done a record album of all the different songs we sang on *M*A*S*H*. I mention this because of the 'peace' song in this episode. There was one episode where Mulcahy is supposed to be singing a song and the writer told me that he just wrote the 'words.' So, I made up the tune."

PA Announcement by Sal Viscuso

Authors' Notes: The scrub room, as seen from the change room in Chapter 2, has only one sink against the wall.

The names on tape over the clothes hooks in Chapter 2's change room are: *Potter, Hawkeye, B.J, Winchester.* Mulcahy's name is not there as in a previous episode, but Mulcahy is.

Potterism: "Bright as a nickel in the well water."

In Chapter 6, Father Mulcahy is looking into Post-Op from the Stage 9 compound, a view rarely seen.

Father John Patrick Francis Mulcahy, as per Hawkeye in Chapter 9.

Another rare sight happens when it snows on the compound, but it's the Stage 9 compound and the tires on the ambulance leave no marks on the new-fallen indoor snow.

B.J. Papa San – 1/1/1979

Season 7 / Episode 163 / Production 149 – T402

Columbia House VHS Tape . . . . Beej (Catalog # 19501)
Fox DVD . . . . Season 7, Disc 2

Alan Alda, Mike Farrell, Harry Morgan
Loretta Swit, David Ogden Stiers, Gary Burghoff, Jamie Farr, William Christopher

Produced by Burt Metcalfe
Executive Script Consultants – Ken Levine & David Isaacs
Written by Larry Balmagia
Directed by James Sheldon

Story Editor – Larry Balmagia
Story Consultant – Ronny Graham
Creative Consultants – Gene Reynolds / Alan Alda
Mariel Aragon. . . . . Kim Sing
Dick O'Neill . . . . Brigadier General Marion Prescott
Shizuko Hoshi . . . . .Korean Mother
Chao-Li-Chi. . . . . Su Sing, Korean Father
Johnny Haymer. . . . . Sergeant Zelmo Zale
Stephen Keep . . . . General's Aide
Copyright 1978 – 20th Century Fox Film Corporation

Non-Credited Appearances. . . . . Kellye Nakahara, Gwen Farrell, Roy Goldman

Chapters

1:	Main Titles / Just Drive	6:	Personal Physician – 12:34
2:	Gold Braid – 3:52	7:	Tracking A Soldier – 15:47
3:	Center of Attention – 5:07	8:	Stung – 17:04
4:	Foot and Wrist Disease – 7:30	9:	It's Not Fair – 20:31
5:	Blackmail – 8:18	10:	Get Me Out / End Titles – 22:56

Closing Stills

1: Freeze – Prescott leaves camp w / blown tire
2: General Prescott in Post-Op
3: Korean mother checks Korean father in their hut
4: B.J. and Kim in the hut
5: Hawkeye on Stage 9 Compound
6: Potter on the phone
7: Margaret
8: Radar carrying boxes
9: Charles
10: Klinger in Post-Op
11: Mulcahy in Post-Op
12: B.J. on Stage 9 Compound

Synopsis: When B.J. helps Su Sing, a Korean local with pneumonia, he becomes more than a doctor when he brings the family food, blankets, and repairs a hole in the hut's roof. Mr. Sing's wife now wants him to find out about their son, who they haven't seen or heard from since the South Korean Army drafted him; a task easier said than done. With a little help, B.J. manages to locate the son and tries to deliver the information only to find an abandoned hut. Back at the 4077th, Brigadier General Marion

Prescott arrives to have his foot looked at and quickly realizes he'd have been safer at the front line.

PA Announcement by Sal Viscuso

Authors' Notes: In Chapter 2, jeep number 18210717 is a Military Police jeep.

Kellye is seen in Chapter 5 giving a haircut to a corpsman on the Ranch compound, in spite of the fact that in Episode 156, "Major Ego," also on the Ranch compound, the barber's tent is clearly seen.

Charles mentions "The Katzenjammer Kids" in Chapter 8. Created by Rudolph Dirks in 1897, *The Katzenjammer Kids* comic strip is the oldest comic strip still in syndication and is today distributed by King Features Syndicate.

Also in Chapter 8, a microphone boom shadow can be seen on the curtain separating the change room and scrub room.

The names over the clothes hooks in the change room are: *Hawkeye, Potter, B.J. , Winchester.*

The view from the change room into the scrub room has changed. In Chapter 9, looking into what was the scrub room in previous episodes, now seen is a curtain where the sink or sinks (depending on the episode) used to be, and there are no visible sinks at all.

As B.J. and Hawkeye are talking outside the hut in Chapter 9, the sound of a single-engine propeller plane is heard flying overhead. However, this does not sound like a military aircraft, or that of 5 O'Clock Charlie from Season 2, but rather a privately owned aircraft out for a leisurely flight that happened to fly over the set as filming was underway.

Inga – 1/8/1979

Season 7 / Episode 164 / Production 167 – T420
Columbia House VHS Tape . . . . Egos, Exorcisms, Etc (Catalog # 22051)
Fox DVD . . . . Season 7, Disc 2

Alan Alda, Mike Farrell, Harry Morgan
Loretta Swit, David Ogden Stiers, Gary Burghoff, Jamie Farr, William Christopher

Produced by Burt Metcalfe
Executive Script Consultants – Ken Levine & David Isaacs
Written and Directed by Alan Alda

Story Editor – Larry Balmagia
Story Consultant – Ronny Graham
Creative Consultants – Gene Reynolds / Alan Alda

Mariette Hartley . . . . .Dr. Inga Halverson
Phyllis Katz . . . . Nurse
Mark Favara . . . . Patient
Copyright 1979 – 20th Century Fox Film Corporation

Non-Credited Appearances. .Kellye Nakahara, Roy Goldman

Chapters

1: Main Titles	6: Apologies – 12:43
2: The Swedish Lady Doctor – 0:55	7: The Right Way and the Wrong Way – 14:59
3: A Little Doctor Talk – 5:02	8: Inga's Opinion – 16:49
4: A New Procedure – 8:30	9: Dancing Partners – 19:09
5: Bested by A Woman – 9:59	10: End Titles – 24:02

Closing Stills

1: Freeze – Hawkeye and Margaret leaving Post-Op
2: Inga in the Officer's Club
3: B.J.
4: Potter in the mess tent
5: Margaret in Post-Op
6: Mulcahy
7: Klinger
8: Charles
9: Hawkeye

Synopsis: Dr. Inga Halverson, a Swedish doctor visiting the 4077th, makes quite an impression when she takes over an operation to show a new procedure, and Hawkeye quickly finds himself in the back row. Slighted by the gesture of a woman who is his equal, Hawkeye's behavior angers Margaret and she lets him know about it in front of everyone in the mess tent. In Post-Op, Charles later diagnoses a patient gasping for air as needing a tracheotomy, but Inga insists it's a reaction to penicillin, and even though she's correct, saving the man from unnecessary surgery, Charles is infuriated. Hawkeye comes to realize that his actions were uncalled for and tries to make it up to Inga, but he's too late as she's being reassigned in a few hours.

PA Announcement by Sal Viscuso

Authors' Notes: This is one of Alan Alda's favorite episodes.

In Chapter 2, Klinger tells Inga he needs two signatures for a Section 8. However, in Season 2, Episode 41, he needs four signatures and in Season 3, Episode 59, he needs three.

Guest star Mariette Hartley, born Mary Loretta in Weston Connecticut, has an extensive list of credits in her fifty-year career, including appearances on *Ben Casey, Dr. Kildare, The Twilight Zone, Star Trek* and 30 appearances in a recurring role on *Peyton Place*. She would soon become even more well-known, playing James Garner's wife in commercials for Kodak. More recently, Hartley has appeared on *Law & Order, S.V.U* and *Navy N.C.I.S.*

The Price – 1/15/1979

Season 7 / Episode 165 / Production 165 – T418

Columbia House VHS Tape. . . . . *Local Color (Catalog # 19506)*
Fox DVD . . . . *Season 7, Disc 3*

Alan Alda, Mike Farrell, Harry Morgan
Loretta Swit, David Ogden Stiers, Gary Burghoff, Jamie Farr, William Christopher
Produced by Burt Metcalfe
Executive Script Consultants – Ken Levine & David Isaacs
Written by Erik Tarloff
Directed by Charles Dubin

Story Editor – Larry Balmagia
Story Consultant – Ronny Graham
Creative Consultants – Gene Reynolds / Alan Alda

Yuki Shimoda . . . . Cho Pak
Johnny Haymer . . . . Sergeant Zelmo Zale
Ken Mochizuki . . . . Ham
Miko Mayama. . . . . Sun Pak
Dennis Sakamoto . . . . R.O.K. Officer
Jeff Maxwell. . . . . .Private Igor
Leigh Kim. . . . . R.O.K. Soldier
Copyright 1979 – 20th Century Fox Film Corporation

Non-Credited Appearances. . . . . Kellye Nakahara, Gwen Farrell, Dennis Troy,
Roy Goldman

Chapters

1: Main Titles	6: Round-Up Time – 13:00
2: Two Cavalry Men – 0:55	7: Days of Glory – 16:01
3: The Shower Spy – 5:05	8: Ham's Choice – 19:25
4: A Worthy Cause – 8:13	9: Honor, Pride & Glory – 21:21
5: Where's Sophie? – 10:29	10: End Titles – 22:42

Closing Stills

1: Freeze – Potter and Klinger in the Officer's Club
2: Cho Pak on Sophie
3: Ham in the Swamp
4: Sun
5: Hawkeye
6: B.J.
7: Margaret in the shower
8: Charles
9: Radar and rubber duck
10: Klinger
11: Potter

Synopsis: Cho Pak, a once proud Colonel in the South Korean Cavalry who fought the Russians to save his village, now considers it a great disgrace at having to do the 4077th's laundry to survive. Later, when Potter goes to see Sophie, all he and Radar find is an empty coral, but it doesn't take long to discover what happened to Potter's horse. Proudly sitting atop Sophie in his old dress uniform, Cho Pak, led by his daughter, rides Sophie into camp. Apologizing for her father, Sun explains what happened but Potter, a former

Calvary man himself understands and let's Cho Pak keep Sophie. When Sun walks into camp the next day alone with the horse, she tells Potter that her father died during the night, and thanks him for making his last few hours memorable ones. In the meantime, Hawkeye and B.J. have kept a 16-year-old Korean boy, who's from the same village as Cho Pak, hidden in the Swamp from the South Korean draft trucks. But Cho Pak's legacy has convinced the boy to return and fight for his village, against the doctor's protests.

Commentary by Erik Tarloff: "Larry Gelbart's absence was key. He was such a powerful presence: once he left, the atmosphere in the production office was different, less charged, less exciting. The writing staff was younger, now, much closer to my age. So, it remained an easy and enjoyable situation for me, in personal terms. It was much more a coming together of equals and peers. There was still a lot of easy laughing during meetings, and we all had sort of the same reference in common that I didn't have with Larry, who was a generation older. I wasn't on especially warm footing with Burt Metcalf. It no longer felt like a master class in the art of comedy writing. It was an assemblage of colleagues doing the best work we could."

PA Announcement by Sal Viscuso

Authors' Notes: Cho Pak and his daughter come to pickup the laundry in Chapter 2. Earlier this season, in Episode 150, "Lil," Radar mentions that Potter took Lil to see the laundry room. As noted in "Lil," we've never seen a laundry room. The laundry was usually picked up and delivered by Korean locals, mostly women.

Klinger's ploy this time is a $10,000 bribe to Potter, but the prospect of 20 years at Leavenworth makes him reconsider.

Potter is wearing a red and gray-stripped robe in Chapter 2. In previous episodes, he also wears a heavy army-green robe.

Also in Chapter 2, there's a picture of what appears to be Potter with a horse, but it's not the 4077th in the background.

Mixed drinks in the Officer's Club cost a whopping 25 cents in Chapter 4.

Klinger has on his tray at the Officer's Club a carton of Chesterfield cigarettes in Chapter 4, and later, is also selling Hawkeye's rubber duck from Episode 154, "None Like it Hot."

The Young and the Restless – 1/22/1979

Season 7 / Episode 166 / Production 168 – T421
Columbia House VHS Tape . . . . *Medical Advances (Catalog # 19499)*
Fox DVD . . . . *Season 7, Disc 3*

Alan Alda, Mike Farrell, Harry Morgan
Loretta Swit, David Ogden Stiers, Gary Burghoff, Jamie Farr, William Christopher

Produced by Burt Metcalfe
Executive Script Consultants – Ken Levine & David Isaacs
Written by Mitch Markowitz
Directed by William Jurgensen

Story Editor – Larry Balmagia
Story Consultant – Ronny Graham
Creative Consultants – Gene Reynolds / Alan Alda
James Canning . . . . Captain Simmons
Copyright 1979 – 20th Century Fox Film Corporation

Non-Credited Appearances. . . . . Kellye Nakahara, Gwen Farrell, Dennis Troy,
Roy Goldman

Chapters

1: *Main Titles*	6: *Drafting Captain Simmons – 7:18*
2: *Potter's Phlebitis – 0:53*	7: *Catching Up – 11:53*
3: *Klinger's Act – 3:05*	8: *Simmons-itis – 14:17*
4: *The Lecture – 4:07*	9: *A Showdown – 19:05*
5: *Incoming Wounded – 6:01*	10: *End Titles – 23:29*

Closing Stills

1: *Freeze – Klinger "busted" in Potter's office*
2: *Captain Simmons*
3: *Potter*
4: *B.J.*
5: *Margaret*
6: *Charles in the mess tent*
7: *Radar in his office*
8: *Mulcahy*
9: *Klinger in a suit and straw hat*
10: *Hawkeye in Post-Op*

Synopsis: When Captain Simmons, a young, almost boyish-looking surgeon lectures the doctors on new heart techniques, Charles becomes more indignant than usual and gives the Captain a difficult time. During surgery, Charles continues to treat Simmons poorly, finding fault with every move he makes, but everyone else is impressed and acknowledges the fact that the young surgeon knows just what he's doing. Simmons being young and up to date on new techniques, plus being stationed at Tokyo General, causes Charles to feel his career as a surgeon is in jeopardy and he promptly gets drunk. Potter, on the other hand, is suffering from phlebitis, and refuses to rest because "if I'm not here, things don't get done." Radar assures him that they're ahead of schedule on paperwork and, since Simmons is only a few minutes away by chopper, Potter is not needed in surgery, and now feels the same effects from "Simmonsitis," and refuses to get out of bed.

Authors' Notes: We see the rarely seen "fourth wall" in Potter's office, again (the wall opposite the wall with the window).

Klinger, in Chapter 3, is wearing a bowling shirt that says "Ernie's All-Stars." The name of the business is Ernie's Pizza Inferno. This might not be a mistake as many businesses have bowling teams with names that differ from the business name.

The names on tape over the clothes hooks in Chapter 5's change room are now: *Hawkeye, Potter, B.J., Winchester.*

Also in Chapter 5, the scrub room is again seen from the change room but this time, the sinks are there and not a curtain as in a previous episode.

B.J. is wearing a heavy dark blue robe in Chapter 7. Earlier in the series, B.J. had a light blue terrycloth robe.

In Chapter 7, Charles mentions "Bobby Shafto." Robert Shafto (sometimes spelled Shaftoe) was an 18th Century British Member of Parliment who was the likeliest subject of a famous North East English folk song and nursery rhyme, "Bobby Shafto."

Hawkeye says the time is 6: 00 AM in Chapter 7. Actually, the time was 5: 50 AM. Close enough.

In Chapter 8, Potter is reading a book *Ride the Man Down,* and refers to Zane Grey as the author, when in fact, it was written in 1942 by another well-known Western writer, Luke Short (November 19, 1908-August 18, 1975), whose real name was Frederick Dilley Glidden. (Not to be confused with the famous gunfighter, Luke Short, 1854-1893.)

Another book Potter is reading in Chapter 8 is *The Hell Benders,* written by Ken Hodgson. Ken Hodgson was born in 1945, which would mean that he wrote this Western between the ages of 5 and 8. Hodgson's first published book was in 1971.

Also in Chapter 8, and for the second time in the series, Charles calls Radar "Peewee." The first time was by Lieutenant Nelson (Mrs. Larry Gelbart) in Episode 70, Season 3's "Payday."

Hot Lips is Back in Town – 1/29/1979

Season 7 / Episode 167 / Production 166 – T419
Columbia House VHS Tape . . . . *Not Released by Columbia House*
Fox DVD . . . . *Season 7, Disc 3*

Alan Alda, Mike Farrell, Harry Morgan
Loretta Swit, David Ogden Stiers, Gary Burghoff, Jamie Farr, William Christopher

Produced by Burt Metcalfe
Executive Script Consultants – Ken Levine & David Isaacs
Teleplay by Larry Balmagia and Bernard Dilbert
Story by Bernard Dilbert and Gary Markowitz
Directed by Charles Dubin

Story Editor – Larry Balmagia
Story Consultant – Ronny Graham
Creative Consultants – Gene Reynolds / Alan Alda
Walter Brooke . . . . Major General Lyle Weiskopf
Peggy Lee Brennan . . . . Lieutenant Linda Nugent
Jan Jorden . . . . Nurse Baker
Enid Kent . . . . Nurse Bigelow
Kellye Nakahara . . . . .Nurse Kellye
Copyright 1979 – 20th Century Fox Film Corporation

Non-Credited Appearances. . . . . .Gwen Farrell, Dennis Troy, Roy Goldman

Chapters

1: *Main Titles / Staff Meeting*
2: *A New Nurse – 3:13*
3: *The Army for Life – 7:33*
4: *Advice for the Lovelorn – 8:46*
5: *Margaret Takes Charge – 10:34*
6: *A Second Opinion – 14:36*
7: *The General Arrives – 16:07*
8: *Getting Aggressive – 18:57*
9: *Date Night – 22:22*
10: *End Titles – 23:58*

Closing Stills

1: *Freeze – Radar dancing w / Lt. Nugent – O. Club*
2: *General Weiskopf*
3: *Lieutenant Nugent*
4: *Radar with Nurses Baker and Bigelow*
5: *Hawkeye in the mess tent*
6: *B.J.*
7: *Potter in bed*
8: *Charles in the mess tent*
9: *Radar*
10: *Klinger*
11: *Mulcahy*
12: *Margaret*

Synopsis: When Margaret's final divorce decree sinks in, she re-dedicates herself to her career, and comes up with a triage procedure that will free the doctors for surgery quicker. Confident that the nursing staff can handle triage themselves, she invites General Weiskopf to the 4077th to see for himself, and angers Potter by not telling him of the General's impending visit before inviting him. The General is impressed with Margaret's nurses and their ability to handle triage, but when he offers Margaret a promotion to lieutenant colonel in exchange for "personal favors," she not only refuses, she throws him out of her tent. Radar tries getting the attention of Lieutenant Linda Nugent, a very pretty nurse who arrives at the 4077th, and when he finally asks her for a date, he's surprised when she accepts.

PA Announcements by Sal Viscuso

Authors' Notes: Hawkeye's jockey shorts can be seen when he gets out of the shower in Chapter 4.

In Chapter 5, Hawkeye says, "Thank you, Kato," a reference to the radio/TV/film/ comic book series *The Green Hornet.* On the captioning, "Kato" is spelled "Cato." The role of Kato was played in the film serial by future *M*A*S*H* alumni, Keye Luke."

In Chapter 7, jeep number 20963388 is now General Weiskopf's jeep, complete with a two-star flag and bumper plate.

In Chapter 8, the month and year on a calendar in the nurses' quarters is December 1950. This puts Season 7 in all three years of the Korean War.

C*A*V*E – 2/5/1979

Season 7 / Episode 168 / Production 170 – T423
Columbia House VHS Tape........ *Hot Lips And Hawkeye (Catalog # 13115)*
Fox DVD .... *Season 7, Disc 3*

Alan Alda, Mike Farrell, Harry Morgan
Loretta Swit, David Ogden Stiers, Gary Burghoff, Jamie Farr, William Christopher

Produced by Burt Metcalfe
Executive Script Consultants – Ken Levine & David Isaacs
Written by Larry Balmagia and Ronny Graham
Directed by William Jurgensen

Story Editor – Larry Balmagia
Story Consultant – Ronny Graham
Creative Consultants – Gene Reynolds / Alan Alda

Basil Hoffman...Bartruff
Mark Taylor... O'Malley
Enid Kent .... Nurse Bigelow
Charles Jenkins ....Private Lovett
Jennifer Davis .... Nurse

Copyright 1979 – 20th Century Fox Film Corporation

Non-Credited Appearances....................... Kellye Nakahara, Dennis Troy

Chapters

1: *Main Titles*	6: *Blood Donor – 14:07*
2: *Caught in the Crossfire – 1:33*	7: *Keeping Watch – 15:13*
3: *Moving Out – 7:01*	8: *Back to Camp – 18:33*
4: *Claustrophobia – 9:17*	9: *Back to Normal – 21:40*
5: *Confining or Cozy? – 11:35*	10: *End Titles – 22:32*

Closing Stills

1: *Freeze – Hawkeye & Margaret in Post-Op beds*
2: *Bartruff on his office phone*
3: *O'Malley in Post-Op*
4: *Potter in the cave*
5: *Charles in the mess tent*
6: *Margaret*
7: *Klinger*
8: *Mulcahy*
9: *B.J.*
10: *Hawkeye in the cave*

Synopsis: With Post-Op at capacity, the 4077th finds itself caught in crossfire and although Colonel Potter tries to get I-Corps to re-direct their line of fire, they think he's Chinese. Left with little choice, the Colonel packs up the bus with the wounded, some supplies and the staff, and heads for a nearby cave where they'll be safe. Hawkeye would rather have taken his chances by remaining at the 4077th when it becomes clear that he suffers from claustrophobia. Even one of his patients who's bleeding into his belly can't keep Hawkeye in the cave more than a few seconds. Not having the necessary equipment to treat the man where they are, Hawkeye, accompanied by Margaret, takes the wounded G.I. back to the 4077th for surgery while shelling continues outside.

Authors' Notes: There are no PA announcements in this episode.

Potter is wearing his heavy dark green robe in Chapter 2. The other robe he wears has red and gray stripes.

When Klinger is under his desk and on the phone with I-Corps in Chapter 2, Hawkeye asks him, "Klinger, you have room for two more?" Klinger answers, "No. I'm wearing a full skirt." But when Klinger finally emerges from under the desk, he's wearing a pink robe and fatigues. No skirt.

For the one and only time in the series, Hawkeye in Chapter 4 suffers from claustrophobia.

Margaret, on the other hand, suffers from loud noises. Although Margaret had mentioned this in Season 6's "Comrades In Arms," one can't help but wonder why someone who fears loud noises would want a military career when the backfire from an automobile frightens her, and shrieks when a bomb explodes outside O.R.

According to Klinger in Chapter 6, Mulcahy and Charles have the same blood type as him, which is B-positive (see Episode 76, Season 4's "It Happened One Night").

For the second time in the series, Hawkeye quotes from the Rudyard Kipling poem "Gunga Din," written in 1892.

Rally Round the Flagg, Boys - 2/14/1979

Season 7 / Episode 169 / Production 172 – T425

Columbia House VHS Tape. . . . . Going Undercover (Catalog # 13119)
Fox DVD . . . . Season 7, Disc 3

Alan Alda, Mike Farrell, Harry Morgan
Loretta Swit, David Ogden Stiers, Gary Burghoff, Jamie Farr, William Christopher

Produced by Burt Metcalfe
Executive Script Consultants – Ken Levine & David Isaacs
Written by Mitch Markowitz
Directed by Harry Morgan

Story Editor – Larry Balmagia
Story Consultant – Ronny Graham
Creative Consultants – Gene Reynolds / Alan Alda

Edward Winter . . . . Colonel Sam Flagg
Neil Thompson . . . . Basgall
James Lough . . . . M.P.
Jerry Fujikawa . . . . Hung Pak , Mayor Of Ouijongbu
Bob Okazaki . . . . Doo Pak, Chief of Police and Hung Pak's younger brother
Roy Goldman . . . . Goldman
Copyright 1979 – 20th Century Fox Film Corporation

Non-Credited Appearances. Kellye Nakahara, Gwen Farrell

Chapters

1: *Main Titles*	6: *Winchester gets Involved – 8:20*
2: *Bridge Night – 0:52*	7: *Snooping – 11:35*
3: *Triage – 2:09*	8: *Interrogation – 16:38*
4: *Speaking Out – 3:39*	9: *A Stakeout – 19:16*
5: *Col. Flagg Investigates – 4:30*	10: *End Titles – 24:03*

Closing Stills

1: *Freeze – Mulcahy & B.J. in Mulcahy's tent*
2: *Flagg*
3: *Basgall in Post-Op*
4: *Charles in the mess tent*
5: *B.J. in Post-Op*
6: *Potter*
7: *Margaret*
8: *Radar in the office*
9: *Klinger*
10: *Mulcahy*
11: *Hawkeye*

Synopsis: Hawkeye is accused of being a Communist sympathizer when he treats a wounded North Korean ahead of a less-seriously wounded American, and the American's buddy, Basgall, isn't going to let him forget it. Worse is the arrival of Colonel Flagg. Flagg suspects Hawkeye as well and to get the proof he needs, he recruits Charles after promising him a cushy post with easy hours at a base in Massachusetts. Feeling guilty after going through Hawkeye's foot locker, Charles quits the spy business, acknowledging that Hawkeye may be obnoxious at times, but he's not a Communist spy or a sympathizer, and comes up with a clever plan that gets Flagg in trouble with the Mayor of Ouijonbu and his brother, the Chief of Police.

Commentary by William Christopher: "Another character that made me laugh was Flagg (Ed Winter). What a wonderful character. Though I wasn't in on any story conferences, I wondered whether Alan felt more interested in going in different directions. Because, it seemed as if Flagg was suddenly dropped, especially after Larry and Gene left. You began to see more of Sidney Freedman. Ed Winter had a great Clark Gable impersonation. I never did much of any scenes with Ed I don't think."

PA Announcement by Sal Viscuso

Authors' Notes: The view from the left window of the office in Chapter 5 shows trees, not the usual side of a corrugated structure.

Potterisms: "Pony pucks," "What the Sam Hill?"

In Chapter 9, we learn that the Mayor of Ouijongbu is Doo Pak, and his brother, Hung Pak is the Chief of Police.

Also in Chapter 9 is a strange occurrence. At 22:33, Flagg shuts the light in the Swamp. Potter says, "Flagg, you nut!" and at 22:36, Hawkeye says, "Colonel, now's our chance to switch decks." Between 22:33 and 22:36 when the lights are off and we hear the dialogue above, the picture freezes. There's no movement for those three seconds while hearing the dialogue.

Preventative Medicine – 2/19/1979

Season 7 / Episode 170 / Production 163 – T416

Columbia House VHS Tape . . . . *A Bird in the Hand (Catalog # 19502)*
Fox DVD . . . . *Season 7, Disc 3*

Alan Alda, Mike Farrell, Harry Morgan
Loretta Swit, David Ogden Stiers, Gary Burghoff, Jamie Farr, William Christopher

Produced by Burt Metcalfe
Executive Script Consultants – Ken Levine & David Isaacs
Written by Tom Reeder
Directed by Tony Mordente

Story Editor – Larry Balmagia
Story Consultant – Ronny Graham
Creative Consultants – Gene Reynolds / Alan Alda

James Wainwright . . . . Colonel Lacy
Larry Flash Jenkins . . . . .Private North *(See Authors' Notes)*
Jeff Maxwell. . . . . .Private Igor
Copyright 1979 – 20th Century Fox Film Corporation

Non-Credited Appearances. .Kellye Nakahara, Roy Goldman

Chapters

1: *Main Titles*	6: *Potter Writes A Letter – 12:32*
2: *About Col. Lacy – 0:53*	7: *Lacy Visits His Men – 14:19*
3: *Klinger's Voodoo – 2:21*	8: *Mixed Drinks – 17:46*
4: *Lacy Arrives – 4:55*	9: *Klinger Confesses – 22:57*
5: *A Bad Impression – 9:48*	10: *End Titles – 23:59*

Closing Stills

1: *Freeze – Mulcahy & Klinger on "9" Compound*
2: *Colonel Lacy in the Swamp*
3: *Private North in Post-Op*
4: *B.J. in Post-Op*
5: *Potter on the Stage 9 Compound*
6: *Margaret*
7: *Radar on Stage 9 Compound*
8: *Mulcahy in Post-Op*
9: *Charles in the mess tent*
10: *Klinger*
11: *Hawkeye in Post-Op*

Synopsis: Colonel Lacy, of the 163rd Infantry, has the highest casualty rate of any battalion commander in the sector, and the wounded men under his command in Post-Op would seem to confirm that statistic; one of which tells the doctors that if he's sent back to Lacy's unit, he'll kill him. Bringing the men their Purple Hearts during a visit does nothing for their morale as one of them refuses to accept it and causes another to go into cardiac arrest. Lacy submits yet another plan to I-Corps in a last attempt to capture the hill he's been trying to take, but this time, permission is denied. Undaunted, Lacy knows a way around I-Corp's order to stay put, and Hawkeye knows a way to keep the Colonel in camp for a couple of weeks and the possibility of Lacy losing his command.

Authors' Notes: For the second time, Hawkeye will perform an unnecessary appendectomy, this time to keep Colonel Lacy off the front lines. The first time Hawkeye did this was in Episode 71, Season 3's "White Gold," to keep Colonel Flagg from leaving with the unit's supply of penicillin. These two episodes remain a point of contention among fans, with this episode getting much of the attention. The difference in the two episodes is Trapper, in "White Gold," had no problem with Hawkeye removing a healthy organ, even covering for him by telling Igor what Hawkeye put in Flagg's coffee was vitamins and had a comedic feel to it. However, in "Preventative Medicine," B.J. takes a very loud and strong stance on Hawkeye cutting into a healthy body, a flagrant violation of the Hippocratic Oath, even calling it "mutilation," and wants nothing to do with it and the seriousness of it is quite evident.

Colonel Lacy was named after Los Angeles Dodgers outfielder, number 34, Lee Lacy.

Corporal North was named after Los Angeles Dodger outfielder, number 4, Billy North.

The 4077th, in this episode, has a 97% survival rate, as per Colonel Lacy.

The sinks in the scrub room in Chapter 8 are side by side, but separated at an angle never seen before.

Also in Chapter 8, Hawkeye returns to the Swamp after removing Lacy's appendix. B.J. tells him that Radar was just there and wounded will be arriving in ten minutes. It's odd that B.J. would gulp down a full martini knowing that wounded will be there in ten minutes.

Klinger's ploy in this episode: Voodoo.

Colonel Lacy and the doctors call North "Corporal North," but in the closing credits, he's listed as "Private North."

A Night at Rosie's – 2/26/1979

Season 7 / Episode 171 / Production 173 – T426

Columbia House VHS Tape . . . . Not Released by Columbia House

Fox DVD . . . . Season 7, Disc 3

Alan Alda, Mike Farrell, Harry Morgan
Loretta Swit, David Ogden Stiers, Gary Burghoff, Jamie Farr, William Christopher

Produced by Burt Metcalfe
Executive Script Consultants – Ken Levine & David Isaacs
Written by Ken Levine & David Isaacs
Directed by Burt Metcalfe

Story Editor – Larry Balmagia
Story Consultant – Ronny Graham
Creative Consultants – Gene Reynolds / Alan Alda

Keye Luke . . . . Cho Kim
Joshua Bryant . . . . Sergeant Jerry Scully *(See Authors' Notes)*
Eileen Saki . . . . Rosie
Joseph Di Reda . . . . Major Frank Dorsett
Richard Lee Sung . . . . Ham Kim
Jim Burk . . . . M.P.
Jennifer Davis . . . . Nurse
Kellye Nakahara . . . . Nurse
Jo Ann Thompson . . . . Nurse

Copyright 1979 – 20th Century Fox Film Corporation

Non-Credited Appearances. . . . . .Gwen Farrell, Dennis Troy, Roy Goldman

Chapters

1:	Main Titles	6:	A Holy Roller – 12:40
2:	A Beer and A Bowl – 0:53	7:	Left Out – 15:08
3:	A.W.O.L. – 2:09	8:	M.P.'s – 18:51
4:	Rosieland – 3:48	9:	The Morning After – 22:20
5:	A Crap Game – 9:50	10:	End Titles – 24:02

Closing Stills

1: Freeze – Hawkeye and B.J. leave Rosie's
2: Scully in Rosie's
3: Rosie
4: Dorsett
5: Cho Kim and Ham Kim
6: Hawkeye
7: B.J.
8: Charles
9: Margaret
10: Klinger
11: Mulcahy (Not in Rosie's)
12: Potter in Rosie's

Synopsis: In an episode filmed entirely at Rosie's, Hawkeye, enjoying a bowl of Rice Krispies and beer for breakfast, meets Sergeant Jack Scully. Scully, who walked off the line after six months of fighting and is now AWOL from his unit hits it off with Hawkeye and they quickly become friends. Potter sends staff members out to look for Hawkeye and one by one, they wind up staying at Rosie's. After B.J. joins Hawkeye and Scully, a vote is taken and Rosie's is declared a new and neutral country called "Rosieland." But when Colonel Potter shows up, he makes it clear to Hawkeye and B.J. that he considers these actions a lack of respect, something he will not tolerate even from them, but promises to get them off the hook after they gag and hog-tie Charles to a chair who now wants to press charges.

Commentary by Ken Levine: "Another last minute episode order by CBS. We wanted to break things up and, in this case, do an entire show in one location that wasn't the camp. This was another script that David and I divided and wrote separately. Interestingly, we had been writing together for so long that you couldn't tell who wrote which act."

Commentary by Josh Bryant: "It was a fascinating project with very talented people. I, like anyone involved with the show, could talk about it ad infinitum. Of the dozens of television shows I appeared in, M*A*S*H and The Mary Tyler Moore Show were certainly the crème of the crop. In 'A Night at Rosie's,' the first episode I did, all the action took place in Rosie's. That set was constructed, as I recall, in one corner of an enormous soundstage on the 20th Century Fox lot. I remember David Ogden Stiers riding around that great, gloomy, empty space between shots on a unicycle. The whimsy of it got me off to a good start and, though he doesn't know it, I've always carried that image with me and smile when I think of it."

Commentary from Richard Lee Sung: "About Jamie Farr and that episode where we had the floating craps game? Key Luke was a wonderful actor and legend in Hollywood. He played my father and I called him 'Pop' because of what Charlie Chan did. He would say 'Hi Pop,' you know. He (Luke) was a wonderful man to work with. I'd known him for years and we had the same agent. I was doing this scene with Jamie Farr, and he's worrying about me, wanting to make sure the camera sees me, and wanting to make sure the light was on me. He said, 'We've got to get the camera on him. He's bigger than me. We've got to make him funny, you know, in a real way.' So, he started tickling me, and that brought the camera to me. It gave me a reason not to fight back because I was ticklish. He said, 'tickling you will be the reason you can't fight back in the scene.' So, he was always thinking. That's so professional and so caring. You know, most people want the camera on them."

Authors' Notes: There are no PA announcements in this episode.
Joshua Bryant, who played Sergeant Jack Scully, is credited as Sergeant "Jerry" Scully.
In this episode, Margaret has fallen for Sergeant Scully. This is the second time she's fallen for someone below the rank of major, despite her earlier claims that she couldn't be with anyone who did not outrank her (not counting Hawkeye in "Comrades In Arms," as the circumstances were much different). The first time was with Captain Tom Greenleigh in "Major Ego." While it was obvious that she admired others of a lesser rank, such as Captain Toby Hill in "An Eye for a Tooth," that admiration did not develop as it did in the two episodes mentioned.
In Chapter 8, as in previous fight scenes at Rosie's, the sound of glass breaking is heard as people crash through the windows, but no glass is seen, as the windows are plastic with wood frames.
Hawkeye says "Rosieland," and B.J. said that's a ballroom. B.J. is correct. "Roseland" began in 1917 in Philadelphia and moved to New York City in 1919. It is still in existence today and appears on *The Late Show with David Letterman* when they tape outdoor segments on West 52nd Street.
Major Dorsett mentions "The Halekulani," the original of which began in 1907.

Ain't Love Grand? – 3/5/1979

Season 7 / Episode 172 / Production 169 – T422

Columbia House VHS Tape. . . . . *Not Released by Columbia House*
Fox DVD . . . . *Season 7, Disc 3*

Alan Alda, Mike Farrell, Harry Morgan
Loretta Swit, David Ogden Stiers, Gary Burghoff, Jamie Farr, William Christopher

Produced by Burt Metcalfe
Executive Script Consultants – Ken Levine & David Isaacs
Written by Ken Levine & David Isaacs
Directed by Mike Farrell

Story Editor – Larry Balmagia
Story Consultant – Ronny Graham
Creative Consultants – Gene Reynolds / Alan Alda

Sylvia Chang. . . . . Sooni
Kit McDonough . . . . Lieutenant Deborah Clark (8063)
Eileen Saki . . . . Rosie
Judy Farrell . . . . .Nurse Able
Michael Williams . . . . Patient
Copyright 1979 – 20th Century Fox Film Corporation

Non-Credited Appearances. . . . . .Kellye Nakahara

Chapters

1:	Main Titles	6:	Poetry and Burgers – 18:32
2:	Unwinding – 0:53	7:	Temporary Quarters – 20:20
3:	Love – 3:06	8:	Good News – 21:01
4:	Familiarity Breeds Contempt – 9:55	9:	Alone Again – 22:57
5:	A Private Rendezvous – 12:47	10:	End Titles – 24:02

Closing Stills

1: Freeze – Charles & Klinger sing "Stormy Weather"
2: Sooni
3: Lieutenant Debbie Clark
4: Rosie
5: Charles
6: Klinger
7: Mulcahy
8: B.J.
9: Margaret
10: Potter in his office
11: Hawkeye

Synopsis: Charles gets more than he bargains for when, after ordering a bottle of Rosie's "finest" wine, a pretty, young local business girl sits at his table and asks him to buy her a burger. At first, Charles gives her a dollar in the hopes she'll go away, but he has a change of heart and tries to bring some of his culture into her life. Unfortunately for Charles, she's more interested in the mess tent food than she is in Tchaikovsky or poetry. A visiting nurse from the 8063rd, wearing regulation fatigues, takes a liking to Klinger, who's wearing a self-made blue dress. While alone in the supply room, she tells Klinger that he's a "gas," but his long-term plans for them is not what she had in mind.

Commentary by Ken Levine: "Another fun episode. I always loved the premise."

Authors' Notes: There are no PA announcements in this episode.

Potter mentions "Looney Tune." "Looney Tunes" or "Toons," is a series of Warner Bros. cartoons that ran in movie theaters from 1930 to 1960.

In Chapter 4, Hawkeye tells B.J., "Let me tell you something, Mr. Clean." "Mr. Clean" did not come out on the market until 1958, three years after the Korean War.

In Chapter 6, Charles quotes from a poem, "She Walks in Beauty," written in 1814 by Lord Byron.

In Chapter 8, Charles quotes, "It is better to have loved and lost…" This quote is from the poem, "In Memoriam A.H.H," written over a 17-year span by Alfred, Lord Tennyson, for his friend, Arthur Henry Hallam.

The Party - 3/12/1979

Season 7 / Episode 173 / Production 171 – T424

Columbia House VHS Tape. . . . . *Over Here (Catalog # 19504)*
Fox DVD . . . . *Season 7, Disc 3*

Alan Alda, Mike Farrell, Harry Morgan
Loretta Swit, David Ogden Stiers, Gary Burghoff, Jamie Farr, William Christopher

Produced by Burt Metcalfe
Executive Script Consultants – Ken Levine & David Isaacs
Written by Alan Alda and Burt Metcalfe
Directed by Burt Metcalfe

Story Editor – Larry Balmagia
Story Consultant – Ronny Graham
Creative Consultants – Gene Reynolds / Alan Alda
Copyright 1979 – 20th Century Fox Film Corporation

Non-Credited Appearances. . . . . Kellye Nakahara, Gwen Farrell, Dennis Troy,
Roy Goldman

Chapters

1: *Main Titles*	6: *The Invitees Respond – 10:47*
2: *Letters from Home – 0:54*	7: *Picking A Date – 15:10*
3: *Evacuation – 4:25*	8: *Group Photo – 18:49*
4: *Depression – 7:10*	9: *Party Reviews – 20:08*
5: *Moving Back – 9:44*	10: *End Titles – 24:03*

Closing Stills

1: *Freeze – Hawkeye, Radar, Charles, BJ in Swamp*
2: *B.J. in the Swamp*
3: *Potter in the office*
4: *Margaret*
5: *Charles*
6: *Radar*
7: *Klinger*
8: *Mulcahy*
9: *Hawkeye*

Synopsis: When Peg Hunnicutt burns a batch of strawberry jam, Potter suggests she write to Mildred to get her recipe for a kumquat-huckleberry combo preserve, thus giving B.J. an idea for a reunion, only this reunion is for everyone's loved ones back home. However, no one wants to write to ask because no one thinks his or her family would attend. Seeing the effect this is having on B.J., Hawkeye gets everyone to write letters home with unexpected results, and once a date is selected, the party is on. After the party, B.J. gets a letter from Peg, which Radar reads out loud in O.R., describing the party as a great success, coupled with some funny and unexpected surprises.

Authors' Notes: There are no PA announcements in this episode.
Charles, in Chapter 2 mentions "Dagwood and Blondie" — a cartoon strip started on September 8, 1930, which still runs today.
As everyone reads the responses from home in Chapter 6, they're seen, two and three at a time, in trucks heading back to the 4077th, but it's the same truck.

The dates selected to choose from for the party are as follows:

February 14, February 21, March 1, March 8, March 15, March 21, and March 28, all supposedly weekends. The only year that these dates fall on a Saturday or Sunday is 1953. 1950-52 contain weekdays.

Going through the dates week-by-week to see when everyone's family could attend the party, they go from February 21 to March 1, seemingly forgetting about February 28, which would then be followed by March 7 (except 1952 due to a leap-year). The date following March 15 should be March 22, not March 21.

The party will be held on March 28, 1953.

Appendix – Season 7

Character Profiles

Hawkeye

Episode 150: Father caught him smoking in bed at 14.
Sucked his thumb until he was 26, then gave it up for bedwetting *(kidding)*.

153: Played Hamlet in college. He was pre-med and the only one who could get his hands on a skull.

168: Father used to play "20 Questions" when on family drives.

173: Father hasn't left Crab Apple Cove in 40 years and delivered most of his patients himself.
When in pre-med, Hawkeye worked part-time for a moving company and could pack a 30-piece set of China in 10 minutes (and less if they didn't mind 60 pieces).

B.J.

Episode 150: Dean of medical school — T.R. Miller.
Favorite comedian — W.C. Fields.
Favorite authors — D.H. Lawrence or T.S. Eliot or S.J. Perelman.
Mother Bea Hunnicutt, Father Jay Hunnicutt.

162: Bought Christmas toys in Tokyo for Erin.

164: He and Peg like to put on "Arioso by Bach" at bedtime.

173: Peg burned a batch of strawberry jam and ruined the stove.
Peg is taking her real estate broker's license exam on March 21.

Colonel Potter

Episode 150: Mildred has a picture of him on the piano.

154: Had Mildred send a palm tree *(small)*.

157: Potterism: "I'll be the son of Princess Papuli" *(see Episode 157, page 493 for alternate spellings of "papuli").*

158: Got his medical training at Fort Sam Houston
35th wedding anniversary was last Saturday *(see Episode 154, page 487 for up-to-date details on this).*

162: Potterism: *"Bright as a nickel in the well water."*
18th Christmas away from Mildred.
Spent a Christmas in the Black Forest; company horse broke a leg; cook tried to pass it off as dark meat; cried all through dinner.

165: Wearing purple satin boxer shorts that Mildred made for him.
Doesn't like starch in his riding britches.

166: Suffers from phlebitis.

167: Grandson Corey weighs 56 pounds — walks like crazy and likes to catch bugs and eat 'em *(according to Radar).*

173: Mildred makes kumquat & huckleberry preserves.

Mildred plays "classical banjo."

Mildred can't make the party on the weekend of March 8th because their grandson Corey's fifth birthday is on the 7th and she'll be in St. Louis that weekend.

Margaret

Episode 156: Law firm of "Whitehurst, Blinn, Blinn, Whitehurst" informed her that the joint savings account with Donald has been tied up until the divorce settlement is finalized.

167: Officially divorced when she receives her final divorce decree.

173: Parents have been separated for over a year.

Parents can't make the party on March 15 because her father meets with his old regiment annually every third Monday in March. He's been doing it for 30 years and refuses to miss it.

Charles

Episode 155: Born in "grandmama's" house on Beacon Hill.

Was always inquisitive as a boy.

Parents gave him nannies, boarding school and a stock portfolio.

By the age of seven, he was dissecting frogs and could put them back together.

Graduated first in his med-school class at Harvard.

Was always a voracious reader.

156: Grants his first interview since graduating from Harvard summa cum laude with one of the highest GPAs ever seen at that institution.

Born in upper Boston where his family has lived for 5 generations. Also attended Choate.

162: Presbyterian.

163: Used to donate one Thursday afternoon a month to the respiratory unit at Massachusetts General.

168: As per Klinger in this episode, Charles has the same blood type as he does, which is B positive *(see Episode 76, page 271).*

169: Lives in Wellesley, Massachusetts with his mother, father and sister, Honoria *(according to Colonel Flagg).*

Has friends in Newport and a few in Martha's Vineyard.

173: Parents can't attend the party on February 14, because his father is to attend a meeting of the Board of Overseers at Harvard.

Radar

Episode 150: Uncle Ed used to give him a quarter to go to the movies when he wanted Radar away from something.

Cousin Raymond went on a picnic with a girl and had to marry her.

Margaret calls him, "Spunky."

Mother is entering her cucumbers in the county fair and his Uncle Ed is a judge *(his mother might win).*

Klinger smells like the raccoon that died under his house.

157: The last time Radar took heaters from the tents, they hid his glasses in the meatloaf.

Chocolate makes his face break out.

Walking backwards always makes him nauseous.

160: Radar's serial number is RA 1949069. In Season 5's "Lieutenant Radar O'Reilly," it was 3911810, and will change again next season *(in Episode 177)*.

162: Edna is his pregnant cow back home
Methodist.

163: Radar's queen bee is, "Isabella" and the other bee is "Blitzen".

165: Radar mentions his skunk *(not seen in this episode, seen in Episode 62)* but doesn't know if it's a boy or girl skunk.

173: Mother makes jam and puts something in it so it won't burn.
Randy, his goat back home tried to kiss a turkey.
Mom & Uncle Ed can't make the party because the finals of the Davenport Midwinter Cattle Competition will be held on February 20 and 21, and they entered Edna's calf.

Klinger

Episode 165: Greed moved his uncle into a cushy job on the Toledo City Council.

166: Brings his bowling ball to Adolph's Sporting Goods.
Bowling team: "Ernie's All-Stars" From Ernie's Pizza Inferno.
Belongs to the Moose Lodge.
Mother's maiden name is "Abodeely."
Social Security number is 556-78-2613.

168: Got his family through 9 evictions.

172: Uncle Ahmed can always buy him a job at City Hall.
The address of the house Klinger was born in is 1215 Michigan Street, Toledo, Ohio.

173: Mother doesn't know he's in Korea — told her he's at Fort Dix in New Jersey because he didn't want her to worry — took almost 100 snapshots of himself at the motor pool, peeling potatoes and getting thrown out of the Officer's Club and has been sending her photos every month.
Uncle got out of WW II wearing women's clothes.
Parents don't speak English but his Uncle Abdul speaks both *(Arabic and English)*.

Father Mulcahy

Episode 158: A little inhibited when it comes to the Southern Baptist service.

162: Used to coach boxing at the C.Y.O.

168: As per Klinger in this episode, Mulcahy has the same blood type as he does, which is B positive *(see Episode 76, page 271)*.

173: Sister "wails" on *Stardust (See Seen, Heard, Mentioned or Referenced – Season 7, page 530)*.
Sister can't make the party on March 1 — her basketball team at the convent won first place in their division and are in the playoffs. She could be named "Most Valuable Sister."

Seen, Heard, Mentioned or Referenced – Season 7

Movies

Episode 148: Hawkeye mentions Captain Bligh from the 1935 movie *Mutiny on the Bounty.*

153: Hawkeye mentions *It Happened One Night* with Clark Gable and Claudette Colbert (1934).

155: B.J. mentions "Doc Holiday," a reference to *My Darling Clementine* (1946).

Charles mentions "Oz" from *The Wizard of Oz* (1939).

156: Hawkeye mentions *Mutiny on the Bounty* (1935).

Klinger mentions *Gone with the Wind* (1939).

Klinger says, "What a dump," a quote from the 1949 Bette Davis movie, *Beyond the Forest.*

Klinger mentions another Bette Davis movie, *Now, Voyager* (1942).

157: Hawkeye mentions *Nanook of the North*, a 1922 silent documentary on Nanook and his family in the Canadian arctic by Robert Flaherty. This is thought to be the first feature-length documentary — however, Flaherty has been criticized for staging some of the sequences, altering the reality of Nanook and his family.

B.J. mentions *Sun Valley Serenade* (1941) and Sonja Henie.

Mulcahy mentions *Song of Bernadette*, a 1943 movie based on the 1942 novel by Franz Werfel.

Hawkeye mentions "Esther Williams meets Dracula" *(not real).*

159: Hawkeye mentions *Death Takes a Holiday* (1934), a romantic fantasy.

164: Hawkeye mentions *Casablanca* (1942).

169: Flagg mentions *Going My Way* (1944) and also the song from this movie. See "Songs" for this episode for details.

Charles mentions "Tin Man," a reference to *The Wizard of Oz* (1939),

Songs

148: "The Anvil Chorus" *(Charles mentions)* Written by Giuseppe Verdi, from Act II, Scene 1 of his Il Trovatore

149: "Reveille" *(Radar plays on the bugle, poorly)* See Episode 9 (page 94) for details.

150: "Harrigan" *(Potter and Lil sing "H-A-double R-I-G-A-N Spells Harrigan…")* Written by George M. Cohan for 1907 musical *50 Miles from Boston.*

"Second-Hand Rose" *(Potter mentions)* Words by Grant Clarke, music by James F. Hanley, circa 1921

"When I'm Calling You" *(Potter sings)* Sung by Nelson Eddy & Jeanette McDonald, between 1929-1941

153: "Tokyo Shoeshine Boy" *(Male Korean or Japanese voice heard over PA in English)* See Episode 1 (page 80) for details.

154: "Anchors Aweigh" *(Hawkeye sings "Anchors aweigh, my friend. Anchors aweigh…")* Song of the United States Navy. Composed in 1906, words by Alfred Hart Miles (who was a lieutenant at the time and had been the Naval Academy Bandmaster since 1887; music by Charles A. Zimmerman. The song was supposed to be a football march.

"1812 Overture" *(Charles mentions, later heard)* Written by Pyotr Ilyich Tchaikovsky to commemorate Russia's 1812 defense against Napoleon's Grande Armée and debuted in the Cathedral of Christ the Saviour in Moscow on August 20, 1882.

156: "Let's Call the Whole Thing Off" *(Hawkeye mentions)* Written by George & Ira Gershwin for 1937 film *Shall We Dance?*
"America the Beautiful" *(B.J. hums)* Words by Kathy Lee Bates, circa 1893, music by Samuel A. Ward (the music was written before the poem, but selected after). The United States national anthem.

157: "Baby, It's Cold Outside" The title of this episode, mentioned again later in the episode. Words and Music by Frank Loesser, 1944.
"Heat Wave" *(All in the mess tent sing, "We're having a heat wave, a tropical heat wave. The temperature is rising, it isn't surprising...")* Written by Irving Berlin in 1933.
"Princess Papuli" *(Potter mentions)* Words and music by Harry Owens, circa 1924. See the Episode Guide listing (page 493) for details.
"I Hear Music" *(Klinger sings "I hear music, mighty fine music.")* Words by Frank Loesser, music by Burton Lane, from the 1940 movie *Dancing On A Dime.*

159: "I've Got You Under My Skin" (Hawkeye mentions) See Episode 46 (page 179) for details.
"Up A Lazy River" *(B.J. mentions, "Epidermis River By the Old Mill Stream," a reference to "Up A Lazy River By the Old Mill Stream.")* Music composed and recorded by Hoagy Carmichael in 1930, words by Sidney Arodin.
"1812 Overture" *(Hawkeye mentions)* See Episode 154 for details.
"Yankee Doodle" *(Kwang mentions)* See Episode 6 (page 90) for details.

161: "It Ain't Gonna Rain No More" *(Hawkeye and B.J. sing "It ain't gonna rain no more, no more, it ain't gonna rain no more..." in the shower)* Song is traditional and anonymous.
"Row, Row, Row Your Boat" *(Hawkeye sings)* An English nursery rhyme and popular children's song, credited to Eliphalet Oram Lyte from the publication *The Franklin Square Song Collection* (1881).

162: "Deck the Halls" *(Instrumental heard on radio, on the PA in Potter's office)* A traditional Yuletide and New Year's carol.
"Dona Nobis Pacem" *(All sing in the mess tent)* Latin for "Give us peace." Set as separate final movement in Bach's "Mass in B Minor."

163: "Figaro" *(Charles sings)* from the French play *The Barber of Seville,* first performed February 23, 1775.
Charles sings an aria from *Don Giovanni,* a play with music written by Mozart (January 27, 1756-December 5, 1791).
"Shave and A Haircut, Two Bits." *(Hawkeye says, "Shave and a haircut, two bits.")* This could be considered the world's shortest complete song, with the first-known occurrence from an 1899 Charles Hale song *At A Darktown Cakewalk.*
"A Pretty Girl is Like A Melody" *(Klinger sings)* Words and music by Irving Berlin, premiered in 1946.
"Night and Day" *(Hawkeye sings, "Night and day, why is it so?")* Words and music by Cole Porter for the 1932 musical play *Gay Divorce.*

164: "When I'm Calling You" *(Hawkeye sings, "When I'm calling you, ooh, ooh, ooh, will you answer true?")* Words by Oscar Hammerstein II, music by Rudolf Friml. Sung by Nelson Eddy and Jeanette MacDonald in the 1936 movie *Rose Marie.*
"Arioso by Bach" *(B.J. mentions, later heard when Hawkeye plays it in the Swamp).*
"Begin the Beguine" *(Hawkeye mentions)* Written by Cole Porter for the 1935 Broadway musical, *Jubilee.*
Inga plays traditional Swedish music in her tent.

165: "I'm an Old Cowhand from the Rio Grande" (Potter sings) Words and music by Johnny Mercer, music also by Harry Warren. The song is from the 1936 movie *Rhythm On the Range.*

"The Caisson Song" *(Margaret sings, "The caissons go rolling along...")* See Episode 67 (page 234) for details.

167: "Old Man River" *(Charles says, "Tote that barge, lift that gurney. Speak your mind, you need an attorney.")* See Episode 139 (page 437) for details.

"Lullaby of Broadway" *(Mulcahy plays on the piano in the Officer's Club)* Words by Al Dubin, music by Harry Warren, published in 1935. (Also a 1951 Doris Day film, in which she sings the song.)

168: Hawkeye mentions "Ave Maria" – Composed by Charles Gounod in 1859 based on Bach's Prelude No. 1 in C Major; is quite popular and has been recorded many times.

169: "Diamonds Are A Girl's Best Friend" *(Hawkeye sings)* Written by Jule Styne for the 1949 Broadway musical *Gentlemen Prefer Blondes* and introduced by Carol Channing.

"Toora, Loora, Loora" *(Flagg mentions)* See Episode 46 (page 179) for details. *(Note: The closed captioning in Episode 169 spells this song as above, but in Episode 46, it's "Too Ra Loo Ra Loo Ral.")*

"Going My Way" *(Flagg mentions)* From the 1944 film of the same name with Bing Crosby and Barry Fitzgerald.

"Carmen" *(Hawkeye mentions)* See Episode 92 (page 301) for details.

170: "Ain't We Got Fun?" *(Hawkeye sings, "In the mornin', in the evenin', ain't we got fun?")* Words by Raymond B. Egan & Gus Kahn, music by Richard A. Whiting, published in 1921.

"Boogie Woogie Bugle Boy" *(Potter says, "boogie woogie bugle beak")* Written by Don Raye and Hughie Prince, recorded at Decca Studios in 1941 and a major hit for The Andrews Sisters.

171: "Some Enchanted Evening" *(Hawkeye, Scully, B.J. sing "Once you have found her never let her go...")* from the song, from the 1949 Rodgers & Hammerstein musical *South Pacific.*

"Home on the Range" *(Hawkeye says, "...And the skies are not cloudy all day.")* See Episode 16 (page 107) for details.

172: Charles plays Beethoven on his record player.

"The Lady is A Tramp" *(Klinger sings "That's why the lady is a tramp...")* Words by Lorenz Hart, music by Richard Rodgers from the 1937 musical *Babes In Arms.*

"It's A Hap-Hap-Happy Day" *(Klinger says)* from *Gulliver's Travels* (1939), and from the 1941 spinoff cartoon short of the same name. Words and music written by Sammy Timberg, Al Neiburg and Winston Sharples.

"Serenade for Strings in C Major, Opus 48" *(Charles plays)* by Pyotr Ilyich Tchaikovsky, premiered in 1880.

"Stormy Weather" *(Charles and Klinger together sing some of the lyrics in the Officer's Club)* See Episode 122 (page 381) for details.

173: "Stardust" *(Mulcahy mentions)* Music by Hoagy Carmichael in 1927, words added in 1929 by Mitchell Parish.

Appearances – Season 7

Aragon, Mariel .... Episode 163 *(Kim Sing)*
Arbus, Allen ....Episode 153 *(Major Sidney Freedman)*
Bates, Laurie .... Episode 159 *(Surgical Nurse)*
Baxley, Marc .... Episode 158 *(The Sergeant)*
Block, Larry .... Episode 159 *(Supply Sergeant Cimoli)*
Brennan, Peggy Lee .... Episode 167 *(Lieutenant Linda Nugent)*
Brooke, Walter .... Episode 167 *(Major General Lyle Weiskopf)*
Bryant, Joshua .... Episode 171 *(Listed as Sergeant Jerry Scully in credits,*
called "Jack" in Episode)
Burk, Jim .... Episode 171 *(M.P.)*
Canning, James ....Episode 166 *(Captain Simmons)*
Cavonis, Paul.. Episode 155 *(Sergeant Cutrifiotis)*
Chi, Chao-Li .... Episode 163 *(Su Sing, Korean Father)*
Chang, Sylvia .... Episode 172 *(Sooni)*
Chung, Byron...Episode 160 *(Myung)*
Clairborne, George .... Episode 160 *(Phelan)*
Clotworthy, Robert ....Episode 159 *(Private Welch)*
Cramer, David...Episode 157 *(Patient)*
Cummins, Don ....Episode 149 *(M.P. Guard)*
Davis, Jennifer... Episode 168, 171 *(Nurse)*
Davis, Todd .... Episode 159 *(Latimer)*
Dean, David .... Episode 156 *(Private Sutton)*
Dever, Tom .... Episode 155 *(M.P.)*
Di Reda, Joseph ....Episode 171 *(Major Frank Dorsett)*
Dozer, David... Episode 159 *(Groves)*
Driscoll, Lawrason.......................................Episode 162 *(Lieutenant Forrester)*
Driscoll, Patrick ....Episode 162 *(Patient)*
Farrell, Judy.. Episode 172 *(Nurse Able)*
Favara, Mark ....Episode 164 *(Patient)*
Fujikawa, Jerry................................ Episode 169 *(Hung Pak, Ouijongbu Chief of Police)*
Gallardo, Edward...Episode 158 *(Medic #1)*
Geer, Kevin .... Episode 153 *(Sergeant Jerry Nielson)*
Gehring, Ted... Episode 154 *(Sergeant Clifford Rhoden)*
Gillan, Hugh.. Episode 149 *(General Tomlin)*
Golden, Roy... Episode 156 *(Corpsman)*
Gorman, Brad .... Episode 158 *(Russell)*
Hagen, Kevin .... Episode 149 *(Major Dean Goss)*
Hartley, Mariette... Episode 164 *(Dr. Inga Halverson)*
Haymer, Johnny .... Episode 154, 160, 163, 165 *(Sergeant Zelmo Zale)*
Hoffman, Basil.. Episode 168 *(Bartruff)*
Hoshi, Shizuko ....Episode 163 *(Korean Mother)*
Jenkins, Charles... Episode 168 *(Private Lovett)*
Jenkins, Larry Flash .... Episode 170 *(Listed as Private North in credits,*
called "Corporal North" in Episode)
Jorden, Jan................................... Episode 148, 154, 157, 158, 167 *(Nurse Baker)*
Katz, Phyllis ....Episode 156 *(Triage Nurse)*
Katz, Phyllis .... Episode 164 *(Nurse)*
Keep, Stephen .... Episode 163 *(General's Aide)*
Kent, Enid.......................................Episode 148, 155, 167, 168 *(Nurse Bigelow)*
Kim, Leigh.. Episode 165 *(R.O.K. Soldier)*
LaGuardia, Michael..Episode 149 *(M.P. Guard)*

Broadcast/Production Order – Season 7

Broadcast	*Production*
148: Commander Pierce *(9/18/1978)*	148: *(T401)* Peace On Us
149: Peace On Us *(9/25/1978)*	149: *(T402)* B.J. Papa San
150: Lil *(10/2/1978)*	150: *(T403)* Baby, It's Cold Outside
151: Our Finest Hour, Part 1 *(10/9/1978)*	151: *(T404)* Commander Pierce
152: Our Finest Hour, Part 2 *(10/9/1978)*	152: *(T405)* The Billfold Syndrome
153: The Billfold Syndrome *(10/16/1978)*	153: *(T406)* Lil
154: None Like It Hot *(10/23/1978)*	154: *(T407)* They Call The Wind KoRea
155: They Call The Wind Korea *(10/30/1978)*	155: *(T408)* Our Finest Hour, Part 1
156: Major Ego *(11/6/1978)*	156: *(T409)* Our Finest Hour, Part 2
157: Baby, It's Cold Outside *(11/13/1978)*	157: *(T410)* None Like It Hot
158: Point Of View *(11/20/1978)*	158: *(T411)* Out Of Gas
159: Dear Comrade *(11/27/1978)*	159: *(T412)* Major Ego
160: Out Of Gas *(12/4/1978)*	160: *(T413)* Dear Comrade
161: An Eye For A Tooth *(12/11/1978)*	161: *(T414)* An Eye For A Tooth
162: Dear Sis *(12/18/1978)*	162: *(T415)* Point Of View
163: B.J. Papa San– 1/1/1979	163: *(T416)* Preventative Medicine
164: Inga– 1/8/1979	164: *(T417)* Dear Sis
165: The Price *(1/15/1979)*	165: *(T418)* The Price
166: The Young And The Restless *(1/22/1979)*	166: *(T419)* Hot Lips Is Back In Town
167: Hot Lips Is Back In Town *(1/29/1979)*	167: *(T420)* Inga
168: C*A*V*E *(2/5/1979)*	168: *(T421)* The Young And The Restless
169: Rally Round The Flagg, Boys *(2/14/1979)*	169: *(T422)* Ain't Love Grand?
170: Preventative Medicine *(2/19/1979)*	170: *(T423)* C*A*V*E
171: A Night At Rosie's *(2/16/1979)*	171: *(T424)* The Party
172: Ain't Love Grand? *(3/5/1979)*	172: *(T425)* Rally Round The Flagg, Boys
173: The Party *(3/12/1979)*	173: *(T426)* A Night At Rosie's

Season 8

Though Season 8 is reminiscent of the previous one, there is something about it that differentiates itself from all preceding seven seasons, and the three that followed. Certainly, this season of M*A*S*H is a stellar one, though quite unlike the Gelbart/Reynolds years in tone. Gary Burghoff had filmed some snippets of scenes that were plugged in to a few of the first shows of this season. His farewell episode, "Goodbye, Radar," aired soon after. Klinger was now out of dresses and semi-permanently into fatigues as he assumed the job of company clerk. From this season on, he became more of a camp operator and schemer. By all accounts, the cast as icing on the cake enjoyed M*A*S*H's eighth season. The show had been on for seven wonderful seasons, and Season 8 was a chance to celebrate it all with more sentimentality. Story ideas were fresh and introspective. The drama became more intense and social messages were more blatant. This is evident in "Guerrilla My Dreams," when Hawkeye calls a South Korean soldier who is preparing to execute an enemy combatant, a "son of a bitch." Margaret was accused of being a Communist sympathizer and was quite far removed from the Hot Lips of earlier years. Potter lost old friends and saluted new ones; BJ missed being home more than ever, and M*A*S*H celebrated April Fool's Day. The blend of comedy and drama was altered. There were lengthy and purely comedic scenes, and lengthy and purely dramatic ones. The contrast became stark. Whole episodes, such as "Dreams," were almost entirely dramatic. Stiers continued to excel at being Charles, and Farrell and Morgan were now at M*A*S*H longer than their predecessors. Notable episodes include "Goodbye Radar," "April Fools," "Dreams," and "The Yalu Brick Road."

Too Many Cooks – 9/17/1979

Season 8 / Episode 174 / Production 174 – S601

Columbia House VHS Tape . . . . Loyalties (Catalog # 22052)
Fox DVD . . . . Season 8, Disc 1

Alan Alda, Mike Farrell, Harry Morgan
Loretta Swit, David Ogden Stiers, Jamie Farr, William Christopher
And Gary Burghoff as Radar

Executive Producer – Burt Metcalfe
Produced by John Rappaport and Jim Mulligan
Written by Dennis Koenig
Directed by Charles S. Dubin

Executive Story Editors – Dan Wilcox & Thad Mumford
Story Consultant – Ronny Graham
Creative Consultants – Gene Reynolds / Alan Alda
John Randolph . . . . Brigadier General Bud Haggerty A.G.
Ed Begly, Jr. . . . . Private Paul Conway
Copyright 1979 – 20th Century Fox Film Corporation

Non-Credited Appearances . . . . Kellye Nakahara, Gwen Farrell, Roy Goldman

Chapters

1: *Main Titles / Funny Bone*
2: *Hard to Reach – 2:33*
3: *Four Letter Word – 4:11*
4: *Ecstasy – 6:32*
5: *True Vacation – 7:20*

6: *Marriage Counselor – 10:30*
7: *Woman to Man – 14:09*
8: *Private Enterprise – 15:40*
9: *Together – 20:36*
10: *Improvisation / End Titles – 23:00*

Closing Stills

1: *Freeze – BJ, Hawk, Charles, Potter - Goat A La King*
2: *General Haggerty in the mess tent*
3: *Conway in the mess tent*
4: *B.J. in the Officer's Club*
5: *Potter*
6: *Margaret in the Officer's Club*
7: *Charles in the Officer's Club*
8: *Klinger in a tuxedo in the mess tent*
9: *Mulcahy in the mess tent*
10: *Radar on leave in Tokyo*
11: *Hawkeye in the Officer's Club*

Synopsis: Private Paul Conway, a klutzy rifleman who's more dangerous to his unit than the enemy, winds up in the hospital with torn ligaments after falling into a foxhole and breaking the collarbones of two of his buddies, who also wind up in the hospital. In civilian life, Conway is a chef and after preparing delicious meals such as "Spam Parmigiana" and "Coq Au Vin," the mess tent is transformed into an upscale eatery, complete with a maitre D', reservations and a line to get in. Although impressed with Conway's talents, Colonel Potter's marriage might be in jeopardy and the very irritable Colonel is not impressed with the staff's attempts to keep Conway at the 4077th.

Commentary by Jeff Maxwell: "You're forgetting my Spam Lamb! Who needed Conway, anyway!"

Authors' Notes: There are no PA announcements in this episode.

This is the first episode with the billing "And Gary Burghoff as Radar."

A rarity in that there's a telephone in the mess tent: this is the second episode where a telephone is seen other than in Radar's or Potter's office, except for the occasional extension into the OR and the compound directly outside the office. The first episode to have a telephone other than the offices is Season 3's "White Gold," when Colonel Flagg hits himself over the head with a telephone in the V.I.P. tent.

According to Margaret in Chapter 7, Potter has been married for 40 years. In the last episode, "The Party," it's been established that the year is 1953. This means that Potter was married in 1913.

The following has been taken from Episode 158, Season 7's "Point of View," as it relates to how long Potter has been married:

In Chapter 8, the date on a letter Private Rich is writing to his folks is [Wednesday] September 12, 1951. According to Potter, his 35th wedding anniversary was last Saturday, making his anniversary September 8, 1916. Although this episode clearly takes place on [Wednesday] September 12, 1951, in Episode 73, Potter took command of the 4077th on [Friday] September 19, 1952 and in Episode 79, he said he and Mildred have been married for 27 years. This means they were married in 1925. His son was born in 1926. However, in Episode 132, he and Mildred were married in 1913 and they will have been married for 38 years "this April." This puts Episode 132 in 1951.

Are You Now, Margaret? - 9/24/1979

Season 8 / Episode 175 / Production 175 – S602

Columbia House VHS Tape . . . . *Up In Arms (Catalog # 21032)*
Fox DVD . . . . *Season 8, Disc 1*

Alan Alda, Mike Farrell, Harry Morgan
Loretta Swit, David Ogden Stiers, Jamie Farr, William Christopher
And Gary Burghoff as Radar

Executive Producer – Burt Metcalfe
Produced by Jim Mulligan and John Rappaport
Written by Thad Mumford & Dan Wilcox
Directed by Charles S. Dubin

Executive Story Editors – Dan Wilcox & Thad Mumford
Story Consultant – Ronny Graham
Creative Consultants – Gene Reynolds / Alan Alda
Lawrence Pressman . . . . R.Theodore Williamson
Jeff Maxwell. . . . . .Igor
Leland Sun . . . . Chinese Patient
Jennifer Davis . . . . Nurse
Copyright 1979 – 20th Century Fox Film Corporation

Non-Credited Appearances. . . . . Kellye Nakahara, Gwen Farrell, Roy Goldman

Chapters

1:	Main Titles / V.I.P. Visitor	6:	…Or Have You Ever Been? – 12:24
2:	Finger on the Pulse – 4:00	7:	No Choice – 16:29
3:	Prankster – 6:02	8:	Hot Lips – 18:10
4:	Let's Get Serious – 6:50	9:	Duped – 19:54
5:	The Direct Approach – 9:45	10:	Love Nest / End Titles – 22:48

Closing Stills

1: *Freeze – BJ, Hawkeye, Charles, Potter, Margaret, Klinger*
2: *Williamson at Margaret's tent door*
3: *Margaret in her tent*
4: *B.J.*
5: *Charles*
6: *Potter*
7: *Klinger in the office*
8: *Mulcahy in the mess tent*
9: *Hawkeye in the Swamp*

Synopsis: The arrival of a congressional aide from Washington, D.C. results in allegations that Margaret is a Communist sympathizer because of a long-ago relationship she had with Wally Crichton. Walter Philip Crichton, after becoming the founding member of "Freedom for Tomorrow," was named a subversive by the House Committee. Margaret doesn't deny her past relationship, even admitting that she liked Wally, but does deny allegations that he's a subversive. R.T. Williamson offers Margaret a choice: she can voluntarily testify before the House Committee and name names, or she can be subpoenaed. Either way, Margaret can handle the public humiliation she's sure to endure, and the end of her army career is almost a certainty, but she cannot handle what this would do to her father, who was very proud of her when she made the rank of major. But Williamson, after learning that Margaret also goes by the name of "Hot Lips," decides to find out if she lives up to her nickname, and falls into a trap that could cause the congressional aide to testify before Mrs. Williamson.

Authors' Notes: There are no PA announcements in this episode.
The picture seems dark until approximately 1:30.
In a few of the "later" episodes, including Chapter 1 in this episode, the view out from the office windows shows the same wood structure and people are seen again milling about (this is also seen in a night scene in Chapter 6).
Colonel Potter usually has two different robes, one is gray and red stripes and the other a heavy dark green, but in Chapter 5, he's wearing the robe usually worn by Henry Blake.
Charles, in Chapter 7, mentions "New Dealer." The term "New Deal" was introduced by President Roosevelt for programs he initiated between 1933 and 1938. These programs were designed to provide relief to the poor, recovery from the Great Depression and to reform the financial system.

Guerilla My Dreams – 10/1/1979

Season 8 / Episode 176 / Production 176 – S603
Columbia House VHS Tape . . . . *Local Color (Catalog # 19506)*
Fox DVD . . . . *Season 8, Disc 1*

Alan Alda, Mike Farrell, Harry Morgan
Loretta Swit, David Ogden Stiers, Jamie Farr, William Christopher
And Gary Burghoff as Radar

Executive Producer – Burt Metcalfe
Produced by Jim Mulligan and John Rappaport
Written by Bob Colleary
Directed by Alan Alda

Executive Story Editors – Dan Wilcox & Thad Mumford
Story Consultant – Ronny Graham
Creative Consultants – Gene Reynolds / Alan Alda

Mako . . . . Lieutenant Hung Lee Park
Josh Bryant . . . . Sergeant Jack Scully
Guerilla Woman . . . . Haunani Minn
George Kee Cheung . . . . 1st Korean Soldier
Marcus Mukai . . . . 2nd Korean Soldier
Conny Izay . . . . Nurse
Copyright 1979 – 20th Century Fox Film Corporation

Non-Credited Appearances . . . . Kellye Nakahara, Gwen Farrell, Roy Goldman

Chapters

1: *Main Titles / Ah, Cognac*	6: *Angel of Mercy – 11:56*
2: *P.O.W. – 3:39*	7: *From the Top – 13:12*
3: *One Tough Cookie – 6:03*	8: *The Winchester Gambit – 14:50*
4: *Jumping the Gun – 8:41*	9: *Just Doing His Job – 17:53*
5: *A Little R&R – 10:38*	10: *Good Work / End Titles – 22:21*

Closing Stills

1: *Freeze – Hawkeye, Margaret, B.J. – Compound*
2: *Scully in Post-Op*
3: *Guerilla Woman*
4: *Lieutenant Hung Lee Park playing chess*
5: *Charles playing chess*
6: *Potter*
7: *Klinger*
8: *Radar in Tokyo*
9: *Margaret in the compound*
10: *Mulcahy*
11: *B.J.*
12: *Hawkeye*

Synopsis: What appears to be a wounded Korean woman turns out to be an enemy guerilla, and a prisoner of Lieutenant Park of the South Korean Army. Hawkeye and B.J. stop the Lieutenant's armed guards from carrying the wounded woman off on a stretcher, even though Lt. Park makes it clear that she's a killer. Hawkeye then makes it clear that he doesn't care who or what she is, because right now, she's his patient and he's going to operate. Also among the wounded is Sergeant Jack Scully, who's aware of Lt. Park's reputation for torturing, and then killing enemy guerillas, and the doctors, including Charles try to prevent that from happening, but are met with limited success. Since Colonel Potter's authority in the matter is also limited, the doctors try to sneak the woman out of camp, but Lt. Park catches them and the situation becomes tense when, after Hawkeye and B.J. try to take the woman back, Park's guards aim their rifles at the doctors.

PA Announcement by Sal Viscuso

Authors' Notes: Some outdoor scenes on the Ranch set in this episode were apparently filmed through chicken wire.

In Chapter 7, B.J. mentions *Truth or Consequences*, a quiz show originally heard on NBC radio by Ralph Edwards between 1940 and 1957, and would later be shown on television with different hosts, including Edwards and Bob Barker.

The view from the office windows shows the same wooden structure, but a little closer than before.

Hawkeye mentions, in Chapter 7, Dorothy Kilgallen (1913-1965), a journalist and a game-show panelist, better known for her coverage of the Sam Sheppard trial.

Hawkeye also mentions, in Chapter 7, Walter Winchell (1897-1972), a newspaper and radio gossip commentator, who was said to have the ability to make or break a career.

In Chapter 8, Charles mentions Ruy Lopez, a 16th century Spanish Bishop and chess player.

Goodbye Radar, Part 1 – 10/8/1979

Season 8 / Episode 177 / Production 183 – S610

Columbia House VHS Tape . . . . *Changing Of The Clerks (Catalog # 19507)*
Fox DVD . . . . *Season 8, Disc 1*

Alan Alda, Mike Farrell, Harry Morgan
Loretta Swit, David Ogden Stiers, Jamie Farr, William Christopher
And Gary Burghoff as Radar

Executive Producer – Burt Metcalfe
Produced by John Rappaport and Jim Mulligan
Written by Ken Levine & David Isaacs
Directed by Charles S. Dubin

Executive Story Editors – Dan Wilcox & Thad Mumford
Story Editor – Dennis Koenig
Creative Consultants – Gene Reynolds / Alan Alda

Johnny Haymer . . . . Sergeant Zelmo Zale
Marilyn Jones . . . . Lieutenant Patty Haven
Michael O'Dwyer . . . . Sergeant Olsen (Air Force)
Tony Cristino . . . . Sergeant Lagrow
Arell Blanton . . . . Private Hough
Sean Fallon Walsh . . . . Forster
Jon St. Elwood . . . . Private Reuss
Richard Lee Sung . . . . Cart Driver

Copyright 1979 – 20th Century Fox Film Corporation

Non-Credited Appearances . . . . Kellye Nakahara, Gwen Farrell, Dennis Troy,
Roy Goldman

Chapters

1: *Main Titles / Lights Out*	6: *Bumped Again – 14:01*
2: *Small World – 4:08*	7: *Magic Suction Machine – 15:22*
3: *Back to Basics – 7:19*	8: *Return of the Hero – 16:08*
4: *Romeo – 9:47*	9: *To Heck in A Hand Basket – 18:07*
5: *Dinner Guests – 12:28*	10: *Going Home / End Titles – 21:23*

Closing Stills

1: *Freeze – Radar finds out he's going home*
2: *Patty*
3: *Zale and Klinger*
4: *Hawkeye*
5: *B.J.*
6: *Potter*
7: *Margaret*
8: *Charles*
9: *Klinger*
10: *Mulcahy in Post-Op*
11: *Radar*

Synopsis: With Radar on R & R, Klinger fills in for him and has a difficult time of it as evidenced by the condition of the office, and it's not going to get easier any time soon as the unit loses electricity during surgery. With orders from Potter, Klinger works with Zale to repair the generator, and after Zale accidentally blows it up, Klinger discovers their backup generator was stolen, and really doesn't want to be the one to tell Potter. Radar returns from R & R, much to the delight of Klinger, but doesn't understand why they couldn't locate a generator since it's only a "three-call finagle." Radar soon finds out that even he can't find a generator, and also finds out that his Uncle Ed passed away, and is headed home.

Authors' Notes: There are no PA announcements in this episode.

Private Hough was named after Los Angeles Dodgers pitcher, # 49, Charlie Hough. Forster was named after Los Angeles Dodgers pitcher, # 51, Terry Forster.

As a clock has been seen in several previous O.R. scenes, the one seen in Chapter 1 in this episode shows both standard and hundred-hour time.

Also in Chapter 1, the Arthur Godfrey (1903-1983) radio program is heard in O.R., and he's talking about powdered soup. "Lipton" was a major sponsor of the very popular radio show and Godfrey was famous for adlibbing the spots.

When Henry, in Season 3's "Life with Father," received his adult movies, he said that they would be screened at midnight in the generator shed. However, in this episode, the generator is clearly seen on the compound. (Stage 9)

Potterisms: "Carolina Cowpies," "Pigeon Pellets."

In Chapter 3, Colonel Potter mentions "Wangensteen suction." This real device was named after its inventor, Doctor Owen H. Wangensteen (1898-1981), who was also a brilliant surgeon, devising several new surgical methods.

Radar's serial number in Chapter 8 is RA 9458063. In Season 5's "Lieutenant Radar O'Reilly," his serial number was 3911810. In Season 7's "Out of Gas," his serial number was RA 1949069.

It would seem that Radar's cow, "Edna," changed her name to "Betsy" for this episode (Chapter 8).

Goodbye Radar, Part 2 – 10/15/1979

Season 8 / Episode 178 / Production 184 – S611
Columbia House VHS Tape . . . . *Changing Of The Clerks (Catalog # 19507)*
Fox DVD . . . . *Season 8, Disc 1*

Alan Alda, Mike Farrell, Harry Morgan
Loretta Swit, David Ogden Stiers, Jamie Farr, William Christopher
And Gary Burghoff as Radar

Executive Producer – Burt Metcalfe
Produced by Jim Mulligan and John Rappaport
Written by Ken Levine & David Isaacs
Directed by Charles S. Dubin

Executive Story Editors – Dan Wilcox & Thad Mumford
Story Editor – Dennis Koenig
Creative Consultants – Gene Reynolds / Alan Alda
Lee De Broux . . . . Major George Van Kirk
Whitney Rydbeck . . . . Sergeant Hondo McKee
David Dozer . . . . Dispatcher
Copyright 1979 – 20th Century Fox Film Corporation

Non-Credited Appearances . . . . Kellye Nakahara, Gwen Farrell, Dennis Troy,
Roy Goldman

Chapters

1: *Main Titles / Recap*
2: *Thrown to the Wolves – 2:00*
3: *Loyalty – 3:56*
4: *Stroke of Genius – 7:16*
5: *Going, Staying – 9:01*

6: *A Real Live Generator – 12:20*
7: *A Damn Good Friend – 15:54*
8: *Godspeed – 17:19*
9: *Whiz-Bang of A Send-Off – 20:14*
10: *Last Goodbye / End Titles – 22:45*

Closing Stills

1: *Freeze – BJ, Hawkeye w/ bear, Potter – Swamp*
2: *Hawkeye*
3: *B.J. – Post-Op*
4: *Potter*
5: *Margaret – Post-Op*
6: *Charles – Post-Op*
7: *Klinger in the office*
8: *Mulcahy*
9: *Radar*

Synopsis: Cleaning out his desk, Radar finds the thermometer given to him by Henry, and his Purple Heart that Hawkeye pinned on him, hardly hearing Klinger's pleas for help. When a call comes in for Radar, he wants Klinger to handle it, then thinks better of it and takes it himself. They can get a generator in exchange for a frozen custard machine, but there probably isn't one in all of Korea. With wounded arriving, and without lights to see at night, Radar wants supply to send all the jeeps and trucks they have. A makeshift operating room is setup in the middle of the compound surrounded by all the vehicles with their headlights on, and the surgeons can finally see what they're doing. Praising Radar for his idea, Potter has a drink with him in the office, and Radar informs him of his decision to stay, infuriating Hawkeye, but even Hawkeye can't change his mind. When another call comes in for Radar, Klinger decides to handle it himself, and winds up going to supply with a case of Scotch in exchange for a generator, but an angry major shows up to claim it instead. After some quick thinking, Klinger gets the generator before anyone else and brings it back to the 4077th, surprising and impressing everyone, including Radar, who now decides he can go home. Radar's farewell party in the mess tent ends before getting started when wounded arrive, forcing quick goodbyes on the compound, and B.J. lets him know that Peg and Erin will meet him at the airport in San Francisco. Taking a last look into the operating room, Hawkeye sees him and salutes his friend, and after returning the salute, Radar is driven out of camp for the last time.

Commentary by Gary Burghoff: "If you look at that last episode, I went from like 160 pounds to 130. I really wanted to get back to my roots."

PA Announcement by Hawkeye seen in the office

Authors' Notes: Potterism: "Hot diggity dog tags."
As per Gary Burghoff's commentary above, he's noticeably thinner in this episode, and he doesn't look or sound like the "Radar" of past episodes.
More and more, Klinger will be seen in regulation fatigues.

Period of Adjustment – 10/22/1979

Season 8 / Episode 179 / Production 177 – S604

Columbia House VHS Tape . . . . *Changing Of The Clerks (Catalog # 19507)*
Fox DVD . . . . *Season 8, Disc 1*

Alan Alda, Mike Farrell, Harry Morgan
Loretta Swit, David Ogden Stiers, Jamie Farr, William Christopher
And Gary Burghoff as Radar

Executive Producer – Burt Metcalfe
Produced by John Rappaport and Jim Mulligan
Written by Jim Mulligan & John Rappaport
Directed by Charles S. Dubin

Executive Story Editors – Dan Wilcox & Thad Mumford
Script Consultant – Ronny Graham
Creative Consultants – Gene Reynolds / Alan Alda

Eileen Saki . . . . Rosie
Jan Jorden . . . . Nurse Baker
Jeff Maxwell. . . . . Igor
Gwen Farrell . . . . Nurse
Copyright 1979 – 20th Century Fox Film Corporation

Non-Credited Appearances. . . . . .Kellye Nakahara, Roy Goldman

Chapters

1:	Main Titles / New Hire	6:	The Same Bozo – 13:46
2:	Mail Call – 2:53	7:	What A Pain – 15:58
3:	In A Bad Mood – 5:07	8:	No Better, No Worse – 18:06
4:	The Letter – 8:13	9:	Missing Out – 19:39
5:	M.I.A. – 11:08	10:	Repairmen / End Titles – 22:39

Closing Stills

1: *Freeze – Hawkeye, Klinger, BJ in the Swamp*
2: *Rosie*
3: *Hawkeye in the Swamp*
4: *B.J. cries*
5: *Potter*
6: *Margaret*
7: *Charles*
8: *Klinger in the Swamp*
9: *Mulcahy*

Synopsis: As Klinger tries to settle into his new position as company clerk, the staff isn't making it easy for him with a constant barrage of insults; worse are the comparisons to Radar, both of which drive him to drink. Meanwhile, B.J. gets a letter from Peg to tell him that she and Erin had spent two or three hours with Radar at the airport and how nice he is. But when she tells B.J. that Erin ran to him and called him "Daddy," it has an adverse effect on him. Upset the first time his daughter calls someone "Daddy" and it wasn't B.J. causes him to become violently drunk, to the point of smashing the still, punching Hawkeye in the face and later, admitting that, although he should be happy for Radar, he isn't and almost hates him.

Authors' Notes: There are no PA announcements in this episode.

"Also Starring Gary Burghoff as Radar" is still in the opening credits, although he's no longer on the show.

The view out of the office windows is on an angle, and the side of a corrugated structure is seen in Chapter 1. Later, in Chapter 7, the angle changes and the wooden structure is seen.

The sign on Margaret's tent door in Chapter 2 is freehand lettering. Sometimes the sign is block lettering.

Potterisms: "Has everybody around here gone dingus?", "What in the name of Sweet Fanny Adams?" Fanny Adams (1859-1867) was murdered by Frederick Baker. Potter's phrase means: "nothing at all."

In Chapter 5, Potter mentions "The Great John L." John L. Sullivan was a heavyweight champ from 1882 to 1892 and beyond. It's also the name of a movie from 1945 which, as a coincidence, was directed by Frank Tuttle.

Mulcahy in Chapter 6 is wearing a brown plaid robe, not the blue plaid or Henry's.

Potter, in Chapter 6 is Presbyterian, even though in Episode 75, Season 4's "Change of Command," he's a Methodist (and hates to sing alone).

Nurse Doctor – 10/29/1979

Season 8 / Episode 180 / Production 181 – S608

Columbia House VHS Tape . . . . Changing Of The Clerks (Catalog # 19507)
Fox DVD . . . . Season 8, Disc 1

Alan Alda, Mike Farrell, Harry Morgan
Loretta Swit, David Ogden Stiers, Jamie Farr, William Christopher
And Gary Burghoff as Radar

Executive Producer – Burt Metcalfe
Produced by Jim Mulligan and John Rappaport
Teleplay by Sy Rosen and Thad Mumford & Dan Wilcox
Story by Sy Rosen
Directed by Charles S. Dubin

Executive Story Editors – Dan Wilcox & Thad Mumford
Story Editor – Dennis Koenig
Creative Consultants – Gene Reynolds / Alan Alda

Alexandra Stoddart . . . . .Lieutenant Gail Harris
Jeff Maxwell. . . . . .Igor
Kellye Nakahara . . . . .Nurse Kellye

Non-Credited Appearances. . . . . .Gwen Farrell, Dennis Troy

Chapters

1: Main Titles / Dry Up	6: Stop! – 15:59
2: Trying to Help – 3:06	7: No Backing Out – 18:36
3: Creamed Everything – 6:07	8: Soap in your Eye – 20:01
4: High Expectations – 7:29	9: A Class By Herself – 21:10
5: Personal Advice – 10:05	10: Stampede / End Titles – 23:04

Closing Stills

1: Freeze – Lieutenant Gail Harris
2: Igor in the mess tent
3: Mulcahy
4: B.J.
5: Potter in the office
6: Margaret in her tent
7: Charles in the mess tent
8: Klinger on mess tent floor after trampled
9: Hawkeye

Synopsis: Grateful for Father Mulcahy's help with studying for a medical aptitude test is Lieutenant Gail Harris, a nurse who wants to become a doctor. Lieutenant Harris is finding out that not everyone is as eager to help her as the good Father is, when, during surgery, she angers Winchester by questioning the use of the instrument he called for. After the session, Margaret lets her know that she alienates people by asking too many questions and offering too many corrections. But the young nurse makes her biggest mistake when she hugs Mulcahy, and might want more than what the priest can offer. Since there's a water shortage in camp, Potter orders the showers off-limits and restricts the use of the remaining water for patient-use only. The temporary drought doesn't seem to affect Charles as he's clean-shaven and his towel is wet and, after following him into the showers, Hawkeye and B.J. find out why.

PA Announcement by Sal Viscuso

Authors' Notes: The second episode with "Also Starring Gary Burghoff as Radar" since he left the show.

Colonel Potter is now seen in Chapter 1 with a fourth robe, similar in design to the one Henry Blake used to wear, but with a light-yellow color. The other three robes he's been seen in are a gray and dark red stripes, a heavy army-green, and the one usually worn by Henry.

In Chapter 7, Potter says "Tempus Fugit" which (usually written on clocks) is Latin for "time flies."

When Charles is in the showers in Chapter 8, there's a brief shot of the top of his jockey shorts.

Gwen Farrell, usually an extra and sometimes credited as a nurse, is seen running out of the mess tent in Chapter 10 after Klinger announces a shower schedule when the water tanks are filled. She's then seen a second time running out from further inside the mess tent.

Private Finance – 11/5/1979

Season 8 / Episode 181 / Production 178 – S605

Columbia House VHS Tape . . . . Not Released by Columbia House
Fox DVD . . . . Season 8, Disc 1

Alan Alda, Mike Farrell, Harry Morgan
Loretta Swit, David Ogden Stiers, Jamie Farr, William Christopher
And Gary Burghoff as Radar

Executive Producer – Burt Metcalfe
Produced by Jim Mulligan and John Rappaport
Written by Dennis Koenig
Directed by Charles S. Dubin

Executive Story Editors – Dan Wilcox & Thad Mumford
Story Consultant – Ronny Graham
Creative Consultants – Gene Reynolds / Alan Alda

Shizuko Hoshi . . . . Mrs. Li
Denice Kumagai . . . . Oksun Li
Mark Kologi . . . . Private Eddie Hastings
Joey Pento . . . . Sergeant Croseti
Philip Simms. . . . . Vitello
Art Evans. . . . . Dolan
Mark Harrison . . . . Soldier
James Emery. . . . . Soldier

Copyright 1979 – 20th Century Fox Film Corporation

Non-Credited Appearances. . . . . Kellye Nakahara, Gwen Farrell, Dennis Troy,
Roy Goldman

Chapters

1: *Main Titles / Saved*
2: *Money Belt – 4:00*
3: *Over – 5:30*
4: *Ill-Gotten Gains – 6:58*
5: *Madam Pitchfork – 8:53*

6: *No Great Loss – 10:49*
7: *Dear Parents – 13:27*
8: *The Cost of War – 15:57*
9: *Community Chest – 20:07*
10: *Do-Gooder / End Titles – 23:03*

Closing Stills

1: *Freeze – Hawkeye, Charles, Klinger, B.J. – toast Eddie*
2: *Mrs. Li with pitchfork*
3: *Oksun Li*
4: *Eddie Hastings*
5: *Klinger*
6: *B.J.*
7: *Potter*
8: *Margaret*
9: *Charles*
10: *Mulcahy*
11: *Hawkeye*

Synopsis: Private Eddie Hastings is seriously wounded, but his main concern is the
money belt he's wearing and won't let Hawkeye take care of him until he promises to
send the money to Hastings' parents if he doesn't make it. In spite of Hawkeye's and

B.J.'s best efforts, Hastings dies on the operating table, and they later discover he had nearly $9,000, not in military scrip, but American cash, from less than honorable sources. Following through on his promise, Hawkeye sends the money to Mr. and Mrs. Hastings with surprising results. When a local Korean woman sees Klinger give her young daughter money, she reaches the wrong conclusion and now wants to put her pitchfork through Klinger's ribs.

PA Announcement by Todd Sussman

Authors' Notes: "Private Finance" is the third episode with the opening credit, "Also Starring Gary Burghoff as Radar" since he left the show.

In the change room in Chapter 4, the order of the names over the hooks has changed to *Hawkeye, Winchester, Potter, B.J.*

Potterism: "What in the name of Beelzebub is going on here?"

Mr. and Mrs. Who? – 11/12/1979

Season 8 / Episode 182 / Production 179 – S606

Columbia House VHS Tape . . . . Not Released by Columbia House

Fox DVD . . . . Season 8, Disc 2

Alan Alda, Mike Farrell, Harry Morgan
Loretta Swit, David Ogden Stiers, Jamie Farr, William Christopher
And Gary Burghoff as Radar

Executive Producer – Burt Metcalfe
Produced by John Rappaport and Jim Mulligan
Written by Ronny Graham
Directed by Burt Metcalfe

Executive Story Editors – Dan Wilcox & Thad Mumford
Story Consultant – Ronny Graham
Creative Consultants – Gene Reynolds / Alan Alda

Claudette Nevins. . . . . Donna Marie Parker

James Keane . . . . Corporal Shaw

Copyright 1979 – 20th Century Fox Film Corporation

Non-Credited Appearances. . . . . Kellye Nakahara, Gwen Farrell

Chapters

1: Main Titles / What Memory?	6: In Shock – 12:18
2: Something to Drink – 3:55	7: What's in A Name – 14:58
3: Korean Fever – 5:58	8: Compliments of the Bride – 19:52
4: Quite A Party – 9:25	9: The Good War – 21:04
5: Complications – 11:23	10: Undo / End Titles – 22:04

Closing Stills

1: Freeze – BJ, Charles, Donna in the mess tent
2: Donna
3: Shaw
4: Hawkeye in Post-Op
5: B.J.
6: Potter in the office
7: Margaret
8: Klinger in the Swamp
9: Mulcahy (S 7 Still)
10: Charles

Synopsis: Returning from R&R, Charles, disheveled and in need of a shave, is hung over from a wild party, and if it weren't for the pictures of him with smiles drawn on his knees, he'd have no memory of the event at all, including his marriage to Mrs. "Chuck" Winchester III. Headache notwithstanding, Charles and the staff is worried about Corporal Shaw's loss of sodium due to Korean Homorganic Fever, and their concern turns to mild panic when a directive prohibits the use of saline solutions. If they go against orders and administer a saline solution, Shaw could die and the staff could be held criminally liable, but if they do nothing, Shaw will die. When the Corporal becomes unconscious from the fever, B.J. comes up with a treatment that hasn't been tried before, and with no options left, Potter allows it.

PA Announcement by Sal Viscuso

Authors' Notes: The fourth episode to have "Also Starring Gary Burghoff as Radar" in the opening credits since he left the show.

The view from the office windows has been fairly consistent, as in Chapter 3, showing the wooden structure and with people milling about

Potterism: "Who in San Juan Hill is that?"

In Chapter 7, Donna Marie Parker says "Come live with me and be my love and we will all the pleasures prove." This quote is from *The Passionate Shepherd to His Love,* written by English poet Christopher Marlowe in the 1590's.

Charles, in Chapter 8, mentions The Mikado, a Gilbert and Sullivan comic opera that opened on March 14, 1885 in London.

Yalu Brick Road – 11/19/1979

Season 8 / Episode 183 / Production 180 – S607

Columbia House VHS Tape . . . . Beej (Catalog # 19501)
Fox DVD . . . . Season 8, Disc 2

Alan Alda, Mike Farrell, Harry Morgan
Loretta Swit, David Ogden Stiers, Jamie Farr, William Christopher
And Gary Burghoff as Radar

Executive Producer – Burt Metcalfe
Produced by John Rappaport and Jim Mulligan
Written by Mike Farrell
Directed by Charles S. Dubin

Executive Story Editors – Dan Wilcox & Thad Mumford
Story Editor – Dennis Koenig
Creative Consultants – Gene Reynolds / Alan Alda

Soon-Teck Oh . . . . Ralph
G.W. Bailey . . . . Rizzo
Byron Chung . . . . North Korean Patrol Leader
Bob Okazaki . . . . Farmer
Jeff Maxwell . . . . .Igor
Kellye Nakahara . . . . .Nurse Kellye
Roy Goldman . . . . Corpsman

Copyright 1979 – 20th Century Fox Film Corporation

Non-Credited Appearances . . . . .Jan Jorden

Chapters

1: *Main Titles / Assassin*
2: *Wrecked – 3:43*
3: *I Surrender – 5:50*
4: *All Hands on Deck – 7:27*
5: *Foreign Relations – 9:52*

6: *A Major Tiff – 13:24*
7: *Farmer in the Dell – 15:15*
8: *On the Ocean – 18:59*
9: *Touchdown – 20:41*
10: *Stuff It / End Titles – 21:58*

Closing Stills

1: *Freeze – Klinger – Stuff it!*
2: *Hawkeye and BJ surrender to Ralph*
3: *Ralph surrenders to Hawkeye and B.J.*
4: *Rizzo in Post-Op*
5: *Igor in Post-Op*
6: *Klinger stuff it!*
7: *Mulcahy*
8: *Charles in a jeep*
9: *Margaret*
10: *Potter*

Synopsis: When an outbreak of salmonella takes hold of the 4077th, it couldn't have come at a worse time. Margaret and Charles are at the 8063rd; B.J. and Hawkeye are at Kansong Battalion Aid, and Potter, temporarily unaffected, is the only doctor left to treat everyone. After getting a rotten turkey from I-Corps Quartermaster, Klinger also gets the blame for the outbreak, but redeems himself when he too becomes stricken with the bacteria. Returning from the 8063rd, Margaret gives Charles a choice: bedpans or laundry and, in spite of his protests, he chooses laundry, and has to do it twice when it doesn't meet Margaret's standards. While B.J. drives back to the 4077th with Hawkeye, he has an accident, forcing them to carry their supplies on foot when they encounter a North Korean soldier, who not only surrenders to the doctors, he saves them from a North Korean platoon on patrol. After helping a hurt Korean farmer, he gives B.J. and Hawkeye an old motorcycle with a sidecar, and, along with their new enemy friend, ride back to camp and directly into the freshly washed linen Charles just hung to dry.

Authors' Notes: There are no PA announcements in this episode.

For the fifth straight episode, the opening credits have "Also Starring Gary Burghoff as Radar," even though he's no longer on the show.

In Chapter 2, Sergeant Rizzo is now wearing Henry Blake's robe.

Also in Chapter 4, a female patient in Post-Op is wearing the robe worn by Trapper.

For the first time, in Chapter 6, there appears to be a laundry room. More of a laundry tent, actually, and not a room, as this has canvas walls like the other tents and not wooden walls usually seen in the scrub room. Also missing are the green bottles of scrubbing soap, the recently added autoclave and the white curtain separating the scrub and change rooms. The door to the tent is clearly seen and there are no double doors leading into the operating room. Just a simple tent with sinks that Charles and Mulcahy use with scrubbing boards on the hospital linen. This tent also appears to be the same one used for Margaret and Mulcahy.

Life Time – 11/26/1979

Season 8 / Episode 184 / Production 182 – S609

Columbia House VHS Tape . . . . Decisions, Decisions (Catalog # 21035)
Fox DVD . . . . Season 8, Disc 2

Alan Alda, Mike Farrell, Harry Morgan
Loretta Swit, David Ogden Stiers, Jamie Farr, William Christopher
And Gary Burghoff as Radar

Executive Producer – Burt Metcalfe
Produced by John Rappaport and Jim Mulligan
Written by Alan Alda and Walter D. Dishell, M.D.
Directed by Alan Alda

Executive Story Editors – Dan Wilcox & Thad Mumford
Story Editor – Dennis Koenig
Creative Consultants – Gene Reynolds / Alan Alda

Kevin Brophy . . . . Roberts
Kellye Nakahara . . . . Nurse Kellye
J.J. Johnston . . . . Chopper Pilot
Jeff Maxwell . . . . Igor
Joann Thompson . . . . Jo Ann
Roy Goldman . . . . Corpsman

Copyright 1979 – 20th Century Fox Film Corporation

Non-Credited Appearances . . . . Gwen Farrell, Dennis Troy, Jan Jorden

Chapters

1: *Main Titles / On the Clock*	6: *Goodbye, My Friend – 13:04*
2: *The Iceman Cometh – 3:39*	7: *One Aorta – 15:59*
3: *Don Quixotes – 6:49*	8: *Such A Good Boy – 17:27*
4: *Don't Let Him Die – 8:12*	9: *Too Late? – 19:37*
5: *Quiet on the Front – 10:05*	10: *Who is He? / End Titles – 21:09*

Closing Stills

1: *Freeze – B.J., Mulcahy, Hawkeye in Post-Op*
2: *Roberts in Post-Op*
3: *Kellye in Post-Op*
4: *B.J. in Post-Op*
5: *Potter in O.R.*
6: *Margaret*
7: *Charles*
8: *Klinger in the office*
9: *Mulcahy*
10: *Hawkeye*

Synopsis: Hawkeye opens a man's chest while still strapped to the chopper and compresses his badly damaged aorta against his spinal column to stem the bleeding. Without proper blood flow, he has only 20 minutes to graft a section of aorta before the man becomes paralyzed. A clock is placed on-screen, further emphasizing a race against time, and it's quickly realized that, of all the grafts taken from those who didn't make it, there is no aorta, and time is running out. The PA announces the arrival of wounded in the compound and while doing triage, B.J. realizes that, although the man is still alive, nothing can be done to keep him alive and that he might have an aorta for Hawkeye in a few minutes. After explaining to the dying man's buddy, also wounded and on the bus, why they're doing what they're doing, B.J. finally has a section of aorta, and the graft is completed, but only after exceeding the time limit by three minutes and 25 seconds.

PA Announcement by Todd Sussman

Authors' Notes: This is now the sixth episode in which "Also Starring Gary Burghoff as Radar" appears, even though he's no longer on the show.

This episode was filmed without a laugh track due to the sensitive nature of the subject matter.

This episode is another of Alan Alda's list of episodes "that worked."

In Chapter 1, Hawkeye tells Klinger to get his canvas bathtub. However, in Season 7's "None Like it Hot," exactly 30 episodes ago, Potter ordered the canvas bathtub gone, and it was traded for ice cream for Radar after having his tonsils removed.

In Chapter 2, the robe usually worn by Henry Blake is on top of Hawkeye's footlocker in the Swamp.

Also in Chapter 2, Nurse Kelly is part Chinese and part Hawaiian.

In Chapter 6, the word "bastard" is used for the second time on the show; the first being in Season 5's "The General's Practitioner."

Dear Uncle Abdul – 12/3/1979

Season 8 / Episode 185 / Production 186 – S613

Columbia House VHS Tape. . . . . *Not Released by Columbia House*
Fox DVD . . . .*Season 8, Disc 2*

Alan Alda, Mike Farrell, Harry Morgan
Loretta Swit, David Ogden Stiers, Jamie Farr, William Christopher

Executive Producer – Burt Metcalfe
Produced by Jim Mulligan and John Rappaport
Written by John Rappaport & Jim Mulligan
Directed by William Jurgensen

Executive Story Editors – Dan Wilcox & Thad Mumford
Story Editor – Dennis Koenig
Creative Consultants – Gene Reynolds / Alan Alda

Richard Lineback . . . . Eddie
Alexander Pitale . . . . Hank
Kelly Ward . . . . .Dave
Copyright 1979 – 20th Century Fox Film Corporation

Non-Credited Appearances. . . . . Kellye Nakahara, Gwen Farrell, Dennis Troy,
Roy Goldman

Chapters

1: *Main Titles / Ceasefire*
2: *Laughter and Song – 3:28*
3: *The Same Joke – 6:59*
4: *Not Too Bright – 9:32*
5: *Everybody's Got A Problem – 11:55*
6: *Heading Home – 13:24*
7: *A Helluva Soldier – 16:26*
8: *Damaged Goods – 18:26*
9: *What's So Funny? – 19:58*
10: *Truce / End Titles – 23:11*

Closing Stills

1: *Freeze – Hawkeye with mustache in the shower*
2: *Eddie*
3: *Hank in Post-Op*
4: *Klinger in dress uniform on Sophie*
5: *B.J. in the Officer's Club*
6: *Potter painting*
7: *Margaret*
8: *Charles in Post-Op*
9: *Mulcahy in the Officer's Club*
10: *Hawkeye*

Synopsis: This episode features multiple storylines, the first of which finds Klinger writing a letter to his Uncle Abdul. Since taking over as company clerk, he finally finds a few minutes to write during a cease-fire, but doesn't get very far as the cease-fire itself seems to have lasted only a few minutes before wounded arrive. Potter, Hawkeye and B.J. take turns singing parodies of well-known WWI songs during surgery, inspiring Father Mulcahy to write his own Korean War song. During some down time, Potter paints a self-portrait as Klinger, sitting on Sophie, poses in the Colonel's dress uniform, and Charles gets a hunting rifle and the proper attire that goes along with it. Now Klinger now finds himself flushing out fowl for the Major to shoot. Hawkeye tells a joke that he thinks is hilarious, but barely gets a rise out of B.J., then gets annoyed when B.J. tells the joke and everyone loves it. The army will only replace Margaret's broken footlocker if it's been destroyed in combat, so she shoots it with Winchester's hunting rifle, and when a soldier wanders into Post-Op looking for his friend, it becomes clear that, while Eddie is a good soldier, the army might have made an error in drafting him.

Authors' Notes: There are no PA announcements in this episode.

This is the seventh episode since Gary Burghoff left the show, and the first without his name in the credits.

As previously seen in earlier episodes, the box containing Potter's art supplies in Chapter 1 has his name in script on it.

Also in Chapter 1, mixed drinks in the Officer's Club are 25 cents, call shots are 20 cents and a beer is 10 cents.

In Chapter 2, B.J. calls Hawkeye "Uncle Miltie" – a reference to Milton Berle, an Emmy-winning comedian and actor.

The sign on Margaret's tent door in Chapter 8 is in freehand, as opposed to block lettering sometimes seen.

Captains Outrageous – 12/10/1979

Season 8 / Episode 186 / Production 187 – S614
Columbia House VHS Tape....... *Command Center Chaos (Catalog # 21037)*
Fox DVD ....*Season 8, Disc 2*

Alan Alda, Mike Farrell, Harry Morgan
Loretta Swit, David Ogden Stiers, Jamie Farr, William Christopher

Executive Producer – Burt Metcalfe
Produced by John Rappaport and Jim Mulligan
Written by Thad Mumford & Dan Wilcox
Directed by Burt Metcalfe

Executive Story Editors – Dan Wilcox & Thad Mumford
Story Editor – Dennis Koenig
Creative Consultants – Gene Reynolds / Alan Alda

John Orchard.	Muldoon
G.W. Bailey.	The G.I.
Paul Cavonis	The Greek
Siri Murad.	The Turk
Eileen Saki	Rosie
Momo Yashima	Suni

Copyright 1979 – 20th Century Fox Film Corporation

Non-Credited Appearances......... Kellye Nakahara, Gwen Farrell, Roy Goldman

Chapters

1: *Main Titles*	6: *No Promotion – 11:59*
2: *Captain's Bars – 0:53*	7: *Love Thy Neighbor... or else – 13:32*
3: *War Zone – 2:41*	8: *Smart for A Bartender – 15:55*
4: *Helping Rosie – 4:37*	9: *The Grumpy Get Promoted – 20:40*
5: *The New Management – 9:03*	10: *Off Limits / End Titles – 22:38*

Closing Stills

1: *Freeze – Klinger, Muldoon, Mulcahy, BJ, Margaret*
2: *Rizzo and B.J. at Rosie's*
3: *G.I. in Post-Op*
4: *The Turk in Post-Op*
5: *Rosie in Post-Op*
6: *Hawkeye*
7: *B.J. in Rosie's*
8: *Potter*
9: *Margaret in Post-Op*
10: *Charles*
11: *Klinger in the office*
12: *Mulcahy in Rosie's*

Synopsis: When Klinger tells Father Mulcahy that a promotion to captain is in the bag, Mulcahy knows better than to get his hopes up since he's already been passed over three times. However, it does little to ease his anger when the promotions list comes out and, for the fourth time, his name isn't on it. Meanwhile, Rosie winds up in the hospital with broken ribs after a brawl breaks out in her bar. Worried over losing her business, the medical staff volunteers to run the bar in her absence. Rosie's main concern is an M.P.

who she allows to drink for free in exchange for keeping her bar open. Unfortunately for Rosie, Charles the bartender doesn't know that, and angers, not only the M.P., but also a G.I. who has something against people who went to college.

Authors' Notes: There are no PA announcements in this episode.

Kellye Nakahara, who is seen in nearly every episode and often credited, is also seen in this one. What isn't seen very often, but is seen here, is Kellye smoking a cigarette.

The view from the office windows in Chapter 4 is of a wooden structure and people are seen, but it's not the same structure seen in the last several episodes going back to Season 7. However, the view will later change in Chapter 7 and again in Chapter 8.

Father Mulcahy, in Chapter 6, is wearing not the blue plaid robe, nor the robe worn by Henry Blake, but the brown plaid robe.

In Chapter 8, and for the second time, Charles is wearing a civilian shirt.

Father Mulcahy finally gets his promotion and in Chapter 9, becomes Captain Mulcahy.

Stars and Stripes – 12/17/1979

Season 8 / Episode 187 / Production 188 – S615

Columbia House VHS Tape. . . . .*Grace Under Pressure (Catalog # 21038)*
Fox DVD . . . .*Season 8, Disc 2*

Alan Alda, Mike Farrell, Harry Morgan
Loretta Swit, David Ogden Stiers, Jamie Farr, William Christopher

Executive Producer – Burt Metcalfe
Produced by Jim Mulligan and John Rappaport
Written by Dennis Koenig
Directed by Harry Morgan

Executive Story Editors – Dan Wilcox & Thad Mumford
Story Editor – Dennis Koenig
Creative Consultants – Gene Reynolds / Alan Alda
Joshua Bryant . . . . Private Jack Scully
Jeff Maxwell. . . . . .Igor
Copyright 1979 – 20th Century Fox Film Corporation

Non-Credited Appearances. . . . . .Kellye Nakahara, Gwen Farrell, Dennis Troy

Chapters

1:	Main Titles	6:	Typical Men – 12:26
2:	A Prestigious Project – 0:55	7:	Team Effort – 15:30
3:	Nothing To Do – 3:03	8:	A New Woman – 17:37
4:	Top Billing – 5:41	9:	Mr. Right Just Left – 21:37
5:	A Lowly Private – 9:12	10:	End Titles – 23:37

Closing Stills

1: Freeze – Margaret and Hawkeye in the O. Club
2: Scully
3: Igor and Hawkeye in the Officer's Club
4: Margaret
5: Margaret in a dress in her tent
6: B.J. and Charles
7: B.J.
8: Charles
9: Potter in the office
10: Klinger
11: Mulcahy
12: Hawkeye

Synopsis: The American College of Surgeons wants B.J. and Charles to write a paper on a surgical procedure they performed together. Once they finish arguing over whose name should go first, that's what they'll do. But when each wants credit for techniques used during the operation, the result is each writing his own separate paper. When Jack Scully returns to the 4077th to see Margaret, she thinks he's wearing someone else's shirt when in fact, it's his. Sergeant Scully, after decking a lieutenant, is now Private Scully, and gets himself into more trouble when he tells Margaret that her rank is honorary and doesn't carry the same weight as a male major.

Authors' Notes: There are no PA announcements in this episode.

The title of this episode on the DVD is "Stars and Stripes," but the DVD booklet lists it as "Stars and Stripe."

This is Joshua Bryant's third and final appearance on *M*A*S*H*.

The wooden structure seen through the office windows in Chapter 2 is the same one seen in several previous episodes, also with people moving about.

In Chapter 3, Kellye, on the Stage 9 compound is giving a haircut to a nurse. We've seen Kellye giving haircuts in several previous episodes. We've also seen in previous episodes a barber's tent on the Ranch compound.

Yessir, That's Our Baby – 12/31/1979

Season 8 / Episode 188 / Production 190 – S617

Columbia House VHS Tape . . . . Grace Under Pressure (Catalog # 21038)
Fox DVD . . . . Season 8, Disc 2

Alan Alda, Mike Farrell, Harry Morgan
Loretta Swit, David Ogden Stiers, Jamie Farr, William Christopher

Executive Producer – Burt Metcalfe
Produced by Jim Mulligan and John Rappaport
Written by Jim Mulligan
Directed by Alan Alda

Executive Story Editors – Dan Wilcox & Thad Mumford
Story Editor – Dennis Koenig
Creative Consultants – Gene Reynolds / Alan Alda

Howard Platt . . . . Major Ted Spector
William Bogert . . . . Rodger Prescott
Elizabeth Farley . . . . Louise Harper
Yuki Shimoda . . . . Chung Ho Kim
Copyright 1979 – 20th Century Fox Film Corporation

Non-Credited Appearances . . . . Kellye Nakahara, Gwen Farrell

Chapters

1: Main Titles	6: Out of Our Hands – 9:15
2: The New Tent Mate – 0:53	7: No Help from Korea – 14:10
3: Our Baby – 2:47	8: Problems with Mr. Prescott – 17:12
4: Auntie Margaret – 4:34	9: The Right Thing – 20:46
5: No Future – 7:02	10: A Small Life / End Titles – 23:15

Closing Stills

1: Freeze – All in O.R.
2: Major Ted Spector
3: Prescott
4: Chung Ho Kim
5: Louise Harper
6: Mulcahy
7: Klinger with baby
8: Charles with baby
9: Margaret with baby
10: Potter in the mess tent
11: B.J.
12: Hawkeye

Synopsis: What Charles calls an "ill-mannered infant" turns out to be abandoned and left at the foot of the Swamp. A note attached to the child explains that, while the mother loves her child, she is unable to care for her, and her father, an American G.I., is gone. The baby girl quickly becomes the center of attention and everyone immediately falls in love with her. But because of her mixed lineage, at best, a miserable existence awaits the little girl, if she's not killed in the name of racial purity. The Red Cross claims that getting the child to the United States is out of their hands, the government of South Korea refuses to help her, and the U.S. consulate in Tokyo won't even discuss it. There's only one option for the little girl, and in the middle of the night, she's taken to a Catholic monastery and placed in a revolving cradle.

Commentary by Howard Platt: "I was contacted by my manager around 10pm the night before filming of my scenes began. I was living in Malibu at the time and knew the messenger would be arriving late with the script. He knocked on my door at 1am and presented it to me. I was exhausted from an active previous day, and fell asleep shortly after reading the title. So, the drive to 20th Century Fox at 6:00 AM was somewhat distracted, what with trying to learn lines while keeping within the appropriate lanes of traffic. Obviously, I was not their first choice for the role. Alan Alda directed that particular episode, and I found him intelligent, kind and easy to understand. He was especially interested in spontaneity when the cameras rolled, so didn't require the perfect rehearsal. I had done a Disney film with Harry Morgan and we shared some hilarious memories of that experience. The M*A*S*H filming, at least my part in it, went off without a hitch. Now, I'm living in Falls Village, Connecticut, in a 174-year old home with a wife and two standard poodles."

Authors' Notes: There are no PA announcements in this episode.

In Chapter 3, Hawkeye implies that the year is 1951 when he calls a surgical glove with milk "Château Moo '51."

Klinger, in Chapter 4, wants to name the baby "Scheherazade." Scheherazade was a famous Persian queen, and the storyteller of One Thousand and One Nights (a collection of stories from various countries and authors).

Potterism: "Mule Muffins."

Bottle Fatigue – 1/7/1980

Season 8 / Episode 189 / Production 191 – S618

Columbia House VHS Tape . . . . Not Released by Columbia House

Fox DVD . . . . Season 8, Disc 2

Alan Alda, Mike Farrell, Harry Morgan
Loretta Swit, David Ogden Stiers, Jamie Farr, William Christopher

Executive Producer – Burt Metcalfe
Produced by John Rappaport and Jim Mulligan
Written by Thad Mumford & Dan Wilcox
Directed by Burt Metcalfe

Executive Story Editors – Dan Wilcox & Thad Mumford
Story Editor – Dennis Koenig
Creative Consultants – Gene Reynolds / Alan Alda

Shelly Long . . . . Nurse Mendenhall
Jeff Maxwell . . . . .Igor
David Hirokane . . . . Chinese Soldier
Shari Saba . . . . Nurse

Copyright 1979 – 20th Century Fox Film Corporation

Non-Credited Appearances . . . . Kellye Nakahara, Dennis Troy, Roy Goldman

Chapters

1: Main Titles	6: Teetotaling Tantrums – 12:33
2: A Two-Ton Bar Tab – 0:53	7: In and Out of the Mood – 15:08
3: Clean and Sober – 2:33	8: A Commie Pineapple – 17:49
4: Military Urgency – 4:38	9: Love, Charles – 20:31
5: Grumpy and Restless – 8:29	10: Needing A Drink / End Titles – 22:01

Closing Stills

1: Freeze – B.J. in Post-Op
2: Nurse Mendenhall
3: Igor
4: Chinese soldier in OR
5: Charles
6: Mulcahy
7: Klinger
8: Margaret
9: Potter in the office
10: B.J. in Post-Op
11: Hawkeye

Synopsis: After learning his bar tab is over $38 at the Officer's Club, not counting Rosie's or how much he's had from the still, Hawkeye decides to take a break from alcohol for a week. Now that he's sober, clean-shaven and feeling great, he's driving everyone else crazy, even chasing a nurse away when he counts how many glasses of wine she's had while on a date with him. Charles, on the other hand, goes on a drinking binge when he learns his sister Honoria is engaged to an Italian man, and B.J. just can't find anywhere quiet enough, including Post-Op, to get some sleep.

PA Announcement by Todd Sussman

Authors' Notes: Potterism: "Hang on to your homburg" (a men's felt hat).

According to Margaret, the sheets in Post-Op are changed every day at 11:30 AM.

In Chapter 5, B.J. mentions "Vic Tanny." Vic Tanny ran a chain of gyms, with several in Los Angeles in 1947. Mr. Tanny's gyms were the first to have carpet and welcome women, as opposed to the old run-down and "stinky" gyms of the day. However, in the mid 60's, his gyms went bankrupt, but the style of the gym continues to flourish today.

In Chapter 7, Hawkeye mentions "J. Fred Muggs." J. Fred Muggs, born on March 14, 1952, was a chimpanzee and mascot for NBC's *Today* show with Dave Galloway, and made his first appearance on January 28, 1953.

It was implied in the previous episode that the year is 1951 when Hawkeye calls a surgical glove with milk "Château '51." Also, if Hawkeye and company were in the final episode, "Goodbye, Farewell and Amen," this would imply that they were in Korea in June 1953. How would they have known about J. Fred Muggs?

Potter mentions "Carrie Nation" (November 25, 1846-June 9, 1911) in Chapter 10. Carrie Nation was a member of the temperance movement opposing alcohol during the pre-prohibition period in the United States. Miss Nation had promoted her views through vandalism, and entering establishments that served alcohol and would attack the bar with a hatchet.

Heal Thyself – 1/14/1980

Season 8 / Episode 190 / Production 189 – S616
Columbia House VHS Tape . . . . Grace Under Pressure (Catalog # 21038)
Fox DVD . . . . Season 8, Disc 3

Alan Alda, Mike Farrell, Harry Morgan
Loretta Swit, David Ogden Stiers, Jamie Farr, William Christopher

Executive Producer – Burt Metcalfe
Produced by John Rappaport and Jim Mulligan
Teleplay by Dennis Koenig
Story by Dennis Koenig and Gene Reynolds
Directed by Mike Farrell

Executive Story Editors – Dan Wilcox & Thad Mumford
Story Editor – Dennis Koenig
Creative Consultants – Gene Reynolds / Alan Alda
Edward Hermann . . . . .Dr. Steven J. Newsome
Copyright 1979 – 20th Century Fox Film Corporation

Non-Credited Appearances. . . . . Kellye Nakahara, Gwen Farrell, Roy Goldman,
Jan Jorden

Chapters

1: Main Titles	6: Insomnia – 13:58
2: The Mumps – 0:54	7: Gargling at 0600 – 14:47
3: Roommates – 3:38	8: Where's Newsome?
4: The Replacement Surgeon – 6:31	9: The Blood Won't Come Off – 21:01
5: Sick Little Soldiers – 10:02	10: Peace & Harmony / End Titles – 23:20

Closing Stills

1: Freeze – Potter, Charles, Klinger in Potter's tent
2: Dr. Newsome
3: Hawkeye in the mess tent
4: Potter
5: Margaret
6: Charles
7: Klinger in the office
8: Mulcahy in Margaret's tent
9: B.J.

Synopsis: Swollen glands, sore throat and a fever have Colonel Potter down with the mumps. Worse still, after making fun of Potter having a childhood malady, Charles, thinking his superior genes render him immune, learns otherwise. Hawkeye and B.J. are left with no choice but to put Charles in Potter's tent, very much against the Colonel's protests. Rest is what they need most, but it's the last thing they get. With much of the nursing staff down with the mumps, Klinger and Father Mulcahy help out in surgery, and Dr. Steve Newsome arrives to stand in for the stricken doctors. A graduate of Johns Hopkins, Newsome, a skilled and talented surgeon with a sense of humor fits right in with his new tent-mates in the Swamp, and seems able to handle the heavy influx of wounded. Suddenly, something goes very wrong with Newsome when he can't decide what the best course of action is while operating on a badly wounded leg, and leaves the operating room.

Authors' Notes: Hawkeye mentions Charles Laughton (July 1, 1899-December 15, 1962) in Chapter 2. An Academy Award-winning actor from England who became a United States citizen in 1950, was best known for playing historical roles.

In Chapter 5, Potter tells Charles that he wants to read a Zane Gray book. However, the book he has in his hands is the same book from Episode 166, Season 7's "The Young and the Restless" named The Hell Benders, written by Ken Hodgson. Ken Hodgson was born in 1945, which would mean that he wrote this Western between the ages of 5 and 8. Hodgson's first published book was in 1971.

Also in Chapter 5, Potter says "If I want a giant, I'll get Mel Ott." Mel Ott (March 2, 1909-November 21, 1958) was a New York Giants (baseball) outfielder. His first game with the Giants was on April 27, 1926, and his last game was on July 11, 1947. Mr. Ott, one the best players of the game, spent his entire Major League career with the New York Giants. He died in an automobile accident at the age of 49.

In this episode, Potter chose to wear his gray and red-stripped robe in Chapter 5, not the heavy green robe or the robe that was originally worn by Henry Blake.

Charles in Chapter 7 mentions "The RCA Building." This famed edifice was built between 1931 and 1933, at 30 Rockefeller Plaza in Manhattan, NY, between West 49th and 50th Streets (also known as 30 Rock). However, the RCA Building is now the GE Building since GE re-acquired the RCA Corporation in 1988. Famous for housing the headquarters of the NBC Television Network, the building was granted official landmark status in 1985.

Old Soldiers – 1/21/1980

Season 8 / Episode 191 / Production 193 – S620

Columbia House VHS Tape . . . . Decisions, Decisions (Catalog # 21035)
Fox DVD . . . . Season 8, Disc 3

Alan Alda, Mike Farrell, Harry Morgan
Loretta Swit, David Ogden Stiers, Jamie Farr, William Christopher

Executive Producer – Burt Metcalfe
Produced by Jim Mulligan and John Rappaport
Written by Dennis Koenig
Directed by Charles S. Dubin

Executive Story Editors – Dan Wilcox & Thad Mumford
Story Editor – Dennis Koenig
Creative Consultants – Gene Reynolds / Alan Alda

Jane Connell . . . . Betty Halpern
Jason Autajay. . . . . Korean Boy
Sally Imamura . . . . Korean Girl

Copyright 1980 – 20th Century Fox Film Corporation

Non-Credited Appearances. . . . . .Kellye Nakahara, Jan Jorden

Chapters

1: Main Titles
2: Bad News from Tokyo – 0:55
3: Orphans in Need – 3:04
4: Overnight Guests – 5:04
5: Breakfast in Bedlam – 7:40

6: Potter's Package – 10:53
7: French Records – 13:35
8: The Last Survivor – 17:36
9: No Starch in the Shorts – 23:04
10: End Titles – 23:41

Closing Stills

1: Freeze – Klinger and Potter in the office
2: Betty Halpern
3: Korean boy
4: Korean girl
5: Hawkeye in the Officer's Club
6: B.J. in the Swamp
7: Margaret
8: Charles in the mess tent
9: Klinger
10: Mulcahy
11: Potter

Synopsis: A phone call at 3:00 AM usually isn't a good sign, as is the case here when Colonel Potter is summoned to Tokyo General to visit a sick friend. Returning to the 4077th, he finds the camp overrun with Korean children being relocated south, but in need of medical attention. Each staff member then receives a personal invitation from the Colonel requesting his or her presence at 1900 hours in his tent, but it's more than a request … it's an order. Going to Tokyo General, returning in what can best be described as an ornery mood, and ordering everyone to his tent causes the staff to think the worst, and although Potter is fine, his four best friends from WWI aren't.

Authors' Notes: There are no PA announcements in this episode.

Potterism: "Who in the name of Annie's Argyles are all these kids?"

For the second time, Potter leaves Hawkeye in command of the 4077th while he goes to Tokyo.

In Chapter 5, Potter mentions "The Dalton Gang." The Dalton Gang was an outlaw group from 1890 to 1892, specializing in train and bank robberies.

The view from the office windows is of the same wooden structure previously seen in several episodes, but in this one, the structure appears a little closer than usual.

Morale Victory – 1/28/1980

Season 8 / Episode 192 / Production 192 – S619

Columbia House VHS Tape . . . . Decisions, Decisions (Catalog # 21035)
Fox DVD . . . . Season 8, Disc 3

Alan Alda, Mike Farrell, Harry Morgan
Loretta Swit, David Ogden Stiers, Jamie Farr, William Christopher

Executive Producer – Burt Metcalfe
Produced by John Rappaport and Jim Mulligan
Written John Rappaport
Directed by Charles S. Dubin

Executive Story Editors – Dan Wilcox & Thad Mumford
Story Editor – Dennis Koenig
Creative Consultants – Gene Reynolds / Alan Alda

James Stephens . . . . Private David Sheridan
G.W. Bailey. . . . . Sergeant Luthor Rizzo
Jeff Maxwell. . . . . Igor

Copyright 1980 – 20th Century Fox Film Corporation

Non-Credited Appearances. . . . . Kellye Nakahara, Gwen Farrell, Dennis Troy,
Roy Goldman

Chapters

1: Main Titles / Movie Madness
2: Morale Officers – 3:18
3: Two Weeks in Toledo – 5:50
4: The Pianist's Problem – 7:46
5: Unhelpful Suggestions – 9:18

6: A Sense of Failure – 12:08
7: Beach Party – 14:20
8: Klinger Comes Through – 16:40
9: On the Other Hand – 19:04
10: His Own Tune / End Titles – 23:04

Closing Stills

1: Freeze – Private Sheridan
2: Roy, Gwen, Rizzo in the mess tent
3: Igor
4: Hawkeye
5: B.J.
6: Potter in the office
7: Mulcahy in his tent
8: Margaret
9: Klinger in the office
10: Charles in Post-Op

Synopsis: During the 12th showing this month of Colonel and Mrs. Potter's favorite movie in the mess tent, Hawkeye and B.J. have had enough and nearly start a riot. Citing low morale, Potter assigns them the unenviable task of morale officers, and they immediately promise a spectacular dinner party. Hawkeye then comes up with the idea of a beach party / cookout, complete with lobsters, crabs and clams. Since Inchon is the nearest location having crabs, Klinger is sent to get them, but when he's late getting back and his footlocker gone, they think he might have gone a bit further than Inchon. The last thing on Charles' mind is a cookout, when in Post-Op, the man he operated on is more concerned with a slight loss of dexterity in his right hand than he is over the fact that Charles saved his leg from amputation. Private Sheridan is, or was, a concert pianist.

Hitting close to home with Charles and his love of classical music, but lacking the "gift" that Sheridan possesses, Charles refuses to let the man give up on himself and displays a side of his personality rarely seen.

Commentary by Jeff Maxwell: "As much as I'd like to take credit for anything and everything, the creaming of the corn must be credited to the prop department and the studio commissary. And now for the dirt: I had a terrible, terrible, terrible hangover the morning we shot that scene and felt creamed myself. As any fine actor should, I used my real, uneasy feelings to help color my dialogue."

PA Announcement by Todd Sussman

Authors' Notes: Potterisms: "Morale here is lower than a gopher's basement," "This place is a cat's whisker from loco."

In Chapter 1, Colonel Potter claims that the movie in the mess tent, *History is Made at Night,* is his and Mildred's favorite, which could possibly mean that it's their favorite movie to watch together because in Episode 119, Season 5's "Movie Tonight," his favorite all-time movie is *My Darling Clementine.*

Father Mulcahy in Chapter 6 is wearing his usual brown plaid robe. He's sometimes seen in blue plaid and Henry Blake's robe.

Something not seen very often is someone actually throwing darts at the dartboard in the Swamp, but in Chapter 7, B.J. is doing just that.

Rizzo mentions "Captain Cook" in Chapter 8. James Cook (1728-1779) was an explorer, navigator and cartographer.

Lend A Hand – 2/4/1980

Season 8 / Episode 193 / Production 194 – S621
Columbia House VHS Tape . . . . .Loyalties (Catalog # 22052)
Fox DVD . . . . .Season 8, Disc 3

Alan Alda, Mike Farrell, Harry Morgan
Loretta Swit, David Ogden Stiers, Jamie Farr, William Christopher

Executive Producer – Burt Metcalfe
Produced by Jim Mulligan and John Rappaport
Written and Directed by Alan Alda

Executive Story Editors – Dan Wilcox & Thad Mumford
Story Editor – Dennis Koenig
Creative Consultants – Gene Reynolds / Alan Alda

Robert Alda. . . . . .Dr. Anthony Borelli
Anthony Alda . . . . Jarvis
Daren Kelly. . . . . Sergeant Herbert
Shari Saba . . . . Nurse
Copyright 1980 – 20th Century Fox Film Corporation

Non-Credited Appearances. . . . . Kellye Nakahara, Gwen Farrell, Dennis Troy,
Roy Goldman

Chapters

1: *Main Titles / Cold and Bored*	6: *Eat the Cheese – 14:13*
2: *Dr. Borelli's Return – 5:00*	7: *Dueling Doctors – 15:51*
3: *Party Themes – 8:54*	8: *In Trouble – 19:49*
4: *Happy Birthday? – 11:12*	9: *Dr. Right & Dr. Left – 21:33*
5: *Duty Calls – 12:02*	10: *Siamese Surgeons / End Titles – 22:56*

Closing Stills

1: *Freeze – Hawkeye and Borelli clapping in O.R.*
2: *Jarvis*
3: *B.J. and Sergeant Herbert*
4: *B.J.*
5: *Potter in the office*
6: *Margaret*
7: *Charles in the mess tent*
8: *Klinger*
9: *Mulcahy in the mess tent*
10: *Hawkeye*

Synopsis: The only one not happy about a surprise birthday party for Hawkeye is Hawkeye, especially since it isn't his birthday. That's the good news. Dr. Anthony Borelli returns to the 4077th, this time to lecture on new nerve graft techniques, but the nit-picking doctor lectures Hawkeye on how to keep warm and how to have a drink. When a Battalion Aid surgeon is badly wounded, they call with an emergency request for a surgeon, and Hawkeye immediately volunteers. Since the wounded surgeon might have nerve damage, Borelli insists on going with him, and the nitpicking continues. But after an exploding shell causes an injury to Hawkeye's left arm and an injury to Borelli's right arm, the bickering surgeons now have to operate as one, each using his good arm.

Authors' Notes: There are no PA announcements in this episode.

Robert Alda, Alan's father, makes his second and final appearance on M*A*S*H as Major Doctor Anthony Borelli, while Anthony Alda, Alan's half-brother, makes his first as Corporal Jarvis. This is the only episode where all three Aldas are together.

In Chapter 2, Potter mentions "Our Gang" (later known in television syndication as *The Little Rascals)*, and the names of Spanky, Alfalfa, Buckwheat and Spot. However, Spot wasn't the dog's name. It was Pete. "Our Gang" was very popular during the 1920's and 30's and remained a favorite until the 1940s; television caused a resurgence of interest and popularity for this multi-child troupe.

Also in Chapter 2, Borelli mentions Dame May Whitty. The captioning has the name "Witty" spelled wrong. Her correct name is "Whitty." Born Mary Whitty, she was the first actress to be vested as a Dame Commander of the Most Excellent Order of the British Empire in 1918 (this is the equivalent to being knighted). However, she didn't receive this for acting, but for her hospital work during WWI. Dame May Whitty first appeared on the English stage in 1862, and her first appearance on film was in 1914.

Good-Bye, Cruel World – 2/11/1980

Season 8 / Episode 194 / Production 195 – S622

Columbia House VHS Tape . . . . *Paging Dr. Freedman (Catalog # 19503)*
Fox DVD . . . .*Season 8, Disc 3*

Alan Alda, Mike Farrell, Harry Morgan
Loretta Swit, David Ogden Stiers, Jamie Farr, William Christopher

Executive Producer – Burt Metcalfe
Produced by John Rappaport and Jim Mulligan
Written by Thad Mumford – Dan Wilcox
Directed by Charles S. Dubin

Executive Story Editors – Dan Wilcox & Thad Mumford
Story Editor – Dennis Koenig
Creative Consultants – Gene Reynolds / Alan Alda

Allen Arbus . . . . Dr. Sidney Freedman
Clyde Kusatsu . . . . .Sergeant Michael Yee
Philip Bruns . . . . .Lieutenant Colonel Burton D. Hedley
James Lough . . . . .Courier
Kellye Nakahara . . . . .Nurse Kellye
David Cramer . . . . .Aide
Copyright 1980 – 20th Century Fox Film Corporation

Non-Credited Appearances. . . . . Gwen Farrell, Roy Goldman

Chapters

1: *Main Titles / Klinger's Crate*	6: *Psychiatric Exam – 14:09*
2: *The Hero – 3:44*	7: *Klinger's Problem – 15:52*
3: *Rummage Sale – 5:10*	8: *Deep-Seated guilt – 17:56*
4: *Suicide Attempt – 8:09*	9: *Tissue of Lies – 20:09*
5: *An Official "Okey-Dokey" – 9:04*	10: *Too Much Swoop / End Titles – 23:04*

Closing Stills

1: *Freeze – Klinger & Potter – too much swoop*
2: *Freedman*
3: *Michael Yee*
4: *Colonel Hedley*
5: *Hawkeye in Post-Op*
6: *B.J. in the Swamp*
7: *Potter in the office*
8: *Margaret*
9: *Charles*
10: *Mulcahy in Margaret's tent (From earlier episode)*
11: *Klinger in the office*

Synopsis: Sergeant Michael Yee, a bona fide hero written up in Stars & Stripes, is taken to the 4077th with a leg wound. Friendly, personable and a sense of humor, the sergeant has an odd reaction to the news that he's going home, and nearly succeeds when he tries to commit suicide by slashing his wrists. Sidney Freedman realizes that the sergeant is not only fighting in Korea, he's also fighting guilt at having to kill fellow Asians who, enemy or not, could very well be members of his family. Klinger's family has sent him a box of personal items and transforms his office into that of a Bedouin's tent, including foul-smelling cheese. Resenting the fact that everyone makes fun of his personal touches, and Potter ordering him to take everything down, he forges Potter's name on discharge papers and sends them to I-Corps. In a twist, Potter apologizes to Klinger for hurting his feelings and signs a three-day pass. All Klinger has to do now is intercept the package he sent to I-Corps, or face a possible stint in the stockade.

Authors' Notes: There are no PA announcements in this episode.

In Chapter 1, Charles said when he turned on a television for the first time, he saw "a seltzer pill named 'Speedy.'" Of course, Charles was talking about Alka Seltzer and their very successful advertising campaign ads. However, the first "Speedy" commercial was taped on March 16, 1953. "Speedy" appeared in 212 commercials between 1954 and 1964.

Potterisms: "Great balls of fire" (a fairly common expression), "Put the twinkle back in your twenty twenties."

For the second time in the series, Poly Adler is mentioned, this time by Colonel Potter in Chapter 1. The first time she was mentioned was in Episode 64, Season 3's "Bulletin Board." And for the second time, Poly Adler ran the most notorious brothel in New York City in the 1920's and 30's.

Sergeant Yee, in Chapter 2, says "Yankees clobbered the 'Whiz Kids'" in four straight games in the 1950 World Series. The "Whiz Kids" were the Philadelphia Phillies and the above World Series statistic is, in fact, correct. The Yankees won the first two games at Shibe Park in Philadelphia, and the second two games at Yankee Stadium.

In Chapter 3, Klinger mentions Better Homes and Gardens. This publication began in 1922.

For the second time in three episodes, darts are being thrown at, or near, the dartboard on the door of the Swamp in Chapter 4. However, this time, there are rubber glove balloons on the door around the dartboard, and Hawkeye, throwing a dart backwards and through his legs, hits a bull's eye in the tent roof.

In Chapter 4, Potter is wearing the robe usually worn by Henry Blake.

At 23:04 in, the picture seems faded on the DVD.

Clyde Kusatsu, who plays Sergeant Michael Lee, makes his third appearance on *M*A*S*H*, the first two in "For Want of A Boot" and "Henry in Love," both from Season 2, and both as Kwang Duk, the bartender in the Officer's Club. With an extensive and impressive list of credits to his name, Mr. Kusatsu will make his fourth and final appearance on **M*A*S*H** in Season 11's "The Joker is Wild," as Captain Paul Yamato.

Dreams – 2/18/1980

Season 8 / Episode 195 / Production 185 – S612

Columbia House VHS Tape............... Not Released by Columbia House

Fox DVD .... Season 8, Disc 3

Alan Alda, Mike Farrell, Harry Morgan
Loretta Swit, David Ogden Stiers, Jamie Farr, William Christopher
And Gary Burghoff as Radar

Executive Producer – Burt Metcalfe
Produced by Jim Mulligan and John Rappaport
Teleplay by Alan Alda
Story by Alan Alda and Jay Rubinifer
Directed by Alan Alda

Executive Story Editors – Dan Wilcox & Thad Mumford
Story Editor – Dennis Koenig
Creative Consultants – Gene Reynolds / Alan Alda

Ford Rainey	General Coogan
Robin Haynes	Taylor
Fred Stuthman	Professor
Rick Waln	Lieutenant Garvey
Catherine Bergstrom	Peg Hunnicutt
Kellye Nakahara	Nurse Kellye
Connie Izay	Connie
Kurtis Sanders	Young Potter
Dennis Troy	Orderly
Ray Lynch	Bridegroom

Copyright 1979 – 20th Century Fox Film Corporation

Non-Credited Appearances............... Gwen Farrell, Roy Goldman, Jan Jorden

Chapters

1: Main Titles	6: The Pontiff's Nightmare – 13:37
2: The Bloody Bride – 0:53	7: Through A Glass Darkly – 16:51
3: Peg of My Dreams – 4:32	8: Arms and the Man – 19:02
4: Better Times – 7:17	9: Perchance to Dream – 22:50
5: Death and Magic – 9:32	10: End Titles – 23:34

Closing Stills

1: Freeze – All in the mess tent
2: Coogan in Post-Op
3: Professor
4: Lieutenant Garvey
5: Peg
6: Margaret
7: B.J.
8: Potter
9: Charles
10: Mulcahy
11: Klinger
12: Hawkeye

Synopsis: The constant pressure of "meatball" surgery, combined with a seemingly endless flow of wounded, has the staff near total exhaustion. Grabbing a few minutes of sleep would normally be a welcome respite, but when the war invades their dreams, they're anything but normal, and a respite they can do without.

PA Announcement by Todd Sussman

Authors' Notes: There is no laugh track in this episode.

Another episode on Alan Alda's list of episodes "that worked."

The first 12 episodes of Season 8 were produced with "Also Starring Gary Burghoff as Radar" in the opening credits. However, the order of production rarely is the same as the order of broadcast. Gary's last on-screen appearance is in "Goodbye Radar, Part 2," the 11th episode produced for Season 8, but the 5th episode to air. "Dreams" is the 12th and final episode to have Gary listed in the opening credits, but it was the 22nd episode to air. This is why Gary's listing in the opening credits is seen in seven episodes after his final appearance.

Margaret mentions "Looney Tunes" in Chapter 2. The Looney Tunes animated Warner Bros. cartoon series ran in movie theaters from 1930 to 1969.

In Episode 92, Season 4's "Some 38th Parallels," there is a yellow sign to the right of the double glass doors, next to the swinging doors that lead to the operating room that says, "WE DELIVER (With minimum purchase) DRINKS NOT INCLUDED IN MINIMUM." There is no sign at all four episodes later. In Episode 105, Season 5's "Dear Sigmund," the yellow sign was replaced with a Red Cross sign. This sign will again be replaced later in the series with one that says "Freedom of speech doesn't mean sloppy talk." However, Chapter 3 in this episode, "Dreams," there is no sign at all.

The view out of the office windows in Chapter 4 is now trees and mountains, instead of the wooden structure previously seen in several episodes.

In Chapter 5, while Charles is dreaming and performing magic tricks, Klinger takes off one large earring and places it in a collection hat being passed around, and then he's seen with both earrings on. Shortly after that, he's seen again, but this time, no earrings at all.

We finally see "Tony Packo's Café" in Chapter 7, located at 1902 Front Street. "Home made chili – ham and live music."

Chapter 8 tells of the 4077th's handling of 211 patients in 33 hours.

War Co-Respondent – 3/3/1980

Season 8 / Episode 196 / Production 197 – S624

Columbia House VHS Tape. . . . . .Loyalties (Catalog # 22052)
Fox DVD . . . . .Season 8, Disc 3

Alan Alda, Mike Farrell, Harry Morgan
Loretta Swit, David Ogden Stiers, Jamie Farr, William Christopher

Executive Producer – Burt Metcalfe
Produced by Jim Mulligan and John Rappaport
Written and Directed by Mike Farrell

Executive Story Editors – Dan Wilcox & Thad Mumford
Story Editor – Dennis Koenig
Creative Consultants – Gene Reynolds / Alan Alda

Susan St. James . . . . .Aggie O'Shea
Brad Wilken . . . . .Private Scott
Calvin Levels. . . . . .Private Jackson
Kellye Nakahara . . . . .Kellye

Copyright 1980 – 20th Century Fox Film Corporation

Non-Credited Appearances. . . . . .Gwen Farrell, Dennis Troy

Chapters

1: Main Titles
2: Aggie O'Shea – 0:54
3: Sticking Close – 4:56
4: Potter's Gallery – 7:47
5: The Direct Approach – 8:52
6: Aggie's Subject – 13:19
7: Close to the Heart – 16:43
8: The Way I Feel – 18:13
9: Live For Tomorrow – 20:34
10: Aggie's Gifts / End Titles – 23:09

Closing Stills

1: Freeze – B.J.
2: Aggie
3: G.I. in Post-Op
4: Potter in the office
5: Margaret in her tent
6: Charles in Post-Op
7: Klinger
8: Mulcahy in his tent
9: B.J.

Synopsis: Accompanying the wounded on the bus is Aggie O'Shea, a famous reporter and sketch artist who's covered everything from the war to sporting events to the succession of the English throne, and who now directs her attention towards B.J. Impressed with his bedside manner and quiet disposition, B.J.'s "lifeline" to Mill Valley prevents their relationship from escalating in spite of the fact that he may be falling in love with her.

PA Announcement by Todd Sussman

Authors' Notes: The wooden structure is seen through the office windows in Chapter 4. In Chapter 4, Aggie O'Shea mentions that Silly Putty came out in 1949. Although the invention of Silly Putty is somewhat in debate, it was invented while researching rubber substitutes in 1943. It was in 1949 that the owner of a toy store marketed the product, and it immediately became the biggest selling item in her catalog.

Aggie also states, in Chapter 5, that she covered the boxing match when Sugar Ray Robinson beat Jake LaMotta. These two world-famous fighters had six matches together. The only time LaMotta lost was the last fight, which took place on February 14, 1951. The fight became known as "The Saint Valentine's Day Massacre."

Other sporting events Aggie covered include the home-run hit by Dick Sisler on the last day of the 1950 baseball season. Sisler's home run that day put the 1950 Philadelphia Phillies in the World Series.

Aggie also covered Florence Chadwick's August 8, 1950 swim in which she crossed the English Channel in 13:20, setting a new record.

B.J. in Chapter 5 mentions Red Barber (February 17, 1908 – October 22, 1992), one of the most well-known sports announcers.

Aggie O'Shea sure gets around. In Chapter 5, she covered the succession of the English throne when George VI died and then-25 year-old Elizabeth II took the throne on February 6, 1952.

Aggie, also in Chapter 5, mentions, Bill Mauldin (October 29, 1921-January 22, 2003), a two-time Pulitzer Prize winning editorial cartoonist best known for his WWII cartoons of American soldiers.

Father Mulcahy and his comical "pitching woo" in Chapter 8: this was an antiquated term meaning to court, make love or flatter.

From the change room in Chapter 8 is a view into the scrub room. The scrub room has one sink against the wall that houses the autoclave (autoclave not seen). The scrub sinks vary in location, sometimes in the middle of the room.

Actress Susan Saint James, probably best known for her roles as Sally McMillan on *McMillan & Wife* (1971-77) with Rock Hudson, and Kate McArdle on *Kate & Allie* (1984-1989), received a star on the Hollywood Walk of Fame on June 11, 2008, and is married to Dick Ebersol, Chairman of NBC Universal Sports and Olympics. Mr. Ebersol was a key NBC executive in launching *Saturday Night Live* in 1975. Their son, Teddy Ebersol, an avid Boston Red Sox fan, died in a plane crash shortly after the Red Sox won their first World Series after an 86-year draught in 2004. The Ebersol's attended the ground breaking of The Teddy Ebersol's Red Sox Fields, located just down the road from Fenway Park.

Back Pay – 3/10/1980

Season 8 / Episode 197 / Production 198 – S625

Columbia House VHS Tape . . . . Over Here (Catalog # 19504)
Fox DVD . . . . Season 8, Disc 3

Alan Alda, Mike Farrell, Harry Morgan
Loretta Swit, David Ogden Stiers, Jamie Farr, William Christopher

Executive Producer – Burt Metcalfe
Produced by John Rappaport and Jim Mulligan
Written by Thad Mumford & Dan Wilcox and Dennis Koenig
Directed by Burt Metcalfe

Executive Story Editors – Dan Wilcox & Thad Mumford
Story Editor – Dennis Koenig
Creative Consultants – Gene Reynolds / Alan Alda

Richard Herd . . . . Captain "Wild Bill" Snyder
Sab Shimino . . . . Doctor Jin
G.W. Bailey . . . . Sergeant Luthor Rizzo
Jerry Fujikawa . . . . Doctor Wu
Peter Kim . . . . Doctor Po

Copyright 1980 – 20th Century Fox Film Corporation

Non-Credited Appearances . . . . Kellye Nakahara, Gwen Farrell, Dennis Troy,
Roy Goldman, Jan Jorden

Chapters

1: Main Titles
2: The "But" Stops Here – 0:54
3: Minimum Rage – 3:20
4: Hawkeye's Bill – 6:28
5: Second Opinion – 9:08
6: For Services Rendered – 11:15
7: One Man's Theft – 14:50
8: Korean Voodoo – 17:13
9: Four Bucks – 22:09
10: Fool and Hardy / End Titles – 23:18

Closing Stills

1: Freeze – B.J. and Hawkeye in the Officer's Club
2: Captain Snyder
3: Jin
4: Rizzo in the office
5: Potter in the office
6: Charles
7: Margaret in the Swamp
8: Klinger
9: Mulcahy
10: B.J.
11: Hawkeye

Synopsis: Hawkeye becomes infuriated after learning about a doctor in Minneapolis averaging $2,000 a day doing X-rays for the Selective Service. Hawkeye now submits a bill to the Surgeon General's Office for more than $38,000, covering 546 bowel resections and all the X-rays he's taken. Captain Snyder arrives from Criminal Investigations to show Hawkeye what they think of his statement by tearing it up, but winds up paying Hawkeye $4.00 for an x-ray after hurting his foot. Charles, meanwhile, is elected to demonstrate surgical techniques to a trio of Korean doctors he equates to The Three Stooges.

Richard Herd appeared as Wild Bill Snyder in "Back Pay" from Season 8.

Being Buddhists, their religion forbids cutting into a human body and they have never seen the inside of one. After throwing his back out, Charles refuses the Koreans when they offer to help, until Colonel Potter orders him to undergo their treatment of acupuncture with surprising results.

Commentary by Richard Herd: "I waited for just the right episode and part for me. I had three offers on other *M*A*S*H* parts, but I knew I'd get just one shot. Wild Bill Snyder was worth waiting to do. I especially enjoyed working with Harry Morgan, with whom I had done a Burt Kennedy western called Kate Bliss and the Ticker Tape Kid. Harry was the last of the breed."

Commentary by Sab Shimono: "It was easier to do this one. I was part of the gang."

Authors' Notes: There are no PA announcements in this episode.
From the beginning of Chapter 2 until 2:08 in, the picture is grainy.
The clothing hooks in the change room are in the order of Winchester, Potter, Hawkeye, and B.J. in Chapter 2. But for some reason in this episode, there's an empty hook between Winchester and Potter and three empty hooks between Hawkeye and B.J. In previous episodes, the hooks and names have all been together.
In the previous episode, "War Co-Respondent," we see the scrub room from the change room and there's only one scrub sink. In Chapter 2 of this episode, there are two scrub sinks side by side.
Hawkeye in Chapter 4 claims he's averaging seven bowel resections a week with a total of 546. This means that Hawkeye has been in Korea exactly 78 weeks, or a year and a half.
Chapter 4 also affords a view from the office windows, and the same wooden structure, also with people milling about, is seen. But in Chapter 6, the structure is seen again and appears to be a little closer.

Potterism: "Jumpin' Jack Armstrong." Possible references to Jack Armstrong that fit the timeline are the *Jack Armstrong, The All American Boy* radio series from 1933-51 and *Jack Armstrong*, a 1947 serial.

A reference to The Three Stooges appears in Chapter 5 when Charles calls the three Korean doctors "Larry, Curly, Moe."

B.J. in Chapter 5 mentions *Don Quixote*, considered one of the most influential works of the Spanish Golden Age, and one of the greatest works of fiction ever published.

In Chapter 8, Potter calls Charles, "Moby" – a reference to *Moby Dick*, the 1851 classic by Herman Melville.

Potter mentions, Hedda Hopper (May 2, 1885-February 1, 1966), but pronounces the name as "Hooper." Hedda Hopper was an actress and a famous gossip columnist.

Actor Richard Herd (born September 26, 1932), a Boston, Massachusetts, native, has played roles ranging from a priest to Starfleet Admiral Owen Paris, father of Lieutenant Tom Paris on *Star Trek: Voyager*. A career that spans over 40 years includes appearances on *The Rockford Files, Streets of San Francisco* (Mr. Herd is sometimes mistaken for series star Karl Malden), and *Eight is Enough*. Herd also played recurring roles on 30 episodes on *T.J. Hooker* as Captain Dennis Sheridan and *Seaquest DSV* in 12 episodes as Admiral Noyce.

April Fools - 3/24/1980

Season 8 / Episode 198 / Production 196 – S623

Columbia House VHS Tape . . . . *A Bird In The Hand (Catalog # 19502)*
Fox DVD . . . . *Season 8, Disc 3*

Alan Alda, Mike Farrell, Harry Morgan
Loretta Swit, David Ogden Stiers, Jamie Farr, William Christopher

Executive Producer – Burt Metcalfe
Produced by John Rappaport and Jim Mulligan
Written by Dennis Koenig
Directed by Charles S. Dubin

Executive Story Editors – Dan Wilcox & Thad Mumford
Story Editor – Dennis Koenig
Creative Consultants – Gene Reynolds / Alan Alda

Pat Hingle . . . . Colonel Daniel Webster Tucker
G.W. Bailey . . . . Sergeant Luthor Rizzo
Roy Goldman . . . . Bartender
Jennifer Davis . . . . Nurse
Copyright 1980 – 20th Century Fox Film Corporation

Non-Credited Appearances . . . . Kellye Nakahara

Chapters

1: Main Titles	6: A Ray of Sunstroke – 13:16
2: The Season to be Silly – 0:53	7: Conduct Unbecoming – 16:17
3: Red, White and Blue Alert – 3:42	8: Cleopatra Klinger – 17:27
4: The Rizzo Secret – 6:58	9: April Fool! – 19:30
5: Bad Timing – 9:22	10: What's So Funny? / End Titles – 22:47

Closing Stills

1: Freeze – "Klingerpatra"
2: Colonel Tucker
3: Rizzo
4: Potter
5: Charles
6: B.J.
7: Margaret
8: Mulcahy
9: Klinger – "Nile"
10: Hawkeye

Synopsis: Colonel Potter orders an immediate end to the practical jokes the staff is playing on each other when he learns of the impending visit of Colonel Daniel Webster Tucker. Coming to observe the 4077th's medical set-up, Tucker, a.k.a., "Lord High Executioner" of the Surgeon General's Office, is a no nonsense by-the-book Colonel who lives for courts martial. But the medical staff can't resist, and after taking the canvas off Margaret's tent, she retaliates by hitting the doctors with a down pillow, just in time for Tucker's arrival. When threatened with court-martials and nothing to lose, the staff plays a practical joke on Tucker himself. But when Tucker appears to suffer a heart attack, he asks to speak to Hawkeye and reveals a stunning practical joke setup weeks before, with the help of his long-time friend, Colonel Potter.

Authors' Notes: There are no PA announcements in this episode.

The change room in Chapter 2 has the clothing hooks in the order of *Hawkeye, Winchester, Potter, B.J.;* but, for some reason, the names start three hooks in from the left and not with the first hook, and an empty hook between Hawkeye and Winchester.

When Charles mentions, "ptomaine au gratin" sitting in the change room in Chapter 2, there's a microphone shadow moving about on the upper left of the white curtain behind Potter.

Immediately following the microphone shadow in Chapter 2 at 1:21 in, there is a one-frame (and extraordinarily quick) shot of what appears to be small white rings on the left side of the frame, and continues partially on B.J. Possibly bubbling from projector bulb heat, or possibly a liquid splatter, but definitely hard to find and freeze.

Potterisms: "Bushwa," "What in the name of Marco Blessed Polo is going on here?", "Peck of pips," "Where in the name of Carrie's corset is your tent?"

Mulcahy, in a rare moment, is seen in Chapter 2 wearing a woman's robe as a result of a practical joke, and isn't too happy about it.

The view from the office windows in Chapter 3 is still the same wooden structure already seen in several episodes. However, in Chapter 4, the scene with Rizzo and Klinger was filmed at the motor pool on the (Stage 9) compound in front of the structure. It appears to be a motor pool supply room as there is a no smoking sign on the door, indicating the possibility of flammable liquids, such as gasoline, being stored inside while Rizzo is under a jeep on a rollaway in front of it.

In Chapter 5, Margaret calls Hawkeye a "tent-napper" after she discovers the canvas missing on her tent, but the captioning says, "tank-napper."

Colonel Tucker arrives in jeep number 18210707 in Chapter 5.

Also in Chapter 5, Potter is wearing his red and gray-stripped robe.

Klinger tells Colonel Tucker in Chapter 5 that he has Cuban cigars for him. Someone did his or her homework for this episode, as the U.S. embargo on Fidel Castro's government took effect on February 7, 1962. But Cuban cigars still might have been available in Korea.

Potter, in Chapter 5, is on the (Stage 9) compound in his pajamas and his robe, but is wearing only one slipper on his right foot. His left foot is bare.

In Chapter 8, Klinger reverts back to his earlier ways and is wearing one of his more memorable outfits: "Klingerpatra"

After Tucker and Potter let the staff in on their practical joke, they're sitting at the bar in the Officer's Club in Chapter 10. As they're sitting there, look at the top left of the picture and see the microphone dip into the frame.

Pat Hingle, born Martin Patterson Hingle on July 19, 1924 in Colorado, had been a popular character actor in the 60's and 70's. A career that spanned 60 years, Mr. Hingle was the 2005 winner of the North Carolina Distinguished Filmmaker Award, and a Tony Award nominee for best supporting or featured actor for the 1958 play *The Dark at the Top of the Stairs.* Appearances include *On The Waterfront* (1954 unaccredited), *Alfred Hitchcock Presents, The Twilight Zone, Dr. Kildare, Medical Center, St. Elsewhere* and *Trapper John, M.D.* Mr. Hingle also appeared in the 2008 movie *Undoing Time* as a judge. He resided with his wife, Julia, in North Carolina, until his death on January 3, 2009.

Appendix – Season 8

Character Profiles

Hawkeye

Episode 177: Hawkeye's radio station back home once held a contest to see how many freckles Arthur Godfrey had.

183: Whenever he and Kathy Harrison wanted to go for a walk or to the movies, her kid brother, Little Ralphie tagged along.

197: In a newspaper article sent by his father, Dr. Hyram R. Ledbetter in Minneapolis earns $5.00 per X-ray for The Selective Service System, and averages $2,000 a day, but "works terribly long hours."
Hawkeye averages seven bowel resections a week, totaling 546. According to these numbers, Hawkeye has been in Korea exactly 78 weeks, or a year and a half. Charging the Army $7.00 per resection totals $3,822, and sends the Army a bill for $38, 215.11, including all the X-rays he's taken. He reduces the total bill to $36,005.00, after claiming a jeep for himself from the Motor Pool.

B.J.

Episode 179: Elwood Einstein — a plumber in Mill Valley.

191: Second grade hall monitor in a one-room schoolhouse.

192: Attended a special dinner party for Lucia Murphy's 14th birthday. They played "spin the bottle" and sent out for Chinese food.

196: Aunt Shirley — likes steamed clams.

Colonel Potter

Episode 174: Mildred plays canasta at Willa Norman's on Tuesday and bridge at Edna Hazeltine's on Thursday, unless Mr. Hazeltine's lumbago is acting up, then they go to Muriel Barlow's, but you have to let the phone ring because Muriel Barlow drinks.
According to Potter, he proposed to Mildred in combat boots.
Potter and Brigadier General Bud Haggerty took basic training together.
Mildred always goes to see her cousin Portia when she needs cheering-up.
Mildred's cousin Portia likes to take her teeth out at parties.

180: Trapped in a small village in France without water, and the only thing to cook with was wine. Men were running for an extra plate of gravy.

185: Sophie is at her best just after breakfast.

188: Potterism: *"Mule Muffins."*

190: Has Tex Ritter 78's at home.

191: Package from "Smith, Smith and Brown — Attorneys at Law."

1917 in France, he and buddies laid low in an old French chateau —
Stein finds a cache of fine brandy and when they got to the last bottle,
the 5 of them made a pledge (Tontine) — whoever is the last survivor
gets the bottle and drinks a toast to his old friends. When Gresky died
in Tokyo, Potter became the last survivor.

The other 4 members of the pledge with Potter are: Ryan, who died in
WWI, Gianelli, who died in WWII, Stein, the joker of the crowd, and
Gresky, Potter's best friend who died in Tokyo.

192: His and Mildred's favorite movie is *History Is Made At Night* (1937).
Mildred loves Charles Boyer *(see Episode 188, page 566 for more
information on Potter's favorite movie).*

194: Mildred has the first Dumont television on the block.

197: Mildred sends swatches, one of which is a butterfly pattern when she
considers reupholstering a chaise lounge. Potter doesn't want to sit on
butterflies.

198: When in the Cavalry, he got "blottoed" and did the Charleston with a
Shetland pony.

Margaret

Episode 175: Hawkeye and B.J. once ran all her underwear up the flagpole *(mentioned).*
Margaret was a student nurse when she dated Walter Philip Crichton
(Wally) in college.

They never went to motels — Wally had a Nash.

Wally, a founding member of "Freedom for Tomorrow," was named a
subversive by the House Committee.

George Pfister, a college friend of Margaret's was president of his
fraternity and "pinned" to four girls at the same time.

Emily Kingsley, a friend from college, majored in chemistry and
collected Russ Colombo records. Russ Colombo, 1908-1934, was a
singer, musician and actor.

Buddy Gurlack was the school chug-a-lug champ.

178: Had a Raggedy Ann (early 1900's) doll when she was a kid

181: Is known to the local Korean laundry girl, Oksun Li, as the "lady with
tiger skin underwear."

187: Margaret wants a man that's 20% her father, 10% Scully, 10% Hawkeye,
3% Frank Burns and 2% Donald reduced to 1% *(the other 56% remains a
mystery).*

Charles

Episode 175: His polo pony was named, "Pegasus."

179: Has a pet mastiff, "Bruno."

180: Four years at Harvard Medical School — five years surgical residency
and the attending staff at Boston General.

182: R & R at the Pink Parasol Nightclub and Bathhouse in Tokyo.
The night after he graduated Harvard Medical School, he distinctly
remembers attempting to swim the Charles River in his cap and gown.
He said since it was named after him, it was his.
"Mrs. 'Chuck' Winchester, III"

184: Blood type is AB negative *(in Episode 168, he has the same blood type as
Klinger, which is B positive, as per episode 76).*
The Winchesters have always given blood in time of crisis, starting with
the Revolutionary War.
A Winchester never accepts charity.

186: Harvard Class of '43 *(Consistent with Episode 142).*
Graduated summa cum laude *(Consistent with Episode 152).*
Lettered in crew and polo.

187: Is so bored that he almost wanted to see pictures of Klinger's Cousin Hakim's nuptials.

189: Sister Honoria engaged to an Italian, but the wedding is off as the Italian man's family forbade her to marry out of her faith. *(However, in Episode 146, Little Sister Honoria ran away from home and married a farmer. She left the farmer; family ostracized her, "of course," and went to live with — not to marry — a shoe clerk).*
Telephone number in Boston is Lawrence 8464
Address is 30 Briarcliff Lane, Boston, Massachusetts

192: More than anything, he wanted to play music, but acknowledged the fact this is one gift he does not possess.

194: First time he turned on a television, he saw an Alka Seltzer commercial featuring "Speedy." *(see Episode 194, page 578 for more information on Alka Seltzer and Speedy).*

Radar

Episode 176: On R&R (rest and reading) at Suzi's Pink Pagoda in Tokyo.

177: Cow back home is Betsy. In Season 7's "The Party," his cow was Edna.
Uncle Ed has a Studebaker that needs water every ten minutes.
Uncle Ed passes away.
Neighbor is Mr. Whitsett.

Klinger

Episode 177: Klinger has been sending MacArthur love letters for over a year.

178: Mother used to pin his bike to his sleeve because he loses things.

191: Cousin Fatima — everything she touches smells like jasmine.

194: Aunt Fatima made the rug he uses for a private room *(see Episode 191, page 572 for more on Cousin Fatima.)*
Father was bowler of the year three times at the height of the depression.
Hangs a lamp in his office that his uncle Hakim got married under twice.
Once sent Colonel Hedley bonbons.
Practiced forging Potter's signature 47 times, but too much swoop on the "T."

Father Mulcahy

Episode 177: Told the story of his cousin Kevin, to Gail Harris, who withdrew from medical school after one month because he didn't have the stomach for it, then became a mortician. His cousin Kevin actually is in roofing and siding.
Francis John Patrick Mulcahy — but his mother always called him "Johnny."

186: Sister about to become Mother Superior.
Captain Mulcahy.

Seen, Heard, Mentioned or Referenced – Season 8

Movies

Episode 174: B.J. mentions *Mildred Pierce* (1945).

177: Klinger calls Zale "Bonzo" (a chimp), a reference to *Bedtime for Bonzo* (1951).

Hawkeye mentions *The Shadow*, a pulp magazine character and a radio show from the 1930's, later a 1933 movie.

179: B.J. says, "The postman always sneers twice," a reference to the 1934 crime-novel *The Postman Always Rings Twice*, and the subsequent movie from 1946.

Potter mentions *The Great John L.*, a movie from 1945, directed by Frank Tuttle.

183: Potter mentions *Snow White* (1937).

187: Hawkeye says "Is Jeanette MacDonald stomping on Nelson Eddy's Mountie hat?" This is a reference to the 1936 movie *Rose Marie* with Jeanette MacDonald and Nelson Eddy (as a Canadian Mountie).

189: B.J. mentions *Naughty Marietta*, a 1935 musical film with Nelson Eddy and Jeanette MacDonald.

192: *History is Made at Night* (1937) seen in the mess tent.

Hawkeye mentions "The Field Pack – Your Canvas Buddy" *(not real)*.

Klinger mentions *Gone with the Wind* (1939).

Potter mentions "Heckle and Jeckle," who first appeared in the animated short *The Talking Magpies* (1946).

Klinger mentions "Terror in the Tiny Town" – the correct name is *The Terror of Tiny Town* (1938), a musical Western with an all-dwarf cast. (The tagline for this film was "Little people with big guns").

198: Hawkeye mentions Perils of Pralines, a reference to *The Perils of Pauline*, first a 1914 silent serial, then a 1933 serial, and movies in 1947 and 1967.

Songs

174: Klinger mentions "Home on the Range" See Episode 16 (page 129) for details.

177: "Heigh-Ho" *(Hawkeye sings "Hi-ho, hi-ho, it's off to work we go...")* From the 1937 classic *Snow White*.

"The U.S. Air Force" *(Sergeant Olsen mentions "Wild Blue Yonder")* See Episode 26 (page 191) for details.

180: "Pop Goes the Weasel" *(Charles whistles)* Associated with jack-in-the-box toys, a jig often sung as a nursery rhyme dating back to 17th century England.

"Ride of the Valkyries" *(Charles hums in the shower)* The beginning of Act III of *Die Walkure* written by Richard Wagner in 1851

181: "Nola" *(Mulcahy plays on the piano in the Officer's Club)* Written by Felix Arndt (1889-1918), a pianist and composer of popular music, in 1915 as an engagement gift to his fiancée, Nola Locke. "Nola" was also a top-ten hit for guitar legend Les Paul in 1950.

"Marie" *(Mulcahy plays on the piano in the Officer's Club)* Written by Tommy Dorsey (1905-1956), a #1 hit in 1937 and #16 in 1938. *(Note: Mulcahy plays the exact same song for "Marie" as he does for "Nola.")*

182: "Happy Days Are Here Again" *(heard over the PA)* See Episode 1 (page 128) for details.

"Shuffle Off To Buffalo" *(Potter mentions)* See Episode 98 and 99 (page 399) for details.

"If You Knew Susie" *(Mrs. "Chuck Winchester" sings, "If you knew sushi like I know sushi...")* Words by B.G. DeSylva, music by Joseph Mayer, published in 1925. Also from the 1948 movie of the same name.

"So Long, It's Been Good to Know You" *(Hawkeye mentions)* Written by Woody Guthrie in 1944. Song is a re-write of Guthrie's "Dusty Old Dust" from 1935.

"Oh Promise Me" *(Mrs. "Chuck Winchester" mentions)* Words by Clement Scott, music by Reginald DeKoven, in 1889-90.

183: "The Mulberry Bush" *(Mulcahy sings "This is the way we wash our sheets so early in the morning...")* A traditional children's nursery rhyme and song (sung with the word "clothes" instead of "sheets").

"The Farmer in the Dell" *(B.J. refers)* Another traditional children's nursery rhyme and song.

185: "Over There" *(Potter sings "Over there, over there...")* One of the best-known songs of WWI, written by George M. Cohan in 1917.

"How Ya Gonna Keep 'Em Down on the Farm (After They've Seen Paree)" *(Hawkeye sings "How ya gone keep 'em down on the farm after they've seen Pusan")* Another well-known WWI song with words written by Joe Young and Sam A. Lewis, music written by Walter Donaldson, published in 1918.

"Mademoiselle from Armentières," *(B.J. sings "Mademoiselle from Panmunjon, Ouijongbu...")* Another well-known WWI song, supposedly popular in the French army during the 1830's. There are different claims as to who wrote this song: words by Edward Rowland, music by Canadian Composer Lieutenant Glitz Rice is one team; Harry Carlton and Joe Tunbridge is another team; and Harry Wincott, a famous British songwriter is another possibility. Also the name of a 1926 movie.

"Marines Hymn" *(Mulcahy mentions "The halls of Montezuma")* The official hymn of the United States Marine Corps, and the oldest official song of the Unites States military. The lyrics date from the 19th Century, but the author remains unknown. The music, written by Jacques Offenbach, is from the opera *Genevieve de Brabant*, which debuted in Paris in 1859.

"A Hunting We Will Go" *(Klinger plays on a kazoo)* Author unknown. Mulcahy sings (with piano: *"Oh, my dear, I can't wait to see ya. But I'm here in South Korea. The picture you sent was quite an eyeful. I've taped it to my trusty rifle."* Mulcahy sings another (with piano): *"There's no one singing war songs now like people used to do. No 'Over There,' no 'Praise the Lord,' no 'Glory Hallelu.' Perhaps at last we've asked ourselves what we should have asked before. With the pain and death this madness brings, what were we singing for?"*

189: "Oh What A Beautiful Morning" *(Hawkeye sings: "There's a bright golden haze in Korea..." twice "The sun is as high as a drunken G.I.")* Lyrics by Oscar Hammerstein, music by Richard Rodgers, from the 1943 musical *Oklahoma*. (The correct lyrics are, "There's a bright golden haze on the meadow...")

"Mockingbird" *(Hawkeye sings "Hush little baby, don't say a word, papa's gonna buy you a mockingbird..." All in O.R. join in)* Written and recorded in 1963 (ten years after the Korean War) by Inez Foxx (born 1942) and her brother, Charlie Foxx (1939–1998).

"Ce' La Luna Mezzo Mare" *(Charles sings "Lucky, lucky lucky me, I'm a lucky son-of-a-gun...")* This song is traditional Italian.

190: "Chicago (That Toddlin' Town)" *(Charles mentions)* Written by Fred Fischer and published in 1922. Probably the best-known version is Frank Sinatra's from the movie *The Joker is Wild* (1957).

191: "Roses of Picardy" *(Potter mentions, also heard on a record player)* A popular song during WWI, words by Frederick E. Weatherly (an English Officer), music in 1916 by Haydn Wood.

193: "For He's A Jolly Good Fellow" *(All sing in the mess tent for Sergeant Herbert)* See Episode 13 (page XX) for details.

"Happy Birthday" *(All sing in the mess tent for Sergeant Herbert)* Standard traditional American song, presently noted by the Guinness Book of World Records as the most well-recognized song in the English language (followed by "For He's A Jolly Good Fellow" and "Auld Lang Syne"). Origins for "Happy Birthday" date back to the late 1800's.

196: "Night and Day" *(PA announcement: "Through the roaring traffic's boom and the silence of your lonely room, night and day, you are the ones.")* Written by Cole Porter for the 1932 musical play, "Gay Divorce." (The correct lyrics are "In the roaring traffic's boom, in the silence of my lonely room.")

"Daisy Bell" *(Hawkeye sings "Daisy, Daisy, give me your answer true...")* Written by Harry Dacre in 1892.

"The Star Spangled Banner" *(Hawkeye says "O'Shea can you see?")*

"Three Little Words" *(Klinger sings "Three little words, that's all I live for...")* Song is words by Bert Kalmer, music by Harry Ruby, published in 1930.

197: "Dixie" *(Margaret says "Whistling Dixie.")* Also known as "I Wish I Was in Dixie" and "Dixie's Land," probably the best-known song to have emerged from the "blackface minstrelsy" in the 1850's. Daniel Decatur Emmett is the most recognized composer, but there are several others who claimed authorship. Making matters worse is Mr. Emmett's inconsistent account of the song's origins and the time he took to have it copyrighted.

"You Do Something to Me" *(Potter says "Do that Voodoo you do so well...")* Written by Cole Porter, 1929.

198: "Ah, Sweet Mysteries of Life" *(Potter says "Sweet cubes of delight," followed by Hawkeye singing "At last I've found you.")* Words by Rida Johnson, music by Victor Herbert, recorded by Nelson Eddy and Jeanette MacDonald for the 1935 movie *Naughty Marietta*.

Appearances – Season 8

Alda, Anthony.. Episode 193 *(Corporal Jarvis)*
Alda, Robert... Episode 193 *(Major Dr. Anthony Borelli)*
Arbus, Allen .... Episode 194 *(Dr. Sidney Freedman)*
Autajay, Jason .... Episode 191 *(Korean boy)*
Bailey, G.W. .... Episode 183, 192, 197, 198 *(Sergeant Luther Rizzo)*
Bailey, G.W. .... Episode 186 *(The G.I., Note: no sergeant's stripes,*
or any other rank insignia in evidence)
Begly Jr., Ed ....Episode 174 *(Private Paul Conway)*
Bergstrom, Catherine.......................................Episode 195 *(Peg Hunnicutt)*
Blanton, Arell.. Episode 177 *(Private Hough)*
Bogert, William .... Episode 188 *(Rodger Prescott)*
Brophy, Kevin.. Episode 184 *(Roberts)*
Bruns, Philip .... Episode 194 *(Lieutenant Colonel Burton D. Hedley)*
Bryant, Joshua... Episode 176 *(Sergeant Jack Scully)*
Cavonis, Paul. .... Episode 186 *(The Greek Soldier)*
Cheung, George Kee................................. Episode 176 *(1st Korean Soldier)*
Chung, Byron................................... Episode 183 *(North Korean Patrol Leader)*
Connell, Jane... Episode 191 *(Betty Halpern)*
Cramer, David..Episode 194 *(Aide)*
Cristino, Tony ....Episode 177 *(Sergeant LaGrow)*
Davis, Jennifer... Episode 175, 198 *(Nurse)*
De Broux, Lee............................. Episode 178 *(Major George Van Kirk)*
Dozer, David..Episode 178 *(Dispatcher)*
Emery, James .... Episode 181 *(Soldier)*
Evans, Art .... Episode 181 *(Dolan)*
Farrell, Gwen .... Episode 179 *(Nurse)*
Farley, Elizabeth.. Episode 188 *(Louise Harper)*
Fujikawa, Jerry...Episode 197 *(Doctor Wu)*
Goldman, Roy.....................................Episode 183, 184 *(Corpsman)*
Goldman, Roy...Episode 198 *(Bartender)*
Harrison, Mark .... Episode 181 *(Soldier)*
Haymer, Johnny .... Episode 177 *(Sergeant Zelmo Zale)*
Haynes, Robin...Episode 195 *(Taylor)*
Herd, Richard .... Episode 197 *(Captain "Wild Bill" Snyder)*
Hermann, Edward .... Episode 190 *(Dr. Steven J. Newsome)*
Hingle, Pat....................Episode 198 *(Colonel Daniel Webster Tucker)*
Hirokane, David...Episode 189 *(Chinese soldier)*
Hoshi, Shizuko .... Episode 181 *(Mrs. Li)*
Imamura, Sally ....Episode 191 *(Korean girl)*
Izay, Connie ....Episode 195 *(Connie)*
Izay, Connie .... Episode 176 *(Nurse)*
Johnston, J.J.. Episode 184 *(Chopper pilot)*
Jones, Marilyn ....Episode 177 *(Lieutenant Patty Haven)*
Jorden, Jan .... Episode 179 *(Nurse Baker)*
Keane, James ....Episode 182 *(Corporal Shaw)*
Kelly, Daren.. Episode 193 *(Sergeant Herbert)*
Kim, Peter ....Episode 197 *(Doctor Po)*
Kologi, Mark.................................. Episode 181 *(Private Eddie Hastings)*
Kumagi, Denice...Episode 181 *(Oksun Li)*
Kusatsu, Clyde .... Episode 194 *(Sergeant Michael Yee)*
Levels, Calvin.. Episode 196 *(Private Jackson)*

Broadcast/Production Order – Season 8

Broadcast	*Production*
174: Too Many Cooks *(9/17/1979)*	*174: (S601)* Too Many Cooks
175: Are You Now, Margaret? *(9/24/1979)*	*175: (S602)* Are You Now, Margaret?
176: Guerilla My Dreams *(10/1/1979)*	*176: (S603)* Guerilla My Dreams
177: Goodbye Radar, Part 1 *(10/8/1979)*	*177: (S604)* Period Of Adjustment
178: Goodbye Radar, Part 2 *(10/15/1979)*	*178: (S605)* Private Finance
179: Period Of Adjustment *(10/22/1979)*	*179: (S606)* Mr. And Mrs. Who?
180: Nurse Doctor *(10/29/1979)*	*180: (S607)* Yalu Brick Road
181: Private Finance *(11/5/1979)*	*181: (S608)* Nurse Doctor
182: Mr. And Mrs Who? *(11/12/1979)*	*182: (S609)* Life Time
183: Yalu Brick Road *(11/19/1979)*	*183: (S610)* Goodbye Radar, Part 1
184: Life Time *(11/26/1979)*	*184: (S611)* Goodbye Radar, Part 2
185: Dear Uncle Abdul *(12/3/1979)*	*185: (S612)* Dreams
186: Captains Outrageous *(12/10/1979)*	*186: (S613)* Dear Uncle Abdul
187: Stars And Stripe *(12/17/1979)*	*187: (S614)* Captains Outrageous
188: Yessir, That's Our Baby *(12/31/1979)*	*188: (S615)* Stars And Stripe
189: Bottle Fatigue *(1/7/1980)*	*189: (S616)* Heal Thyself
190: Heal Thyself *(1/14/1980)*	*190: (S617)* Yessir, That's Our Baby
191: Old Soldiers *(1/21/1980)*	*191: (S618)* Bottle Fatigue
192: Morale Victory *(1/28/1980)*	*192: (S619)* Morale Victory
193: Lend A Hand *(2/4/1980)*	*193: (S620)* Old Soldiers
194: Goodbye, Cruel World *(2/11/1980)*	*194: (S621)* Lend A Hand
195: Dreams *(2/18/1980)*	*195: (S622)* Goodbye, Cruel World
196: War Co-Respondent *(3/3/1980)*	*196: (S623)* April Fools
197: Back Pay *(3/10/1980)*	*197: (S624)* War Co-Respondent
198: April Fools *(3/24/1980)*	*198: (S625)* Back Pay

Season 9

The final three seasons of *M*A*S*H* continue to set a high standard for anything on television. They are also quite unlike any of the early seasons. This is no wonder, as different people were running the show. The cast moved through episodes of this, and subsequent seasons, in a more cohesive pattern. Plot lines from the ninth season were certainly interesting. Margaret's father, though mentioned as deceased in "Hot Lips and Empty Arms" from Season 2, pays a very stoic visit. Hawkeye bets he can go a whole day without joking. The O.R. gets a cement floor. Klinger starts a camp newspaper. Sidney Freedman returns, as does Colonel Baldwin, who sent Charles to the 4077th in Season 6. The trend towards heavier drama continued. "Death Takes a Holiday" was the show's third Christmas episode. In contrast to the first one, "Dear Dad" from Season 1, the members of the 4077th seemed genuinely battle weary by this holiday installment. Episodes like "No Sweat," "Depressing News" and "No Laughing Matter" were quite humorous, and moved along at a lively pace.

The Best of Enemies – 11/17/1980

Season 9 / Episode 199 / Production 202 – Z404

Columbia House VHS Tape . . . . *Not Released by Columbia House*
Fox DVD . . . . *Season 9, Disc 1*

Alan Alda, Mike Farrell, Harry Morgan
Loretta Swit, David Ogden Stiers, Jamie Farr, William Christopher

Executive Producer – Burt Metcalfe
Produced by John Rappaport
Written by Sheldon Bull
Directed by Charles S. Dubin

Executive Script Consultants – Thad Mumford & Dan Wilcox
Executive Story Editor – Dennis Koenig
Creative Consultants – Gene Reynolds / Alan Alda

Mako . . . . Li Han

Copyright 1980 – 20th Century Fox Film Corporation

Non-Credited Appearances . . . . .Kellye Nakahara, Roy Goldman

Chapters

1: Main Titles / 24 Hour Pass	6: The Big Game – 12:03
2: Grudge Match – 2:39	7: Something to Live For – 13:45
3: Dressed to be Killed – 5:07	8: A Whole New Game – 15:09
4: Looking for a Partner – 6:42	9: A Soldier's Burial – 19:14
5: The Soldier's Friend – 10:24	10: Breakfast in Bed / End Titles – 22:09

Closing Stills

1: *Freeze – Hawkeye asleep in the Swamp*
2: *Li Han*
3: *B.J. in the Officer's Club*
4: *Potter in the Officer's Club*
5: *Margaret in her tent*
6: *Charles in the Officer's Club*
7: *Klinger*
8: *Mulcahy in his tent*
9: *Hawkeye*

Synopsis: When Hawkeye's jeep breaks down on his way to Seoul, he quickly finds himself being held at gunpoint by a North Korean soldier. He orders Hawkeye out of the jeep with his medical bag and brings him to his badly wounded friend who needs more attention than Hawkeye is able to provide in a field. Unable to convince the man that the equipment needed to save his friend is back at the 4077th, and still being held at gunpoint, Hawkeye tries to save him, but his head wounds are too extensive and the man dies. Acknowledging Hawkeye's efforts, the enemy soldier allows him to leave, takes out a large knife and starts digging a grave. Seeing this, Hawkeye turns back and helps the man bury his friend. Back at camp, Potter boasts about Mildred and her partner taking first prize in the Hannibal Missouri bridge tournament. In a game of one-upmanship, Charles and his sister are four-time champions of the Beacon Hill Bridge Society, and the challenge between Potter and Winchester is on. But first, they have to find suitable partners, which proves more difficult than surgery.

Authors' Notes: There are no PA announcements in this episode.

It seems Hawkeye has a new civilian shirt in Chapter 1, similar to but not the same as Trapper's yellow shirt.

In Chapter 2, Potter mentions Primo Carnera (October 26, 1906-June 29, 1967), an Italian boxer who stood at 6'7", weighing 270 pounds, and a former heavyweight champion.

The sign on Margaret's tent door is in freehand in Chapter 4. Sometimes, the sign is in block lettering.

B.J. mentions Frankie Laine in Chapter 4. Frankie Laine (March 30, 1913-February 6, 2007) was a musician and a singer / songwriter who enjoyed a lengthy career. His first concerts took place in 1931 and his final performance was in 2005.

In Chapter 6, Potter mentions Charlie Goren. Born Charles Henry Goren (March 4, 1901-April 3, 1991), he was a world champion bridge player and best-selling author on the subject.

In Chapter 6, Klinger is wearing a Toledo Mudhens baseball jersey and cap. The cap is blue with a red bill and has the letter "T" on the front. Some Mudhens caps have the "T" on the front, but also have a "Mudhen" over it. Mudhens batting practice caps have only the bird. The baseball cap Klinger is wearing is that of the Texas Rangers Baseball Club, not the Toledo Mudhens. Interestingly, The Texas Rangers, formerly the Washington Senators in 1961, did not become the Texas Rangers until the team moved to Arlington, Texas in 1972. The Texas Ranger's cap Klinger is seen in is from the 70's and 80's (the previous Washington Senators became the Minnesota Twins after they left Washington D.C. at the end of the 1960 season). By the way, the Toledo Mudhens are the AAA affiliate of baseball's Detroit Tigers.

Potterisms: "What the Sam Hill?" (said previously as well), "Beaver biscuits."

Charles mentions "Doodles Weaver" in Chapter 8. Winstead Sheffield "Doodles" Weaver (May 11, 1911-January 17, 1983) was a radio and television comedian, the brother of NBC television executive Pat Weaver, and the uncle of actress Sigourney Weaver.

In Chapter 9, the wounded North Korean soldier dies, and Li Han allows Hawkeye to go. When Hawkeye gets up to leave, he walks away leaving his medical bag and all the surgical instruments on the man's chest.

Letters – 11/24/1980

Season 9 / Episode 200 / Production 201 – Z403

Columbia House VHS Tape . . . . *War Stories (Catalog # 21043)*
Fox DVD . . . . *Season 9, Disc 1*

Alan Alda, Mike Farrell, Harry Morgan
Loretta Swit, David Ogden Stiers, Jamie Farr, William Christopher

Executive Producer – Burt Metcalfe
Produced by John Rappaport
Written by Dennis Koenig
Directed by Charles S. Dubin

Executive Script Consultants – Thad Mumford & Dan Wilcox
Executive Story Editor – Dennis Koenig
Creative Consultants – Gene Reynolds / Alan Alda

Richard Paul . . . . Captain William Bainbridge
Larry Cedar . . . . Mike The Soldier
Michael Currie . . . . Dr. Breuer
Eileen Saki . . . . Rosie
Copyright 1980 – 20th Century Fox Film Corporation

Non-Credited Appearances. . . . . Kellye Nakahara, Gwen Farrell, Roy Goldman,
Jennifer Davis

Chapters

1: *Main Titles / Gray Skies*
2: *Irving the Lush – 2:59*
3: *Hate Mail – 5:27*
4: *Breeding Farm – 7:29*
5: *Getting Close – 9:12*

6: *On the Job Training – 11:29*
7: *Crisis of Conscience – 14:18*
8: *Hoops Potter – 16:02*
9: *Fall Color – 19:27*
10: *Providence / End Titles – 21:11*

Closing Stills

1: *Freeze – Potter, Klinger, Hawkeye, B.J., Charles in Swamp*
2: *Captain Bainbridge*
3: *G.I.*
4: *Rosie*
5: *Margaret*
6: *B.J.*
7: *Mulcahy*
8: *Potter*
9: *Charles*
10: *Klinger*
11: *Hawkeye*

Synopsis: A fourth-grade teacher, and a friend of Hawkeye's from Crabapple Cove, has her class write letters to the 4077th on topics that range from saving lives to jealousy over camping out every day and eating army food. Some of the kids' letters are inquisitive, some funny, and one fourth-grader finds the exercise boring and would rather be playing dodge ball. Margaret's letter stirs up her emotions when she's reminded of a badly wounded G.I. with only a couple of hours to live, and Charles is genuinely touched after receiving a letter containing a leaf from a birch tree during the fall season in New England. But Hawkeye's letter from a young boy named Ronnie is filled with hate, and has him rattled.

Commentary by Larry Cedar: "*M*A*S*H* was, at the time, the hottest show on television and, being very young and barely out of college, I was more than a bit star struck in the presence of both the legendary Hot Lips and Hawkeye (I'm somewhat embarrassed to admit that I asked a rather surprised Ms. Swit for her autograph between takes). But everyone couldn't have been kinder or more professional. Loretta, with whom I did my scene, was charming and focused on the work. Alan Alda was brimming with intelligence and wit. We were, however, just coming off an extended actors' strike and I recall one somewhat tense exchange between Loretta, who was very supportive of The Screen Actors Guild action, and a particular member of the crew, many of whom had been temporarily put out of work by the extended negotiations. But overall, everyone on the set, including myself, was thrilled to be working on such a successful and acclaimed program."

Authors' Notes: There are no PA announcements in this episode.

Mildred was to send Colonel Potter a "Cloverine" salve for his "barking bunions" in Chapter 1. The Cloverine salve has been in existence since 1890.

In Chapter 4, Potter mentions "Brogans." Brogan usually refers to a heavy ankle-high boot; more specifically, boots worn by soldiers in the American Civil War. This style of boot is available today.

Larry Cedar's character in Chapter 5, "The Soldier," is actually named Mike.

In Chapter 8, Colonel Potter debuts a new robe. Similar in color to the earlier red and gray-stripped robe, the one seen here has much wider stripes.

In Chapter 9, B.J. mentions "Captain Nemo," a character from one of the best known literary works in Jules Verne's *20,000 Leagues Under the Se*a (1870).

Potterism: "Hot sausage."

Potter sets a new camp free-throw record of 32, breaking the old record by one in Chapter 10.

Cementing Relationships – 12/1/1980

Season 9 / Episode 201 / Production 199 – Z401
Columbia House VHS Tape............. Major Margaret (Catalog # 22048)
Fox DVD .... Season 9, Disc 1

Alan Alda, Mike Farrell, Harry Morgan
Loretta Swit, David Ogden Stiers, Jamie Farr, William Christopher

Executive Producer – Burt Metcalfe
Produced by John Rappaport
Written by David Pollock and Elias Davis
Directed by Charles S. Dubin

Executive Script Consultants – Thad Mumford & Dan Wilcox
Executive Story Editor – Dennis Koenig
Creative Consultants – Gene Reynolds / Alan Alda
Joel Brooks .... Ignazio De Simone
Alan Toy .... Private Cochran
Mel Harris... The Driver
Eileen Saki .... Rosie
Copyright 1980 – 20th Century Fox Film Corporation

Non-Credited Appearances.......... Kellye Nakahara, Dennis Troy, Roy Goldman

Chapters

1: Main Titles / Jilted	6: Two Ships – 12:33
2: Culture and Breeding – 3:52	7: Wrong Proportions – 13:56
3: That's Amore – 4:14	8: Prisoner of Love – 18:00
4: The Genghis of Con – 7:19	9: The Ribbon Cutting – 21:52
5: Day Laborers – 11:18	10: Nice Sound / End Titles – 23:31

Closing Stills

1: Freeze – Surgical instrument on cement floor
2: Ignazio
3: Cochran (G.I.)
4: Charles
5: Potter
6: B.J.
7: Margaret
8: Mulcahy
9: Klinger in the office
10: Hawkeye in Post-Op

Synopsis: A wood floor in the operating room is a breeding ground for bacteria, and the source of Private Cochran's staph infection. A cement floor would prevent this from happening, but because the "M" in MASH means "mobile," the Army Corps of Engineers won't do it, leaving the 4077th to do it themselves. Klinger is able to get the necessary materials to make the floor, and since he's the only one that knows how to do it, he appoints himself as foreman and oversees the project. Twice. In Post-Op with a leg wound is Ignazio DeSimone, who, after getting a "Dear Gianni" letter, falls in love with Margaret. As much as Margaret tries to discourage any relationship with the jilted Ignazio, she's less than successful and now can't get rid of him.

Commentary by David Pollock: "This was our first one. They called us in and gave us the story. Burt was the boss and Gene was the consultant. I remember talking to Dr. Walter Dishell, bothering him up at Lake Tahoe, to ask about staph infections. We'd write the script, and then ask him for help. We had to figure out what type of concrete to use."

Authors' Notes: There are no PA announcements in this episode.

In Chapter 1, Hawkeye, after learning of a man's temperature says, "101.6? You're into the FM dial." What Hawkeye says is accurate, as the FM band at the time extended from 88 to 108 MHz, as it does today, but no station would have been assigned that frequency, as they start at 88.1 and are spaced 0.2 MHz apart, so there is always an odd digit after the decimal point in the United States. Even though "101.6" would be in the FM band, FM radio had not yet really caught on, and there wasn't much listening at that time, making Hawkeye's line improbable at best.

Also in Chapter 1, a wounded Italian man, Ignazio DeSimone, is in post-op recovering from a leg wound. Becoming a member of the United Nations in 1955, two years after the Korean War ended, Italy did not send any ground troops to Korea. However, Italy did send a Red Cross Field Hospital # 68 that contained 150 beds, a medical staff of 131 and treated 14,041 in-patients. In this episode, Mr. DeSimone has, along with a patch that says "ITALY" on his left upper sleeve, a Red Cross patch underneath. Also, he's wearing Red Cross insignia on his collar. It's plausible that he would be in Korea. We can only speculate as to why he was being treated at the 4077th as opposed to his own hospital.

Jeep number 18210717 is seen driving Ignazio from the 4077th in Chapter 6.

In Chapter 7, Father Mulcahy is singing, and B.J. refers to him as "der Bingle," a nickname given to Bing Crosby (May 3, 1903–October 14, 1977), presumably from German fans.

Father's Day – 12/8/1980

Season 9 / Episode 202 / Production 203 – Z405

Columbia House VHS Tape. . . . . *Major Margaret (Catalog # 22048)*
Fox DVD . . . . *Season 9, Disc 1*

Alan Alda, Mike Farrell, Harry Morgan
Loretta Swit, David Ogden Stiers, Jamie Farr, William Christopher

Executive Producer – Burt Metcalfe
Produced by John Rappaport
Written by Karen L. Hall
Directed by Alan Alda

Executive Script Consultants – Thad Mumford & Dan Wilcox
Executive Story Editor – Dennis Koenig
Creative Consultants – Gene Reynolds / Alan Alda

Andrew Duggan . . . . Colonel Alvin Houlihan
Jeffrey Kramer. . . . . Sergeant Ronnie Morgove
Art La Fleur . . . . M.P.

Copyright 1980 – 20th Century Fox Film Corporation

Non-Credited Appearances. . . . . Kellye Nakahara, Gwen Farrell, Dennis Troy,
Roy Goldman, Jennifer Davis

Chapters

1: *Main Titles / Daddy!*	6: *Three Ring Circus – 11:47*
2: *Prime Stuff – 2:20*	7: *The Four Musketeers – 14:17*
3: *Top Notch – 3:34*	8: *Finding Fault – 17:57*
4: *Naked Cow – 6:21*	9: *Wetting the Appetite – 20:22*
5: *Light-Hearted Atmosphere – 8:21*	10: *No Beef / End Titles – 22:33*

Closing Stills

1: *Freeze – Margaret and the M.P. (Beef)*
2: *Colonel Alvin Houlihan*
3: *G.I. in Post-Op*
4: *Hawkeye*
5: *B.J.*
6: *Potter*
7: *Charles in the Swamp*
8: *Klinger*
9: *Mulcahy*
10: *Margaret*

Synopsis: Colonel Alvin "Howitzer" Houlihan, now a civilian military advisor, is coming to the 4077th, and Margaret wants everything and everyone to be perfect, but it's not enough. Howitzer Al seems uncomfortable around Margaret, and would rather unpack his bags in the VIP tent than talk to his daughter. Potter and Colonel Houlihan hit it off at the Officer's Club, having a drink together, until Hawkeye and B.J. sit at their table. Howitzer Al is not impressed with the civilian attire the doctors wear and although they're respectful of the Colonel, he lets them know what he thinks and knocks over the table on his way out. After Potter tells an infuriated Margaret that the fracas was her father's fault and not the doctors', he then tells the Colonel what he thinks about the way he's treating his daughter. The doctors do however have something to hide…an entire side of beef rerouted from a general and replaced with canned liver, sent as a thank you from Sergeant Morgove, a former patient who works in Food Requisition and Disbursements.

PA Announcement by Klinger

Authors' Notes: In Episode 38, Season 2's "Hot Lips and Empty Arms," Margaret told Henry that he looks like her father just before he died. But in this episode, he makes a full recovery as Colonel Alvin "Howitzer" Houlihan comes to the 4077th to visit his daughter. Since the Colonel's divorce, he's taken a position as a civilian military advisor.

We see the wall in front of Klinger's desk in this episode, a view rarely seen.

On the Ranch compound in Chapter 1, Kellye is giving someone a haircut. We've seen Kellye do this several times in the past, but rarely on the Ranch compound. We've also seen, in previous episodes, a barber's tent on the Ranch set.

Hawkeye has a new civilian shirt in Chapter 6: blue with pineapples.

Interestingly, Charles in Chapter 7 is holding soap on a rope.

In Chapter 9, Father Mulcahy is wearing his previously seen brown plaid robe.

A fifty-year career that began in the 1940s, Andrew Duggan (December 28, 1923-May 15, 1988) has over 200 credits to his name. Appearances include *Hawaii Five-0* (6 episodes), *Lou Grant, CHiPS,* nine episodes of *Disneyland, The Streets of San Francisco,* and a recurring role in 20 episodes on the 1968-70 Western, *Lancer.*

Art LaFleur (born September 9, 1943) began his 40-year career with one of his earliest appearances in this episode of *M*A*S*H.* Other appearances include *Hill Street Blues, Northern Exposure, Home Improvement, The Practice* and *House.* Mr. LaFleur had a role in the 1989 hit movie *Field of Dreams* as Chick Gandil, the first baseman for the 1919 Chicago White Sox, the central figure behind the "Chicago Black Sox Scandal."

Death Takes A Holiday – 12/15/1980

Season 9 / Episode 203 / Production 206 – Z408

Columbia House VHS Tape . . . . *Major Margaret (Catalog # 22048)*
Fox DVD . . . . *Season 9, Disc 1*

Alan Alda, Mike Farrell, Harry Morgan
Loretta Swit, David Ogden Stiers, Jamie Farr, William Christopher

Executive Producer – Burt Metcalfe
Produced by John Rappaport
Teleplay by Mike Farrell – John Rappaport – Dennis Koenig
Story by Thad Mumford & Dan Wilcox and Burt Metcalfe
Directed by Mike Farrell

Executive Script Consultants – Thad Mumford & Dan Wilcox
Executive Story Editor – Dennis Koenig
Creative Consultants – Gene Reynolds / Alan Alda

Keye Luke . . . . Choi Sung Ho
G.W. Bailey. . . . . .Sergeant Luthor Rizzo
Kelley Nakahara . . . . Kellye
Jeff Maxwell. . . . . .Igor
Sally Imamura . . . . Girl
Yoshiki Hoover . . . . .Boy
Perren Page . . . . .Driver
Copyright 1980 – 20th Century Fox Film Corporation

Non-Credited Appearances. . . . . Dennis Troy, Jennifer Davis

Chapters

1: *Main Titles / A Hexed Christmas*   6: *Alive Through Christmas – 15:26*
2: *Scrooge Winchester – 3:15*   7: *Rice and Cabbage – 16:54*
3: *An Anonymous Gift – 7:01*   8: *An Old Family Tradition – 20:24*
4: *Choi's Children – 10:30*   9: *It's Over – 21:30*
5: *Black Market Candy – 13:58*   10: *A Special Present / End Titles – 23:23*

Closing Stills

1: *Freeze – Mulcahy, Margaret, Hawkeye and B.J.*
2: *Rizzo*
3: *Choi*
4: *Hawkeye*
5: *Mulcahy*
6: *Potter Clause*
7: *Margaret*
8: *Klinger*
9: *Charles*
10: *B.J.*

Synopsis: As the staff prepares and decorates the mess tent for a Christmas party with the orphans, some are reminded of Christmas celebrations when they were children while others carry out family traditions of anonymous benevolence. The children are welcomed by all and they're treated to fudge and food, some of which is good, some, "blech." But not everyone is at the party. Hawkeye, B.J. and Margaret are desperately trying to prevent a badly wounded soldier from dying on Christmas day so his children won't have to think of Christmas as the day their father died.

Authors' Notes: There are no PA announcements in this episode.

Charles, in Chapter 1 mentions "Tiny Tim," a reference to the fictional character from the Charles Dickens classic, A Christmas Carol, published on December 19, 1843.

Potter, in Chapter 1, says "a smorgasbord like the Kiwanis back home." The Kiwanis, since 1915, is dedicated to helping children and, in 1939, began providing grants and assistance.

Sergeant Rizzo is using the engine compartment of jeep number 18210717 in Chapter 2 as a pillow.

Potter mentions "A&P" in Chapter 2. The Great Atlantic & Pacific Tea Company (A&P) was founded in 1859 in New York City. Today, with 456 stores on the East Coast of the United States, their headquarters are in Montvale, New Jersey.

Charles mentions Popular Mechanic in Chapter 5. The enthusiast magazine began publication in 1902.

In Chapter 7, a clock on the wall with a dual display of times, one standard and one in hundred hours, is the same one seen in the O.R. in previous episodes.

For the second time, in Chapter 10, it's snowing on Stage 9.

Also in Chapter 10, everyone in the mess tent is singing "Silent Night." When the episode ends with the freeze-frame of Margaret, Father Mulcahy, Hawkeye and B.J., the song continues.

Margaret, in Chapter 10, is about to falsify an official record by entering the time of death for a patient at 12:05 AM, December 26, as opposed to the actual time of death at 11:25 PM, December 25. This will be the first time in her career that she will falsify a record as it would prevent the man's family having to think of Christmas as the day their father died. Hawkeye, B.J. and Father Mulcahy all agree that this is the right thing to do.

A War for All Seasons – 12/29/1980

Season 9 / Episode 204 / Production 207 – Z409

Columbia House VHS Tape . . . . Not Released by Columbia House
Fox DVD . . . . Season 9, Disc 1

Alan Alda, Mike Farrell, Harry Morgan
Loretta Swit, David Ogden Stiers, Jamie Farr, William Christopher

Executive Producer – Burt Metcalfe
Produced by John Rappaport
Written by Dan Wilcox & Thad Mumford
Directed by Burt Metcalfe

Executive Script Consultants – Thad Mumford & Dan Wilcox
Executive Story Editor – Dennis Koenig
Creative Consultants – Gene Reynolds / Alan Alda

Jeff Maxwell . . . . Igor
Carl Freed . . . . Patient
Laurie Bates . . . . Nurse

Copyright 1980 – 20th Century Fox Film Corporation

Non-Credited Appearances . . . . Kellye Nakahara, Gwen Farrell, Dennis Troy,
Roy Goldman, Jennifer Davis

Chapters

1: Main Titles / A Toast	6: Gold Mine – 12:13
2: A Catalog – 2:48	7: Sausage Link – 14:36
3: In the Springtime – 3:49	8: Pennant Race – 17:33
4: Kidneying Themselves – 6:38	9: Auld Lang Syne – 20:30
5: Independence Day – 8:56	10: Highlight / End Titles – 22:07

Closing Stills

1: Freeze – Charles slices the movie screen
2: Hawkeye
3: Charles
4: Margaret
5: B.J. in the Swamp
6: Klinger in the office
7: Mulcahy
8: Potter as "1951"

Synopsis: A year in the life of the 4077 begins with a New Year's Eve celebration, and the hope of being home before the next one. A mail order catalog helps lift their spirits as the staff orders a few personal effects like seeds and gardening tools, knitting material and baseball gloves. Even an electric fireplace, complete with electric logs, can help battle the bitter-cold Korean winters, but after setting it up in the Swamp, it only serves as a reminder of an unbearably hot Korean summer. Hawkeye realizes that the catalog can also be used to order some parts to make a crude kidney machine for a patient whose kidneys have shut down. When a Fourth of July party gets underway, Father Mulcahy is anxious to serve his freshly grown corn on the cob. However, the good Father is not only disappointed: he's infuriated after learning Igor did the unthinkable to his corn. It's now fall, the end of the baseball season is nearly at hand, and Charles picked the wrong season to expand the Winchester fortune.

PA Announcement by Sal Viscuso
Baseball Announcer for the Brooklyn Dodgers and the New York Giants playoff game

Authors' Notes: Chapter 1 is the third time snow is seen on the compound (Stage 9). Potter, in Chapter 1, is "Father Time" for the year 1950, while Klinger is "1951." This presents a monumental task in keeping with the timeline. All three years of the Korean War have already been established in many previous episodes.

In Chapter 3, Colonel Potter is wearing the same colorful civilian shirt he wore in Season 7, Episode 150, "Lil." This is the second time he's worn this shirt.

Also in Chapter 3, Potter mentions "Goobers," a very popular chocolate-coated peanut snack made by the Blumenthal Chocolate Co. in 1925 and acquired by Nestle in 1984.

In Chapter 3, Klinger mentions "Newcombe," "Erskine," "Roe" and Branca," and is correct. Don Newcombe, right-handed pitcher # 36; Ralph Branca, right-handed pitcher # 13; Carl Erskine, right-handed pitcher # 17; Preacher Roe, left-handed pitcher # 28: all four of these very well-known pitchers played for the 1951 Brooklyn Dodgers.

Potter mentions "Stan the Man" in Chapter 3, a reference to Stan Musial, outfielder for the St. Louis Cardinals, # 6. Stan Musial, one of the greatest to play the game, spent his entire 22-year career with the St. Louis Cardinals and finished with a .331 batting average, an on-base percentage of .417 and a .559 slugging percentage.

On a side note, the 1951 Brooklyn Dodgers, as noted by Klinger, did have a 13-game lead in the National League in late August. A late dive in the standings, and a red-hot streak by the New York Giants, led to one of the most famous three-game playoff series' in baseball history between the two teams. It took all three games, with game three in the 9th inning to decide the pennant winner. Pitching for the Dodgers was Ralph Branca, and at the plate for the Giants was Bobby Thompson, whose 9th inning home run off Branca not only won the pennant for the Giants, but became known as "The Shot Heard 'Round the World."

Charles mentions "Cracker Jacks" (correct pronunciation is Cracker Jack). Introduced by F.W. Rueckheim and his brother Louis at the World's Columbian Exposition (at Chicago's first World's Fair in 1893), the Cracker Jack name was trademarked in 1896.

B.J. in Chapter 4 mentions "Cheerios." First introduced in 1941 as Cheeri Oats, it was the first ready-to-eat oats cereal. In 1945, the name of the cereal became "Cheerios."

B.J. also mentions sending in Cheerios box tops. According to Cathy at the General Mills call center, the General Mills "Box Tops for Education" did not go into effect until 1996.

Also in Chapter 4, B.J. credits Dr. Kolff as the inventor of the kidney machine.

In 1943, Dr. Willem Kolff was the first to build a working dialyzer. Two years later, after 11 hours of hemodialysis with his machine, a 67-year-old woman regained consciousness from a uremic coma and became the first person to be successfully treated with Dr. Kolff's dialyzer.

B.J. (who mentions much in this episode) also mentions "The new kid for the Giants, Willie Mays." This is also correct. Willie Mays began his illustrious career with the New York Giants on May 25, 1951 and played his final season with the New York Mets during the 1972-73 season. Willie Mays was a 21-time All-Star selection, World Series Champion in 1954, 12-time Gold Glove winner, two-time National League MVP, two-time All Star Game MVP, Roberto Clemente Award winner in 1971 and his number 24 was retired by the Giants. Mr. Mays was the Rookie of the Year in 1951 and was elected to the baseball Hall of Fame in 1979 with nearly 95 % of the votes on his first ballot.

According to Margaret in Season 2, Episode 32, "The Trial of Henry Blake," it was against air raid regulations to have rocks painted white because enemy planes can see them at night. Igor was ordered to paint only the tops of the rocks and "turn 'em over at night." But in this episode, during a July 4th celebration, large, loud and brightly colored fireworks are exploding in the night sky.

Potter mentions two Zane Grey books in Chapter 7, *30,000 On the Hoof* (1940) and *Thundering Herd* (1925).

The view out of the office windows in Chapter 7 is of the same wooden structure, but this time, the chain link fence is visible with the Motor Pool sign.

Your Retention, Please – 1/5/1981

Season 9 / Episode 205 / Production 204 – Z406

Columbia House VHS Tape . . . . Not Released by Columbia House

Fox DVD . . . . Season 9, Disc 1

Alan Alda, Mike Farrell, Harry Morgan
Loretta Swit, David Ogden Stiers, Jamie Farr, William Christopher

Executive Producer – Burt Metcalfe
Produced by John Rappaport
Written by Erik Tarloff
Directed by Charles S. Dubin

Executive Script Consultants – Thad Mumford & Dan Wilcox
Executive Story Editor – Dennis Koenig
Creative Consultants – Gene Reynolds / Alan Alda

Barry Corbin . . . . Sergeant Joe Vickers
Sam Weisman . . . . Sergeant Barney Hutchinson
Jeff Maxwell . . . . Igor

Copyright 1981 – 20th Century Fox Film Corporation

Non-Credited Appearances . . . . Kellye Nakahara, Dennis Troy

Chapters

1: Main Titles / Heartbreak	6: Vulture – 12:13
2: Opening the Mind – 3:24	7: Escape Clause – 13:29
3: War to War Salesman – 4:37	8: Not A Free Man – 17:21
4: Man's Best Friend – 7:35	9: The Oath – 20:30
5: Unique Opportunity – 10:24	10: Godiva / End Titles – 21:56

Closing Stills

1: Freeze – Klinger breaks jukebox record in the Officer's Club
2: Sergeant Vickers
3: Sergeant Hutchinson in Post-Op
4: Igor
5: Hawkeye
6: B.J.
7: Potter
8: Margaret in Post-Op
9: Charles in Post-Op
10: Mulcahy (still From Season 7)
11: Klinger Godiva

Synopsis: When Klinger gets a letter from Laverne, he thinks she wants him back. But all she wants is to tell him she's leaving Morty and marrying Gus Nagy, Klinger's best friend. While drowning his sorrows in the Officer's Club, he meets the area retention officer, who takes advantage of Klinger's inebriated state and convinces him to do the unthinkable…re-enlist. Sergeant Hutchinson, a male nurse as qualified and skilled as any other nurse, is angry that the army won't promote him to lieutenant like the rest of the nursing staff. Agreeing with Hutchinson, Margaret, unofficially, promotes him to lieutenant for the remainder of his tour at the 4077th.

Authors' Notes: There are no PA announcements in this episode.

It's not unusual to see Father Mulcahy with an issue of The Ring Magazine, probably the best-known magazine dedicated to the sport of boxing, of which Mulcahy is a fan. In Chapter 1, Mulcahy is indeed seen holding a copy of the magazine. The only problem with this: the issue he has in his hands is from December 1969, with Rocky Marciano and Jersey Joe Walcott on the cover. If you look carefully, midway up on the right side of the magazine, there's a black square covering the area where the year "1969" is printed.

Klinger mentions "Nero Wolfe" in Chapter 1. Nero Wolfe was a fictional detective created in 1934 by Rex Stout. The first radio broadcast of Nero Wolfe was on the New England Network from April 7 to June 30, 1943.

Although not very often, nurses have held open surgical textbooks to help guide the doctors through difficult procedures in the operating room, and that device is seen again in Chapter 2 of this episode. What makes it noteworthy now: this time, the surgeon is Charles.

In Chapter 5, Potter mentions "Katzenjammer." As noted in a previous episode after Charles mentions this, The Katzenjammer Kids was a cartoon strip, which first appeared on December 12, 1897 in a Sunday supplement of the New York Journal. The German immigrant Rudolph Dirks created the strip.

In Chapter 9, Potter is wearing the robe worn by Henry Blake.

Also in Chapter 9, Potter is still reading what he previously says is a Zane Grey western, Ride the Man Down. However, as noted earlier, Luke Short, another popular Western writer in 1942, wrote Ride the Man Down (not to be confused with Luke Short, the noted gunfighter of the late 1800's).

Potterism: "What in the name of George Armstrong Custer?"

Klinger in Chapter 10 is riding Sophie, and is dressed (or undressed in this case) as Lady Godiva. The Countess wanted her husband, Earl Leofric, to repeal heavy taxes for the people of Coventry. After he requested her to ride her horse naked from one end of town to the other, in the market where all can see her, he would honor her request. Covering her body with her long tresses, she carried out the request, and her husband lived up to his word and freed the people of Coventry from the heavy taxes (circa 1080).

If you look closely at Klinger up on the horse, the top of his jockey shorts can be seen.

Tell it to the Marines – 1/12/1981

Season 9 / Episode 206 / Production 208 – Z410

Columbia House VHS Tape . . . . *Not Released by Columbia House*
Fox DVD . . . . *Season 9, Disc 2*

Alan Alda, Mike Farrell, Harry Morgan
Loretta Swit, David Ogden Stiers, Jamie Farr, William Christopher

Executive Producer – Burt Metcalfe
Produced by John Rappaport
Written by Hank Bradford
Directed by Harry Morgan

Executive Script Consultants – Thad Mumford & Dan Wilcox
Executive Story Editor – Dennis Koenig
Creative Consultants – Gene Reynolds / Alan Alda

Michael McGuire . . . . Colonel Mulholland
Denny Miller. . . . . M.P.
Stan Wells . . . . Private Jost Van Liter
James Gallery . . . . Murray Thompson
Copyright 1981 – 20th Century Fox Film Corporation

Non-Credited Appearances. . . . . Kellye Nakahara

Chapters

1: *Main Titles / Pro Tem*	6: *Freedom of Suppress – 14:32*
2: *A Mere Week – 3:04*	7: *A Larger Audience – 15:33*
3: *King Charles I – 4:27*	8: *Back in the Saddle – 18:41*
4: *Shame, Shame, Shame – 7:58*	9: *21-Day Flu – 20:40*
5: *Taken Away – 12:16*	10: *Dutch Treat / End Titles – 22:18*

(Note: Chapter 10 on the DVD is listed only as, "Dutch Treat." It should be, "Dutch Treat / End Titles.")

Closing Stills

1: *Freeze – Charles in the office*
2: *Colonel Mulholland*
3: *M.P.*
4: *Private Jost Van Liter in Post-Op*
5: *U.N. man*
6: *B.J. in the Swamp*
7: *Potter in the office*
8: *Margaret in Post-Op*
9: *Charles*
10: *Klinger*
11: *Mulcahy*
12: *Hawkeye*

Synopsis: When Mrs. Van Liter divorces her American husband, she faces deportation back to Holland, and the Marines won't allow her son to be discharged a week early to see her before she leaves. Hawkeye tries to get Stars & Stripes to run an article to stir public opinion, but Colonel Mulholland, Private Van Liter's no-nonsense Commanding Officer, prevents it. While Mulholland can control the military press, he cannot control the civilian press, and with B.J., Hawkeye heads for the press train in Munsan and stirs up a little more than public opinion. On the flip side, Potter assigns Charles the task of temporary C.O. when he leaves for a week to meet with The 38th Parallel Medical Society. As Commanding Officer, Charles appropriates military personnel, and Klinger becomes his personal purveyor of, among other items, silk bed sheets.

Authors' Notes: There are no PA announcements in the episode.

Potter mentions "Dr. Scholl" in Chapter 1. William Mathias School (1882-1968) graduated Illinois Medical School in 1904 as a podiatrist. He opened his first foot-care store in 1928 and is now one of the largest and best-known foot-care chains in the United States.

Klinger in Chapter 3 mentions "Homer and Jethro." "Homer" was guitarist Henry D. Haynes (1920-1971) and "Jethro" was mandolin player Kenneth C. Burns (1920-1989). Also known as "The Thinking Man's Hillbillies," Homer and Jethro enjoyed a long and fruitful career spanning more than 30 years, as a country music duo specializing in comedy records and satirical versions of popular songs.

In Chapter 4, B.J. uses a Superman catch phrase, "Truth, Justice and the American Way." Superman's first appearance was in Action Comics # 1, 1938. This comic book is considered to be the most valuable of its kind.

B.J. also references Lionel Trains in Chapter 7. Joshua Lionel Cowen (later Cohen) invented his train in 1901.

When Potter returns to camp in Chapter 8, Klinger, with a mouthful of water, accidentally sprays the Colonel. When the scene cuts away from Potter and then returns, the water splatter is much larger and different than the original.

Charles in Chapter 8 mentions, "Trigger," a reference to The Lone Ranger. The Lone Ranger television show debuted on September 15, 1949 and ran until June 6, 1957. The show continued in reruns until 1961.

Taking the Fifth – 1/19/1981

Season 9 / Episode 207 / Production 205 – Z407
Columbia House VHS Tape. . . . . Not Released by Columbia House
Fox DVD . . . . Season 9, Disc 2

Alan Alda, Mike Farrell, Harry Morgan
Loretta Swit, David Ogden Stiers, Jamie Farr, William Christopher

Executive Producer – Burt Metcalfe
Produced by John Rappaport
Written by Elias Davis & David Pollock
Directed by Charles S. Dubin

Executive Script Consultants – Thad Mumford & Dan Wilcox
Executive Story Editor – Dennis Koenig
Creative Consultants – Gene Reynolds / Alan Alda
Charles Hallahan . . . . Corporal Colin Turnbull
Margie Impert. . . . . Nurse Palmer
Judy Farrell . . . . .Nurse Able
Jan Jorden . . . . Nurse Baker
Copyright 1981 – 20th Century Fox Film Corporation

Non-Credited Appearances. . . . . Kellye Nakahara, Gwen Farrell, Roy Goldman

Chapters

1: Main Titles	6: An Interleague Trade – 10:06
2: No More Curare – 0:55	7: Dear Hawkeye – 13:28
3: Klinger's Canadian Friend – 2:32	8: Off the Wagon – 18:24
4: French Wine – 4:55	9: The Winner – 20:50
5: In A Class By Yourself – 7:53	10: The Cat's Pajamas / End Titles – 23:35

Closing Stills

1: Freeze – Hawkeye and Margaret in O.R.
2: Klinger and Colin Turnbull
3: Hawkeye and nurses in the office
4: B.J. in the Swamp
5: Charles in the Swamp
6: Margaret
7: Mulcahy (From Season 7)
8: Klinger
9: Potter
10: Hawkeye

Synopsis: In exchange for some fruit cocktail, Klinger gets a bottle of French wine, but gives it to Hawkeye in exchange for the $5 he owes him. However, Hawkeye's search for a nurse to share his wine is less than successful, until he gets a positive reply to his advertisement on the bulletin board. A rendezvous is arranged in the supply room, but Hawkeye gets more than he bargains for. Since the Army banned the use of Curare, getting wounded anesthetized is not only proving difficult, it's also slowing the pace. In an unusual move, Potter breaks orders and arranges a trade with a Canadian medical unit, the same unit in which Klinger's wine originated. Klinger's friend Colin has five more bottles and will trade them for more fruit cocktail. With Curare and wine in hand, Potter and Klinger head back to camp, but not before the jeep overheats. Not having water to fill the radiator, they have no choice but to use the five bottles of the '47 Bordeaux that Klinger was going to sell to Charles for $150.

Commentary by David Pollock: "One of the ideas that we came in with in 1973, was that someone in the unit saves a French soldier. In turn, the soldier gives a case of wine to the doctors, as a gift. Our original idea was to follow the story of each bottle of wine. Eight years later, we brought it up again, and Burt liked it. But to follow what happened to each bottle was too cumbersome. So, we followed the story of what happened to one bottle."

PA Announcement by Todd Sussman

Authors' Notes: Corporal Colin Turnbull is a member of the 2nd Princess Pat Battalion in Chapter 3. The 2nd Battalion, Princess Patricia's Canadian Light Infantry, received the Distinguished Unit Citation from the President of The United States for its stand near Kapyong, Korea, in April 1951. The authors recognize the efforts of The 2nd Battalion, Princess Patricia's Canadian Light Infantry.

B.J. wears Converse sneakers and they've been seen many times in several episodes, just as they're seen in Chapter 3 of this episode. The unusual thing is they always seem to be brand new and never look like they've "gone through a war," as opposed to Hawkeye's, or anyone else's, boots.

In Chapter 4, Charles recognizes Klinger's (now Hawkeye's) bottle of wine as a "'47 Bordeaux" from the "Haute Meddoc." The Haute Meddoc is an Appellation d' Origine Controlee (AOC) for wine in the Bordeaux wine region of Southwest France and was established in 1936.

In Chapter 5, Klinger is in the shower. This is a rarity. Not to say that Klinger doesn't shower, we just hardly ever see him under the spray of the showerhead.

For the first time in a while, Klinger is wearing a dress from Bonwit Teller in Chapter 7.

Potterism: "Bushwa."

Jeep number 18210707 is the lucky recipient of five bottles of a '47 Bordeaux.

Operation Friendship – 1/26/1981

Season 9 / Episode 208 / Production 210 – Z412

Columbia House VHS Tape . . . . *War Stories (Catalog # 21043)*
Fox DVD . . . . *Season 9, Disc 2*

Alan Alda, Mike Farrell, Harry Morgan
Loretta Swit, David Ogden Stiers, Jamie Farr, William Christopher

Executive Producer – Burt Metcalfe
Produced by John Rappaport
Written by Dennis Koenig
Directed by Rena Down

Executive Script Consultants – Thad Mumford & Dan Wilcox
Executive Story Editor – Dennis Koenig
Creative Consultants – Gene Reynolds / Alan Alda
Tim O'Connor . . . . Dr. Norman Traeger
Copyright 1981 – 20th Century Fox Film Corporation

Non-Credited Appearances . . . . Kellye Nakahara, Gwen Farrell

Chapters

1: *Main Titles / Forgetful*	6: *Prima Donnas – 12:58*
2: *Steambath – 2:53*	7: *A Fine Line – 16:20*
3: *Silver Lining – 5:37*	8: *Turf War – 17:49*
4: *Not A Scratch – 7:45*	9: *Best Man for the Job – 20:23*
5: *A Debt of Honor – 9:26*	10: *Confetti / End Titles – 23:20*

Closing Stills

1: *Freeze – Klinger – Charles – confetti in the office*
2: *Dr. Norman Traeger*
3: *Hawkeye in the Swamp*
4: *Klinger in bed with broken nose*
5: *Mulcahy (From Season 7)*
6: *Potter in the Swamp*
7: *Margaret*
8: *Charles*
9: *B.J.*

Synopsis: When Klinger sees the autoclave about to explode, he pushes Charles out of the way and breaks his nose in the process. B.J. walks in seconds before the explosion and takes the brunt of it, knocking him into the wall. In an attempt to repay Klinger for possibly saving his life, Charles takes over as company clerk while Klinger recuperates, and offers himself for anything Klinger needs, a decision Charles may later come to regret. B.J insists he's fine, that he doesn't need medical attention and x-rays seem to confirm his diagnosis. But after dropping a martini glass, Hawkeye knows there's something wrong. B.J.'s temporary replacement is also a specialist and if he doesn't operate on B.J.'s hand, he could lose all function.

PA Announcement by Todd Sussman
PA Announcement by Klinger

Authors' Notes: Potter, in Chapter 1, mentions "Dixie Cups." The Dixie Cup was invented in 1908. At the time, shared-use cups were banned, as it was a source for spreading germs.

Names written on tape over clothing hooks in the change room are: Winchester – Potter – Hawkeye – B.J. – Mulcahy in Chapter 1. As previously seen, names do not follow any particular pattern and are sometimes separated by a hook or two, and sometimes Mulcahy's name is not there at all.

Also in Chapter 1, Potter mentions "Wheatena" and "Fruit of the Looms." "Wheatena" was invented by George H. Hoyt on Mulberry Street in New York City (circa 1879). "Fruit of the Loom" was founded in 1851.

The sinks in the scrub room in Chapter 3 are in the middle, side by side.

Chapter 4, Potter mentions waxing the LaSalle with Mildred's new pedal-pushers. The LaSalle was a General Motors automobile made from 1927 until 1940.

Klinger implies that the unit has real eggs in Chapter 5 by telling Charles that he likes "three-minute eggs." Sometimes eggs were a precious commodity and rarely seen in camp. Other times, eggs were plentiful.

The Mickey Spillane book, I the Jury, seen in Chapter 5, was written in 1947. At the time, this paperback sold for 35 cents.

No Sweat – 2/2/1981
Season 9 / Episode 209 / Production 200 – Z402

Columbia House VHS Tape . . . .*Letting Loose (Catalog # 21040)*
Fox DVD . . . .*Season 9, Disc 2*

Alan Alda, Mike Farrell, Harry Morgan
Loretta Swit, David Ogden Stiers, Jamie Farr, William Christopher

Executive Producer – Burt Metcalfe
Produced by John Rappaport
Written by John Rappaport
Directed by Burt Metcalfe

Executive Script Consultants – Thad Mumford & Dan Wilcox
Executive Story Editor – Dennis Koenig
Creative Consultants – Gene Reynolds / Alan Alda

Kellye Nakahara . . . . Kellye
Jeff Maxwell. . . . . .Igor
W. Perren Page . . . . .Driver
Copyright 1981 – 20th Century Fox Film Corporation

Non-Credited Appearances. . . . . .Joanne Thompson

Chapters

1: Main Titles	6: Heat Frustration – 10:39
2: In the Heat of the Night – 0:53	7: Prickly Situations – 13:22
3: Debt and Taxes – 3:51	8: Potter on Parade – 15:21
4: Emergency – 6:47	9: The Big Broadcast – 20:20
5: Waking Colonel Potter – 9:04	10: Butt Out / End Titles – 22:01

Closing Stills

1: *Freeze – Margaret and Potter in the mess tent*
2: *Potter*
3: *Hawkeye*
4: *B.J. in the Swamp*
5: *Klinger*
6: *Mulcahy*
7: *Charles*
8: *Margaret*

Synopsis: Unable to sleep in the unbearable heat, Charles uses the mess tent to put the vast Winchester fortune, and all its paperwork, in order, while Klinger takes apart the PA system to learn electronics. Much to Margaret's dismay, she learns there is no ointment in camp to sooth a case of prickly heat she developed on her derriere, and has a difficult time ordering any since Potter is fast asleep after taking a sleeping pill. Angry at not being home to help Peg clean the rain gutters, it's B.J. keeping Hawkeye up, not the heat.

Commentary by Jeff Maxwell: "The Stage 9 cement floor was covered in some kind of rubbery, sound-muffling material. After nine years of walking on it, I grew fond of its elasticity. I think the OR was just the bare cement floor."

Accidental PA conversation between Margaret and Potter

PA Announcement by Klinger

Authors' Notes: Potterisms: "Great Caesar's Salad," "Heat's enough to melt the spots off a pinto."

In Chapter 2, Potter mentions "vicuna." The vicuna is related to the llama and alpaca, and produces small amounts of extremely fine wool and is very expensive. Shorn every three years, vicunas are found in the high alpineous Andes and are considered endangered.

In Chapter 2, Potter mentions "Motorola." Started as Galvin Manufacturing Corporation in 1928, the Motorola name came from the founders, Paul and Joseph Gavin, when the company began making car radios.

Hawkeye mentions "Andy Grump" in Chapter 5. Andy Grump Incorporated has been is business over 50 years in Southern California and the greater Los Angeles area providing portable sanitation, septic systems, etc. However, it is a borderline inconsistency in the timeline with "over 50 years."

Charles mentions "The Calgary Stampede" in Chapter 8. The Calgary Stampede, or "The Greatest Outdoor Show on Earth" is, for ten days every summer in July, a large festival, exhibition and rodeo. The annual event is held in Calgary, Alberta, Canada and the first such event was held in 1912.

Depressing News – 2/9/1981

Season 9 / Episode 210 / Production 209 – Z411

Columbia House VHS Tape . . . . *Not Released by Columbia House*
Fox DVD . . . . *Season 9, Disc 2*

Alan Alda, Mike Farrell, Harry Morgan
Loretta Swit, David Ogden Stiers, Jamie Farr, William Christopher

Executive Producer – Burt Metcalfe
Produced by John Rappaport
Written by Dan Wilcox & Thad Mumford
Directed by Alan Alda

Executive Script Consultants – Thad Mumford & Dan Wilcox
Executive Story Editor – Dennis Koenig
Creative Consultants – Gene Reynolds / Alan Alda

William Bogert . . . . Captain Maurice Allen
David Dozer . . . . The Delivery Man
Rodney Saulsberry . . . . Oldham

Copyright 1981 – 20th Century Fox Film Corporation

Non-Credited Appearances . . . . Jeff Maxwell, Kellye Nakahara, Dennis Troy

Chapters

1: *Main Titles / Bored*	6: *Monument to Stupidity – 13:23*
2: *Muckraker – 3:06*	7: *Leaning Tower of Peace – 16:11*
3: *Snafu – 4:53*	8: *Tribute to the Fallen – 18:32*
4: *Skin Deep – 7:23*	9: *To Kingdom Come – 21:41*
5: *Depressed – 9:51*	10: *Memento / End Titles – 23:26*

Closing Stills

1: *Freeze – Painting of Hawkeye and tower*
2: *Captain Allen*
3: *Delivery man and Potter*
4: *B.J. in the Swamp*
5: *B.J.*
6: *Mulcahy*
7: *Charles*
8: *Margaret*
9: *Potter*
10: *Hawkeye*

Synopsis: With some down time, Margaret does her laundry, Colonel Potter paints and Klinger becomes a newspaper publisher with the help of a mimeograph machine. Charles will write a column on food and dining while Margaret agrees to write a column on beauty tips. But the "big" story is about a monument Hawkeye builds after the 4077th gets a delivery of 500,000 tongue depressors, with each one used bearing the name of wounded who've passed through. Army Information sends a representative with a photographer from Stars and Stripes, but when Captain Allen mentions that Hawkeye's monument will be good for recruitment, Hawkeye makes use of Primacord, an explosive left behind by a demolitions expert being shipped home.

Commentary by Rodney Saulsberry: "I had just finished playing the role of Carl the Boxer in an episode of Taxi titled, 'Alex Jumps Out of an Airplane.' So I'm on the set rehearsing with Alan Alda and the rest of the cast and I keep whistling the theme song from Taxi. It was really just nervous energy I guess because I was so happy to be working with the *M*A*S*H* cast. I probably thought I was whistling the M*A*S*H theme. Anyway, at some point Mr. Alda gives me a look like, 'Hey buddy what gives?' I got the point and stopped. I had a great time and they treated me with the utmost respect. It's a wonderful scene that I appeared in and the set was so life like, I didn't have any problem getting into character." (Learn about Rodney Saulsberry's career at *rodneysaulsberry.com* and see his *MySpace* page for some good music)

Authors' Notes: There are no PA announcements in this episode.

In Chapter 1, The Laundry Room makes its second appearance in this, the 210th episode.

Klinger, in Chapter 2, mentions "William Randolph Scott." Randolph Scott (January 23, 1898-March 2, 1987) was an actor whose motion picture career began in 1928 and lasted until 1962. Klinger most likely confused William Randolph Scott for William Randolph Hearst (April 29, 1863-August 14, 1951), the famous newspaper publisher.

In Chapter 4, Hawkeye appears to be wearing blue running shoes from the 70's or later.

The sign on Margaret's tent door in Chapter 4 is in the freehand style. Sometimes, this sign is in block lettering.

Igor's last name is mentioned for the first time in Chapter 5: "Straminsky."

In Chapter 10, the view from the office windows shows people, but no building previously seen in several episodes of the "later" seasons.

No Laughing Matter – 2/16/1981
Season 9 / Episode 211 / Production 211 – Z413

Columbia House VHS Tape . . . . *Not Released by Columbia House*
Fox DVD . . . . *Season 9, Disc 2*

Alan Alda, Mike Farrell, Harry Morgan
Loretta Swit, David Ogden Stiers, Jamie Farr, William Christopher

Executive Producer – Burt Metcalfe
Produced by John Rappaport
Written by Elias Davis & David Pollock
Directed by Burt Metcalfe

Executive Script Consultants – Thad Mumford & Dan Wilcox
Executive Story Editor – Dennis Koenig
Creative Consultants – Gene Reynolds / Alan Alda

Robert Symonds . . . . Colonel Horace Baldwin
Eileen Saki . . . . Rosie
Jeff Maxwell. . . . . .Igor
Mae Hi . . . . Korean Woman
Nathan Jung . . . . .Korean Man
Kellye Nakahara . . . . .Kellye
Copyright 1981 – 20th Century Fox Film Corporation

Non-Credited Appearances. . . . . .Roy Goldman

Chapters

1:	Main Titles / Gagholic	
2:	Platitudes – 3:37	
3:	It's A Bet – 6:50	
4:	Do Unto Others – 7:59	
5:	Speaking of Tokyo – 11:03	

6:	For A Shy Friend – 12:54	
7:	Slight Misunderstanding – 16:26	
8:	Through His Teeth – 20:02	
9:	Back to Abnormal – 22:31	
10:	On Principle / End Titles – 23:28	

Closing Stills

1: Freeze – Charles and Margaret in the Officer's Club
2: Colonel Baldwin in the Officer's Club
3: Charles in the Officer's Club
4: B.J. in the Officer's Club
5: Potter in the office
6: Klinger
7: Mulcahy (From Season 7)
8: Margaret in Post-Op
9: Hawkeye in the office

Synopsis: An impending visit from Colonel Horace Baldwin, the person responsible for Charles being at the 4077th, prompts Colonel Potter to make sure Charles doesn't do anything that he'll regret. In a complete "about-face," Charles is nothing but warm and welcoming to his former employer, even letting him win in cribbage. But when Baldwin is accused of improper behavior, he offers Charles a position in Tokyo if he'll lie (which will ruin a friend's career). Meanwhile, B.J. thinks Hawkeye's insecurity is the reason he jokes all the time. Annoyed at B.J.'s diagnosis, Hawkeye bets him $10 that he can go 24 hours without joking, and finds it's not as easy as he might have thought.

PA Announcement by Hawkeye

Authors' Notes: B.J. is reading a copy of *Reader's Digest* in Chapter 1. The popular magazine was founded in 1922.

The view out of the office windows in Chapter 2 is that of the wooden structure, determined earlier to be the Motor Pool Supply. This time, it's closer to the window.

In Chapter 4, Potter mentions "Joe Palooka." *Joe Palooka* is a comic strip heavyweight boxer created by Ham Fisher in 1921.

Also in Chapter 4, Potter mentions "Smilin'Jack." Not only a Season 4 episode of the same name, *Smilin' Jack*, created by Zack Mosely, appeared in the *Chicago Tribune* from October 1, 1933 through April 1, 1973. It was the longest running aviation comic strip. Mr. Mosely was a 27-year-old aviation enthusiast when he created the strip.

In Chapter 4, Charles mentions "Tokyo Rose." The name "Tokyo Rose" was the name given to any number of about a dozen English speaking female broadcasters of Japanese propaganda during WWII by the Allied Forces in the South Pacific. Iva Toguri D'Aquino is the woman most associated with the name of "Tokyo Rose."

Potter is wearing his red and gray-stripped robe in Chapter 8.

Oh, How We Danced – 2/23/1981
Season 9 / Episode 212 / Production 212 – Z414
Columbia House VHS Tape . . . . *Not Released by Columbia House*
Fox DVD . . . . *Season 9, Disc 2*

Alan Alda, Mike Farrell, Harry Morgan
Loretta Swit, David Ogden Stiers, Jamie Farr, William Christopher

Executive Producer – Burt Metcalfe
Produced by John Rappaport
Written by John Rappaport
Directed by Burt Metcalfe

Executive Script Consultants – Thad Mumford & Dan Wilcox
Executive Story Editor – Dennis Koenig
Creative Consultants – Gene Reynolds / Alan Alda

Yuki Shimoda . . . . Key Long Lu
Arlen Dean Snyder . . . . Major Finch
Catherine Bergstrom. . . . . Peg
Michael Cho . . . . Soon Chi Lu
Jennifer Davis . . . . Nurse
Shari Saba . . . . Nurse
Copyright 1981 – 20th Century Fox Film Corporation

Non-Credited Appearances. . . . . Kellye Nakahara

Chapters

1: *Main Titles / Fractured*	6: *Self Defense – 10:22*
2: *One Missing Name – 2:15*	7: *Third Degree – 12:47*
3: *Parting Thoughts – 4:38*	8: *Just One Harmonica – 14:51*
4: *The Little Things – 6:05*	9: *Happy Anniversary – 18:39*
5: *Unfair! – 8:41*	10: *Mule Kick / End Titles – 23:23*

Closing Stills

1: *Freeze – Hawkeye, Potter and B.J.*
2: *Key Long Lu*
3: *Major Finch*
4: *Soon Chi Lu*
5: *Hawkeye*
6: *Margaret*
7: *Charles*
8: *Mulcahy*
9: *Klinger*
10: *Potter*
11: *B.J.*

Synopsis: Peg Hunnicutt was eight months pregnant with Erin on their last wedding anniversary, and the next will be the first that she and B.J. are apart. With the help of Charles' tape recorder and hiding the microphone, Hawkeye gets B.J. to talk about some of the things he does when at home and what he and Peg would do on their anniversary. After sending the tape to Peg, she records a home movie of her and Erin and is seen during a surprise anniversary party for Peg and B.J. in Colonel Potter's office. Potter, on the other hand, sent Charles to a nearby combat unit to give them their sanitation inspection which, according to Charles, the unit failed miserably. To show his appreciation of the report, Major Finch comes to the 4077th and knocks out one of Charles' teeth.

Authors' Notes: There are no PA announcements in this episode.

The names on tape in the change room in Chapter 1 are: Winchester – Potter – Hawkeye – B.J. – Mulcahy. This changes from episode to episode. Sometimes Mulcahy's name is there, other times it's missing.

In Chapter 3, B.J. mentions that Pork Chop Hill has already been taken. As noted in an earlier episode, The Battle of Pork Chop Hill took place during the spring and summer of 1953. This puts "Oh, How We Danced" in 1953.

As Hawkeye was imitating Charles in Chapter 3, he says, in a "Charles voice," to "spread my ashes over Robert Taft." Robert Alphonso Taft (September 8, 1889-July 31, 1953) was a Republican Senator and staunch opponent of the New Deal from 1939 to 1953 in the Senate (see "Are You Now, Margaret?" in Season 8 for information on The New Deal). Taft was a major supporter of the foreign policy of non-intervention.

In Chapter 8, Hawkeye is practicing golf in the Swamp with a putter, and Klinger refers to him as "Bantam Ben," a reference to Ben Hogan (August 13, 1912-July 25, 1977). Mr. Hogan turned pro in 1929 and finished in the top ten in 241 out of 292 PGA Tour events and is considered one of the greatest golfers in the history of the game.

B.J. is again throwing darts at the dartboard in the Swamp in Chapter 9.

Also in Chapter 9, B.J.'s pink shirt looks purple in Potter's office.

B.J.'s home movie of Peg and Erin is seen in Chapter 9.

Bottoms Up – 3/2/1981

Season 9 / Episode 213 / Production 213 – Z415
Columbia House VHS Tape............... Not Released by Columbia House
Fox DVD ....Season 9, Disc 3

Alan Alda, Mike Farrell, Harry Morgan
Loretta Swit, David Ogden Stiers, Jamie Farr, William Christopher

Executive Producer – Burt Metcalfe
Produced by John Rappaport
Written by Dennis Koenig
Directed by Alan Alda

Executive Script Consultants – Thad Mumford & Dan Wilcox
Executive Story Editor – Dennis Koenig
Creative Consultants – Gene Reynolds / Alan Alda

Gail Strickland ....Captain Helen Whitfield
Jeff Maxwell..Igor
Kellye...Nurse Kellye
Shari Saba... Nurse
Laurie Bates .... Nurse
Bill Snider.. Corpsman
Jimmy Baron .... Patient

Copyright 1981 – 20th Century Fox Film Corporation

Non-Credited Appearances...............Jan Jorden, Dennis Troy, Roy Goldman

Chapters

1: Main Titles
2: Houlihan & Whitfield – 0:53
3: Buns Away – 3:41
4: The Wretched Harlequin – 5:13
5: Old Funny Pants – 9:06
6: Whitfield's Secret – 12:21
7: A Drinking Problem – 14:17
8: Say, "Cheesecake" – 18:12
9: Keeping Her Word – 21:38
10: To the Last Laugh / End Titles – 23:02

Closing Stills

1: Freeze – Hawkeye, Charles in the Officer's Club
2: Nurse Whitfield
3: Igor
4: Margaret
5: Charles
6: B.J.
7: Mulcahy
8: Klinger
9: Potter
10: Hawkeye

Synopsis: B.J., the master practical joke manipulator, helps Hawkeye play a joke on Charles in the operating room. When the joke proves to be in poor taste, B.J. lets Hawkeye alone suffer the wrath of the entire camp and refuses to acknowledge any participation. After convincing Charles that he didn't act alone, Hawkeye teams up with him to turn the tables on B.J. leaving him in a most uncomfortable position, in front of the entire camp. Captain Helen Whitfield, one of Margaret's best friends, is assigned to the 4077th, and also has a history of drinking. A mistake in O.R. and being found in the supply room alone and drunk forces Margaret to make the difficult decision to pull her friend from O.R. and assign her to the lab instead.

PA Announcements by Sal Viscuso

Authors' Notes: The view from the office windows in Chapter 6 shows the same wooden structure with people milling about, determined earlier to be Motor Pool Supply. But this time, it seems much closer.

Potterism: "Tougher than a two-bit steak."

In Chapter 9, Potter mentions the "DT's" after Helen Whitfield displays the symptoms. The "DT's," or delirium tremens, occur from withdrawal from alcohol after long-term habitual drinking.

The Red / White Blues – 3/9/1981

Season 9 / Episode 214 / Production 214 – Z416

Columbia House VHS Tape . . . . *War Stories (Catalog # 21043)*
Fox DVD . . . . *Season 9, Disc 3*

Alan Alda, Mike Farrell, Harry Morgan
Loretta Swit, David Ogden Stiers, Jamie Farr, William Christopher

Executive Producer – Burt Metcalfe
Produced by John Rappaport
Written by Elias Davis & David Pollock
Directed by Gabrielle Beaumont

Executive Script Consultants – Thad Mumford & Dan Wilcox
Executive Story Editor – Dennis Koenig
Creative Consultants – Gene Reynolds / Alan Alda

Roy Goldman . . . . Roy
Kellye. . . . . .Nurse Kellye
Jeff Maxwell. . . . . .Igor
Frank Pettinger . . . . Corpsman
Joann Thompson . . . . Nurse
Jimmy Baron . . . . Patient
Copyright 1981 – 20th Century Fox Film Corporation

Non-Credited Appearances. . . . . Gwen Farrell, Jan Jorden

Chapters

1: Main Titles	6: Fun, Fun, Fun – 12:01
2: Under Pressure – 0:54	7: Malaria? – 15:13
3: 165 Over 93 Good Reasons – 3:00	8: The Mystery Disease – 17:38
4: A Hard Pill to Swallow – 6:47	9: In A Tizzy – 20:41
5: Disaster Area – 10:19	10: Klinger's Weekend / End Titles – 22:55

Closing Stills

1: Freeze – Klinger and Roy
2: Potter in the office
3: B.J. in the Officer's Club
4: Charles in the Officer's Club
5: Margaret
6: Mulcahy (From Season 7)
7: Klinger
8: Hawkeye

Synopsis: High blood pressure could lead to more serious medical conditions, and for Colonel Potter, it could also mean the end of his long military career. With two weeks to go before his medical report is due, his physician, Hawkeye, bans salt, caffeine, liquor and cigars. But the one thing they might not be able to shield him from is aggravation. According to HQ, all of Klinger's morning reports for the past 60 days are completely wrong, and he has only three days to correct them. Suffering the side effects of Primaquine (a drug used in the treatment of malaria), Klinger's attempt at correcting the reports results in the office becoming a complete shambles, and the staff now has to keep Potter away so his blood pressure doesn't boil over.

Commentary by David Pollock: "That came out of research. We built on it."

Authors' Notes: There are no PA announcements in this episode.

Potterisms: "What in Hanna's hell" ("have you done now?"), "Geez, Louise," "What in Samuel Hill" ("hit this place?"). Potter has said this previously, but with a slight variation: "What in Sam Hill?"

In Chapter 4, Potter mentions feeling like a "Don McNeill Breakfast Clubber." Don McNeill (December 23, 1907-May 7, 1996) was the creator and host of a radio show called *The Breakfast Club.* The early-morning radio show premiered in 1933 on the NBC Blue Network, which later became ABC Radio, and ran for 30-plus years.

A flashback to Season 4's "Smilin' Jack" when, in the Officer's Club in Chapter 6, a sign is seen above the door that says "Dangerous Dan was here 6/22/51."

Igor, in Chapter 6, offers Potter a "pure Havana" cigar. This is possible since the United States Embargo against Cuba went into effect on February 7, 1962. It's also possible that, even if the embargo was in effect during the Korean War, a "pure Havana" could have been gotten in Korea.

For the second time in the series, "Carrie Nation" is mentioned, this time by Charles. The first time she was mentioned was by Colonel Potter in Episode 189, Season 8's "Bottle Fatigue," and that's where you'll find information about who she was.

The tape over the hooks in the change room in Chapter 8 is the same as episode 212: *Winchester, Potter, Hawkeye, BJ, Mulcahy*

In Chapter 9, B.J. says, "Congratulations, Maxwell. Your blood is good to the last drop." "Good to the Last Drop" became a very popular advertising slogan for Maxwell House Coffee in 1917.

The view from the office window in Chapter 9 is on an angle and not a direct view out. Crates and people moving about are seen.

Bless You, Hawkeye – 3/16/1981

Season 9 / Episode 215 / Production 215 – Z417

Columbia House VHS Tape . . . . *Not Released by Columbia House*

Fox DVD . . . . *Season 9, Disc 3*

Alan Alda, Mike Farrell, Harry Morgan
Loretta Swit, David Ogden Stiers, Jamie Farr, William Christopher

Executive Producer – Burt Metcalfe
Produced by John Rappaport
Written by Dan Wilcox & Thad Mumford
Directed by Nell Cox

Executive Script Consultants – Thad Mumford & Dan Wilcox
Executive Story Editor – Dennis Koenig
Creative Consultants – Gene Reynolds / Alan Alda

Allen Arbus . . . . Dr. Sidney Freedman
Barry Schwartz . . . . Private Joe Caputo
Dennis Troy . . . . Driver
Pamela Coleman . . . . Nurse

Copyright 1981 – 20th Century Fox Film Corporation

Non-Credited Appearances . . . . Kellye Nakahara, Jan Jorden

Chapters

1: Main Titles	6: I'm Dying – 9:05
2: If the Sneeze Fits… – 0:53	7: Sidney Steps In – 10:16
3: How Goes the Nose – 4:04	8: Cousin Billy – 15:09
4: Physician Non Grata – 5:18	9: Three Queens – 23:14
5: Fuzz and Pollen – 7:25	10: End Titles – 24:11

Closing Stills

1: Freeze – Hawk and Sidney in the Officer's Club
2: Sidney
3: Hawkeye in bed
4: Potter in the office
5: B.J. in the Swamp
6: Margaret
7: Charles in the office
8: Klinger
9: Mulcahy (From Season 7)
10: Hawkeye in the office

Synopsis: Hawkeye might be allergic to something and begins getting rid of things in the Swamp that might be causing his violent sneezing, including a bottle of cologne given to Charles by his mother. Showering has no effect and all allergy tests prove negative. But when Hawkeye enters the office with severe itching, rashes on his neck and feeling like he's going to die, it becomes apparent to Colonel Potter that Hawkeye's problems might not be physical, and a call is placed to Sidney Freedman.

PA Announcements by Sal Viscuso

Authors' Notes: A corpsman in Chapter 2 is wearing Henry Blake's robe.

It is somewhat odd seeing Potter in Chapter 2 wearing a white with black polka dots nightgown.

In Chapter 2, Potter mentions the "lab keys doing a Judge Crater on us." Judge Joseph Force Crater (January 5, 1889 – date of death unknown) was a New York City judge who, on August 6, 1930, left a restaurant, got into a taxi and was never seen again. One of the most famous disappearances in American history, Judge Crater became known as "The Missingest Man in New York."

For the first time in several episodes, the view out of the office windows in Chapter 2 has changed from the wooden motor pool supply to a different structure showing a corrugated right side and no visible door.

In chapter 4, Potter tells Mildred to keep snow tires on the Hudson year-round. The Hudson Motor Car Company made cars in Detroit from 1909 to 1954.

In Chapter 7, Margaret mentions "Benadryl," a popular medicine for hay fever, and it fits in the M*A*S*H timeline.

Blood Brothers – 4/6/1981

Season 9 / Episode 216 / Production 219 – Z421
Columbia House VHS Tape............... Not Released by Columbia House
Fox DVD .... Season 9, Disc 3

Alan Alda, Mike Farrell, Harry Morgan
Loretta Swit, David Ogden Stiers, Jamie Farr, William Christopher

Executive Producer – Burt Metcalfe
Produced by John Rappaport
Written by David Pollock & Elias Davis
Directed by Harry Morgan

Executive Script Consultants – Thad Mumford & Dan Wilcox
Executive Story Editor – Dennis Koenig
Creative Consultants – Gene Reynolds / Alan Alda

Patrick Swayze ....Gary Sturgis
Ray Middleton ....Cardinal Reardon
G.W. Bailey..Sergeant Luthor Rizzo
Jeff Maxwell...Igor
Tom Kindle...G.I.
Robert Balderson..Captain Bratton
Roy Goldman ....Roy
Dennis Troy...Dennis
Copyright 1981 – 20th Century Fox Film Corporation

Non-Credited Appearances................................Kellye Nakahara

Chapters

1: Main Titles	6: Cardinal Reardon – 13:04
2: Sturges's Friend – 0:53	7: Nothing I Can Do – 15:31
3: The Cardinal's Coming – 2:09	8: Tokyo Can Wait – 17:06
4: A Den of Iniquity – 6:21	9: About Two Men – 19:02
5: Bad Blood – 8:25	10: An Inspirational Visit / End Titles – 23:22

Closing Stills

1: Freeze – Charles, Marg, Potter, Mulcahy, Klinger, B.J.
2: Sturgis
3: Cardinal Reardon
4: Rizzo
5: Klinger in the Officer's Club
6: Hawkeye
7: B.J. in Post-Op
8: Potter in the Officer's Club
9: Margaret
10: Charles
11: Klinger
12: Mulcahy

Synopsis: An impending visit from Cardinal Reardon has Father Mulcahy frazzled trying to clean up the camp, a task easier said than done. It's payday and Rizzo's crap game is in full swing, and those not playing are packed into the Officer's Club, along with a poster of a scantily clad woman. Angry and frustrated, Mulcahy seeks comfort with

Hawkeye in the mess tent, but Hawkeye doesn't feel much like talking. After his patient offers to give blood to his seriously wounded friend, Hawkeye, while cross matching, discovers the man has leukemia, and that's the easy part. The difficult part is telling him and knowing that, as a doctor, there's nothing he can do about it.

Commentary by Elias Davis: "I do like this story, and have told it a few times when teaching comedy writing at USC Film School."

Commentary by David Pollock: "We were nominated for the Humanitas Award for this one. We lost to *WKRP in Cincinnati.*"

Authors' Notes: There are no PA announcements in this episode.
Gary Sturgis' name in the captioning and end titles is spelled S-T-U-R-G-I-S.
Gary Sturgis' name in the Chapter Titles is spelled S-T-U-R-G-E-S.
There are what appear to be two pictures of Potter's granddaughter in his tent in Chapter 3.
Mulcahy in Chapter 6 is wearing his brown plaid robe.
Potter in Chapter 6 is wearing the robe usually worn by Henry Blake.
Patrick Swayze, who played Gary Sturgis in this episode was born on August 8, 1952 and is best known for his role in the 1987 hit movie *Dirty Dancing.* Mr. Swayze, ironically, played a GI who finds out he has leukemia and sadly, died from pancreatic cancer on September 14, 2009.

The Foresight Saga – 4/13/1981

Season 9 / Episode 217 / Production 220 – Z422

Columbia House VHS Tape. . . . . Not Released by Columbia House

Fox DVD . . . . Season 9, Disc 3

Alan Alda, Mike Farrell, Harry Morgan
Loretta Swit, David Ogden Stiers, Jamie Farr, William Christopher

Executive Producer – Burt Metcalfe
Produced by John Rappaport
Written by Dennis Koenig
Directed by Charles S. Dubin

Executive Script Consultants – Thad Mumford & Dan Wilcox
Executive Story Editor – Dennis Koenig
Creative Consultants – Gene Reynolds / Alan Alda

Philip Sterling. . . . .(Captain) Dr. Myron "Bud" Herzog

Rummel Mor . . . . .Park Sung

Jeff Maxwell. . . . . .Igor

Copyright 1981 – 20th Century Fox Film Corporation

Non-Credited Appearances. . . . . .Kellye Nakahara, Roy Goldman

Chapters

1: Main Titles / Letter from Radar	6: Wounded Villagers – 11:00
2: Klinger's Crack-Up – 3:45	7: A New Roommate – 12:22
3: Park Sung's Present – 4:56	8: Herzog's Girl – 15:21
4: Dr. Herzog – 7:06	9: Person-to-Little person – 18:00
5: Dear Pudd'n'head – 8:37	10: Aloha, Park Sung / End Titles – 22:50

Closing Stills

1: Freeze – B.J., Hawkeye, Park Sung – mess tent
2: Dr. Herzog
3: Park Sung in the mess tent
4: Igor
5: Margaret in her tent
6: B.J. in the Officer's Club
7: Potter
8: Charles in the Swamp
9: Klinger
10: Mulcahy
11: Hawkeye in the Officer's Club
12: Mulcahy

Synopsis: Not used to being a civilian human again, in a letter to his friends at the 4077th, Radar tells of good fortune on the farm. Looking ahead to his best year ever with corn coming out of his ears, Radar stands to make a lot of money, but misses everyone, including Charles. The 4077th misses him as well, so Colonel Potter places a call to Ottumwa, Iowa, only to find out from Mrs. O'Reilly that Radar might have been exaggerating a little, that the farm isn't doing well at all and was embarrassed to say anything. A local Korean boy with a green thumb has provided the 4077th with fresh vegetables to make coleslaw, and Potter thanks him by providing an eye doctor and arranges for the boy to get a new pair of glasses. With Park Sung's skills at farming and Radar needing help, B.J. comes up with a plan to send the boy to Ottumwa.

PA Announcement by Todd Sussman

Authors' Notes: In Chapter 2, the view out of the office windows shows a wooden structure with a door, but it's a lot closer than before

Hawkeye mentions "Oliver Twist" in Chapter 6. Oliver Twist (1838) was Charles Dickens' second novel.

The view out the same office windows in Chapter 9 changes to a wooden structure out the left window and a partly corrugated structure out the right window, then changes to a corrugated structure out the right

In Chapter 9, we learn Mrs. O'Reilly's name is Edna, same as his cow.

Hawkeye, in Chapter 10, mentions "the Boston Braves." From 1912 until 1952, this Major League Baseball team was known as the Boston Braves (not to be confused with the Boston Red Sox). The team relocated to Milwaukee in 1953, becoming the Milwaukee Braves and relocated once again in 1965 to become the Atlanta Braves, which is where they remain today in the Eastern Division of the National League.

The Life You Save – 5/4/1981

Season 9 / Episode 218 / Production 216 – Z418
Columbia House VHS Tape . . . . Not Released by Columbia House
Fox DVD . . . . Season 9, Disc 3

Alan Alda, Mike Farrell, Harry Morgan
Loretta Swit, David Ogden Stiers, Jamie Farr, William Christopher

Executive Producer – Burt Metcalfe
Produced by John Rappaport
Written by John Rappaport & Alan Alda
Directed by Charles S. Dubin

Executive Script Consultants – Thad Mumford & Dan Wilcox
Executive Story Editor – Dennis Koenig
Creative Consultants – Gene Reynolds / Alan Alda

Val Bisoglio . . . . The Cook
Andrew Parks . . . . The Dying Soldier
G.W. Bailey. . . . . .Sergeant Luthor Rizzo
Jim Knaub . . . . .Private Markham
Arthur Taxier. . . . . Surgeon
Jim Boeke . . . . Sergeant Chiaverini
Jack Kearney . . . . Soldier
Paul Ventura . . . . Soldier
Wayne Morton . . . . Enlisted Man
Meshach Taylor. . . . . .Orderly
Shari Saba . . . . .Shari
Roy Goldman . . . . .Roy
Gwen Farrell . . . . Gwen
Dennis Troy. . . . . Dennis

Copyright 1981 – 20th Century Fox Film Corporation

Non-Credited Appearances. . . . . .Kellye Nakahara

Chapters

1:	Main Titles	6:	Stolen Trays – 12:44
2:	Sniper – 0:53	7:	Motor Pool Madness – 15:06
3:	Additional Duties – 2:41	8:	Plusses and Minuses – 18:09
4:	French Toast – 4:54	9:	Death's Witness – 19:27
5:	Close to Death – 8:03	10:	The Army Way / End Titles – 23:26

Closing Stills

1: Freeze – Klinger, Hawkeye, Margaret
2: The cook in the kitchen
3: M.P. in the mess tent
4: Wounded G.I.
5: Hawkeye
6: Potter
7: B.J.
8: Margaret
9: Klinger in the mess tent
10: Mulcahy
11: Charles

Synopsis: Helping B.J. resuscitate a patient while under fire on the compound, Charles soon realizes his own near-death experience when he finds a bullet hole in his hat. Obsessed with finding out what happens when death is at hand, he talks to B.J.'s patient in Post-Op, who doesn't understand what Charles wants, and angers B.J. in the process when he sees Charles talking to him. But Charles reveals a tragic event that took place when he was very young, an event that for months had a lingering effect on him. Meanwhile, Hawkeye is the new Mess Tent Officer. While instructing the cook on how to make homemade French toast, he soon discovers that he might be arrested for missing trays...from the 8063rd.

Authors' Notes: There are no PA announcements in this episode.
Chapter 10 on the DVD is listed only as "The Army Way," not listing "End Titles."
A corpsman in Chapter 2 is wearing Henry Blake's robe.
The names on the tape over the clothes hooks in the change room are: *Winchester, Potter, Hawkeye, B.J.* and *Mulcahy* (sometimes, Mulcahy's name isn't there, even if he is).
The laundry room makes yet another appearance in Chapter 4.
Hawkeye, in Chapter 6, refers to Eggs Benedict when he says, "Eggs Benzedrine." Doctors, to perk up patients before breakfast, used Benzedrine. Used as a bronchodilator and appetite suppressant, Benzedrine and the amphetamines derived from it were used as a stimulant for armed forces in WWII and Viet Nam. The Federal Drug Administration made it a prescription drug in 1959.
In Chapter 8, the Garbage Depot makes its debut.
In Chapter 9, Charles, in a rare display, cries while talking to a patient who's near death at an aid station, still wanting to know what the experience is like.

Appendix – Season 9

Character Profiles

Hawkeye

Episode 199: Has a picture of his father and little Cousin Martin at the annual sugaring-off dinner.

200: Amy Clark, a teacher and friend in Crabapple Cove.

According to Hawkeye, there are 400 people in Crabapple Cove.

202: Has a new civilian shirt: blue with pineapples.

203: Lumberjack shirt.

Family always used to put up a Nativity scene.

One year he got a set of electric trains and laid the track all around a village with three wise men in the caboose. As the conductor, he would say, "Next stop, Bethlehem."

215: Alludes to being a Methodist when talking about his childhood in Maine — a lobster in every pot and two Methodists in every garage.

He and his cousin Billy used to go to a swimming hole up the road to fish and swim and wade looking for pollywogs.

He was six and cousin Billy was 12 — the older brother he never had and Billy was yo-yo district champ.

Used to read Billy's father's *Police Gazettes* in the garage.

Delivered prescriptions on his bike for Ballinger's Drug Store even though he didn't like Mr. Ballinger but made a enough tip money to buy a Savings Bond.

At seven years old, he went fishing with Billy on a pond in a borrowed rowboat and Billy pushed him into the water, then pulled him out — then blacked out — woke smelling like a wet burlap sack and he hated Billy for that which is why he started violently sneezing in the episode after a patient arrives smelling like that burlap sack.

B.J.

Episode 199: Has Frankie Laine records with him in Korea.

203: As a child, his father would put him on his shoulders so he could put the Christmas angel on top of the tree and did this until he was 11 years old. If he weren't in Korea, Erin would be on his shoulders.

209: Peg writes and tells him the rain gutters need to be cleaned.

Has a ladder in the garage, but the third rung is broken and he didn't tell Peg.

B.J.'s neighbor Eddie Hoffman is "bagged" most of the time while his other neighbor, Old Man Wallerstein, is 83.

Rain overflows into the window well and floods his cellar. The water rises and puts out the furnace pilot light.

Won't call Carl, the handyman. Carl is 6'4", works out with weights, has huge arms and wears skintight tee shirts with the sleeves cut off. Better looking than Errol Flynn.

212: Wedding anniversary is May 25.

Last anniversary Peg was eight months pregnant — this is the first anniversary apart — would probably have dinner in Sausalito or a candlelit dinner at home.

Colonel Potter

Episode 199: Mildred and her partner took first prize in the Hannibal, MO, Bridge Tournament.

Potter and Mildred are the best mixed-doubles bridge team in the entire "Show Me" state, according to Potter.

200: In WWI, it rained "cats and dachsunds" for 37 straight days.

Mildred was to send Cloverine salve for his "barking bunions."

"Hoops Potter" breaks the camp record of 31 straight free throws by one.

203: Potter's niece sent a sugar-cured ham.

209: Has a cat.

210: Should have taken the severance pay in 1928 and started a dude ranch, but didn't because of the "damn zoning laws."

211: He and Mildred have complete abridged *Reader's Digest* library.

212: Once owned a mule.

214: The best physical he ever had was back in WW I from a pretty French girl in a French farmhouse. It was the only time his reflexes were checked without a hammer.

His blood pressure is 165 over 93, but by episode's end it was reduced to 137 over 88.

When he was a kid, he hated eating dinner with "the little people" and was always stuck at a rickety card table.

215: Spent seven years in medical school.

Told Mildred to keep snow tires on the Hudson year round.

217: When he first arrived at the 4077th, Radar broke his "trusty" pocket watch. Radar felt bad and ran into the office every 15 minutes to tell him the time.

Mildred calls him "Puuddin' Head" and misses the sweet way he whistles when he snores.

Margaret

Episode 202: Since her father's divorce, he's taken a position as a civilian military advisor.

203: Margaret is about to falsify an official record by entering the time of death for a patient at 12:05 A.M., December 26, as opposed to the actual time of death at 11:25 P.M., December 25. This will be the first time in her career that she will falsify a record as it would prevent the man's family having to think of Christmas as the day their father died. Hawkeye, B.J. and Father Mulcahy all agree that this is the right thing to do.

209: Prickly heat on her derriere.

218: Has leopard underwear *(seen).*

Charles

Episode 199: Past Master Bridge Champion
Charles and sister Honoria are four-time champions of the Beacon Hill Bridge Society.

200: Answers a letter that contained a leaf from a birch tree during the fall season in New England.

202: Is seen on his way to the showers holding soap on a rope

203: It's a Winchester Christmas tradition to leave gifts at places such as the orphanage in this episode. For this to be a true gift of charity, the gift must remain anonymous.
Earliest childhood recollections are associated with his mother, father and sister as Mr. Wallingford hand wraps each piece of chocolate, then wiping a hole in the frost of the car window to watch his father leave the package.

209: As of last Tuesday, Charles' accountant was incarcerated on five counts of fraud, two counts of embezzlement and "countless counts concerning accounts for which he cannot account."
The Internal Revenue Service is curious about the Winchesters and the Emersons.
Mulcahy implies, after looking at some of Charles' documents, that the Winchesters have Swiss bank accounts.
Charles has a $681.78 medical deduction.

212: In a tape-recorded letter home, Charles grants power of attorney to his father for the disposition of all his real estate and gives his mother proxy, never to be used to vote for Cousin Alfred. He also leaves, to his sister Honoria, his butterfly collection, knowing that she really doesn't want it, but Cousin Alfred does.

214: Doesn't do volunteer work, except the occasional fundraising for the Boston Symphony.

215: Bottle of cologne that Hawkeye tossed out of the Swamp was a gift from his mother.

218: When he was very young, his little brother passed away and he couldn't pass his room for months after the accident without fear and tingling in his chest and arms.

Klinger

Episode 200: Klinger's "Chinchilla Villa Breeding Farms." Too bad he didn't know the two chinchillas are both male.

201: Spent two summers working for his Uncle Amos who was in the birdbath business. Klinger poured the cement molds.

205: According to Hawkeye, Klinger files X-rays under "E."
Klinger's best friend is (was) Gus Nagy.

206: At Uncle Abdul's wedding, all the ushers wore silk bed sheets

208: Likes for breakfast 3-minute eggs, lightly buttered toast with the crusts trimmed off.

210: 7199199 is Klinger's uncle.
Has an Uncle Bustaffa.
Is "Aunt Sadie," a column for the lovelorn in his newspaper.

214: During his weekend in Tokyo, he got sick on raw fish, a sumo wrestler fell on him, was thrown out of a geisha house for leaving a ring around the bath and "flattened" by a hit and run rickshaw driver.

Father Mulcahy

Episode 199: According to Mulcahy, Margaret is an excellent bridge player.

200: Name in this episode is Francis J. Mulcahy *(his name in the Pilot episode was John P. Mulcahy, and his name in Episode 176 was Francis John Patrick Mulcahy).*

208: Once forgot the words to the 23rd Psalm. "Or was it the 22nd?"

209: Back in 1941, wrote a check for $1,297 instead of $12.97.

Seen, Heard, Mentioned or Referenced – Season 9

Movies
Episode 206: Hawkeye mentions "Grumpy" See Episode 67 (page 234) for details.
207: Nurse Baker mentions *Gone with the Wind* (1939)

Songs
199: "Top Hat, White Tie and Tails" *(Hawkeye sings "Puttin' on my top hat, tyin' on my white tie, brushin' off my tails, doin' up my shirt front...")* See Episode 109 (page 360) for details.
"Dream (When You're Feeling Blue)" *(Hawkeye sings "Dream when you're feeling blue, dream, that's the thing to do...")* Words and music by Johnny Mercer, 1944.
"In My Merry Oldsmobile" *(Hawkeye sings "Come away with me Lucille, in my merry Oldsmobile, down the road of life we'll fly...")* Words by Vincent P. Bryan, music by Gus Edwards, 1905.
"Mule Train" *(Charles mentions)* Written by Johnny Lange, Hy Heath & Fred Glickman, recorded by Frankie Laine on October 2, 1949. On the Billboard charts for 13 weeks, peaking at #1 (also recorded by others).
200: "Zip-a-Dee-Doo-Dah" *(Klinger sings "Zip-a-dee-doo-dah, zip-a-dee ay, my oh my, what a wonderful day...")* From the 1946 Disney movie *Song of the South*, words by Ray Gilbert, music by Allie Wrubel. Won the Academy Award in 1947 for "Best Song."
201: "Cement Mixer" *(Mulcahy sings "Cement mixer, putti, putti...a puddle o' gooty, puddle o'vooty, puddle o'scooty...")* Words by Sam Gaillard, music by Lee Ricks, 1945.
203: "Santa Claus is Coming to Town" *(Hawkeye sings "Santa gauze is coming to town.")* Words by Haven Gillespie, music by J. Fred Coots. First sung on Eddie Cantor's radio show in November, 1934.
"Deck the Halls" *(B.J. sings "Deck the halls with balls of cotton...")* A traditional Christmas and New Year's Carol, used by Mozart for a violin and piano duet. Original lyrics in Welch, English used today dates to the 19th Century.
"Jingle Bells" See Episode 12 (page 129) for details.
"O Holy Night" *(All sing in the mess tent "Long lay the world in sin and error pining...")* A Christmas carol written by Adolphe Adam in 1847 to the French poem by Placide Cappeau (1808-1877)
"Silent Night" *(All sing in the mess tent.)* This popular Christmas carol, with words by Father Josef Mohr and music by Franz Xaver Gruber, was first performed in the Church of Nicholas in Oberndorf, Austria on December 24, 1818.
"The 12 Days of Christmas" *(Klinger hums)* An English carol, it's a cumulative song with verses built on previous verses and one of the most popular and recorded songs in the U.S. and Europe in the past century.
205: "Harbor Lights" *(Instrumental heard in the Officer's Club)* Words by Jimmy Kennedy, music by Hugh Williams (Wilhelm Grosz). Published in 1950 and said to have originated in 1937 England.
"Home on the Range." *(Hawkeye says "Where the buffalo wouldn't roam.")* See Episode 16 (page 129) for details.
206: "Whistle While You Work." *(Klinger whistles)* See Episode 146 (page 470) for details.
"I'm Back in the Saddle Again." *(Potter sings)* See Episode 66 (page 259) for details.

207: "The Star Spangled Banner" *(Hawkeye says "Land of the free and the home of depraved...")* See Episode 56 (page 258) for details.

"Alouette" *(Potter wishes Colonel LaFleur a "Jaunty Allowetter.")* A popular Canadian children's song. American soldiers in France during WWI had learned this song and returned home with it.

"Love for Sale" *(Hawkeye sings "Love for sale. Appetizing young love for sale...")* Written by Cole Porter. This song, considered to be in bad taste, even scandalous at the time, is from the musical *The New Yorkers*, which opened on Broadway in 1930.

208: "The Anvil Chorus" (Charles hums) See Episode 148 (page 530) for details.

"Reveille" *(Klinger hums)* See Episode 9 (page 129) for details.

209: "When Johnny Comes Marching Home" *(Klinger makes a reference)* A Civil War song, written by Louis Lambert in 1863.

212: "The Desert Song" *(Klinger mentions)* Lyrics and book by Otto Harbach and Oscar Hammerstein II, music by Sigmund Romberg. An operetta, the show opened in 1926 at The Broadway theater and was made into a movie in 1929, 1943 and 1953.

"The Anniversary Waltz" *(Korean Boy plays on a harmonica)* Words by Al Dubin, music by Dave Franklin, published in 1941.

217: "For He's A Jolly Good Fellow" *(All sing in the mess tent)* See Episode 13 (page 129) for details.

Appearances – Season 9

Arbus, Allen .... Episode 215 *(Dr. Sidney Freedman)*
Bailey, G.W. ....Episode 203, 216, 218 *(Sergeant Luther Rizzo)*
Balderson, Robert ....Episode 216 *(Captain Bratton)*
Baron, Jimmy .... Episode 213, 214 *(Patient)*
Bates, Laurie .... Episode 204, 213 *(Nurse)*
Bergstrom, Catherine..Episode 212 *(Peg Hunnicutt)*
Bisoglio, Sal... Episode 218 *(The Cook (Sergeant)*
Boeke, Jim .... Episode 218 *(Sergeant Chiaverni)*
Bogert, William ....Episode 210 *(Captain Maurice Allen)*
Brooks, Joel ....Episode 201 *(Ignazio DeSimone)*
Cedar, Larry .... Episode 200 *(credited as "The Soldier," but his name is Mike)*
Cho, Michael ....Episode 212 *(Soon Chi Lu)*
Coleman, Pamela .... Episode 215 *(Nurse)*
Corbin, Barry .... Episode 205 *(Sergeant Joe Vickers, Area Retention Officer)*
Currie, Michael... Episode 200 *(Dr. Bruer)*
Davis, Jennifer..Episode 212 *(Nurse)*
Dozer, David .... Episode 210 *(The Delivery man)*
Duggan, Andrew..................... Episode 202 *(Colonel Alvin "Howitzer" Houlihan)*
Farrell, Gwen ....Episode 218 *(Gwen)*
Farrell, Judy .... Episode 207 *(Nurse Able)*
Freed, Carl ....Episode 204 *(Patient)*
Gallery, James... Episode 206 *(Murray Thompson)*
Goldman, Roy..Episode 214 *(Corporal Roy Goldman)*
Goldman, Roy... Episode 216, 218 *(Roy)*
Hallahan, Charles .... Episode 207 *(Corporal Colin Turnbull,*
2nd Princess Pat Battalion, Canada)
Harris, Mel..Episode 201 *(The Driver)*
Hi, May... Episode 211 *(Korean Woman)*
Hoover, Yoshiki .... Episode 203 *(Korean Boy)*
Imamura, Sally .... Episode 203 *(Korean Girl)*
Impert, Margie..................................... Episode 207 *(Nurse Sandra Palmer)*
Jorden, Jan .... Episode 207 *(Nurse Baker)*
Jung, Nathan .... Episode 211 *(Korean Man)*
Kearney, Jack .... Episode 218 *(Soldier)*
Kindle, Tom ....Episode 216 *(G.I.)*
Knaub, Jim .... Episode 218 *(Private Markham)*
Kramer, Jeffrey .... Episode 202 *(Sergeant Ronnie Morgove)*
La Fleur, Art .... Episode 202 *(M.P.)*
Luke, Keye .... Episode 203 *(Choi Sung Ho)*
Mako .... Episode 199 *(Li Han)*
Maxwell, Jeff ....Episode 203, 204, 205, 209, 211, 213, 214, 216, 217 *(Igor)*
McGuire, Michael ....Episode 206 *(Colonel Mulholland)*
Middleton, Ray..................................... Episode 216 *(James Cardinal Reardon)*
Miller, Denny .... Episode 206 *(M.P.)*
Mor, Rummel... Episode 217 *(Park Sung)*
Morton, Wayne..Episode 218 *(Enlisted Man)*
Nakahara, Kellye .... Episode 203, 209, 211 *(Kellye)*
Nakahara, Kellye .... Episode 213, 214 *(Nurse Kellye)*
O'Connor, Tim ....Episode 208 *(Doctor Norman Traeger)*
Page, Perrin .... Episode 203 *(Driver)*
Page, Perrin W. .... Episode 209 *(Driver)*

Broadcast/Production Order – Season 9

Broadcast	Production
199: The Best Of Enemies *(11/17/1980)*	*199: (Z401)* Cementing Relationships
200: Letters *(11/24/1980)*	*200: (Z402)* No Sweat
201: Cementing Relationships *(12/1/1980)*	*201: (Z403)* Letters
202: Father's Day *(12/8/1980)*	*202: (Z404)* The Best Of Enemies
203: Death Takes A Holiday *(12/15/1980)*	*203: (Z405)* Father's Day
204: A War For All Seasons *(12/29/1980)*	*204: (Z406)* Your Retention, Please
205: Your Retention, Please *(1/5/1981)*	*205: (Z407)* Taking The Fifth
206: Tell It To The MaRines *(1/12/1981)*	*206: (Z408)* Death Takes A Holiday
207: Taking The Fifth *(1/19/1981)*	*207: (Z409)* A War For All Seasons
208: Operation Friendship *(1/26/1981)*	*208: (Z410)* Tell It To The Marines
209: No Sweat *(2/2/1981)*	*209: (Z411)* Depressing News
210: Depressing News *(2/9/1981)*	*210: (Z412)* Operation Friendship
211: No Laughing Matter *(2/16/1981)*	*211: (Z413)* No Laughing Matter
212: Oh, How We Danced *(2/23/1981)*	*212: (Z414)* Oh, How We Danced
213: Bottoms Up *(3/2/1981)*	*213: (Z415)* Bottoms Up
214: The Red / White Blues *(3/9/1981)*	*214: (Z416)* The Red / White Blues
215: Bless You, Hawkeye *(3/16/1981)*	*215: (Z417)* Bless You, Hawkeye
216: Blood Brothers *(4/6/1981)*	*216: (Z418)* The Life You Save
217: The Foresight Saga *(4/13/1981)*	*217: (Z419)* That's Show Biz, Part 1*
218: The Life You Save *(5/4/1981)*	*218: (Z420)* That's Show Biz, Part 2*
	219: (Z421) Blood Brothers
	220: (Z422) The Foresight Saga
	221: (Z423) Identity Crisis*
	222: (Z424) Rumor At The Top*

Although produced during Season 9, Z419, Z420, Z423 and Z424 were held over for broadcast in Season 10.

Season 10

Despite all of the changes in front of and behind the camera, *M*A*S*H* had survived for an impressive tenth season. And though the tone and style had changed dramatically, the writers were certainly not at a loss for story ideas. In Season 10, viewers got to see the newer *M*A*S*H* crews take on early season subject matter. "Showtime" aired at the end of Season 1, but now, "That's Showbiz" took a different slant on a visiting USO troupe: this time around, the entertainers didn't just provide a backdrop to the story, but were part of it. "Divided We Stand" was the Season 2 opener, but "Rumor At The Top" gave audiences a chance to see how the gang from Season 10 of *M*A*S*H* would be on their best or worst behavior for a visiting official. Racism, wills and communication with the dead were all subjects that Season 10 tackled. Hy Averback, a wonderful director from classic television and the early years of *M*A*S*H*, returned to direct "Snap Judgment" and "Snappier Judgment." In the latter episode, Charles shines in the courtroom scene. There had been talk within the *M*A*S*H* ranks that this might be the last season. But, the promise of doing a final movie lured everyone into doing one last year of the show.

That's Show Biz – 10/26/1981

Season 10 / Episode 219 and Episode 220
Production 217 and Production 218 – Z419-Z420

Columbia House VHS Tape . . . . *Not Released by Columbia House*
Fox DVD . . . . *Season 10, Disc 1*

Alan Alda, Mike Farrell, Harry Morgan
Loretta Swit, David Ogden Stiers, Jamie Farr, William Christopher

Executive Producer – Burt Metcalfe
Produced by John Rappaport
Written by David Pollock & Elias Davis
Directed by Charles S. Dubin

Executive Script Consultants – Thad Mumford & Dan Wilcox
Executive Story Editor – Dennis Koenig
Creative Consultants – Gene Reynolds / Alan Alda

Gwen Verdon . . . . Brandy Doyle (Brenda Delinski)
Danny Dayton. . . . . Fast Freddie Nichols
Gail Edwards. . . . . Marina Ryan
Karen Landry . . . . Sarah Miller
Amanda McBroom . . . . Ellie Carlyle
Richard Molnar. . . . . Michael Nowicki
Kellye Nakahara . . . . Kellye
Freddie Dawson . . . . Patient
Bryan Byers. . . . . Patient

Copyright 1981 – 20th Century Fox Film Corporation

Non-Credited Appearances. . . . . Dennis Troy, Roy Goldman

Chapters

1:	Main Titles	11:	Road Block – 23:32
2:	Arrival of the U.S.O. Tour – 0:55	12:	Freddie's Dilemma – 25:06
3:	There's Going to be A Show! – 4:44	13:	Passing Time – 26:02
4:	Hometown Heroes – 8:19	14:	Ballet Shoes – 28:12
5:	A Treat for Colonel Potter – 11:38	15:	I Like Apples, Too – 29:59
6:	This One is for Winchester – 13:53	16:	The Women of the U.S.O. – 31:30
7:	Klinger's Debut – 14:58	17:	Everyone's A Comedian – 37:40
8:	Sweet Molly Malone – 16:17	18:	Healing Scars – 39:53
9:	Getting to Know Brandy Doyle – 18:43	19:	Fond Farewells – 45:00
10:	The Fast Freddie Effect – 21:19	20:	The Show's Over / End Titles – 47:50

Closing Stills

1: Freeze – Hawkeye, CEW, Klinger w/ accordion
2: Brandy Doyle
3: Fast Freddie
4: Marina Ryan
5: Sarah Miller
6: Ellie Carlyle
7: Patient in Post-Op
8: Hawkeye
9: B.J.
10: Margaret

11: *Charles*
12: *Mulcahy*
13: *Klinger in the office*
14: *Potter*

Synopsis: The last hour-long episode of the series focuses on individual relationships that develop between the staff and the members of a U.S.O. troupe. Although no one was wounded when they came under fire, the troupe makes an unscheduled stop at the 4077th when one of the members needs an emergency appendectomy. The staff and the U.S.O Troupe take an instant liking to each other, and when they're forced to stay in camp because of travel restrictions, the troupe puts on a show in Post-Op for everyone. Relationships of love, comedy, music and compassion are explored, some with happy endings, some not so.

Commentary by David Pollock: "Because of the actor's strike, this was done in Season 9 and shelved. When we wrote it, we didn't know Gwen Verdon would be in it. So, we were thrilled to get her. You could only film at the Fox Ranch during daylight savings time. During standard time, we'd film inside, at Stage 9."

Commentary by Gail Edwards: "*M*A*S*H* taught me the vast difference between being a series regular and a guest-star, especially in a film situation. When an actor appears as a guest-star on film, they are lucky to get one decent take to deliver their close-up, whereas the series regulars (the regular cast), can take as many as they'd like or need. What stunned me was, here I had a ten-page intimate scene with Alan Alda, a real actor's dream come true, and he didn't know any of his lines! At first, I didn't know what to do. I took to heart the danger of an actor's repetitive performance getting stale, but then felt confident that I was good enough to get around it — hence, I volunteered to rehearse my scenes with Alan. Many actors would have had a line-reader step in. But, for me, the lack of Alan knowing his lines allowed me to rehearse with him, over and over; therefore, I really got to know him, like him, and 'love him,' as I needed to do in our scene. And, finally, after his 25 takes…I got my one. Guest starring on *M*A*S*H* offered one great experience after another, but what was extra-special for me was, when I was young and in love with musicals, my mom took me to New York City where I saw an incredible performance of *Sweet Charity*, staring Gwen Verdon. What a thrill it was, years later, to be in the same show of *M*A*S*H* with her! (Used with permission. *Note: Videos clips of Ms. Edwards' appearances on* M*A*S*H, Taxi, Benson, Blossom, Doogie Houser, Full House, *and many other shows, plus information about each, can be found at www.gailedwards.com.*)

PA Announcement by Todd Sussman

Authors' Notes: As noted by David Pollock, this episode (both parts 1 and 2) was produced in Season 9 and aired as the Season 10 opener. The following two episodes, "Identity Crisis" and "Rumor at the Top," were also produced in Season 9 and broadcast in Season 10 as the second and third episode after "That's Show Biz."
Potterism: "Not a snowball's chance in the South of Hades."
In Chapter 4, Potter claims to have caught Brandy Doyle's act in the Gaiety Theater in Kansas City. There is/was a Gaiety Theater in Boston and two in New York City (at different time periods) and some around the world, including Dublin, Ireland. But Potter's claim of the Gaiety Theater in Kansas City cannot be verified either way.
While performing in Chapter 6, Brandy Doyle swings part of her costume and hits the Post-Op lamp above her.
In Chapter 12, Fast Freddie Nichols mentions "Toast of the Town." *Toast of the Town* was a very popular television variety show hosted by Ed Sullivan. For 23 years, *Toast of the*

Town aired every Sunday night at 8:00 PM on CBS. *The Ed Sullivan Show* became the show's official name on September 25, 1955. Famous performances include Elvis Presley (first appearance September 9, 1956), The Beatles (first appearance February 9, 1964), The Rolling Stones (on January 15, 1967, with Mick Jagger's famous "eye roll," when he changed a line in a song to comply with CBS censors), and The Doors' very controversial and only appearance on September 17, 1967, when the band said they would change a line in their song to comply with CBS censors, and Jim Morrison sang the original line. They were never invited back.

In Chapter 13, Marina Ryan, the troupe member who needed an appendectomy, is playing cards with some of the wounded. Behind her is a white curtain. On the right side of the curtain, a boom shadow appears.

Eleanor "Ellie" Carlyle in Chapter 16 mentions Dvorak and Brahms. Antonin Leopold Dvorak (September 8, 1841-May 1, 1904) was a composer of Czech romantic music and folk dances, and Johannes Brahms (May 7, 1833-April 3, 1907) was a German composer during the Romantic period and Hungarian folk dances.

Hawkeye, in Chapter 20, says "We barred the door, Katie." On February 20, 1437, Catherine (or Kate) Douglas, in an effort to protect King Kames I from assassins, put her arm through the staples of a door to bar entry, but the assassins pushed in, breaking her arm in the process, and killed the King. She then took the surname "Barlass." *The King's Tragedy*, a poem by Dante Gabriel Rossetti, recounts the incident and has the line, "Catherine, keep the door!" which could be the origin of the phrase, "Katy, bar the door," a warning of trouble approaching.

Identity Crisis – 11/2/1981

Season 10 / Episode 221 / Production 221 – Z423

Columbia House VHS Tape . . . . Mistaken Identities (Catalog # 22044)
Fox DVD . . . . Season 10, Disc 1

Alan Alda, Mike Farrell, Harry Morgan
Loretta Swit, David Ogden Stiers, Jamie Farr, William Christopher

Executive Producer – Burt Metcalfe
Produced by John Rappaport
Written by Dan Wilcox & Thad Mumford
Directed by David Ogden Stiers

Executive Script Consultants – Thad Mumford & Dan Wilcox
Executive Story Editor – Dennis Koenig
Creative Consultants – Gene Reynolds / Alan Alda

Dirk Blocker . . . . James Mathes
Squire Fridell. . . . . Alvin Rice
Joe Pantoliano . . . . Gerald Mullen
Jeff Maxwell. . . . . Igor
Kellye Nakahara . . . . Nurse Kellye
Jo Ann Thompson . . . . Nurse
Shari Saba . . . . Nurse
Bill Snider . . . . Driver

Copyright 1981 – 20th Century Fox Film Corporation

Chapters

1: Main Titles
2: A Nobody – 0:55
3: Opportunity Knocks – 3:53
4: Corporal Levin – 6:42
5: Levin's Confession – 8:34
6: The Corporate Corporal – 13:47
7: A Possible Solution – 14:49
8: The Silent Treatment – 17:10
9: Letters from Home – 18:52
10: Healed! / End Titles – 23:06

Closing Stills

1: Freeze – B.J. and Charles
2: Mathes in Post-Op
3: Alvin Rice
4: Mullen in Post-Op
5: Igor and Hawkeye
6: Hawkeye
7: B.J.
8: Potter
9: Margaret
10: Charles
11: Klinger in the office
12: Mulcahy

Synopsis: Among the wounded is a patient suffering from a broken heart, another whose goal is to sell everyone mutual funds and securities, and Corporal Joshua Levin. B.J. thinks a mistake on Levin's dog tags is the reason he's having a bad reaction to a transfusion, but the dog tags are in fact correct. In Post-Op, Levin, who claims to be an Orthodox Jew, asks that a conversation with Father Mulcahy be treated as a confession. Since Levin is not the first non-Catholic to make this request, Mulcahy is not surprised and obliges him. What does surprise him is Levin insisting he wear his stole, and then giving himself the Sign of the Cross before confessing that Joshua Levin, who was scheduled to go home in a couple of weeks, was killed in action, that his real name is Gerald Mullen, and has assumed Levin's identity in order to use his travel orders.

Commentary by Father Frank Toste: "From the first time Gary (Burghoff) called me at the high school where I was teaching, the kids would get all excited when the phone rang, assuming a star was calling. There was always a big rush to answer the phone after that. Well, one day this new kid answered the phone. He returns to the theater and says, 'You ready for this? Some guy on the phone wants to talk to you. He says he's Alan Alda.' All of the other kids were saying things like, 'It is!' 'It IS Alan Alda!' The student had told Alan that I was not to be disturbed when I was directing a production and could he ask who's calling. When he said, 'This is Alan Alda,' my student didn't believe him, and replied, 'Well listen, Pius the 12th is here too, do you want to talk to him?' At the time, I think Alan was calling about an episode where a soldier takes a dead soldier's dog tags to assume his identity. The dead soldier was scheduled to be sent home, and this soldier wanted to take his place. He confesses this to Father Mulcahy. Technically, the soldier was not a Catholic, so it wasn't a valid sacramental confession. The script had Father Mulcahy, the next day, approaching the soldier in the mess tent and saying, 'I would like to talk to you about your confession.' I said, 'No, no, no! A priest cannot do that. He cannot talk about anything heard in confession, outside the confessional.' So, I asked them to revise the scene so that, after hearing his confession, Father Mulcahy says to him, 'May I have your permission to talk to you about this outside of confession?' And this is how it was filmed."

Authors' Notes: There are no PA announcements in this episode.
This is the third episode produced during Season 9 and held for broadcast in Season 10.
In Chapter 5, we learn that Igor met his girlfriend at the slaughterhouse. They worked side by side on the stun line (we hope his wife doesn't find out).
Mulcahy is wearing his brown plaid robe in Chapter 5.
In Chapter 7, Potter mentions his grandson "Skip." However, in Season 7, Episode 167, "Hot Lips is Back in Town," his grandson is "Corey," who weighs 56 pounds and likes to catch bugs and eat them.
Potter mentions Popular Mechanics magazine in Chapter 7. The first issue of the popular magazine was January 11, 1902.
Potterism: "What's buzzin' in your bonnet?"
Also in Chapter 7, *Death of a Salesman* is mentioned. This began as a successful Broadway play and was a feature film in 1951. Four television movies were broadcast in the years 1966, 1985, 1996 and 2000.
In Chapter 9, while reading a letter, Mulcahy mentions "Anna May Wong." Anna May Wong (January 3, 1905-February 2, 1961) was the first Chinese American movie star and the first Asian American international star. *(Note: The reference to Anna May Wong was made while talking about gifts bought in Tokyo, Japan.)*
Joe Pantoliano, born in Hoboken, New Jersey on September 12, 1951, has an extensive list of credits to his name, but is probably best known for his 26 appearances on the HBO hit series *The Sopranos* as Ralph Cifaretto. Other appearances include *Trapper John, M.D., Hill Street Blues, Hart to Hart* and three appearances on *NYPD Blue.*
Mr. Pantoliano has started an organization, "No Kidding, Me Too!" Please visit their web site, *www.nkm2.org* for more information.
"No Kidding, Me Too!" is a nonprofit organization comprised of entertainment industry members united in an effort to educate Americans about the epidemic related to brain disease in all forms. Through this enlightenment we will teach those suffering from it, and their loved ones who are victims of it, to talk about it openly. The goal is to tear this

stigma out of the closet so these people will be surprised to find millions of others like themselves and say, "No Kidding, Me Too!" *(courtesy of www.nkm2.org).*

Rumor at the Top – 11/9/1981

Season 10 / Episode 222 / Production 222 – Z424

Columbia House VHS Tape . . . . Not Released by Columbia House
Fox DVD . . . . Season 10, Disc 1

Alan Alda, Mike Farrell, Harry Morgan
Loretta Swit, David Ogden Stiers, Jamie Farr, William Christopher

Executive Producer – Burt Metcalfe
Produced by John Rappaport
Written by David Pollock & Elias Davis
Directed by Charles S. Dubin

Executive Script Consultants – Thad Mumford & Dan Wilcox
Executive Story Editor – Dennis Koenig
Creative Consultants – Gene Reynolds / Alan Alda

Nicholas Pryor . . . . Major Nathaniel Burnham
Jeff Maxwell . . . . Igor
Roy Goldman . . . . Roy

Copyright 1981 – 20th Century Fox Film Corporation

Non-Credited Appearances . . . . Kellye Nakahara

Chapters

1: Main Titles / A Visitor
2: How Rumors Begin – 3:23
3: Anticipating A Breakup – 5:06
4: An Accessory to A Fabrication – 8:03
5: Major Burnham – 12:59

6: Putting on A Show – 15:10
7: The Missing Patient – 17:07
8: Leaving in A Huff – 18:48
9: The Truth is Revealed – 19:20
10: Father Mulcahy's Portrait /
     End Titles – 22:01

Closing Stills

1: Freeze – Hawkeye and Mulcahy in the office
2: Major Burnham
3: Igor
4: Charles
5: Potter
6: Margaret
7: Klinger
8: Mulcahy
9: B.J. in the shower
10: Hawkeye

Synopsis: When Logistics & Support sends Major Burnham to the 4077th, the staff believes it's for the purpose of recruiting members for a new M*A*S*H. To make sure that doesn't happen, they display behavior that, even for them, is bizarre. Not wanting Potter to go, Margaret and Father Mulcahy make him look like a doddering old man, Hawkeye and B.J. imply that they're having the camp dog for dinner, and Klinger becomes a religious fanatic. However, the reason why Burnham is there isn't what they expected and Colonel Potter is the only one who knows that.

Commentary by David Pollock: "The idea here was that we always thought it was great poking fun at army bureaucracy. We thought it would be funny if you suddenly had no record of a GI on paper. But, they had done something similar. So, we had the doctors 'pretend' to lose the guy on paper. We flipped the idea around. Instead of having the guy vanish, we had the guy vanish on paper."

PA Announcement by Todd Sussman

Authors' Notes: This is the fourth and final episode produced in Season 9 and held for broadcast in Season 10.

In Chapter 1, Potter said that he and General "Torgy" Torgeson came out of the Cavalry together, and then they both went into medical school. Four years later, Potter was a doctor and Torgeson was washed up. However, in Season 9, Episode 215, "Bless You, Hawkeye," Potter said he was in medical school for seven years. In Season 3, Episode 63, "Bombed," Trapper said he was in medical school for 10 years.

The captioning in Chapter 2 does not capitalize the word "Manhattan."

Hawkeye in Chapter 3 is reading a magazine seen in early seasons: Fun.

In Chapter 4, we learn that Henry Blake was already at the 4077th when Margaret and Mulcahy were assigned there.

The sign on Margaret's tent door is in the freehand style. Sometimes it's block lettering.

Klinger's serial number in Chapter 4 is US 19571782 – a far cry from his serial number in Episode 70, Season 3's "Payday," when his number was 36-24-36.

Once again, a nurse is giving a corpsman a haircut on the compound (Stage 9) in Chapter 4. Usually it's Kellye, but this time, while he's getting a haircut, Kellye is giving him a manicure. The barber's tent, along with the barber's pole has been seen in several previous episodes on the Ranch set.

In Chapter 5, Charles mentions "the next Saddler-Pep bout." Gugliermo Papaleo (September 19, 1922-November 23, 2006), better known as Willie Pep, had 229 wins (65 by knockout) and 11 losses, being knocked out six times and one draw, for a total of 241 fights consisting of 2,026 rounds. Joseph "Sandy" Saddler (June 23, 1926-September 18, 2001) had 144 wins (103 by knockout) and 16 losses, being knocked out once and two draws for a total of 162 fights consisting of 929 rounds. The two featherweights squared off four times:

October 29, 1948 at Madison Square Garden. Saddler won the featherweight title with a 4th round knockout.

February 11, 1949 at Madison Square Garden when Pep won his title back with a 15-round unanimous decision. This fight was the Ring Magazine "Fight of the Year," and one of the most brutal matches ever held.

September 8, 1950 at Yankee Stadium when Saddler took the title once again as Pep was unable to answer the bell for the 8th round due to a separated shoulder sustained at the end of Round 7.

September 26, 1951 at the Polo Grounds in New York City. Saddler retains the title when the referee stopped the fight in the 9th Round due to Pep's right eye swelling. This was a very dirty fight involving eye gouging, thumbing, tripping and every other dirty trick they were aware of. Because of the illegal tactics used in this fight, the New York State Athletic Commission briefly suspended both fighters.

The four fights between these two featherweights remain as some of the best and brutal fights in the history of the sport.

The fact that Charles mentions "the next Saddler-Pep fight" means that it's possible that this episode takes place between the September 1950 and September 1951 fights, or even after the 1951 fight. Considering the fact that the series has episodes that place it in all three years of the Korean War, it's difficult to place anything, even with dates.

In Chapter 7, the scrub room sinks are in the middle, side by side.

Also in Chapter 7, B.J. mentions "Dr. Kildare." The first screen appearance of Dr. Kildare was in the 1937 movie *Interns Can't Take Money* starring Joel McCrea as Dr. Kildare. *Dr. Kildare* became a radio series in the early 1950s and a very popular television series from 1961 to 1966 starring Richard Chamberlain in the title role.

The view out of the office windows in Chapter 10 is the Motor Pool Supply seen in many previous episodes.

Father Mulcahy's portrait by Potter appears in this episode in Chapter 10.

Give 'Em Hell, Hawkeye – 11/16/1981

Season 10 / Episode 223 / Production 223 – 1-G01

Columbia House VHS Tape . . . . *Mistaken Identities (Catalog # 22044)*
Fox DVD . . . . *Season 10, Disc 1*

Alan Alda, Mike Farrell, Harry Morgan
Loretta Swit, David Ogden Stiers, Jamie Farr, William Christopher

Executive Producer – Burt Metcalfe
Supervising Producer – John Rappaport
Written by Dennis Koenig
Directed by Charles S. Dubin

Producers – Dan Wilcox / Thad Mumford / Dennis Koenig
Executive Script Consultants – David Pollock & Elias Davis
Story Eidtor – Karen Hall
Creative Consultants – Gene Reynolds / Alan Alda

Stefan Gierasch	Colonel Ditka
Lance Toyoshima	Kim Han
Ed Vasgerian	Captain Broz
John Lavachielli	Young Turk
Xander Berkeley	Marine
Kellye Nakahara	Kellye
Mae Hi	Korean Woman

Copyright 1981 – 20th Century Fox Film Corporation

Non-Credited Appearances. . . . . Roy Goldman, Dennis Troy

Chapters

1: *Main Titles / Truce Talks*	6: *An Epidemic – 10:33*
2: *A Letter to the President – 2:39*	7: *Peace Talks Continue – 13:43*
3: *Colonel Ditka – 3:39*	8: *American Eyes – 15:24*
4: *The Beautification Program – 5:55*	9: *Turks in the Military – 19:55*
5: *Kim Han – 9:14*	10: *The Bedpan Fountain / End Titles – 21:38*

Closing Stills

1: *Freeze – Klinger and the fountain*
2: *Colonel Ditka*
3: *Kim Han (The Korean boy)*
4: *Margaret*
5: *B.J.*
6: *Potter*
7: *Charles in the Officer's Club*
8: *Klinger*
9: *Mulcahy in the Mess Tent*
10: *Hawkeye*

Synopsis: The first anniversary of the truce talks inspires Hawkeye to write another letter to President Harry S. Truman to offer a solution: "Stop the war." Hawkeye also promises President Truman that if he ends "this fiasco," he'll purchase all of his daughter Margaret's recordings, even offering to pick them up on his way home. The 4077th has its own problems to deal with, and needs a higher capacity water heater, a wooden ramp and a bigger O.R. refrigerator. Colonel Ditka is there to discuss the unit's needs and will help them, but they must first implement a beautification program to spruce up the compound. With the supplies on hand, they use green paint to simulate grass and make use of bedpans in a way they've never been used before. A young Korean boy, infatuated with American movies and women, wants B.J. to perform plastic surgery to make his eyes look more American so American women will be attracted to him.

PA Announcement by Todd Sussman

Authors' Notes: In Chapter 1, Hawkeye makes mention of the first anniversary of the peace talks. The peace talks began on July 10, 1951. This clearly places this episode in the summer of 1952, but it doesn't seem to be very hot at the 4077th.

The view from the office windows in Chapter 3 shows a wooden structure, but a different configuration than the previously seen Motor Pool Supply.

Hawkeye, in Chapter 3, says "Better Homes and Hovels." Hawkeye also said this line early in the series.

In Chapter 8, Hawkeye dumps what's left on his food tray in a trashcan, and then dunks the tray in a 55-gallon drum of water before placing it in the tray pile. We've seen, several times, people dumping leftovers in the trash, but this is the first time anyone has ever dunked a tray in water afterward.

In Chapter 9, Charles mentions "Clyde Beatty." Clyde Beatty (June 10, 1905-July 19, 1965) began his circus career as a cage cleaner, then went on to become a very well-known lion tamer and animal trainer. Mr. Beatty's show had merged with the Cole Brothers and became the Clyde Beatty – Cole Brothers Circus.

Charles mentions "Oscar Wilde" in Chapter 9. Oscar Fingal O'Flahertie Wills Wilde (October 16, 1854-November 30, 1900) was an Irish playwright, novelist and poet, who was also one of the most successful playwrights of his time.

Also in Chapter 9, Hawkeye gives his finished letter to Kellye to mail for him. However, in Chapter 10, he continues writing his letter to Harry S. Truman.

Potterism: "Worked harder than a woodpecker in a petrified forest."

Mary Margaret Truman-Daniel (February 17, 1924-January 29, 2008) was the only child of President Harry S. Truman and Bess Truman, had an active singing career, and was also the author of 32 books.

Wheelers and Dealers – 11/23/1981

Season 10 / Episode 224 / Production 224 – 1-G02
Columbia House VHS Tape . . . . Not Released by Columbia House
Fox DVD . . . . Season 10, Disc 1

Alan Alda, Mike Farrell, Harry Morgan
Loretta Swit, David Ogden Stiers, Jamie Farr, William Christopher

Executive Producer – Burt Metcalfe
Supervising Producer – John Rappaport
Written by Thad Mumford & Dan Wilcox
Directed by Charles S. Dubin

Producers – Dan Wilcox / Thad Mumford / Dennis Koenig
Executive Script Consultants – David Pollock & Elias Davis
Story Eidtor – Karen Hall
Creative Consultants – Gene Reynolds / Alan Alda

G.W. Bailey. . . . . .Sergeant Luthor Rizzo
Anthony Charnota. . . . . Sergeant Verbanic
Tony Becker. . . . . Private Brown
Jeff Maxwell. . . . . .Igor
Chris Peterson. . . . . .Second Recruit
Shari Saba . . . . Nurse
Copyright 1981 – 20th Century Fox Film Corporation

Non-Credited Appearances. . . . . .Kellye Nakahara

Chapters

1: Main Titles / Paperwork VS Poker	6: Bluffing – 9:08
2: Money Trouble – 4:25	7: Test Results – 11:25
3: Driving School – 5:50	8: The Gambling Bug – 13:36
4: The Poker Game – 7:33	9: The Hustler – 17:10
5: Sleeping in Class – 7:56	10: The Make-Up Test / End Titles – 19:53

Closing Stills

1: Freeze – Potter on Sophie
2: Rizzo
3: Margaret and Verbanic playing poker
4: Igor
5: Hawkeye
6: B.J.
7: Margaret
8: Charles
9: Klinger
10: Mulcahy
11: Potter

Synopsis: When Peg takes a job as a hostess in the coffee shop she and B.J. used to eat in, B.J. becomes incensed, especially now that she'll be serving their friends. Making matters worse, she took the job to help payoff their second mortgage, due in six months, and B.J. takes out his anger and frustration at being in Korea on anyone crossing his path. Becoming cutthroat in a friendly game of poker to hustling nickels at the pinball machine, B.J. becomes intolerable, until Margaret sets him straight. A speeding ticket results in

Colonel Potter having to take a driving class and, according to the instructor, Sergeant Rizzo, he does something nobody has ever done before: he fails the written exam.

Commentary by Thad Mumford: "I liked how Mike (Farrell) played out the emotions in this one. It reflected the male chauvinism of the times."

Authors' Notes: There are no PA announcements in this episode.

In Chapter 1, Potter says "Promises to keep and piles to go before you sleep." This is a reference to *Stopping by Woods on A Snowy Evening*, a poem by Robert Frost (March 16, 1874-January 29, 1963), written in 1922 and published in 1923. It was Frost's favorite of his poems.

Potter also says, in Chapter 1, "Never put off till tomorrow what you can do today." This quote is attributed to Thomas Jefferson (April 13, 1743-July 4, 1826), the third President of the United States.

Potterism: Sufferin' buffalo chips."

In Chapter 3, Rizzo is in jeep number 18210707. Later, the same jeep is parked in front of the hospital.

Also in Chapter 3, there's a quick microphone shadow on top of Rizzo's hat on the Ranch compound.

At the poker game in Chapter 6, B.J. is using Military Payment Certificates (MPC). While it was certainly possible for B.J. to bet 10 and 20 dollars with MPCs, the ones he has in his hand are the 25¢ denomination, as are the certificates in the pot plus a 50¢ certificate. (And you thought nobody was looking, eh?)

One of the main reasons Military Payment Certificates were originally invented was to prevent having to use large amounts of US dollars overseas. This would prevent legal tender US dollars from ever being captured by the enemy and used against the USA. Following WWII regular MPC notes were issued. Another reason for issuing MPC was that it helped combat black-market activities. A soldier dealing in the black market would be hampered trying to get his ill-gotten gains back home. Only those personnel authorized to have MPC when C-Day, or Conversion Day, rolled around, had the chance to convert their soon to be worthless MPC to the newly issued MPC and retain their value. No notice would be given when a C-Day would come. Bases would be closed, no passes were issued, in essence a lockdown, and on that single day you had to convert your current MPC or risk "losing your money" (see Episode 131, Season 6, "Change Day"). MPC was printed in denominations of 5¢, 10¢, 25¢, 50¢, $1, $5, $10 and $20. Some series do not contain all the denominations. (This information is copyright Brad Peacock and used with permission. For a complete history and breakdown on Military Payment Certificates, or if you are a collector of these historical notes, please visit Brad's web site, www.c-day.com.)

Rizzo's driving lecture in Chapter 5: "The Army Driver: Ambassador with A Clutch."

Hawkeye in Chapter 6 mentions Jujubes and Milk Duds. Jujubes were produced before 1920 and Milk Duds are a circa-1928 creation.

The pinball machine in the Officer's Club in Chapter 9 is a Gottlieb & Company SPOT-A-CARD. Gottlieb & Company, in business from 1931 to 1977, had manufactured two different SPOT-A-CARD pinball machines. The first was manufactured in 1941 and certainly fits in the M*A*S*H timeline. However, that's not the machine in the Officer's Club. The Gottlieb & Company SPOT-A-CARD pinball machine seen in the Officer's Club was made in 1960, seven years after the Korean War ended. The two machines have completely different back glass and playfields.

Also in Chapter 9, Margaret mentions "Diamond Jim." James Buchanan Brady (August 12, 1856-April 13, 1917), was an American businessman, philanthropist and financier and a highly successful salesman for a railroad supply company. Known for liking diamonds and precious stones, Mr. Brady's collection was worth more than $2 million. In today's market, the value of his collection would be approximately $60 million. Diamond Jim is also a biographical film of Mr. Brady from 1935.

Communication Breakdown – 11/30/1981
Season 10 / Episode 225 / Production 225 – 1-G03
Columbia House VHS Tape. . . . . *Mistaken Identities (Catalog # 22044)*
Fox DVD . . . . *Season 10, Disc 1*

Alan Alda, Mike Farrell, Harry Morgan
Loretta Swit, David Ogden Stiers, Jamie Farr, William Christopher

Executive Producer – Burt Metcalfe
Supervising Producer – John Rappaport
Written by Karen Hall
Directed by Alan Alda

Producers – Dan Wilcox / Thad Mumford / Dennis Koenig
Executive Script Consultants – David Pollock & Elias Davis
Story Eidtor – Karen Hall
Creative Consultants – Gene Reynolds / Alan Alda

Byron Chung.	Lieutenant Yook
James Saito	Park
Jeff Maxwell.	Igor
Kwang Ho Paek.	Kim
Kellye Nakahara	Kellye
Roy Goldman	Goldman
Joanne Thompson	Nurse
Abigail Nelson.	Nurse

Copyright 1981 – 20th Century Fox Film Corporation

Non-Credited Appearances. . . . . Dennis Troy, Gwen Farrell

Chapters
1:	Main Titles / No Second Class Mail	6:	My Brother, The Enemy – 12:44
2:	Winchester's Newspapers – 2:26	7:	Tit for Tat – 16:00
3:	A Li'l Abner Update – 5:07	8:	An Unfortunate Error – 19:26
4:	Newspaper Panic – 6:39	9:	The Same Blood – 22:20
5:	Attention, All Vermin – 10:50	10:	A Fine Mess / End Titles – 23:37

Closing Stills
1: *Freeze – Charles and mess tent crashing down*
2: *Lieutenant Yook*
3: *Park*
4: *Patient in Post-Op*
5: *Hawkeye*
6: *B.J.*
7: *Potter on microphone in the office*
8: *Margaret*
9: *Klinger on the microphone in the office*
10: *Mulcahy*
11: *Charles on the microphone in the office*

Synopsis: A newspaper is a precious commodity at the 4077th, and Charles gets a week's worth of the Boston Globe. Promising to make them available to everyone after he reads them first, he discovers one of his newspapers missing. Not only does he change his mind about sharing them, he launches a blistering verbal assault on the entire unit over the PA, and becomes the most hated person in camp. In an act of vengeance, the very unpopular Charles attempts to use a jeep to collapse a packed mess tent, until Potter stops him after learning what happened to the missing newspaper. During the newspaper snafu, Hawkeye learns that the wounded North Korean soldier he operated on is the brother of the South Korean Soldier guarding him, and the two have not seen or spoken to each other for nearly two years. The South Korean brother explains how this came to be and if they're seen talking to each other, the implications could be disastrous.

PA Announcement by Todd Sussman
PA Announcements by Charles and Potter
Potter reads Li'l Abner cartoon strip over the PA

Authors' Notes: Joanne Thompson is credited as a nurse in this episode. However, her name is spelled "Jo Ann" in several previous episodes.

Although the option is available in this episode to turn off the laugh track, by now, many episodes like this one did not feature it. The producers did not favor a laugh track, and would occasionally eliminate it or tone it down to such a degree as it sounded like only two or three people were laughing ... quietly.

Potter's robe in Chapter 1 has the wide red and gray stripes.

Potter, again in Chapter 1, mentions "Li'l Abner," a cartoon strip written and drawn by Alfred Gerald Caplin (September 28, 1909-November 5, 1979), better known as Al Capp. *Lil Abner* ran from 1934 to 1977.

Henry Blake's robe is now being worn by a corpsman in Chapter 1.

In Chapter 2, Charles mentions Joseph Alsop. Joseph Alsop (October 11, 1910-August 28, 1989) was an American journalist and syndicated newspaper columnist from the 1930s to the 1970s.

A corpsman in Chapter 4 mentions Louella Parsons (August 6, 1881-December 9, 1992), a famed gossip columnist.

Here's a switch ... In Chapter 5, Roy Goldman is giving a haircut on the Stage 9 compound. Later in the episode in a scene shot on the Ranch, the barber's pole is seen (actually, a flat board painted with the colored spiral of a barber's pole). More often than not, Kellye was the "compound barber."

Charles calls Klinger "Fur Face" in Chapter 5, but the term is not in the captioning,

In Chapter 4, while everyone in camp congregates around Mulcahy and Charles, there's a woman off to the side standing in front of the post-op doors on the Ranch set wearing a blue shirt standing there with her arms folded and she's alone. While she's also wearing white pants, she appears to be someone other than a member of the 4077th.

The Ranch compound in earlier episodes had the shower times posted on a pole just in front of the showers, but in Chapter 7 in this episode, there are no times posted on the Ranch set.

Also in Chapter 7, Charles mentions the B-29. This fits in the M*A*S*H timeline. The first flight of the B-29 was September 21, 1942 and introduced on May 8, 1944. The B-29 was retired on June 21, 1980, except for those in air-museums.

More often than not, quick shots of the tops of jockey shorts can be seen when someone would enter or leave the showers. But in Chapter 7, when Charles has to "cover up" with newspapers, this time, there really is nothing underneath.

Just before Potter reads the "Lil' Abner" cartoon strip over the PA in Chapter 8, he said that he was going to take a page from that "Fiorello fellow." Fiorello Enrico LaGuardia (December 11, 1882-September 20, 1947) was one of the great and popular Mayors of New York City. First elected in 1934, he served three terms until 1945. Among his many triumphs were his tough stance on issues ranging from organized crime to his massive public works programs, which created jobs for thousands of unemployed New Yorkers. However, one of the things he's best remembered for was reading newspaper comics over WNYC radio during a 1945 newspaper strike.

Snap Judgment – 12/7/1981

Season 10 / Episode 226 / Production 226 – 1-G04

Columbia House VHS Tape . . . . *Not Released by Columbia House*
Fox DVD . . . .*Season 10, Disc 1*

Alan Alda, Mike Farrell, Harry Morgan
Loretta Swit, David Ogden Stiers, Jamie Farr, William Christopher

Executive Producer – Burt Metcalfe
Supervising Producer – John Rappaport
Written by Paul Perlove
Directed by Hy Averback

Producers – Dan Wilcox / Thad Mumford / Dennis Koenig
Executive Script Consultants – David Pollock & Elias Davis
Story Eidtor – Karen Hall
Creative Consultants – Gene Reynolds / Alan Alda

Peter Jurasik. . . . . Captain Alvin Triplett
Richard Winters . . . . M.P. # 1
Micky Jones. . . . . M.P. # 2
Jeff Maxwell. . . . . .Igor
George Chung. . . . . .Peddler # 1
Richard Lee Sung . . . . .Peddler # 2
Monty Bane . . . . M.P. # 3
Eileen Saki . . . . Rosie
Copyright 1981 – 20th Century Fox Film Corporation

Non-Credited Appearances. . . . . Kellye Nakahara, Roy Goldman, Gwen Farrell

Chapters

1: *Main Titles*
2: *Horseshoe Ringers – 0:55*
3: *Developing Arguments – 2:01*
4: *Polaroid Problems – 3:29*
5: *The Stolen Camera Caper – 5:22*

6: *Little Chicago – 10:22*
7: *Under Arrest – 13:13*
8: *Wiseguys for the Prosecution – 14:42*
9: *All Wrapped Up – 18:11*
10: *The Official Recommendation /
End Titles – 23:15*

Closing Stills

1: *Freeze – Klinger*
2: *Triplett*
3: *M.P.'s*
4: *Hawkeye*
5: *Charles*
6: *B.J.*
7: *Margaret*
8: *Potter in the office*
9: *Mulcahy in the mess tent*
10: *Klinger in a jeep*

Synopsis: Grateful for the operation and treatment his son received at the 4077th, a camera storeowner from Illinois sends a Polaroid Land Camera addressed to the "Chief Surgeon." Since Hawkeye and B.J. both operated on the man's son, and after a minor argument, they agree to share the prized possession. All they need to do now is figure out how to use it, but the problem is solved when, during surgery, the camera is stolen from the Swamp. Klinger fills out a report, but an investigation never takes place because instead of sending the paperwork, he sent the carbon paper by mistake. Klinger gets some information on where the camera can be found and after getting it back, he's arrested for possession of stolen property and faces six months of hard labor, a dishonorable discharge and the loss of his vet benefits.

Authors' Notes: There are no PA announcements in this episode.

After a long absence, Hy Averback returns to direct this episode.

From 0:55 until 1:43 in, the picture seems dark, and then brightens.

In Chapter 2, the microphone is visible, for one shot, when the doctors are playing horseshoes.

Also in Chapter 2, Klinger mentions "mukluks." Mukluks, originally worn by the Inuit and Yupik Arctic natives, are a soft boot made of either reindeer or sealskin and were designed for cold weather.

The doctors get a Polaroid camera in Chapter 3. It appears to be either Model 95, 95 A or 95 B. Since the Model 95 was introduced in late 1948, this would fit in the timeline. However, the Model 95 B, which is the same as the Model 95 except for very small modifications, was produced between 1957 and 1961. In this case, we'll give this episode the benefit of the doubt since it's very difficult to tell exactly which model this camera is. *Note: Thanks to Jim Skelton for helping identify the Polaroid camera seen in this episode. Please visit "Jim's Polaroid Camera Collection" at http://www.polaroids.theskeltons. org for a historical timeline of Polaroid cameras with photos and complete details and specs for each listing.*

Hawkeye, in Chapter 3 mentions "David and Sheba's bath." Bathsheba was the wife of Uriah the Hittite and later, King David of the United Kingdom of Israel and Judah. Her son, Solomon, succeeded David as King, according to the Hebrew Bible.

Charles, in Chapter 4, mentions the fact that he has Rolleiflex and Leica cameras. Rolleiflex cameras were introduced circa 1928 and Leica in 1925. Both of these very fine cameras are available today.

In Chapter 4, Potter said he has a Brownie Hawkeye. These cameras, which produced pictures sized 2 ¼" by 2 ¼", were available from May 1949 to July 1961.

In Chapter 4, B.J. mentions Pinky Lee (May 2, 1907-April 3, 1993), whose real name was Pincus Leff. He was the host of a children's television show in the early 1950's, The Pinky Lee Show. Before his television show, he was a burlesque comic and during the 1940s he was heard on several radio programs.

Hawkeye mentions "Kelly Girls" in Chapter 5: this remains one of the best-known temporary staffing agencies since 1946.

Rosie mentions "Gimbels" in Chapter 7. A competitor of Macy*s, Gimbels was in business from 1887 to 1987.

In several episodes, we see various people using jeeps for one reason or another. Often, we'd see a jeep being driven to a destination having one serial number, and on the return trip, a different serial number. Back in Chapter 6, the jeep Klinger uses to get the camera back from "Little Chicago" (possibly a nod to Larry Gelbart since he's originally from Chicago) is number 18210717. Oddly enough in Chapter 7, and as rare as it is, Klinger is driving the same jeep on the return trip to camp.

Klinger identifies a "Lady Benrus" watch that was stolen from him in Chapter 6. Benjamin, Ralph and Oscar Lazrus founded the Benrus Watch Company in 1921. The name Benrus is a combination of Benjamin and Lazrus.

The spirit of Henry Blake lives on. In Chapter 8, Potter is wearing the robe usually worn by Henry.

Charles mentions Crime and Punishment in Chapter 9, a novel by the Russian author, Fyodor Dostoevsky (1866).

Captain Arvin Triplett mentions Champion, the Wonder Horse in Chapter 9. This was a children's television series set in the Old West, airing only 26 episodes from 1955 to 1956, after the Korean War ended.

The view out of the office windows in Chapter 10 is the wooden structure seen several times. But this time, it seems much cleaner and closer than before.

Potter in Chapter 10 mentioned being a buck private digging a trench at Vimy Ridge. The Battle of Vimy Ridge was a Canadian offensive in WWI against the German 6th Army, and took place from April 9 to April 12, 1917. Why would Potter be digging a trench there?

Peter Jurasik has appeared in dozens of movies, plays and television shows, including *Barney Miller, Hill Street Blues, Night Court, Taxi* and *NYPD Blue*. Mr. Jurasik is well known for his portrayal of Londo Mollari in the Emmy Award winning sci-fi series, *Babylon 5*.

Snappier Judgment – 12/14/1981

Season 10 / Episode 227 / Production 227 – 1-G05

Columbia House VHS Tape............... *Not Released by Columbia House*
Fox DVD ....*Season 10, Disc 2*

Alan Alda, Mike Farrell, Harry Morgan
Loretta Swit, David Ogden Stiers, Jamie Farr, William Christopher

Executive Producer – Burt Metcalfe
Supervising Producer – John Rappaport
Written by Paul Perlove
Directed by Hy Averback

Producers – Dan Wilcox / Thad Mumford / Dennis Koenig
Executive Script Consultants – David Pollock & Elias Davis
Story Eidtor – Karen Hall
Creative Consultants – Gene Reynolds / Alan Alda

Peter Hobbs..Colonel Drake
Jack Blessing ....Lieutenant Rollins
Jim Boeke ....M.P.
Monty Bane ....Crooked M.P.

Copyright 1981 – 20th Century Fox Film Corporation

Non-Credited Appearances...........Jeff Maxwell, Kellye Nakahara, Roy Goldman,
Gwen Farrell

Chapters

1: *Main Titles*
2: *When Last We Met – 0:56*
3: *Win with Winchester! – 2:08*
4: *Hot Bibles – 5:25*
5: *Baiting Hooks – 7:49*

6: *On His Side – 10:36*
7: *Better Doctor than Lawyer – 12:13*
8: *Klinger's Darkest Recess – 17:51*
9: *Caught in Sixty Seconds – 18:43*
10: *About those Bibles / End Titles – 23:25*

Closing Stills

1: *Freeze – Mulcahy, Charles, M.P. in the compound*
2: *Colonel Drake*
3: *Prosecutor*
4: *Hawkeye*
5: *B.J.*
6: *Margaret*
7: *Potter in the office*
8: *Mulcahy in the mess tent*
9: *Klinger*
10: *Charles*

Synopsis: With little choice, Klinger agrees to let Charles defend him against the charge of grand theft at a court-martial, where the star witnesses for the prosecution will be Hawkeye and B.J. Under oath, Hawkeye's reluctant testimony serves to make matters worse for Klinger. But his testimony also makes him realize that the rash of thefts is occurring during O.R. sessions, thus giving him an idea designed to catch the real thief. It's not surprising that his plan works, but the identity of the real culprit is, and comes just in time as Klinger is about to be found guilty.

Commentary by Jeff Maxwell: "Hy Averback came from the days of I Love Lucy. He was a comic actor and adored, appreciated and respected funny. And he was a very nice man. He knew what I was doing and let me do it. I went to his house once for advice, and he had little to offer other than to do what I was doing and enjoy it every second. So I did."

PA Announcement by Todd Sussman

Authors' Notes: After a recap of "Snap Judgment," from 2:11 to 2:50 of Chapter 3, the DVD picture is grainy, and then clears up.

The view out of the office windows in Chapter 3 is the same as the previous episode as this is where the story resumes.

Father Mulcahy, in Chapter 4, mentions The Seoul Plaza Hotel. While this is a real hotel located in the heart of Seoul, it first opened its doors in 1976.

In Chapter 9, Klinger mentions Pepsi-Cola, which trademarked the name on June 16, 1903.

'Twas the Day After Christmas – 12/28/1981

Season 10 / Episode 228 / Production 228 – 1-G06

Columbia House VHS Tape..........*Madness and Miracles (Catalog # 22045)*
Fox DVD ....*Season 10, Disc 2*

Alan Alda, Mike Farrell, Harry Morgan
Loretta Swit, David Ogden Stiers, Jamie Farr, William Christopher

Executive Producer – Burt Metcalfe
Supervising Producer – John Rappaport
Written by Elias Davis & David Pollock
Directed by Burt Metcalfe

Producers – Dan Wilcox / Thad Mumford / Dennis Koenig
Executive Script Consultants – David Pollock & Elias Davis
Story Eidtor – Karen Hall
Creative Consultants – Gene Reynolds / Alan Alda

Val Bisoglio ....Sergeant Salvatore Pernelli
Michael Ensign..Major Cass
Leo Lewis .... Sergeant Barnstable
Kellye Nakahara ....Kellye
Jeff Maxwell..Igor
Roy Goldman ....Enlisted Man
Bill Snider...Enlisted Man
Copyright 1981 – 20th Century Fox Film Corporation

Non-Credited Appearances.........................Dennis Troy, Gwen Farrell

Chapters

1: *Main Titles*	6: *Infection – 14:17*
2: *Our Own Boxing Day – 0:54*	7: *Maximizing the Minimums – 15:43*
3: *Colonel for A Day – 6:10*	8: *Private Winchester's Complaint – 18:16*
4: *Chef Winchester – 8:39*	9: *Emergency – 21:09*
5: *How the Other Half Lives – 10:13*	10: *Changed Attitudes / End Titles – 23:20*

Closing Stills

1: *Freeze – Charles, Hawkeye, B.J. in the mess tent*
2: *Sergeant Pernelli*
3: *Major Cass*
4: *Sergeant Barnstable*
5: *Klinger and Kellye*
6: *B.J.*
7: *Margaret*
8: *Charles*
9: *Mulcahy (Previously seen still)*
10: *Potter*
11: *Hawkeye*

Synopsis: In an episode where the lower ranks trade places with higher-ranking officers, Sergeant Pernelli now has someone to command in the kitchen, and Private Winchester is not happy about it. Nurse Kellye is now Major Kellye and in charge of the nursing staff and Corporal Potter's new commanding officer is Colonel Klinger. With the proverbial shoe on the other foot, things run fairly well at the 4077th, until Colonel Klinger finds himself out of his league when an emergency arises and asks for advice from Corporal Sherman T. Potter.

Commentary by David Pollock: "We started with, 'Wouldn't it be a good story to see how you could operate in a snowstorm.' So, here's an example of where we 'backed in' to a story. We started out with the fun aspect, and then built the medical part of the story around it."

Authors' Notes: There are no PA announcements in this episode.

In Chapter 3, as Colonel Klinger is handing out new assignments, he refers to Kellye as "Head Nurse Nakahara."

In Chapter 5, B.J. mentions Michelin taking away a star. Andre Michelin, in 1900, started a guide to France. This guide was to help drivers maintain their cars and find places to rest and eat. The star rating first appeared in 1926 to note good cooking. More stars were added in the 1930s.

Klinger mentions Archie Comics and Walnettos in Chapter 5. Archie's first appearance was in Pep Comics, # 22 in 1941. Walnettos, a walnut-flavored caramel, is from 1919.

Potter mentions Daffy Duck in Chapter 8. The famous cartoon duck's first appearance was in Porky's Duck Hunt from 1937.

Potterism: "Prunes in his poncho."

B.J. in Chapter 9 says "as thin as 3.2 beer." In the U.S., 3.2 beer is considered a non-alcoholic beer containing less than 0.5 % alcohol by volume.

The scrub room makes a return in Chapter 9 and the sinks are in the middle of the room, side by side.

Also in Chapter 9, and for the fourth time in the series, it's snowing.

Follies of the Living
Concerns of the Dead – 1/4/1982

Season 10 / Episode 229 / Production 229 – 1-G07

Columbia House VHS Tape. . . . . *Life Or Death (Catalog # 21034)*
Fox DVD . . . . *Season 10, Disc 2*

Alan Alda, Mike Farrell, Harry Morgan
Loretta Swit, David Ogden Stiers, Jamie Farr, William Christopher

Executive Producer – Burt Metcalfe
Supervising Producer – John Rappaport
Written and Directed by Alan Alda

Producers – Dan Wilcox / Thad Mumford / Dennis Koenig
Executive Script Consultants – David Pollock & Elias Davis
Story Eidtor – Karen Hall
Creative Consultants – Gene Reynolds / Alan Alda

Kario Salem. . . . . Private Jimmy Weston
Randall Patrick . . . . Franklin Hicks
Jeff Tyler . . . . Soldier
Perren Page . . . . Driver
Copyright 1982 – 20th Century Fox Film Corporation

Non-Credited Appearances. . . . . Kellye Nakahara, Gwen Farrell, Dennis Troy,
Roy Goldman

Chapters

1: Main Titles / Klinger's Visions	6: On Being Invisible – 14:52
2: Arriving Casualties – 2:01	7: A Letter – 17:18
3: A Wandering Ghost – 3:05	8: A Toast – 19:27
4: Memories – 8:07	9: Fading Away – 20:51
5: Private Weston's Friend – 10:59	10: Feeling Better / End Titles – 22:39

Closing Stills

1: Freeze – Klinger in bed in Post-Op
2: Private Weston
3: Hicks in Post-Op
4: Hawkeye
5: B.J. in the Swamp
6: Charles
7: Margaret
8: Mulcahy
9: Potter in Post-Op
10: Klinger
11: Hawkeye

Synopsis: As Father Mulcahy administers the Last Rites to Private Weston, his spirit rises from his body and Klinger, with a temperature of nearly 105, is the only one who can see and talk to it. Watching Mulcahy administer his own Last Rites, Weston questions it since he doesn't feel dead. Wandering through the camp and unsuccessful at getting anyone's attention, he observes the process of his personal effects and hears a letter to his parents written by his buddy informing them of his death. As his vision and hearing start to diminish, he realizes that he is indeed dead, and is called to walk with other spirits.

PA Announcement by Sal Viscuso

Authors' Notes: There is no laugh track in the episode.
Some of Klinger's hallucinations are actually quite funny. Slow motion photography was used for a third time, as the spirit of a soldier walks through camp.
In Chapter 3, the tape over the clothing hooks (nails, actually) is, from left to right: *Mulcahy, Potter, B.J., Hawkeye, Winchester.* It also seems that Winchester has two hooks (nails).
The sinks in the scrub room in Chapter 3 are in their usual position: in the middle of the room and side by side.

The Birthday Girls – 1/11/1982

Season 10 / Episode 230 / Production 230 – 1-G08

Columbia House VHS Tape.........*Madness and Miracles (Catalog # 22045)*
Fox DVD ....*Season 10, Disc 2*

Alan Alda, Mike Farrell, Harry Morgan
Loretta Swit, David Ogden Stiers, Jamie Farr, William Christopher

Executive Producer – Burt Metcalfe
Supervising Producer – John Rappaport
Written by Karen Hall
Directed by Charles S. Dubin

Producers – Dan Wilcox / Thad Mumford / Dennis Koenig
Executive Script Consultants – David Pollock & Elias Davis
Story Eidtor – Karen Hall
Creative Consultants – Gene Reynolds / Alan Alda

Jerry Fujikawa .... Lee Seung-Chul, Farmer
Kellye Nakahara .... Lt. Kellye Nakahara

Copyright 1982 – 20th Century Fox Film Corporation

Non-Credited Appearances........................ Roy Goldman, Gwen Farrell

Chapters

1: Main Titles / Going to Tokyo
2: A War Victim – 2:47
3: Change of Plans – 4:05
4: Negotiations – 5:47
5: A Lottery – 7:24
6: To the Plane – 11:23
7: The Lecture – 12:59
8: Jeep Trouble – 14:28
9: A Demonstration – 18:44
10: A Quiet Celebration / End Titles – 20:01

Closing Stills

1: Freeze – Klinger and Margaret in the mess tent
2: Mulcahy and the farmer
3: Kellye
4: Hawkeye
5: B.J.
6: Potter
7: Charles
8: Klinger
9: Mulcahy (still previously seen)
10: Margaret

Synopsis: When a farmer brings his wounded cow for treatment at the 4077th, he tells the doctors she's also pregnant, and Klinger organizes a betting pool for the calf, but Margaret has other plans for Klinger. She convinces Charles to take her place and give a lecture to the nurses, then insists Klinger drive her to Kimpo. Going against Klinger's better judgment, she orders him to take a shortcut and the jeep breaks down. Now stuck at night in the middle of nowhere, Margaret confesses that it's her birthday, and she wanted to spend an evening in Tokyo with a general. Back in camp and after speaking with a veterinarian, the doctors celebrate another birthday by delivering a healthy calf.

Authors' Notes: There are no PA announcements in this episode.
For the second time, Kellye is mentioned by her last name, "Lieutenant Nakahara."

The view from the office windows in Chapter 2 is the same wooden structure previously seen in several episodes of the later seasons. Although the scenery changed from episode to episode in the earlier seasons, sometimes changing in mid-scene, the structure seen in the later seasons has, for the most part, remained in place.

In Chapter 3, a veterinarian, "Dr. Landau," is mentioned. Rarely ever mentioned in the series, there were veterinarians in the Korean War.

Sometimes, the times for showers were listed, usually men from 1600 to 1630 and women from 1630 to 1700. But in Chapter 5 in this episode, the shower tent has no sign indicating times.

Blood and Guts - 1/18/1982

Season 10 / Episode 231 / Production 231 – 1-G09

Columbia House VHS Tape. . . . . *Not Released by Columbia House*
Fox DVD . . . .*Season 10, Disc 2*

Alan Alda, Mike Farrell, Harry Morgan
Loretta Swit, David Ogden Stiers, Jamie Farr, William Christopher

Executive Producer – Burt Metcalfe
Supervising Producer – John Rappaport
Written by Lee H. Grant
Directed by Charles S. Dubin

Producers – Dan Wilcox / Thad Mumford / Dennis Koenig
Executive Script Consultants – David Pollock & Elias Davis
Story Eidtor – Karen Hall
Creative Consultants – Gene Reynolds / Alan Alda

Gene Davis . . . . Clayton Kibbee
Bret Cullen . . . . Thomas Anthony McKegney
Rita Wilson. . . . . .Lieutenant Nurse Lacey

Copyright 1982 – 20th Century Fox Film Corporation

Non-Credited Appearances. . . . . Kellye Nakahara, Roy Goldman, Dennis Troy

Chapters

1: *Main Titles / Waiting for Kibbee*	6: *Hawkeye is Incensed – 13:23*
2: *Meeting A Legend – 3:08*	7: *A Bike Ride – 16:30*
3: *B.J. Gets A Bike – 5:06*	8: *Clay's Complaint – 18:36*
4: *The Ladie's Man – 9:23*	9: *The Missing Motorbike – 19:39*
5: *Poetic License – 11:35*	10: *The Truth / End Titles – 23:31*

Closing Stills

1: *Freeze – B.J. and Hawkeye in the mess tent*
2: *Clayton Kibbee*
3: *McKegney in Post-Op*
4: *Nurse Lacey*
5: *B.J. in Post-Op*
6: *Potter*
7: *Margaret*
8: *Charles*
9: *Klinger in the office*
10: *Mulcahy*
11: *Hawkeye*

Synopsis: Clayton Kibbee, a well-known journalist, comes to the 4077th to write about the recipients of blood donated by his readers. Everyone in camp is anxious to meet the famous newspaperman, who's covered everything from Louis/Walcott boxing matches to Saber Jets during the war. When Hawkeye finds out that a nurse he wants to spend time with has plans with Kibbee instead, Hawkeye becomes annoyed. He becomes downright angry when, listening to Kibbee phone in a story, embellishments are added to make the story more exciting, even though none of it happened that way. Even B.J. becomes angry with the gruff journalist when, after repairing a motorcycle, a drunken Clayton Kibbee takes the bike for a ride, has an accident with it, and then lands on a pile of broken glass that Hawkeye has to remove from his rear.

Commentary by Jeff Maxwell: "If Roy (Goldman) hadn't been quite so intimidated by the camera, I would be auditioning for a part on his show."

Authors' Notes: There are no PA announcements in this episode.

Klinger mentions "Brilliantine" in Chapter 1. This was a hair grooming product by Ed Pinaud, circa 1900.

Klinger also mentions "Beau Brummelness" and Andy Varipapa in Chapter 1. George Bryan Brummell (June 7, 1778-March 30, 1840) was an authority on men's fashion in Regency, England. Andy Varipapa (March 31, 1891-August 25, 1984) was a world-famous professional and trick bowler. Mr. Varipapa was famous for, among other bowling tricks, converting 7-10 splits with a ball in each hand simultaneously and a "boomerang" ball. Rolled slowly, the ball would come back to him.

Clayton Kibbee arrives in jeep number 18210707 in Chapter 1. Later, in Chapter 3, that same jeep arrives from the front with a different driver.

Klinger in Chapter 3 mentions Indian Motorcycles. Indian, Harley Davidson and Triumph produced motorcycles for the military during both World Wars and Korea, and were made to Pentagon specifications. Harley Davidson alone produced 90,000 motorcycles for WWII.

In Chapter 4, Kibbee mentions covering the first Joe Louis (May 13, 1914-April 12, 1981) – Jersey Joe Walcott (January 31, 1914-February 25, 1994) fight, which took place in 1947 at Yankee Stadium in New York City. Walcott knocked down Louis twice, but lost a disputed decision. They had a rematch in 1948, also at Yankee Stadium, and Walcott again knocked down Louis. Joe Louis won the fight after knocking out Walcott in the 11th round.

Note: In a total of 72 fights, Joe "The Brown Bomber" Louis' record was 69 wins (55 by knockout) and three losses. His defeat of Max Schmeling in a rematch in 1938 is one of the most famous boxing matches ever, held in Yankee Stadium before a crowd of more than 73,000 and broadcast over the radio around the world. Mr. Louis served in WWII and was one of the most popular boxers in history. When he died in 1981, President Reagan waived the eligibility rules for burial in Arlington National Cemetery and on April 21, 1981, Joe Louis was buried there with full military honors. In 1982, he was awarded the Congressional Gold Medal, the highest award given by the U.S. Legislative branch. Congress stated that he "did so much to bolster the spirit of the American people during one of the most crucial times in American history and which have endured throughout the years as a symbol of strength for the nation."

In Chapter 5, Kibbee mentions "Sabre jets." The F-86 Sabre, although developed in the 1940s, was adaptable and used during the Korean War and were very successful against the Russian built MiGs. The first swept-wing airplane in the U.S. fighter inventory, the F-86 scored consistent victories over Russian-built MiG fighters during the Korean War, accounting for a final ratio of 10-to-1. All 39 United Nations jet aces won their laurels in Sabres.

Boy's Life was mentioned in Chapter 5. First published by George S. Barton in 1911, this was a Boy Scouts of America publication.

A Holy Mess – 2/1/1982

Season 10 / Episode 232 / Production 232 – 1-G10

Columbia House VHS Tape. . . . .*Madness and Miracles (Catalog # 22045)*
Fox DVD . . . .*Season 10, Disc 2*

Alan Alda, Mike Farrell, Harry Morgan
Loretta Swit, David Ogden Stiers, Jamie Farr, William Christopher

Executive Producer – Burt Metcalfe
Supervising Producer – John Rappaport
Written by David Pollock and Elias Davis
Directed by Burt Metcalfe

Producers – Dan Wilcox / Thad Mumford / Dennis Koenig
Executive Script Consultants – David Pollock & Elias Davis
Story Editor – Karen Hall
Creative Consultants – Gene Reynolds / Alan Alda

Cyril O'Reilly . . . . Private Nick Gillis
David Graf . . . . Lieutenant Spears
Val Bisoglio . . . . Sergeant Sal Pernelli
Roy Goldman . . . . Goldman
Ed Ramirez . . . . .Wounded G.I.
Bill Snider . . . . G.I.
Dennis Troy. . . . . G.I.
Leland Sun . . . . G.I.
Kip Curtis . . . . G.I.

Copyright 1982 – 20th Century Fox Film Corporation

Non-Credited Appearances. .Kellye Nakahara, Jennifer Davis

Chapters

1: *Main Titles*
2: *The Best News Possible – 0:55*
3: *Remembering Eggs – 2:33*
4: *Private Nick Gillis – 4:57*
5: *Sunday Morning – 7:44*

6: *Sanctuary – 13:44*
7: *Benefit of the Doubt – 15:42*
8: *Demanding Brunch – 18:22*
9: *Father Mulcahy's Good Deed – 21:09*
10: *Powdered Eggs / End Titles – 23:06*

Closing Stills

1: *Freeze – Hawkeye, Mulcahy, B.J. in the mess tent*
2: *Nick Gillis*
3: *Sergeant Pernelli, the cook*
4: *Lieutenant Spears*
5: *Hawkeye*
6: *Potter*
7: *Margaret*
8: *Charles*
9: *B.J.*
10: *Klinger*
11: *Mulcahy*

Synopsis: Private Nick Gillis walks off the line and right into the 4077th's mess tent, but his troubles go deeper than just being AWOL. While having a drink in the Swamp,

Gillis tells of a letter congratulating him on the birth of his child. But Gillis has been in Korea over a year, his wife had never mentioned anything about this in her letters and he desperately wants to get home. When Lieutenant Spears finds him attending Father Mulcahy's services and wants to take him back to his unit, Gillis asks for and receives sanctuary. I-Corps however, doesn't recognize the mess tent as a proper facility for a church and subsequently denies Gillis' request. When Lieutenant Spears tries to take Gillis back, Gillis holds his rifle on Mulcahy. While this is happening, the rest of the camp prepares for a rare treat: Real eggs. As a way of thanking local G.I.'s after saving his farm, a farmer donates an entire day's production of eggs, but they won't necessarily make it to anyone's tray.

Commentary by David Pollock: "During one interview we did, a *M*A*S*H* surgeon went on and on about some operation he performed. Suddenly, after this long description, he said he remembered that day because they got a shipment of eggs. That's what we picked up on for our story."

Authors' Notes: There are no PA announcements in this episode.

Although real eggs were a rare treat in this episode, there were several earlier episodes where real eggs weren't a problem. Real eggs were used to throw at Radar and other times used as part of a practical joke on Frank Burns. Frank even applied for a Purple Heart when an "egg shell" fragment wounded him, and Charles had real hard-boiled eggs for lunch.

Potter mentions "Argosy" in Chapter 5. The Golden Argosy started as a general information magazine first published on December 2, 1882 and aimed for the "boys adventure" demographic. The first issue was eight pages and cost five cents.

David Graf (April 16, 1950-April 7, 2001) was probably best known as Cadet, then Sergeant Eugene Tackleberry in the *Police Academy* movies. Mr. Graf also appeared in *Star Trek Voyager, Star Trek Deep Space Nine* and *The West Wing.* While attending a family wedding in Arizona, Mr. Graf died of a heart attack only nine days short of his 51st birthday. His father and great grandfather also died of sudden heart attacks at the age of 51. Graf is survived by his wife and two sons.

The Tooth Shall Set You Free – 2/8/1982

Season 10 / Episode 233 / Production 233 – 1-G11

Columbia House VHS Tape . . . . *Letting Loose (Catalog # 21040)*
Fox DVD . . . . *Season 10, Disc 2*

Alan Alda, Mike Farrell, Harry Morgan
Loretta Swit, David Ogden Stiers, Jamie Farr, William Christopher

Executive Producer – Burt Metcalfe
Supervising Producer – John Rappaport
Written by David Pollock and Elias Davis
Directed by Charles S. Dubin

Producers – Dan Wilcox / Thad Mumford / Dennis Koenig
Executive Script Consultants – David Pollock & Elias Davis
Story Eidtor – Karen Hall
Creative Consultants – Gene Reynolds / Alan Alda

Tom Atkins	Major Weems
Jason Bernard	Major Rockingham
Larry Fishburne	Corporal Dorsey
Bill Snider	Corpsman
Kellye Nakahara	Kellye
John Fujioka	Duc Phon Jong

Copyright 1982 – 20th Century Fox Film Corporation

Chapters

1:	Main Titles / Night Operations	6:	Incoming Wounded – 10:26
2:	Toothache Remedy – 3:22	7:	Alternative Medicine – 11:19
3:	Inspection – 5:24	8:	Questioning Weems – 16:38
4:	Self Medication – 6:57	9:	The Bigot – 19:08
5:	Corporal Dorsey – 8:32	10:	The Dentist / End Titles – 23:09

Closing Stills

1: *Freeze – Rockingham, Charles and Hawkeye*
2: *Weems in the mess tent*
3: *Rockingham*
4: *Corporal Dorsey*
5: *Hawkeye*
6: *Potter in the mess tent*
7: *Margaret*
8: *Klinger on the phone.*
9: *Mulcahy in the mess tent*
10: *B.J.*
11: *Charles*

Synopsis: Major Weems wants one of his wounded men to be shipped home, even though he's not seriously wounded, citing reasons of hardship. When Hawkeye talks to the man, he gets a completely different story. More wounded arrive from Weem's unit and when the doctors realize they're all black, they become suspicious and do a little research. Only 11% of Weem's unit is black but they make up 46 % of the unit's casualties. Weems wants them out of his unit and sends them out on dangerous missions, even if it means getting them killed. When Potter cleverly gets Weems to admit he does not want blacks in his unit, they introduce him to Quentin Rockingham, a black Major who offers Weems a choice: Court-Martial or resigning his commission. Major Rockingham also has a surprise for Charles, when, suffering with a toothache and refusing to see a dentist, Potter brings a dentist to Charles: Captain Quentin Rockingham, DDS.

Commentary by Tom Atkins: "I had a wonderful time shooting my single episode of *M*A*S*H*. The episode was titled 'The Tooth Shall Set You Free,' at least that's what I think I see on my little residuals that come, from time to time. And, they get littler each time. My episode, or at least the part I was in, was shot entirely on the sound stage at 20th Century Fox. I made no trips to the exterior at the ranch. Gary was gone from the show by the time I appeared, but I had a great time working with Alan Alda, Harry Morgan and Mike Farrell. I played this wonderfully bigoted artillery officer who commanded a company of almost entirely black men, and I purposely put them in harm's way to get them wounded or killed and out of the company. A despicable guy, and a joy to play. I remember a scene outside a tent with Alan and Harry. In the rehearsal break, I told a story and Alan said, 'Oh, that's a great line. Put that in the scene.' And, I did. Something about burnt toast. They were all terrific to work with; the regulars, and all at the top of their game, not at all jaded or ho hum about any of it. And this was their ninth year. I was given a coffee mug, which says on the side '*M*A*S*H*, The 9th Great Year.' Now, it may have been sitting around from the year before, so maybe it was actually the 10th Great Year I was on, I'm not sure. I do know, these many years later, I still have a cup of tea in the mug on cold winter days. I also remember, at the time, that David Ogden Stiers and myself had the same agent. I remember her telling me, one day, that David had been offered a recurring role on *M*A*S*H*, but that it had been running four or five years so it probably wouldn't tie him up for long. I think he was happily tied up for seven more years."

Commentary by David Pollock: "It was only years later that we made the connection that it was Lawrence Fishburne in this episode. He wasn't a big star back then."

PA Announcement by Todd Sussman

Author's Notes: In Chapter 1, Potter is wearing his wide-stripped gray and red robe. Sometimes he wears a heavy dark green robe, at other times, Henry Blake's robe.

Potterism: "A twinge in your tusk?"

Hawkeye, in Chapter 7, mentions *Uncle Tom's Cabin,* also known as "Life Among the Lowly," written by Harriet Beecher Stowe in 1852.

In Chapter 9, Potter says the Civil War was nearly a hundred years ago. The American Civil War, or The War Between the States, was in effect from 1861-1865.

Pressure Points – 2/15/1982

Season 10 / Episode 234 / Production 234 – 1-G12

Columbia House VHS Tape . . . . Not Released by Columbia House

Fox DVD . . . . Season 10, Disc 3

Alan Alda, Mike Farrell, Harry Morgan
Loretta Swit, David Ogden Stiers, Jamie Farr, William Christopher

Executive Producer – Burt Metcalfe
Supervising Producer – John Rappaport
Written by David Pollock and Elias Davis
Directed by Charles S. Dubin

Producers – Dan Wilcox / Thad Mumford / Dennis Koenig
Executive Script Consultants – David Pollock & Elias Davis
Story Eidtor – Karen Hall
Creative Consultants – Gene Reynolds / Alan Alda

Allen Arbus . . . . Dr. Sidney Freedman
John O'Connell . . . . Captain Schnelker
Gene Pietragallo . . . . Corporal Fisher
William Rogers . . . . Corporal Logan
Roy Goldman . . . . Goldman

Copyright 1982 – 20th Century Fox Film Corporation

Non-Credited Appearances. . . . . .Kellye Nakahara, Jennifer Davis

Chapters

1: Main Titles
2: Good Catch – 0:53
3: Second-Hand Surgeon – 3:18
4: Fall's New Weapons Line – 4:29
5: Summoning Sidney – 5:44

6: On the Edge – 7:53
7: Room Service – 13:40
8: The Colonel's Concerns – 17:10
9: What He Does Best – 22:45
10: I'm A Surgeon / End Titles – 23:22

Closing Stills

1: Freeze – Potter shaves Charles (with Sidney and Hawkeye)
2: Sidney
3: Captain Schnelker
4: Charles
5: Hawkeye
6: B.J.
7: Margaret
8: Mulcahy (Still previously seen)
9: Klinger
10: Potter

Synopsis: When Colonel Potter returns from the 8063rd, he learns that Hawkeye had to operate on one of his patients because he missed a piece of shrapnel the first time. While attending a meeting in the office to bring the medical staff up to date on new and improved enemy weaponry, Potter first loses his cool with the medical staff, and then yells at the visiting captain who's informing them of the new technology. Potter confides in Sidney Freedman that he's worried about losing his ability to perform surgery, and that's the only kind of doctor he ever wanted to be. But Potter isn't the only one to "let off steam" as the doctors in the Swamp begin trashing each other's property while the camp looks on.

Authors' Notes: The view out of the office windows in Chapter 4 has remained fairly consistent in the later seasons as the same wooden structure is seen.

In Chapter 8, Potter says, "DiMaggio just hung up # 5." Joe DiMaggio (November 25, 1914-March 8, 1999), "The Yankee Clipper," was one of the greatest baseball players of all-time. He spent his entire 13-year career with the New York Yankees, was a nine-time world champion, three-time American League M.V.P. and played in 11 All-Star games. Between May 15 and July 16, 1941, DiMaggio set a Major League-record 56 consecutive game hitting streak, a record that still stands today and one that will be very difficult to break. During what has become known simply as "The Streak," DiMaggio, during those 56 games, had a batting average of .409. Starting his Major League career with the Yankees on May 3, 1936, he played his last game on September 30, 1951. In 1952, the Yankees retired his number 5 and in 1955 was inducted into the Baseball Hall of Fame.

Where There's A Will, There's A War – 2/22/1982

Season 10 / Episode 235 / Production 235 – 1-G13

Columbia House VHS Tape......... Last Will & Testament (Catalog # 22046)

Fox DVD ....Season 10, Disc 3

Alan Alda, Mike Farrell, Harry Morgan
Loretta Swit, David Ogden Stiers, Jamie Farr, William Christopher

Executive Producer – Burt Metcalfe
Supervising Producer – John Rappaport
Written by David Pollock and Elias Davis
Directed by Alan Alda

Producers – Dan Wilcox / Thad Mumford / Dennis Koenig
Executive Script Consultants – David Pollock & Elias Davis
Story Eidtor – Karen Hall
Creative Consultants – Gene Reynolds / Alan Alda

Dennis Howard	Captain Rackley
Larry Ward	General Kratzer
Jim Borelli	The G.I.
James Emery	The Corpsman
Jeff Maxwell	Igor
Kellye Nakahara	Kellye
Brian Fuld	G.I.
Ned Bellamy	G.I.
Dennis Flood	Driver
Tom Valentino	G.I.
Corkey Ford	G.I.

Copyright 1982 – 20th Century Fox Film Corporation

Chapters

1:	Main Titles	6:	To Margaret Houlihan – 11:14
2:	The Front Lines – 0:53	7:	To Sherman Potter – 15:04
3:	The Will – 3:02	8:	To Maxwell Q. Klinger – 19:06
4:	To Charles Emerson Winchester, III – 6:44	9:	To Erin Hunnicut – 21:27
5:	To Father Francis Mulcahy – 9:01	10:	Glad You're Back / End Titles – 23:23

Closing Stills

1: Freeze – Charles and Hawkeye in the Swamp
2: Captain Rackley
3: General Kratzer
4: B.J.
5: Potter
6: Mulcahy
7: Margaret
8: Charles
9: Klinger
10: Hawkeye

Synopsis: B.J. returns to the 4077th after getting a haircut and a manicure, only to discover Hawkeye was sent to a battalion aid station in his place. Once there, he learns that
the previous surgeon was killed by mortar fire and now finds himself under heavy shelling.
Caught up with the wounded but still under fire, Hawkeye takes cover and starts making

out his last will and testament. In this Humanitas Award-winning episode, flashbacks help Hawkeye decide what to leave his friends at the 4077th, but has a difficult time trying to decide what to leave his best friend, B.J. He finally decides to leave something, not to B.J., but something very special to Erin Hunnicutt.

Commentary by David Pollock: "We won our first Humanitas Award for this one. People seemed to like this one. It was a variation of the Dear Dad letters that Gelbart started."

PA Announcement by Todd Sussman

Authors' Notes: Charles in Chapter 2 mentions "Pork Chop Hill." As in earlier episodes, Pork Chop Hill places this episode in the spring and summer of 1953. In the previous episode, "Pressure Points," Potter mentions Joe DiMaggio "just hung up # 5," placing "Pressure Points" towards the later part of 1951.

Also in Chapter 2, a not-often-seen photograph of Peg bathing Erin Hunnicutt is seen in the Swamp.

Hawkeye wills a copy, given to him by his father, of The Last of the Mohicans to Potter. In Episode 59, Season 3's "Adam's Ribs," Hawkeye mentioned that The Last of the Mohicans was the only book his father ever read. At the time, however, it had not yet been established that the senior Mr. Pierce was a doctor. Now that we know he is indeed a doctor, Hawkeye mentions that The Last of the Mohicans was his favorite book.

In Chapter 8, Klinger gives Hawkeye an issue of Life magazine with a photo spread of Muscongus Bay in Maine. The title of the spread is "The Shores of Maine. Aerial Pictures Display Its Rocky Beauty. Photographed for Life by Laurence Lowry."

It has been determined that this issue of Life is from August 4, 1952 and cost, at the time, 20 cents. This particular issue of Life has another connection with *M*A*S*H* because on the cover is Democratic Presidential Nominee Adlai Stevenson, third cousin of McLean Stevenson, "Lovable Colonel Henry Blake." McLean, or "Mac" as he was known, was Adlai's press secretary for both of his 1952 and 1956 presidential campaigns.

Promotion Commotion – 3/1/1982

Season 10 / Episode 236 / Production 236 – 1-G14

Columbia House VHS Tape . . . . Not Released by Columbia House
Fox DVD . . . . Season 10, Disc 3

Alan Alda, Mike Farrell, Harry Morgan
Loretta Swit, David Ogden Stiers, Jamie Farr, William Christopher

Executive Producer – Burt Metcalfe
Supervising Producer – John Rappaport
Written by Dennis Koenig
Directed by Charles S. Dubin

Producers – Dan Wilcox / Thad Mumford / Dennis Koenig
Executive Script Consultants – David Pollock & Elias Davis
Story Eidtor – Karen Hall
Creative Consultants – Gene Reynolds / Alan Alda

G.W. Bailey. . . . . .Sergeant Luthor Rizzo
John Matuszak . . . . Corporal Elmo Hitalski
Deborah Harmon . . . . Nurse Webster
Jim Reid Boyce . . . . .Danielson
Richard Fullerton . . . . Soldier
Cameron Dye . . . . Soldier
Jeff Maxwell. . . . . .Igor
Kellye Nakahara . . . . .Kellye
Roy Goldman . . . . Corpsman
Bill Snider . . . . .Corpsman # 2

Copyright 1982 – 20th Century Fox Film Corporation

Chapters

1:	Main Titles	6:	Standing on His Principles – 9:14
2:	Chairman of the Board – 0:54	7:	Name, Rank and Phone Number – 12:25
3:	Promotion Kiss-Ups – 2:51	8:	Next Stop, E.O.D. – 14:55
4:	Bedside Professional – 6:25	9:	Hitalski's Promotion – 16:10
5:	An Unveiled Threat – 7:54	10:	Lonely at the Top / End Titles – 23:28

Closing Stills

1: Freeze – B.J. and Hawkeye on chow line
2: Rizzo
3: Charles and Hitalski
4: G.I. in Post-Op
5: Potter
6: Igor
7: B.J. in the Swamp
8: Margaret
9: Klinger
10: Mulcahy
11: Hawkeye in the Swamp
12: Charles in the Officer's Club

Synopsis: Word gets out that Hawkeye and B.J. are on the promotions board, and people start behaving differently, not knowing what to do first to please them. But as chairman, it's Charles who is threatened by Elmo Hitalski, a six-foot, eight-inch, 280 pound corporal whose father, an Army career man, wants to know why he hasn't made sergeant yet. Even if Hawkeye and B.J. agree to recommend Hitalski for a promotion, the corporal's history and arrest record would not be overlooked by I-Corps. As the board quizzes candidates for promotion, Igor and Rizzo prove less than promising, while Klinger impresses them. When the promotion list finally comes out, some are disappointed, others are ecstatic, and one very large and very angry corporal hunts down Charles. Not everyone is concerned with promotions as Potter befriends Danielson, a young soldier in Post-Op whose father died when he was a baby and who is razzed by others in his outfit.

Authors' Notes: There are no PA announcements in this episode.

In Chapter 6, when asked if he has any children, Potter says he has one daughter. In Episode 87, Season 4's "Mail Call, Again," Potter mentions his son, the dentist who was born at City General in 1926. Next season (Season 11) in episode 251, "Strange Bedfellows," Potter mentions his daughter, Evie.

Igor is called "Private Straminsky" in Chapter 7. This is the second time "Straminsky" in mentioned.

In Post-Op, Danielson mentions being "razzed" by others in his unit, who are now with him in Post-Op. They trick him into playing poker in Chapter 8 with a deck of cards depicting nude women. When Danielson sees the cards, he gets angry, throws the cards down and says, "very funny." However, when he says "very funny," there is no lip or mouth movement.

Also in Chapter 8, Corporal Maxwell Q. Klinger has been promoted to Sergeant.

John Matuszak (October 25, 1950-June 17, 1989), a 6' 8" defensive end for the Oakland Raiders of the National Football League, was a 1973 first round draft pick and the #1 pick. Going by the nickname "Tooz," under which he wrote his autobiography, he was also known for the role of "Sloth" in the 1985 movie Goonies. Mr. Matuszak died of heart failure allegedly due to the use of anabolic steroids.

Heroes – 3/15/1982

Season 10 / Episode 237 / Production 237 – 1-G15
Columbia House VHS Tape . . . . *Letting Loose (Catalog # 21040)*
Fox DVD . . . . *Season 10, Disc 3*

Alan Alda, Mike Farrell, Harry Morgan
Loretta Swit, David Ogden Stiers, Jamie Farr, William Christopher

Executive Producer – Burt Metcalfe
Supervising Producer – John Rappaport
Written by Thad Mumford & Dan Wilcox
Directed by Nell Cox

Producers – Dan Wilcox / Thad Mumford / Dennis Koenig
Executive Script Consultants – David Pollock & Elias Davis
Story Eidtor – Karen Hall
Creative Consultants – Gene Reynolds / Alan Alda

Earl Boen . . . . Major Robert Hatch
Pat McNamara . . . . Gentleman Joe Cavanaugh
Gerard Castillo . . . . Reporter
Jay Gerber . . . . Reporter
Matthew Faison . . . . Bill Stitzel
Britt Leach . . . . Dan Blevik
Al Rossi . . . . Reporter
Tierre Turner . . . . Patient
Hennen Chambers . . . . Patient
Eddie Frescas . . . . Patient
David Orr . . . . Patient
Richard Cummings . . . . Soldier
Copyright 1982 – 20th Century Fox Film Corporation

Non-Credited Appearances . . . . Dennis Troy/ Roy Goldman, Kellye Nakahara,
Joann Thompson

Chapters

1: *Main Titles*
2: *Special Announcement – 0:55*
3: *"Gentleman" Joe Cavanaugh – 3:06*
4: *Steak Dinner – 6:41*
5: *Big News Around These Parts – 9:33*
6: *The Press Corp. – 11:59*
7: *The Price of Fame – 14:15*
8: *Saying Goodbye to A Hero – 16:25*
9: *Homemade Defibrillator – 19:47*
10: *Memo / End Titles – 23:24*

Closing Stills
1: *Freeze – Klinger and Potter in the office*
2: *Major Hatch*
3: *Potter, Cavanaugh and Mulcahy*
4: *B.J. in the shower*
5: *Potter*
6: *Margaret*
7: *Charles*
8: *Klinger*
9: *Mulcahy*
10: *Hawkeye*

Synopsis: Nobody is more excited than Father Mulcahy after learning that Gentleman Joe Cavanaugh is coming to the 4077th. Now a restaurant owner in Hollywood, Cavanaugh, the undefeated middleweight champion for nine years, is on a good will tour of medical units in Korea to meet the wounded. Somewhat gruff and demanding of the Army Information Officer assigned to schedule the champ's appearances, his presence in Post-Op is a welcome respite. During a banquet in Cavanaugh's honor, complete with T-bone steaks for everyone, the former champ gets up to say a few words and suffers a severe stroke. When word gets out, a busload of reporters from the press train in Munsan arrive and Hawkeye, who is treating Cavanaugh, is thrust into the spotlight to report that Cavanaugh's chances are not good. Neither are the chances for B.J.'s patient when his heart starts fibrillating during surgery, until Klinger builds an experimental device from a magazine B.J. has in the Swamp.

PA Announcement by Todd Sussman

Authors' Notes: Margaret in Chapter 2 mentions "Joe Palooka," a comic strip by Ham Fisher that debuted on April 19, 1930.

The view has changed out of the office windows in Chapter 2 to a different looking wooden structure.

In Chapter 3, jeep number 18210717 is now "Cavanaugh's Caravan," transporting the champ around.

Also in Chapter 3, Cavanaugh mentions "Bugs Bunny." The famous cartoon rabbit made his first appearance in A Wild Hare in 1940 (the USA release was The Wild Hare). The voice of Bugs Bunny, as well as several other well-known voices, was the equally famous Mel Blanc (May 30, 1908-July 10, 1989) who first did Bugs' voice in 1940 and continued through hundreds of other Bugs cartoons until shortly before his death in 1989.

Cavanaugh also mentions, in Chapter 3, "Billy Soose," who held the world middleweight title in 1941. Mr. Soose (August 2, 1915-September 5, 1998) adorned the cover of The Ring Magazine for June 1941. His professional career record is 34 wins (13 by knockout), six losses and one draw for a total of 312 rounds. Billy Soose never defended the title, and retired in 1942 after losing to Jimmy Bivens.

Potter mentions Theda Bara in Chapter 4. Born Theodosia Burr Goodman (July 29, 1885-April 13, 1955), Bara was one of the most popular silent film stars and one of the earliest sex symbols.

Potter also mentions George Jessel in Chapter 4. Jessel (April 3, 1898-May 23, 1981) was an actor, singer, songwriter and an Academy Award-winning movie producer.

Potter is wearing Henry Blake's robe in Chapter 5.

Hawkeye tells the press that he attended Absorbine Jr. College in Chapter 6. "Absorbine" is a natural formula of herbs and oils used for treating lame and overworked horses. In 1892, Wilbur F. Young and his wife Mary developed the formula and named it "Absorbine Veterinary Liniment." As the product continued gaining popularity, it was soon realized that it also relieved muscle pain in farmers, and Mr. Young developed Absorbine Jr. specifically for humans. This product, still in use today, remains one of the most popular pain relievers.

When B.J.'s patient's heart begins to fibrillate in Chapter 9, he sends Klinger to the Swamp for a magazine, which shows a defibrillator and how to build one. Somehow, all the necessary parts happen to be in camp and a defibrillator is built and used successfully on the patient. In previous episodes, devices were used and proper credit was given to the inventor of the device, such as Dr. Owen Wangensteen. But in this episode, "Heroes," it seems as if credit is given to B.J. for inventing this machine and its successful operation. In spite of the fact that Hawkeye knows the design and plans for the defibrillator were obtained from a magazine, he tells a reporter that B.J. invented it. However, the inventor of the defibrillator was not B.J. Hunnicutt, but Doctor Claude S. Beck (1894-1971), a cardiac surgeon. In 1947, Dr. Beck had been operating on a 14-year-old boy who went into cardiac arrest when his chest was being closed. Dr. Beck reopened the chest, hand-massaged the boy's heart for 45 minutes before using the defibrillator, which he designed and then was built by James Rand, a friend of the surgeon. Dr. Beck applied the paddles to the boy's heart and successfully brought the heart out of fibrillation. The 14-year-old boy had made a full recovery. Doctor Claude S. Beck retired in 1965 and suffered a fatal stroke in 1971.

Potterism: "Great logs of limburger."

Sons and Bowlers – 3/22/1982
Season 10 / Episode 238 / Production 238 – 1-G16
Columbia House VHS Tape . . . . Not Released by Columbia House
Fox DVD . . . . Season 10, Disc 3

Alan Alda, Mike Farrell, Harry Morgan
Loretta Swit, David Ogden Stiers, Jamie Farr, William Christopher

Executive Producer – Burt Metcalfe
Supervising Producer – John Rappaport
Written by Elias Davis & David Pollock
Directed by Hy Averback

Producers – Dan Wilcox / Thad Mumford / Dennis Koenig
Executive Script Consultants – David Pollock & Elias Davis
Story Editor – Karen Hall
Creative Consultants – Gene Reynolds / Alan Alda
Dick O'Neill . . . . Colonel Pitts USMC
William Lucking . . . . Sergeant Marty Urbancic USMC
Roger Hampton . . . . The Second Marine
Kellye Nakahara . . . . Kellye
Copyright 1982 – 20th Century Fox Film Corporation

Non-Credited Appearances . . . . Roy Goldman

Chapters

1:	Main Titles	6:	Pre-Game Jitters – 10:33
2:	Sore Losers – 0:34	7:	A Father vs A Dad – 12:19
3:	Important Phone Call – 2:25	8:	The Bowling Tournament – 15:26
4:	Where Did You Learn to Bowl? – 5:35	9:	Happy Endings – 20:40
5:	Bad News – 6:46	10:	Victory Party / End Titles – 23:25

Closing Stills
1: Freeze – Charles and Hawkeye toasting each other in the Officer's Club
2: Colonel Pitts
3: Marty Urbancic
4: Kellye and Margaret in the Officer's Club
5: Potter in the Officer's Club
6: B.J.
7: Klinger
8: Mulcahy
9: Hawkeye
10: Margaret

Synopsis: Tired of consistently losing to the Marines, Potter needs to find an event they can win, and bowling might just be the one. Since Margaret is the reason they lost the softball game, Potter rejects her as the fourth member of the bowling team. However, when Klinger learns the Marines have a ringer, Potter calls on Margaret's talents as a woman to keep the man busy. Insulted at first, she reconsiders and with the help of Methylene Blue, Marty Urbancic, after teaching Margaret how to bowl while filling up on beer, sees colors in the latrine he's not accustomed to seeing, causing the ringer to be rung. Hawkeye has a different problem. After getting a letter from his father written two weeks ago to tell him he needs an operation, Hawkeye places a call to the hospital back home. Learning of his father's condition leads him to think the worst, and finds comfort and support from an unlikely source: Charles.

Commentary by David Pollock: "Here, we had some fun pointing out the lunacy of the army, in trying to get a bowling alley to a unit. The idea of having guys delivering a bowling alley and getting pinned down by the enemy was absurd to us. We always had the 'Methylene Blue' idea and decided to plug it in to this episode. It preceded the bowling idea, sort of the tail wagging the dog."

PA Announcement by Todd Sussman

Authors' Notes: This is Episode 238, and the first in which the closing theme is used for the opening. Although the same song, it's a faster tempo and a slightly different arrangement. The standard opening is usually 53 seconds. By using the faster closing theme for the opening and editing out the clip of B.J. and Hawkeye doing triage on the chopper pad now makes the opening 33 seconds, thus extending the show by 20 seconds. One possible reason for using this device would be to prevent something conducive to the story line from being edited out.

For the fourth and final time on *M*A*S*H*, slow motion photography is used as Margaret tosses the bowling ball.

In Chapter 3, Klinger mentions "Methylene Blue," which is used to treat urinary tract infections and as a diagnostic tool because of its blue staining properties. One of the side effects of Methylene Blue causes urine, stools and skin to turn a green-blue color. However, it's to be expected and will disappear when the medication is stopped.

For the first time, in Chapter 5, we learn the senior Doctor Pierce's name is Daniel.

Picture This – 4/5/1982

Season 10 / Episode 239 / Production 239 – 1-G17
Columbia House VHS Tape . . . . *Not Released by Columbia House*
Fox DVD . . . . *Season 10, Disc 3*

Alan Alda, Mike Farrell, Harry Morgan
Loretta Swit, David Ogden Stiers, Jamie Farr, William Christopher

Executive Producer – Burt Metcalfe
Supervising Producer – John Rappaport
Written by Karen Hall
Directed by Burt Metcalfe

Producers – Dan Wilcox / Thad Mumford / Dennis Koenig
Executive Script Consultants – David Pollock & Elias Davis
Story Eidtor – Karen Hall
Creative Consultants – Gene Reynolds / Alan Alda
Jeff Maxwell. . . . . .Igor
John Fujioka . . . . .Peasant
Copyright 1982 – 20th Century Fox Film Corporation

Non-Credited Appearances. . . . . .Kellye Nakahara

Chapters

1: *Main Titles*	6: *A Portrait in Pieces – 11:46*
2: *Stolen Goods – 0:34*	7: *Bodies, But No Souls – 14:53*
3: *The Colonel's Gift – 4:24*	8: *The Go-Betweens – 15:34*
4: *Pierce Move Out – 6:56*	9: *Staying for Good – 20:16*
5: *Kind of Lonely – 8:58*	10: *Tuning Out / End Titles – 23:25*

Closing Stills

1: *Freeze – Hawkeye, B.J. and Charles in the Swamp*
2: *Igor*
3: *B.J. in the Swamp*
4: *Charles in the Swamp*
5: *Potter painting*
6: *Margaret*
7: *Klinger*
8: *Mulcahy*
9: *Hawkeye*

Synopsis: Hawkeye becomes enraged when he finds his last pair of socks, pilfered from his footlocker, on B.J.'s feet. Complaining about privacy, he moves out of the Swamp to a nearby shack. The bickering continues between Charles and B.J. over music and Erin Hunnicut's toilet training is making things difficult for Potter. The Colonel wants to paint a portrait of the staff as a birthday present for Mrs. Potter, but getting everyone to cooperate at the same time is no easy task. Potter finds a solution by having the staff pose, two at a time, and the staff finds a solution to get Hawkeye to move back into the Swamp. However, both solutions are met with limited success.

Authors' Notes: There are no PA announcements in this episode.
This is the second consecutive episode in which the closing theme is used for the opening. Although the same song, it's a faster tempo and a slightly different arrangement.

The standard opening is usually 53 seconds. By using the faster closing theme for the opening and editing out the clip of B.J. and Hawkeye doing triage on the chopper pad now makes the opening 33 seconds, thus extending the show by 20 seconds. One possible reason for using this device would be to prevent something conducive to the story line from being edited out.

Potterism: "Hot hushpuppies."

When Colonel Potter took command of the 4077th, he told Radar that the photo of Mrs. Potter (actually, the photo is of then Mrs. Harry Morgan) always goes on the right side of his desk. In this episode, it would seem the Colonel has rearranged his desk. The photo of Mrs. Potter is now on the left side of his desk and a different photo (unidentified) is on the right. Both photos are aligned on an angle aimed towards the middle so when Potter is sitting at his desk, he can see both photos. While Potter tries to paint the staff, one scene has the right-side photo aimed towards the middle of the desk, but when the scene cuts away and cuts back, the photo is in a different position.

In Chapter 4, and for the second time, Hawkeye moves out of the Swamp, this time, renting an "apartment" for $8.00 a month.

It's increasingly difficult trying to keep up with the Potters. In Episode 87, Season 4's "Mail Call, Again," weighing in at 8 ½ pounds, born on the 23rd, was Sherry Pershing Potter, his granddaughter. In Episode 143, Season 6's "Mail Call, Three," Mildred had sent poorly taken photographs of his grandson, Corey. In this episode, "Picture This," Potter mentions his grandson having his first pony ride. Remembering his anniversary would seem to be the least of his concerns.

That Darn Kid – 4/12/1982

Season 10 / Episode 240 / Production 241 – 1-G19

Columbia House VHS Tape........Last Will and Testament (Catalog # 22046)
Fox DVD ....Season 10, Disc 3

Alan Alda, Mike Farrell, Harry Morgan
Loretta Swit, David Ogden Stiers, Jamie Farr, William Christopher

Executive Producer – Burt Metcalfe
Supervising Producer – John Rappaport
Written by Karen Hall
Directed by David Ogden Stiers

Producers – Dan Wilcox / Thad Mumford / Dennis Koenig
Executive Script Consultants – David Pollock & Elias Davis
Story Eidtor – Karen Hall
Creative Consultants – Gene Reynolds / Alan Alda

G.W. Bailey...Sergeant Luthor Rizzo
John P. Ryan ....Major Van Zandt
Richard Lee Sung ....The Farmer, Peddler
Kellye Nakahara ....Kellye
Tom Kindle..The G.I.
Copyright 1982 – 20th Century Fox Film Corporation

Non-Credited Appearances.........................Dennis Troy, Roy Goldman

Chapters

1: Main Titles
2: The Fuller Junk Man – 0:55
3: Paymaster Pierce – 3:27
4: Getting His Goat – 5:31
5: Simple Compound Interest – 7:58

6: The Noose Before the Gavel – 11:32
7: The Bank of Rizzo – 15:17
8: A Goat of A Chance – 17:36
9: Butting Heads – 21:03
10: A Vicious Cycle / End Titles – 22:34

Closing Stills

1: Freeze – Rizzo and Charles at the Officer's Club bar
2: Rizzo
3: Major Van Zandt
4: The Farmer
5: Charles
6: Potter
7: Margaret in the Officer's Club
8: B.J. in the Swamp
9: Mulcahy (Still previously seen)
10: Klinger in the Officer's Club
11: Hawkeye in the Swamp

Synopsis: The first time Hawkeye was paymaster almost landed him in the stockade over a $3,000 discrepancy. This time as paymaster, the experience could follow him for the duration of his military service and well into his civilian life when Klinger's goat eats over $22,000 in yet-to-be-distributed pay. Without any conclusive proof, Hawkeye's earnings could be garnished until every penny is paid back to the United States Army, no matter how long that might take. But a few of the enlisted were paid before wounded arrived and Rizzo is more than happy to lend Charles $50 for a vase he thinks is hundreds of years old and worth a lot more than $50. Since Rizzo is a "friend," he offers Charles a $50 loan with a moderate interest rate of 100 % compounded daily. Charles accepts Rizzo's generous offer, a decision he will come to regret.

PA Announcement by Todd Sussman
PA Announcement by Hawkeye

Authors' Notes: In Chapter 3, Potter said that the combination to the company safe is Mildred's measurements and nobody will know this information. However, in Episode 85, Season 4's "Soldier of the Month," it was revealed that the combination and Mildred's measurements are 42-36-42.

Potter, in Chapter 4, is wearing his red wide-stripped robe.

Appendix – Season 10

Character Profiles

Hawkeye

Episode 226: Golf clubs were stolen.
Scratches his initials, "B.F.P." in the Polaroid camera that also belongs to B.J.

234: Magazine *Sun Worshipper's Monthly.*

235: Likes fishing, but hasn't done any in a long time.
Once caught a "Blue Fin" [tuna] but it took over an hour to land it.
He and his father mostly fished for salmon in the Saint Croix River — biggest catch was a 30-pounder.
According to B.J. Hawkeye uses vertical mattress stitches with white cotton sutures.

238: When he was 10, his father made breakfast — a bowl of Corn Flakes — told Hawkeye his mother wasn't feeling well, but it was nothing. When he made scrambled eggs and bacon, his mother was in the hospital and there was nothing to worry about. By the time his father made French toast and sausages, his mother was gone.

B.J.

Episode 224: Peg sent rum cookies
Peg took a job as a hostess at Papaneck's Coffee Shop to help pay the second mortgage, which is due in six months. Peg and BJ used to eat there, now she'll be waiting on their friends.
Peg put BJ through medical school.
Ned Gradinger — "All American Hero" from Stanford got a medical deferment signed by Dr. Ned Gradinger Sr.
B.J. turned down a medical deferment.

232: Likes his eggs fried up (Sunnyside up)

238: Had the third highest average in his bowling league, but it was a while ago.

239: Electricity went off while Peg was at work — the ice cream melted all over everything in the freezer and had to throw out everything. She did manage to save the pork chops.
Manager of a restaurant brought Erin a big chocolate milkshake to celebrate her having to "go potty." Erin was so excited about it that she wet herself on the way home.

Colonel Potter

Episode 221: Bought 25 shares of Security Fidelity from Corporal Alvin Rice of Whedon, Webber and Dunsmuir for his grandson, Skip *(see Episode 221, page 655 for information on Potter's grandson).*
Has never locked a door and he's not going to start in Korea.
Has a picture of himself alongside his new barbecue at home that he built himself with complete plans taken from an old *Popular Mechanics* magazine.
Barbecue tilts to the left and told Mildred that it keeps smoke away from the house — uses toothpicks to keep burgers from sliding off.
After grandson Skip sampled candied yams, Mildred had to change her blouse.

222: Potter and General "Torgy" Torgeson came out of the Cavalry together, then both went to medical school. Four years later, Potter was a doctor and Torgeson was washed up *(in Episode 215, Potter said he was in medical school for 7 years. In Episode 34, "The Sniper," Frank said it took twice as long to become a doctor because he flunked out of two medical schools, but no mention of how many years were needed in medical school to become a doctor. In Episode 63, "Bombed," Trapper said he was in medical school for 10 years).*

223: Once had a C.O. who made them shine the soles of their boots.

224: Two more payments and the DuMont is theirs.
Grandma Mavis.
Mildred's sister uses a walker and can go faster than 15 MPH *(reference to his speeding ticket).*
Emma Potter — The Colonel's mother.

225: Went 19 Saturdays during WW I without an *[Saturday] Evening Post.*

226: Only Mildred could "whup" him in horseshoes.
He and Mildred were on Heavenly Hill *(many locations claim the name of Heavenly Hill).*
Said he was a buck private digging a trench at Vimy Ridge. The Battle of Vimy Ridge was a Canadian offensive in WW I against the German 6th Army, and took place from April 9 to April 12, 1917. *(Why would Potter be digging a trench there?)*

228: Spent the winter of '44 in the Ardennes.

231: Mildred likes Cesar Romero. Cesar Julio Romero Jr. was a film and TV actor known for playing the Joker on *Batman* (February 15, 1907-January 1, 1994).

232: Mildred clipped a recipe from *Argosy (see Episode 232, page 680 for information on Argosy magazine).*

234: 62 years old.
In Hannibal, Missouri, he had an uncle Roy who was a veterinarian and took Potter on rounds with him. He operated on a colicky horse and from that point forward, the only kind of doctor he ever wanted to be was a surgeon.
At the Kiwanis picnic, he used to put the beer in the creek to keep it cold.

235: Was in "Gay Paree" when the Armistice was signed for WWI in 1918 and celebrated in an "all-night establishment."
As a fisherman, standing hip-deep in a freezing river might've been the best training he ever had for standing for long periods at O.R. tables.

236: Like to go fly-casting for trout in the White River in Arkansas.
Ties his own flies.

239: Got Mildred fleece lined mukluks for her last birthday.

Mildred is not too fond of watercolor landscapes when she can open the drapes and see the real thing.

Grandson had his first pony ride *(see Episode 239, page 695 for details On Potter's Grandchildren).*

Margaret

Episode 221: Bought 60 shares of Security Fidelity from Corporal Alvin Rice of Whedon, Webber and Dunsmuir.

222: According to Margaret, Henry Blake was already at the 4077th when she and Father Mulcahy were assigned there.

Once met General Torgeson at a meeting.

230: As an "army brat," Margaret never went to the same school two years in a row. She would make new friends and have to move out again.

Charles

Episode 225: Sister Honoria sent a week's worth of the *Boston Globe* parcel post.

Reads one and only one newspaper per day; can take an hour or two.

Bought a "lovely" kimono in Tokyo for his sister.

238: At the evening meal, the Winchesters would have intimate discussions. Every night at 7:15 all would gather at the dinner table. During soup, his father would say, "Tell us what you did today, Charles."

240: Once took an elective course in Oriental art.

Klinger

Episode 221: Cousin Num-Num — has photo of her in her roller derby uniform taken the day she was voted, "Miss Hell On Wheels."

In grade school, Num-Num was a bouncer in the cafeteria.

Has "great" action shots of his grandmother's bowling team.

226: Identifies a "Lady Benrus" watch that was stolen from him at "Little Chicago" because it says Max Klinger on the back.

227: Uncle Harry — The best whiplash man in Toledo, but is tied up right now for 10 years to life.

Files rectal thermometer invoice under "Business Equipment."

229: Develops a temperature of 104.5

Uncle Yusef stole melons — grandmother knows — she read the future in dust balls under the bed.

Passes a kidney stone.

230: Cousin Adeeb.

Once in the same grade two years in a row.

213: Got an autographed copy of Andy Varipapa's biography, *Life Is A 7-10 Split.*

236: Sergeant Maxwell Q. Klinger.

Is the second most successful member of the Klinger family behind Hassan, the Enforcer.

Father Mulcahy

Episode 221: Saw *The Jazz Singer (See Seen, Heard, Mentioned or Referenced for Season 10, Episode 216, page 703).*

225: Only vice is curiosity.

229: Had a "sweetheart" in school — Patricia Duggan — no matter where she sat, at 12, he was the "spin the bottle champ" and could put just the right amount of English on the bottle to make it point to her. She has six kids now.

237: Had met Gentleman Joe Cavanaugh 20 years earlier after his fight with
Galligan at the Convention Hall in Philadelphia. He stuck his head in
the car window and waved.
Had two heroes growing up: Gentleman Joe Cavanaugh and Plato.
He was small growing up and wore thick glasses. At 12, his father
dragged him to his first fight, Gentleman Joe vs. Tony Giovanetti.

Seen, Heard, Mentioned or Referenced – Season 10

Movies
Episode 216: Mulcahy saw *The Jazz Singer* (1927, 1952, 1980).
    217: B.J. mentions "Dr. Kildare." The first Dr. Kildare movie, *Interns Can't Take Money,* debuted in 1937.
    223: Fox MovieTone News reel.
    Margaret says "You just put your lips together and blow," a line from *To Have and Have Not* with Humphrey Bogart and Lauren Bacall (1944).
    224: Klinger mentions the O.K. Corral, probably best known from *My Darling Clementine* (1946) and other films of the famous gunfight.
    Mulcahy mentions, during a poker game in the Swamp, that he once saw Joel McCrea do what B.J. just did with regard to gambling. This could be a reference to the movie *Gambling Lady* (1934), with Barbara Stanwyck and Joel McCrea.
    232: Mulcahy mentions *Samson and Delilah* (1922, 1949, 1984, 1996).
    Mulcahy mentions *Mr. Belvedere Goes to College* (1949).
    B.J. combines those two movies: "Samson and Mr. Belvedere Go to Delilah."
    233: Hawkeye mentions "Gone with the Weems," a reference to *Gone with the Wind* (1939).
    Hawkeye mentions "Yank in Korea" – reference to *A Yank in Korea* (1951, a borderline reference in the *M*A*S*H* timeline).
    234: B.J. mentions "Stanley Kowalski" – a character in the Tennessee. William's 1947 play *A Streetcar Named Desire,* and a 1951 movie.
    237: Hawkeye mentions *Francis, the Talking Mule* featured in a series of movies beginning in 1950.
    238: B.J. mentions *Blues in the Night* (1941). See "Songs," Episode 238 (page 705) for details.

Songs
Episode 219: "Cuddle Up A Little Closer, Lovely Mine" *(Gwen Verdon, as Brandy*
and 220: Doyle sings) Words by Otto Harbach, music by Karl Hoschna. Published in 1908, from the Broadway musical, *The Three Twins.*
    "Sweet Molly Malone" *(Karen Landry, as Sarah Miller plays guitar and sings)* An Irish folk song published by Francis brothers and Day in 1884.
    "Shuffle Off to Buffalo" *(Hawkeye says "Shuffle off, Buffalo")* See Episode 98 (page 399) for details.
    "Swan Lake" *(Hawkeye mentions)* Written by Pyotr Ilyich Tchaikovsky in 1875-76.
    "The Star Spangled Banner" *(Hawkeye says "Since dawn's early light…")* The national Anthem of The United States, written by Francis Scott Key in 1814.
    222: "Got A Date with an Angel" *(Hawkeye sings)* Words by Clifford Gray & Sonny Miller, music by Jack Waller & Joseph Tunbridge (1931).
    223: "Old Man River" *(Klinger says "Lift that shovel, tote that hoe…")* See Episode 139 (page 470) for details. *(Note: This is the second time Klinger has referenced this song.)*
    224: "Shave and A Haircut, Two Bits" *(Hawkeye says "Shave and a haircut, three times" and "Shave and a haircut, two bits.")* See Episode 163 (page 531) for details.

"Matilda" *(Hawkeye sings)* Recorded circa 1930 by Norman Span, also known as King Radio, later recorded by Harry Belafonte in 1953. Written by Harry Thomas (sometimes, additional people are given writing credit, including Mr. Belafonte). *(Note: There is also a song called "Waltzing Matilda," referred to as the unofficial national anthem of Australia and written by Banjo Paterson in 1895. This song has its own museum, The Waltzing Matilda Centre, located in Winton, Queensland.)*

225: "Pictures at an Exhibition" *(Charles hums)* Written by Russian composer Modest Petrovich Mussorgsky (1839-1881). This well-known piano piece describes paintings in sound. The piece was performed and recorded live by British rock group Emerson, Lake and Palmer for their 1971 album of the same name (which made it even more famous).

226: "You Ought to be in Pictures" *(Klinger sings "You ought to be in pictures, you're beautiful to see...")* See Episode 102 (page 399) for details.
"Chattanooga Choo-Choo" *(instrumental heard in Rosie's)* See Episode 1 (page 128) for details.

227: "1812 Overture." *(B.J. mentions)* See Episode 154 (page 530) for details.
"(I'd Like to Get You On A) Slow Boat to China" *(Hawkeye sings "I'm gonna get you on a slow boat to China...")* Written by Frank Loesser and published in 1947.
"Chattanooga Choo-Choo" *(instrumental heard in Rosie's)* See Episode 1 (page 128) for details.

228: "Jingle Bells" *(All sing in the mess tent)* See Episode 12 (page 129) for details.
"We Wish You A Merry Christmas" A 16th Century English carol, and one of the few that mentions the New Year.
"Hey Diddle Diddle" (also "Hi Diddle Diddle") *(B.J. says "Cow jumped over the moon...")* A reference to the English nursery rhyme of the same name.
"Gloria in Excelsis Deo" *(Mulcahy sings)* Latin for Glory to G-d in the highest. An Angelic hymn, the name is sometimes shortened to "Gloria in Excelsis" or just "Gloria."

230: Charles is listening to Mussorgsky in the Swamp (an airy piano piece). Charles mentions the Beethoven Emperor Piano Concerto and likes the Schnabel performance of 1932 better than the 1947 performance. *(Note: Popularly referred to as the Emperor Concerto, it's actually The Piano Concerto No. 5 in E flat major, and was Beethoven's last piano concerto.)* The piece was written between 1809 and 1811 in Vienna.

231: "Over There" *(Clayton Kibbee sings "I won't be back till it's over, over there.")* See Episode 185 (page 593) for details.

232: "The Doxology" *(Mulcahy sings "Praise God from whom all blessing flow."* Written by Thomas Ken, a priest in the Church of England, in 1674.

234: "Along the Santa Fe Trail" *("When the moon is burning brightly along the Santa Fe Trail..." plays on Potter's record player)* Words by Al Dubin & Edwina Coolidge, music by Wilhelm (Will) Grosz, 1940 .
"Tumbling Tumbleweeds" *(Also on Potter's record player, he sings along)* Written by Bob Nolan and released circa 1934.

236: "Begin the Beguine" *(Klinger attempts to play on the accordion)* Written by Cole Porter and introduced by June Knight in the 1935 Broadway musical *Jubilee.*

238: "Marines Hymn" *("If the Army and the Navy ever look on Heaven's scene, they will find the streets guarded by U.S. Marines..." sung by the Marines in the Officer's Club.)* See Episode 185 (page 593) for details.

"Happy Days are Here Again" *(Father Mulcahy plays on piano in the Officer's Club.)* See Episode 1 (page 128) for details.

"Blues In the Night" *(B.J. mentions)* From the movie of the same name. Words by Johnny Mercer, music by Harold Arlen, 1941.

239: "Me and My Shadow" *(Hawkeye sings, "Me and my shadow strolling down the avenue...")* Words by Billy Rose and Al Jolson, music by Dave Dreyer, 1927.

Appearances – Season 10

Arbus, Allan .... Episode 234 *(Dr. Sidney Freedman)*
Atkins, Tom .... Episode 233 *(Major Weems 358th Combat Engineers)*
Bailey, G.W. ....Episode 224, 236, 240 *(Sergeant Luthor Rizzo)*
Bane, Monte...Episode 226 *(M.P. 3)*
Bane, Monte.. Episode 227 *(Crooked M.P.)*
Becker, Tony...Episode 224 *(Private Brown)*
Bellamy, Ned ....Episode 235 *(G.I.)*
Berkeley, Xander .... Episode 223 *(Marine)*
Bernard, Jason .... Episode 233 *(Major – Captain Quenten Rockingham, DDS)*
Bisoglio, Val.. Episode 228, 232 *(Sergeant Salvatore Pernelli)*
Blessing, Jack.. Episode 227 *(Lieutenant Rollins)*
Blocker, Dirk .... Episode 221 *(James Mathes)*
Boeke, Jim .... Episode 227 *(M.P.)*
Boen, Earl .... Episode 237 *(Major Robert Hatch)*
Borelli, Jim .... Episode 235 *(The G.I.)*
Boyce, Jim Reid.. Episode 236 *(Danielson)*
Byers, Bryan .... Episode 219 & 220 *(Patient)*
Castillo, Gerard...Episode 237 *(Reporter)*
Chambers, Hennen..Episode 237 *(Patient)*
Charnota, Anthony.................................... Episode 224 *(Sergeant Charnota)*
Chung, Byron.. Episode 225 *(Lieutenant Yook)*
Chung, George ....Episode 226 *(Peddler #1)*
Cullen, Bret... Episode 231 *(Thomas Anthony McKegney)*
Cummings, Richard... Episode 237 *(Soldier)*
Curtis, Kip ....Episode 232 *(G.I.)*
Davis, Gene..Episode 231 *(Clayton Kibbee)*
Dawson, Freddie .... Episode 219 & 220 *(Patient)*
Dayton, Danny................................ Episode 219 & 220 (Fast Freddy Nichols)
Dye, Cameron .... Episode 236 *(Soldier)*
Edwards, Gail... Episode 219 & 220 *(Marina Ryan)*
Emory, James ....Episode 235 *(The Corpsman)*
Ensign, Michael.. Episode 228 *(Major Cass)*
Faison, Matthew .... Episode 237 *(Bill Stitzel)*
Fishburn, Larry .... Episode 233 *(Corporal Dorsey)*
Flood, Dennis .... Episode 235 *(Driver)*
Ford, Corkey ....Episode 235 *(G.I.)*
Frescas, Eddie ....Episode 237 *(Patient)*
Fridell, Squire.. Episode 221 *(Corporal Alvin Rice)*
Fujikawa, Jerry.................................... Episode 230 *(Lee Seung-Chul, the farmer)*
Fujioka, John .... Episode 233 *(Duc Phon Jong)*
Fujioka, John .... Episode 239 *(Peasant, "Real Estate Broker")*
Fullerton, Richard .... Episode 236 *(Soldier)*
Fuld, Brian ....Episode 235 *(G.I.)*
Gerber, Jay..Episode 237 *(Reporter)*
Gierasch, Stefan ....Episode 223 *(Colonel Ditka)*
Goldman, Roy... Episode 222, 234 *(Roy)*
Goldman, Roy.. Episode 225, 232 *(Goldman)*
Goldman, Roy...Episode 228 *(Enlisted man)*
Goldman, Roy... Episode 236 *(Corpsman)*
Graf, David ....Episode 232 *(Lieutenant Spears)*
Hampton, Roger ....Episode 238 *(The 2nd Marine)*

Broadcast/Production Order – Season 10

Broadcast	Production
219: That's Show Biz, Part 1 *(10/26/1981)* *	*223: (1-G01)* Give 'Em Hell, Hawkeye
220: That's Show Biz, Part 2 *(10/26/1981)* *	*224: (1-G02)* Wheelers And Dealers
221: Identity Crisis *(11/2/1981)* *	*225: (1-G03)* Communication Breakdown
222: Rumor At The Top *(11/9/1981)* *	*226: (1-G04)* Snap Judgment
223: Give 'Em Hell, Hawkeye	*227: (1-G05)* Snappier Judgment
(11/16/1981)	
224: Wheelers And Dealers *(11/23/1981)*	*228: (1-G06)* 'Twas The Day After Xmas
225: Communication Breakdown	*229: (1-G07)* Follies of the Living –
(11/30/1981)	Concerns of the Dead
226: Snap Judgment *(12/7/1981)*	*230: (1-G08)* The Birthday Girls
227: Snappier Judgment *(12/14/1981)*	*231: (1-G09)* Blood And Guts
228: Twas The Day After Christmas	*232: (1-G10)* A Holy Mess
(12/28/1981)	
229: Follies of the Living –	*233: (1-G11)* The Tooth Shall Set You
Concers of the Dead *(1/4/1982)*	Free
230: The Birthday Girls *(1/11/1982)*	*234: (1-G12)* Pressure Points
231: Blood And Guts *(1/18/1982)*	*235: (1-G13)* Where There's a Will,
	There's a War
232: A Holy Mess *(2/1/1982)*	*236: (1-G14)* Promotion Commotion
233: The Tooth Shall Set You Free	*237: (1-G15)* Heroes
(2/8/1982)	
234: Pressure Points *(2/15/1982)*	*238: (1-G16)* Sons And Bowlers
235: Where There's a Will, There's a War	*239: (1-G17)* Picture This
(2/22/1982)	
236: Promotion Commotion *(3/1/1982)*	*240: (1-G18)* Who Knew? *
237: Heroes *(3/15/1982)*	*241: (1-G19)* That Darn Kid
238: Sons And Bowlers *(3/22/1982)*	*242: (1-G20)* The Moon Is Not Blue †
239: Picture This *(4/5/1982)*	*243: (1-G21)* Hey, Look Me Over †
240: THat Darn Kid *(4/12/1982)*	*244: (1-G22)* Foreign Affairs †
	245: (1-G23) Settling Debts †
	246: (1-G24) The Joker Is Wild †

Episodes 219, 220, 221 and 222 were produced during Season 9, but held over for broadcast in Season 10.

†*Although produced during Season 10, 1-G18, 1-G20, 1-G21, 1-G22, 1-G23, and 1-G24 were held over and broadcast in Season 11.*

Season 11

There was great anticipation for Season 11 of *M*A*S*H*, as people from the show and audiences alike knew this was the final season. There are fans of the early years of *M*A*S*H*, fans of the middle years, fans of the later years, and fans of all the seasons. Whatever the season or the preference, it's all part of *M*A*S*H* history. Nurse Kellye finally gets the spotlight in Season 11's "Hey Look Me Over." There's homage to practical jokes in "The Joker's Wild" and there is even a Halloween episode, "Trick or Treatment." Then, there's "As Time Goes By." This half-hour installment was the last episode to air before the final movie, but was the last show filmed. The plot has members of the 4077th burying a time capsule. Some of the *M*A*S*H* actors mirrored this event by burying their own time capsule on the 20th Century Fox lot, which was inadvertently dug up by a Fox employee. The final scene to be filmed was not the closing tag of the show, but the previous scene. In it, everyone is gathered around the time capsule. Based on press coverage at the time, Jamie Farr was a bit disappointed that his character had gone off camera just before the scene ended. As a result, Farr wasn't in close proximity of his cast mates as the director yelled, "that's a wrap." In February 1983, the final two-and-a-half-hour *M*A*S*H* finale aired. It had been scheduled to run two hours, but the *M*A*S*H* gang asked for and was given an extra half an hour to tell their story. "Goodbye, Farewell and Amen" had the Korean War ending, and everyone going home. "GFA," as it's known among *M*A*S*H* fans, broke all ratings records, a feat which has yet to be surpassed. Immediately after "GFA" aired, there was another record broken. New York City registered a sudden, huge and dramatic increase in water usage. Apparently, millions of viewers had put off going to the bathroom until the show was over, and flushed in unison. When watching the *M*A*S*H* Pilot and "GFA" back to back, it's almost like watching two different shows. Whatever the preferences are for the various stages of *M*A*S*H*, it's only a testament to the depth of passion that still exists for the show, to this very day.

Hey, Look Me Over – 10/25/1982

Season 11 / Episode 241 / Production 243 – 1-G21
Columbia House VHS Tape . . . . *Not Released by Columbia House*
Fox DVD . . . . *Season 11, Disc 1*

Alan Alda, Mike Farrell, Harry Morgan
Loretta Swit, David Ogden Stiers, Jamie Farr, William Christopher

Executive Producer – Burt Metcalfe
Supervising Producer – John Rappaport
Written by Alan Alda & Karen Hall
Directed by Susan Oliver

Producers – Dan Wilcox / Thad Mumford / Dennis Koenig
Executive Script Consultants – David Pollock & Elias Davis
Story Editor – Karen Hall
Creative Consultants – Gene Reynolds / Alan Alda

Kellye Nakahara . . . . Kellye
Peggy Feury. . . . . Colonel Bucholtz
Deborah Harmon . . . . Nurse Webster
Peggy Lang . . . . Sandler
Rita Wilson. . . . . Nurse Lacey
Gary Grubbs . . . . Lieutenant Geyer
Shari Saba . . . . Shari
Jeff Maxwell. . . . . Igor

Copyright 1982 – 20th Century Fox Film Corporation

Non-Credited Appearances. . . . . .Roy Goldman

Chapters

1: *Main Titles*
2: *Packing – 0:54*
3: *The Nurses Return – 2:05*
4: *Under Margaret's Command – 5:18*
5: *Volunteering – 8:42*

6: *Kellye's Crush – 10:11*
7: *Trouble During Inspection – 12:56*
8: *Compassion – 18:01*
9: *Major Change of Heart – 20:18*
10: *Satisfactory Rating / End Titles – 22:36*

Closing Stills

1: *Freeze – Hawkeye and Kellye dancing*
2: *Kellye in the office*
3: *Colonel Bucholz and Margaret in Post-Op*
4: *Potter in bed*
5: *Margaret*
6: *B.J. in the mess tent*
7: *Charles in Potter's office*
8: *Klinger*
9: *Mulcahy*
10: *Hawkeye*

Synopsis: When the nurses return after shipping out, they return to an operating room in complete and utter disarray. Worse still is news of an inspection of the nursing staff by a no-nonsense colonel who wants to see how they do after returning from a bug out. While everyone helps to get everything ready, Hawkeye makes passes at some of the nurses, and then complains to Kellye that he doesn't understand why his tactics aren't working. Kellye tells him they would work on her, but it seems Hawkeye has no interest, hurting her feelings in the process. Kellye then displays a side of her personality never seen before as she lets Hawkeye know, in no uncertain terms, just what she thinks of him chasing tall, blonde nurses, neither of which apply to Kellye.

Commentary by Jeff Maxwell: "She (Kellye) was a good friend through the show years. We were pals then, and we're pals now."

Authors' Notes: There are no PA announcements in this episode.

This is the first of six episodes produced during Season 10's production and held over for broadcast in Season 11.

In Chapter 3, Charles is applying a plaster cast on a patient's left shoulder with a good amount of plaster on the left side of the man's face. The scene cuts away from this, but when it cuts right back, the patient's face is perfectly clean and spotless.

Also in Chapter 3, Kellye mentions Patti Page. Born Clara Ann Fowler on November 8, 1927, she became one of the best-known female artists in traditional and pop music. Ms. Page signed with Mercury Records in 1947 and in 1950, had a million-seller and has sold 100 million records to date.

In Chapter 4, Colonel Potter just loves his books about the Old West. This time, he's reading a book titled *Two Rangers from Texas (Rangers is Powerful Hard to Kill)*, written by Caddo Cameron in 1950. This would seem to fit in the timeline, as it would have been possible for Mildred to send it to him.

Trick or Treatment – 11/1/1982

Season 11 / Episode 242 / Production 247 – 9-B01
Columbia House VHS Tape. . . . . . . Last Will And Testament (Catalog # 22046)
Fox DVD . . . . Season 11, Disc 1

Alan Alda, Mike Farrell, Harry Morgan
Loretta Swit, David Ogden Stiers, Jamie Farr, William Christopher

Executive Producer – Burt Metcalfe
Supervising Producer – John Rappaport
Written by Dennis Koenig
Directed by Charles S. Dubin

Producers – Dan Wilcox / Thad Mumford
Executive Story Consultant – Karen Hall
Creative Consultants – Gene Reynolds / Alan Alda

George Wendt. . . . . Private La Roche
Richard Lineback . . . . .Private Scala
Andrew Clay . . . . .Corporal Hrabosky
James Lough . . . . .Private Crotty
Herman Poppe . . . . M.P.
R.J. Miller . . . . Graves Registration Driver
Arnold Turner . . . . Graves Registration Assistant
Arlee Reed. . . . . Soldier
Terry Brannon. . . . . Marine
John Otrin. . . . . Ambulance Attendant
Copyright 1982 – 20th Century Fox Film Corporation

Non-Credited Appearances. . . . . Kellye Nakahara, Gwen Farrell

Chapters

1: *Main Titles*
2: *Halloween Spirit – 0:53*
3: *Winchester's Bedside Manner – 3:18*
4: *Party Crashers – 5:44*
5: *Ghost Story – 9:34*
6: *The Wounded Keep Coming – 11:50*
7: *Learning to Live with It – 15:26*
8: *During Last Rites – 19:29*
9: *Saving A Life – 20:56*
10: *This One's for Charles / End Titles – 22:46*

Closing Stills

1: *Freeze – Charles in the Swamp*
2: *Private LaRoche*
3: *Patient in Post-Op*
4: *Charles*
5: *B.J. in a clown costume*
6: *Potter*
7: *Mulcahy*
8: *Margaret*
9: *Klinger*
10: *Hawkeye*

Synopsis: It's Halloween at the 4077th, but trying to keep in the spirit proves difficult when wounded arrive. While the staff exchanges eerie stories about ghost ships and spirits during surgery, Charles takes care of a Marine who shows what not to do with a billiard ball. Among the never-ending stream of wounded are more Marines, and one of

Hawkeye's patients, suffering from malnutrition, refuses to eat. But this time, it's Father Mulcahy who saves a man's life while administering the Last Rites…prematurely.

Commentary by Jeff Maxwell: "Charles Dubin came from a classy background, but he loved funny too. A bit more erudite than the others, but friendly and warm nevertheless and that was important to my daily life. Igor showed up in a number of his scripts so we were used to and comfortable with each other."

PA Announcement by Todd Sussman

Authors' Notes: In Chapter 3, Charles calls Private LaRoche "Private Mosconi," a reference to billiards legend, Willie Mosconi (June 27, 1913-September 12, 1993). William Joseph Mosconi, a member of the Billiard Congress of America Hall of Fame, won the BCA World Championship 15 times between 1941 and 1957, a record unmatched.

In Chapter 5, Hawkeye says he's taking 1954 off. This would seem to imply that the year is currently 1953. But later in Chapter 7, a G.I. says he was up at Heartbreak Ridge. The Battle of Heartbreak Ridge, with the Army's 2nd Infantry Division teaming with a French Battalion against the North Korean Army, took place in 1951.

In Chapter 6, Kellye is helping with triage on the compound (Stage 9). While on-screen helping, her voice is heard in the background at the same time.

Foreign Affairs – 11/8/1982

Season 11 / Episode 243 / Production 244 – 1-G22

Columbia House VHS Tape .Visitors (Catalog # 22047)
Fox DVD . . . . .Season 11, Disc 1

Alan Alda, Mike Farrell, Harry Morgan
Loretta Swit, David Ogden Stiers, Jamie Farr, William Christopher

Executive Producer – Burt Metcalfe
Supervising Producer – John Rappaport
Written by David Pollock & Elias Davis
Directed by Charles S. Dubin

Producers – Dan Wilcox / Thad Mumford / Dennis Koenig
Executive Script Consultants – David Pollock & Elias Davis
Story Eidtor – Karen Hall
Creative Consultants – Gene Reynolds / Alan Alda

Soon -Teck Oh . . . . Joon - Sung
Jeffrey Tambor. . . . . .Major Reddish
Melinda Mullins . . . . Martine LeClerc
Byron Chung. . . . . .Lieutenbant Chong –Wha Park
Buddy Farmer . . . . M.P.
Patrick Romano. . . . . French Soldier
Joann Thompson . . . . Nurse
Dennis Troy. . . . . Corpsman

Copyright 1982 – 20th Century Fox Film Corporation

Non-Credited Appearances. . . . . Kellye Nakahara, Roy Goldman, Gwen Farrell

Chapters

1:	Main Titles	6:	Wooing Martine – 9:17
2:	America's Newest Hero? – 0:53	7:	Early Morning Upset – 11:40
3:	French Invasion – 3:20	8:	Differences that Matter – 15:47
4:	Good Conversation – 6:03	9:	The Happy Turncoat – 21:40
5:	Not Lost in Translation – 7:27	10:	The Going Away Gift / End Titles – 23:40

Closing Stills

1: Freeze – Lieutenant Chong-Wha Park
2: Major Reddish
3: Martine LeClerc
4: Joon-Sung
5: Lieutenant Chong-Wha Park
6: Hawkeye
7: Potter in Post-Op
8: Margaret in the Officer's Club
9: Mulcahy in Post-Op
10: Klinger in the mess tent
11: B.J. in Post-Op
12: Charles

Synopsis: Major Reddish, Assistant Chief of Public Information, arrives at the 4077th to inform a wounded North Korean pilot that he's America's newest war hero. General Clark offered a reward of $50,000 to any North Korean pilot who safely landed a Russian

MiG in friendly territory. Because Lieutenant Chong-Wha Park was the first, he's being awarded an extra $50,000 and a trip to the United States complete with citizenship. The pilot refuses the offer because his landing in friendly territory was accidental and would rather be sent to a POW camp. When a French Red Cross volunteer arrives to visit wounded French soldiers, a serious relationship develops between her and Charles. In a rare display of emotion, Charles, tearfully, ends the relationship after he learns of something in her past that he, nor the Winchester family, can accept.

Commentary by David Pollock: "We were always desperate for ideas. I picked up a 1950s almanac and it said a guy in charge of the Far East command would offer $100,000 for the first North Korean who flew a Soviet jet to South Korea and surrendered. He would also get U.S. citizenship. It was a fun story to write. Tambor was a public information officer and I had actually 'gone' to army information school in Fort Slocum, New York."

Authors' Notes: There are no PA announcements in this episode.
This is the second episode produced during Season 10's production and held over for broadcast in Season 11.
This is the third episode in which the closing theme is used for the opening. Although the same song, it's a faster tempo and a slightly different arrangement. The standard opening is usually 53 seconds. By using the faster closing theme for the opening and editing out the clip of B.J. and Hawkeye doing triage on the chopper pad now makes the opening 33 seconds, thus extending the show by 20 seconds. One possible reason for using this device would be to prevent something conducive to the story line from being edited out.
In Chapter 2, Kellye is helping Hawkeye with triage and, as in previous episodes, her voice is heard in the background while she's on-screen. This time, it's the Ranch compound.
Major Reddish in Chapter 2 tells of a $50,000 reward to any North Korean pilot who safely lands a Russian MiG in friendly territory. Dubbed "Project Moolah," more than one million leaflets were dropped by B-29s on the night of April 26, 1953 along the Yalu River, offering $50,000 and political asylum to any Korean, Russian and Chinese pilot who landed his jet at Kimpo Airfield. An extra $50,000 would be given to the first man to accomplish this. On the nights of May 10 and May 18, 1953, another 500,000 leaflets were dropped over Sinujiu and Uiju Airfields. Radio broadcasts of "Project Moolah" were done in Russian, Chinese and Korean. However, the effort was less than successful as no Communist pilot landed a plane as a result of the offer. A North Korean lieutenant defected after the war on September 21, 1953, but claimed to have never heard about the $100,000 he was going to receive, possibly not wanting to admit otherwise.
This episode is clearly set in 1953.
The Eversharp-Schick mentioned by Major Reddish in Chapter 7 fits into the M*A*S*H time line.
Colonel Potter said in Chapter 8 that he spent the better part of the Battle of the Marne with a French woman in Soissons. However, there were two Battles of the Marne in WWI. The first, also known as "Miracle of Marne," took place from September 5 to September 12, 1914. A Franco-British victory ended a month-long German offensive that opened WWI and began trench warfare for four years on the Western front.
The second Battle of the Marne, also known as "Battle of Riems," took place from July 15 to August 5, 1918 and was the last German offensive on the Western front. An Allied counterattack led by French forces overwhelmed the Germans and inflicted severe casualties.
The good Colonel also said that the woman he was with was "an older woman of 20." We know that this episode is clearly set in 1953 as stated above, and we'll assume Potter was 19. If he were with the French woman of 20 in the first Battle of the Marne

in 1914, this would imply his year of birth was 1895. As he sits in the Officer's Club, he's 58 years old. If Potter were with the French woman of 20 during the second Battle of the Marne in 1918, this would imply his year of birth was 1899 and is 54 years old. In Season 4, Episode 75, "Change of Command," Potter said he was 15 years old in WWI (lied about his age to join).

Let's assume he's 15 years old, and was with the 20-year-old French woman in 1914 (the beginning of WWI). This would mean he was born in 1899, and would make him 54 years old in this episode. If Potter was with the French woman in 1918, the second Battle of the Marne, this would mean he was born in 1903 and he would be 50 years old in this episode.

In Season 10, Episode 234, "Pressure Points," Potter tells Sidney Freedman he's 62 years old.

Trying to remember his anniversary in Season 7, Episode 158, "Point of View," seems to be the least of his worries.

Also in Chapter 8, we see the "Dangerous Dan was here" sign again above the exit door of the Officer's Club.

In Chapter 9, B.J. mentions "John Cameron Swayze." Mr. Swayze (April 4, 1906-August 15, 1995) was a popular news commentator and game show panelist during the 1950s. He's also known for his Timex Watch commercials, and is a distant cousin of actor (and M*A*S*H alumnus) Patrick Swayze.

Jeffrey Michael Tambor was born in 1944 in San Francisco and has an extensive list of credits in his 40-plus year career. Included are appearances on Kojak, Barney Miller, The Love Boat, 15 episodes of Hill Street Blues and more recently, 53 episodes of Arrested Development.

The Joker is Wild – 11/15/1982

Season 11 / Episode 244 / Production 246 – 1-G24
Columbia House VHS Tape . . . . Not Released by Columbia House
Fox DVD . . . . Season 11, Disc 1

Alan Alda, Mike Farrell, Harry Morgan
Loretta Swit, David Ogden Stiers, Jamie Farr, William Christopher

Executive Producer – Burt Metcalfe
Supervising Producer – John Rappaport
Written by John Rappaport and Dennis Koenig
Directed by Burt Metcalfe

Producers – Dan Wilcox / Thad Mumford / Dennis Koenig
Executive Script Consultants – David Pollock & Elias Davis
Story Eidtor – Karen Hall
Creative Consultants – Gene Reynolds / Alan Alda

Clyde Kusatsu . . . . Captain Paul Yamato
David Haid . . . . Private Leightman
Jeff Maxwell. . . . . Igor
Jin-Taek-Yi . . . . Korean Soldier
Terry Moyer . . . . Nurse
Copyright 1982 – 20th Century Fox Film Corporation

Non-Credited Appearances

Chapters

1: Main Titles	6: Paranoia – 11:44
2: Off on the Wrong Foot – 0:54	7: Not A Joke – 13:50
3: The Good Old Days – 2:51	8: Klinger Goes Down – 17:01
4: Let the Games Begin – 5:10	9: The Joke's on Hawkeye – 19:47
5: Dr. Paul Yamato – 10:04	10: Not Over Yet / End Titles – 23:26

Closing Stills

1: Freeze – B.J. with half a moustache
2: Captain Paul Yamato
3: Private Leightman in Post-Op
4: B.J. in the Swamp
5: Potter in Post-Op
6: Margaret
7: Charles in the office
8: Mulcahy in the mess tent
9: Klinger in the office
10: Hawkeye in the Swamp

Synopsis: Having his practical jokes called stupid and dumb, coupled with high praise for the classics pulled by Hawkeye and Trapper, B.J. comes up with a plan to "get" each member of the staff within a 24-hour period. Those who have been gotten would then have to do a striptease on a mess tent table while singing "You're the Tops." But when B.J. tells Hawkeye that whoever would pull this off would want to get Hawkeye most of all, Hawkeye becomes paranoid to the point of a visiting doctor thinking he's lost his mind.

Commentary by Jeff Maxwell: "Mess tent, Igor bits were usually shot first thing in the morning. It was a regular practice of mine, and others, to snack on those steam table goodies during rehearsals and between shots. As the scene progressed, and the same pieces of food were used repeatedly for different takes, the snacking ceased. I know that the cast did swallow some of those meals, but they did not inhale."

Authors' Notes: There are no PA announcements in this episode.

This is the third episode produced during Season 10's production and held for broadcast in Season 11.

In Chapter 3, Father Mulcahy tells of a practical joke pulled by Trapper on Henry Blake. Since Trapper's last character profile was in Season 3, the only place to mention this is here: Trapper had taken a pair of Henry's shorts that were hanging on a line and flew them on a kite into enemy territory.

Potterisms: "Great Mother Machree!" *(See Season 11 –Song List, Episode 244),* "Polishing the pearlies."

In Chapter 6, Igor calls beans "has-beans." This is the second time this line has been used. The first was in Season 4, Episode 76, "It Happened One Night."

Who Knew? – 11/22/1982

Season 11 / Episode 245 / Production 240 – 1-G18
Columbia House VHS Tape . . . . Life Or Death (Catalog # 21034)
Fox DVD . . . . Season 11, Disc 1

Alan Alda, Mike Farrell, Harry Morgan
Loretta Swit, David Ogden Stiers, Jamie Farr, William Christopher

Executive Producer – Burt Metcalfe
Supervising Producer – John Rappaport
Written by Elias Davis & David Pollock
Directed by Harry Morgan

Producers – Dan Wilcox / Thad Mumford / Dennis Koenig
Executive Script Consultants – David Pollock & Elias Davis
Story Editor – Karen Hall
Creative Consultants – Gene Reynolds / Alan Alda

Kellye Nakahara . . . . Kellye
Enid Kent . . . . Nurse Bigelow
Shari Saba . . . . Shari
Joanne Thompson . . . . Jo Ann
Terry Moyer . . . . Nurse
Copyright 1982 – 20th Century Fox Film Corporation

Chapters

1:	Main Titles	6:	Simple Things – 11:34
2:	Lover Boy – 0:54	7:	The Diary – 14:39
3:	News of Death – 5:25	8:	Tearing Up A Dream – 17:49
4:	A Good Nurse – 4:54	9:	The Eulogy – 19:03
5:	Getting to Know Millie – 10:13	10:	Great Ideas / End Titles – 23:25

Closing Stills

1: Freeze – Charles flings a "Frisbee"
2: Kellye
3: Bigelow, Kellye, Hawkeye and a nurse in the nurse's tent
4: Nurse
5: B.J.
6: Potter
7: Margaret
8: Charles
9: Klinger
10: Mulcahy
11: Hawkeye

Synopsis: Hawkeye is hit hard by the death of a nurse he was dating and tries to learn more about her for a eulogy. Talking to the nurses, the only thing he learns is that nobody knew her well enough to offer much information. But when he reads her diary, what he learns about her shakes him and causes him to express his love for the people closest to him, before it's too late. Klinger, on the other hand, has come up with an idea that could potentially pay off, and turns to Charles for financial backing.

Commentary by David Pollock: "This was the third time we were nominated for the Humanitas Award, and we won."

Commentary by Karen Hall: "The people on *M*A*S*H* were the best. Maybe because we all knew how lucky we were to be there, but I think it was also just an exceptionally fine collection of people, for whatever reason."

Authors' Notes: There are no PA announcements in this episode.

This is the fourth episode produced during Season 10's production and held for broadcast in Season 11.

Starting as a writer in Season 9's "Father's Day," the Emmy and WGA Award winner Karen L. Hall went on to not only write future episodes, but to become the story editor for Seasons 10 and 11.

The view out the office windows in Chapter 6 is the same as it has been in several previous episodes showing the same wooden structure. For some reason, this has been consistent throughout the later seasons, quite unlike the earlier seasons with vastly different backdrops that would sometimes change mid-scene.

Also in Chapter 6, and still unexplained, is Mrs. Potter's picture on the left side of the Colonel's desk. It has been established in Season 4, Episode 75, "Change of Command," that the Colonel always puts her picture on the right side of his desk. It would appear he's had a change of heart, or scenery.

The Colonel has a "Shmoo" in his office in Chapter 6. The "Shmoo" is a character who made its first appearance in August, 1948 in the Al Capp comic strip, *Li'l Abner. (See Season 10 Episode 225, "Communication Breakdown" for details on* Li'l Abner.)

In Chapter 7, Father Mulcahy is wearing his brown plaid robe and not the blue plaid seen in earlier episodes.

According to Hawkeye, Millie Carpenter was the head nurse of thoracic surgery at "Letterman." Dr. Jonathan Letterman (December 11, 1824-March 15, 1872), also known as "The Father of Battlefield Medicine," is credited as the originator of modern methods for medical organization in armies. Dr. Letterman was responsible for the recovery and treatment of thousands of men during the Civil War.

In this episode, Klinger has come up with an idea for a new toy in which a large hoop is spun around the waist. In Season 5, Episode 105, "Dear Sigmund," Klinger said he would wear "Hula Hoops" as earrings if they would get him out of the army. The Hula Hoop proper came about in 1957, four years after the Korean War. This is one of the better-known inconsistencies and has been noted by a great number of fans. Often, this episode, "Who Knew?" is also mentioned when discussing Klinger and Hula Hoops. However, there is a big difference between the two episodes. While Klinger mentions Hula Hoops in "Dear Sigmund," the product name is never mentioned in "Who Knew?" It's not unreasonable to suggest that Klinger had come up with the idea of the hoop as a toy, but due to circumstances and the lack of funding, it never materialized. It's also not unreasonable to suggest that someone else, four years later, had the same idea and capitalized on it.

Bombshells – 11/28/1982

Season 11 / Episode 246 / Production 248 – 9-B02

Columbia House VHS Tape . . . . Not Released by Columbia House
Fox DVD . . . . Season 11, Disc 1

Alan Alda, Mike Farrell, Harry Morgan
Loretta Swit, David Ogden Stiers, Jamie Farr, William Christopher

Executive Producer – Burt Metcalfe
Supervising Producer – John Rappaport
Written by Dan Wilcox & Thad Mumford
Directed by Charles S. Dubin

Producers – Dan Wilcox / Thad Mumford
Executive Story Consultant – Karen Hall
Creative Consultants – Gene Reynolds / Alan Alda

Gerald O'Loughlin . . . . Brigadier General Franklin Schwerin
Allen Williams . . . . Lieutenant Priore
Michael Bond . . . . Captain Hobart
Stu Charno . . . . Corporal Sonneborn
Michael Carmine . . . . Patient
Robert Townsend . . . . Patient
Ken Neumeyer . . . . Patient
Paul Tuerpe . . . . I-Corps Courier
Bill Snider . . . . Corpsman
Natasha Bauman . . . . Nurse

Copyright 1982 – 20th Century Fox Film Corporation

Non-Credited Appearances . . . . Roy Goldman, Kellye Nakahara, Dennis Troy

Chapters

1:	Main Titles	6:	Operation Bombshell – 11:09
2:	People Will Believe Anything – 0:54	7:	Movie Talk – 15:03
3:	The Rumor Mill – 4:19	8:	The Telegram – 18:16
4:	Leaving A Man Behind – 6:52	9:	A Soldier Now – 20:22
5:	The Excitement Builds – 8:33	10:	Bronze Star / End Titles – 23:28

Closing Stills

1: Freeze – B.J. in Post-Op
2: General Schwerin
3: Lieutenant Priore
4: Corporal Sonneborn
5: Hawkeye
6: Potter in the office
7: Margaret
8: Charles in the office
9: Klinger in the office
10: Mulcahy in the mess tent
11: B.J. in Post-Op

Synopsis: Colonel Potter once said scuttlebutt was common in the army and it would seem the Colonel was correct. To prove the point that people will believe anything, Hawkeye starts a rumor that Marilyn Monroe is coming for a visit and word spreads quickly. Unfortunately for Hawkeye, the word might have spread a little too far when Brigadier General Schwerin cancels a three-day trip to Tokyo so he can meet the famous and beautiful movie star himself. The General also has another reason to visit the 4077th. Because of actions taken by B.J. on a chopper in an attempt to save a wounded soldier, the pilot put B.J. in for the Bronze Star, and General Schwerin is to present it to him. But other actions taken by B.J. will have a profound effect on him and the last thing he wants is a medal.

Commentary by Karen Hall: "I especially remember 'the wall' — which began as the door and became the wall – whenever someone (writers) said something funny that wasn't related to the script, someone would write it on an index card and tack it to the door. We filled the door and kept going. It used to drive Burt Metcalfe nuts because we were having a great time with the wall and none of the jokes were going into the script. At the end of the year, Dan Wilcox took all the index cards somewhere and had them made into a wall plaque. I still have mine somewhere. A lot of stupid things people said ended up on the wall. I remember I had a dentist appointment one day and I was griping about it, and the guys were telling me that I was a wimp, and I said, 'I just don't like pain in my mouth.' That ended up on the wall. And my favorite things on the wall were the jokes people pitched that made no sense. A lot of those lines are still in my head. Two of my favorites were 'United Nations? I love your cookies.' I won't embarrass the writer by telling you who pitched that, but I'll tell you that he then spent half an hour arguing with us, trying to get it into the script, even though he had an entire writing staff telling him that the line made NO sense. Another line like that was, 'The only thing square about you are your bed and your purse.' I have no idea what that was supposed to mean, and it's not because a lot of years have passed."

PA Announcement by Todd Sussman

Authors' Notes: Father Mulcahy in Chapter 2 mentions Ted Williams leaving Korea due to an ear and throat infection, and the Marines are sending him to a military hospital in the States. This is essentially correct. The Boston Red Sox slugger was a Marine pilot and flew 38 missions before being pulled due to an old ear infection acting up in June 1953.

In Chapter 3, Colonel Potter tells of a rumor in WWI in which he got word the war was over because Kaiser Wilhelm was entering the priesthood. Prince Frederick William Victor Albert of Prussia (January 27, 1859-June 4, 1941) was the last German Emperor and King of Prussia ruling both the German Empire and the kingdom of Prussia from June 15, 1888 until November 9, 1918.

It's been previously noted early on that jeeps seen at the 4077th had multiple owners. For example, in "Welcome to Korea," Hawkeye reaches a checkpoint on the way to Kimpo with Radar. One of the jeep's serial numbers is 2A401. This is also the same jeep that Hawkeye steals from the General and the same jeep Potter first arrives in.

In this episode, "Bombshells," a jeep is seen in Chapter 5, but where a serial number would normally be, it says "U.S. ARMY" instead.

In Chapter 6, Charles mentions "Kresge's." Founded in 1899, the S. S. Kresge Company in Detroit, Michigan became the better known K-Mart in 1962.

Potterism: "A flat tire on your hayride."

B.J. is awarded The Bronze Star for bravery.

Settling Debts – 12/6/1982
Season 11 / Episode 247 / Production 245 – 1-G23
Columbia House VHS Tape . . . .*Life or Death (Catalog # 21034)*
Fox DVD . . . . *Season 11, Disc 1*

Alan Alda, Mike Farrell, Harry Morgan
Loretta Swit, David Ogden Stiers, Jamie Farr, William Christopher

Executive Producer – Burt Metcalfe
Supervising Producer – John Rappaport
Written by Thad Mumford & Dan Wilcox
Directed by Michael Switzer

Producers – Dan Wilcox / Thad Mumford / Dennis Koenig
Executive Script Consultants – David Pollock & Elias Davis
Story Editor – Karen Hall
Creative Consultants – Gene Reynolds / Alan Alda

Jeff East . . . . Lieutenant Pavelich
Guy Boyd . . . . Sergeant Lally
Michael Lamont . . . . .Corporal
Jack McCulloch. . . . . Soldier
Jennifer Davis Westmore. . . . . Nurse
Copyright 1982 – 20th Century Fox Film Corporation

Non-Credited Appearances. . . . . .Roy Goldman, Kellye Nakahara

Chapters

1: *Main Titles*	6:	*Injured Lieutenant – 10:52*
2: *Security – 0:54*	7:	*Stalling Colonel Potter – 11:50*
3: *A Letter from Mrs. Potter – 2:56*	8:	*All's Fair in Love and War – 14:20*
4: *Party Planning – 4:31*	9:	*Home Sweet Home – 19:55*
5: *Mildred in Trouble – 8:01*	10:	*Goodnight / End Titles – 22:55*

Closing Stills

1: *Freeze – Charles passed out in Potter's bed*
2: *Lieutenant Pavelich*
3: *Sergeant Lally*
4: *Margaret in the office*
5: *B.J. in the Swamp*
6: *Mulcahy*
7: *Klinger*
8: *Charles*
9: *Potter in the office*
10: *Hawkeye*

Synopsis: When Colonel Potter tries to find out why Mildred wrote a letter to Hawkeye, his curiosity turns to anger when all he learns is, "it's a surprise." Furious that Mildred withdrew $800 from the bank and possibly bought a houseboat, he can't wait to get her on the phone. The staff finds it increasingly difficult keeping the surprise a secret and keeping Potter from entering his tent as they prepare a surprise party. But when he finally does enter, he realizes he had jumped to the wrong conclusion. When Sergeant Lally drives his wounded lieutenant to the 4077th, he's unaware of how seriously wounded the man really is. When he finds out that Lieutenant Pavelich may never walk again, Sergeant Lally draws his gun, cocks the trigger and aims it at the wounded North Korean responsible.

Commentary by Guy Boyd: "When I asked Alan Alda (as Hawkeye) what happened to my lieutenant, he was supposed to answer 'chord shock' (meaning a spinal injury) but, he turned to me and said 'shord cock.' It took us 17 takes without someone going into total hysterics. It was a great day."

Commentary by Thad Mumford: "I loved that show. I loved Harry (Morgan)."

Authors' Notes: There are no PA announcements in this episode.
This is the fifth episode produced during Season 10's production and held for broadcast in Season 11

In Chapter 2, Father Mulcahy mentions *The Joe Miller Joke Book.* Joe Miller (Joseph or Josias) (1684-1738) was an English actor who first appeared in Committee by Sir Robert Howard in 1709. John Mottley (1692-1750) came out with a book after Miller died called *Joe Miller's Jests* in 1739. The first edition was a thin paperback of 247 coarse witticisms. Later editions were called *Joe Miller's Joke Book.*

This episode has added to the increasingly difficult task of keeping track of Colonel Potter's wedding anniversary. In Chapter 4, he said his anniversary is Groundhog's Day, which is February 2. He picked this day so he wouldn't forget it. It didn't work. Episode 158, Season 7's "Point of View," his anniversary was determined to be September 8, 1916 and Episode 132, Season 6's "Images," he'll be married 38 years "this April."

The framed photo of Mrs. Potter in Chapter 5 is still on the left side of his desk, only this time, the telephone is on the right side where a previously unidentified picture had been.

Evidently, Potter throws with his left hand in Chapter 5 when he throws a cup at the wall with his left hand.

The view from the office window in Chapter 5 is still the wooden structure determined to be the Motor Pool supply.

In Chapter 5, Father Mulcahy mispronounces Margaret's name as "Major Houlihand." This is the second time in the series in which this occurs. The first time was by Frank Burns when, in Season 1, Episode 10's "I Hate A Mystery," he says, "Major Houlihand."

The view from the office windows in Chapter 7 remains the same wooden structure.

In Chapter 7, there's a rarely seen picture of Mrs. Potter in the Colonel's tent. It's the same-framed photo as the one on his desk.

Potterism: "Slow as a summer time hound dog."

Also in Chapter 7, Charles mentions "Becky Thatcher," a character and reference to the Mark Twain classic *The Adventures of Tom Sawyer* (1876). On a side note, there are two connections that can be made between Colonel Potter and The Adventures of Tom Sawyer. Becky Thatcher, the girl who inspired the character of the same name, who Tom Sawyer fell in love with, lived across the street from Mark Twain's boyhood home in Hannibal, Missouri (Ms. Thatcher's home is now a landmark). Another connection is also another character of Mark Twain's, Muff Potter, a fisherman who likes helping kids fix their kites, but who is sometimes drunk.

The Moon is not Blue – 12/13/1982

Season 11 / Episode 248 / Production 242 – 1-G20

Columbia House VHS Tape . . . . Not Released by Columbia House
Fox DVD . . . . Season 11, Disc 1

Alan Alda, Mike Farrell, Harry Morgan
Loretta Swit, David Ogden Stiers, Jamie Farr, William Christopher

Executive Producer – Burt Metcalfe
Supervising Producer – John Rappaport
Written by Larry Balmagia
Directed by Charles S. Dubin

Producers – Dan Wilcox / Thad Mumford / Dennis Koenig
Executive Script Consultants – David Pollock & Elias Davis
Story Editor – Karen Hall
Creative Consultants – Gene Reynolds / Alan Alda

Hamilton Camp . . . . .Major T Frankenheimer
Sandy Helberg. . . . . .Corporal Bannister
Larry Ward . . . . .General Rothaker
Jeff Maxwell. . . . . .Igor
Jan Jorden . . . . Nurse Baker
Copyright 1982 – 20th Century Fox Film Corporation

Non-Credited Appearances. . . . . .Kellye Nakahara

Chapters

1: Main Titles	6: Hollywood Style – 9:32
2: Film Critics – 0:53	7: Tempers Flare – 13:15
3: Speakeasy Under Fire – 2:54	8: The Klinger Connection – 16:03
4: Declared Prohibition – 5:06	9: The Moon is not Blue – 18:43
5: Placebo – 8:33	10: For Reel / End Titles – 22:20

Closing Stills

1: Freeze – B.J. and Mulcahy at the movie in the mess tent
2: Major Frankenheimer
3: Corporal Bannister
4: General Rothaker
5: B.J.
6: Potter in the mess tent
7: Charles in the Swamp
8: Margaret
9: Klinger
10: Mulcahy (Still previously seen)
11: Hawkeye in the office

Synopsis: An unbearably hot Korean summer only gets worse with the showing of the movie Sahara, and a diminishing supply of codeine is replaced with a shipment of placebos. Worse still, General Rothaker, recovering in Post-Op, officially bans alcohol and declares the 4077th dry. Hawkeye, however, finds a practical use for the placebos. First he gives some to Klinger telling him the new "medicine" will protect him from the effects of the heat, and gives some to a corporal at Special Services who breaks out into a panicked sweat at the mere thought of talking to a woman. The placebos have the desired effect on both men, and the only thing Hawkeye wants in return is for the Special Services corporal to send the 4077th a copy of a racy movie that was banned in Boston, *The Moon is Blue*. After telling Corporal Bannister that he's been taking placebos, he sends the 4077th a movie, but not exactly the "sexually explicit" film they were expecting.

Commentary by Karen Hall: "I remember that John Rappaport's nickname was 'Rap' and Dan Wilcox was 'Disco Dan,' because he was always the most serious — the one who was always trying to get the rest of us back to work when we were being silly. So we gave him that name as a way of giving him a hard time about it."

PA Announcement by Todd Sussman

Authors' Notes: This is the sixth and final episode produced during Season 10's production and held for broadcast in Season 11.

Charles in Chapter 5 mentions Pinocchio, the very well known children's tale by Carlo Collodi (1853).

In Chapter 6, Hawkeye mentions "Busby Berkeley." William Berkeley Enos (November 29, 1895-March 14, 1976) was a highly influential Hollywood movie director and musical choreographer.

When Hawkeye and B.J. return to camp in Chapter 8, they do so in jeep number 18210717.

Potterisms: "Sung a few choruses of the four-letter serenade," "Monkey muffins."

Run for the Money – 12/20/1982

Season 11 / Episode 249 / Production 249 – 9-B03

Columbia House VHS Tape.................... *Visitors (Catalog # 22047)*
Fox DVD ....*Season 11, Disc 2*

Alan Alda, Mike Farrell, Harry Morgan
Loretta Swit, David Ogden Stiers, Jamie Farr, William Christopher

Executive Producer – Burt Metcalfe
Supervising Producer – John Rappaport
Teleplay by Elias Davis & David Pollock
Story by Mike Farrell and Elias Davis & David Pollock
Directed by Nell Cox

Producers – Dan Wilcox / Thad Mumford
Executive Story Consultant – Karen Hall
Creative Consultants – Gene Reynolds / Alan Alda

Phil Brock... Private Walt Palmer
Thomas Callaway... Captain Sweeny
Barbara Tarbuck .... Major Judy Parker
William Schilling .... Sergeant Jessup McFarland
Robert Alan Browne ....Colonel Crocker
Kellye Nakahara .... Kellye
Mark Anderson.........................Earl "Jackrabbit" LeMasters
Michael Conn .... G.I.
Ken Wright.. G.I.
Juney Smith... G.I.
Ron Karpa..Driver
Copyright 1982 – 20th Century Fox Film Corporation

Non-Credited Appearances...................................Dennis Troy

Chapters

1:	Main Titles	6:	In Training – 9:32
2:	Staying in Shape – 0:54	7:	Race Day – 13:33
3:	Place Your Bets – 3:06	8:	It's Personal – 16:26
4:	The Ringer Unfortunately – 5:09	9:	For the Orphanage – 20:15
5:	Confronting Captain Sweeny – 8:07	10:	All Bets are Off / End Titles – 22:47

Closing Stills

1: *Freeze – Klinger on the phone*
2: *Private Palmer in Post-Op*
3: *Captain Sweeny in the Officer's Club*
4: *Margaret and Major Parker*
5: *Hawkeye*
6: *B.J.*
7: *Potter*
8: *Margaret*
9: *Charles*
10: *Klinger*
11: *Mulcahy*

Synopsis: When a world-class sprinter is assigned to the 4077th, Klinger wants to race him against the 8063rd's ringer, and nobody wants to beat them more than Margaret and Potter. But when the runner finally arrives, it isn't exactly who they thought he would be, and the only person left with any chance at all of beating the 8063rd is Father Mulcahy. It's clear right from the start that LeMaster, the ringer from the 8063rd, is bigger, in much better condition and much faster than Mulcahy, but that doesn't necessarily mean he'll win. Charles is preoccupied with a patient he's taken a special interest in. Private Walt Palmer was not only wounded, he suffers from an affliction that hits close to home with Charles, and it's later revealed that his sister, Honoria, suffers from the same affliction.

Commentary by William Christopher: "I used to run with my son, all the time. Part of his program, when he lived at home, was to run. So, I'd run with him. But, the running didn't get in the show because I was a runner. I remember shooting that show. I'd been very busy and kept hoping I'd remember my lines."

Commentary by David Pollock: "Mike Farrell did the story, but we actually did the teleplay. Just last year, we won an award from the National Stutterer's Association for this one. Here it is 20 years later, and we won an award."

Authors' Notes: There are no PA announcements in this episode.
In Chapter 3, Margaret mentions the USS Coral Sea. Commissioned on October 1, 1947, the ship's length was 968 feet, with 932 of those feet an armored flight deck. Engines delivered 212,000 horsepower and were capable of 33 knots. The Coral Sea boasted a crew of over 3,500, housed 125 aircraft, and carried enough fuel oil to heat 3,000 homes for a year with enough horsepower to supply electricity to a city of 1,000,000. The Battle of the Coral Sea, which took place from May 4 to May 8, 1942, repelled a Japanese attack on the Australian Port Moresby, the anniversary of which is still commemorated in Australia. The USS Coral Sea was decommissioned on April 20, 1990. For more information and a complete and extensive history of the USS Coral Sea and those who served on her, please visit Bob Dorais's remarkable web site, USSCORALSEA.NET.
On the Ranch compound in Chapter 4, as Jessup McFarland gets off the truck, there's a microphone shadow on the right side of the back canvas.
Hawkeye gets a letter in Chapter 4 addressed to "B.F. Pierce – 4077th MASH – APO 175 – NYC NY." The return address is "C. Traim – 12 W 84 Street – NY NY."
Potter implies he has a Studebaker automobile in Chapter 7, but two episodes ago in "Settling Debts," he has a Hudson.
In Chapter 8, Honoria Winchester mentions guest artist "Piatigorsky."
Gregor Pavlovich Piatigorsky (April 17, 1903-August 6, 1976) was a Ukrainian-American cellist.

U.N., the Night and the Music – 1/3/1983

Season 11 / Episode 250 / Production 252 – 9-B06
Columbia House VHS Tape . . . . Visitors (Catalog # 22047)
Fox DVD . . . . Season 11, Disc 2

Alan Alda, Mike Farrell, Harry Morgan
Loretta Swit, David Ogden Stiers, Jamie Farr, William Christopher

Executive Producer – Burt Metcalfe
Supervising Producer – John Rappaport
Written by Elias Davis & David Pollock
Directed by Harry Morgan

Producers – Thad Mumford / Dan Wilcox
Executive Story Consultant – Karen Hall
Creative Consultants – Gene Reynolds / Alan Alda

George Innes . . . . .Dr. Randolph Kent
Dennis Holahan . . . . .Per Johannsen
Kavi Raz . . . . Rammurti Lal
David Packer . . . . .Private Lumley
Kellye Nakahara . . . . .Kellye
Bill Snider . . . . Bartender
Shari Saba . . . . .Shari
Brigitte Chandler . . . . Nurse

Copyright 1983 – 20th Century Fox Film Corporation

Chapters

1:	Main Titles	6:	To Tell the Truth – 13:37
2:	The U.N. Tour – 0:34	7:	Growing Closer – 14:32
3:	Remembering Home – 2:48	8:	Outclassed by the Butler's Son – 19:10
4:	Cultural Differences – 4:26	9:	Bravery – 21:31
5:	Uncomfortable Situations – 8:39	10:	Farewell / End Titles – 23:03

Closing Stills

1: Freeze – Hawkeye and Margaret
2: Dr. Randolph Kent
3: Per Johannsen
4: Rammurti Lal
5: Private Lumley
6: Charles
7: Margaret
8: Potter
9: Mulcahy (Still previously seen)
10: B.J.
11: Klinger
12: Hawkeye

Synopsis: As part of a U.N. delegation, representatives from three different countries arrive to see how a M*A*S*H unit operates, and all three have an impact on some of the staff. An English physician appears to share a similar background as Charles with a penchant for the finer things in life, but appearances can be deceiving. The U.N. representative from India demonstrates meditation to Colonel Potter and Klinger as a way to relieve stress. But it's the U.N. representative from Sweden that Margaret falls for, even though he tries to avoid relationships ever since an unfortunate wound has left him impotent. Operating on a man's leg, after the man has been lying in mud for hours, B.J. doesn't have time to socialize, and might have spoken too soon when he assures him he's going home with both legs.

Commentary by Kavi Raz: "My work on *M*A*S*H* was during my very early years in Hollywood. I still felt like this wide-eyed kid who found himself living out a dream he thought would never be possible. I had just signed on for *St. Elsewhere* as a regular, playing Dr. V.J. Kochar and then the greatest moment of my life: to appear on a show as a guest star that I have watched in awe for so many years. To share frame space with legends that I had aspired to learn from was indeed a Godly intervention for me in a career that was just taking its first steps. And what first steps. I am indebted to *M*A*S*H* for being such an important part of my life. I will cherish this forever and hopefully be able to share those moments with my grandchildren...oh my, what stories an old man can weave."

Authors' Notes: There are no PA announcements in this episode.

Three previous episodes, "Sons and Bowlers" and "Picture This" in Season 10, and "Foreign Affairs" in Season 11, all ran the closing theme for the opening. Although the same song, it's a faster tempo and a slightly different arrangement. The standard opening is usually 53 seconds. By using the faster closing theme for the opening and editing out the clip of B.J. and Hawkeye doing triage on the chopper pad now makes the opening 33 seconds, thus extending the show by 20 seconds. One possible reason for using this device would be to prevent something conducive to the story line from being edited out.

This episode, "U.N., the Night and the Music," also ran a 33-second opening instead of the usual 53 seconds, but was the first episode in which the regular opening theme is used with B.J. and Hawkeye doing triage on the chopper pad edited out and again, extended the show by 20 seconds. It's a mystery why the faster closing theme was used when the regular opening theme, with the edit, also ran for 33 seconds.

In Chapter 2, Colonel Potter mentions "Rosie, the Riveter," who was closely associated with Rose Will Monroe (1920-1997). Monroe worked as a riveter at the Willow Run Aircraft Factory in Ypsilanti, Michigan, where she helped build B-29 and B-24 bombers for the Army Air Forces. She starred in a promotional film about the war effort at home, and was featured in a poster campaign. In 1943, Rosie the Riveter was released and Redd Evans and John Jacob Loeb wrote the song. Rose Will Monroe closely resembled the workers depicted in the song.

Potterisms: "Great gopher holes," "Extra innings with the sandman" (on sleeping late).

Hawkeye, in Chapter 2, mentions "Captain Video." Captain Video and his Video Rangers was the first sci-fi series on American television and broadcast on the Dumont TV Network from June 27, 1949 until April 1, 1955.

The photo of Mildred Potter in Chapter 5 is still on the left side of the desk and not the original right side.

Margaret mentions Hans Christian Anderson (April 2, 1805 – August 4, 1875) in Chapter 5. From Denmark, the author and poet is probably best known for his fairy tales *The Little Mermaid, The Ugly Duckling* and *Thumbelina.*

A rarity in Chapter 8 as Charles smokes a cigar.

Loretta Swit and actor Dennis Holahan, who played the part of Per Johannsen, were married on December 21, 1983. They divorced 12 years later.

Strange Bedfellows – 1/10/1983

Season 11 / Episode 251 / Production 253 – 9-B07
Columbia House VHS Tape . . . . *Charles In Charge (Catalog # 22049)*
Fox DVD . . . . *Season 11, Disc 2*

Alan Alda, Mike Farrell, Harry Morgan
Loretta Swit, David Ogden Stiers, Jamie Farr, William Christopher

Executive Producer – Burt Metcalfe
Supervising Producer – John Rappaport
Written by Karen Hall
Directed by Mike Farrell

Producers – Thad Mumford / Dan Wilcox
Executive Story Consultant – Karen Hall
Creative Consultants – Gene Reynolds / Alan Alda
Dennis Dugan . . . . Bob Wilson
Copyright 1983 – 20th Century Fox Film Corporation

Non-Credited Appearances . . . . Kellye Nakahara

Chapters

1: *Main Titles*
2: *Up All Night – 0:33*
3: *Colonel Potter's Son-in-Law – 2:46*
4: *Caught in the Act – 4:39*
5: *Father Mulcahy's Advice – 9:37*
6: *A Winchester's Fear – 13:27*
7: *A Father's Love – 16:33*
8: *Confronting Charles – 18:13*
9: *Bob's Betrayal – 19:25*
10: *Now What? / End Titles – 23:38*

Closing Stills

1: *Freeze – Hawkeye and Charles in the Swamp*
2: *Bob Wilson*
3: *Potter*
4: *Charles*
5: *B.J. in the mess tent*
6: *Margaret*
7: *Klinger*
8: *Mulcahy*
9: *Hawkeye*

Synopsis: While Bob Wilson is in Tokyo on business, he makes a side trip to visit his father-in-law: Colonel Potter. The reunion is a happy one and, although it might have taken a little while, their relationship appears to be on solid ground. But after getting a disturbing phone call about Bob, Potter decides to call his daughter to let her know about her husband's indiscretions. What's disturbing to Hawkeye and B.J. is the fact that Charles' snoring is keeping them awake. Unfortunately, Charles doesn't believe that someone of his ilk and stature snores and confides in Father Mulcahy that he's worried about being worthy of the Winchester name, and the possibility that he's like everyone else. The good Father is less than sympathetic.

Authors' Notes: There are no PA announcements in this episode.
This is the second episode in which an abbreviated opening theme is used. By editing out B.J. and Hawkeye doing triage at the chopper pad, the opening is 33 seconds and not

the usual 53 seconds. It remains a mystery why the faster closing theme was used when the regular opening theme, with the edit, also ran for 33 seconds.

This is also the second episode to feature Dennis Dugan. His first appearance was in Season 3's "Love and Marriage."

Potterisms: "Hot po-taters," "Spiffier than a petunia in a patch of chigger weed."

In Chapter 4, Potter gets a phone call from the Imperial Hotel in Tokyo. The Imperial Hotel in Tokyo was founded in 1890. In 1923, a new Imperial Hotel, designed by architect Frank Lloyd Wright, had opened. On that day, a devastating earthquake struck Tokyo and Yokohama, destroying whole sections of both cities and killing over ten thousand people. However, the newly designed Imperial Hotel suffered minimal damage and was left intact. This beautiful hotel thrives today and is certainly worthy of a "Winchester."

We learn in Chapter 4 that Bob Wilson works for the "Rapahanak" Import Company. In Season 4, Episode 84, "Of Moose and Men," we learned that Colonel Potter is one-fourth Cherokee Indian. Although the name "Rapahanak" is misspelled in the captioning for "Strange Bedfellows," is it coincidence that "Rappahannock" (correctly spelled) is an American Indian tribe? The land of the Rappahannock Indians is "the place where water rises and falls." The Rappahannock's land stretches from the Northern Neck of the Rappahannock River to the Mattaponi River and as far north as Fredericksburg, Virginia. A fascinating history of the thriving Rappahannock Indian tribe can be found at *www.rappahannockindiantribe.org.*

In Chapter 5, Bob Wilson said that he and Evy took their son Stuart to a horse show in Dry Fork (West Virginia).

It would seem the Colonel's wedding anniversary isn't the only thing he has trouble keeping up with. In Episode 87, Season 4's "Mail Call, Again," Potter gets a letter from his son (now his daughter) telling him of the birth of his granddaughter, Sherry Pershing Potter. In Episode 100, Season 5's "Margaret's Engagement," his newborn granddaughter is five years old. Also in Season 5, Episode 105, "Dear Sigmund," only five episodes later, his five-year-old granddaughter is now eight years old. My, how quickly they grow up. However, in Season 6, Episode 143, "Mail Call Three," his granddaughter Sherry is now his grandson, Cory, of which Mildred sent pictures, but you can't see the little guy. Moving along to this episode in Season 11, Potter's grandson Cory is now his grandson Stuart.

Say No More – 1/24/1983
Season 11 / Episode 252 / Production 254 – 9-B08
Columbia House VHS Tape . . . . Charles In Charge (Catalog # 22049)
Fox DVD . . . . Season 11, Disc 2

Alan Alda, Mike Farrell, Harry Morgan
Loretta Swit, David Ogden Stiers, Jamie Farr, William Christopher

Executive Producer – Burt Metcalfe
Supervising Producer – John Rappaport
Written by John Rappaport
Directed by Charles S. Dubin

Producers – Thad Mumford / Dan Wilcox
Executive Story Consultant – Karen Hall
Creative Consultants – Gene Reynolds / Alan Alda

John Anderson. . . . . .Major General Addison Collins
Michael Horton . . . . .Lieutenant Curt Collins
James Karen. . . . . Dr. Steven Chesler
Chip Johnson . . . . .Captain Sterne
Jeff Maxwell. . . . . .Igor
Kellye Nakahara . . . . .Kellye
Jeff Chapman . . . . .Maloney
Norman Garrett . . . . Patient
Dennis Troy. . . . . Corpsman

Copyright 1983 – 20th Century Fox Film Corporation

Non-Credited Appearances. . . . . Jan Jorden, Shari Saba

Chapters
1: Main Titles
2: Just Another Day – 0:53
3: Collins and Collins – 5:00
4: Say No More – 7:02
5: The General is Moving In – 8:39
6: Important Phone Calls – 10:18
7: A Visit From Dr. Chesler – 14:18
8: The Worst News – 16:23
9: This Man's Son – 20:49
10: End Titles – 23:14

Closing Stills
1: Freeze – Charles and Margaret in the mess tent – after kiss
2: General Collins
3: Lieutenant Collins in Post-Op
4: Doctor Chesler
5: Igor in the mess tent
6: Margaret in her tent
7: Charles on the phone
8: B.J. in Post-Op
9: Mulcahy in Post-Op
10: Klinger
11: Potter
12: Hawkeye

Synopsis: Doctor Steven Chesler, an expert on emergency care, had once written an article which inspired Margaret to expand the nurses' duties in triage, and now the renowned surgeon is giving a lecture in Seoul. Deeply disappointed at having to cancel her trip due to laryngitis, she has Charles phone Dr. Chesler to express her regrets. Charles, however, unbeknownst to Margaret, manages to have Margaret meet the famous surgeon, but it won't be in Seoul. Arriving with the wounded is Lieutenant Curt Collins, whose father is Major General Addison Collins. After visiting with his son in Post-Op, Hawkeye has the unpleasant duty of informing the General that due to complications from surgery, his son didn't make it. Touched by the softer side of the gruff General, Hawkeye accepts his offer to have a drink with him in his son's memory, but when the General gets a phone call in his private trailer, it causes Hawkeye to wonder if he misjudged the man.

PA Announcement by Todd Sussman
PA Announcement by Klinger

Authors' Notes: In earlier episodes, a sign over the shower tent had listed the times available for men and women to shower, but in Chapter 2 of this episode, all it says is "Showers. Keep it clean."

B.J. mentions "Goldilocks" in Chapter 2. A widely known children's story, *Goldilocks and the Three Bears* was written by Robert Southey in 1837.

Also in Chapter 2, Potter mentions "Dizzy Dean." Jerome Hanna "Dizzy" Dean (January 16, 1910-July 17, 1974) made his Major League Baseball debut on September 28, 1930 for the St. Louis Cardinals. His final game was on September 28, 1947 for the St. Louis Browns. Dean boasted a win / loss record of 150 – 83, an Earned Run Average of 3.02 and 1,163 strikeouts. Dizzy Dean played his career with the St. Louis Cardinals (1930, 1932-37), the Chicago Cubs (1938-41) and the St. Louis Browns (1947). He was an All Star selection in 1934-37, a World Series Champion in 1934, and was the National League MVP in 1934. The St. Louis Cardinals retired Dizzy Dean's number 17 and on the ninth ballot, with 79% of the votes, Dean was elected to the Baseball Hall of Fame in 1953.

Igor mentions "Wheaties" in Chapter 2. What would become "The Breakfast of Champions" began in 1924.

The serial number on General Collins' jeep appears to be BC 4990, a new number not seen before.

General Collins mentions "Kumsong Bulge" in Chapter 3, and clearly puts this episode where it should be chronologically...

The Battle of the Kumsong (River) Salient.

On July 13, 1953, the Chinese People's Volunteer Army or Chinese Communist Forces (CCF) launched its third attack of their summer campaign. The attack was focused southward at the center of the Korean peninsula primarily at the ROK (Republic of Korea) Army that was supported by the UN (United Nation) military forces. The Chinese called it "The Golden City Campaign," while the Americans would call this final bloody battle of the Korean War, "The Battle of the Kumsong Salient."

This was the Chinese Army's largest and most violent attack since the Spring Offensive of May 1951. By July 14, 150,000 Chinese had pressed savagely against the six ROK Divisions in the Kumsong Bulge and had practically destroyed the ROK Capitol Division and much of the ROK 3rd Division. They had fought on the flanks of the narrow 20-mile bulge. Casualties on both sides were extremely heavy, because it was a stand-up fist fight directly on the main line of resistance with direct (human wave) assaults by the Communists into the heart of the stubborn ROK defensive positions. After the slug match, retreat, reinforcement, and counter attacks, the major fighting finally sputtered to a halt by the 20th of July. The ROK Army, who bore the brunt of the fighting, called this "The Battle of the Kumsong River." *(This battle brief by John R. Carpenter.)*

For an in-depth account of part of The Battle of the Kumsong Salient, please visit: *members.cox.net/lostbastards/july1953.htm.* See also *www.koreanwar.org.*

We would also like to acknowledge Richard L. "Dick" Carpenter, who as a young US Army soldier served with the ROK Capital Division during that trying time in July 1953. A memorial plaque at the Mount Soledad War Memorial in La Jolla, California, in honor of Dick Carpenter reads: "A 'Lost Bastard' who earned a Battlefield Commission during the Battle of the Kumsong River with the ROK Capitol Division while surrounded by enemy forces. After discharge, he re-enlisted and became an officer again, after OCS." Dick Carpenter was a rare "Double Mustang" of distinction and honor.

In Chapter 4, Charles tells Margaret that the cause of her laryngitis was due to being out in the cold with wet hair. It should be noted that going outside with wet hair does not cause one to get sick. Germs do. This is an "old wives tale" that has since been debunked.

Way back in "Requiem for A Lightweight," Episode 3 from Season 1, a PA announcement is made by actor Jimmy Lydon, yet the captioning credits Klinger as making the announcement, even though Klinger had not yet appeared on M*A*S*H. Ironically, when Klinger makes his PA announcement in Chapter 6, of this episode, the captioning reads: "Man on PA."

In Chapter 6, Hawkeye mentions "Simoniz," a trademark for a car wax that was originated in 1935 by Union Carbide.

Another "tip of the hat" to the Marx brothers when, in Chapter 6, B.J. mentions "Harpo."

For the second time in the series, "Son of a bitch" is said, this time by General Collins in Chapter 8.

In several previous episodes, a photograph of a man in a suit (head shot) with what appears to be very thinning hair has been seen in the Swamp next to Hawkeye's bunk. In Chapter 8, inside General Collins' trailer, hangs the very same photograph.

At 23:16 of Chapter 10, the picture seems quite dark.

Friends and Enemies – 2/7/1983

Season 11 / Episode 253 / Production 251 – 9-B05

Columbia House VHS Tape . . . . *Not Released by Columbia House*

Fox DVD . . . . *Season 11, Disc 2*

Alan Alda, Mike Farrell, Harry Morgan
Loretta Swit, David Ogden Stiers, Jamie Farr, William Christopher

Executive Producer – Burt Metcalfe
Supervising Producer – John Rappaport
Written by Karen Hall
Directed by Jamie Farr

Producers – Thad Mumford / Dan Wilcox
Executive Story Consultant – Karen Hall
Creative Consultants – Gene Reynolds / Alan Alda

John McLiam . . . . .Colonel Woody Cooke
Jim Lefebvre . . . . Sergeant Zurilli
Kellye Nakahara . . . . .Kellye
Matthew Price . . . . .Corporal Marsh
Jeff Maxwell . . . . .Igor
Jack Yates . . . . .Large Enlisted Man
Roy Goldman . . . . .Roy
Bill Snider . . . . .Snider
Joann Thompson . . . . Nurse
Jennifer Davis . . . . Nurse

Copyright 1983 – 20th Century Fox Film Corporation

Chapters

1: *Main Titles*
2: *Mail Call – 0:55*
3: *Old Friend – 2:46*
4: *Healing Hunnicutt – 4:35*
5: *About Colonel Cooke – 8:18*

6: *Height of Frustration – 9:53*
7: *Truth Revealed – 14:13*
8: *Turning the Tables – 18:18*
9: *Friends No More – 20:50*
10: *Appreciation / End Titles – 23:41*

Closing Stills

1: *Freeze – Hawkeye and Potter on the compound (Stage 9)*
2: *Colonel Woody Cooke*
3: *Sergeant Zurilli*
4: *Corporal Marsh*
5: *Charles*
6: *B.J.*
7: *Potter*
8: *Margaret*
9: *Mulcahy*
10: *Klinger*
11: *Hawkeye*

Synopsis: Among the wounded is Colonel Woody Cooke, a long-time friend of Potter's; a friendship that began in WWI has endured three wars, but some of the wounded in Post-Op blame Colonel Cooke for their injuries. Hawkeye tries to tell Potter about his friend, but Potter only gets angry and dismisses him. Talking to the unit's sergeant in Post-Op, Potter realizes that, although a close friend for many years, he has to be truthful in his report which could mean the end of his friendship with Woody. Friendship not withstanding, Charles' music is irritating B.J. to the point where, when alone, he damages the needle on Charles' record player. But with a little help from Margaret, Charles does get his revenge.

Commentary by Karen Hall: "One day we spent some time procrastinating by comparing the strangest thing we'd ever been called in a mass mailing. Several people ended up with nicknames that stuck and are still in use. Thad Mumford became Thadogis and Dennis Koenig became Kodak. Those are the only two I remember. I didn't have a nickname."

PA Announcement by Todd Sussman

Authors' Notes: In Chapter 2, Charles plays a record of Gustav Mahler. If you look closely, you can see that the record is warped.

In many previous episodes, two names can be seen on the lower left of the Red Cross sign in the Officer's Club, just as they're seen in Chapter 6 of this episode. Those two names are "Pat and Larry Marshall." Those two names are also a reference to Larry Gelbart and his wife, Pat Marshall. Pat Marshall appeared in Episode 70, Season 3's "Payday" as Lieutenant Nelson. The names "Pat and Larry Marshall" were an inside joke.

Give and Take – 2/14/1983
Season 11 / Episode 254 / Production 255 – 9-B09
Columbia House VHS Tape . . . . *Not Released by Columbia House*
Fox DVD . . . . *Season 11, Disc 2*

Alan Alda, Mike Farrell, Harry Morgan
Loretta Swit, David Ogden Stiers, Jamie Farr, William Christopher

Executive Producer – Burt Metcalfe
Supervising Producer – John Rappaport
Written by Dennis Koenig
Directed by Charles S. Dubin

Producers – Thad Mumford / Dan Wilcox
Executive Story Consultant – Karen Hall
Creative Consultants – Gene Reynolds / Alan Alda

Craig Wasson . . . . Private Kurland
G.W. Bailey. . . . . Sergeant Luther Rizzo
Jeff Maxwell. . . . . Igor
Kellye Nakahara . . . . Kellye
Sagan Lewis . . . . Nurse Armstrong
Dereck Wong . . . . Korean Soldier
Alberta Jay. . . . . Nurse
Joann Thompson . . . . Nurse
Jennifer Davis . . . . Nurse
Copyright 1983 – 20th Century Fox Film Corporation

Non-Credited Appearances. . . . . Roy Goldman, Dennis Troy

Chapters
1: *Main Titles*
2: *Charitable Assignment – 0:54*
3: *Bribe – 3:39*
4: *Passing the Buck – 5:44*
5: *Billy Bubba Needs Shoes – 7:33*
6: *Blackmail and Apology – 10:43*
7: *Klinger Takes Over – 13:07*
8: *Back to Where We Started – 17:39*
9: *A Soldier's Remorse – 21:40*
10: *Mission Accomplished / End Titles – 23:03*

Closing Stills
1: *Freeze – Potter and Charles in the office*
2: *Private Kurland*
3: *Rizzo*
4: *Igor*
5: *Charles*
6: *Potter*
7: *B.J.*
8: *Margaret*
9: *Mulcahy*
10: *Klinger*
11: *Hawkeye*

Synopsis: Colonel Potter assigns Charles as the Charity Collection Officer, and tells him the best time to separate a G.I. from his money is payday. Since Charles neglected to do this, the task is now much more difficult. However, Charles finds a way to pass the task off to Margaret, and the first of a long line of deals is made between the staff. The last person to try his hand at collecting charity money is Father Mulcahy. But after some investigating, he discovers who was originally assigned the unenviable task and hands the job right back to Charles, who, in a few hours, will have to turn in an empty ledger to Potter. Private Kurland is not happy that the North Korean soldier he shot, is now in the bed next to him, and makes his feelings known. The Private has a change of heart though when he finds out why the North Korean was trying to steal his boots.

Commentary by Jeff Maxwell: "Consider yourself thrown on the set of *M*A*S*H* with little rehearsal and a lot of pressure to perform in front of 85-plus people with thousands of dollars a minute flying by. Think of it as you showing up at your job and realizing you forgot to wear pants."

Authors' Notes: There are no PA announcements in this episode

In Chapter 2, Potter is not wearing a watch on his left wrist, and the tan lines are visible.

In Chapter 3, and for the second time in the series, the word "bastard" is said, this time by Private Kurland. The first time this was said was by Hawkeye in Season 5, Episode 118, "The General's Practitioner."

Margaret mentions Sonnets of the Portuguese by poet Elizabeth Barrett Browning (1806 – 1861) in Chapter 3. (*See Margaret's Season 11 Profile for more details.*)

In Chapter 6, Klinger hands out Hershey's Chocolate Bars to some of the wounded, including the North Korean in Post-Op. However, a UPC bar code is clearly visible on the chocolate bars. While the idea of bar-coding dates back to the 1930s, it was during the 1970s when retail history was made. On June 26, 1974, a cashier at Marsh's Supermarket in Troy, Ohio is credited as having scanned the very first UPC bar code on a 10-pack of Wrigley's Juicy Fruit gum. The gum is now on display at the Smithsonian Institution in Washington, D.C.

Something of an oddity in Chapter 7 as both main doors on the inside of the mess tent are covered with roll-down canvas.

In Chapter 10, the view out of the office windows, even at night, is the same as it has been for most of the recent episodes: the Motor Pool Supply.

Also in Chapter 10, and also in Potter's office, is Mildred's picture, still on the left side of his desk, and not the right where it's been all along up until the past few episodes.

As Time Goes By – 2/21/1983

Season 11 / Episode 255 / Production 256 – 9-B10

Columbia House VHS Tape . . . . Charles In Charge (Catalog # 22049)
Fox DVD . . . . Season 11, Disc 2

Alan Alda, Mike Farrell, Harry Morgan
Loretta Swit, David Ogden Stiers, Jamie Farr, William Christopher

Executive Producer – Burt Metcalfe
Supervising Producer – John Rappaport
Written by Dan Wilcox & Thad Mumford
Directed by Burt Metcalfe

Producers – Thad Mumford / Dan Wilcox
Executive Story Consultant – Karen Hall
Creative Consultants – Gene Reynolds / Alan Alda

G.W. Bailey . . . . Sergeant Luthor Rizzo
Rosalind Chao . . . . Soon-Lee
Mark Herrier . . . . Corporal Stoddard
Michael Swan . . . . Lieutenant Brannum
Kellye Nakahara . . . . Kellye
Jeff Maxwell . . . . Igor
Wesley Thompson . . . . Corpsman
Chao Li Chi . . . . Korean Husband
Oksun Kim . . . . Korean Wife
Jo Ann Thompson . . . . Nurse # 1
Brigitte Chandler . . . . Nurse # 2
Copyright 1983 – 20th Century Fox Film Corporation

Non-Credited Appearances . . . . Roy Goldman, Dennis Troy

Chapters

1: Main Titles
2: Up to No Good – 0:53
3: Unlikely Prisoner – 3:25
4: Meaningful Artifacts – 5:26
5: Begging for Freedom – 9:02

6: Lost and Found – 10:47
7: Good Deeds – 14:11
8: Failed Reunion – 19:06
9: The Time Capsule – 19:49
10: Ongoing Joke / End Titles – 23:01

Closing Stills

1: Freeze – Hawkeye, Charles and B.J.
2: Rizzo
3: Soon-Lee
4: Corporal Stoddard
5: Klinger
6: Potter
7: Charles
8: B.J. in the shower
9: Mulcahy
10: Margaret
11: Hawkeye

Synopsis: The main focus in this episode is Margaret wanting to bury a time capsule in the hopes that, if dug up in a hundred years, people will know why they were in

Korea and what they were doing there. Members of the 4077th are eager to contribute, but Margaret's version of meaningful artifacts isn't the same as everyone else's. Sergeant Rizzo, on the other hand, has a dummy hand-grenade, and uses it to perfection causing B.J. to run out of the shower naked. But when Rizzo tries to use the dummy grenade with Charles, Charles does something that will truly humble Rizzo and put him in a state of disbelief. A chopper pilot flying a wounded soldier to the 4077th is 24 hours late. When Potter questions the pilot, all he says is "engine trouble." It isn't until after the pilot leaves that the wounded man tells the story of how the pilot flew his chopper, damaged by enemy fire, to the 4077th 200 yards at a time. A young Korean woman is brought to the 4077th in handcuffs after it's believed she shot an American soldier. The woman tries to plead her case, denying she shot anyone, and all she wants to do is find her parents who might have been taken to a refugee center. But the longer the woman is handcuffed to a tent post, the further away her parents will be, lessening the chances of finding them.

Commentary by Karen Hall: "I was famous for shooting down everything that anyone pitched, which often prompted Thad to say, in a very thick southern accent (mocking mine), 'Ah hate it, ah hate it, ah hate it.'"

Commentary by Jeff Maxwell: "Our prop man worked very hard at keeping track of all the props. As soon as a scene was over, anything that could be lifted was put safely away. He was a friend, and taking a prop on his watch would have been a serious violation of our friendship. Even if that hadn't been the case, behaving like a 'slickie boy' just wasn't in me. It was more comfortable and rewarding to say "so long" to it all than to take small pieces home in a bag. My mind was on the future, not stealing props from the studio."

PA Announcement by Todd Sussman

Authors' Notes: This was the final episode to be filmed. The cast actually buried its own time capsule, which was subsequently dug up some time later.
  According to Larry Gelbart, he returned to the set during this episode for the first time since he left after Season 4.
  In Chapter 3, Potter says "I ain't here to model bathrobes." Good thing, especially since he's wearing the bathrobe usually worn by Henry Blake.
  In Chapter 4, Potter mentions a Zane Grey novel, The Last of the Plainsmen. As in some previous episodes, Potter mentions books written by Zane Grey that were, in fact, written by others. The book he has and mentions in this episode is, in fact, a Zane Grey novel from 1908.
  At approximately 8:43 of Chapter 4, there's a microphone shadow above and to the left of the door inside the Swamp.
  Another microphone shadow, this time at approximately 10:36 of Chapter 5, inside the tent where Soon-Lee is handcuffed to the tent post, across the top.
  For the third time in the series, Kellye, in Chapter 9, is called "Lieutenant Nakahara."
  Henry Blake, Radar and Frank Burns are mentioned in this episode, but not Trapper.

This Episode was dedicated to the memory of
Connie Izay, R.N.
Technical Advisor
1977 - 1982

Goodbye, Farewell and Amen – 2/28/1983

Season 11 / Two-Hour Special / Production 250 – 9-B04

Columbia House VHS Tape.... Goodbye, Farewell And Amen (Catalog # 21041)
Fox DVD ....*Season 11, Disc 3*

Alan Alda, Mike Farrell, Harry Morgan
Loretta Swit, David Ogden Stiers, Jamie Farr, William Christopher

Guest Starring – Allen Arbus, G.W. Bailey, Rosalind Chao

Film Editors – Stanford Tischler, A.C.E. / Larry L. Mills, A.C.E.
Art Director – John Leimanis
Director of Photography – Dominic R. Palmer, Jr.
Supervising Producer – John Rappaport
Executive Producer – Burt Metcalfe

Written by
Alan Alda, Burt Metcalfe, John Rappaport
Dan Wilcox & Thad Mumford
Elias Davis & David Pollock
Karen Hall
Directed by Alan Alda

Producers – Thad Mumford / Dan Wilcox
Executive Story Consultant – Karen Hall

John Shearin	Chopper Pilot
Kellye Nakahara	Nurse Kellye
Jeff Maxwell	Private Igor Straminsky
Lang Yun	Korean Woman on the Bus
John Van Ness	Truman
Kevin Scannell	MacArthur
Arthur Song	Korean Man
Judy Farrell	Nurse Able
Jan Jorden	Nurse Baker
Enid Kent	Nurse Bigelow
June Kim	Woman with Shawl
Scott Lincoln	G.I.
Herb L. Mitchell	1st M.P.
Blake Clark	2nd M.P.
David Orr	Soldier
Mark Cassella	Jeep Driver
John Otrin	Ambulance Driver
Dennis Flood	Corpsman
Nurses	Shari Saba, Joann Thompson, Brigitte Chandler, Gwen Farrell, Natasha Bauman, Jennifer Davis

Corpsmen ....Roy Goldman, Dennis Troy, Bill Snider

Chinese Musicians .... Lawrence Soong, Byron Jeong, Jen-Chia Chang
Jim Lau, Frank Zi-Li Peng

Copyright 1983 – 20th Century Fox Film Corporation

Synopsis: Not all wounds are physical, as Hawkeye can attest to when he finds himself in a hospital he calls a "wacketeria," under the care of Dr. Sidney Freedman. Angry and not fully understanding why he's there, Sidney tries to get him to talk about the events that ultimately led to his stay in Ward D but, for now, the only thing Sidney learns is that more sessions are needed. Hawkeye comes to realize just what a nervous disorder is and what brought him to the ward in the first place. Sidney tells him he's ready to leave and Hawkeye thinks he's going home. Sidney has other ideas, and sends Hawkeye back to the 4077th.

As word quickly spreads that peace may finally be near, the camp is bustling with local civilian activity, a pen with enemy POWs, and Charles has an encounter in which he finds himself surrounded by five Chinese soldiers. Reaching for what Charles thinks is a weapon turns out to be a violin, and the Chinese soldiers turn out to be musicians. Taking them under his wing to teach them Mozart, the Chinese musicians will later have an impact on Charles and his love of classical music, while B.J. gets the news that he, along with nearly everyone else, has been waiting for: he's going home. When he finally gets a ride to Kimpo, and for the second time, Hawkeye's best friend goes home without leaving a note. Unfortunately for B.J., he'll have an opportunity to correct that.

Margaret's father pulls a few strings to help his daughter land an administrative assignment in Tokyo that doesn't involve nursing, designed to increase her chances of promotion. Margaret, on the other hand, pulls a few strings of her own in an effort to help Charles become the chief of thoracic surgery at Boston Mercy.

Meanwhile, Klinger searches the countryside looking for Soon-Lee and when he finally finds her, he tells her he loves and wants to marry her. Although she agrees, she refuses to leave Korea until she finds her family and, amazingly, Klinger winds up staying in Korea.

Returning from a bug-out after a fire threatens the entire camp, a "last supper" takes place in the mess tent giving others the chance to tell what they'll do after the war. Father Mulcahy had wanted to coach boxing for the C.Y.O., but is now interested in working with the deaf, and is also saddened that he might not be able to hear confessions again. Mildred has the Colonel's itinerary all planed out with a very long list of things to do around the house and Hawkeye just wants to take it easy for a while. Jokingly, B.J. wants to run off with a girl named "Cookie," whom he met in a bar in Guam, while Kellye has put in for an assignment at Triplet Army Hospital in Honolulu so she can be with her family. Igor will finally have an opportunity to do a job in which people won't yell at him all the time...a pig farmer. Rizzo plans to breed frogs for French restaurants. Dennis will work on his father in law's ranch in Colorado and Roy, well, Roy doesn't know what he's going to do.

Father Mulcahy's last official task is to marry Klinger and Soon-Lee, and then the newlyweds ride off in search of her family. After saying their goodbyes to each other, the members of the 4077th leave camp for the last time, but not before Hawkeye and Margaret engage in a 35-second kiss goodbye and in a show of respect, Hawkeye and B.J. salute Colonel Potter. Now that B.J. has an opportunity to say a proper goodbye to his friend Hawkeye, they both realize what they have meant to each other with promises of reuniting back in the States. B.J. rides off on a motorcycle that had once belonged to the Chinese musicians and Hawkeye leaves in a chopper. Once in the air, both Hawkeye and the viewer see one final message from B.J. written out in rocks: "GOODBYE."

Commentary by Larry Gelbart: "My idea would have been to do that last episode of the season, then have the camera pull back, back, back. Suddenly, we realize that we're watching a television show all along. Then Alan would come on and tell the audience that this had always been just a show, that there was no way in the world anybody could really convey this kind of war experience and what it meant to those people who lived it."

Commentary by Thad Mumford: " 'Goodbye, Farewell, and Amen' was team-written, like a relay race. I wasn't really crazy about the story, at first. I thought it was a little heavy. But, by the time we were working on it, the ball was already rolling."

Commentary by David Pollock: "We all sat in the conference room, for days, and then came up with the story, but in paragraph form. Then, each writer or writing team wrote a half an hour. Alan wrote with all of the writers. We, with Alan, wrote the first half hour."

Commentary by Karen Hall: "The night the last episode aired, we had a special screening of it and then we went to a Moroccan restaurant for dinner (writers, producers and Alan...I don't remember if any other actors went, you should check with the other guys). At some point during the dinner, Alan picked up his napkin (a big white linen napkin because we were eating with our hands) and flung it at someone. This started a napkin fight that lasted for a while, with napkins flying all over the restaurant and people chasing each other down to get a good shot. The waiters didn't know what to make of us, but we had a great time."

PA Announcements by Todd Sussman
PA Announcement by Klinger
Armed Forces Radio announcement by Robert Pierpoint over the PA with news of the end
of the Korean War and the grim statistics that go along with it.

Authors' Notes: Approximately 125 million people watched as *M*A*S*H* said "Goodbye," setting a new record. Since the arrival of cable and satellite television, bringing with them hundreds of channels, it would be very difficult to get that many people to watch the same program at the same time to break this record.

This is the only showing of *M*A*S*H* in which the title appears on-screen.

"Goodbye, Farewell and Amen" on DVD also lists the names of the chapters, as well as their time.

During the filming of "Goodbye, Farewell and Amen," the all-too-common wildfires of California ravaged the hills of Malibu. Sadly, the outdoor set of *M*A*S*H* at Malibu Creek State Park was directly in the path of the fires, and was destroyed. According to accounts at the time, even the metal hospital building melted beyond recognition. The *M*A*S*H* producers and writers decided to incorporate the fires into the final tele-movie. The fires that caused the *M*A*S*H* personnel to temporarily "bug out" were, according to Colonel Potter, caused by incendiary bombs. The real fires destroyed so much of the outdoor set that a bit of a new, fire ravaged but recognizable set had to be built.

For the first time, Hawkeye is seen in a blue robe while in Ward D.

According to Father Mulcahy, in Chapter 9, there are 40 orphans at Sister Theresa's Orphanage.

Potterisms: "I've got North Koreans up to my Southern border," "Biggest dunce since the monkey wrapped his tail around the flagpole," "The ravine latrine."

In Chapter 10, Hawkeye mentions that he has the same boots he got when he first got to the 4077th. What a coincidence, since Alan Alda wore the same pair of boots for the entire run of the show, and took them home when the series ended.

In Chapter 11, Hawkeye mentions Arizona Magazine, founded in 1925.

For the third time in the series, and the second by Hawkeye, he says "Son of a bitch" in Chapter 11.

In Chapter 12, Potter is wearing Henry Blake's robe.

The chopper pilot in Chapter 12 mentions Dr. Pepper. Dr. Pepper was invented and began sales in Waco, Texas, in 1885.

Once in a while, the end doors of the mess tent are used to enter, as they are in Chapter 13 in this episode.

In a jeep that's been on the show from the beginning, Hawkeye returns to the 4077th in number 18210717 in Chapter 14.

When Hawkeye returns to camp, he realizes B.J. left without leaving a note, as did Trapper.

In Chapter 15, an ambulance with a different serial number is seen. The numbers are in big block type and have not been seen before.

While the trash dump has been mentioned and seen, in Chapter 16 we see, for the first time, a sign stating "4077th Trash Dump."

The barber's tent has been seen in previous episodes filmed at the Ranch. In Chapter 17, we see it close up as a G.I. pulls the striped barber's sign down while bugging out.

Margaret, in Chapter 19, is wearing a blue colorful shirt that corpsmen wore in previous episodes.

In Chapter 20, Sidney arrives by jeep to check on Hawkeye. What's unusual about this is Sidney arrives in a jeep clearly marked, "MASH 4077."

In Chapter 20, the PA announcement states that hostilities will end in twelve hours at 10:00. In a different announcement, the time is given as 2:00. It's doubtful the military would announce times that way. It's much more likely the military would say 2200 hours or 1400 hours. Although during the course of the series, standard times were used every now and then and Robert Pierpont was a civilian war correspondent.

Colonel Henry Blake's bathrobe sure gets around. Potter was wearing it in Chapter 12, as noted above, and now here in Chapter 20, a corpsman is wearing it.

Strange that in Chapter 26, Klinger marries Soon-Lee wearing a tuxedo that's a perfect fit. We can assume Hawkeye gave him the tuxedo his father sent and Klinger could have done the alterations himself.

Robert Pierpoint was a broadcast journalist for CBS who covered the Korean War before becoming a CBS White House correspondent. Pierpoint was on the first edition of *See it Now* (1951) and also covered the State Department for CBS. Mr. Pierpoint is not only known for his work with CBS, he's also remembered as the voice over Armed Forces Radio in "Goodbye, Farewell and Amen," a role in which he played himself. As a White House correspondent, he covered six presidential administrations from Eisenhower to Carter, and published his memoirs from that time in his book, *At the White House*, in 1981.

Appendix - Season 11

Character Profiles

Note: GFA is "Goodbye, Farewell and Amen"

Hawkeye

Episode 242: His uncle was out at sea with a broken compass, no radio and a storm approaching. Uncle sees a boat through the fog with the name, "Luck of the Irish" and follows it back to port. He later found out that the "Luck of the Irish" sank 20 years ago.

255: Gives the chopper pilot's broken fan belt and Radar's bear for the time capsule.

GFA: Wearing the same boots he got when he first got to the 4077th. Found chewing gum under the seat at the Rialto in Kennebunkport. Once drove a jeep through the wall of the Officer's Club and ordered a double bourbon, according to Sidney, and that morning, wanted to operate on a patient without anesthetic — accused the anesthetist of trying to smother him with the mask.

When he gets home, he wants a banana and a piece of chocolate cake and also wants to take it easy for a while.

Hawkeye gives Margaret something to remember him by…a 35-second kiss. It's doubtful they'll forget each other.

B.J.

Episode 242: Selma is his father's sister.

244: Roomed with Captain Paul Yamato in Army Medical Training School.

254: The kid B.J. defeated for the marble championship of the second grade was Earl Flagen.

255: Gives a fishing lure for the time capsule that once belonged to Henry Blake.

GFA: Erin's second birthday is next week.

Looking forward to cleaning the garage, rain gutters and pruning the lemon tree.

B.J. says he makes $300 a month. *(Something is wrong here. In Episode 33, Hawkeye mentions earning $413.50 a month. In Episode 47, Margaret tells Frank that she earns $400 a month. Henry mentioned earning $831.75 a month in Episode 70, most likely due to his being the commanding officer. Why is it that Hawkeye earn $113.50 more a month than B.J.? The bigger question is how does Margaret earn $100 a month more than B.J.?)*

Wants to run off with a woman he met in Guam (when he thought he was going home) named "Cookie."

Colonel Potter

Episode 241: During WWII, he spent three weeks in a field hospital without a nurse in sight.

242: In 1939, Mildred dreamt her brother Calvin came into the room, sat at the foot of the bed and shook his head at her, sadly. She got a phone call in the morning that Calvin had died of a heart attack. She called her sister Louise, and Louise knew it was bad news.

243: Spent the better part of The Battle of the Marne with an "older" 20-year-old French woman who worked in boulangerie in Soissons, France. They hung onto each other behind the bread racks — she made him feel safe and Mildred can't understand why he gets misty-eyed every time he cracks open French bread *(see Episode 243, page 716 for details on the two battles of the Marne).*

245: Mildred has been all over Missouri looking for a Shmoo for their grandson.
Potter got a Shmoo from the Kimpo PX.

247: Mildred always uses that old fountain pen that makes everything look like it was written by a monk.
Mildred bought her stationary at the Sisters of Mercy tag sale last summer.
Mildred scrimped and saved and paid off their mortgage six months early, as read by Hawkeye in a letter from Mildred.
"You're gonna love it" is what Mildred told Potter when she put leopard-skin seat covers on the Hudson. Potter never felt safe getting into the car without a whip and a chair, according to the Colonel.
Doesn't want a houseboat and doesn't want to move to Florida. "Nobody over 60 should go to scuba school."
Mildred withdrew $800 of his hard earned money this month.
Got nervous when Mildred opened a charge account at the pharmacy.
Mildred's cousin Portia, who has been mentioned earlier in the series and lives in Florida, now has a last name: Nelson.
According to Hawkeye, Potter bought his house in the 1930's.

249: The Studebaker should last another couple of years *(See Episode 247, page 725 for the Hudson he has).*
Double clutching is good for Mildred's rheumatism.

251: Bob Wilson is Potter's son-in-law and is in the import business. He gives Potter horse-shaped bookends for his Zane Grey collection.
Wilson came to the house one night in a new suit and was friendly and polite. He called Potter, "Sir," but the Colonel didn't buy it for a minute.
Potter gets a phone call from the Imperial Hotel in Tokyo and learns that "Mrs. Wilson" left a silk nightgown in the room. The real "Mrs. Wilson," is back home.
Wilson works for the "Rapahanak" Import Company *(see Episode 251, page 733 for more on the name "Rapahanak").*
Evy and Bob took their son, Stuart, to a horse show in Dry Fork (West Virginia) *(See Episode 251, page 733 for more on Potter's Grandchildren).*
Finishing up his residency, he was about to start his first job at a VA hospital in Springfield (Missouri). Mildred went ahead to setup housekeeping while he stayed in St. Louis. Coming off a late shift with a nurse, they went to get something to eat and a nightcap at her place. Things got friendlier than they should have and couldn't look Mildred in the face for a week.

252: Mildred put up turnips in the summer.

253: Potter and Colonel Woody Cooke go back to WWI and was one of the best friends Potter ever had — Cooke was injured when he went to check a fuel snafu after only two months behind a desk and 34 years without "skinning his knees."

Potter and Cooke went to their old unit's costume party — Potter was Roy Rogers and Cooke was Dale Evans because "he had better legs.."

255: Gives a Zane Grey novel, The Last of the Plainsmen (1908), for the time capsule.

GFA: Mildred sent a list *(long)* of things they can do together when he gets home, like fixing the holes in the screens and weeding Mildred's nasturtiums.

Once saw a similar orange glow in the Ardennes to the glow he sees now. A fire was started by incendiary bombs.

Misses fresh corn — any style.

As per Father Mulcahy's request, and the fact that he can't take Sophie home, he'll give her to the orphans. In between work, she can give them rides.

Margaret

Episode 243: Father stationed at Fort Bliss when she was seven years old — mother used to take her to the art museum in El Paso.

254: According to Margaret, "the most beautiful words ever written" were Elizabeth Barrett Browning's "Sonnets from the Portuguese" *(see Episode 254, page 740 for details on Elizabeth Barrett Browning).*

255: Gives a Nurses' Manual for the time capsule.

GFA: Uncle Robert Harwell – Chairman of the Board of Boston Mercy Hospital. Aunt Betsy Harwell.

Father lined up a better assignment than Tokyo. He knows someone who can get her assigned to NATO headquarters in Belgium.

Catches Soon-Lee's bouquet.

Charles gives her his leather-bound copy of "Sonnets from the Portuguese," a favorite of hers, to remember him by.

Hawkeye gives Margaret a 35-second long kiss. It's doubtful they'll forget each other.

Charles

Episode 243: Likes Tom & Jerry (MGM cartoon series from the 1940s and 1950s)

Has a bottle of Château Petrus purchased from Geller Brothers' Liquors on Commonwealth Ave. in Boston. *(Château Petrus is one of the most highly rated and expensive wines in the world.)*

247: When the Winchesters bought their first house, the first thing they did was fire the staff.

249: Honoria Winchester is afflicted with stuttering.

Gives a leather-bound copy of Moby Dick to Private Walt Palmer (Herman Melville, 1851).

250: Has a summer place in the Berkshires — a "baton's throw away from Tanglewood."

Has eaten in a restaurant in France called "Le Pied du Chevac" in Bordeaux.

Was in Elewijt standing in the house where Rubens painted his "most wonderful" masterpiece, "The Rape of the Daughters of Leucippus," according to Charles. Peter Paul Rubens (June 28, 1577-May 30, 1640) was a 17th Century Flemish Baroque painter.

255: Gives a bottle of 100-year-old cognac for the time capsule.

GFA: Informed by a friend that his application to be chief of thoracic surgery at Boston Mercy might be turned down.

Dr. Torborg is the Chief Administrator of Boston Mercy hospital.

As Charles helps during triage, he discovers one of the seriously wounded is a Chinese musician from the group of Chinese musicians he befriended. Unfortunately, this Chinese friend dies while Charles is looking on. He goes back to the Swamp and plays the record of Mozart he was trying to teach them but instead, takes the record and angrily smashes it on a table.

The incident with the five Chinese musicians and the impact it had on Charles will alter his perception of refuge. Whereas before, his music was his refuge, now it will serve as a reminder.

Gives Margaret the book she loves, his leather-bound Sonnets from the Portuguese.

Klinger

Episode 242: Wearing a Zoot Suit given to him by his Uncle Habib, who had a "business setback" of one to five years.

244: Lived through four Toledo gang wars and a father with a short temper and a quick jab.

245: Uncle Amir is "on his butt" ever since his door-to-door pita bread business went "belly-up."

Uncle Amir's address is: Mr. Amir Abdullah, 1329 S. 15th Street, Toledo, Ohio.

255: Originally wanted to give his Scarlet O'Hara dress for the time capsule, but decided the black sequined "designer original from Mr. Sid of Toledo" was the better way to go.

GFA: Uncle Jameel used to say, "If you wanna hide in the desert, you gotta look like sand."

Eddie Fahey is a kid Klinger grew up with — "crazy as a fruitcake" — ran into a light post and wound up wearing a steel plate in his head — used to wear a "Scottie" black and white dog magnet on his forehead.

In the old country, Uncle Jameel was a camel rustler.

Marries Soon-Lee and since she refuses to leave Korea until she finds her family, he's staying in Korea to help her.

Father Mulcahy

Episode 249: Stays in shape by running and to work off stress.

251: Was thrown out of the seminary dorm for snoring.

254: Took a course in the seminary on how to "put the bite" on prisoners for monetary contributions for charity.

255: Gives boxing gloves for the time capsule.

Seen, Heard, Mentioned or Referenced – Season 11

Note: GFA is "Goodbye, Farewell and Amen"

Movies

Episode 244: Potter mentions *The O.K. Corral*. See Episode 224 (page 703) for details.

246: Mulcahy mentions *Sorrowful Jones*, a 1949 remake of the 1934 Shirley Temple film *Little Miss Marker*.

248: *Sahara* (1943) mentioned, then seen in the mess tent
Hawkeye says "By the light of the silvery moonshine" – a reference to *By the Light of the Silvery Moon*, a 1953 Doris Day movie See "Songs," Episode 248 for details.
B.J. reads from the newspaper about *The Moon is Blue* with David Niven, William Holden and Maggie McNamara, directed by Otto Preminger (whose brother, Ingo Preminger, produced the film *M*A*S*H*, and was executive consultant for the series Pilot episode.) *(Note: The movie was released on July 8, 1953, a borderline inconsistency in the* M*A*S*H *timeline).*
Hawkeye mentions "Babette Meets the Fleet" *(Not real)*
Major Frankenheimer mentions *High Noon* (1952)

GFA: Hawkeye tells of Charles Boyer trying to drive Ingrid Bergman crazy in *Gaslight* (1944).

Songs

241: "Unforgettable" *(Hawkeye sings "Unforgettable, that's what you are...")* Written by Irving Gordon, sung by Nat King Cole, and published in 1951.
"Hey Good Lookin'" *(Hawkeye sings "Hey good lookin', watcha got cookin'")* Written by Hank Williams, from 1951.
"Rag Mop" (sometimes referred to as "Ragg Mopp") *(Kellye says "R-A-G-G-M-O-P-P")* Written by Deacon Anderson and Johnnie Lee Wills. Published in 1949, made popular by The Ames Brothers. (Note: "Rag Mop" is also heard in Season 9's "A War For All Seasons.")

242: "Heat Wave" *(Hawkeye sings, "We're having a party, a Halloween party..." to the melody)* Written by Irving Berlin in 1933 for the Broadway musical *As Thousands Cheer*. "Heat Wave" is also sung in Season 7's "Baby, It's Cold Outside."
"The Marines' Hymn" *(Charles says "Pool halls of Montezuma," a reference to The Halls of Montezuma.)* See Episode 185 (page 593) for details.

244: "Happy Days are Here Again" *(Korean female voice, heard over PA)* See Episode 1 (page 128) for details.
"You're the Top" *(Mentioned by B.J., later sung by Hawkeye)* See Episode 104 (page 399) for details.
"Mother Machree" *(Potter exclaims "Great Mother Machree")* Words by Rida Johnson Young, music by Chauncey Olcott & Earnest Ball, from 1910. (Also a 1928 silent film.)

246: "Don't Get Around Much Anymore" *(Charles mentions)* A jazz standard with music written by Duke Ellington, words by Bob Russell. The original title for this song was "Never No Lament," recorded by Mr. Ellington in 1940 as an instrumental. The lyrics and a new title were added in 1942.
"Hooray for Hollywood" *(Potter mentions, later heard by a military band on the Ranch compound)* Words by Richard A. Whiting, music by Johnny Mercer from the 1937 film *Hollywood Hotel*.

248: "You Make Me Feel So Young" *(Instrumental heard on the jukebox in the Officer's Club)* See Episode 1 (page 130) for details.
"Our State Fair" *("Our state fair is a great state fair...")* From the 1945 movie *State Fair*, words by Oscar Hammerstein II, music by Richard Rodgers. See also Season 11 "Movies."
"By the Light of the Silvery Moon" *(Hawkeye says "By the light of the silvery moonshine")* Words by Edward Madden, music by Gus Edwards. (Also a 1953 Doris Day movie.)

250: "Rosie the Riveter" *(Potter mentions)* a song written by Redd Evans and John Jacob Loeb in 1943. See Episode 250 in the Episode Guide (page 731) for more information.
"Trout" (also known as "The Trout Quintet) *(Heard on Charles' record player)* Franz Schubert composed the Piano Quintet in A Major in 1819 at the age of 22, but the piece wasn't published until 1829, a year after his death.
"Oh, My Papa" *(Klinger mentions)* The German "O Mein Papa" was written by Paul Burkhard in 1939 for the musical *Der Schwarze Hecht*. The song was adapted into English by John Turner and Geoffrey Parsons. Recorded by Eddie Fisher, the song became a number 1 hit on the U.S. Billboard Hot 100 Chart in 1954.

252: "Let A Smile be your Umbrella" *(Margaret sings "Let a smile be your umbrella on a rainy, rainy day...")* Words by Irving Kahal and Francis Wheeler, music by Sammy Fain, published in 1927.

253: Charles received and listened to composer Gustav Mahler's "Kindertotenlieder." In English, "Songs on the Death of Children." The words were poems written by Friedrich Rukert in 1833 and 1834. Gustav had taken five poems from a group of 425 (the original Kindertotenlieder) written by Rukert after suffering the loss of two of his children in a 16-day period. Gustav composed them in 1901 and 1904.
"Your Feets Too Big" *(Klinger mentions)* Written by Fred Fisher (September 30, 1875-January 14, 1942). Fisher was inducted into the Songwriter's Hall of Fame in 1970.
"It's A Long Way to Tipperary" *(Potter and Woody Cooke sing)* A British music hall and marching song written by Jack Judge and Harry Williams on January 30, 1912.

255: "M-O-T-H-E-R" *(Igor sings "M is for the many things she gave me...")* Words by Howard Johnson, music by Theodore F. Morse, published in 1915.

GFA: "Quintet for Clarinet and Strings (K.581)" by Mozart *(Charles plays a recording, and teaches the five Chinese musicians).*
"California, Here I Come" *(B.J. sings)* Written by Buddy DeSylva and Joseph Meyer, and recorded by Al Jolson in 1924.
"Row, Row, Row Your Boat" *(Sung on the bus)* English nursery rhyme and children's song. Credited to Eliphalet Oram Lyte in the Franklin Square Song Collection, 1881
"Oh! Susanna" *(Chinese musicians play)* Written by Stephen Foster, published on February 25, 1848.
"Chattanooga Choo-Choo" *(Male Japanese voice, heard over the PA)* See Episode 1 (page 128) for details.
"Home On the Range" *(all sing, in the mess tent)* See Episode 16 (page 129) for details.

Appearances – Season 11

Note: GFA is "Goodbye, Farewell and Amen"

Anderson, John..Episode 252 *(Major General Addison Collins)*
Anderson, Mark..Episode 249 *(Earl "Jackrabbit" LeMasters)*
Arbus, Allen..GFA *(Major Sidney Freedman)*
Bailey, G.W...................................... Episode 254, 255, GFA *(Sergeant Luther Rizzo)*
Bauman, Natasha..Episode 246, GFA *(Nurse)*
Bond, Michael.. Episode 246 *(Captain Hobart)*
Boyd, guy..Episode 247 *(Sergeant Lally)*
Brannon, Terry.. Episode 242 *(Marine)*
Brock, Phil..Episode 249 *(Private Walt Palmer)*
Brown, Alan Robert.. Episode 249 *(Colonel Crocker)*
Callaway, Thomas..Episode 249 *(Captain Sweeny)*
Camp, Hamilton.. Episode 248 *(Major T. Frankenheimer)*
Carmine, Michael..Episode 246 *(Patient)*
Cassella, Mark..GFA *(Jeep Driver)*
Chandler, Brigitte..Episode 250, GFA *(Nurse)*
Chandler, Brigitte..Episode 255 *(Nurse Number 2)*
Chang, Jen-Chia..GFA *(Chinese Musician)*
Chao, Rosalind.. Episode 255, GFA *(Soon-Lee)*
Chapman, Jeff..Episode 252 *(Maloney)*
Charno, Stu..Episode 246 *(Corporal Sonneborn)*
Chung, Byron.. Episode 243 *(Lieutenant Chong-Wha Park)*
Clark, Blake.. GFA *(2nd M.P.)*
Clay, Andrew.. Episode 242 *(Corporal Hrabosky)*
Conn, Michael..Episode 249 *(G.I.)*
Davis, Jennifer.. Episode 253, 254, GFA *(Nurse)*
Dugan, Dennis..Episode 251 *(Bob Wilson)*
East, Jeff.. Episode 247 *(Lieutenant Pavelich)*
Farmer, Buddy.. Episode 243 *(M.P.)*
Farrell, Gwen..GFA *(Nurse)*
Farrell, Judy.. GFA *(Nurse Able)*
Feury, Peggy..Episode 241 *(Colonel Bucholz)*
Flood, Dennis..GFA *(Corpsman)*
Garrett, Norman..Episode 252 *(Patient)*
Goldman, Roy..GFA *(Corpsman)*
Goldman, Roy.. Episode 253 *(Roy)*
Grubbs, Gary.. Episode 241 *(Lieutenant Geyer)*
Haid, David..Episode 244 *(Private Leightman)*
Holahan, Dennis.. Episode 250 *(Per Johannsen)*
Horton, Michael.. Episode 252 *(Lieutenant Curt Collins)*
Harmon, Deborah..Episode 241 *(Nurse Webster)*
Helberg, Sandy..Episode 248 *(Corporal Bannister)*
Herrier, Mark.. Episode 255 *(Corporal Stoddard)*
Innes, George..Episode 250 *(Doctor Randolph Kent)*
Jay, Alberta.. Episode 254 *(Nurse)*
Jeong, Byron..GFA *(Chinese Musician)*
Johnson, Chip..Episode 252 *(Captain Sterne)*
Jorden, Jan.. Episode 248, GFA *(Nurse Baker)*
Karen, James..Episode 252 *(Doctor Steven Chesler)*
Karpa, Ron.. Episode 249 *(Driver)*
Kent, Enid..Episode 245, GFA *(Nurse Bigelow)*

Turner, Arnold .... Episode 242 *(Graves Registration Assistant)*
Van Hess, John .... GFA *(Truman)*
Ward, Larry .... Episode 248 *(General Rothaker)*
Wasson, Craig .... Episode 254 *(Private Kurland)*
Wendt, George .... Episode 242 *(Private LaRoche)*
Westmore, Jennifer Davis .... Episode 247 *(Nurse)*
Williams, Allen .... Episode 246 *(Lieutenant Priore)*
Wilson, Rita .... Episode 241 *(Nurse Lacey)*
Wong, Dereck .... Episode 254 *(Korean Soldier)*
Wright, Ken .... Episode 249 *(G.I.)*
Yates, Jack .... Episode 253 *(Large enlisted man)*
Yi, Jin-Taek .... Episode 244 *(Korean Soldier)*
Yun, Lang .... GFA *(Korean Woman on the Bus)*
Zi-Li, Frank .... GFA *(Chinese Musician)*

Broadcast/Production Order - Season 11

Broadcast	Production
241: Hey, Look Me Over *(10/25/1982)**	*247: (9-B01)* Trick Or Treatment
242: Trick Or Treatment *(11/1/1982)*	*248: (9-B02)* Bombshells
243: Foreign Affairs *(11/8/1982)**	*249: (9-B03)* Run For The Money
244: The Joker Is Wild *(11/15/1982)**	*250: (9-B04)* Goodbye, Farewell and Amen
245: Who Knew? *(11/22/1982)**	*251: (9-B05)* Friends And Enemies
246: Bombshells *(11/28/1982)*	*252: (9-B06)* U.N, The Night and the Music
247: Settling Debts *(12/6/1982)**	*253: (9-B07)* Strange BedFellows
248: The Moon Is Not Blue *(12/13/1982)**	*254: (9-B08)* Say No More
249: Run For The Money *(12/20/1982)*	*255: (9-B09)* Give And Take
250: U.N, The Night and the Music *(1/3/1983)*	*256: (9-B10)* As Time Goes By
251: Strange Bedfellows *(1/10/1983)*	
252: Say No More *(1/24/1983)*	
253: Friends And Enemies *(2/7/1983)*	
254: Give And Take *(2/14/1983)*	
255: As Time Goes By *(2/21/1983)*	
Goodbye, Farewell and Amen *(2/28/1983)*†	

* Episodes 241, 243, 244, 245, 247 and 248 were produced during Season 10 but held over for broadcast in Season 11.

† Although most people refer to "Goodbye, Farewell and Amen" as the final episode, it's actually a 2½ hour "special."

Interviews

Enid Kent Sperber

Enid Kent, as she was billed, made her debut as Nurse Bigelow in "Out of Sight, Out of Mind" in Season 4, with several memorable subsequent appearances.

"My first job in television in Los Angeles was the episode 'Out of Sight, Out of Mind.' Previously I had worked on stage, in television commercials and limited roles in films mostly in New York and San Francisco. I got the job on *M*A*S*H*, as I recall, because my mother knew Gene Reynolds and Burt Metcalfe. My mother was actress Irene Tedrow and had known Gene since he was a child actor in radio. 'Out of Sight, Out of Mind' was memorable particularly because of Tom Sullivan, the blind actor who was the guest star. One of the things he was noted for was having dived into a swimming pool to rescue his young daughter. Alan (Alda) and Mike (Farrell) were having a conversation with him when he bragged that he

761

could 'see!' 'What do you mean?' they said. 'Hold up fingers to my face and I will tell you how many fingers you are holding up,' he challenged. Mike held up three fingers and without missing a beat, Tom said 'three.' 'How did you do that?' They wanted to know. He explained that since he was totally blind his other senses had been heightened and he was able to 'see' Mike's fingers by body heat. The cast of *M*A*S*H* was the friendliest cast I ever worked with in my subsequent years in television. Alan took the lead by striding up to new cast members and thrusting his hand out to introduce himself, 'I'm Alan Alda.' I have worked many shows where the stars took no notice of the day players and we remained anonymous to everyone on the set. *M*A*S*H* was more like a theatrical company. There was a concerted effort to create a community because of the nature of the program. The *M*A*S*H* unit was in the same place in Korea for all those years. They used the same extras and brought the same day players giving them the same character names in order to create that reality on screen. Each week Gene, Burt and Alan would get together on a Wednesday evening after work and discuss the show for the following week making sure there was that continuity of the same people working the same jobs in the unit week after week. I have worked on a number of series and been called back to re-appear a number of seasons. Sometimes I would appear as a different character on each episode and other times I would have the same character name but my personality would have undergone a complete overhaul. That never happened in all the years I appeared on *M*A*S*H*. That is one of the things that made the show so special not only for those of us who worked on it but for the audience who watched it. I have small recollections of many of my fellow actors. Larry Linville and I used to chat about theater all the time. Harry Morgan was an old friend of my mother's having been in the business longer than almost everyone on the set. Harry was a cut up. He was so familiar with the camera and so comfortable with what he had been doing all these years that he didn't always need time to get into character. I remember one day where Harry, Alan and I were preparing to shoot a short scene. The soundman yelled, 'Speed.' Harry told a fun joke as the director called, 'In five, four, three, two and action.' In that short time Harry got serious and Alan and I had to look as if we were not cracking up. David Ogden Stiers, the consummate professional, had a passion for music and conducting. He owned my recordings of the same symphonies conducted by different artists. He loved to listen to these recording and practice conducting 'in the style of.' He loved the fact that our stage at Twentieth Century Fox was near the famous scoring stage presided over in various years by the illustrious Newman composing family. I do have fond memories of him jumping on the board and announcing to the stage manager that he was heading over to the score stage. At this point this tall lanky fellow would glide out the large open door to the sound stage and ride over to hear live music. One of my favorite people on the set was not an actor. It was Terry Miles, the head make-up artist. Terry had been in the business all his life. His father was an actor in silents. Sitting in his chair was an education. He had the best stories about a make-up artist at MGM in the late thirties and forties. He was quite skilled in his craft and because we were a hospital unit out in the boonies we were not supposed to look as if we had make-up on. One year I was lucky to get a job on Macmillan and Wife with Rock Hudson at Universal Studios. I was excited to get the Universal make-up studio treatment and hoped to look terribly glamorous. I couldn't wait to see the show to see how I looked. What a disappointment. I looked awful and painted. It was then that I realized the skill of Terry Miles. He made us all look real and frankly very glamorous with great artistry and he never took very long to do it. One day I was hanging around and looked across the stage to where Alan was talking to a very handsome charismatic gentleman. I couldn't take my eyes off this man. I couldn't figure out who he was. Was he a 'suit' from the studio? Was he Alan's agent? I had to know. So I went up to one of the grips and asked, 'Who is that man that Alan is talking to?' The guy looked at me as if I was crazy and said. 'That is Alan's Dad!'"

Melinda Mullins
Guest Star in "Foreign Affairs," in Season 11

"Guess what? I live with (and am profoundly in love with) another *M*A*S*H* veteran, Josh Bryant. He played Sergeant Scully. In fact, I believe we worked on *M*A*S*H* the very same year, but we only met and fell in love twenty years later. I have a slightly interesting story about my episode, because I had to *pretend* to be French during the whole week of shooting, because that's how I got the job in the first place. More on that later. It turned out to be a rather amusing week, and truly astonishing for me because I had grown up watching *M*A*S*H* and there I was, at 21, guest-starring on my favorite show in the world. Very heady. I had been living in Europe (Paris) though I'm American, and had just decided 6 months before to move back to America and be a movie star. I had been doing some modeling and looking for an agent, and then I did a silly play in Pasadena and got nice and pudgy because I didn't know that you couldn't eat pizza every night after the show and stay thin. Anyhow, there I was I had a third- or fourth-rate agent (whom I had picked because their name was French) and I was working as an assistant to the President of a computer corporation. Then the agent called and told me about the part on *M*A*S*H* and how he submitted my name but they had said I wasn't old enough to play the love interest for David Ogden Stiers. He suggested that I go to 20th Century and take a photo of myself and look as old as possible. It sounded like a good gutsy plan to me. So I dressed in my most mature-looking clothes (earrings and all) and hand-delivered my photo. Of course, they wanted an authentic French person (easy for me because I'd been brought up bilingual). So, when I gave my photo to the secretary, I handed it over with all the heavily French-accented English at my command. It worked. The secretary did a double take and asked me to wait. Right then she got me in to read for, I think, the casting director and then I was asked to return that afternoon and read for the producer (Burt Metcalfe) and read with David. I was excited beyond belief. I had never done a film or TV show in my life. I went to the phone booth on the lot and called my mom! We were both huge *M*A*S*H* fans. I went in that afternoon and made up some silly story about how I was 100% French but just visiting Los Angeles or something. I heard who the competition was for the part...Sylvie Vartan, the bleach-blonde pop singer. For some reason that didn't intimidate me. The reading went well, I gather. Everybody thought I was French anyway. And, maybe being pudgy made me look older and/or more appropriate for working with Monsieur Stiers. So I had to wait over a long weekend and then got the part! What was now required was going to the first read-through etc., and always pretending to be French. The read-through went great. I couldn't believe I was at a big table with all these people whom I had idolized for the previous ten years. And boy was I nervous, but I think I hid it pretty well. They asked me for help with the French-ness of the script, of Martine's part and I was able to deliver. Finally, came the first day of shooting. Everybody was spectacularly nice. Don't forget, I had never worked in front of a camera before. Loretta Swit had to tell me what a 'mark' was. She was very kind, as was everyone. Charles Dubin was the director and he also spoke a lot of French and enjoyed speaking with me in French. Thank God, I really was bi-lingual. Then after a few days, it all started to unravel, in a nice way. I got accepted to the Julliard Theater School in New York. David Ogden Stiers had been there as well. So, I told him my good news. I could hardly contain myself. He, of course, expressed some surprise that they would accept a foreigner with such a heavy accent. Then, a sort of spontaneous game cropped up between us, between takes. He would do an accent (Indian, lets say) and I would do it back at him. And on around the globe we went until he realized, (duh!), that I was probably faking the French accent. But he didn't say anything or put me on the spot. That day at the commissary, the famous 20th Century Fox commissary, I shared the truth with Harry Morgan and David Stiers. They agreed to keep my secret. Very nice. In the meantime, Alan Alda developed some kind of suspicions, because he would ask me out of the blue the French word for something...or the words to the French national anthem. Scary stuff. I think he saw through me a bit, but he was still very nice. The one day we shot on location, I had to be in make-up at 4am, and I remember some nice person asking me if I wanted some coffee. And, to my utter horror, I heard myself say 'you bet I would' in a heavy (sleepy) American accent. They didn't seem to notice, Thank God. The week of shooting went well. David Ogden Stiers was very kind and kept my secret and even took me with him at a lunch break to watch an orchestra scoring some film or other. (Stiers is a conductor in one of his many alternate lives). At the pizza festivities the day we wrapped, I went up to Burt Metcalfe (being the ambitious actress that I was) and said, in my usual American accent, that if he ever needed an *American* actress for a part, would he please call me. I don't think he was altogether thrilled that he'd been tricked. I don't blame him. So, that was my *M*A*S*H* experience. Then, I went off to Julliard in New York that fall and left behind, for the most part, LA-LA Land, and all it does or doesn't have to offer. Josh would like to add that everyone was extremely nice to him and working on the show was a great pleasure and honor. He also remarked at how good everyone was on that show, even down to all the extras (the nurses, the guy who served food on the chow line). Voila!"

PHOTO COURTESY RICHARD LEE SUNG

Richard Lee Sung

First credited appearance was in "Officr of the Day," in Season 3

"There are several stories, but the one I want to tell most is about Alan Alda. The cast was a wonderful cast. They were professionals and really great human beings, all of them. That's why they worked so well together. And when I joined them, they went hysterical with me over the 'Kim Luck' thing (from 'Officer of the Day'). The crew and everyone went hysterical over the scene and my one line, 'this is me.' It was my first experience where the crew was applauding and having a heck of a time. So, it was just a wonderful moment for me. See, Asian American actors don't get a chance to be human beings. We are caricatures and stereotypes of what Hollywood thinks we should be. For 37 years I've been playing those roles. It was a shock when we were doing 'Dear Mildred,' and Alan Alda came up to me. I think it was the second day of filming and he said to me 'you know, I couldn't sleep last night and decided you should forget the accent. Portray this man as lost in the war, and well educated. He's a businessman. Just play him as a human being.' I was so shocked. They usually want a certain image, and for Alan Alda to tell me that, was a shock. No one had ever done that in Hollywood in all the years I'd worked. I haven't worked that much because I have to wait for Asian roles. *Kung Fu* and *M*A*S*H* were where all the Asian American actors got to work. So, that was a story I really wanted to tell. I wish the whole world knew how wonderful Alan Alda is...how caring in trying to make things right. I went to see a play Alan Alda was in called 'Art,' about a painting that has nothing on it and went for $40,000. It was funny from the first moment on. I went backstage with my daughter and he was kind enough to let us in and spend 15 or 20 minutes with us. It made me feel really good in front of my daughter. And he was just so gracious. I enjoyed that moment with him. The whole cast of *M*A*S*H* was that way. Another incident...I was at 20th Century trying to audition for a job and I saw Loretta Swit's trailer. I wondered what she was doing and thought I'd drop in to say hello. All of a sudden, out of the clear blue sky, here comes Loretta yelling 'Curly's here!!' That's what they call me. And, she introduced me to everybody. I felt like I was a movie star for the first time in my life. After so many years, she remembered me. She is such a warm, beautiful person. For an Asian American actor who rarely gets that kind of treatment. We were aliens in Hollywood. It's difficult until you realize that that's the way it is and it involves money. But, if you love the business you stay with it and hope, one day, you'll get that role where you don't have to be that caricature...that image. I'm also a veteran of the Korean War. I fought the real war in the Marines. So, I fought the real war, and fought it in Hollywood. I'm also part Mexican. Nobody ever knew. Two years ago, I was at a reunion in San Antonio and I was on the news. One of the crewmembers recognized me from *M*A*S*H* and he put me on the news. I spoke Spanish and he got a big kick out of that and put me on the Spanish news. They put that on as a follow up to a rerun of 'Dear Mildred.' The Korean War is the forgotten war, you know. We still forget the loss of American life. I'm a hawk and a dove at the same time. I hate wars, yet when our guys are dying and you don't support them...that's support you're giving the enemy. That's the way I feel because that's what happened to us in Korea. I was just so shocked I got out of Inchon. It was 65 degrees below zero and we lost a lot of men out there. I was lucky, and now I'm getting disability. Someone above me said it just wasn't my time. I'm very happy I'm here and able to tell my story about what *M*A*S*H* did for me and Asian American actors. I had an incident where I had some in-laws coming in from Australia. I asked if they wanted to visit the studio and they said that would be great. The whole cast was so nice to these people. They let them have one of the Martini glasses as a souvenir. Stiers, Christopher and Harry Morgan were all there, and made my relatives feel so good. They still remember, and have the glass in a special glass case. Gary Burghoff, of course, was wonderful. He was the first actor I worked with on that 'Kim Luck' episode. One time, I got a chance to talk to him when he was leaving the show. I realized what turmoil he was going through about leaving the cast. We started talking and…I joke alot, you know. I told him there's nothing like being happy in what you're doing in life. Sometimes, money's not important. It's very difficult to leave a hot show. I want to tell him how much that lunch with him meant to me, when he was going through that turmoil in trying to decide which way to go concerning leaving *M*A*S*H*. He'd been on it so long, with the original movie and all. It gets to you after a while. You want to go in different directions. There's more to Gary Burghoff than Radar. I always admired him for what he did. It was pretty gutsy. In my first *M*A*S*H* segment, I didn't realize what a great thing it would be for me. It paid my rent for that year. I did this one scene…I think we shot it only two or three times. Gene Reynolds was so happy with the way the scene ran. My ego was out of control. I don't think I worked with Wayne Rogers. I came on after him, mostly. I was on *City of Angels* with him, that's right. They just needed a good-looking Oriental guy. They couldn't find any others. It's like the Marine Corps. Here I am trying to replace John Wayne, and the next thing you know I'm in Korea. Getting my job was just one of those cattle calls. Joyce Robinson was very nice. We did a nice interview. And, they kept calling me back. The *M*A*S*H* people were so good to me. They were quite a talented bunch of people. But Alan Alda was the leader. The way he worked, they worked. It made a wonderful ensemble. One time, I was at a children's benefit. One of the writers snuck up behind me and thanked me for the way I read the lines in 'Dear Mildred.' He tapped me on the shoulder and said 'I just want to say thank you for reading my lines.' It's an ego trip because I don't think of myself as a movie star. As a sex symbol…yes, but not as a movie star. I have a wonderful mentor by the name of Kathleen Freeman. She got nominated for the musical *The Full Monty* and she was my mentor for many years. As both an actor and human being, she was one of the nicest people you'd ever want to meet. You could run into her with your jaw hanging down to your knees and she would turn everything around. Thanks to her, I'm happy with what I've done, and no longer feel sorry for myself. That's a waste of time. Racism is going to be here as long as we live and…just as long as they don't hate bald-headed people. (Laughs) I was working with Lou Gossett and we were talking about how Kareem (one of the Lakers) was worried about the bald spot he had. And Gossett was trying to convince him to shave his hair off because when you do that, you become 10 years younger. As you get older, all bald headed people look younger and sexier. That's where I get the label that's so frustrating. You know, they say bald headed people are sexy and have to point, constantly. Here's a funny story. I'm in a 7/11 store near a theater where I got a lot of my training. I went in for a cup of coffee and there were six Mexican kids making their 99-cent hot dogs. One of the kids said to the others, in Spanish...not knowing I was part Mexican and spoke Spanish, 'look at that ugly, bald headed guy.' So, I took two steps and turned around and said 'yeah, but my mother loves me.' And the other Mexicans were in hysterics and shock because they didn't know I spoke Spanish. Then, in Chinatown, there were three girls selling oranges. I walked by and they said the same thing... 'look at that ugly, bald headed guy.' Again, I turned around and said, 'yeah, but my mother loves me.' They started screaming and hollering and couldn't believe it. People see the negative but they don't see the person. I think that's what makes these *M*A*S*H* people so warm. They treated us all with respect. I know I could do a better job of acting now than 20 years ago, but Hollywood doesn't. It's so difficult not to be able to work as often as you want to. I see so many people working for money or fame, but when you find someone who really loves their work, there's no stopping them. Look at Alan Alda. Every time I run into him he's a real, wonderful human being. And he gives the same respect to everyone; whether you're an oriental actor from Texas who thinks he's John Wayne or whatever. I got to love the business so much, I wanted to be a art of it...no matter what they gave me. I had another mentor, Mako, who also worked on *M*A*S*H*. He was the head of the East/West Theater group I belong to. And he advised us, 'if you don't take it, somebody else will.' And so, these Chinaman roles, I always try to make them as human as possible. One of the cast members has the bust I did in 'Dear Mildred.' You know what *I* wanted to save? That grungy old jacket... with all the...Hitler's pencil box, watches, etc. I made a big, 2 x 3' blow up of that photo of all of us with the wooden bust and gave it to Harry Morgan for Christmas. He was very wonderful to me. To me, Harry Morgan is a legend. (Here, this author reminded Curly that he's a legend, too.) Oh, c'mon...you sound like my mother. (Laughs). I had all these one-liners. Like when they auctioned off the garbage and asked how much we would pay for it and I said 'one buck.' I hold up a piece of wood and say 'used to be round.' I'm very grateful to *M*A*S*H*. They give small residuals but it pays for my haircuts. You know, I'm thinking of going into a new business. I'm going to make shampoo for bald headed people. Or hairdryers for noses and ears. I just lost a dear friend who was 87 years old. I used to tell him dying is so easy but living is the only way to go. We're all going to get a shot at dying, so there's no sense in wasting any energy on it or being afraid of it. Enjoy the life we have and make the best of it. One of my buddies, Jack Granger from *Rebel Without a Cause*, was in Korea with me. We were aboard ship and he did a song and dance number for entertainment. Well, he fainted after his song and dance and fell into my arms. I said 'you're supposed to be ready to go to war!' People never die, especially when you remember them. And Kathleen Freeman will always be remembered. She was a special lady and worked right up until that last minute. She was born on the stage and went out the same way. *M*A*S*H* was the best thing that ever happened to me. I did a film which I was real proud of, too, and worked one month in Moscow. It was never shown, though. I'm going to Rome sometime this year, and will look up that Italian production company to find out what happened. I'm very close to a friend of mine named Herb Jeffries. He was the first black cowboy, supposedly. Anyway, he's a dear friend and is 93 now. He's got a star on the Walk of Fame. So, it's all attitude. I don't think old, I don't act old, I don't want people to talk to me about being old…it's all attitude. We put so much emphasis on age and weight. We never like ourselves and only see the bad. Never think old. Don't worry about age. Keep doing what you love. My son is a principal of a school and I keep telling him to tell the kids that this is a time to make mistakes and to learn from them. As far as Asian Americans go, we don't get the opportunity to grow. We don't get enough chances to do roles that are really, you know, important. And when we do, it's really great…like *The Killing Fields*. There are some Asian Americans who want to work in the film industry, but they don't because they see no future in it. And that's what I'm upset about because I like to see the young people get a chance to do whatever they want…if given the opportunity. You won't see me in x-rated movies. And the parts are too small for me anyway *(really laughs)*. You know, my son asked me to talk to some kids about acting, so he sent me to the school where he works. Anyway, I decided to start off with…I'd never met the teacher or anything, so I pulled out my pack of cigarettes and said 'you know, this is my favorite sport…this is what I do (chuckles).' And she nearly fainted. I continued, 'now it costs me five dollars a pack and I enjoy it so. But, I hope if you take up smoking, you'll go to college and get a good medical degree so that you can earn enough to take care of your medical problems because smoking is so good for you, and I'm smoking 10 packs a day, now.' And the teacher let out a big sigh of relief because she knew the point I was making. I got the habit in Korea. They say it was 65 below zero where we were at, at the Manchurian border. I caught a very bad cold and somebody gave me a pack of cigarettes, and that helped a lot…you know, when you're traveling in the snow…ten miles a day. I didn't think I would get hooked on the habit because I got seasick on the way home and never wanted to smoke again. But they drew me back. It's 54 years later and I'm trying to stop. The way I live my life, I don't get much adulation. When I got my first fan letter…I think you were first. So, I hope the book becomes a great success. Once they know I'm in the book, most of your bald-headed people will want to buy it. I have the same trouble with Hollywood. I'm right here, and better looking every day. I understand what acting is all about. But no calls. It's a shame. Think of what the world is missing (laughs at himself). I'm upset for the young people. I never got serious about acting because there was no future. It cost me $300 to join the Guild at the time and that was a lot of money to me. With three children, I wanted extra income. It seems like every time I'd work as an extra, they'd make me a...I'll tell you a funny story. I had done work as an extra in *Around the World in 80 Days*. 20th Century Fox had a beautiful location set of Hong Kong and had a hundred foot dragon. One day, I was in Chinatown and my buddy says, 'I want you to meet somebody.' He took me over to this Mexican fellow and it was Cantinflas (1911-1993). He was famous all over the world, except for here, and was sitting there. I was thinking how I grew up watching his movies. He's like the Charlie Chan of Mexico. And he was so gracious and wonderful. I met him years later, and said how we had worked in *Around the World in 80 Days*. He didn't really remember yet, so I said 'remember the dragon in that movie? Well I was the fourth leg.' He got the biggest kick out of that. He was like a legend to me. I want my story told about Alan Alda...my superhero in Hollywood. I couldn't get out of that character I had already been working on, but was trying so hard to avoid the Chinaman thing, and worked so hard to get ready for the shot. This was about an hour, or so, before we were to shoot the scene. I wasn't that good enough to make the switch, and turn the character around, you know. I ended up doing some of it, but not as much as I could have to get away from the stereotype. I was still thinking of what I thought Hollywood wanted me to do. You try so hard to give them what you think they want. They'll tell you (Hollywood) 'you've got to squint your eyes so you look more Oriental.' But it was a great group of people on *M*A*S*H*, and I'm very grateful to all of them. I put myself under a lot of stress to do better, but they all made my stay there a lot of fun. There are some directors who think they know how to tell an Asian American actor how to talk and look more Oriental. You have to wait for the Oriental roles. You can never be doctors, lawyers or teachers. After years of this, it still goes on. We try to say we are here, we are American and can play other roles. In real life, you see the diversity. There used to be a show, *Hawaii Five-0*, and even on that show there were never many Asians. You can't walk five steps in Hawaii without walking into an Asian American. This is a problem I wish I could do something about. Maybe your book will reach some people; who knows. Let them read what Alan Alda said, 'They are human beings.' Well, you think you've got enough? Imagine me writing all that I just said (laughs). It would be five years before I mailed a letter. Mark O'Neill... hmmm. It's not very Chinese, but I'll deal with it (laughs). I'd love a copy of the book. If there's a cost, let me know...I'll just cut down on my haircuts. Oh, and I just want to say that I completely understand if you decide to put me on the cover of the book."

Harvey J. Goldenberg
Captain Kaplan, Dentist in "Major Fred C. Dobbs" and "Ceasefire," in Season 1

"When I was five and living in NYC, a younger lad said to me, 'Hey, mister, would you help me cross the street.' I was highly insulted. I said, 'I'm not a mister, I'm a boy.' The great thing about being ancient looking from a young age is I seemed eligible for senior discounts without requesting them twenty years prior to the time I was actually a senior. Going to the movies and eating places allow you to have discounts without any question, no matter how young you are."
(His web site is at http://www.geocities.com/hollywood/set/5657.)

PHOTO COURTESY STUART MARGOLIN

Stuart Margolin
*Guest Star in "Bananas, Crackers and Nuts," in Season 1
and "Operation Noselift," in Season 2*

"The thing that I remember most, that I've never forgotten and I speak of most often, is the first segment I did, the psychiatrist in season one. What comes to mind is we came in to read around the table, as you often get on a half-hour show. Most shows were a multi-camera. But, as you know, this was a one-camera show. Everybody sat around and read the script. And Larry Gelbart was there, along with Gene. The thing that I remember, I've never forgotten and I've never seen anybody do it since, was that there was quite a bit of dissatisfaction with the script. There were problems, as there often are in a first read. And so, Larry said, 'Ok, everybody go to lunch, then come back, and we'll begin blocking or whatever.' So, we all went to lunch and when we came back there was an entirely new script! Of 35 pages, there were probably 30 that were re-written. I've never seen anything like that in my life. And the script was superb. So, I've always thought of Larry Gelbart as being some kind of a superman when it came to re-writing scripts. That's my main memory. It was a lot of fun, and all the actors were great fun. I'm trying to remember which show it was where I kind of jumped on Loretta Swit; I think that may have been the second show. Well, we had a lot of fun doing that. Burt Metcalfe was the casting director. I had done a show called *Occasional Wife* and, in fact, it's funny, because I was just beginning and I kept doing serious roles. I said to my agent, 'Gee, if we could get a comedy role, I'd love it.' And, he got me a reading for *Occasional Wife* and I got the part. And that was because of Burt Metcalfe. And, I've done nearly all comedies since then. But, it was because of Burt Metcalfe that I got the part on *M*A*S*H*. The script had the jokes and the situations that made it funny, but I don't recall anybody saying, 'Play it this way.' Usually, on TV, when you're a guest, they pretty much only direct you when you're going off in the wrong direction. And having directed a few, that's my recollection. You know, you hire the people you believe in and then you give them the space to let them do what they do best. And that's how I remember it. This is kind of a sidebar, but for a while I lived in Natchez, Mississippi. But, somebody was at some kind of an antique show and ran into Gary Burghoff and he sent me a card with his name on it, a very kind little note. And I've since lost the card because we lose so much. And very often, I've wondered where he is and what he's doing. (Author's note: they did, indeed, catch up with each other.) He kind of withdrew from the scene. I left in '80, and went to Canada. I moved to an island. Fortunately, I had begun to direct. In directing, you didn't need to be on the scene quite as much as if you're an actor. Alan Alda was helpful and encouraging. As the kind of actor he is, he was encouraging to somebody trying to do a certain kind of character role. He wasn't, you know, 'here, let me help you.' And Gary, very much so (encouraging). I'm trying to remember, it was McLean at the time. And he was just funny. Everybody was welcoming. Loretta was great. And Larry Linville was awfully nice, too. If there was (any discussion about bringing me back on the show), I didn't hear about it. I had done in '71 a show called *Nichols* (with James Garner). Well, see, it's a very interesting thing. We shot 24 of them, and in 1980, the TV station in Dallas had an interest in showing them. They contacted Warner's, who had no interest in showing them. And, I've asked Jim (Garner) about them. It's reached the stage, according to Jim…and I want to be careful not to mischaracterize this, that it really is a question of who really owns those now. It's very odd. Because a lot of people want to see them. There was actually somebody who taught them in a course at the University of Toronto. It became a course. Frank Pearson was the head writer. At any rate, I did that in '71. Then I did *M*A*S*H*. About the same time I did *Mary Tyler Moore*. Then Jim Garner and Meta Rosenberg, who was the executive producer on *Nichols*, came and said they had a new idea for a show (*The Rockford Files*). I do recall when we rehearsed, or maybe even when we did a take where I leap on Hot Lips that it broke the crew up. I did the same thing in both of my episodes? I think it was the first one, then. I remember jumping her in the dark. I remember the crew breaking up. I'm trying to remember the other guest stars I might have worked with. There was the actor whose nose I did the work on. Todd. Hy Averback, the director of 'Operation Noselift,' gave me my first job I ever had. My first professional job. It was *The Gertrude Berg Show*. It was called 'Mrs. G Goes to College.' If *M*A*S*H* is on I certainly watch if I'm in a community where they're showing it. And you never know. I'd have to say I haven't seen myself on *M*A*S*H* in I can't tell you how long. It's been a few decades. Most of the ones I see seem to have Mike Farrell instead of Wayne. Right now (June 2006), I'm doing 'The Cherry Orchard' in western New York. I did 'All My Sons' here, last year. It's an exciting theater to work in, the material's very good. The two artistic directors are a married couple, Ethan McSweeney and Vivian Benesch. My co-actor from 'All My Sons' is an actress named Lisa Harrow. She worked many years with the Royal Shakespeare Company in England, and won an Australian Academy Award. There's also Joel Friedman, and DJ Wilson. The other actors are the cream of the crop of the graduate schools across the country. I've just finished my final draft of a novel I've been working on for too many years. It's now being read by an agent. I've never done this before. It's taken an embarrassing amount of time. I finished, probably, two years ago…but the rewrites. At any rate, that's big for me. And I'm trying to get a film made from a script from a good friend of mine, a Canadian writer named Tom Gallant. The script is called 'The Last Hunt.' And Jim Garner has agreed to do it. And we're now trying to find an actor to play his son, and an actress to play the co lead. It's a small film, awfully good script. But that doesn't necessarily get a film made. It's an odd time. But, it's a script I believe in. I'm working on two musicals. I'll work on them wherever I am with a computer and, hopefully, a piano nearby. At this point, I'm still working on the book. Hopefully, the musicals are for New York."

PHOTO COURTESY FATHER FRANK TOSTE

Father Frank Toste

Technical Advisor for the Father Mulcahy character

"I had known Gary Burghoff since he starred in 'You're a Good Man, Charlie Brown,' and would often visit him on the *M*A*S*H* set. During one of those visits, Larry Gelbart and Gene Reynolds came up to me. Larry said, 'Father, this Jewish boy does not know if Father Mulcahy can say these lines. Will you help me out?' As a result, I became the technical advisor. When there was any question about religious actions, dialogue for Father M, theological questions, Mulcahy's spiritual direction to a penitent or plain priestly advice, my phone would ring. 'Alcoholics Anonymous' is my favorite episode. I was used as an extra, and am sitting in the mess tent listening to Mulcahy's sermon. But I'm on the end, and you only see me if you watch the actual, original film on a projector. By far, Gary Burghoff is an excellent actor who has a firm grasp of his craft and always strives to do his best, as an actor and contributor to the entire production. The first year Harry Morgan played Potter, before I left the house to go to the set, my dad gave me a message for him. During lunch I told Harry that my father told me to tell him that he is really a great actor with tremendous talent. Harry's eyes surveyed all of us at the table, took a puff on his cigar and said, 'Father's father is a man with class.'"

Larry Hama

Appeared in "The Korean Surgeon," in Season 5, as a North Korean soldier.

Ed Solomonson: Everyone we've contacted has said the same thing about appearing on *M*A*S*H*. That the cast was warm and welcoming, knew exactly what they were doing and treated everyone with respect. It's remarkable that these sentiments run through all 11 seasons. Was this the case with you as well?

Larry Hama: I found everyone connected with the show to be incredibly kind, professional and supportive. The warmth and graciousness of Mr. Alda and Mr. Linville stands out particularly. They were, (in actor's parlance) exceedingly generous — that is, they gave to the ensemble rather than trying to dominate a scene. The crew was just as nice. Being up at the ranch was very surrealistic since just about everything there was G.I. Most of the crew wore Army fatigues and everything was housed in O.D. tents. The mess tent actually functioned and everyone ate lunch off metal trays stamped U.S. It created some very *deja-vu* moments for me.

ES: The scene with you, Robert Ito and Larry Linville, from the time Major Burns approaches the jeep in the compound until you and Mr. Ito throw him out (Go back to your camp. It's the best thing you can do for our side) remains, until this day, a fan favorite, including me. How was it working with those two gentlemen?

LH: They are two total pros. Very relaxed and confident. I was pretty stressed as I had blown out a tire on the way to the Malibu ranch and had to change the flat in pre-dawn darkness on the Ventura Freeway, just barely making the make-up call on time. The make-up people looked at my greasy hands and face and said, "that's great, you already look like you've been in the field for weeks!" On the set, Mr. Linville and Mr. Ito were so laid back and friendly that it put me at ease immediately. Those guys were very serious about the craft, but never preten-tious. Light-hearted, but well-prepared and ready to go as soon as the camera was rolling. It's almost impossible to convey how thrilling and satisfying it is to be part of such a well-oiled and precise machine like that even for the brief amount of time I was there.

ES: By the time "The Korean Surgeon" was in production, sometime around the end of 1975 and the beginning of 1976, *M*A*S*H* had established itself as one of the best and highest rated shows on television. How was it to have gotten the part?

LH: I was amazed that I had got the part. I was in LA working in the first production of Stephen Sondheim's "Pacific Overtures" at the Dorothy Chandler. Alvin Ing, who was also in the show set me up with agent Guy Lee (of Bessie Loo Agency) and said I should try to pick up some TV work while I was in town. That's how I got the gig. I don't think I ever actually read for much else. I visually didn't fit a lot of slots since I had hair down to my waist at the time. (On *M*A*S*H* it was tied back and hidden down into my jacket collar and covered up by the helmet.)

ES: Lastly, the questions I ask of people who appeared on *M*A*S*H* are fairly general. What we're looking for are light-hearted anecdotes, never before published stories, and any comments one would care to make.

LH: It took a long time to nail the first shot where Bob Ito and I first drive up in the jeep. There were a lot of elements that had to hit their marks at the same time and it took a while to reset between takes. So I had time to shoot the breeze with Bob. During one of these breaks, Bob asked me if I was going to try out for the new medical show. He said he was reading for it next week and I should get Guy to get me an audition. I asked him what the show was about exactly, and he said it was about a medical examiner — a guy who did autopsies. I thought, "Ugh, a show about a guy who cuts up bodies? Who's gonna watch *that?*" So, I thanked Bob and never called Guy Lee about it. It turned out to be *Quincy* and of course Bob got the gig!

Interviews: The Writers

Ken Levine
writer

"David (Isaacs) and I were in the Army Reserves (which is where we met) so we both had a real feel for the military and its absurd world. If we hadn't had that experience I don't think we could have written for the show. David and I pretty much wrote every show in season seven. I think we wrote ten ourselves and rewrote most of the others. By the end of the 7th season we had pretty much picked through the bones of the research. Since *M*A*S*H* was locked into a time and place we really couldn't branch out with the show, which was a little frustrating. We would routinely do two or three stories in every episode. That meant between 50 and 75 episodes a season. By this point in the series we had done every hot show, cold show, visiting general, everyone slept with everyone else, Klinger wore every kind of costume, every activity had been interrupted by choppers, we did every mystery disease…you get the idea. We were offered the chance by NBC to develop our own show and decided it was time to try something new. I do still watch *M*A*S*H*, particularly the Larry Gelbart years. The show was at its peak during the Gelbart-Reynolds era. 'Point of View' is my favorite of the ones we wrote. 'The More I See You' from the 4th season is my all time favorite. Frank and Hawkeye were my favorite characters to write for. The glory days of *M*A*S*H* were the Larry Gelbart years. We just got to drive the car for a few years. But it was his car. After we left the show evolved and focused more on sensitivity, reflecting Alan's sensibility. We wanted to move the camp one year, put them in an old burned out schoolhouse just to shake up the look. It was felt that that might be too radial. Maybe they're right. We'll never know."

(Ken Levine has his own website and blog at http://kenlevine.blogspot.com.)

Thad Mumford
writer

"The season before getting our job on *M*A*S*H*, we had been working on *The Waverly Wonders*. John Rappaport and Burt Metcalfe were working on *M*A*S*H* and we pitched an idea and they wanted to bring us on board. We wrote the bulk of 'Are You Now, Margaret,' overnight. This was the idea we had pitched. Here was this crew that had been writing for this awful show was now writing for *M*A*S*H*. I had decided I wanted to write jokes because of seeing *The Tonight Show* in 1969 as an NBC page. *The Electric Company* was my first actual staff job (1971). Because of *The Tonight Show*, I met Joan Rivers. She used some of my jokes, at six dollars a joke. That led to my association with the William Morris Agency. They told me that there was to be a sort of spin off of *Sesame Street* called *The Electric Company*. And I was hired. I had tried to write for *Saturday Night Live*, but they didn't want me. One day I got a call from them. Jesse Jackson was going to be a guest star and they wanted to bring me on as a writer. They wanted a black writer for when he came on. I really let them have it. I told them how phony, insulting, and hypocritical it was that they only wanted me for this reason. Then I said, 'How much will you pay me?' It turned out to be a good experience.

I met Burt (Metcalfe) in 1973. Larry Gelbart was doing *Roll Out* with Gene Reynolds and I met them too. They came into the office and Burt said, 'I've heard some nice things about you.' And I said, 'I wish I could say the same.' Gene and Larry cracked up and they hired me as a writer. Larry is like Uncle Larry to me...a real genuine guy. I talked to Larry about turning *Roll Out* as a movie, a couple of years ago, but we both got involved in other things. I felt that the black aspect that the show focused on had been largely ignored. Larry and I wrote a lot together on *Roll Out*. It was fine (working with a partner), in the beginning. We wrote an episode of *That's My Mama*. Dan had been writing for *Fernwood Tonight*. I had really wanted to write for *Maude*. I was finally given an audition script and worked on it. I finished the script, well almost, and the next day had an offer to be a story editor on the show. Dan helped me write on *Roots*, but wasn't getting any credit...even though I paid him, myself. They wanted a "black" writer...not one who was part of a team. I watch (*M*A*S*H*) once in a while, but I'm out of the habit of watching television. Colonel Potter and Hawkeye were my favorite characters to write for, of course. We were trying hard to write the show the way Larry had written it, and I've told him this. We realized the characters changed because the actors changed. At first, this was very frustrating because it wasn't the same Hawkeye anymore. In the season before, Hawkeye and Margaret had made love. You just couldn't go back to the way things were because it would have looked ridiculous. I realized, in watching reruns that we went too far with Potter's way of speaking. It was funny when we'd come up with something like 'horse hockey' at the roundtable, but we ended up making Potter sound like Gabby Hayes. We were trying to write like Larry, and it couldn't be as zany as it was in its early years. There were so many (episodes) during Larry's years that were just hysterical. I like 'Bottle Fatigue' and 'Are You Now, Margaret,' for nostalgic reasons. Winchester was another character who was fun to write for. Stiers was so willing to play silliness, especially if his character was under the influence. I hate cheese. Smells like feet to me. So in the episode where Klinger has taken over for Radar, and wants to add his personal touches to the clerk's office, the cheese was my suggestion. And I don't know if this is one I wrote, but there was an episode about a racist soldier, Tom Atkins, who tries to get rid of the black soldiers in his command by giving them dangerous duty. The dentist, in that episode, was named after my father. ('The Tooth Shall Set You Free.'). I liked how Mike (Farrell) played out the emotions in this one episode where he's upset about Peg taking a job ('Wheelers and Deelers'). It reflected the male chauvinism of the times. I also liked the one where Potter paid off his mortgage ('Settling Debts'). I loved that show. I loved Harry."

David Pollock
writer

"Elias Davis and I had been writing other shows. We'd started as pages at CBS when Gelbart was doing *The Danny Kaye Show*. We had been writing for *Mary Tyler Moore*, which was very popular. We came in and pitched an episode in 1973, but it was never shot. We actually wrote the script...called 'The Tub.' The story just didn't seem to work right. We met with Gelbart and Lawrence Marks to discuss a story about the doctors getting a bathtub. One of the shows we pitched, that we actually did several years later. The one we always talked about was 'Iron Guts Kelly.' Years later, I've shown that episode to students when I lecture at The University of Michigan. Sid Dorfman and Gelbart wrote it. We watched a lot (of *M*A*S*H*, before writing) to get the rhythm of the characters. We were pretty familiar with the early episodes and were sorry we never got to write for Linville, Stiers and Rogers. I remember hearing Hy (Averback) on the radio as a kid. Any joke you put in, any line you wrote, you knew Alan would give it 100 percent. Writing for Potter was fun, but I would have liked to have written for Blake. I've always worked with a partner. We did a couple of years with Steve Allen. You have horrible time constraints. We, with Alan, wrote the first half-hour of 'Goodbye, Farewell and Amen.' I had always remembered 'The Moon is Blue' when it came out. It was pretty big news then, and we thought that if Hawkeye and BJ knew about it, they'd want to get it. It was only dirty because they used the word 'virgin' in it. We got Larry Balmalgia in on the script. This is one we worked on, but didn't get writing credit for. We worked on all the scripts but wanted the teleplay writer to get his credit. I always liked 'Adam's Rib.' An idea that we always wanted to do was that Hawkeye hears that Stalin dies. Out of an act of loyalty to Russia, our old WWII ally, Hawkeye tries to get a leave to attend Stalin's funeral. In our idea, he would never get there, but his wanting to would make a statement."

Erik Tarloff
writer

"Larry Gelbart was *the most brilliant* writer I had worked with. It was always exciting to see how fast his mind worked, and with what unerring accuracy he went straight to the right development or the most interesting attitude or the perfect joke. Also, how quickly and completely he grasped what other writers were trying to accomplish. He was a good listener as well as a good talker, which is rare in someone so talented. In a formal sense, working with Larry was like working with any other writer/producer on any other show. You offered your ideas, you discussed them with him, you refined and altered them in accordance with his suggestions, and you left his office with a script to write. It was the quality of his ideas and the high level of free-ranging merriment that made the experience different and memorable and so much fun. And it was a challenge, in the best sense, because you felt an obligation to try to keep up with him as best you could. Sort of like enjoying a casual chess game with Gary Kasparov. I should add here that Gene Reynolds's presence in the room was an important factor. He may not have had Larry's awesome facility, no one does, but his story instincts were excellent. He was inclined to ask the common-sense questions the rest of us often preferred to ignore if they were inconvenient when a promising story was being developed. And he was a gentleman who could be counted on to smooth over any rough patches or personal awkwardness. And very funny in his own unassuming style. He was a crucial element in the chemistry of the show in the early years. Larry's absence was key. He was such a powerful presence, once he left the atmosphere in the production offices was different, less charged, less exciting. The writing staff was younger now, much closer to my age, so it remained an easy and enjoyable situation for me purely in personal terms. Much more a coming together of equals, of peers. There was still a lot of easy laughing during meetings, and we had all sorts of references in common that I didn't have with Larry, who was a generation older. I wasn't on an especially warm footing with Bert Metcalfe. But I guess I'd have to say the main difference was, it no longer felt like a master class in the art of comedy writing; it was an assemblage of colleagues doing the best work we could. More generally, I believe the quality of the writing on the show remained quite high after Larry's departure. McLean Stevenson and Harry Morgan were very different actors with very different voices; distinctive enough so that it wasn't at all difficult to write for either one of them. It was relatively easy to hear their voices in your head, but they were different enough, as characters so that the lines you would give one wouldn't necessarily translate for the other. I don't mean only in terms of diction, but also attitude. (The same of course goes for the Frank Burns and Charles Winchester characters.) Whereas BJ, although he gradually emerged as a more individualized character, could, at least at first, be given something approximating Trapper's lines and it wouldn't be inappropriate or jarring. BJ and Trapper had approximately the same function in the show, which was to be Hawkeye's friend and ally and partner in mayhem. Their other qualities were secondary. I had nothing to do with casting. But I happened to meet Stuart Margolin a few months afterward. I was on a date at Musso & Franks, and he was having dinner there at the same time. The woman I was with knew him and greeted him and then introduced us. That was one of the first times in my life I was able to say to an actor, 'You were in something I wrote.' It was a thrill to me back then, when I was in my 20s. I occasionally visited the set, and was introduced to all or at least most of them when that happened. Pleasant, but perfectly perfunctory. A few years later I wrote several episodes of *House Calls*, and talked a bit with Wayne Rogers during that experience. And, many years after my sitcom-writing days were essentially over, I met Alan Alda and his wife, socially, in a totally different setting, on a totally different coast, and have seen them a few times since. We've reminisced about *M*A*S*H* only very briefly; there are lots of other things to talk about."

Burt Prelutsky
writer

"It was very easy working with both Larry and with Gene Reynolds. Unlike many TV producers, they didn't feel compelled to leave their fingerprints all over a freelancer's script. They were all pretty good characters (to write for) and a good cast to write for. I never wrote for Trapper John because Wayne Rogers left the show before I ever wrote for it. However, at the time I was writing 'Quo Vadis, Capt. Chandler,' it was thought that Rogers would still return to the show. So, I was writing for his character. By the time they shot the episode, they had replaced him with Mike Farrell. The script remained the same, but because Farrell was a much different actor and B.J. was a much softer character, the words came out sounding different. I also never wrote for McLean Stevenson because he, too, had jumped ship before I came aboard. I liked writing for Colonel Potter because I had always been a fan of Harry Morgan, and had written a bunch of *Dragnet* scripts when he was playing Gannon opposite Jack Webb's Friday. I did miss writing for Frank Burns after Larry Linville left the show. There were times when I was writing scenes set in the O.R. when the rhythm of the scene called for Frank's saying something totally boorish, and it just wasn't the same thing writing for David Ogden Stiers' Winchester. From what I hear (starting in season 6), Gene, who'd gone off to produce *Lou Grant*, would come in on Saturdays and look over the scripts, and discuss things with Alan Alda. I missed working with Gelbart, who left after the first season I wrote for the show. To begin with, I only had to deal with he and Gene and, to a much lesser extent, Burt Metcalfe. But when Larry left, they replaced him with, as I recall, three other guys. By that time, I had begun writing TV movies, which I much preferred to writing episodes. One, it paid better. Two, there were fewer meetings. Three, the meetings did not involve an entire mob. And, four, the characters were your own. Producers and network executives could say they didn't like a scene or a bit of dialogue, but at least the days of people telling me that Joe Friday or Hawkeye Pierce or Rhoda Morgenstem wouldn't say a particular line were over. Writing for the character of Charles Emerson Winchester was tough. When I began my episode (The Grim Reaper), Greenbaum and Fritzell were busy writing the show that would introduce Winchester. For my initial draft, I was told to write Winchester as if he were extremely wealthy. When I turned in the draft, Everett and Jim were still working away. But, I was told that instead of being rich, in the re-write I should make him the biggest snob in the world. By the time I had finished the second draft, I was told in the polish to make him very witty, able to hold his own against Hawkeye and B.J., and an excellent surgeon, but aloof...not really cut out to be a *M*A*S*H* doctor. I still recall saying that it seemed to me that if he was a great surgeon and able to trade barbs with the two resident smart alecks, they'd be wise to consider changing the name of the show to 'Winchester.' Frankly, I never did think his character really worked. He wasn't fish or fowl. For the most part, I thought he just took up room. I liked 'Quo Vadis' a lot. I thought 'The Novocain Mutiny' was very funny. I thought 'Hawkeye's Nightmare' was first-rate. Also it gave me the opportunity to name an unpleasant, off-camera character Vanderhaven, which was the name of my fifth grade teacher, whom I detested. I thought 'The General's Practitioner' was okay. I didn't think 'Souvenirs' was any good. It seemed preachy and not at all funny. I thought 'Images' was a stinkeroo. This idea came from the staff, and I told them it made no sense to me. I felt that Hot Lips was entirely right to come down on the young nurse like a ton of bricks. A nurse who keeps breaking down in the O.R. and then self-righteously defends her lack of professionalism was more than I could stomach. But the powers-that-be insisted they wanted to show Hot Lips seeing the error of her ways. It was a strange situation because the only lines that made any sense to me were those that were supposed to make Hot Lips look insensitive and tyrannical. I liked the B-story, though, because it gave me the opportunity to make my anti-tattoo jokes. I thought 'The Light That Failed' was funny, and was probably the best use I ever got out of Winchester. I watched a few of them (*M*A*S*H* episodes) years after I had written them. The biggest surprise was seeing Brian Dennehy pop up in one as an M.P. The only occasion when I required help as a writer was when I was writing an episode in which I needed to know things about Toledo so I could write some background for Klinger. Jamie Farr, one of the nicest people in the world, and is known as Mr. Toledo in certain circles, was a cornucopia of information. I would probably say the earlier ones (scripts) were easier to write because there were fewer people in the office to read them and make suggestions. Once we had agreed on the basic story, it took a few days to write a script. On one occasion, I wrote a script overnight. I guess something must have screwed up the pipeline and it was a rush job. I recall being home watching an episode from, I believe season seven. In it, Radar was off for some r&r and a shell hit near his jeep. He was brought back to the *M*A*S*H* unit for surgery. We had already seen that Hawkeye had been working for something like 36 straight hours, and had just sacked out before Radar was brought in. The next morning, as Hawkeye was walking his rounds in post-op, he comes across Radar, who starts bawling him out. Radar is steamed because even though the surgery went well, as I recall, Potter performed what was obviously a pretty minor operation. His hero wasn't on duty. Now, keep in mind that Radar was, if I'm not mistaken, a corporal, and Pierce was a captain. And although Pierce never pulled rank and made a point of not wearing his bars, he was an officer. As I sat there watching the silly story unfold, I recall thinking that the show had obviously run out of gas, and would soon be off the air. In later years, this sort of thing came to be known as jumping the shark. And of course, as usual, I was right...the show only stayed on the air another five years! After that (my) first year, they depended on the staff to write the arc of the season. The staff writers would come up with the bare bones for an episode and then they would assign a certain number to freelancers who would then flesh out the stories, get feedback from the staff, and then go off and write the scripts. *M*A*S*H* was a very good place for a freelancer. Even on those episodes I didn't much care for, I was given a pretty free hand. As a rule, the only way that the episode differed from the final polish was when it ran long, and had to be cut in the editing process. However, on my very first show, I had written a different tag for 'Quo Vadis.' In my script, Hawkeye and B.J. were walking across the compound the day after sending Chandler out of harm's way when they spot Klinger walking towards them. He is dressed like a tart. When Hawkeye asks him what he's up to, he explains that he is Mary Magdalene. After all, if it worked for 'Christ,' it should work for him. Hawkeye and B.J. exchange looks, Hawkeye says, 'Let he who is without sin cast the first stone,' and we *freeze* as they both bend over to pick up rocks to throw at Klinger. Well, believe me, I was shocked when I sat with friends watching the episode at home...and along comes Klinger dressed in a robe, wearing a fake beard and carrying a tablet. Suddenly he's Moses, and Hawkeye and B.J. are talking about parting the China Sea or some such thing. Unfortunately, the show aired on Friday or Saturday and I had to wait until Monday to call Gene Reynolds and find out what had happened. He explained that the tech advisor for the Father Mulcahy character, a Catholic priest named Toste, had read the script and said my version would offend Catholics. I guess they figured that nothing ever offends Jews. I told him that it made no sense for Klinger to be out of drag, and that if they had only told me there was a problem, I would have written a different tag. As it was, I didn't think it was funny and I didn't think it made any sense. I should probably add that I was very grateful for the opportunity to write so many episodes of a show that people are still enjoying thirty years later. Although I'm tempted not to mention it, I must confess that whenever I'm introduced to people as a guy who wrote for *M*A*S*H*, I inevitably ask them to name their favorite episodes...and not once in all these years has anyone ever mentioned a single one that I wrote!"

Captain Chandler & Me

"Recently, I received an e-mail from a young associate pastor in Maryland. Re introduced himself as an avid fan of *M*A*S*H*. He said that one of his favorite episodes had been one I wrote, 'Quo Vadis, Captain Chandler?', and that he was considering using the show as an inspiration for an upcoming sermon. He wanted to know how I had come up with the idea. He also wanted to know how my own faith and understanding of God or Christ had informed my writing. I must confess that I am not usually given to thinking of my writing in such grandiose terms, and it shocked me to find a man of the cloth doing so. It took some thinking on my part, especially as the writing took place over 30 years ago. At the time, my TV writing career was at a standstill. Because my agents were a man and wife team who were well meaning, but highly ineffective, it appeared that things weren't likely to change for the better any time soon. Fortunately, I was still a print journalist, writing a weekly humor column for the L.A. Times. I would occasionally mention having gone to Fairfax High School, and was invited to host an event celebrating the 50th anniversary of the school's founding. As part of the event, someone representing each of the five decades would reminisce about their years of internment. Larry Gelbart, writer-producer of *M*A*S*H*, spoke about the 1940s. I did double duty, hosting and talking about life at Fairfax in the 50s. One day, some months later, I got a call from my female agent. She wanted me to know that they'd taken in a third partner. The new guy would specialize in sit-com writers. She suggested I come down and meet him. I did, and regretted it almost immediately. The guy was totally obnoxious. It seemed he wanted to be a producer more than he wanted to be an agent. He proposed that I should write up his ideas. I pointed out he didn't seem too crazy about the way I wrote up my own. He said that was true, but this time he would be around to help. I told him that I would think about it, but in the meantime I had a family to support. He asked me what shows appealed to me. I mentioned *Bob Newhart, Mary Tyler Moore* and *M*A*S*H*. He looked at me as if I were insane. 'You're only talking about the hottest shows on the air.' I told him I was fully aware of that fact, but those were the ones I wanted to write for, and, besides, I was merely answering his question. I told him that, in as much as I had to earn a living, I would gladly write for any shows that would have me. He told me that at least now I was being realistic. When I got home, my wife told me I had a phone call from Larry Gelbart. I called him back. He started out by thanking me for having mentioned him in a column I had written that past Sunday in which I argued that for a quarter of a century the best comedy in America wasn't in books or movies or on Broadway, but, rather, on TV. I then mentioned ten of the anonymous talents who were most responsible for writing *Sgt. Bilko, The Sid Caesar Show, Mr. Peepers, The Honeymooners* and *M*A*S*H*. Gelbart was one of the ten. He went on to say that when he and his wife had attended the Fairfax event months earlier, they had assumed they'd be bored to tears, but that I had been very funny, and that he felt remiss for not having dropped me a note. I thanked him for the kind words and was ready to hang up when he said, 'By the way, I hear on the grapevine that you sometimes write for TV. If you ever get a notion for a *M*A*S*H* episode, please send it along.' Some of you will wonder why I hadn't broached the possibility of my writing a *M*A*S*H* script. It's not as if it didn't occur to me, but I would have considered it impolite. I mean, Gelbart was calling to pay me a compliment and to thank me for mentioning him in my column. Taking advantage of his courtesy to ask him for a job simply struck me as rude. In any case, as soon as we hung up, I called my new agent and told him he was now my ex-agent, and that *M*A*S*H* apparently wasn't as locked up as he'd insisted it was half an hour earlier. For a few seconds, I felt just great. Then it hit me that I was not only unemployed, but now I didn't even have an agent. Talk about your Pyrrhic victories! In a panic, I sat down in a chair with a steno notebook and my pen and hoped (prayed?) that a terrific idea would magically appear on the page. The idea that arrived within minutes was that a wounded soldier would show up at the *M*A*S*H* unit without dog tags, claiming to be Jesus Christ. I took another twenty minutes or so to fill in the details pitting good Dr. Freedman and evil Col. Flagg in a battle for the man's body and soul. I even came up with a title, 'Quo Vadis, Captain Chandler?' I typed it up and mailed it to Gelbart at 20th Century-Fox. A day or two later, he called to say that he and his producing partner, Gene Reynolds, loved the idea. The final script got nominated for a Humanitas Prize, and led to my writing seven more *M*A*S*H* episodes, and totally resuscitated my TV career. At the time and to this day, although I am a non-observant Jew, I felt the idea was divinely inspired. How could I not? After all, when I sat down with pad and paper, I had no reason to suspect that Jesus Christ was going to wind up in a sit-com episode. Although there is no way to really explain how the creative process works, typically a notion buzzes around in a writer's head until the opportunity to use it comes along. But that was certainly not the case here. With 'Captain Chandler,' there was no notion, no buzzing, just a timely Christmas miracle. I must confess that when I first saw the actor they had cast as Chandler, I thought they had badly missed the mark. But I came to see that he was perfect, especially in that quiet moment before he entered the ambulance. I believe at the time I dropped Alan Fudge a note letting him know how much I had enjoyed his performance. And I thought Larry Gelbart did a very nice job of direction. At the time, I was unaware that writers had to submit their own scripts for EMMY consideration. In fact, it was several years before I became aware of that fact. Considering how regularly *M*A*S*H* scripts were nominated, I always felt that at least a couple of mine would have made it to the finals. But I was under the impression that the producers did the submitting. I was mistaken. I hated the original movie, with its stupid sex scenes and its boring football game/pot smoking orgy. It struck me as just another service comedy for a generation too young to have seen the earlier ones or to understand that it was no more anti-establishment, anti-war, than the likes of 'Don't Go Near the Water' or 'Operation Petticoat.' All it had going for it was Altman's pomposity. Before its release, everybody connected with the movie thought they had a bomb of their hands. And if there had been any justice in the world, they would have been right. I tried watching the 2 1/2 hour series ender, but I couldn't stay awake. What a pretentious mish-*M*A*S*H!*"

(Burt Prelutsky is the author of The Secret of Their Success, *a new book which features 78 interviews. These include ones with Jamie Farr and Larry Gelbart, as well as Gerald Ford, Billy Wilder, Sid Caesar, Henry Mancini, George Carlin, Gene Kelly, Randy Newman, Art Linkletter, Ginger Rogers and Norman Lear. His web site is http://www.burtprelutsky.com.)*

Elias Davis
writer

"I have one anecdote that may be of interest to you; then again, it may not be. It might require your doing some research. I was in Aspen, Colorado, a couple of years ago. My wife was in the hospital after a skiing accident. She's okay, by the way. A *M*A*S*H* episode was playing on the waiting room TV. I never watch reruns but in this case I was intrigued. I had a feeling that David and I had worked on the episode that was running, but had no idea whether or not we had written the episode. Then, reference was made by one of the *M*A*S*H* characters to a patient named Rothaker. I knew, immediately, that we'd written the episode — or at the least had a hand in rewriting it, because I went to high school with a kid named Bob Rothaker. I thought it to be an interesting name and so I'd used it in a few scripts through the years. I don't remember the name of the episode but I do think it is one that Dave and I wrote. I do like the story Blood Brothers, and have told it a few times when teaching comedy writing at USC Film School. My first job in show business was as an usher at CBS Television City in Los Angeles. That's where I met David — we were both ushers. Well, actually I was an assistant Usher's Supervisor. But I don't like the word to get around about that! During the short time I was on the usher staff, one of the shows that was on CBS and taped at TV city was *The Danny Kaye Show*. I had gotten my usher's job thanks to a family friend Sheldon Keller who was a writer for Danny Kaye. (As a side note: I believe Shelly wrote some *M*A*S*H* episodes during the early seasons.) This was the 1963 TV season, by the way, and a story I heard from Sheldon was that a friend had gone to an ophthalmologist for an eye exam accompanied by another friend. The Doctor asked the second friend, since he was there, if he'd like to have his eyes examined also. When the doctor looked into the second friend's eyes he found cancer. I was floored by that story — wow. Life is like that. Capricious and cruel and ironic. The story stayed with me and many years later ('Blood Brothers,' season 9), as we were talking about a healthy GI and a wounded GI coming to the *M*A*S*H* unit and the healthy GI wanting to give blood, that whole story popped into my head and I said something like 'and they look at the healthy GI's blood so they can do a match, but he has leukemia.' I don't remember a lot about the genesis of stories but I do remember that one very well. 'The Tub' — oh, brother — it was terrible. I don't know if David told you this but when we worked on *M*A*S*H* we mentioned 'The Tub' to Burt Metcalfe, who was our boss. Dave and I had thought 'The Tub' was pretty good when we wrote it and were very disappointed it hadn't been shot. Burt found a copy and asked us to look it over and see if it could be used. We read 'our' script and *hated it*. We felt that Larry had been right to toss it in the trash. And that's where it remains to this day."

Missing in Action

Not all episodes of the series featured each member of the main cast — only Alan Alda would appear in every episode of M*A*S*H. What follows is a list of the episodes in which cast members *did not* appear.

Alan Alda
Seasons 1 through 11: *The only cast member to appear in all 255 episodes plus the 2½ hour finale.*

Wayne Rogers
Seasons 1 through 3: *Appeared in all 72 episodes of the first three seasons.*

McLean Stevenson
Seasons 1 through 3: *Did not appear in Season 3 Episodes 51 & 57.*

Loretta Swit
Seasons 1 through 11: *Did not appear in Season 1 Episodes 5 & 9, Season 3 Episodes 59, 60, 62 & 68, Season 4 Episodes 76, 78, 90, 92, 94 & 96, Season 5 Episode 110, Season 7 Episode 165 and Season 10 Episode 227.*

Larry Linville
Seasons 1 through 5: *Did not appear in Season 1 Episode 5, Season 2 Episode 36, and Season 4 Episodes 90 & 94.*

Gary Burghoff
Seasons 1 through 8: *Did not appear in Season 4 Episodes 76 & 90, Season 5 Episodes 106, 118 & 119, Season 6 Episodes 127, 128, 131, 132, 133, 135, 136 & 137, Season 7 Episodes 152, 155, 157, 160, 164 & 168 and Season 8 Episode 171. (Note: Although Season 8 contains Episodes 170 through 194, Gary Burghoff's last on-screen appearance was Episode 174, "Goodbye Radar, Part 2," and would not appear in the subsequent episodes of Season 8.)*

Jamie Farr
Seasons 1 through 11: *Did not appear in Season 1 Episodes 1, 2, 3, 5, 6, 7, 8, 9, 10, 11, 13, 14, 15, 16, 17, 21, 22 & 24, Season 2 Episodes 28, 29, 34, 35, 36, 38, 40, 42, 46 & 48, Season 3 Episodes 52, 56, 61, 62 & 68, Season 4 Episodes 78, 79, 83 & 90, Season 5 Episode 98, Season 6 Episode 141, Season 7 Episodes 159 & 165 and Season 9 Episode 202.*

William Christopher
Seasons 1 through 11: *Did not appear in Season 1 Episodes 1, 2, 4, 5, 6, 7, 11, 13, 14, 16, 21 & 22, Season 2 Episodes 28, 29, 32, 34, 36, 38, 39, 40 & 41, Season 3 Episodes 55, 60, 61, 62 & 69, Season 4 Episodes 75, 76, 78, 80, 83, 90 & 93, Season 5 Episodes 98, 99, 102,*

106, 110, 112, 114 & 119, Season 7 Episodes 147 & 160, Season 8 Episode 172 and Season 10 Episode 229.

Mike Farrell

Seasons 4 through 11: *Did not appear in Season 4 Episode 90.*

Harry Morgan

Seasons 4 through 11: *Did not appear in Season 4 Episode 90. (Note: Credited as Colonel Sherman T. Potter for Seasons 4 through 11, Harry Morgan guest starred in Episode 49, the Season 3 opener as General Bartford Hamilton Steele.)*

David Ogden Stiers

Seasons 6 through 11: *Did not appear in Season 7 Episode 147*

Broadcast History

M*A*S*H Time Slots on CBS

Season 1 / 1972-73 / Sunday
7:30 – *Anna and the King*
8:00 – *M*A*S*H*
8:30 – *The Sandy Duncan Show*
(None of these shows finished in the Top 30)

Season 2 / 1973-74 / Saturday
8:00 – *All In the Family* – 31.2 Rating *(Finished 1st)*
8:30 – *M*A*S*H* – 25.7 Rating *(Finished 4th)*
9:00 – *The Mary Tyler More Show* – 23.1 Rating *(Finished 9th)*

Season 3 / 1974-75 / Tuesday
8:00 – *Good Times* – 25.8 Rating *(Finished 7th)*
8:30 – *M*A*S*H* – 27.4 Rating *(Finished 5th)*
9:00 – *Hawaii Five-0* – 24.8 Rating *(Finished 10th)*

Season 4 / 1975-76 / Friday
8:00 – *Big Eddie (Did not finish in the Top 30)*
8:30 – *M*A*S*H* – 22.9 Rating *(Finished 14th, tied with* The Waltons *on CBS)*
9:00 – *Hawaii Five-0 (Did not finish in the Top 30)*

Season 5 / 1976-77 / Tuesday
8:00 – *The Tony Orlando and Dawn Rainbow Hour (Did not finish in the Top 30)*
9:00 – *M*A*S*H* – 25.9 Rating *(Finished 4th)*
9:30 – *One Day At A Time* – 23.4 Rating *(Finished 8th, tied with* The ABC Sunday Night Movie *and* Baretta *on ABC)*

Season 6 / 1977-78 / Tuesday
8:00 – *The Fitzpatricks (Did not finish in the Top 30)*
9:00 – *M*A*S*H* – 23.2 Rating *(Finished 8th, tied with* Alice *on CBS)*
9:30 – *One Day At A Time* – 23.0 Rating *(Finished 10th)*

Season 7 / 1978-79 / Monday
8:30 – *People (Did not finish in the Top 30)*
9:00 – *M*A*S*H* – 25.4 Rating *(Finished 7th)*
9:30 – *One Day At A Time* – 21.6 Rating *(Finished 18th)*

Season 8 / 1979-80 / Monday
8:00 – *The White Shadow (Did not finish in the Top 30)*
9:00 – *M*A*S*H* – 25.3 Rating *(Finished 4th, tied with* Alice *on CBS)*
9:30 – *WKRP In Cincinnati* – 20.7 Rating *(Finished 22nd)*

Season 9 / 1980-81 / Monday
8:30 – *Ladies' Man (Did not finish in the Top 30)*
9:00 – *M*A*S*H* – 25.7 Rating *(Finished 4th)*
9:30 – *House Calls* – 22.4 Rating *(Finished 8th)*

Season 10 / 1981-82 / Monday
8:30 – *Two of Us (Did not finish in the Top 30)*
9:00 – *M*A*S*H* – 22.3 Rating *(Finished 9th)*
9:30 – *House Calls* – 19.2 Rating *(Finished 23rd)*
Season 11 / 1982-83 / Monday
8:30 – *Private Benjamin (Did not finish in the Top 30)*
9:00 – *M*A*S*H* – 22.6 Rating *(Finished 3rd)*
9:30 – *Newhart* – 20.0 Rating *(Finished 12th, tied with* The Jeffersons*)*

M*A*S*H Ratings

September 17, 1972 – February 28, 1983 / CBS

Season 1 / 1972-73
(Did not finish in the Top 30)

Season 2 / 1973-74
25.7 Rating *(Finished 4th)*
All In the Family (CBS) / 31.2 Rating *(Finished 1st)*

Season 3 / 1974-75
27.4 Rating *(Finished 5th)*
All In the Family (CBS) / 30.2 Rating *(Finished 1st)*

Season 4 / 1975-76
22.9 Rating *(Finished 14th, tied with* The Waltons *on CBS)*
All In the Family (CBS) / 30.1 Rating *(Finished 1st)*

Season 5 / 1976-77
25.9 Rating *(Finished 4th)*
(Happy Days (ABC) / 31.5 Rating *(Finished 1st)*

Season 6 / 1977 – 78
23.2 Rating *(Finished 8th, tied with* Alice *on CBS)*
Laverne & Shirley (ABC) / 31.6 Rating *(Finished 1st)*

Season 7 / 1978 – 79
25.4 Rating *(Finished 7th)*
Laverne & Shirley (ABC) / 30.5 Rating *(Finished 1st)*

Season 8 / 1979 – 80
25.3 Rating *(Finished 4th, tied with* Alice *on CBS)*
60 Minutes (CBS) / 28.4 Rating *(Finished 1st)*

Season 9 / 1980 – 81
25.7 Rating *(Finished 4th)*
Dallas (CBS) / 34.5 Rating *(Finished 1st)*

Season 10 / 1981 – 82
22.3 Rating *(Finished 9th)*
Dallas (CBS) / 28.4 Rating *(Finished 1st)*

Season 11 / 1982-83
22.6 Rating *(Finished 3rd)*
60 Minutes (CBS) / 25.5 Rating *(Finished 1st)*

After M*A*S*H

House Calls

Though McLean Stevenson and Larry Linville continued to act following their tenure on M*A*S*H, it was M*A*S*H alumnus Wayne Rogers who came closest to working near the 4077th, again.

As M*A*S*H started its eighth season, so too premiered a TV version of the Walter Matthau movie, *House Calls*. However, *House Calls*, the TV series, would star Wayne Rogers as a doctor working in a hospital, and the series' time slot would be right after M*A*S*H. As a 1979 *TV Guide* ad announced for the premiere of both shows, Alan Alda and Wayne Rogers were back to back. *House Calls* ran for three years, and featured a great supporting cast, consisting of Lynn Redgrave (later replaced by Sharon Gless, as Redgrave had a dispute with Universal), David Wayne and others. The comedy show was filmed like M*A*S*H, with a single camera and not before a studio audience. Jeff Maxwell, who played Igor on M*A*S*H, even appeared in one episode. For some episodes, Hy Averback *(M*A*S*H alumnus)* directed, and even Erik Tarloff *(M*A*S*H writer)* returned to write one episode. The show was quite funny, and Rogers's character of Dr Charley Michaels was likeable, humorous and reminiscent of Trapper John McIntire. The show utilized two different theme songs, the first of which was quite catchy. This author recalls, in particular, excitedly thinking how Wayne Rogers was so close to being back on M*A*S*H, but so far.

Trapper John, M.D.

Also premiering in 1979 was a sort of spin off of M*A*S*H, called *Trapper John, M.D.* This would be a modern-day approach to the character from M*A*S*H but ironically, would not feature Wayne Rogers. Instead, Pernell Roberts took over the role of the seasoned doctor in the hour-long hospital show. Though a drama, *Trapper John, M.D.* was sprinkled with bits of comedy or comedic characters. At the time, many TV shows were attempting to copy the winning formula of M*A*S*H. *Trapper John, M.D.* was no exception. There was Trapper and his counterpart, a Frank Burns type character, and even a nurse named "Ripples," reminiscent of "Hot Lips." The formula aspects of the show were toned down in time, and the show ran for several seasons. There was very little in the way of references to M*A*S*H on Trapper John, M.D., and no M*A*S*H regulars ever appeared on the show. Though the studio claimed that Trapper John, M.D. existed separately from M*A*S*H, they were none-too-thrilled when, as a joke, one of the M*A*S*H producers sent them a M*A*S*H script that featured Hawkeye receiving word that his old buddy, Trapper, had been killed in a motor vehicle accident back home. Some of the M*A*S*H crew contributed to this series, including Jack Sonntag, Mark Evans, Lionel Newman (music supervision), and even Jackie Cooper (director).

AfterM*A*S*H

During the later seasons of M*A*S*H, cast members such as Jamie Farr and Harry Morgan began to wonder what they would do after the show. Alan Alda wondered what would happen to all of the patients that were treated and sent home. That notion triggered an idea, and AfterM*A*S*H premiered in 1983. The show would follow up on the lives of some of the M*A*S*H crew following the Korean War, would feature Harry Morgan, Jamie Farr and William Christopher in their M*A*S*H characters, and would take place in a VA Hospital in Missouri. For this half-hour follow-up to M*A*S*H, Larry Gelbart returned. Gelbart had an interest in the franchise, as he was the genius behind the original show.

Commentary by Larry Gelbart: "The show was far less than brilliant. I take full responsibility for its failure. When I learned that M*A*S*H was going off the air, the first thought I had was that any sequel would have to be AfterM*A*S*H. If I hadn't been so in love with the title, I might have thought out the show to go with it in a more objective way. I knew the series would inherit Potter, Mulcahy, and Klinger. I knew, too, that good as these people are, a leading player was going to be necessary. There was an attempt to build up a central character, a doctor who had lost his leg in Korea, and played wonderfully by David Ackroyd, but other attempts at making a show with its own tone, style and intent were not as successful. Probably, an hour show would have been a better format. One which did not try to emulate M*A*S*H, one with more drama than comedy. Oh, well, you win some and you lose some (except on TV you lose in front of a whole lot of people)."

Other M*A*S*H producers, writers and technical alumni returned for the show, including Burt Metcalfe, Ken Levine, David Isaacs, Dennis Koenig, Everett Greenbaum, Larry Mills, and Stanford Tischler. Even Colonel Flagg and Radar O'Reilly returned (a la Edward Winter and Gary Burghoff) for a few episodes. Rosalind Chao played Klinger's wife, as she did in "Goodbye, Farewell and Amen." Barbara Townsend played Dr. Potter's wife, a reasonable facsimile of Harry Morgan's then real wife, who's portrait was seen on Colonel Potter's desk on *M*A*S*H*. Very little mention was made, on the show, of other *M*A*S*H* characters, with the exception of Hawkeye and Charles. *AfterM*A*S*H* premiered in the former time slot of *M*A*S*H*, and actually did better in the ratings than the first season of *M*A*S*H*, finishing in the top fifteen.

Unfortunately, the show was moved opposite *The A-Team*, and lasted only one more season.

W*A*L*T*E*R

In 1984, *W*AL*T*E*R* premiered, starring Gary Burghoff as his old *M*A*S*H* character. The half-hour comedy picked up with Walter (no longer "Radar") O'Reilly having moved to Missouri following his mother's death. He becomes, of all things, a police officer. Only one episode of the series aired, and interestingly, it featured Clete Roberts playing the interviewer he had played on *M*A*S*H*. Everett Greenbaum, a former *M*A*S*H* alumnus, returned to do some writing.

"Hawkeye would have become a right wing conservative. BJ would be on his third marriage. Trapper John and his wife would be celebrating their 40th. Houlihan would be living with a woman partner. Radar would be a taxidermist. Klinger would be a Congressman. Potter would be deceased. So would I".

— Larry Gelbart, on where M*A*S*H people would be, now.

Related Ratings

AfterM*A*S*H
September 26, 1983 / December 18, 1984 / CBS

Season 1 / 1983-84
20.1 Rating *(Finished 15th)*
Dallas (CBS) / 25.7 Rating *(Finished 1st)*

Season 2 / 1984
(Did not finish in the Top 30)

House Calls
December 17, 1979 / September 13, 1982 / CBS

Season 1 / 1979-80
22.1 Rating *(Finished 14th, tied With* Real People *on NBC)*
60 Minutes (CBS) / 28.4 Rating *(finished 1st)*
M*A*S*H (CBS) / 25.3 Rating *(finished 4th)*

Season 2 / 1980-81
22.4 Rating *(Finished 8th, tied with* Three's Company *on ABC)*
Dallas (CBS) / 34.5 Rating *(Finished 1st)*
M*A*S*H (CBS) / 25.7 Rating *(Finished 4th)*

Season 3 / 1982
19.2 Rating *(Finished 23rd)*
Dallas (CBS) / 28.4 Rating *(Finished 1st)*
M*A*S*H (CBS) / 22.3 Rating *(Finished 9th)*

Trapper John, M.D.
September 23, 1979-September 4, 1986 / CBS

Season 1 / 1979-80
21.2 Rating *(Finished 19th)*
60 Minutes (CBS) / 28.4 Rating *(Finished 1st)*
M*A*S*H (CBS) / 25.3 Rating *(Finished 4th)*
House Calls (CBS) / 22.1 Rating *(Finished 14th)*

Season 2 / 1980-81
20.7 Rating *(Finished 17th, tied with* Fantasy Island *on ABC and* Diff'rent Strokes *on NBC)*
Dallas (CBS) / 34.5 Rating *(Finished 1st)*
M*A*S*H (CBS) / 25.7 Rating *(Finished 4th)*
House Calls (CBS) / 22.4 Rating *(Finished 8th)*

Season 3 / 1981-82
21.1 Rating *(Finished 15th, tied with* Hart To Hart *on ABC)*
Dallas (CBS) / 28.4 Rating *(Finished 1st)*
M*A*S*H (CBS) / 22.3 Rating *(finished 9th)*
House Calls (CBS) / 19.2 Rating *(finished 23rd)*

Season 4 / 1982-83
18.7 Rating *(Finished 18th, tied with* Gloria *on CBS)*
60 Minutes (CBS) / 25.5 Rating *(Finished 1st)*
M*A*S*H (CBS) / 22.6 Rating *(Finished 3rt)*

Season 5 / 1983-84
17.0 Rating *(Finished 30th)*
Dallas (CBS) / 25.7 Rating *(Finished 1st)*
AfterM*A*S*H (CBS) / 20.1 Rating *(Finished 15th)*

Season 6 / 1984-85
16.8 Rating *(Finished 29th)*
Dynasty (ABC) / 25.0 Rating *(Finished 1st)*

Season 7 / 1985-86
(Did not finish in the Top 30)

Awards

Emmy Award Nominations
Academy of Television Arts and Sciences
(Awards won are in **bold.***)*

1973
Outstanding Achievement in Film Editing for Entertainment Programming:
    Stanford Tischler, ACE / Fred W Berger, ACE, Editors
Outstanding Comedy Series:
    M*A*S*H Gene Reynolds, Producer
Outstanding Continuing Performance by an Actor in a Leading Role in a Comedy Series:
    Alan Alda
Outstanding Directorial Achievement in Comedy:
    "Pilot" Gene Reynolds, Director
Outstanding New Series:
    M*A*S*H Gene Reynolds, Producer
Outstanding Performance by an Actor in a Supporting Role in Comedy:
    Gary Burghoff, McLean Stevenson
Outstanding Writing Achievement in Comedy:
    "Pilot" Larry Gelbart, Writer

1974
Actor of the Year – Series:
    Alan Alda
Best Directing in Comedy:
    "Carry On Hawkeye" Jackie Cooper, Director
Best Directing in Comedy:
    "Deal Me Out" Gene Reynolds, Director
Best Film Editing For Entertainment Programming:
    Stanford Tischler, ACE / Fred W Berger, ACE, Editors
Best Lead Actor in a Comedy Series:
    Alan Alda
Best Supporting Actor in Comedy:
    Gary Burghoff, McLean Stevenson
Best Supporting Actress in Comedy:
    Loretta Swit
Best Writing In Comedy:
    "Hot Lips and Empty Arms" Linda Bloodworth and Mary Kay Place, Writers
    "The Trial of Henry Blake" McLean Stevenson, Writer
Outstanding Comedy Series:
    M*A*S*H Gene Reynolds / Larry Gelbart, Producers

1975

Outstanding Achievement in Cinematography:
"Bombed" William Jurgensen, Cinematographer
Outstanding Comedy Series:
M*A*S*H Gene Reynolds / Larry Gelbart, Producers
Outstanding Continuing Performance by a Supporting Actor in a Comedy Series:
Gary Burghoff, McLean Stevenson
Outstanding Continuing Performance by a Supporting Actress in a Comedy Series:
Loretta Swit
Outstanding Directing in a Comedy Series:
"O.R." Gene Reynolds, Director
Outstanding Directing in a Comedy Series:
"Bulletin Board" Alan Alda, Director
"Alcoholics Unanimous" Hy Averback, Director
Outstanding Film Editing For Entertainment Programming:
"The General Flipped At Dawn"
Stanford Tischler, ACE / Fred W Berger, ACE, Editors
Outstanding Lead Actor in a Comedy Series:
Alan Alda
Outstanding Single Performance by a Supporting Actor in a Comedy or Drama Series:
"The General Flipped At Dawn" Harry Morgan

1976

Outstanding Achievement in Cinematography for Entertainment Programming for a Series:
"Hawkeye" William Jurgensen, Cinematographer
Outstanding Comedy Series:
M*A*S*H Gene Reynolds / Larry Gelbart, Producers
Outstanding Continuing Performance by a Supporting Actor in a Comedy Series:
Gary Burghoff, Harry Morgan
Outstanding Continuing Performance by a Supporting Actress in a Comedy Series:
Loretta Swit
Outstanding Directing in a Comedy Series:
"Welcome To Korea" Gene Reynolds, Director
Outstanding Directing In a Comedy Series:
"The Kids" Alan Alda, Director
Outstanding Film Editing For Entertainment Programming For a Series:
"Welcome to Korea" Stanford Tischler, ACE / Fred W Berger, ACE, Editors
Outstanding Lead Actor in a Comedy Series:
Alan Alda
Outstanding Writing In a Comedy Series:
"The More I See You" Larry Gelbart / Gene Reynolds, Writers
Outstanding Writing In a Comedy Series:
"Hawkeye" Larry Gelbart / Simon Muntner, Writers

1977

Outstanding Cinematography in Entertainment Programming for a Series:
"Dear Sigmund" William Jurgensen, Cinematographer
Outstanding Comedy Series:
M*A*S*H Gene Reynolds, Executive Producer – Allan Katz / Don Reo / Burt Metcalfe, Producers
Outstanding Continuing Performance by a Supporting Actor in a Comedy Series:
Gary Burghoff

Outstanding Continuing Performance by a Supporting Actor in a Comedy Series:
  Harry Morgan
Outstanding Continuing Performance by a Supporting Actress in a Comedy Series:
Loretta Swit
Outstanding Directing in a Comedy Series:
  "Dear Sigmund" Alan Alda, Director
Outstanding Directing in a Comedy Series:
  "The Nurses" Joan Darling, Director
  "Lt. Radar O'Reilly" Alan Rafkin, Director
Outstanding Film Editing In a Comedy Series:
  "Dear Sigmund" Samuel E. Beetley, ACE / Stanford Tischler, ACE, Editors
Outstanding Lead Actor in a Comedy Series:
  Alan Alda
Outstanding Writing In a Comedy Series:
  "Dear Sigmund" Alan Alda, Writer

1978
Outstanding Comedy Series:
  M*A*S*H Burt Metcalfe, Producer
Outstanding Continuing Performance by a Supporting Actor in a Comedy Series:
  Gary Burghoff, Harry Morgan
Outstanding Continuing Performance by a Supporting Actress in a Comedy Series:
  Loretta Swit
Outstanding Directing In a Comedy Series:
  "Comrades In Arms, Part 1" Burt Metcalfe / Alan Alda, Directors
Outstanding Film Editing In a Comedy Series:
  "Fade Out, Fade In" Stanford Tischler, ACE / Larry L Mills, Editors
Outstanding Lead Actor in a Comedy Series:
  Alan Alda
Outstanding Writing In a Comedy Series:
  "Fallen Idol" Alan Alda, Writer

1979
Outstanding Comedy Series:
  M*A*S*H Burt Metcalfe, Producer
Outstanding Directing In a Comedy or Comedy-Variety or Music Series:
  "Dear Sis" Alan Alda, Director
  "Point Of View" Charles S. Dubin, Director
Outstanding Film Editing For a Series:
  "The Billfold Syndrome" Larry L. Mills / Stanford Tischler ACE, Editors
Outstanding Lead Actor in a Comedy Series:
  Alan Alda
Outstanding Supporting Actor in a Comedy or Comedy-Variety or Music Series:
  Gary Burghoff, Harry Morgan
Outstanding Supporting Actress in a Comedy or Comedy-Variety or Music Series:
  Loretta Swit
Outstanding Writing in a Comedy or Comedy-Variety or Music Series:
  "Inga" Alan Alda, Writer
Outstanding Writing in a Comedy or Comedy-Variety or Music Series:
  "Point Of View" Ken Levine / David Isaacs, Writers

1980

Outstanding Achievement in Film Editing for a Series:
"The Yalu Brick Road" Larry L. Mills / Stanford Tischler ACE, Editors
Outstanding Comedy Series:
M*A*S*H Burt Metcalfe, Executive Producer; Jim Mulligan / John Rappaport, Producers
Outstanding Directing in a Comedy Series:
"Dreams" Alan Alda, Director
"Period of Adjustment" Charles S. Dubin, Director
"Bottle Fatigue" Burt Metcalfe, Director
"Stars and Stripe" Harry Morgan, Director
Outstanding Lead Actor in a Comedy Series:
Alan Alda
Outstanding Supporting Actor in a Comedy or Comedy-Variety or Music Series:
Harry Morgan
Outstanding Supporting Actor in a Comedy or Comedy-Variety or Music Series:
Mike Farrell
Outstanding Supporting Actress in a Comedy or Comedy-Variety or Music Series:
Loretta Swit
Outstanding Writing in a Comedy Series:
"Goodbye Radar, Part 2" David Isaacs / Ken Levine, Writers

1981

Outstanding Achievement in Film Editing for a Series:
"Death Takes A Holiday" Stanford Tischler, ACE / Larry L. Mills, ACE, Editors
Outstanding Comedy Series:
M*A*S*H Burt Metcalfe, Executive Producer; John Rappaport, Producer
Outstanding Directing in a Comedy Series:
"The Life You Save" Alan Alda, Director
"No Laughing Matter" Burt Metcalfe, Director
Outstanding Informational Special:
"Making M*A*S*H" Michael Hirsh, Producer (PBS)
Outstanding Lead Actor in a Comedy Series:
Alan Alda
Outstanding Supporting Actor in a Comedy or Variety or Music Series:
Harry Morgan, David Ogden Stiers
Outstanding Supporting Actress in a Comedy or Variety or Music Series:
Loretta Swit
Outstanding Writing In a Comedy Series:
"Death Takes A Holiday"
Mike Farrell, John Rappaport, Dennis Koenig, Teleplay
Thad Mumford, Dan Wilcox, Burt Metcalfe, Story

1982

Outstanding Comedy Series:
M*A*S*H Burt Metcalfe, Executive Producer; John Rappaport, Supervising Producer; Thad Mumford, Dan Wilcox, Dennis Koenig, Producers
Outstanding Directing In a Comedy Series:
"When There's A Will, There's A War" Alan Alda, Director
"Sons And Bowlers" Hy Averback, Director
"Pressure Points" Charles S Dubin, Director
"Picture This" Burt Metcalfe, Director

Outstanding Lead Actor in a Comedy Series:
Alan Alda
Outstanding Supporting Actor in a Comedy or Variety or Music Series:
Harry Morgan, David Ogden Stiers
Outstanding Supporting Actress in a Comedy or Variety or Music Series:
Loretta Swit
Outstanding Writing in a Comedy Series:
"Follies Of The Living, Concerns Of The Dead" Alan Alda, Writer

1983
Outstanding Comedy Series:
M*A*S*H Burt Metcalfe, Executive Producer; John Rappaport, Supervising
Producer; Dan Wilcox, Thad Mumford, Producers
Outstanding Directing in a Comedy Series:
"Goodbye, Farewell, and Amen" Alan Alda, Director
"The Joker Is Wild" Burt Metcalfe, Director
Outstanding Film Editing for a Series:
"Goodbye, Farewell, and Amen" Stanford Tischler, ACE / Larry L. Mills, ACE,
Editors
Outstanding Film Sound Editing for a Series:
"Goodbye, Farewell, and Amen" Ed Rossie, Supervising Sound Editor; William
Hartman, David Ice, Don V. Isaacs, Godfrey Marks, Richard A Sperber, Sound
Editors
Outstanding Individual Achievement – Costumers:
"Goodbye, Farewell, and Amen" Albert A Finkel, Men's Costumer; Rita Bennett,
Women's Costumer
Outstanding Lead Actor in a Comedy Series:
Alan Alda
Outstanding Supporting Actor in a Comedy, Variety, or Music Series:
Harry Morgan
Outstanding Supporting Actress in a Comedy, Variety, or Music Series:
Loretta Swit

Golden Globe Award Nominations
Hollywood Foreign Press Association
*(Awards won are in **bold**.)*

1972
Best Television Series – Musical or Comedy:
M*A*S*H
Best Actor in a Leading Role – Musical or Comedy:
Alan Alda

1973
Best Actor in a Leading Role – Musical or Comedy:
Alan Alda
Best Actor in a Supporting Role – Series, Mini-Series or Television Movie:
McLean Stevenson
Best Actress in a Supporting Role – Series, Mini-Series or Television Movie:
Loretta Swit

1974
Best Actor in a Leading Role – Musical or Comedy:
Alan Alda

1975
Best Actor in a Leading Role – Musical or Comedy:
Alan Alda

1976
Best Television Series – Musical or Comedy:
M*A*S*H
Best Actor in a Leading Role – Musical or Comedy:
Alan Alda

1977
Best Actor in a Leading Role – Musical or Comedy:
Alan Alda

1978
Best Actor in a Leading Role – Musical or Comedy:
Alan Alda

1979
Best Television Series – Musical or Comedy:
M*A*S*H
Best Actor in a Leading Role – Musical or Comedy:
Alan Alda
Best Actress in a Leading Role – Musical or Comedy:
Loretta Swit

1980
Best Television Series – Musical or Comedy:
M*A*S*H
Best Actor in a Leading Role – Musical or Comedy:
Alan Alda

1981
Best Television Series – Musical or Comedy:
M*A*S*H
Best Actor in a Leading Role – Musical or Comedy:
Alan Alda
Best Actress in a Leading Role – Musical or Comedy:
Loretta Swit

1982
Best Television Series – Musical or Comedy:
M*A*S*H
Best Actor in a Leading Role – Musical or Comedy:
Alan Alda
Best Actress in a Supporting Role – Series, Mini-Series or Television Movie:
Loretta Swit

People's Choice Awards
Hollywood Foreign Press Association
*(Awards won are in **bold**.)*

1975
Favorite Male Television Performer:
Alan Alda

1978, 1979, 1980, 1981, 1982
Favorite Television Comedy Series:
M*A*S*H

Director's Guild of America
Outstanding Directorial Achievement In Television
*(Awards won are in **bold**.)*

1972
"Pilot"
   Gene Reynolds, Director
   Wes McAfee, Unit Production Manager and First Assistant Director
   Ron Schwary, Second Assistant Director

1973
"Deal Me Out"
   Gene Reynolds, Director
   Ted Butcher, Unit Production Manager
   Leonard Smith, First Assistant Director
   George Batcheller, Second Assistant Director

1974
"Alcoholics Unanimous"
   Hy Averback, Director
   Ted Butcher, Unit Production Manager
   Len Smith, First Assistant Director
   George Batcheller, Second Assistant Director

1975
"Bombed"
   Hy Averback, Director
   Len Smith, First Assistant Director
   George Batcheller, Second Assistant Director

1976
"Dear Sigmund"
   Alan Alda, Director
   Ted Butcher, Unit Production Manager
   David Hawks and Lisa Hallas, Assistant Directors

1979
"Period Of Adjustment"
   Charles S Dubin, Director
   David Hawks, Unit Production Manager and First Assistant Director
   Catherine Kinsock, Second Assistant Director

1981
"The Life You Save"
    Alan Alda, Director
    David Hawks, Unit Production Manager and First Assistant Director
    Catherine Kinsock, Second Assistant Director

1982
"Where there's a Will, there's a War"
    Alan Alda, Director
    David Hawks, Unit Production Manager and First Assistant Director
    Catherine Kinsock, Second Assistant Director

Eddie Awards
American Cinema Editors
Best-Edited Episode from a Television Series
(Awards won are in **bold.***)*

1973
M*A*S*H "Pilot" Stanford Tischler
"Bananas, Crackers And Nuts" Fred W Berger

1974
"The Trial Of Henry Blake" Fred W Berger, Stanford Tischler

1975
"A Full, Rich Day" Fred W Berger, Stanford Tischler

1976
"Welcome To Korea" Stanford Tischler, Fred W Berger

1977
"Dear Sigmund" Samuel E Beetley, Stanford Tischler

1978
"Fade Out / Fade In" Larry L Mills, Stanford Tischler

1979
"The Billfold Syndrome" Larry L Mills, Stanford Tischler

1980
"The Yalu Brick Road" Larry L Mills. Stanford Tischler

1981
"Dreams" Larry L Mills, Stanford Tischler

Humanitas Prize Winners

1976: Larry Gelbart "The Interview"
1980: Alan Alda
1982: David Pollock & Elias Davis
1983: Elias Davis & David Pollock

Production Codes

One of the most frequently asked questions about *M*A*S*H* is "How many episodes are there?" Well, that depends on whom you ask. The majority of fans will tell you there are 251 episodes, but this is inaccurate. While there are 251 titles, there are actually 255 episodes plus the 2½ hour special, "Goodbye, Farewell and Amen." Each 30-minute episode (approximately 26:00 minutes of actual show without commercials) has its own production code. For instance, Episode 36, Season 2's "The Incubator," is a single half-hour episode with the production code K412. The first episode of Season 4, "Welcome to Korea," was the series' first hour-long broadcast. The first half of this episode has the production code G504, and the second half has the production code G506, technically making this two episodes. Season 5's "Bug Out" was the second hour-long broadcast with the first part having the production code U801 and the second part having U802. "Fade Out / Fade In" from Season 6, "Our Finest Hour" from Season 7 and "That's Show Biz" from Season 10 are the other hour-long broadcasts with production codes for each of the two halves. The series finale, "Goodbye, Farewell, and Amen" is a 2½ hour special; however, most people will refer to this as the final episode. The first three episodes from Season 10, "That's Show Biz," "Identity Crisis" and "Rumor at the Top," were produced during Season 9's production and held over for broadcast in Season 10. Six episodes in Season 11, "Who Knew?" "The Moon is not Blue," "Hey, Look Me Over," "Foreign Affairs," Settling Debts" and "The Joker is Wild," were produced during Season 10 and held for broadcast in Season 11.

Afterword

Ed Solomonson and Gary Burghoff.

Eddie Solomonson

The United States was still involved in Viet Nam when *M*A*S*H* aired on September 17, 1972, which was five months away from my 18th birthday and an appointment to register with the Selective Service System. I had started paying close attention to Eyewitness News at 6:00, and I can still hear the anchor saying, "Good evening. I'm Roger Grimsby, here now, the news." At the time, the lead stories were almost always updates on the war, including wounded and killed in action, usually accompanied with filmed coverage of the fighting. Arguably, the most unpopular war in American history.

I saw an ad for a new television comedy based on a movie about an army hospital three miles from the front lines during the Korean War. I hadn't seen the movie yet, and I was trying not to think about the very real prospect of being sent to Viet Nam. What could be funny about wounded soldiers being brought to a mobile army hospital in a war zone? Why would I want to see this when, in just a few months, it could be me on the stretcher had I been fortunate enough to make it that far? I tuned in anyway, thinking there's nothing funny about wounded soldiers and nothing funny about operating on them.

Driving golf balls into a minefield? Wearing civilian shirts? Martinis? Who are these guys and just what are they doing? The answers to all my questions came quickly as I realized that these guys were actually highly skilled surgeons displaying a flippant attitude towards war and those who run them. In the operating room, it became quite clear to me that they were as dedicated to saving lives as they were skilled, and I was hooked. It almost seemed like two different shows. One was a comedy with anti-war, anti-military captains who detested where they were and why they were there, who chased after nurses and lived to party, even if it meant breaking orders, while the other show was about surgeons who would break their backs to save a life. So impressive were these surgeons, the chief medical officer of the Seoul Sector, a brigadier general who wanted to arrest Hawkeye and Trapper for breaking orders, changed his mind.

But was *this* the right time to debut this type of comedy? Yes. The time was right for a television "sitcom" with a strong anti-war sentiment shared by a great many people at the time, and after seeing the Pilot, I couldn't wait for the next episode.

*M*A*S*H* was speaking for me, saying what I wasn't able to say, and it said it loud and clear. But then, *M*A*S*H* was speaking *to* me, drawing me in. I felt as if I was in the Swamp having a martini, that I was the one operating and saving someone's life, and feeling the profound impact of losing one. No other television show had this effect on me, and given my situation at the time, this was remarkable. Week after week, *M*A*S*H* had stayed true to itself; never trivializing war, never making light of the wounded and then, a little more than half-way through the first season, aired a pivotal episode that was never done before on a sitcom. 36 years later, "Sometimes You Hear the Bullet" remains one of the most talked-about episodes of this or any other series, and helped set the tone of this show in cement by having Hawkeye's friend die on his table in OR.

While *M*A*S*H* had helped define the term "dramedy," the drama was only one ingredient in this unique show. The other key ingredients were brilliant writing and the nearly flawless delivery and comedic timing of what proved to be an extremely talented cast. One minute you're brought to tears from laughter, and the next, you're brought to tears from the reality of death and destruction. To this day, the prospect of being sent to Viet Nam and the irony of finding comfort in *M*A*S*H* continues to fascinate me.

Eddie Solomonson was born in 1955 in Brooklyn, New York, and remains a life-long "Brooklyn Boy" who still lives there with his wife and daughter. Studying electronics and appliance repairs, Eddie's passion as a musician is only rivaled by his passion for M*A*S*H. *Having read all the books he could find about M*A*S*H, they left him wanting more. To that end, he decided to write what he calls "The most complete and comprehensive book ever written about the show." Knowing full well that what he had in mind was a monumental challenge, he also knew he needed help and found Mark O'Neill, "whose enthusiasm matched my own. When he told me he contacted William Self, I knew I had teamed up with the right person."*

Afterword

Mark O'Neill, his wife, Ann and Gary Burghoff.

PHOTO COURTESY MARK O'NEILL

Mark O'Neill

We moved to Connecticut in 1977, when I was 12. I was the new kid on the block, and didn't have many friends. Every day, I would come home from school and watch a syndicated episode of *M*A*S*H* at 3:30 pm. *M*A*S*H* became my friend. "The Incubator" was the first episode I remember watching, savoring.

Then, I realized that new episodes of *M*A*S*H* were still airing, so I tuned in. Comparing and contrasting older seasons versus new became a fascination with me. I was hooked. And even at age 12, I quickly realized that seeing the name Larry Gelbart in the opening credits meant it was a classic episode.

Back in the late 70's, there was no Internet and there were no Hollywood gossip programs. So, it was next to impossible to find even a tidbit of information on *M*A*S*H* (or any other program), much less a photo. I would write to the local affiliates that aired *M*A*S*H*, and ask if they had any photos from the show. They sent me a couple. I got greedy and wrote again. More photos. I'd wait a few months and write again...until they finally caught on to the *M*A*S*H* addict in Preston. To this day, I have a magazine clipping which announced that Gary Burghoff was leaving *M*A*S*H*.

In 1980, *Making M*A*S*H* aired on PBS. For the first time, I saw the extended footage of the opening credits used in the Pilot, which had been edited out for syndication. I experienced ecstasy. That same year, my sainted mom won a *M*A*S*H* contest at the local affiliate. As a result, she got to introduce an episode of her choice ("The Interview"), in a 30-second spot. The producer marveled at

Joan Katheryn Spindler O'Neill (Mark O'Neill's mom) introducing "The Interview" on a local station after winning a contest in 1980. Mrs. O'Neill did a 30-second spot, and did it perfectly in one take.

how she did it on one flawless take, and with no script.

This was also a time before videos and DVDs. I would get in bed at night, and quietly get out my cassette player, and secretly listen to the one episode of *M*A*S*H* I had taped, "White Gold." Over and over again. "Appears tired in class" on my report card can be blamed on *M*A*S*H*.

In 1983, my parents — God love them — paid for me to visit Hollywood and Stage 9. *M*A*S*H* had ended filming a month earlier, but I did get to see the outside of Stage 9, and got a script from Burt Metcalfe's office.

A year earlier, a friend had given me the phone number of Stage 9, so I called. In as grown up a voice as I could muster, I asked for Jamie Farr. Imagine how I almost fainted when he actually came on. He was so very polite.

Over two decades and a zillion viewings of *M*A*S*H* later, I found myself contacting *M*A*S*H* alumni for interviews for this book. It was surreal to start receiving responses via phone, mail or e-mail. Joan Van Ark (guest star) was the very first to respond, and was so nice. Then, Gene Reynolds left a message. Then,

Gary Burghoff called, and three minutes into the conversation, I felt like I was talking to an old college buddy. And the list went on. There were some *M*A*S*H* alumni I was sure I'd never be able to locate, much less get an interview from. I was always sorry that Wayne Rogers left *M*A*S*H*. To hear from him was such a thrill. And thanks to Larry Gelbart, I was put in touch with Stuart Margolin, one of my favorite character actors. One *M*A*S*H* alumni I was sure I'd never find was Richard Lee Sung, who played the character famous for sculpting a bust of Colonel Potter. Imagine how thrilled I was when he not only called me, but enthusiastically recited some of his classic lines like, "This is me!"

Gary Burghoff's THE HOME ©

Above: Gary Burghoff was kind enough to invite Mark O'Neill to collaborate on his idea for a comic strip.

Right: A caricature drawn by Mark O'Neill of Richard Lee Sung. Mr. Sung, known to many as "Curly," has incorporated this into his personal letterhead. Richard Lee "This is me" Sung remains one of the most popular and talked about guest stars to appear on M*A*S*H.

God works in mysterious ways and, on many occasions, Gary Burghoff (who I've become friends with) has either called me or I've called him…just when one of us needed to chat. Similarly, Richard Lee Sung (Curly) has called me just when I was at my lowest. Both of my parents passed to Heaven this year, and Curly — not entirely aware of this — called a few different times at just the right time and was so kind, wise, supportive and utterly positive. One night, I happened to be watching *M*A*S*H* and one of the cast members called me. The TV was muted, but I would be watching a character's lips move while hearing that very actor's voice on the phone. Utterly surreal.

I like *M*A*S*H* at its zaniest. It's not that I'm trivializing the destruction of war. In my mind, rather, the zaniest episodes of *M*A*S*H* remind me of my belief that whatever the tough or awful situation, it is entirely possible to remain positive in it, with faith, and even humor. Episodes like "Divided We Stand," "Crisis," "Deal Me Out" and "Operation Noselift" shine like pure gold to me. The lines roll out of Hawkeye and Trapper's mouths like they just thought of them. Episodes like "The Light That Failed" and "None Like It Hot," from later seasons, also capture that zany *M*A*S*H* feel.

I'm a fan of the use of background music on *M*A*S*H*, and can't imagine the opening scenes of "The Incubator" or "White Gold" without it. Nor can I imagine Hawkeye walking through camp naked, without that slightly jazzy background music playing. I'm also a staunch fan and defender of the laugh track. When watching *M*A*S*H* alone, it makes me feel like other people are laughing with me.

I thought I knew everything *M*A*S*H*, until I met Eddie Solomonson. I call him "The Encyclopedia" because he knows all things *M*A*S*H*. We worked hard on this book, and hope you enjoy reading it. In Heaven, "A hundred years from now," please see me for a copy of part two of this book. Up there, I intend to get interviews from those *M*A*S*H* greats who have gone on ahead of us, like McLean Stevenson, Larry Linville, Ed Winter, Johnny Haymer, Sorrell Booke, Mary Wickes, Logan Ramsey and many more.

Mark O'Neill was born in 1965 in Rochester, New York, and has lived in Preston, Connecticut, for the past 31 years. One of his comic strips, "Potluck Parish," was with United Feature Syndicate for three years. He continues to work on it, as well as one he's hoping to get syndicated with Gary Burghoff called "Gary Burghoff's...The Home." Mark has written humor columns and done cartoons for The Thames River Times (a small local paper), and has children's books he's trying to get published. He has a sweet sweet wife and they're expecting their new son, John James O'Neill.

Index of Episodes

* Hour-long Broadcast
** Part Two Continued the following week

Index